Lecture Notes in Computer Sci

Commenced Publication in 1973
Founding and Former Series Editors:
Gerhard Goos, Juris Hartmanis, and Jan van Leeuwen

Leonard Bolc
Ryszard Tadeusiewicz
Leszek J. Chmielewski
Konrad Wojciechowski (Eds.)

Computer Vision
and Graphics

International Conference, ICCVG 2012
Warsaw, Poland, September 24-26, 2012
Proceedings

 Springer

Volume Editors

Leonard Bolc
Polish-Japanese Institute of Information Technology, Warsaw, Poland

Ryszard Tadeusiewicz
AGH University of Science and Technology, Krakow, Poland
E-mail: rtad@agh.edu.pl

Leszek J. Chmielewski
Warsaw University of Life Sciences (SGGW), Warsaw, Poland
E-mail: leszek_chmielewski@sggw.pl

Konrad Wojciechowski
Silesian University of Technology, Gliwice, Poland
and
Polish-Japanese Institute of Information Technology, Warsaw, Poland
E-mail: konrad.wojciechowski@polsl.pl

ISSN 0302-9743   e-ISSN 1611-3349
ISBN 978-3-642-33563-1   e-ISBN 978-3-642-33564-8
DOI 10.1007/978-3-642-33564-8
Springer Heidelberg Dordrecht London New York

Library of Congress Control Number: 2012947146

CR Subject Classification (1998): I.4.1-10, I.3.5, I.3.8, I.5.3-4, I.2.10

LNCS Sublibrary: SL 6 – Image Processing, Computer Vision, Pattern Recognition, and Graphics

Typesetting: Camera-ready by author, data conversion by Scientific Publishing Services, Chennai, India

Printed on acid-free paper

Springer is part of Springer Science+Business Media (www.springer.com)

Preface

The International Conference on Computer Vision and Graphics, organized since 2002, is the continuation of the International Conferences on Computer Graphics and Image Processing, GKPO, held in Poland every second year from 1990 to 2000. The founder and organizer of these conferences was Prof. Wojciech Mokrzycki. The main objective of ICCVG is to provide an environment for the exchange of ideas between researchers in the closely related domains of computer vision and computer graphics.

ICCVG 2012 brought together more than 100 authors. The proceedings contain 89 papers, each accepted on the grounds of at least two independent reviews. During the conference a special session on Visual Surveillance and a workshop on Medical Image Analysis with the Open Source Software CreaTools were organized.

The content of the book has been divided into three parts. The first two are devoted to the main topics of the conference, namely Computer Vision and Computer Graphics, respectively. The third part is related to the special session, mentioned above, containing four chapters.

ICCVG 2012 was organized by the Association for Image Processing, Poland (Towarzystwo Przetwarzania Obrazów – TPO), the Faculty of Applied Informatics and Mathematics, Warsaw University of Life Sciences (WZIM SGGW), and the Polish-Japanese Institute of Information Technology (PJWSTK).

The Association for Image Processing integrates the Polish community working on the theory and applications of computer vision and graphics. It was formed between 1989 and 1991.

The Faculty of Applied Informatics and Mathematics, established in 2008 at Warsaw University of Life Sciences, offers two programs of study: Informatics, and Informatics and Econometrics. Its main advantage is merging technical education with applied sciences, including the application of computer sciences to the management and analysis of the agricultural industry.

The Polish-Japanese Institute of Information Technology founded in 1994 by the Computer Techniques Development Foundation under the agreement of the Polish and Japanese governments is one of the leading, non-state (private) Polish universities. We are very grateful that the institute hosted and supported the conference.

We would like to thank all the members of the Scientific Committee, as well as the additional reviewers, for their help in ensuring the high quality of the papers. We would also like to thank Grażyna Domańska-Żurek for her excellent work on technically editing the proceedings, and Dariusz Frejlichowski, Bernadeta Bonio, Paweł Wieman, Henryk Palus, Marcin Bator, and Artur Wiliński for their engagement in the conference organization and administration.

September 2012

Leonard Bolc
Ryszard Tadeusiewicz
Leszek J Chmielewski
Konrad Wojciechowski

Organization

- Association for Image Processing (TPO)
- Polish-Japanese Institute of Information Technology (PJWSTK)
- Faculty of Applied Informatics and Mathematics,
  Warsaw University of Life Sciences (WZIM SGGW)

Conference General Chairs

J.L. Kulikowski (Poland)
L.J. Chmielewski (Poland)
K. Wojciechowski (Poland)

Scientific Committee

Ivan Bajla (Slovakia)
Ewert Bengtsson (Sweden)
Maria Berndt-Schreiber (Poland)
Prabir Bhattacharya (USA)
Gunilla Borgefors (Sweden)
Adam Borkowski (Poland)
Leszek Chmielewski (Poland)
László Czúni (Hungary)
Silvana Dellepiane (Italy)
Marek Domański (Poland)
Paweł Forczmański (Poland)
Dariusz Frejlichowski (Poland)
Maria Frucci (Italy)
André Gagalowicz (France)
Duncan Gillies (UK)
Marcin Iwanowski (Poland)
Adam Jóźwik (Poland)
Heikki Kälviäinen (Finland)
Andrzej Kasiński (Poland)
Włodzimierz Kasprzak (Poland)
Bertrand Kerautret (France)
Nahum Kiryati (Israel)
Reinhard Klette (New Zealand)
Józef Korbicz (Poland)
Witold Kosiński (Poland)

Witold Malina (Poland)
Krzysztof Marasek (Poland)
Andrzej Materka (Poland)
Nikolaos Mavridis (United Arab Emirates)
Paweł Mikołajczak (Poland)
Wojciech Mokrzycki (Poland)
Heinrich Niemann (Germany)
Mariusz Nieniewski (Poland)
Sławomir Nikiel (Poland)
Lyle Noakes (Australia)
Antoni Nowakowski (Poland)
Maciej Orkisz (France)
Krzysztof Okarma (France)
Arkadiusz Orłowski (Poland)
Henryk Palus (Poland)
Wiesław Pamula (Poland)
Jan Piecha (Poland)
Maria Pietruszka (Poland)
Piotr Porwik (Poland)
Artur Przelaskowski (Poland)
Przemysław Rokita (Poland)
Khalid Saeed (Poland)
Gerald Schaefer (UK)
Andrzej Śluzek (United Arab Emirates)
Maciej Smiatacz (Poland)

Table of Contents

Computer Graphics

Computer Vision

Visual Surveillance

Video Summarization:
Techniques and Classification

Muhammad Ajmal, Muhammad Husnain Ashraf, Muhammad Shakir,
Yasir Abbas, and Faiz Ali Shah

COMSATS Institute of Information Technology
M.A. Jinnah Building Defence Road, Off Raiwind Road, Lahore, Pakistan
{rajmal,fashah}@ciitlahore.edu.pk

Abstract. A large number of cameras record video around the clock,
producing huge volumes. Processing these huge chunks of videos demands plenty of resources like time, man power, and hardware storage etc. Video summarization plays an important role in this context.
It helps in efficient storage, quick browsing, and retrieval of large collection of video data without losing important aspects. In this paper,
we categorize video summariztion methods on the basis of methodology
used, provide detailed description of leading methods in each category,
and discuss their advantages and disadvantages. Moreover, we discuss the
situation in which each method is most suitable to use. The advantage of
this research is that one can quickly learn different video summarization
techniques, and select the method that is the most suitable according to
one's requirements.

1 Introduction

Recently, digital video technology is growing at a rapid rate. Due to advancement
in technology, it becomes very easy to record huge volume of videos. A huge
bulk of digital contents such as news, movies, sports, and documentaries etc.
is available. Moreover, the need for surveillance has increased significantly due
to increase in the demand of security especially after 9/11. Thousands of video
cameras can be found at public places, public transport, banks, airports, etc.
resulting in large amount of information which is difficult to process in real
time. Furthermore, storage of huge amount of video data is not that easy. It is
very important to quickly retrieve and browse huge volume of data efficiently
because end user want to get all important aspects of data. To solve this problem,
numerous solutions are provided in literature [1,2,3,4,5,6]. Video summarization
plays an important part in this regard, as it helps the user to navigate and
retrieve through a large sequence of videos. In recent years, video summarization
has become an emerging field of research. But pratical implementation is far
behind due to complexity of mehtods. The purpose of our work is to provide a
brief and categorized overview of video summarization techniques according to
advantages, drawbacks, and methodology used. One can easily grasp the idea of
different techniques and can choose the technique of his/her choice.

L. Bolc et al. (Eds.): ICCVG 2012, LNCS 7594, pp. 1–13, 2012.

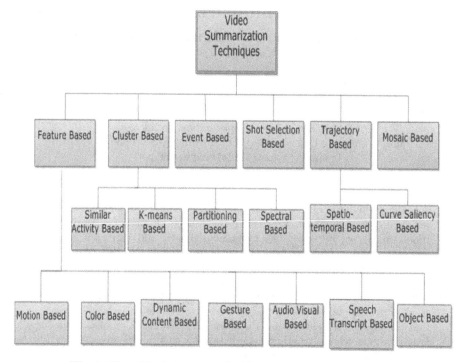

Fig. 1. Hirarchical structure of video summarization techniques

Surveys on video summarization techniques are already conducted that provides an overview and classification in different ways as video skims, highlights [7], still image and moving image abstracts [8,9], and video summarization techniques for mobile applications [10]. Techniques are based on features [11,12,13], clustering [14,15,16,17], event [12,15,18], shot selection [19,20], mosaic [21,22,23,24], and trajectory analysis [25,26,27]. Figure 1 represents a hierarchical classification of these techniques. As can be seen from the figure, we categorize video summarization techniques in 6 major categories based on mechanism and overall process. A detailed overview of these techniques is given in the following sections.

2   Feature Based Video Summarization

Digital video contains many features like color, motion, and voice etc. These techniques work well if user wants to focus on features of video. For example, if user wants to see color features then its good to pick color based video summarization techniques. As can be seen from the Figure 1, feature based video summarization techniques are classified on the basis of motion, color, dynamic contents, gesture, audio-visual, speech transcript, object. These techniques are described below.

2.1 Motion Based Video Summarization

It is always difficult to summarize video based on motion only . The task becomes more complex when camera motion is also involved. The concept of motion for key frame extraction was first used in [11]. After that, [1,2,28] also used motion for key frame extraction. A novel technique involving camera motion as well as object motion is presented in [29]. The changes in dominant image motion lead to temporal segmentation of video. The residual contents (i.e. after subtracting the camera motion from global image motion) of the video are identified. The extraction of meaningful dynamic events is done by statistical motion model. The technique described in [30] focuses on constant speed motion and generates summary by using the concept of relative motion. It also preserves the spatial and motional information for further analysis. Motion based approach are good when there is medium-level motion in a video. In contrast, it fails to do well for videos containing huge motion or no motion at all. Surveillance videos are good candidate for motion based approach.

2.2 Color Based Key Frame Extraction

Color is considered an important aspect of video. Thats why it has been used quite often for video summarization. A nice color based technique is proposed in [3]. Color histogram is used to store color information of a shot. By using probability model, different shots having color change patterns are identified. Utterance of a shot is also identified. Finally, integration of these utterances leads to the meaningful summary of video. Zhang also proposed color based techniques in [4,13], in which key frames are selected based on color and texture properties. The first frame within a shot is considered as key frame. Color histogram difference is used to identify next key frame. At the end, we have a collection of key frames. Color based summarization techniques are very simple and easy to use. However, their accuracy is not reliable, as color based techniques may consider noise as part of summary.

2.3 Dealing with Dynamic Contents

Such kind of techniques use motion, color, and audio features for video summarization [12,13]. In particular, a novel approach towards preserving dynamic contents was proposed in [31]. Firstly, it does color and motion based segmentation and then classifies dynamic and static segments. The next step is clustering of dynamic and static segments and then the selection of summary segments which results in a meaningful summary. This technique is very useful for videos containing rich visual, graphic, and audio contents as well as for moving camera, but summary is not generated as camera is zooming or panning.

2.4 Gestures Based Key Frame Extraction

Gestures are very important in real life. Recently, some studies have focused on gestures considering it a very important aspect of video. A compact framework for summarizing lecture video using hand gestures recognition is presented in [32]. Similarly, the method proposed in [33] summarizes video on the basis of gestures like hand, head, and legs movement etc. The gesture energy is calculated using Zernike movement and then local maxima and minima are monitored for key frames. It is not a threshold dependent technique so the number of key frames extracted may vary. This technique is very useful for videos of sign language communication, human computer interaction and even for robot guidance. Accurate classification and segmentation of different gestures is a difficult task, due to which it may fail to produce a meaningful summary.

2.5   Audio-Visual Based Approach

Nowadays, music companies put their music online for business. The customers who want to buy music would like to see highlights first. Several methods for music video summarization has been proposed [34,35]. Most of which are for MIDI data. MIDI data summarization cannot be applied to real music videos. Music video structure consists of audio data that depicts what we see on the screen (visual data). Lectures and sports videos are also rich with audio-visual features. Moreover, many surveillance applications also use audio-visual features for summarization. The synchronization between audio and video is really crucial in this regard, so the summarization must be audio centric and image centric. To ensure synchronization, summary must be generated by choosing video segments that correspond to some audio segments. Such kind of techniques use audio-visual features alone or in combination with some other features like motion, color, and depth etc. A nice approach is used in [36] for summarizing movies to produce clips or trailers. A video summarization technique, which is specific to music videos, is proposed in [37]. The technique is based on the methods of video highlights. Using audio-visual features for key frames extraction is efficient. But this technique lacks efficiency when audio from a video is missing.

2.6   Speech Transcript Based Approach

In [38,39] frequency of word is used for creating summary of long video. This type of videos do not contain the close-caption text. First of all whole video is segmented into small coherent segments and audio pause boundary detection is done through temporal analysis of pauses between words. Segment boundary is declared between these words. But before doing this, speech transcript is generated using speech recognition systems such as IBM Via voice [40], and a shot table is generated. Ranking of each segment is done by detecting dominant word pairs using an adaptation method [41]. The rank of those segments increases that contain the first 30 of dominant word pairs. Video skims are generated by selecting those segments that maximize the cumulating score of summary and the duration of summary is provided by user. This technique is useful for those videos that contain gradual pauses between speech of the speaker, while the audience is silent. It fails in noisy videos and also for those in which there is continuous talking.

2.7 Object Based Approach

These techniques are used when user concerns more about objects in the video. Content change in video can be detected by appearance and disappearance of such objects [12,42,43,44]. Generally, such techniques are based on detecting, tracking, and keeping history of objects lifetime. However, different studies use different approaches to deal with each of the step described earlier. For example, technique of temporal segmentation to extract key frames is proposed in [45]. First of all, the temporal sub regions are defined and analysis is done on each sub region. Then motion signature for each sub region is defined and indexing is done. After indexing, key frames are extracted, that represents important stages in each object's life time. Object based approach is mostly used in surveillance applications. However, some non-surveillance applications also use this approach, but it depends on the application domain and interest of end users. One needs to be very careful using object based approach at rush places, as false objects may lead to a false summary.

3 Video Summarization Using Clustering

Clustering is most frequently used technique when we encounter similar characteristics or activities within a frame. It also helps to eliminate those frames which have irregular trends. As discussed earlier, other methods for video summarization enable more efficient way of browsing video, but create summary either too long or confusing. Video summarization based on clustering is classified into similar ctivities, K-means, partitioned clustering, and spectral clustering (Figure- 1).

3.1 Similar Activities Based Clustering

Video synopsis created by displaying similar activities which can be performed in different time periods is an effective way to present video data in summarized form [46]. First of all activity is defined; activity is a dynamic object appearing in multiple frames and defined by sequence of object masks in those frames. Activities are divided into subparts called tublets. A comparison is done on tublets and activity features are extracted. Next step is to determine similarity between activities and distance between activities is used for clustering. Then play time is assigned to objects within each cluster and play time is assigned to each cluster. At last, desired clusters are selected for summarization. Clustered summaries are very clear, easy to access. Moreover, irregular activities are easy to detect and presents a structured browsing of objects. Wrong perception about activity may lead to false summary.

3.2 K-means Clustering

K-means clustering uses k-means algorithm for clustering of key frames [47,48]. A method, using concept of histogram computation in combination with k-means algorithm is proposed in [31]. It splits the input file into k segments and takes first frame of each segment, as a representative of this segment. It then computes histograms from these frames and cluster the histogram using k-means algorithm. Desired segments are selected and inserted into a list. Finally, lists are joined to generate desired summary. This technique is not very good for videos, in which scene remain static for long time as it selects repeated segments.

3.3   Partitioned Clustering

This technique works by removing the visual content redundancy that exists among the video frames [16,17]. First of all, the whole video is grouped into clusters such that each cluster contains frames of similar visual content. This clustering is done using partition clustering technique [49]. Cluster validity analysis is done in order to find the number of clusters that is optimal for the given sequence. Finally, key frames are concatenated to produce the video summary which is dependent on the number of shots that are contained in the video. It fails to generate good video summary for those videos where change in scene is rapid and every frame of video presents a different view.

3.4   Spectral Clustering

Spectral clustering uses the spectrum of similarity matrix of data in order to reduce dimensions for clustering. Spectral clustering technique for video summarization is proposed in [15]. There is also a novel technique based on human face detection and spectral clustering [50]. Human face detection is done to compute the location, size, and number of faces. Spectral clustering is used to cluster the desired key frames. This technique is useful in videos where our concern is only humans only. But in video which contains multiple faces in each frame this algorithm does not work well. Moreover, hidden faces may mislead to false summary.

4   Event Based Key Frame Selection

The most difficult task in such kind of techniques is the description and detection of interesting events [12,18]. Event detection consists of two steps; in first step, difference between pixel intensities of current and reference frame is calculated and absolute value of this difference is taken. Then for each difference frame, energy is calculated. In second step, finding of those frames is done that are showing some events. Then with respect to this frame, reference frame will be refreshed. Then these frames are used as input for spectral clustering algorithm.

Spectral clustering algorithm is used to create short video skims for dynamic summary and key frames are used for static browsing. Each cluster is used to create summary for some duration and more than one segment - that representing the events - from one cluster includes in the summary [15]. This technique is most suitable for those videos that are captured from static camera. The reason is that in static camera environment, the background remains same, so reliability of event detection increases. This technique is not good for those videos where background is changing, since this change may be considered as event.

5   Shot Selection Based Approach

A shot is important component of a video, that is contiguous in appearance and time space. There are many techniques to segment video into shots [6,38]. Key frame selection from a shot [20] is also very challenging task. First important shots are measured. For example in film shooting, camera shifted from one actor to other, it consists of two shots. Hierarchical clustering methods exist in which each frame in video is considered as unique cluster and by merging two closest clusters, number of clusters is reduced. Many techniques are available for measuring distance between frames such as the color histogram distance [14], and transformation co-efficient distance [51]. Hierarchical structuring will result in a tree form, such as individual frames on the leaves of tree. Important clustered are determined by assigning weight to each cluster. Greedy algorithm or dynamic programming can be used to find optimal layout. But [19] proposed a frame packing algorithm to find best layout and this algorithm is better than dynamic programmig and greedy approach. This algorithm packs best sequence of frame in a block. Best sequence is found by finding all possible ways for a block. Iteratively it packs the blocks until all blocks are packed. So, by applying frame packing algorithm, it organizes the shots and make summary of long videos. This technique is suitable, when end user's focus is to select important shots of video. It is used only with moving camera, because it makes selection on shot boundary detection.

6   Video Summarization Using Trajectory Analysis

When it comes to analyzing dynamic environment in a video, this technique is equally efficient. In most of the surveillance applications, camera is fixed and background does not change. In this type of environment, the important element for video generalization is to detect the behavior of moving objects with respect to time.

6.1   Spatio-temporal Based Approach

Moving objects can be traced in three dimensional space (x,y,t). Here (x,y) is spatial dimension and (t) is time dimension. Summary is being generated by extracting and analyzing the trajectory. This technique is based on the identification of nodes in these trajectories and marks it as critical points in the video. [26,27] presented a decent approach towards trajectory analysis. The time corresponding to a node provide respective frame. Nodes are assigned with respect to spatio-temporal behavior, if spatio-temporal breakpoint occurs then more nodes are assigned and if motion is smooth then fewer nodes are assigned [52]. Self organization map is used for node placement. Number of nodes is selected for controlling the generalization of video. Generalization of nodes and trajectories of objects make a hierarchical tree data structure which is used to describe the movement of objects in a scene. Spatio-temporal approach is highly useful in surveillance applications. However, it fails when camera motion is also involved.

6.2   Curve Simplification Approach

Curve simplification algorithms [5,28] are best choice to analyze motion, because they use the spatial data of moving objects. In first step, important frames are determined by curve saliency. In second step, finalized key frames are selected by clustering. Mesh saliency algorithms which takes important part of mesh can also be used for curve simplification [25].

Curve saliency is done by computing Gaussian weighted average. Reduction process is done if excessive number of frames has values greater than average. The key frames are selected by each angle of curve. In final step, those key frames are deleted having least importance among nearest key frames and the selected key frames make the summary of long video. This method deletes the redundant key frames and represents the motion capture sequence by only small percentage of all captured frames.

7   Mosaic Based Approach

Mosaic based approach is used to generate a panoramic image from a large number of consecuetive frames having some important content. This technique is proposed in [21,22,23,24,53,54] and known by different names as salient stills, video sprits, and video layers. Two fundamental steps that are used in these studies are: In first step, a global motion model is fitted between two successive motion frames and then a panoramic image is generated using motion model [55]. The drawback of this technique that it represents only static background information, but does not contain any information about moving objects. In order to deal with this drawback, [56] proposed a technique in which two types of mosaics are defined, static background mosaic and synopsis mosaic. In static background mosaic, the focus is on background scenes, whereas in synopsis mosaic, visual summary is generated by analyzing the trajectory of moving objects. After this, combination of these two mosaics is used to generate single panoramic image. This technique is ideal for situations in which multiple cameras are used and background is static.But it fails when background/foreground is rapidly changing.

8   Analysis

This study presents numerous techniques of video summarization and also classifies them into different categories based on methodology and characteristics.

Table 1. Suitable video summarization techniques in different domains

Types of videos	Summarization techniques
Sports videos	Motion based approach
	Color based approach
	Clustering
	Event based approach
	Object based approach
Music videos	Audio-visual based approach
	Clustering
Traffic videos	Motion based approach
	Object based approach
	Event based approach
	Clustering
Surveillance videos	Color based approah
	Motion based approach
	Event based approach
	Clustering
	Trajectory analysis
Movie highlights	Audio-visual based approach
	Similar activity based approach
	Motion based approach
	Shot selection based
	Mosaic based approach
Phone calls	Audio-visual based approach
Sign language communication	Gesture based approach
Rushy videos	Motion based approach
	Clustering
	Audio-visual based approach
	Shot selection based approach
Documentary	Motion based approach
	Shot selection based approach
	Mosaic based approach
	Clustering
News videos	Audio-visual based approach
	Mosaic based approach
	Gesture based approach
Rushy videos	Gesture based approach
	Audio-visual based approach

In Table 2, techniques are classified according to static summary, dynamic summary, fixed camera, moving camera, having knowledge of significant contents, and without knowledge of significant contents. Some techniques work well when camera is fixed and in contrast, others are good with moving camera. For example, spatio-temporal based approach is used with static camera and shot selection based approach is used with a moving camera. Similarly, mosaic based approach is a good choice, when the focus is on detailed and quick overview of entire scene. However, it is difficult to extract only few key frames representing whole scene.

Table 2. Quick analysis of video summarization techniques

Techniques	Static summary	Dynamic summary	Fixed camera	Moving camera	Significant contents knowledge	Without significant contents knowledge
Motion based	No	Yes	Yes	Yes	No	Yes
Color based	Yes	No	Yes	Yes	No	Yes
Dynamic contents based	No	Yes	Yes	Yes	Yes	Yes
Gesture based	Yes	No	Yes	Yes	Yes	No
Audio-Visual based	No	Yes	Yes	Yes	Yes	No
Speech transcript based	No	Yes	Yes	Yes	Yes	No
clustering based	Yes	Yes	Yes	Yes	Yes	Yes
Event based	Yes	No	Yes	No	Yes	No
Shot selection based	Yes	No	No	Yes	No	Yes
Trajectory based	Yes	No	Yes	No	Yes	No
Mosaic based	Yes	No	No	Yes	No	Yes

Different domains require different approaches towards video summarization. Some techniques do fit in more than one situations while others are specific to a single situation. Table 1 presents techniques with respect to application area. Each technique contains specific prons and cons regarding a specific situation. For example trajectory analysis technique outperforms in surveillance applications but it does not produce good results for non-surveillance applications as camera motion is very high. However, the presented techniques tend to save time and cost as well as reduce efforts needed for browsing of long sequence of videos.

9   Conclusion

The fast evolution of video technology has brought huge volume of video data. There is need to browse, retrieve and store this video data efficiently. Nowadays, people have no time to spend on watching whole videos. People want to see only important content of videos. So there is need of efficient video summarization techniques to facilitate users of all categories. Table 2 represents suitable techniques for specific domain. It will save time and cost as one can quickly select the most suitable technique according to one's need. Although, a lot of effort is done to efficiently store, retrieve and browse large video streams, but still there are many deficiencies in video summarization techniques that need to be addressed.

References

1. Divakaran, A., Peker, K.A., Sun, H.: Video Summarization Using Motion Descriptors. In: Conf. on Storage and Retrieval from Multimedia Databases (2001)
2. Ju, S.X., Black, M.J., Minneman, S., Kimber, D.: Summarization of Video-Taped Presentations: Automatic Analysis of Motion and Gestures. IEEE Transactions on CSVT (1998)

3. Fujimur, K., Honda, K., Uehara, K.: Automatic Video Summarization by Using Color and Utterance Information. In: Proceedings 2002 IEEE International (2002)
4. Zhang, H.J., Low, C.Y., Smoliar, S.W.: Video parsing and browsing using compressed data. Multimedia Tools and Applications 1, 89–111 (1995)
5. DeManthon, D., Kobla, V., Doermann, D.: Video Summarization by Curve Simplification. In: Proceedings of the Sixth ACM International Conference on Multimedia (1998)
6. Koskela, M., Sjberg, M., Laaksonen, J., Viitaniemi, V., Muurinen, H.: Rushes Summarization with Self-Organizing Maps. In: Proceedings of the International Workshop on TRECVID Video Summarization (2007)
7. Truong, B.T., Venkatesh, S.: Video Abstraction: a Systematic Review and Classification. ACM Transactions on Multimedia Computing, Communications, and Applications 3(1) (2007)
8. Li, Y., Zhang, T., Tretter, D.: An Overview of Video Aabstraction Techniques. Technical Report HPL (2001)
9. Barbieri, M., Agnihotri, L., Dimitrova, N.: Video summarization: methods and landscape. In: Proceedings of SPIE, vol. 5242, p. 1 (2003)
10. Adami, N., Benini, S., Leonardi, R.: An Overview of Video Shot Clustering and Summarization Techniques for Mobile Applications. In: Proceedings of the 2nd International Conference on Mobile Multimedia Communications (2006)
11. Wolf, W.: Key frame selection by motion analysis. In: ICASSP, vol. 2, pp. 1228–1231 (1996)
12. Wang, F., Ngo, C.W.: Summarizing rushes videos by motion, object and event understanding. IEEE Transactions on Multimedia 14 (2012)
13. Zhang, H.J., Wu, J., Zhong, D., Smoliar, S.W.: An integrated system for content based video retrieval and browsing. Pattern Recognition 30, 643–658 (1997)
14. Chheng, T.: Video Summarization Using Clustering. Department of Computer Science University of California, Irvine (2007)
15. Damnjanovic, U., Fernandez, V., Izquierdo, E.: Event Detection and Clustering for Surveillance Video Summarization. In: Proceedings of the Ninth International Workshop on Image Analysis for Multimedia Interactive Services. IEEE Computer Society, Washington, USA (2008)
16. Hanjalic, A., Zhang, H.: An integrated scheme for automated video abstraction based on unsupervised cluster-validity analysis. IEEE Transactionson Circuits and Systems for Video Technology 9, 1280–1289 (1999)
17. Vctor Valdes, J.M.M.: On-Line Video Skimming Based on Histogram Similarity. In: Proceedings of the International Workshop on TRECVID Video Summarization (2007)
18. Li, B., Sezan, M.I.: Event Detection and Summarization in Sports Video. In: Content-Based Access of Image and Video Libraries, CBAIVL IEEE Workshop (2001)
19. Uchihachi, S., Foote, J., Wilcox, L.: Automatic Video Summarization Using a Measure of Shot Importance and a Frame Packing Method. United States Patent 6, 535,639, March 18 (2003)
20. Evangelopoulos, G., Rapantzikos, K., Potamianos, A., Maragos, P., Zlatintsi, A., Avrithis, Y.: Movie Summarization Based on Audio-Visual Valiency Detection. In: IEEE Intl Conf. Image Processing (ICIP), San Diego, CA (2008)
21. Wang, J., Adelson, E.: Representing moving images with layers. IEEE Transactions on Image Processing 3 (1994)
22. Pope, A., Kumar, R., Sawhney, H., Wan, C.: Video abstraction: Summarizing video content for retrieval and visualization (1998)

23. Aner, A., Kender, J.R.: Video Summaries through Mosaic-Based Shot and Scene Clustering. In: Heyden, A., Sparr, G., Nielsen, M., Johansen, P. (eds.) ECCV 2002, Part IV. LNCS, vol. 2353, pp. 388–402. Springer, Heidelberg (2002)

24. Sawhney, H., Ayer, S.: Compact representation of video through dominent and multiple motion estimation. IEEE Trans. on Pattern. Analysis and Machine Intelligence 18 (1996)

25. Lee, C.H., Varshney, A., Jacob, D.W.: Mesh saliency. ACM Transaction on Graphics, 659–666 (2005)

26. Ngo, C.W., Ma, Y.F., Zhang, H.J.: Automatic Video Summarization by Graph Modeling. In: Proceedings of the 9th IEEE International Conference on Computer Vision (2003)

27. Qiu, X., Jiang, S., Liu, H., Huang, Q., Cao, L.: Spatial temporal attention analysis for home video. In: IEEE International Multimedia and Expo, vol. 23 (2008)

28. Bulut, E., Capin, T.: Key Frame Extraction from Motion Capture Data by Curve Saliency. In: Proceedings of 20th Annual Conference on Computer Animation and Social Agents, Belgium (2007)

29. Peyrard, N., Bouthemy, P.: Motion-Based Selection of Relevant Video Segments for Video Summarization 26(3) (2005)

30. Li, C., Wu, Y.T., Yu, S.S., Chen, T.: Motion-focusing key frame extraction and video summarization for lane surveillance system. In: 16th IEEE International Conference on Image Processing (ICIP), pp. 7–10 (2009)

31. Chen, F., Cooper, M., Adcock, J.: Video Summarization Preserving Dynamic Content. In: Proceedings of the International Workshop on TRECVID Video Summarization (2007)

32. Adnan, H., Mufti, M.: Video Summarization Based Handout Generation from Video Lectures: A Gesture Recognition Framework. In: 5th WSEAS International Conference on Signal Processing, Computational Geometry and Artificial Vision (2005)

33. Kosmopoulos, D.I., Doulamis, A., Doulamis, N.: Gesture-based video summarization. In: ICIP IEEE International Image Processing, pp. 11–14 (2005)

34. Furini, M., Ghini, V.: An Audio-Video Summarization Scheme Based on Audio and Video Analysis. In: IEEE CCNC (2006)

35. Divakaran, A., Peker, K., Radhakrishnan, R., Xiong, Z., Cabasson, R.: Video summarization using mpeg7 motion activity and audio descriptors. In: Video Mining, vol. 91 (2003)

36. Evangelopoulos, G., Rapantzikos, K., Potamianos, A., Maragos, P., Zlatintsi, A., Avrithis, Y.: Movie Summarization Based on Audiovisual Saliency Detection. In: ICIP (2008)

37. Shao, X., Xu, C., Maddage, N.C., Kankanhalli, M.S., Jin, J.S., Tian, Q.: Automatic summarization of music videos. ACM Transactions on Multimedia Computing,Communications and Applications (TOMCCAP) 2 (2006)

38. Taskiran, C.M., Amir, A., Ponceleon, D., Delp, E.J.: Auto-mated video summarization using speech transcripts. In: Proceedings of SPIE Conference on Storage and Retrieval for Media Databases volume, San Jose, CA, pp. 20–25 (2002)

39. Taskiran, C.M., Pizlo, Z., Amir, A., Ponceleon, D., Delp, E.J.: Automated video program summarization using speech transcripts. IEEE Transactions on Multimedia (2006)

40. Bahl, L.R., Aiyer, S.B., Bellegarda, J.R., Franz, M., Gopalakrisnan, P.S., Nahamoo, D., Novak, M., Padmanabhan, M., Picheny, M.A., Roukos, S.: Performance of the IBM Large Vocabulary Continuous Speech Recognition System on the ARPA Wall Street Journal Task. In: Proceedings of IEEE International Conference on Acoustic, Speech and Signal Processing, Detroit, MI (1995)

41. Dunning, T.E.: Accurate methods for the statistics of surprise and coincidence. Computational Linguistics 19(1), 61–74 (1993)

42. Liu, D., Chen, T., Hua, G.: A hierarchical visual model for video object summarization. IEEE Transactions on Pattern Analysis and Machine Intelligence 32 (2010)

43. Kim, C., Hwang, J.N.: An Integrated Scheme for Object-Based Video Abstraction. In: Proceedings of the 8th ACM International Conference on Multimedia (2000)

44. Lee, Y.J., Ghosh, J., Grauman, K.: Discovering Important People and Objects for Egocentric Video Summarization. In: Proceedings of the IEEE Conference on Computer Vision and Pattern Recognition, CVPR (2012)

45. Ferman, A.M., Gunsel, B., Tekalp, A.M.: Object-Based Indexing of MPEG-4 Compressed Video. In: Proceedings of IS&T/SPIE Symp. on Electronic Imaging (1997)

46. Pritch, Y., Ratovitch, S., Hendel, A., Peleg, S.: Clustered synopsis of surveillance video. In: 6th IEEE Int Conf. on Advance Video and Signal Base Selection (AVSS 2009), Genoa, Italy, pp. 2–4 (2009)

47. Ali Amiri, M.F.: Hierarchical key frame-based video summarization using qr-decomposition and modified k-means clustering. EURASIP Journal on Advaces in Signal Processing (February 2010)

48. Farin, D., Effelsberg, W., Peter, H.N.: Robust Clustering Based Video Summarization with Integration of Domain Knowledge. In: Proceedings 2002 IEEE International Conference (2002)

49. Jain, A.K., Dubes, R.C.: Algorithms for Clustering Data. Prentice-Hall, Englewood Cliffs (1988)

50. Peker, K.A., Bashir, F.I.: Content-Based Video Summarization using Spectral Clustering. Mitsubishi Electric Research Laboratories Cambridge, MA. University of Illinois at Chicago, Chicago, IL (2009)

51. Girgensohn, A., Foote, J.: Video Frame Classification Using Transform Coefficients. In: ICASSP 1999 (1999)

52. Stefanidis, A., Partsinevelos, P., Peggy Agouris, P.D.: Summarizing Video Datasets in the Spatiotemporal Domain (2000)

53. Massey, M., Bender, W.: Salient stills: Process and practice. IBM Systems Journal 35 (1996)

54. Lee, M., Chen, W., Lin, C., Gu, C., Markoc, T., Zabinsky, S., Szeliski, R.: A layered video object coding system using sprite and affine motion model. IEEE Transactions on Circuits and Systems for Video Technology (1997)

55. Vasconcelos, N., Lippman, A.: A Spatio Temporal Motion Model for Video Summarization. In: Proceedings of IEEE Computer Society Conference on Computer Vision and Pattern Recognition (1998)

56. Iran, M., Anandan, P.: Video indexing based on mosaic representation. IEEE Computer Society (1998)

Discrete Geometric Modeling
of Thick Pelvic Organs with a Medial Axis

Thierry Bay, Romain Raffin, and Marc Daniel

Aix-Marseille University, LSIS UMR 7296
Avenue Escadrille Normandie-Niemen, 13397 Marseille Cedex, France
{thierry.bay,romain.raffin,marc.daniel}@lsis.org

Abstract. Modeling of soft pelvic organs and their thicknesses is a difficult task, especially when inputs are noisy and scattered. In order to define the geometric step for a global pelvic surgery simulator, we define a new method based only on geometry while considering the problem of error transfer between outer and inner organ surfaces. We compare this approach with a parametric formulation and a mass-spring system.

Keywords: Offset, parametric surface, discrete mesh, medial axis.

1 Introduction and Motivations

Our work is part of the construction of a realistic simulator for pelvic surgery, to evaluate mechanically the consequences of the surgical gesture. The starting point of our study is a series of medium quality and noisy MRI images. A first step, which does not concern this paper, consists in segmenting the image to outline the organs of interest. All these organs have a thickness, like the uterus whose internal walls are nearly into contact, or the bladder which has a large cavity. After our geometric reconstruction, a finite element calculation (in charge of the organs deformation) has to take into account this thickness (possibly variable) and can not just consider a homogeneous mesh describing the organs.

Our goal is to generate a volume mesh which describes geometrically the thick wall of the pelvic organs (with hexahedra), but can not be comprehended from the current state of the input images. Obtaining *in vivo* this information is currently not realistic, and depends therefore on clinical data [8]. We work with a fixed thickness, but we will see later that variable ones do not raise problems. The segmentation of the input data allowed us to obtain a reliable external model, built from C^2 closed B-splines [1]. Our first approach was to offset the data to the desired thickness and to reconstruct the same model [2]. However, keeping the parametric representation to build an *offset surface* leads to two major problems. On the one hand, local and even global self-intersections are created if the *offset distance* between the two surfaces is too large regarding the radii of curvature (cf. Figure 1(a)). On the other hand, modifying a mesh to avoid intersections could require to increase locally the thickness to ensure a value superior to the *offset distance* everywhere (cf. Figure 1(b)). Different

L. Bolc et al. (Eds.): ICCVG 2012, LNCS 7594, pp. 14–21, 2012.

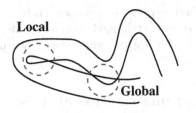
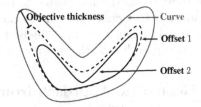

(a) Local/global self-intersections.   (b) Two offsets without intersections.

Fig. 1. Problems raised by offset constructions

modifications will lead to different offsets, which makes it difficult to obtain an internal cavity faithful to a physiological reality.

First, related work, presented in Section 2, describe solutions to build internal offsets. We propose a new geometric method in Section 3 from a non-linear medial axis. We compare our results in Section 4 and conclude in Section 5.

2   Related Work

We aim at building a mesh of hexahedra without *flat or crossed elements*. The management of self-intersections is clearly considered in parametric methods, according to a direct control on the surface: continuity, parameterization, projections on the tangent plane [3–5]. Some methods exist to deal with the self-intersections: removing the loops by working on each line and column [6] (for ordered datasets), curvature reduction by an iterative repositioning of the control points [11], or parametric restriction [9]. A common drawback of these methods is that they may not detect small self-intersections, such as in Figure 1.

Models based on active contours could also be used [13]. The parameterization of a B-spline surface makes it possible to control easily the discretization density, so that a quality conformal mesh is created. However, the usage of active contours is to make a seed evolve with a set of forces, without considering the connections with the external mesh. The drawback in our specific context comes from automatic feedbacks of the physical step that requires modifications in the surface sampling (local density change, holes, ...) when high deformations are performed. This involves an expensive update of the mesh connections with the internal non-parameterized mesh to avoid crossed hexahedra. Finally, the discrete representation can directly use a conformal mesh and correct the self-intersections. The mesh tension can be managed with the elastic forces of a MSS for example. Its principle consists in a lattice for the configuration of the springs network [7], forces that interoperate and a numerical scheme to solve the equations of Newtonian dynamics [10, 12]. Besides, a particle-centered method would facilitate the use of variable thicknesses on the same organ, without complexifying the model unlike parametric and implicit approaches.

The above methods have in common that they dismiss noise or non-described parts of the data. An offset construction based on the external mesh would transfer the errors towards the internal mesh. The method we propose in Section 3 is based on a medial axis (organs shape are 0-genus) to preserve a relation between the outer surface and the inner layers. A qualitative and quantitative comparison between our new approach and other methods is then achieved.

3   Geometric Approach from a Parametric Medial Axis

Our requirement is to acquire an internal mesh located at an *offset distance*, to avoid *self-intersections* and to position *properly the inner cavity*. We introduce a Medial Axis Approach (MAA) estimating an initial cavity evolving outwards.

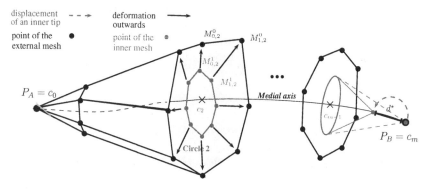

Fig. 2. Example of an inner mesh construction around the medial axis

Further to the dataset acquisition by the segmentation step with Itk-Snap [13], the clinician highlights erroneous parts in the shape of the organs. Although the general distribution should be used as a guideline, the use of high frequencies amounts to consider artifacts for the internal mesh. To overcome this issue, the model is based on a curvilinear medial axis of the initial point cloud D. An inner mesh initialized as a basic extrusion generalized cylinder embedded in the dataset is positioned along this axis, and will evolve outwards to build the internal cavity (cf. Figure 2). The following four steps process details its construction.

The first step is the construction of the curvilinear medial axis, computed as described in [2]: a parametric fitting is applied on the dataset with a Bézier curve C. The curve has two tips (P_A and P_B) which belongs to D. The axis $P_A P_B$ describes the main direction (obtained by a PCA) of the point cloud.

The second step positions circles along this axis to initialize the inner mesh. To know how many circles we need, we consider the sampling of the parametric surface S. Let $\{M_{i,j}^0\}_{i,j=0}^{n,m}$ be the external mesh (a uniform discretization of C^2 surface S). One of the parametric direction starts from one tip P_A to the second tip P_B. The second sampling direction can be considered *orthogonal* to the travel direction of the organ. We will build therefore $(m+1)$ circles, orthogonally to the medial axis (the normal to each circle is parallel to the tangent vector where the circle is positioned). In order to build a conformal mesh, each circle will have $(n+1)$ points like the mesh M^0. A 1 mm radius is applied for each circle (threshold chosen to define a minimum value for the thickness of the internal cavity of the organs). We first need to calculate the $(m+1)$ centers. Let $\{M^1_{i,j}\}^{n,m}_{i,j=0}$ be the internal mesh to compute and $lbrace c_j\}^m_{j=0}$ the centers. For $0 < j < m$, the center c_j is determined as the projection of the isocurve barycenter created from the points $M^0_{.,j}$ on the curve C, calculated with Equation 1:

$$c_j = C \left(\arg\min_s \left(\left\| \frac{\sum^n_{i=0} M^0_{i,j}}{n+1} - C(s) \right\|^2 \right) \right). \tag{1}$$

The parameter value s_j associated to each center c_j positions the jth circle on the curve. A special case concerns the centers c_0 and c_m. Indeed, to close the external mesh, the set $\{M^0_{i,0}\}^n_{i=0}$ is degenerated in a point $C(0) = P_A$. Similarly, $\{M^0_{i,m}\}^n_{i=0}$ is degenerated in a point $C(1) = P_B$. The solution of Equation 1 for c_0 is obviously $s = 0$, i.e. $\{M^1_{i,0}\}^n_{i=0} = C(s = 0) = P_A$. In the same way, the solution for c_m is $s = 1$, i.e. $\{M^1_{i,m}\}^n_{i=0} = C(s = 1) = P_B$. The two sets $\{M^1_{i,0}\}^n_{i=0}$ and $\{M^1_{i,m}\}^n_{i=0}$ are respectively replaced at a distance $d^\star$ from P_A and P_B on the curvilinear medial axis ($d^\star$ is determined such that $d^\star \leq d_o$, with d_o the *offset distance*). Without this operation, the meshes M^0 and M^1 would be into contact at the tips P_A and P_B. This mandatory modification is transmitted to the other centers c_j so that the sequence $(c_i)^m_{i=0}$ remains ordered along the medial axis.

The third step consists in moving the points $\{M^1_{.,j}\}^n_{i=0}$ of each circle j to avoid a crossed mesh between M_0 and M_1. For the jth circle, we initialize uniformly the points $\{M^1_{i,j}\}^n_{i=0}$. We orientate the circle to have the shortest Euclidean distance between $M^0_{0,j}$ and $M^0_{0,j}$, then we calculate the total length between each segment of $M^0_{.,j}$. Each point of $M^1_{i,j}$ with $i \geq 1$ is repositioned so that to the length $\|M^1_{i,j}M^1_{i+1,j}\|$ is proportional to $\|M^0_{i,j}M^0_{i+1,j}\|$ regarding the total length of $M^0_{.,j}$.

The fourth step is finally the iterative deformation of the initialized inner mesh outwards. The system is governed by the satisfaction of the following constraints to authorize the displacement of a point according to Equation 2. If one condition is not satisfied, the displacement of $M^1_{i,j}$ is rejected:

1. *Local intersection*: quadrangles associated with $M^1_{i,j}$ are not crossed;
2. *Global intersection*: segment $[M^0_{i,j}M^1_{i,j}]$ does not cross quadrangle of M^1;
3. *Test of distance*: distance from $M^1_{i,j}$ to its projection on S is inferior to d_o.

Newton-type orthogonal projection method is used. The process ends when all vertices are stationary. The new position at time $t + \Delta t$ for $M^1_{i,j}$ is computed as follows, with $\Delta x > 0$ the displacement step:

$$M_{i,j}^1(t + \Delta t) = M_{i,j}^1(t) + \Delta x \frac{\overrightarrow{M_{i,j}^1(t)M_{i,j}^0(t)}}{\|M_{i,j}^1(t)M_{i,j}^0(t)\|} . \tag{2}$$

A volume mesh without boundaries and with an internal cavity is therefore created. According to FEM experts, deformation calculations would be more accurate with nearly uniform hexaedral elements like cubes in the mesh. Since the thickness is not neglected, the distance between the outer and the inner meshes is too large compared to the constant discretization step. Several layers are generated by cutting the connections between the two meshes according to a used-defined distribution function.

According to Equation 2, the thickness is used as stopping criterion, implying that a thickness map could be integrated easily in the process. We could thus obtain a generalized offset.

4   Results and Comparisons

We compare results of B-spline, MSS and MAA constructions of offsets. The simulations were performed with an Intel Core i7 M620 (2.67 GHz, 4 GB RAM). The chosen thickness is 5.5 mm for the bladder and the rectum [8]. The point clouds describing the bladder and the rectum have respectively 45K points and 21K points. To evaluate our approach, we propose first to compare it with a B-spline parametric offset obtained by surface fitting of *offset points* [2] (each sample point of the outer B-spline surface is shifted of the *offset distance* along the normal vector and the new set of points is smoothed with a C^2 closed B-spline surface) and second to work on a full discrete method with a MSS [7] (whose lattice is given Figure 3).

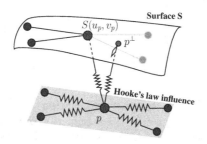

Fig. 3. The six-springs lattice of the MSS

Comparison 1 highlights the difference of reconstruction quality between the parametric approach and the MSS to build a rectum. The first one is based on the least squares, which enables us to average the errors between the approximating surface and the *offset points* to fit. However, a proper offset can not be built due to overlaps of the hexaedra in case of high curvature (cf. Figure 4(a)).

The MSS is based on an elastic regularization for each sampled point p of the inner mesh through a six-springs lattice and three internal forces: a stretching force defined from the Hooke's law is represented by four springs between p and its 1-neighborhood on the inner mesh; a linking force moderates the *sliding* of the internal mesh inside the shape, by associating each point p and the point on S with the same parametric location (u_p, v_p); an orthogonal force pulls the internal mesh in an orthogonal direction in spite of the *sliding*, and corresponds to an orthogonal projection $p^\perp$ of p on S (dynamically modified). In the MSS case, poor quality quadrangles are corrected easily by increasing locally the tension with the springs stiffness (the increase is thresholded to avoid degeneration of the whole mesh). The inner mesh contracts and a mesh without self-intersections is obtained (cf. Figure 4(b)). Finally, the B-spline approach is more time- consuming with 34 seconds, while the MSS performs in 10 seconds.

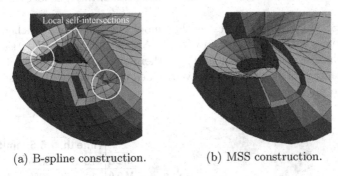

(a) B-spline construction.   (b) MSS construction.

Fig. 4. Volume mesh of a rectum with three layers

Comparison 2 insists on the difference of robustness and stability between the MSS and the MAA to build a bladder (which has a shape which is relatively near to a sphere). Figures 5(a) and 5(b) show the evolution of the thickness of the inner mesh over computation time. We can notice that the MAA is very stable all along the iterations. *A contrario*, the standard deviation for the MSS fluctuates a lot, even for this simple shape. MSS systems are difficult to control. With the lattice described in Figure 3, we have $12(n+1) \times (m+1) + 3$ parameters for a set of $(n + 1) \times (m + 1)$ particles (mainly coming from stiffness and rest length of the springs). As a consequence, the thickness for the MSS is farther from the 5.5 mm objective thickness than the MAA.

Comparison 3 emphasizes the difference of reconstruction quality between the MSS and the MAA with a rectum. Indeed, the MSS in Figure 6(a) manages the self-intersections by contracting the inner mesh with the springs stiffness. Figure 6(b) illustrates the fact that the organs have a direction of travel (associated with their physiological function). We consider that the cavity has to cover the maximum of the travel, and does not have to be too far from the ends. This distance can be managed with d^* in the MAA, but such a control is not possible

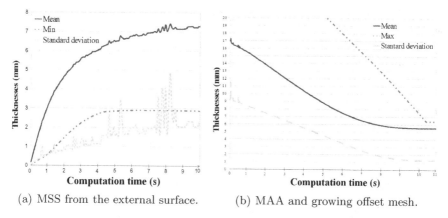

(a) MSS from the external surface.   (b) MAA and growing offset mesh.

Fig. 5. Evolution of the thickness over time for a 5.5 mm thick bladder construction

with the MSS. Figure 6(c) indicates that more elements have reached the expected thickness with the MSS than with the MAA. But our medial axis method maximizes the travel in the organ and goes therefore in narrower areas (implying a lower percentage of elements that have reached the objective thickness) so that it is closer to physiological reality.

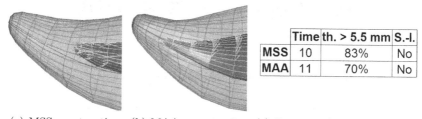

	Time	th. > 5.5 mm	S.-I.
MSS	10	83%	No
MAA	11	70%	No

(a) MSS construction. (b) MAA construction. (c) Statistics (mm and seconds).

Fig. 6. Extremity of two rectum meshes and quantitative comparison between the MSS and the MAA (S.-I.: self-intersections, th.: thickness)

5   Conclusions and Future Works

In our method, we have avoided errors transfers inwards from the surface describing the organs by building the inner cavity directly from the point cloud. The method is not based on *a priori* knowledge. The cavity expands without self-intersections until it reaches the appropriate volume. Our MAA approach estimates the positioning of the cavity, which yields a necessary but not sufficient heuristic to overcome the lack of knowledge about the inside of the organs.

About the future works, the first improvement would transform the process into a variational approach to have a convergent method. The second one would be to obtain a thickness map in order to improve our physiological accuracy. We could then build the set uterus/vagina (very different in terms of thickness and indissociable in the MRI images), and evaluate the results on all pelvic organs.

Acknowledgements. This work is supported by the French National Research Agency, under reference "ANR-09-SYSC-008".

References

1. Bay, T., Chambelland, J.C., Raffin, R., Daniel, M., Bellemare, M.E.: Geometric modeling of pelvic organs. In: IEEE EMBS (ed.) 33rd Annual International Conference of the IEEE EMBS, Boston, USA, pp. 4329–4332 (2011)
2. Bay, T., Chen, Z.W., Raffin, R., Daniel, M., Joli, P., Feng, Z.Q., Bellemare, M.E.: Geometric modeling of pelvic organs with thickness. In: Baskurt, A.M., Sitnik, R. (eds.) Three-Dimensional Image Processing and Applications II, Burlingame, USA, vol. 8290, pp. 82900I–1–82900I–14 (2012)
3. Farouki, R.: The approximation of non-degenerate offset surfaces. In: CAGD, vol. 3, pp. 15–43. Elsevier Science Publishers B. V, Amsterdam (1986)
4. Hoschek, J., Schneider, F.J., Wassum, P.: Optimal approximate conversion of spline surfaces. In: CAGD, vol. 6, pp. 293–306. Elsevier Science Publishers B. V (1989)
5. Kulczycka, M.A., Nachman, L.J.: Qualitative and quantitative comparisons of B-spline offset surface approximation methods. In: CAD, vol. 34, pp. 19–26. Elsevier Science Publishers B. V (2002)
6. Kumar, G.V.V.R., Shastry, K.G., Prakash, B.G.: Computing non-self-intersecting offsets of NURBS surfaces. In: CAD, vol. 34, pp. 209–228 (2002)
7. Provot, X.: Deformation Constraints in a Mass-Spring Model to Describe Rigid Cloth Behavior. In: Graphics Interface, pp. 147–154 (1996)
8. Schuenke, M., Schulte, E., Schumacher, U., Voll, M., Wesker, K.: Neck and Internal Organs, vol. 20, ch. 2. Thieme Medical Publishers (2010)
9. Seong, J.K., Elber, G., Kim, M.S.: Trimming local and global self-intersections in offset curves/surfaces using distance maps. In: CAD, vol. 38, pp. 183–193. Butterworth-Heinemann, Newton (2006)
10. Shinya, M.: Theories for Mass-Spring Simulation in Computer Graphics: Stability, Costs and Improvements. IEICE - Transactions on Information and Systems E88-D, 767–774 (2005)
11. Sun, Y.F., Nee, A.Y.C., Lee, K.S.: Modifying free-formed NURBS curves and surfaces for offsetting without local self-intersection. In: CAD, vol. 36, pp. 1161–1169 (2004)
12. Volino, P., Magnenat-Thalmann, N.: Comparing efficiency of integration methods for cloth simulation. In: Ip, H.H.S., Magnenat-Thalmann, N., Lau, R.W.H., Chua, T.S. (eds.) Computer Graphics International Proceedings, pp. 265–274. IEEE Computer Society (2001)
13. Yushkevich, P., Piven, J., Hazlett, H., Smith, R.G., Ho, S., Gee, J., Gerig, G.: User-guided 3D active contour segmentation of anatomical structures: Significantly improved efficiency and reliability. In: NeuroImage, vol. 31, pp. 1116–1128. Academic Press Inc Elsevier Science, San Diego (2006)

An Evolutionary-Neural Algorithm
for Solving Inverse IFS Problem for Images
in Two-Dimensional Space

Marzena Bielecka[1] and Andrzej Bielecki[2]

[1] Chair of Geoinformatics and Applied Computer Science
AGH University of Science and Technology
Al. Mickiewicza 30, 30-059 Kraków, Poland
[2] Institute of Computer Science, Jagiellonian University
Łojasiewicza 6, 30-348 Kraków, Poland
bielecka@agh.edu.pl, bielecki@ii.uj.edu.pl

Abstract. In this paper an approach based on hybrid, evolutionary-neural computations to the IFS inverse problem is presented. Having a bitmap image we look for an IFS having the attractor approximating of a given image with a good accuracy. A method using IFSes consisting of a variable number of mappings is proposed. A genom has hierarchical structure. A number of different operators acting on various levels of the genome are introduced. The algorithm described in [7] is aided by multilayer neural networks. Such improved algorithm is less time consuming.

1 Introduction

Complex visual structures usually require a huge amount of data to be kept in order to be able to represent such structures. There is a number of methods used to compress an image so that it is smaller and thus easier to store, process and transfer. One of such methods is a fractal compression, where the encoded image is represented by a set of affine functions, called Iterated Function System (IFS), being its attractor. Applications of fractal sets to computer graphics were originated by Mandelbrot, Barnsley, Demko and Sloan ([1,2,3,9]). However, the problem consists in finding an IFS for a given image. In papers [4,5,6,7,11] a certain evolutionary strategy has been proposed. It is effective as the way of finding the IFS encoded the given pattern properly, but is extremely time consuming. In this paper the improving, consisting in aiding the primal algorithm by neural networks is introduced. It turns out, that the new version of the algorithm allows to save at least 10% of the time.

2 Theoretical Basis

Let us briefly recalled the theoretical basis if the algorithm. The first systematic accounts of iterated function schemes seems to be that of Hutchinson and Barnsley [1]. The theory is based on contractive mappings on metric spaces. Here we briefly recall definitions and results that are essential to our method.

L. Bolc et al. (Eds.): ICCVG 2012, LNCS 7594, pp. 22–29, 2012.

Let (X, d) be a metric space. A transformation $g : X \to X$ is called *contractive mapping* if there exists a constant $s \in [0, 1)$ such that $d(g(x), g(y)) \leq s \cdot d(x, y)$ for each $x, y \in X$. The number s is called the contractive factor of g. If the point $x \in X$ is such that $g(x) = x$ then it is called the *fixed point* of the mapping g. Let $(\mathcal{H}(X), h)$ be the space of nonempty compact subsets of a space X with the Hausdorff metric h on it, generated by the metric d. Let $g_i : X \to X$, $i = 1 \ldots n$ be a set of contractive mappings on (X, d). Let's define $F_i : \mathcal{H}(X) \to \mathcal{H}(X)$, $i = 1 \ldots n$ as $F_i(A) = \{g_i(p) : p \in A\}$. It can be easily shown that if g_i is a contractive mapping on the space X with a contractive factor s_i then F_i is contractive on $\mathcal{H}(X)$ with the same contractive factor. The Barnsley operator $F : \mathcal{H}(X) \to \mathcal{H}(X)$ is defined in the following way

$$F(A) = \bigcup_{i=1}^{n} F_i(A).$$

If every g_i, $i = 1, ..., n$, and F_i as a consequence, are contractive mappings with the contractive factors s_i, respectively, then the Barnsley operator F is contractive on $(\mathcal{H}(X), h)$ with the contractive factor $s = \max\{s_1, ..., s_n\}$. Thus, having an IFS which is defined as a finite set of contractive mappings on a metric space IFS $:= \{(X, d), g_1, ..., g_n\}$ the Barnsley operator is generated univocally and is continuous as a contractive mapping.

The Barnsley operator on the Hausdorff space satisfies assumptions of Banach Contraction Principle. Therefore, the operator has a unique fixed point, say A^*, and a sequence of iterations of the operator converges to A^* for every starting point $A \in \mathcal{H}(X)$. Formally, $F^0(A) := A$, $F^n(A) := F(F^{n-1}(A))$ and $\lim_{n \to \infty} F^n(A) = A^*$, for each $A \in \mathcal{H}(X)$. Thus the fixed point A^* is the global attractor of F.

The important property of any IFS, especially in graphical applications, is the fact that attractor is independent from the starting point A. This means that the attractor A^* is fully defined by the set of mappings g_i constituting the operator F and can be generated iteratively by the Barnsley operator for any starting point, including one-element set $\{x\} \in \mathcal{H}(X)$.

By the continuity of a Barnsley operator its attractor is also continuous. This means in turn that small changes in parameters of mappings g_i result in small changes of the attractor.

Finding an IFS which attractor is a good approximation of a given computer image is a non-trivial task. For images which can be easily decomposed into separate parts, such that each one is an image of the whole attractor transformed by one of mappings g_i, the Collage Theorem can be effectively applied [1]. Otherwise, if the analyzed image is more complex no effective algorithm able to find an IFS for such image is known. This paper deals with such a problem.

Thus, by adjusting parameters, we can move closer to the IFS whose attractor is similar enough to a desired image. The existence of such IFS is guaranteed by the Collage Theorem [1].

In computer graphics and image processing most often are used IFSes founded on the Euclidean plane with affine functions

$$g_i(p) = g_i(x_1, x_2) = \begin{pmatrix} y_1^{(i)} \\ y_2^{(i)} \end{pmatrix} = \begin{pmatrix} a_i x_1 + b_i x_2 + e_i \\ c_i x_1 + d_i x_2 + f_i \end{pmatrix} = \begin{pmatrix} a_i & b_i \\ c_i & d_i \end{pmatrix} \cdot \begin{pmatrix} x_1 \\ x_2 \end{pmatrix} + \begin{pmatrix} e_i \\ f_i \end{pmatrix}.$$

In such a case both the Barnsley operator and its attractor are fully defined by the set of parameters $\{a_i, b_i, c_i, d_i, e_i, f_i, \ i = 1, ..., n\}$.

3   Evolutionary-Neural Algorithm

The evolutionary part of the algorithm is described in details in [7]. Here, only indispensable facts are briefly recalled.

Different types of genetic operators are applied at different levels of the hierarchical genotype representation. The following genetic operators are used - see [7] for details.

- Arithmetic crossover.
- Vector one-point crossover.
- Interspecies crossover.
- Reasortment - a crucial operator ([4,5,6,7,11]) based on mechanism of replication of an influenza A virus - see [13]. The above mentioned mechanism would be effective for a class of problems showing the following properties. First of all, unlike in classical genetic algorithms in which genomes consist of a single segment [8]), the genotype should have a hierarchical structure. Furthermore, various types of phenotypes, encoded by various types of genotypes, should exist. Additionally, it it should not be known a priori, which type of genotype contains a solution. Moreover, the exchange of genetic material is possible on various levels of hierarchy. An inverse problem for IFS has all the properties described above.
- Self creation - operator used for creation a new type of IFS, utilizing the vector of probabilities distribution VD, describing the fitness distribution in the current population.
- Three types of mutation operators.

Selection is based on a standard fitness proportional procedure in which the fittest individual is most likely to be selected as a parent but it is modified so that it takes into account the existence of many subpopulation (species). Moreover the elitism is used in which the fittest individual of each subpopulation may survive to the next generation. Although in a number of approaches a Hausdorff distance of a target image and an attractor of IFS being evaluated is considered, its computational time makes it impractical. In this paper a fitness function of an IFS is based on the relative points coverage of the target image. To evaluate how well the attractor covers an image we calculate the number of differences: the number of points that are in the image but not in the attractor - N_{ND} (not drawn points) and the number of points present in the attractor but not in the

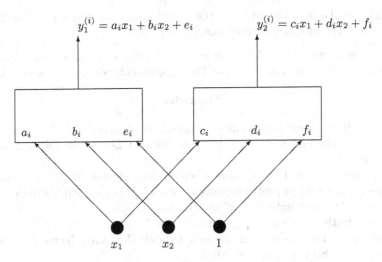

Fig. 1. A multi-layer artificial neural network representing a singel

image -N_{NN} (points not needed). If we denote by N_A the number of points in the attractor and by N_I - in the image then $RC = N_{ND}/N_I$ is the relative coverage of the attractor and $RO = N_{NN}/N_A$ calculates how many points of an attractor are outside the image. Thus the smaller each of this values the better the solution. Two combine both values we use the fitness function defined as $(1 - RC) + (1 - RO)$. This function has to be maximized. The points produced by an IFS outside the image rectangle are also classified as points not needed thus leading to low fitness and fast elimination of such functions. In such a fitness function an equal importance is given to the number of points drawn correctly and points drawn outside. It seems useful to first eliminate IFSes drawing too many points outside the image and then concentrating on improving point coverage. This requires replacing this fitness function with its modified version $p_{rc} \cdot (1 - RC) + p_{ro} \cdot (1 - RO)$ and changing parameters p_{rc} and p_{ro}. The convergence of probabilistic algorithms such as evolutionary strategies is slow. Therefore, hybrid algorithms, in which the probabilistic part of the algorithm is aided by deterministic procedure, are widely used. In our approach, the evolutionary strategy is aided by neural networks. Each *singel* g_i in a given IFS can be represent by a simple multi-layer artificial neural network (ANN) consisting of two linear neurons - see, for instance [12], where information concerning ANNs can be found. The ANN's input consists of three components. Two of them correspond to the point p coordinates x_1 and x_2 and the third one is always equal to 1. The weights of the first neuron correspond to coefficients a, b and e in the *singel* g whereas the weights of the second neuron correspond to coefficients c, d and f in the *singel* g - see Fig.1. Since neurons are linear, the two-componental output of the neural network is given as $y_1 = ax_1 + bx_2 + e$, $y_2 = cx_1 + dx_2 + f$. Thus, the IFS consisting of n *singels* is represented by n ANNs, each having two linear neurons. The weights are modified using back-propagation algorithm. The error is calculated in such a way that for the given pattern the point (u_1, u_2)

belonging to the pattern and being the closest one to the point x_1, x_2 is chosen. The error is the distance between these two points.

The neural part of the algorithm is activated if the activation conditions are satisfied - see discussion in Section 4. The improved algorithm is presented below.

Algorithm

1. Generate a genetic universum - an initial set of *singels*.
2. Generate the first population using an initial VD and the self-creation operator.
3. For each individual in the current population calculate its fitness function.
4. Adapt the vector of probability distribution VD proportionally to the fitness value of the best individual of each degree.
5. Generate the new empty population.
6. Put to the new population the best individual of each degree if its fitness value is above threshold Th value.
7. Generate N_1 individuals in the following way
   - select a species according to vector VD
   - select two individuals according to fitness proportional selection;
   - select the operator to produce offsprings (either arithmetic or vector crossover);
   - produce two offsprings by the selected operator;
   - put the produced offspring to the new population.
8. Generate N_2 individual by the self-creation operator using adapted VD and add them to the new population.
9. Generate N_3 individuals in the following way
   - select a species according to vector VD;
   - select a second species according to vector VD and distance from the first species;
   - select two individuals according to fitness proportional selection; one from each selected species;
   - produce two offsprings by the inter-species crossover operator;
   - put the produced offspring to the new population.
10. Generate N_4 individuals in the following way
    - select two individuals according to fitness proportional selection;
    - produce two offsprings by the reasortment operator;
    - put the produced offspring to the new population.
11. For each element of the new population perform mutation with probability p_m.
12. Activate the neural part of the algorithm if the activation condition is satisfied.
13. Update the VC vector
14. Remove weakest species if they fall below a threshold
15. Remove species with population below 5% of total
16. Create new species
17. If the stop condition is not satisfied go to 3.

4   Results

The fern and the Durer pentagon (see Fig.2) were used as fractal patterns being recognized. They are encoded, respectively, by four and five componental IFSes, given by the following vectors $v_i = (a_i, b_i, c_i, d_i, e_i, f_i)$ of coefficients of g_i :

$$\begin{pmatrix} < 0.0, 0.0, 0.0, 0.16, 0.0, 0.0 > \\ < 0.85, 0.04, -0.04, 0.85, 0.0, 1.6 > \\ < 0.2, -0.26, 0.23, 0.22, 0.0, 1.6 > \\ < -0.15, 0.28, 0.26, 0.24, 0.0, 0.44 > \end{pmatrix}$$

$$\begin{pmatrix} < 0.382, 0.0, 0.0, 0.382, 0.0, 0.0 > \\ < 0.382, 0.0, 0.0, 0.382, 0.618, 0.0 > \\ < 0.382, 0.0, 0.0, 0.382, 0.809, 0.588 > \\ < 0.382, 0.0, 0.0, 0.382, 0.309, 0.951 > \\ < 0.382, 0.0, 0.0, 0.382, -0.191, 0.588 > \end{pmatrix} \, .$$

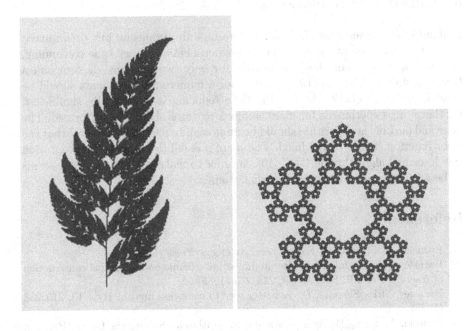

Fig. 2. The fern and Durer pentagon

Tests shown that the condition of neural part activation was crucial for the time optimization of the algorithm. If the neural aiding was activated regularly every n iterations the time of the algorithm performing was greater than for algorithm without neural aiding. This phenomenon was independent of n. The best results were obtained if the neural part was activated when the best individual achieved the value of fitness equal to 1 and then the activation was turn on every 40 iterations. After achieving fitness value equal to 1.3, the neural aiding was activated every 30 iterations. The results presented below were achieved for the above condition of the neural part activation.

For the fern pattern the evolutionary algorithm reconstructed the pattern satisfactorily after 4000 iterations. The improved, neuronal aided algorithm, for the same parameters used in the evolutionary part of the algorithm and the same starting population, reconstructed the pattern after 3200 iterations. For the Durer pentagon pattern satisfied results were achieved after 3400 and 2900 iterations respectively. This means that in the hybrid algorithm the number of generations was reduced reduced by 15% ÷ 20%. According to the fact that the iteration is more complex if the neural algorithm is performed, the time consumption was reduced by 10% ÷ 15%. The computer having 512 MB of RAM, 1800 MHz frequency of processor and operating system XP Windows was used for experiments. The algorithm was implemented in JAVA. One task was performed in about 75 hours.

5   Concluding Remarks

It should be stressed that the described results are promising but preliminary. First of all, because of the fact that the experiments are very time consuming, only w few experiments have been done for only two patterns - a fern and a Durer pentagon. The statistical analysis for a numerous experiments should be done in order to check whether the time reducing is statistically significant. Furthermore, experiments for more complex patterns should be performed. The neuronal part of the algorithm should be improved. In particular it seems that the error function should be modified. Testing of possibilities of the implementation the described algorithm on GPU [10], in order to make it highly parallel, seems to be an interesting idea for the further studies.

References

1. Barnsley, M.F.: Fractals Everywhere. Academic Press (1988)
2. Barnsley, M.F., Demko, S.G.: Iterated function schemes and the global construction of fractals. Proc. R. Soc. A 399, 243–275 (1985)
3. Barnsley, M.F., Sloan, A.D.: A better way to compress images. Byte 13, 215–233 (1988)
4. Bielecki, A., Strug, B.: An Evolutionary Algorithm for Solving the Inverse Problem for Iterated Function Systems for a Two Dimensional Image. In: Kurzyński, M., Puchała, E., Woźniak, M. (eds.) Computer Recognition Systems. AISC, vol. 30, pp. 347–355. Springer, Heidelberg (2005)
5. Bielecki, A., Strug, B.: A Viral Replication Mechanism in Evolutionary Algorithms. In: Proc. of ICAISC 2006, pp.175–180. IEEE Computational Intelligence Society (2006)
6. Bielecki, A., Strug, B.: Evolutionary Approach to Finding Itarated Function Systems for a Two Dimensional Image. In: Computational Imaging and Vision, pp. 512–520. Springer, Berlin (2006)

7. Bielecki, A., Strug, B.: Finding an Iterated Function Systems based representation for complex visual structures using an evolutionary algorithm. Machine Graphics and Vision 16, 171–189 (2007)
8. Holland, J.H.: Adaptation in Natural and Artificial Systems. University of Michigan Press, Ann Arbor (1975)
9. Mandelbrot, B.: The Fractal Geometry of Nature. Freeman, New York (1982)
10. Owens, J.D., Houston, M., Luebke, D., Green, S., Stone, J.E., Philips, J.C.: GPU computing. Proc. IEEE 96, 879–899 (2008)
11. Strug, B., Bielecki, A., Bielecka, M.: Evolutionary Viral-type Algorithm for the Inverse Problem for Iterated Function Systems. In: Wyrzykowski, R., Dongarra, J., Karczewski, K., Wasniewski, J. (eds.) PPAM 2007. LNCS, vol. 4967, pp. 579–588. Springer, Heidelberg (2008)
12. Tadeusiewicz, R.: Neural Networks. Akademicka Oficyna Wydawnicza, Warszawa (1993) (in Polish)
13. Taubenberger, J.K., Reid, A.H., Fanning, T.G.: Capturing a killer flu virus. Scientific American 292, 62–71 (2005)

Euler's Approximations to Image Reconstruction

Dariusz Borkowski

Faculty of Mathematics and Computer Science, Nicolaus Copernicus University
Chopina 12/18, 87-100 Toruń, Poland
dbor@mat.umk.pl
http://www.mat.umk.pl

Abstract. In this paper we present a new method to reconstruction of images with additive Gaussian noise. In order to solve this inverse problem we use stochastic differential equations with reflecting boundary (in short reflected SDEs). The continuous model of the image denoising is expressed in terms of such equations. The reconstruction algorithm is based on Euler's approximations of solutions to reflected SDEs.

We consider a classical Euler scheme with random terminal time and controlled parameter of diffusion. The reconstruction time of our method is substantially reduced in comparison with classical Euler's scheme. Our numerical experiments show that the new algorithm gives very good results and compares favourably with other image denoising filters.

1   Introduction

Let D be a bounded, convex domain in $\mathbf{R}^2$, $u : \overline{D} \to \mathbf{R}$ be an original image and $u_0 : \overline{D} \to \mathbf{R}$ be the observed image of the form $u_0 = u + \eta$, where η stands for a white Gaussian noise. We assume that u and u_0 are appropriately regular. We are given u_0, the problem is to reconstruct u. This is a typical example of an inverse problem [2].

The inverse problem of restoration of noisy image by automatic and reliable methods belongs to the most intensively studied topics of image processing. Various techniques of noise removal were proposed to tackle this problem. One may quote the linear filtering, wavelets theory, variational/PDE-based approaches and stochastic modelling [5].

Stochastic methods generally are based on the Markov field theory, however some papers [4,7,13,14] involve advanced tools of stochastic analysis such as: stochastic differential equations, stochastic differential equations with reflection, backward stochastic differential equations. The weakest point of this approach in the case of images denoising is the necessity of using Monte Carlo method. In particular, we have to do multiple simulations of trajectories of the diffusion process. Euler's approximation [11] is a classical method of diffusion simulations. This scheme gives good results only for small time-step discretization but unfortunately, reconstruction takes very long time. In [3] the Euler scheme was improved for applications to image processing by adding a controlled parameter. This new numerical scheme considered for a constant terminal time T is

L. Bolc et al. (Eds.): ICCVG 2012, LNCS 7594, pp. 30–37, 2012.
© Springer-Verlag Berlin Heidelberg 2012

called a modified diffusion (in short MD) and gives good results for long time-step discretization and reconstruction is about 50 times faster than the Euler's approximation.

In this paper we introduce a numerical scheme based on Euler's approximations with random terminal time. We consider the modified diffusion method with terminal time which depends on geometry of the reconstructed image and therefore it is random. These modifications of the classical Euler scheme lead to the new algorithm of denoising images: modified diffusion with random terminal time (in short MDRTT), which compares favourably with modified diffusion method [3] and other classical denoising filters such as Perona-Malik (in short PM) [8], total variation (in short TV) [9], minimal surfaces (in short MS) [1].

2 Mathematical Preliminaries

The reconstruction of images is based on two advanced tools of stochastic analysis: stochastic differential equations (in order to model image diffusion) and Skorokhod problem (in order to constrain diffusion to domain image).

First we will define the Skorokhod problem. Let $D \subset \mathbf{R}^n$ be a domain with closure $\overline{D}$ and boundary ∂D. Let $T > 0$ and by $\mathbf{C}([0,T];\mathbf{R}^n)$ we denote the set of continuous functions $f : [0,T] \to \mathbf{R}^n$.

Definition 1. Let $y \in \mathbf{C}([0,T];\mathbf{R}^n)$, $y_0 \in \overline{D}$. A pair $(x,k) \in \mathbf{C}([0,T];\mathbf{R}^{2n})$ is said to be a solution to the Skorokhod problem associated with y and D if

1. $x_t = y_t + k_t$, $t \in [0,T]$,
2. $x_t \in \overline{D}$, $t \in [0,T]$,
3. k is a function with bounded variation $|k|$ on $[0,T]$, $k_0 = 0$ and

$$k_t = \int_0^t n_s \, d|k|_s, \quad |k|_t = \int_0^t 1_{\{x_s \in \partial D\}} \, d|k|_s, \quad t \in [0,T],$$

where $n_s = n(x_s)$ is an inward normal unit vector at $x_s \in \partial D$.

It is known that if D is a convex set, then there exists a unique solution to the Skorokhod problem [12].

Definition 2. Let $(\Omega, \mathcal{F}, \mathcal{P})$ be a probability space.

1. An n-dimensional stochastic process $X = \{X_t; t \in [0,T]\}$ is a parametrised collection of random variables defined on a probability space $(\Omega, \mathcal{F}, \mathcal{P})$ with values in $\mathbf{R}^n$.
   For each fixed $\omega \in \Omega$ the function $X_t(\omega)$, $t \in [0,T]$ is called a trajectory of X and is denoted by $X(\omega)$.
2. A filtration $(\mathcal{F}_t) = \{\mathcal{F}_t; t \in [0,T]\}$ is a nondecreasing family of sub-σ-fields of $\mathcal{F}$ i.e. $\mathcal{F}_s \subseteq \mathcal{F}_t \subseteq \mathcal{F}$ for $0 \le s < t \le T$. By $(\mathcal{F}_t^X)$ we denote a filtration generated by process X, i.e.
   $\mathcal{F}_t^X = \sigma(X_s; 0 \le s \le t)$.

3. *A stochastic process X is adapted to the filtration $(\mathcal{F}_t)$ (X is $(\mathcal{F}_t)$ adapted) if for each $t \in [0,T]$, X_t is $\mathcal{F}_t$ - measurable random variable.*

Definition 3. *Let Y be $(\mathcal{F}_t)$ adapted process with continuous trajectories, $Y_0 \in \overline{D}$. We say that a pair (X, K) of $(\mathcal{F}_t)$ adapted processes is a solution to the Skorokhod problem associated with Y and D, if for almost every $\omega \in \Omega$, $(X(\omega), K(\omega))$ is a solution to the Skorokhod problem associated with $Y(\omega)$ and D.*

In what follows, by $W = \{W_t; t \in [0,T]\}$ we will denote a Wiener process starting from zero. We assume that we are given a point $x_0 \in \overline{D}$ and some function $\sigma : \mathbf{R}^n \to \mathbf{R}^n \times \mathbf{R}^m$.

Definition 4. *Let Y be an $(\mathcal{F}_t)$ adapted process. A pair $(X, K^{\overline{D}})$ of $(\mathcal{F}_t)$ adapted processes is called a solution to reflected SDE*

$$X_t = x_0 + \int_0^t \sigma(X_s)\,dW_s + K_t^{\overline{D}}, \ t \in [0,T], \tag{1}$$

if $(X, K^{\overline{D}})$ is a solution to the Skorokhod problem associated with

$$Y_t = x_0 + \int_0^t \sigma(X_s)\,dW_s, \ t \in [0,T] \ \text{ and } \ D.$$

The process X is called the process with reflection. The proof of existence and uniqueness of the solution to reflected SDEs can be found in [12].

3   Stochastic Representation of Solution to the Heat Equation

Before presenting a general method, we will illustrate our ideas by constructing a model which is equivalent to a commonly used filter, namely, the convolution of the noise image with two-dimensional Gaussian mask. The construction of our model is based on construction of the process X. We suppose for a while that the image is given by a function defined on the whole plane. Put $X_t = W_t^x$, $t \in [0,T]$, where W^x is a two-dimensional Wiener process starting from $x \in \overline{D}$.
    Then

$$\mathbf{E}[u_0(X_T)] = \int_{\mathbf{R}^2} \frac{1}{2\pi T} e^{-\frac{|x-y|^2}{2T}} u_0(y)\,dy = \int_{\mathbf{R}^2} G_{\sqrt{T}}(x-y)u_0(y)\,dy, \tag{2}$$

where $G_{\sqrt{T}}(x) = \frac{1}{2\pi T} e^{-\frac{|x|^2}{2T}}$ is two-dimensional Gaussian mask.

    The reconstructed pixel $u(x)$ is defined as the mean value $\mathbf{E}[u_0(X_T)]$. Therefore, by (2) the image is the convolution of the noise image with two-dimensional Gaussian mask.

    Since we want to consider the image as a function defined on the bounded convex set, we have to introduce a new assumption on the process X. It is natural to assume that the process X is a stochastic process with reflection with values in $\overline{D}$. In this case process X is given by a Wiener process with reflection, i.e. it can be written as $X_t = W_t^x + K_t^{\overline{D}}$ (see Definition 4).

4   Image Denoising

The model constructed in the previous section is equivalent to the convolution of the noisy image with two-dimensional Gaussian mask. This filter removes noise and blurs edges. In this section we follow by [8] and provide a construction with the following properties: noise is removed and image has sharp edges.

In a neighbourhood of an edge, the image exhibits a strong gradient. In order to preserve this edge, we should diffuse along it. At locations where the variations of the brightness are weak (low gradient), we would like to encourage smoothing, the same in all directions. We expect that process X will have the property of the Wiener process. These conditions may be achieved by imposing (see [15])

$$X_t = x + \int_0^t \sigma(X_s)\, dW_s + K_t^{\overline{D}}, \tag{3}$$

where $\sigma(X_t) =$

$$
\begin{bmatrix}
-\lambda_1(|\nabla(G_\gamma * u_0)(X_t)|)\frac{(G_\gamma * u_0)_{x_2}(X_t)}{|\nabla(G_\gamma * u_0)(X_t)|}, & \lambda_2(|\nabla(G_\gamma * u_0)(X_t)|)\frac{(G_\gamma * u_0)_{x_1}(X_t)}{|\nabla(G_\gamma * u_0)(X_t)|} \\
\lambda_1(|\nabla(G_\gamma * u_0)(X_t)|)\frac{(G_\gamma * u_0)_{x_1}(X_t)}{|\nabla(G_\gamma * u_0)(X_t)|}, & \lambda_2(|\nabla(G_\gamma * u_0)(X_t)|)\frac{(G_\gamma * u_0)_{x_2}(X_t)}{|\nabla(G_\gamma * u_0)(X_t)|}
\end{bmatrix}
$$

$$\lim_{s \to 0} \lambda_1(s) > 0,\ \lim_{s \to 0} \lambda_2(s) > 0,\ \lim_{s \to 0} \frac{\lambda_1(s)}{\lambda_2(s)} = 1,\ \lim_{s \to +\infty} \lambda_1(s) > 0,\ \lim_{s \to +\infty} \lambda_2(s) = 0.$$

To avoid false detections due to noise, u_0 is convolved with a Gaussian kernel G_γ (3×3 Gaussian mask). As an example of λ_1 and λ_2 we can use functions which are shown in Fig. 1.

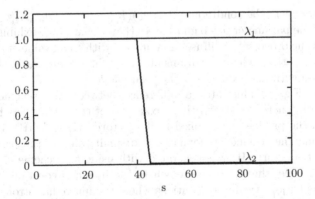

Fig. 1. Example of functions λ_1 and λ_2

5   Euler's Approximations

Consider the following numerical scheme

$$X_0^m = X_0, \ X_{t_k}^m = \Pi_{\overline{D}}[X_{t_{k-1}}^m + \sigma(X_{t_{k-1}}^m)(W_{t_k} - W_{t_{k-1}})], \ k = 1, 2, ..., m, \quad (4)$$

where $t_k = kh$, $h = \frac{T}{m}$, $k = 0, 1, ..., m$ and $\Pi_{\overline{D}}(x)$ denotes a projection of x on the set $\overline{D}$. Since D is convex, the projection is unique.

Theorem 1. *Let* $(X, K^{\overline{D}})$ *be the solution to the reflected SDE (1). If there exists* $C > 0$ *such that* $\|\sigma(x) - \sigma(y)\|^2 \le C|x - y|^2$, *then*

$$\lim_{m \to +\infty} |X_T^m - X_T| = 0 \quad \text{almost surely.}$$

The proof of the above theorem can be found in [11].

6   Modified Diffusion

Recall that the reconstructed pixel $u(x)$ is the mean value $\mathbf{E}[u_0(X_T^m)]$. The numerical scheme (4) gives good results, but only with small value of time-step parameter $h = \frac{T}{m}$ (for example $h = 0.05$). Calculating the mean value using Monte Carlo method for small h is not effective and takes a long time. To omit this problem, we improve the scheme (4) by adding a controlled parameter p [3].

$$X_0^m = X_0, \ H_{t_k}^m = \Pi_{\overline{D}}[X_{t_{k-1}}^m + \sigma(X_{t_{k-1}}^m)(W_{t_k} - W_{t_{k-1}})],$$

$$X_{t_k}^m = \begin{cases} H_{t_k}^m, & \text{if } \Theta, \\ \\ X_{t_{k-1}}^m, & \text{elsewhere,} \end{cases} \qquad k = 1, 2, ..., m, \qquad (5)$$

where by Θ we mean the condition $|(G_\gamma * u_0)(H_{t_k}^m) - (G_\gamma * u_0)(X_{t_{k-1}}^m)| < p$.

Note that, the parameter $p > 0$ guarantees that, if the image exhibits a strong gradient then the process X^m diffuses as a process with small value of the parameter h and at locations where variations of the brightness are weak, the process X^m can diffuse with large value of h (for example $h = 4$).

The figure Fig. 2. illustrates a difference between the scheme (4) and the scheme (5). There are shown three examples of trajectories of the process $u_0(X_t^m)$ from the pixel A to the pixel B. Trajectories (I) and (III) were generated with using the scheme (4) for large and small value of the parameter h, respectively. Trajectory (II) was generated with using the scheme (5) for large h. It is easy to see, that at locations where the image is constant, trajectory (II) diffuses as trajectory (I). At locations where the image has strong gradient, the trajectory (II) is similar to the trajectory (III).

For small h or $p = +\infty$ (in practice $p > 255$) the numerical scheme (5) is equivalent to the scheme (4).

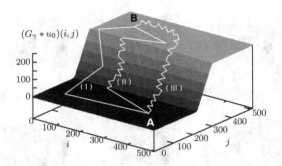

Fig. 2. Example of trajectories of the process $(G_\gamma * u_0)(X_t^m)$ from pixel A to B: (I) – with using the scheme (4) and large h, (II) – with using the scheme (5) and large h, (III) – with using the scheme (4) and small h.

7   Modified Diffusion with Random Terminal Time

The numerical scheme (5) can be rewritten as

$$X_0^m = X_0, \quad H_{t_k}^m = \Pi_{\overline{D}}[X_{t_{k-1}}^m + \sigma(X_{t_{k-1}}^m)(W_{t_k} - W_{t_{k-1}})],$$

$$X_{t_k}^m = \begin{cases} H_{t_k}^m, & \text{if } \Theta \\ X_{t_{k-1}}^m, & \text{elsewhere,} \end{cases} \quad k = 1, 2, ..., \tau_m, \text{ where } \tau_m = m.$$

At locations where gradient is strong in all directions it is possible that condition Θ does not hold enough times than we would expect. This situation is presented in Fig. 3. In the picture a) and b) we can see the original image and the noisy image respectively. The noisy image has been denoised by running MD algorithm and result is presented in figure e). On the right side and top of the image we can see a pixel (noise), which should be removed. The reason of this situation is that diffusion at this pixel has stopped. To avoid this we propose the following modification of the numerical scheme:

$$X_0^m = X_0, \quad H_{t_k}^m = \Pi_{\overline{D}}[X_{t_{k-1}}^m + \sigma(X_{t_{k-1}}^m)(W_{t_k} - W_{t_{k-1}})],$$

$$X_{t_k}^m = \begin{cases} H_{t_k}^m, & \text{if } \Theta, \\ X_{t_{k-1}}^m, & \text{elsewhere,} \end{cases} \quad k = 1, 2, ..., \tau_m, \tag{6}$$

where $\tau_m = \min\{k; k \geq m \text{ and } \Theta \text{ is true } m \text{ times}\}$.

Terminal time τ_m guarantees that the numerical simulation of the diffusion trajectory gives at least m values of $X_{t_k}^m$ which differ from the value in previous step. Observe, that the scheme (6) works well only, if the model of the digital image $G_\gamma * u_0$ is continuous. In practice, we can use linear interpolation to get value of the image $G_\gamma * u_0$, for any point $x \in \overline{D}$.

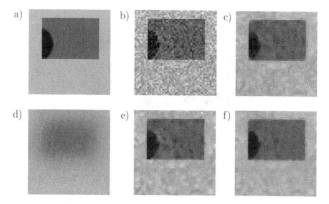

Fig. 3. a) Original image: 50×50 pixels b) Noisy image: standard deviation of the noise $\rho = 25$ c) Euler's scheme: $T = 40$, $h = 0.05$ (480 seconds) d) Euler's scheme: $T = 40$, $h = 4$ (7 seconds) e) MD: $T = 40$, $h = 4$ (12 seconds) f) MDRTT: $T = 40$, $h = 4$ (14 seconds)

The picture Fig. 3 presents comparison of reconstruction results with using the Euler's approximation with long and short time-step discretization MD and MDRTT. We can see that the image f) is comparable to c) which is the result of classical Euler's scheme with short-time discretization. The reconstruction time of MDRTT was substantially reduced.

8   Experimental Results

Some results from our evaluation experiments regarding the modified diffusion with random terminal time and classic PDE-based methods (minimal surfaces,

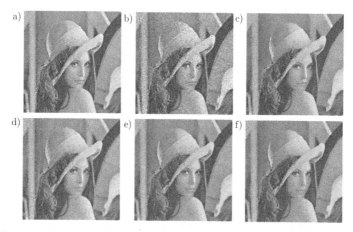

Fig. 4. a) Original image: 512×512 pixels b) Noisy image: $\rho = 25$ c) MS: PSNR=29.92, d) PM: PSNR=30.92, e) TV: PSNR=31.42 f) MDRTT: PSNR=31.69.

Perona-Malik, total variation) are presented in Fig. 4. Figure presents images with maximum values of PSNR obtained after applying methods MS, PM, TV and MDRTT. It can be observed that the image created by the MDRTT algorithm performs better and is visually more pleasant than PDE approaches.

9   Conclusion

In this paper we have presented a new denoising method based on Euler's approximation of reflected SDEs. The obtained results demonstrate the efficiency of the proposed approach, compared with classical Euler scheme.

References

1. Aubert, G., Barlaud, M., Charbonnier, P., Blanc-Féraud, L.: Two Deterministic Half-Quadratic Regularization Algorithms for Computed Imaging. In: Image Processing, Proceedings ICIP 1994, pp. 168–172 (1994)
2. Aubert, G., Kornprobst, P.: Mathematical problems in image processing. Springer, New York (2002)
3. Borkowski, D.: Modified diffusion to image denoising. Adv. Soft Comp. 45, 92–99 (2007)
4. Borkowski, D.: Smoothing, Enhancing Filters in Terms of Backward Stochastic Differential Equations. In: Bolc, L., Tadeusiewicz, R., Chmielewski, L.J., Wojciechowski, K. (eds.) ICCVG 2010, Part I. LNCS, vol. 6374, pp. 233–240. Springer, Heidelberg (2010)
5. Chan, T.F., Shen, J.J.: Image Processing and Analysis – Variational, PDE, wavelet, and stochastic methods. SIAM, Philadelphia (2005)
6. El Karoui, N., Mazliak, L. (eds.): Backward stochastic differential equations. Pitman Research Notes in Mathematics Series. Longman (1997)
7. Juan, O., Keriven, R., Postelnicu, G.: Stochastic Motion and the Level Set Method in Computer Vision: Stochastic Active Contours. Int. J. Comput. Vision 69(1), 7–25 (2006)
8. Perona, P., Malik, J.: Scale-space and edge detection using anisotropic diffusion. IEEE Trans. Pattern Anal. Mach. Intell. 12(7), 629–639 (1990)
9. Rudin, L.I., Osher, S., Fatemi, E.: Nonlinear total variation based noise removal algorithms. Physica D 60(1-4), 259–268 (1992)
10. Saisho, Y.: Stochastic differential equations for multidimensional domain with reflecting boundary. Probab. Theory Rel. 74(3), 455–477 (1987)
11. Słomiński, L.: Euler's approximations of solutions of SDEs with reflecting boundary. Stoch. Proc. Appl. 94, 317–337 (2001)
12. Tanaka, H.: Stochastic differential equations with reflecting boundary condition in convex regions. Hiroshima Math. J. 9(1), 163–177 (1979)
13. Unal, G., Krim, H., Yezzi, A.: Stochastic differential equations and geometric flows. IEEE Trans. Image Process. 11(12), 1405–1416 (2002)
14. Unal, G., Ben-Arous, G., Nain, D., Shimkin, N., Tannenbaum, A., Zeitouni, O.: Algorithms for stochastic approximations of curvature flows. In: Image Processing, Proceedings ICIP 2003, vol. 2–3, pp. 651–654 (2003)
15. Weickert, J.: Theoretical Foundations Of Anisotropic Diffusion In Image Processing. Computing Supplement 11, 221–236 (1996)

Application of Backward Stochastic Differential Equations to Reconstruction of Vector-Valued Images

Dariusz Borkowski[1] and Katarzyna Jańczak-Borkowska[2]

[1] Faculty of Mathematics and Computer Science,
Nicolaus Copernicus University Chopina 12/18, 87-100 Toruń, Poland
dbor@mat.umk.pl

[2] Institute of Mathematics and Physics, University of Technology and Life Sciences
al. prof. S. Kaliskiego 7, 85-789 Bydgoszcz, Poland
kaja@utp.edu.pl

Abstract. In this paper we explore the problem of reconstruction of vector-valued images with additive Gaussian noise. In order to solve this problem we use backward stochastic differential equations. Our numerical experiments show that the new approach gives very good results and compares favourably with deterministic partial differential equation methods.

1 Introduction

Let D be a bounded, convex domain in $\mathbf{R}^2$, $u : \overline{D} \to \mathbf{R}^3$ be an original colour image and $u_0 : \overline{D} \to \mathbf{R}^3$ be a noisy observation of the form: $u_0 = u + \eta$, where η means white Gaussian noise. Having u_0 we have to reconstruct an original image u. Presented problem is a classic example of an inverse problem [3].

Problem of denoising colour images using fully automatic and reliable methods is one of the most important issues of digital image processing and computer vision. Efficient and effective reconstruction of images is an essential element of most image processing and recognizing algorithms. Algorithms of reconstruction allow us to make initial treatment of data for further analysis, which is very important especially in astronomy, biology and medicine.

The four most popular methods in reconstruction of images are statistic methods, linear filtration, methods based on partial differential equations and stochastic methods. Stochastic methods of denoising images mostly base on theory of random Markov fields. Backward stochastic differential equations give us a new approach to stochastic image processing. In bibliography one can only find theoretical bases of usage of backward stochastic differential equations to image reconstruction [1] and some practical results in the case of grey images [4].

A novel look on the reconstruction problem of gray images with using backward stochastic differential equations was fruitful and gave results that are usually better than existing methods. The idea of this paper is to generalize these results to images with values in $\mathbf{R}^n$, in particular to colour images.

L. Bolc et al. (Eds.): ICCVG 2012, LNCS 7594, pp. 38–47, 2012.

The paper is organized as follows. Section 2 contains definitions and fundamental facts of stochastic analysis. In Section 3 we recall basic ideas from [4]. Section 4 provides new results to reconstruction of colour images. Section 5 is devoted to presenting experimental results and comparing with PDE methods.

2   Mathematical Preliminaries

Let $D \subset \mathbf{R}^n$ be a domain with closure $\overline{D}$ and boundary ∂D. Let $T > 0$ and by $\mathbf{C}([0,T];\mathbf{R}^n)$ denote the set of continuous functions $f : [0,T] \rightarrow \mathbf{R}^n$.

Definition 1. *Let $y \in \mathbf{C}([0,T];\mathbf{R}^n)$, $y_0 \in \overline{D}$. A pair $(x,k) \in \mathbf{C}([0,T];\mathbf{R}^{2n})$ is called a solution to the Skorokhod problem associated with y and D if*
1. $x_t = y_t + k_t$, $t \in [0,T]$,
2. $x_t \in \overline{D}$, $t \in [0,T]$,
3. k is a function with bounded variation $|k|$ on $[0,T]$, $k_0 = 0$ and

$$k_t = \int_0^t n_s \, d|k|_s, \; t \in [0,T], \; |k|_t = \int_0^t 1_{\{x_s \in \partial D\}} \, d|k|_s, \; t \in [0,T],$$

where $n_s = n(x_s)$ is an inward normal unit vector at $x_s \in \partial D$.

It is known that if D is a convex set, then there exists a unique solution to the Skorokhod problem [11].

Definition 2. *Let $(\Omega, \mathcal{F}, \mathcal{P})$ be a probability space.*
1. An n-dimensional stochastic process $X = \{X_t; t \in [0,T]\}$ is a parametrised collection of random variables defined on $(\Omega, \mathcal{F}, \mathcal{P})$ with values in $\mathbf{R}^n$.
2. For each fixed $\omega \in \Omega$ the function $X_t(\omega)$, $t \in [0,T]$ is called a trajectory of X and is denoted by $X(\omega)$.
3. A filtration $(\mathcal{F}_t) = \{\mathcal{F}_t; t \in [0,T]\}$ is a nondecreasing family of sub-σ-fields of $\mathcal{F}$ i.e. $\mathcal{F}_s \subseteq \mathcal{F}_t \subseteq \mathcal{F}$ for $0 \leq s < t \leq T$.
4. A process X is $(\mathcal{F}_t)$ adapted if for each $t \in [0,T]$, X_t is $\mathcal{F}_t$ - measurable random variable.

Definition 3. *Let Y be an $(\mathcal{F}_t)$ adapted process with continuous trajectories, $Y_0 \in \overline{D}$. We say that a pair (X,K) of $(\mathcal{F}_t)$ adapted processes is a solution to the Skorokhod problem associated with Y and D, if for almost every $\omega \in \Omega$, $(X(\omega), K(\omega))$ is a solution to the Skorokhod problem associated with $Y(\omega)$ and D.*

Definition 4. *Assume that we are given $x_0 \in \overline{D}$ and $\sigma : \mathbf{R}^n \rightarrow \mathbf{R}^n \times \mathbf{R}^n$. Let Y be an $(\mathcal{F}_t)$ adapted process and by $W = \{W_t; t \in [0,T]\}$ denote an n-dimensional Wiener process. A pair $(X, K^{\overline{D}})$ of $(\mathcal{F}_t)$ adapted processes is called a solution to reflected stochastic differential equation (in short reflected SDE)*

$$X_t = x_0 + \int_0^t \sigma(s, X_s) \, dW_s + K_t^{\overline{D}}, \; t \in [0,T], \tag{1}$$

if $(X, K^{\overline{D}})$ is a solution to the Skorokhod problem associated with
$$V_t = x_0 + \int_0^t \sigma(s, X_s) \, dW_s, t \in [0,T] \text{ and } D.$$

The proof of existence and uniqueness of the solution to reflected SDEs can be found in [11]. The process X satisfying (1) is a diffusion process with values in domain $\overline{D}$. The process X is called the process with reflection.

Let $(\mathcal{F}_t^W)$ be a filtration generated by an l-dimensional Wiener process W, $\xi \in \mathbf{L}^2(\Omega, \mathcal{F}_T, P, \mathbf{R}^k)$ be a square integrable random variable and let $f : \Omega \times [0, T] \times \mathbf{R}^k \to \mathbf{R}^k$ be a Lipschitz continuous function in the space variable.

Definition 5. *A solution to the backward stochastic differential equation (BSDE) associated with ξ and f is a pair of $(\mathcal{F}_t^W)$ adapted processes (Y, Z) with values in $\mathbf{R}^k \times \mathbf{R}^{k \times l}$ satisfying* $\mathbf{E}\left[\int_0^T \|Z_s\|^2 \, ds\right] < \infty$ *and*

$$Y_t = \xi + \int_t^T f(s, Y_s) ds - \int_t^T Z_s \, dW_s, \quad t \in [0, T].$$

See [7] for the proof of existence and uniqueness of the solution to BSDEs.

3   Reconstruction of Gray Levels Images

A general model of the image reconstruction is the following:

$$\begin{cases} X_t = x + \displaystyle\int_0^t \sigma(s, X_s) \, dW_s + K_t^{\overline{D}}, \\ Y_t = \xi + \displaystyle\int_t^T f(s, Y_s, X_s) ds - \int_t^T Z_s \, dW_s, \quad t \in [0, T], \end{cases}$$

where ξ depends on u_0 and the process X.

Note that, the process X has values in domain of the image $\overline{D}$ and is driven by a function σ, the process Y has values in codomain of the image and is driven by a function f. Moreover, the value of the process Y at time $t = 0$ is the reconstructed pixel $u(x)$.

3.1   Stochastic Representation of Solution to the Heat Equation

Before presenting a general method, we will illustrate our ideas by constructing a model which is equivalent to a commonly used filter, namely, the convolution of the noise image with two-dimensional Gaussian mask. We suppose for a while that the image is given by a function defined on the whole plane. Put

$$\begin{cases} X_t = W_t^x, & t \in [0, T], \\ Y_t = u_0(X_T) - \displaystyle\int_t^T Z_s \, dW_s, & t \in [0, T], \end{cases} \tag{2}$$

where W^x is two-dimensional Wiener process starting from $x \in \overline{D}$. From (2) we deduce

$$\begin{cases} X_t = W_t^x, \quad t \in [0, T], \\ Y_0 = u_0(X_T) - \displaystyle\int_0^T Z_s \, dW_s = \mathbf{E}\left(u_0(X_T)\right) = \int_{\mathbf{R}^2} \frac{1}{2\pi T} e^{-\frac{|x-y|^2}{2T}} u_0(y) \, dy. \end{cases} \tag{3}$$

A value of the process Y at time $t = 0$ is the reconstructed pixel $u(x)$. Therefore, by (3) the image is the convolution of the noisy image with two-dimensional Gaussian mask.

While discussing the above example, we assumed that the image is the function given on the whole plane. Since we want to consider the image as a function defined on the bounded, convex set, we have to introduce a new assumption for X. We assume that X is a stochastic process with reflection with values in $\overline{D}$. In this case X is a Wiener process with reflection, which we can write as

$$\begin{cases} X_t = W_t^x + K_t^{\overline{D}}, & t \in [0, T], \\ Y_t = u_0(X_T) - \displaystyle\int_t^T Z_s \, dW_s, & t \in [0, T]. \end{cases}$$

3.2 Anisotropic Diffusion

In the case of smoothing filters we will consider BSDEs associated with $\xi = u_0(X_T)$ and $f(t, y) = 0$, where X is a diffusion process with reflection. Following [13] we provide a construction of a model where process X diffuses along edges. This condition may be achieved by imposing

$$\begin{cases} X_t = x + \displaystyle\int_0^t \begin{bmatrix} -\frac{(G_\gamma * u_0)_{x_2}(X_s)}{|\nabla(G_\gamma * u_0)(X_s)|}, & 0 \\ \frac{(G_\gamma * u_0)_{x_1}(X_s)}{|\nabla(G_\gamma * u_0)(X_s)|}, & 0 \end{bmatrix} dW_s + K_t^{\overline{D}}, \\ Y_t = u_0(X_T) - \displaystyle\int_t^T Z_s \, dW_s, & t \in [0, T] \end{cases} \qquad (4)$$

where $u_{x_i}(y) = \frac{\partial u}{\partial x_i}(y)$. In particular $Y_0 = \mathbf{E}\,[u_0(X_T)]$.

To avoid false detections due to noise, u_0 is convolved with a Gaussian kernel $G_\gamma(x) = \frac{1}{2\pi\gamma^2} e^{-\frac{|x|^2}{2\gamma^2}}$ (in practice 3×3 Gaussian mask).

3.3 Backward Diffusion

In the case of enhancing images we will consider BSDEs associated with $\xi = u_0(x)$ and $f(t, y) = c(y - u_0(X_t))$, where X is a Wiener process with reflection and $c > 0$ is some constant. In accordace with Theorem 3 in [4] the reconstructed image $u(x)$

$$u(x) = Y_0^m = \sum_{k=0}^{m-1} a_k \mathbf{E}\left[u_0(W_{t_k}^x + K_{t_k}^{\overline{D}})\right], t_k = \frac{kT}{m}$$

is a combination of convolutions of the noisy image and two dimensional Gaussian mask with coefficients a_k where $a_0 > 0$, $a_k < 0$, for $k = 1, ..., m - 1$ and $\sum_{k=0}^{m-1} a_k = 1$. This mean that the kernel of filtering is made up of positive weight for central pixel and negative weights for neighborhood pixels and finally is a model of enhancing filter. As it was shown in [4] if parameter c is greater than the result is more enhancing.

4   Reconstruction of Vector-Valued Images

Now we concentrate on images with values in $\mathbf{R}^3$. A very common idea to re-store vector-valued images is to use scalar diffusion on each channel of a noisy image. But one fastly notices that this scheme is useless, since each image channel evolves independently with different smoothing geometries. To avoid this blending effect, the regularization process have to be driven in a common and coherent way for all the vector image channels. In order to execute that we use Di Zenzo geometry [5,6].

Let $u : D \to \mathbf{R}^3$ be a vector-valued image and $x \in D$ be fixed. Consider the function $F_x : V \to \mathbf{R}$, $F_x(v) = \left| \frac{\partial u}{\partial v}(x) \right|^2$, where $V = \{v \in \mathbf{R}^2; |v| = 1\}$. We are interested in finding the arguments $\theta_+(u,x), \theta_-(u,x)$ and corresponding values $\lambda_+(u,x) = F_x(\theta_+(u,x))$, $\lambda_-(u,x) = F_x(\theta_-(u,x))$ which maximize and minimize the function F_x, respectively.

Note that F_x can be rewritten as $F_x(v) = F_x([v_1, v_2]^T) = v^T \mathbf{G}(x) v$, where

$$
\mathbf{G}(x) = \begin{bmatrix} \displaystyle\sum_{i=1}^{3} \left(\frac{\partial u_i}{\partial x_1}(x) \right)^2, & \displaystyle\sum_{i=1}^{3} \frac{\partial u_i}{\partial x_1}(x) \frac{\partial u_i}{\partial x_2}(x) \\ \displaystyle\sum_{i=1}^{3} \frac{\partial u_i}{\partial x_1}(x) \frac{\partial u_i}{\partial x_2}(x), & \displaystyle\sum_{i=1}^{3} \left(\frac{\partial u_i}{\partial x_2}(x) \right)^2 \end{bmatrix}.
$$

The interesting point about $\mathbf{G}(x)$ is that its positive eigenvalues $\lambda_+(u,x)$, $\lambda_-(u,x)$ are the maximum and the minimum of F_x while the orthogonal eigenvectors $\theta_+(u,x)$ and $\theta_-(u,x)$ are the corresponding variation orientations.

Three different choices of vector gradient norms $N(u,x)$ have been proposed in the literature $N(u,x) = \sqrt{\lambda_+(u,x)}$, $N(u,x) = \sqrt{\lambda_+(u,x) - \lambda_-(u,x)}$, $N(u,x) = \sqrt{\lambda(u,x) + \lambda_-(u,x)}$. In presented examples we have used $N(u,x) = \sqrt{\lambda_+(u,x)}$ as a natural extension of the scalar gradient norm viewed as the value of maximum variations.

4.1   Anisotropic Diffusion

Replacing in equation (4) $|\nabla(u,x)|$ and $[u_{x_1}(x), u_{x_2}(x)]^T$ respectively by $N(x,u)$ and $\theta_+(u,x) = [\theta_+^1(u,x), \theta_+^2(u,x)]^T$ we obtain the following model of anisotropic diffusion for vector-valued images:

$$
\begin{cases} X_t = x + \displaystyle\int_0^t \begin{bmatrix} -\frac{\theta_+^1(G_\gamma * u_0, X_s)}{N((G_\gamma * u_0)(X_s))}, & 0 \\ \frac{\theta_+^2(G_\gamma * u_0, X_s)}{N((G_\gamma * u_0)(X_s))}, & 0 \end{bmatrix} dW_s + K_t^{\overline{D}}, \\ Y_t = u_0(X_T) - \displaystyle\int_t^T Z_s\, dW_s, \qquad t \in [0, T] \end{cases} \tag{5}
$$

and in particular $u(x) = Y_0 = \mathbf{E}\left[u_0(X_T)\right]$.

4.2 Backward Diffusion

Theorem 1. *Let $u_0 : \mathbf{R}^2 \to \mathbf{R}^n$, $x \in \mathbf{R}^2$, $f(t,y) = c(y - u_0(W_t^x))$, where W^x is two-dimensional Wiener process starting from x, $c > 0$. If (Y, Z) is a solution to BSDE associated with $\xi = u_0(x)$ and f then*

$$\lim_{m \to +\infty} Y_0^m = \lim_{m \to +\infty} \sum_{k=0}^{m-1} a_k \mathbf{E}\left[u_0(W_{t_k}^x)\right] = \lim_{m \to +\infty} \sum_{k=0}^{m-1} a_k (G_{\sqrt{t_k}} * u_0)(x) = Y_0,$$

where $a_0 = \left(1 + \frac{cT}{m}\right)^m - \frac{cT}{m}$, $a_k = -\frac{cT}{m}\left(1 + \frac{cT}{m}\right)^k$, $t_k = \frac{kT}{m}$, $k = 0, 1, ..., m-1$ ($G_0 \equiv \delta$ is a Dirac function) and $\sum_{k=0}^{m-1} a_k = 1$.

The above theorem is a generalization of results from [4] and its proof is silmilar to the proof of Theorem 3 in [4].

Since the image is a function defined on the bounded set we have to consider Wiener process with reflection with values in domain $\overline{D}$. Finally we have the following model of backward diffusion for vector-valued images:

$$u(x) = Y_0^m = \sum_{k=0}^{m-1} a_k \mathbf{E}\left[u_0(W_{t_k}^x + K_{t_k}^{\overline{D}})\right], \tag{6}$$

where Y^m is process with values in $\mathbf{R}^n$.

5 Experimental Results

Some results from our evaluation experiments regarding BSDE method and classic PDE methods: total variation [9] (in short TV) and Perona-Malik [8] (in short PM) for colour images [5,10] are presented in: Table 1, Table 2 and Fig. 1, Fig. 2. The results refer to RGB images: *Lenna*, *house* and *peppers* corrupted

Table 1. SSIM

Image Method\Standard deviation	*Lenna* $\rho = 30$	*Lenna* $\rho = 40$	*house* $\rho = 30$	*house* $\rho = 40$	*peppers* $\rho = 30$	*peppers* $\rho = 40$
PM	0.8422	0.8203	0.7528	0.7291	0.8373	0.8073
TV	0.8723	0.8333	0.7884	0.7550	0.8692	0.8249
BSDE (5)	**0.8823**	**0.8449**	**0.7896**	**0.7566**	**0.8705**	**0.8342**

Table 2. PSNR

Image Method\Standard deviation	*Lenna* $\rho = 30$	*Lenna* $\rho = 40$	*house* $\rho = 30$	*house* $\rho = 40$	*peppers* $\rho = 30$	*peppers* $\rho = 40$
PM	29.0295	27.6992	28.7392	27.4461	28.6412	27.3377
TV	**29.4952**	28.2040	29.2119	27.7876	**28.8832**	27.5218
BSDE (5)	29.3037	**28.2205**	**29.5891**	**28.2195**	28.7124	**27.5597**

Fig. 1. a) Original *Lenna* image b) Noisy image: $\rho = 40$ c) PM d) TV e) BSDE (5) f) Original *peppers* image g) Noisy image: $\rho = 30$ h) PM i) TV j) BSDE (5) k) BSDE (6): $c = 0.6$, SSIM=0.8641, PSNR=28.2813 l) BSDE (6): $c = 0.8$, SSIM=0.8561, PSNR=27.5979

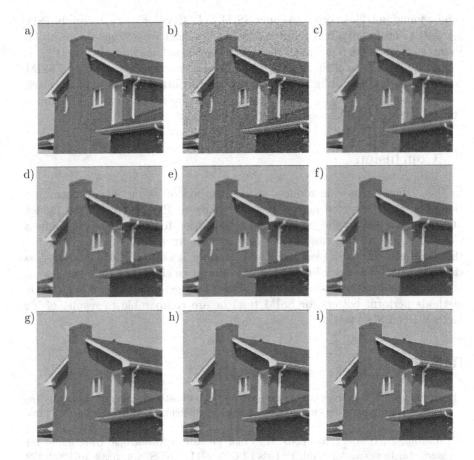

Fig. 2. a) Original *house* image b) $\rho = 30$, c) PM d) TV e) BSDE (5) f) BSDE (6): $c = 0.4$: SSIM=0.7762, PSNR=29.5289 g) BSDE (6): $c = 0.6$, SSIM=0.07589, PSNR=29.1452 h) BSDE (6): $c = 0.8$, SSIM=0.7270, PSNR=28.2127 i) BSDE (6): $c = 1$, SSIM=0.6760, PSNR=26.8126

(independent all channels) with the Gaussian noise with standard deviation ρ. Noisy images have been reconstructed with using vector analysis in RGB space. The maximum values of SSIM and PSNR are given in tables. PSNR is defined by the following formula:

$$\mathrm{PSNR}(U, \hat{U}) = 10 \log_{10} \left(\frac{255^2}{\mathrm{MSE}(U, \hat{U})} \right),$$

$$\mathrm{MSE}(U, \hat{U}) = \frac{\sum_{i=1}^{M} \sum_{j=1}^{N} \|U(i,j) - \hat{U}(i,j)\|^2}{3 \cdot N \cdot M}, \quad \|(r, g, b)\| = \sqrt{r^2 + g^2 + b^2},$$

where M, N are the image dimensions, $U(i,j)$ and $\hat{U}(i,j)$ denote the original and the restored RGB vector, respectively. Definition of SSIM error to gray scale can be found in [12]. In order to count SSIM to RGB color space, we apply SSIM measure to each individual color component and next we average the result [2]. Parameters of SSIM were set to the default values as recommended by [12].

Fig. 1 c,d,e,h,i,j, and Fig. 2 c,d,e, show images with maximum value of SSIM. In Fig. 1 k,l, and Fig. 2 f,g,h,i, we can see results obtained after applying backward diffusion (6) to Fig. 1 j, and Fig. 2 e, respectively. It is clear that if parameter c is greater than the result is more enhancing.

6 Conclusion

In this paper we have introduced a new method of colour image reconstruction. The idea presented here is the alternative to PDE vector-valued models and provide a new methodology based on advanced tools of stochastic analysis. Comparing figures one can observe that images created by the stochastic methods are visually more pleasant. The reason for it is that PDE methods show clear evidence of a block image, but this stair-case effect is reduced in our algorithm. Moreover analysing the measuring of image quality shows that BSDE methods perform better (for SSIM test) or are comparable to results of TV method (for PSNR test).

References

1. Abraham, R., Riviere, O.: Forward-backward stochastic differential equations and PDE with gradient dependent second order coefficients. ESAIM P&S 10, 184–205 (2006)
2. Åström, F., Felsberg, M., Lenz, R.: Color Persistent Anisotropic Diffusion of Images. In: Heyden, A., Kahl, F. (eds.) SCIA 2011. LNCS, vol. 6688, pp. 262–272. Springer, Heidelberg (2011)
3. Aubert, G., Kornprobst, P.: Mathematical problems in image processing, 2nd edn. Applied Mathematical Sciences, vol. 147. Springer (2006)
4. Borkowski, D.: Smoothing, Enhancing Filters in Terms of Backward Stochastic Differential Equations. In: Bolc, L., Tadeusiewicz, R., Chmielewski, L.J., Wojciechowski, K. (eds.) ICCVG 2010, Part I. LNCS, vol. 6374, pp. 233–240. Springer, Heidelberg (2010)
5. Deriche, R., Tschumperlé, D.: Diffusion PDE's on vector-valued images: local approach and geometric viewpoint. IEEE Signal Processing Magazine 19(5), 16–25 (2002)
6. Di Zenzo, S.: A note on the gradient of a multi-image. Comput. Vis. Graph. Image Process. 33(1), 116–125 (1986)
7. Pardoux, É.: Backward stochastic differential equations and viscosity solutions of systems of semilinear parabolic and elliptic PDEs of second order. In: Stochastic Analysis and Related Topics, VI, Geilo, vol. 42, pp. 79–127 (1998)
8. Perona, P., Malik, J.: Scale-space and edge detection using anisotropic diffusion. IEEE Trans. Pattern Anal. Mach. Intell. 12(7), 629–639 (1990)
9. Rudin, L.I., Osher, S., Fatemi, E.: Nonlinear total variation based noise removal algorithms. Physica D 60(1–4), 259–268 (1992)

10. Sapiro, G., Ringach, D.L.: Anisotropic diffusion of multivalued images with applications to color filtering. IEEE Trans. Image Process. 5(11), 1582–1585 (1996)
11. Tanaka, H.: Stochastic differential equations with reflecting boundary condition in convex regions. Hiroshima Math. J. 9(1), 163–177 (1979)
12. Wang, Z., Bovik, A.C., Sheikh, H.R., Simoncelli, E.P.: Image quality assessment: From error visibility to structural similarity. IEEE Trans. Image Process. 13(4), 600–612 (2004)
13. Weickert, J.: Theoretical Foundations Of Anisotropic Diffusion In Image Processing. Computing Suppement 11, 221–236 (1996)

Batch Neural Gas with Deterministic Initialization for Color Quantization

M. Emre Celebi[1], Quan Wen[2], Gerald Schaefer[3], and Huiyu Zhou[4]

[1] Department of Computer Science, Louisiana State University, Shreveport, LA, USA
ecelebi@lsus.edu
[2] School of Computer Science and Engineering
University of Electronic Science and Technology of China, Chengdu, P.R. China
quanwen@uestc.edu.cn
[3] Department of Computer Science, Loughborough University, Loughborough, UK
gerald.schaefer@ieee.org
[4] The Institute of Electronics, Communications and Information Technology
Queen's University Belfast, Belfast, UK
h.zhou@ecit.qub.ac.uk

Abstract. Color quantization is an important operation with many applications in graphics and image processing. Clustering methods based on the competitive learning paradigm, in particular self-organizing maps, have been extensively applied to this problem. In this paper, we investigate the performance of the batch neural gas algorithm as a color quantizer. In contrast to self-organizing maps, this competitive learning algorithm does not impose a fixed topology and is insensitive to initialization. Experiments on publicly available test images demonstrate that, when initialized by a deterministic preclustering method, the batch neural gas algorithm outperforms some of the most popular quantizers in the literature.

Keywords: Color quantization, clustering, competitive learning, batch neural gas.

1 Introduction

True-color images typically contain thousands of colors, which makes their display, storage, transmission, and processing problematic. For this reason, color quantization (CQ) is commonly used as a preprocessing step for various graphics and image processing tasks. In the past, CQ was a necessity due to the limitations of the display hardware, which could not handle the 16 million possible colors in 24-bit images. Although 24-bit display hardware has become more common, CQ still maintains its practical value [1]. Modern applications of CQ include: (i) compression, (ii) segmentation, (iii) text localization/detection, (iv) color-texture analysis, (v) watermarking, (vi) non-photorealistic rendering, and (vii) content-based retrieval.

The process of CQ is mainly comprised of two phases: palette design (the selection of a small set of colors that represents the original image colors) and

L. Bolc et al. (Eds.): ICCVG 2012, LNCS 7594, pp. 48–54, 2012.

pixel mapping (the assignment of each input pixel to one of the palette colors). The primary objective is to reduce the number of unique colors, N', in an image to K ($K \ll N'$) with minimal distortion. In most applications, 24-bit pixels in the original image are reduced to 8 bits or fewer. Since natural images often contain a large number of colors, faithful representation of these images with a limited size palette is a difficult problem.

CQ methods can be broadly classified into two categories: image-independent methods that determine a universal (fixed) palette without regard to any specific image and image-dependent methods that determine a custom (adaptive) palette based on the color distribution of the images. Despite being very fast, image-independent methods usually give poor results since they do not take into account the image contents. Therefore, most of the studies in the literature consider only image-dependent methods, which strive to achieve a better balance between computational efficiency and visual quality of the quantization output.

Numerous image-dependent CQ methods have been developed over the past three decades. These can be categorized into two families: preclustering methods and postclustering methods [1]. Preclustering methods are mostly based on the statistical analysis of the color distribution of the images. Divisive preclustering methods start with a single cluster that contains all N' image colors. This initial cluster is recursively subdivided until K clusters are obtained. Well-known divisive methods include median-cut [2], octree [3], variance-based method [4], greedy orthogonal bipartitioning [5], center-cut [6], and rwm-cut [7]. On the other hand, agglomerative preclustering methods [8,9] start with N' singleton clusters each of which contains one image color. These clusters are repeatedly merged until K clusters remain. In contrast to preclustering methods that compute the palette only once, postclustering methods first determine an initial palette and then improve it iteratively. Essentially, any data clustering method can be used for this purpose. Since these methods involve iterative or stochastic optimization, they can obtain higher quality results when compared to preclustering methods at the expense of increased computational time. Clustering algorithms adapted to CQ include maxmin [10], k-means [11], fuzzy c-means [12], and self-organizing maps [13].

In this paper, we adapt a recent competitive learning algorithm, the batch neural gas algorithm [14], to the problem of CQ. The rest of the paper is organized as follows. Section 2 describes the online and batch neural gas algorithms. Section 3 presents the comparison of the batch neural gas algorithm with other CQ methods. Finally, Section 4 gives the conclusions.

2   Neural Gas Algorithm

Neural gas (NG) [15] is an online clustering algorithm based on the competitive learning paradigm. The algorithm starts with an initial set of N prototype vectors (cluster centers) $W = \{\mathbf{w}_1, \mathbf{w}_2, \ldots, \mathbf{w}_N\} \in \mathbb{R}^D$. Each time a data vector $\mathbf{x} \in \mathbb{R}^D$ is presented, the "neighborhood-ranking" of the prototype vectors $(\mathbf{w}_{(1)}, \mathbf{w}_{(2)}, \ldots, \mathbf{w}_{(N)})$ is determined with $\mathbf{w}_{(k)}$ being the k-th nearest prototype to $\mathbf{x}$. Let $k_i(\mathbf{x}, \mathbf{w})$ denote the rank of the prototype $\mathbf{w}_i$, the adaptation step for adjusting this prototype is given by:

$$\mathbf{w}_i(t+1) = \mathbf{w}_i(t) + \epsilon(t) \cdot h_\lambda(k_i(\mathbf{x}, \mathbf{w})) \cdot (\mathbf{x} - \mathbf{w}_i(t)) \tag{1}$$

where, the learning rate $\epsilon \in [0, 1]$ determines the overall extent of the modification and $h_\lambda(k) = \exp(-k/\lambda)$ is a Gaussian shaped curve with a characteristic decay constant λ. Typically, ϵ and λ monotonically decrease with time according to an exponential schedule, i.e. $\epsilon(t) = \epsilon_0(\epsilon_f/\epsilon_0)^{t/T}$ and $\lambda(t) = \lambda_0(\lambda_f/\lambda_0)^{t/T}$, where T is the maximum number of iterations, $\epsilon_0 > \epsilon_f$ are the initial and final learning rates and $\lambda_0 > \lambda_f$ are the initial and final decay constants.

It can be shown that the dynamics of the prototype vectors obeys a stochastic gradient descent on the cost function [15]:

$$E(W, \lambda) = \frac{1}{2C(\lambda)} \sum_{i=1}^{N} \int h_\lambda(k_i(\mathbf{x}, \mathbf{w})) \|\mathbf{x} - \mathbf{w}_i\|^2 P(\mathbf{x}) d^D x \tag{2}$$

where $P(\mathbf{x})$ represents the probability distribution of the data vectors, $C(\lambda)$ is a normalization factor given by $\sum_{i=1}^{N} h_\lambda(k_i)$, and $\| \|$ is the Euclidean norm.

NG is a simple and highly effective clustering algorithm due to its simple adaptation rule (1), independence of a prior lattice, and insensitivity to initialization [14]. However, because of its online formulation, NG has several drawbacks. First, it has high computational requirements since the prototypes need to be updated after the presentation of each data vector. Second, it is sensitive to noise. Third, it is order-dependent, that is different presentation orders of the data vectors induce different partitions. In order to address these issues, Cottrell et al. [14] proposed a batch variant of NG, in which the prototypes are updated only after the presentation of all data vectors. This variant minimizes the same cost function (2) and, in most cases, converges after a few iterations since it can be interpreted as the Newton's method. The adaptation steps for batch NG (BNG) are given as:

(1) Determine $k_{ij} = k_i(\mathbf{x}_j, \mathbf{w})$ as the rank of prototype $\mathbf{w}_i$.
(2) Update the prototype $\mathbf{w}_i$ by setting it to

$$\mathbf{w}_i = \frac{\sum_{j=1}^{M} h_\lambda(k_{ij}) \cdot \mathbf{x}_j}{\sum_{j=1}^{M} h_\lambda(k_{ij})}$$

where M denotes the number of data vectors.

The algorithm operates as follows. In each iteration, the prototypes are first ranked in ascending order with respect to their distance to each data vector. Each prototype is then updated as a weighted average of all the data vectors with the weights determined by the rank of the prototype using the $h_\lambda(.)$ function.

3   Experimental Results and Discussion

The BNG quantization method was compared to 11 well-known CQ methods: median-cut (MC) [2], octree (OCT) [3], variance-based method (WAN) [4], greedy orthogonal bipartitioning (WU) [5], center-cut (CC) [6], self-organizing

Table 1. Comparison of the CQ methods on Hats

Method	N			
	32	64	128	256
MC	587.9	206.6	123.2	77.3
OCT	292.5	132.0	65.4	34.0
WAN	623.7	311.3	105.7	53.1
WU	212.9	102.7	51.7	29.6
CC	284.1	152.9	88.6	52.3
SOM	214.3	96.3	44.6	27.6
RWM	210.4	105.4	58.3	36.7
MMM	281.6	141.9	92.6	51.1
PWC	180.9	91.8	52.5	33.6
SAM	179.9	95.4	54.3	33.5
CY	247.0	123.6	66.7	38.9
BNG-MC	156.0	78.6	40.6	21.5
BNG-OCT	155.7	**76.9**	**40.5**	**21.3**
BNG-WAN	**154.9**	84.0	40.8	**21.3**
BNG-WU	161.7	82.1	**40.5**	21.4

Table 2. Comparison of the CQ methods on Motocross

Method	N			
	32	64	128	256
MC	437.6	254.0	169.4	114.3
OCT	300.5	158.9	96.2	54.2
WAN	445.6	292.1	168.7	92.4
WU	268.1	147.2	86.7	51.0
CC	335.1	202.0	122.6	74.9
SOM	301.7	134.7	70.3	44.2
RWM	251.4	150.1	83.7	51.0
MMM	407.9	276.9	138.2	85.6
PWC	214.2	126.4	73.9	46.4
SAM	238.1	138.5	81.8	53.5
CY	248.0	146.6	89.3	53.2
BNG-MC	201.9	**108.4**	**63.6**	**38.0**
BNG-OCT	196.7	112.1	64.0	38.4
BNG-WAN	**196.6**	111.8	64.3	38.1
BNG-WU	197.2	112.4	64.4	38.2

Table 3. Comparison of the CQ methods on Flowers & Sill

Method	N			
	32	64	128	256
MC	271.3	143.1	92.9	56.4
OCT	155.2	88.0	47.4	25.9
WAN	198.1	97.8	56.8	37.4
WU	133.9	71.2	40.4	25.5
CC	206.5	112.8	69.9	40.0
SOM	188.9	80.1	35.1	22.2
RWM	149.4	74.7	41.3	28.1
MMM	175.2	119.1	58.1	34.8
PWC	120.0	67.7	39.4	27.6
SAM	141.5	85.3	48.2	30.8
CY	141.4	78.1	42.5	29.1
BNG-MC	**99.3**	54.1	31.3	**18.2**
BNG-OCT	100.4	**53.5**	**30.8**	**18.2**
BNG-WAN	102.9	55.1	31.1	**18.2**
BNG-WU	101.1	54.6	31.1	**18.2**

Table 4. Comparison of the CQ methods on Parrots

Method	N			
	32	64	128	256
MC	441.0	265.1	153.6	112.3
OCT	342.4	191.2	111.2	63.8
WAN	376.0	233.4	153.4	92.2
WU	299.2	167.3	95.4	58.3
CC	398.8	246.5	148.7	78.9
SOM	279.4	151.5	82.2	47.7
RWM	296.5	171.0	99.8	60.6
MMM	352.1	194.8	128.7	68.5
PWC	262.3	151.3	88.7	55.5
SAM	282.4	157.5	92.4	58.8
CY	313.2	178.6	106.7	64.5
BNG-MC	233.9	128.0	73.5	43.6
BNG-OCT	**231.8**	128.6	73.7	43.6
BNG-WAN	233.8	129.3	**73.3**	43.3
BNG-WU	**231.8**	**127.4**	73.4	**43.1**

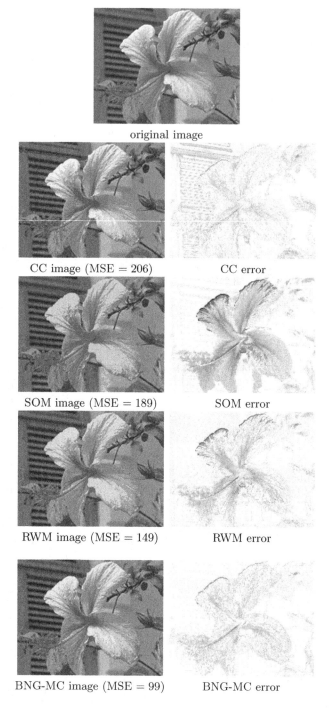

original image

CC image (MSE = 206)   CC error

SOM image (MSE = 189)   SOM error

RWM image (MSE = 149)   RWM error

BNG-MC image (MSE = 99)   BNG-MC error

Fig. 1. Sample CQ results for Flowers & Sill ($N = 32$)

map (SOM) [13], rwm-cut (RWM) [7], modified maxmin (MMM) [10], pairwise clustering (PWC) [8], split and merge (SAM) [9], and Cheng and Yang (CY) [16].

In the experiments, following [14], parameters of BNG were set to $\lambda_0 = N/2$, $\lambda_f = 0.01$, and $T = 100$. The convergence of the algorithm was controlled by the disjunction of two criteria: the number of iterations reaches a maximum of $T = 100$ or the relative improvement in the cost function (2) between two consecutive iterations drops below a threshold, i.e. $(E_{i-1} - E_i)/E_i \leq \varepsilon$, where E_i denotes the cost function value at the end of the i-th ($i \in \{1, 2, \ldots, 100\}$) iteration. The convergence threshold was set to $\varepsilon = 0.001$.

One of the most important factors that influences the performance of a batch clustering algorithm such as BNG is the selection of the initial prototypes [11]. Due to their gradient descent formulation, in many of these algorithms, the initial prototypes are typically chosen uniformly at random from the data vectors. Such a random initialization is undesirable as there are often no performance guarantees and thus it is common practice to perform multiple randomly initialized runs and take the output of the run that produces the minimum cost function value. In this study we avoid this problem by initializing BNG using the four most commonly used deterministic preclustering methods, namely MC, OCT, WAN, and WU.

Tables 1–4 show the Mean Squared Error (MSE) values obtained by the CQ methods on Hats, Motocross, Flowers & Sill, and Parrots, respectively (these images are taken from the *Kodak Lossless True Color Image Suite* [17]). The best (lowest) MSE values are shown in **bold**. It can be seen that the BNG variants obtain significantly lower average distortion when compared to the other methods. Interestingly, despite significant differences among MC, OCT, WAN, and WU, the BNG variants that are initialized by these preclustering methods exhibit negligible variation, which demonstrates the insensitivity of BNG to initialization.

Figure 1 shows sample CQ results for Flowers & Sill and the corresponding error images. The error image for a particular CQ method was obtained by taking the pixelwise absolute difference between the original and quantized images. In order to obtain a better visualization, pixel values of the error images were multiplied by 4 and then negated. It can be seen that the proposed method obtains visually pleasing results with less prominent contouring. Furthermore, it achieves the highest color fidelity, which is evident by its clean error image.

4   Conclusions

In this paper, an effective and deterministic CQ method based on the batch neural gas algorithm was introduced. When compared to self-organizing maps, this competitive learning algorithm does not impose a fixed topology and is insensitive to initialization. Experiments on a set of publicly available test images demonstrated that the presented method outperforms state-of-the-art methods with respect to distortion minimization.

Acknowledgments. This publication was made possible by grants from the Louisiana Board of Regents (LEQSF2008-11-RD-A-12), US National Science Foundation (0959583, 1117457), and National Natural Science Foundation of China (61050110449, 61073120).

References

1. Brun, L., Trémeau, A.: Color Quantization. In: Digital Color Imaging Handbook, pp. 589–638. CRC Press (2002)
2. Heckbert, P.: Color Image Quantization for Frame Buffer Display. ACM SIGGRAPH Comp. Graph 16, 297–307 (1982)
3. Gervautz, M., Purgathofer, W.: A Simple Method for Color Quantization: Octree Quantization. In: New Trends in Computer Graphics, pp. 219–231. Springer (1988)
4. Wan, S., et al.: Variance-Based Color Image Quantization for Frame Buffer Display. Color Res. Appl. 15, 52–58 (1990)
5. Wu, X.: Efficient Statistical Computations for Optimal Color Quantization. In: Graphics Gems, vol. II, pp. 126–133. Academic Press (1991)
6. Joy, G., Xiang, Z.: Center-Cut for Color Image Quantization. Visual Comput. 10, 62–66 (1993)
7. Yang, C.Y., Lin, J.C.: RWM-Cut for Color Image Quantization. Comput Graph 20, 577–588 (1996)
8. Velho, L., et al.: Color Image Quantization by Pairwise Clustering. In: Proc SIBGRAPI, pp. 203–210 (1997)
9. Brun, L., Mokhtari, M.: Two High Speed Color Quantization Algorithms. In: Proc CGIP, pp. 116–121 (2000)
10. Xiang, Z.: Color Image Quantization by Minimizing the Maximum Intercluster Distance. ACM T. Graphic 16, 260–276 (1997)
11. Celebi, M.E.: Improving the Performance of K-means for Color Quantization. Image Vision Comput 29, 260–271 (2011)
12. Wen, Q., Celebi, M.E.: Hard vs. Fuzzy C-Means Clustering for Color Quantization. Eurasip. J. Adv. Sig. Pr. 2011(1), 118–129 (2011)
13. Dekker, A.: Kohonen Neural Networks for Optimal Colour Quantization. Network-Comp. Neural 5, 351–367 (1994)
14. Cottrell, M., et al.: Batch and Median Neural Gas. Neural Networks 19, 762–771 (2006)
15. Martinetz, T., et al.: Neural-Gas Network for Vector Quantization and its Application to Time-Series Prediction. IEEE T. Neural Networ. 4, 558–569 (1993)
16. Cheng, S., Yang, C.: Fast and Novel Technique for Color Quantization Using Reduction of Color Space Dimensionality. Pattern Recogn. Lett. 22, 845–856 (2001)
17. Franzen, R.W.: Kodak Lossless True Color Image Suite (1999), http://www.r0k.us/graphics/kodak/

CreaTools: A Framework to Develop Medical Image Processing Software: Application to Simulate Pipeline Stent Deployment in Intracranial Vessels with Aneurysms

Eduardo E. Dávila Serrano[1], Laurent Guigues[1], Jean-Pierre Roux[1],
Frédéric Cervenansky[1], Sorina Camarasu-Pop[1], Juan G. Riveros Reyes[2],
Leonardo Flórez-Valencia[2], Marcela Hernández Hoyos[3], and Maciej Orkisz[1]

[1] Université de Lyon, CREATIS; CNRS UMR5220; INSERM U1044; INSA-Lyon,
Université Lyon 1, France
eduardo.davila@creatis.insa-lyon.fr,
http://www.creatis.insa-lyon.fr/site/en
[2] Grupo Takina, Pontificia Universidad Javeriana, Bogotá, Colombia
[3] Grupo Imagine, Grupo GIB, Universidad de los Andes, Bogotá, Colombia

Abstract. The paper presents a collaborative project that offers stand-alone software applications for end-users and a complete open-source platform to rapidly develop/prototype medical image processing work-flows with sophisticated visualization and user interactions. It builds on top of a flexible cross-platform framework (Linux, Windows and MacOS) developed in C++, which guarantees an easy connection of heterogeneous C++ modules and provides the user with libraries of high-level components to construct graphical user interfaces (GUI) including input/output (file management), display, interaction, data processing, etc.

In this article, we illustrate the usefulness of this framework through a research project dealing with the study of thrombosis in intra-cranial aneurysms. Algorithms developed by the researchers, such as image segmentation, stent model generation, its interactive virtual deployment in the segmented vessels, as well as the generation of meshes necessary to simulate the blood flow through thus stented vessels, have been implemented in a user-friendly GUI with 3D visualization and interaction.

1 Introduction

Medical images increasingly become 3-dimensional (3D) or more, if we consider temporal sequences of 3D images or multi-spectral 3D images. At the same time, publication of new medical image processing methods increasingly requires extensive validation on large datasets, which involves physicians non familiar with computer science. At each stage of the development (tests, visual debugging, periodic evaluation, demonstration) and clinical validation of new methods, an appropriate graphical user interface (GUI) is needed to visualize the images and

L. Bolc et al. (Eds.): ICCVG 2012, LNCS 7594, pp. 55–62, 2012.

the results, as well as to interact with them. While creating such GUIs for 2D images is relatively straightforward, the visualization of 3D images and user-friendly interaction with them is a matter for experts in computer graphics and human-machine interfaces. Although some specialists in image processing possess this expertize, for most of them, and particularly for PhD/MSc students and trainees involved in medical image processing projects, it is highly preferable to focus on developing new image processing algorithms rather than spending time to acquire high-level knowledge necessary to develop the corresponding GUIs. Several initiatives from academia and/or industry, such as MeVisLab, GIMIAS, MAF or XIP (see the ToolKit page of the European Network of Excellence VPH [1]), have been proposed with the aim to bridge the gap and provide the researchers in medical image processing with easy to use high-level visualization and interaction tools. Each of them has its own advantages and limitations (e.g. portability issues, data format restrictions, difficulties to customize the tools). Most of them share the choice of underlying libraries widely used in the community, such as Kitware's open-source Visualization ToolKit (VTK) and Insight ToolKit (ITK), as well as Qt. In this paper, we describe a more recent initiative that shares the same choices but has the ambition to overcome the above-mentioned limitations. It is also proposed within the VPH NoE ToolKit [2]. After presenting CreaTools, this paper illustrates its usefulness via a European project Thrombus [3].

2   Presentation of CreaTools

CreaTools [4] is a collaborative project initiated at CREATIS laboratory and developed with contributions from los Andes and Javeriana universities, Bogotá, Colombia. It offers a complete open-source platform to rapidly develop/prototype medical image processing work-flows with sophisticated visualization and user interactions. It builds on top of bbtk (black-box toolkit), a flexible cross-platform framework (Linux, Windows and MacOS) developed in C++, which guarantees an easy connection of heterogeneous C++ modules and provides the user with libraries of high-level components to construct GUIs including input/output (file management), display, interaction, data processing, etc. Beyond Thrombus, research projects where the CreaTools have been or are being successfully used, include cardio-vascular studies (Fig. 1), the analysis of maxillofacial bones, the segmentation of corals and the quantification of cerebral perfusion, visceral adipose tissue, pulmonary ventilation, etc. Publications related to scientific projects using the CreaTools are listed on the PLUME-FEATHER project page [5]. The CreaTools can be used, modified and redistributed under the terms of the French license CeCILL abiding the distribution rules of free software. They are protected by the French Agency for the Protection of Programs (IDDN.FR.001.250014.000.S.P.2010.000.20700).

Several types of CreaTools users can be identified, namely: end-users of stand-alone applications and tools, users building prototypes from available boxes and developers of new boxes, libraries and packages. End-users have access to various mini-tools, such as interactive rigid alignment of 2D and 3D images, image

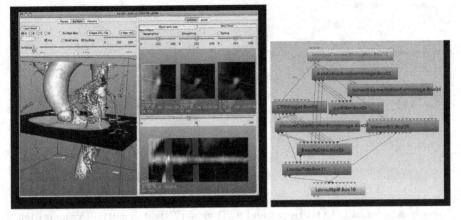

Fig. 1. GUI used to study coronary arteries (segmentation and lesion detection) and the corresponding **bbtk** pipeline

clipping, resampling, etc., and full applications such as an advanced interactive 3D viewer including volume rendering and surface rendering with multiple iso-values, as well as `creaContours`, an interactive contour tracer in N-dimensional images. The latter allows the user to create various contour shapes (B-splines, circles, rectangles, rings...) and thus extract information from the image: calculate local statistical parameters within thus defined regions of interest and on their contours and/or obtain pixel-wise data of the region of interest, to be used in custom computations. The application also provides tools for contour propagation in 3D and basic automatic segmentation.

Both prototypers and developers take advantage of **bbtk** that allows the user to quickly design small applications, particularly demonstrators, which include high-level components: graphical user interface metawidgets (combinations of windows, buttons, sliders...), high-level readers/writers, image/mesh viewers, interactors, etc. Its plug-in and auto-documentation mechanisms contribute to easily capitalize and share new black boxes. It is also used as an educational tool. One of the main features of **bbtk** is its flexibility: any `C++` class can be wrapped into a black box and connected with appropriate inputs/outputs of other black boxes, provided that it meets the definition of a filter, i.e. is defined by its function, inputs and outputs. More than 300 black boxes are currently available. These boxes are mainly based on third-party libraries: `VTK`, `ITK`, `wxWidgets` and `Qt`. The latter are open-source libraries used in numerous medical image processing projects worldwide, which guarantees their quality and foresees potential interoperability between the CreaTools and other toolboxes and software. One of them, `gdcm`, widely used to manage (read/parse and write) DICOM files, has been developed at CREATIS.

An application (prototype, demonstrator ...) is obtained by interconnecting black boxes into a pipeline, which can be done using **bbs**, a very simple scripting language composed of a dozen of commands to include appropriate libraries, instantiate the necessary classes, initialize constants, connect outputs to inputs

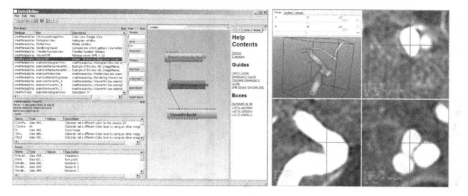

Fig. 2. bbEditor prototyping environment. Left: example of a simple pipeline including a directory selector, a DICOM reader and a 3D viewer. Right: aneurysm visualization using ViewerNV: 3D surface representation and orthogonal slices of the image.

and run the whole. The script is interpreted by a custom interpreter called bbi. Script editing and testing can be performed within an environment called bbStudio, which also provides an on-line help, examples and all necessary documentation of the existing black boxes. Recently, we developed a graphical editor called bbGEditor, which greatly facilitates the creation and editing of pipelines and generates appropriate scripts. In some cases, when the application involves very high level components, the corresponding pipeline can be extremely simple (see example Fig. 2 left). When executing this example, a dialog box is displayed to select a directory containing medical images, then a DICOM reader opens the selected image files and sends them to a 3D viewer (Fig. 2 right).

Another very important and useful feature of bbtk is the possibility to create complex boxes. A complex box actually is a pipeline that demonstrated its usefulness and is likely to be reused in other applications. A very simple mechanism transforms such a pipeline into a black box that can be used like any other box, thus simplifying the networks and capitalizing the developers' efforts. This can be illustrated by the Cropping box developed for the Thrombus project. The purpose of this box is to interactively select an image subvolume of interest (VOI), to clip it and create the necessary data structure so that the VOI can be used in the sequel of the workflow. It involves a number of visualization and interaction tools together with necessary synchronization, which gave rise to a quite complex network with many atomic black boxes (Fig. 3). After defining the inputs and the outputs of this pipeline, the newly created Cropping box has been added to the bank of existing boxes. It is now used as any other atomic box, which greatly simplifies the pipeline creation, understanding and editing.

In addition to using the existing black boxes, developers can create new ones. To this purpose, the base library of the CreaTools suite, called crea, provides a very useful utility called creaNewProject that generates the whole structure of a new C++ project, including the necessary third-party libraries and access to bbtk packages. This structure is based on CMake and allows the user to generate

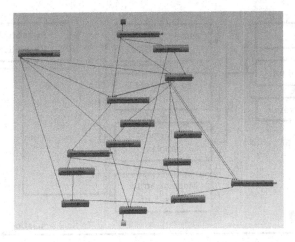

Fig. 3. Internal structure of the `Cropping` complex black box. The squares (red and green) respectively materialize the input and the output of the complex black box.

projects for the target platforms. Tools necessary to wrap `C++` classes into new black boxes are also available, as well as other `CMake` macros and `C++` resources.

In addition to already cited major CreaTools components, let us mention other two important libraries. `creaImageIO` is dedicated to manage and index image files. It provides a high-level widget called `Gimmick!` (*Give me my medical images quick!*) that reads standard image formats (jpg, tif, ...) and medical ones (mhd, hdr, dcm, ...), displays the selected files in a previewer and allows the user to organize images into various trees (default is DICOM tree: patient — series — images) that are stored in SQL databases, hence can be quickly retrieved. `creaMaracasVisu` manages the visualization (2D, 3D) of medical images. Furthermore, it provides various interaction techniques and viewers, which help analyzing the images and the results of their processing. For example, it is possible to use geometric transformations (rotation, translation, scaling), volume rendering, surface rendering and so on, in order to get relevant information from the object of study. At the same time, different 2D slices and 3D views of the same object can be displayed and binary objects (typically segmentation results) can be combined with the original image within the same scene.

3   CreaTools for Thrombus

The Thrombus project aims at modeling multiscale interactions between biological and hemodynamic processes to better understand the thrombosis mechanisms in intracranial aneurysms and how blood-flow diverting stents can influence the healing process. Here we only describe the part of the project related to virtual insertion of the stent into the patient's vessels. This part can be subdivided into three steps that will be described in the sequel, namely: preprocessing, generation of stent geometrical characteristics and virtual stent deployment (Fig. 4).

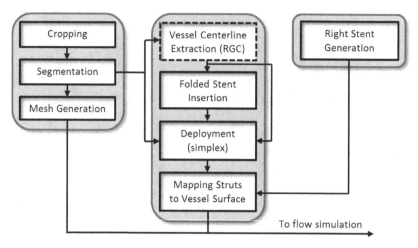

Fig. 4. Workflow to simulate stenting

The preprocessing begins by selecting a volume of interest (VOI) within the original image, both to facilitate the visualization and interaction at the subsequent stages of the workflow and to reduce the computational time. This is performed by the already mentioned Cropping tool. Subsequently, a segmentation separating aneurysm and vessels from the remaining tissues, is performed within the VOI. Various vessel segmentation algorithms can be tested at this stage. We have implemented a method based on optimal thresholding [6] and two alternative versions of the level-sets approach, Chan and Vese [7] and Holtzman-Gazit et al. [8], which require an interactive definition of an initial point within the aneurysm. The separation between the aneurysm and the vessels is performed by an improved version of the subjective-surface method from Sarti et al. [9]. The segmentation algorithms have been wrapped into new black boxes and the necessary interaction tools have been implemented within a GUI. The segmentation results are to be used by fluid dynamics simulation software, which requires a mesh representation of the vascular surface. To transform the segmented volume into a mesh, standard VTK classes have been wrapped into black boxes.

Before simulating the insertion of a stent into vascular structures, it was necessary to generate a representation of a right stent, i.e. with an axis represented by a straight line. The algorithm implemented in C++ has been wrapped into a black box and connected to a dedicated GUI, which allowed the researchers to set the parameters (length and diameter of the stent, number and thickness of the struts etc.), to visually assess the resulting interlaced structure and to validate the correctness of the algorithm. This GUI can now be used as demonstrator, but is not needed in the final integrated software. Conversely, the black box enclosing the algorithm is reused within the workflow.

Simulating the stent deployment requires the following inputs: the surface of the vessels and aneurysm, resulting from the segmentation stage, and the model of a right stent generated as described above. In its current implementation, the process also needs the vessel centerline as a guide wire. The availability of the centerline depends on the segmentation algorithm used at the previous stage, namely the selected level-sets algorithms do not directly provide a centerline. We have therefore implemented an optional centerline extraction process that uses a binary representation of the vessels separated from the aneurysm. The extraction algorithm is based on a generalized cylinder model (RGC) [10,11], which couples a continuous centerline and a continuous surface calculated from a stacking of discrete contours. It has been wrapped into appropriate black boxes. As it requires an interactive definition of the end points, the necessary interaction has been implemented in the GUI, as well as the interaction that allows the user to slide the folded stent model along the centerline and to choose the delivery location. The model is then transformed into a simplex deformable mesh in order to display an animation of the actual deployment, until the stent fits the vessel shape and size [12,13]. The final radius, length and axial shape of the simplex model are used to calculate the actual spatial coordinates to represent the interlaced struts by thin cylinders (Fig. 5). The resulting mesh representation is combined with the mesh representing the vascular surface, so that the whole can be used to simulate the blood flow modified by the presence of the stent.

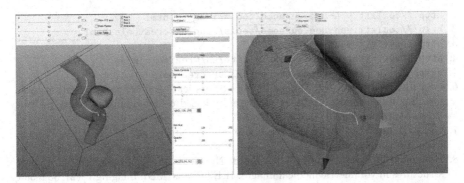

Fig. 5. GUI used to simulate the stent deployment. Left: vessel, aneurysm and folded stent placed along the centerline. Right: unfolded stent within the vessel.

4   Conclusions and Perspectives

The example of the Thrombus project shows several ways in which the CreaTools are used. Existing boxes corresponding to various widgets are used to construct prototype GUIs and demonstrators for image visualization and processing tasks. New algorithms are wrapped into new atomic black boxes, so as to be tested using the appropriate GUIs. Missing visualization and interaction techniques and the corresponding tools are implemented and either added as new boxes or used to enrich the existing widgets. Thoroughly tested reusable sub-pipelines are transformed into complex boxes enriching the whole ToolKit shared within the VPH NoE and beyond, according to the open-source nature of the CreaTools.

The goal of this presentation of the CreaTools project is to encourage the researchers in image processing to download, install and use our software suite. We want to create a real community of users who report bugs, contribute to develop new black boxes and document the existing ones. Simultaneously with debugging, documenting and adding new functionalities, we are working on interoperability. At first, we want to guarantee the connection between BBTK and Slicer3D/CTK, and include Matlab in the workflows. The second development axis is related to distributed computing. We want to provide the image processing workflows with a direct access to computing resources such as clusters and grids. The third axis is virtual reality. We are trying to facilitate the interaction with 3D images, by use of stereovision and remote control devices.

Acknowledgements. This work has been partly funded by ECOS Nord C11S01, Uniandes Interfacultades 06-2010 and Colciencias 1204-519-28996 grants, as well as by the European Community via VPH STREP Thrombus FP7-ICT-2009-6-269966.

References

1. http://toolkit.vph-noe.eu/home/tools/imaging.html
2. http://toolkit.vph-noe.eu/home/tools/imaging/creatools.html
3. http://www.thrombus-vph.eu/
4. http://www.creatis.insa-lyon.fr/site/en/CreaTools_home
5. https://www.projet-plume.org/en/relier/creatools
6. Gan, R., Wong, W.C.K., Chung, A.C.S.: Statistical cerebrovascular segmentation in three-dimensional rotational angiography based on maximum intensity projections. Med. Phys. 32(9), 3017–3028 (2005)
7. Chan, T.F., Vese, L.A.: Active contours without edges. IEEE Trans. Image Proc. 10(2), 266–277 (2001)
8. Holtzman-Gazit, M., Kimmel, R., Peled, N., Goldsher, D.: Segmentation of thin structures in volumetric medical images. IEEE Trans. Med. Imaging 15(2), 354–363 (2006)
9. Sarti, A., Malladi, R., Sethian, J.A.: Subjective surfaces: a geometric model for boundary completion. Int J. Comput. Vision 46, 201–221 (2002)
10. Orkisz, M., Flórez-Valencia, L., Hernández Hoyos, M.: Models, algorithms and applications in vascular image segmentation. Mach. Graph. Vision 17(1/2), 5–33 (2008)
11. Flórez Valencia, L., Azencot, J., Orkisz, M.: Algorithm for Blood-Vessel Segmentation in 3D Images Based on a Right Generalized Cylinder Model: Application to Carotid Arteries. In: Bolc, L., Tadeusiewicz, R., Chmielewski, L.J., Wojciechowski, K. (eds.) ICCVG 2010, Part I. LNCS, vol. 6374, pp. 27–34. Springer, Heidelberg (2010)
12. Flórez-Valencia, L., Montagnat, J., Orkisz, M.: 3D graphical models for vascular-stent pose simulation. Mach. Graph. Vision 13(3), 235–248 (2004)
13. Flórez-Valencia, L., Montagnat, J., Orkisz, M.: 3D models for vascular lumen segmentation in MRA images and for artery-stenting simulation. Innov. Tech. Biol. Med. - RBM 28(2), 65–71 (2007)

Visualization of Multidimensional Data in Explorative Forecast

Diana Domańska[1], Marek Wojtylak[2], and Wiesław Kotarski[1]

[1] Institute of Computer Science, University of Silesia
Będzińska 39, 41200 Sosnowiec, Poland
ddomanska@poczta.onet.pl, kotarski@ux2.math.us.edu.pl
[2] Institute of Meteorology and Water Management (IMGW)
Bratków 10, 40039 Katowice, Poland
monitoring.katowice@imgw.pl

Abstract. The aim of this paper is to present a new way of multidimensional data visualization for explorative forecast built for real meteorological data coming from the Institute of Meteorology and Water Management (IMGW) in Katowice, Poland. In the earlier works two first authors of the paper proposed a method that aggregates huge amount of data based on fuzzy numbers. Explorative forecast uses similarity of data describing situations in the past to those in the future. 2D and 3D visualizations of multidimensional data can be used to carry out its analysis to find hidden information that is not visible in the raw data e.g. intervals of fuzziness, fitting real number to a fuzzy number.

1 Introduction

Knowledge exploration from large sets of data is a challenging task. Additional difficulties arise when the data is multidimensional. Illustrative visualization techniques can help to solve many problems of pattern recognition, image processing, etc. The two classical methods Principal Component Analysis (PCA) [7] and multidimensional scaling (MDS) [13] are used to the reduction of data dimension. Basic PCA is suitable for linear data [14], whereas MDS uses the data distances to the visualization, e.g. Sammon's mapping [11] which minimizes the difference between the inter-point distance in the input space and the corresponding distance in the output space. Neural networks [9] provide another kind of methods for mapping multidimensional data. Also fuzzy set theory and fuzzy techniques [15] have found a promising field of application in digital image analysis. Fuzziness is an intrinsic quality of images and a natural outcome of many imaging techniques [3]. The visualization of multidimensional data, in particular of huge sets of meteorological data, is very difficult task. To show data in an accessible way and simultaneously not to loose too many information we apply different techniques, e.g. [12]. Data visualization using fuzzy numbers allows to present multidimensional medical data [10], meteorological data [4]. Method presented in the paper can also be used for visualization of clustered data, e.g. with multidimensional data clustering methods [8]. Presented solution is innovatory,

L. Bolc et al. (Eds.): ICCVG 2012, LNCS 7594, pp. 63–70, 2012.

easy to use for multidimensional data. Additionally, there exist the possibility of choosing some parameters in the algorithm by an expert, e.g. the accuracy of the obtained outcome data. The visualization presented in the paper is used for explorative forecast. The explorative forecast is understood as the forecast with the use of similarity between the analysed data and the historical data. The forecast of pollution concentrations with the use of the past and present weather forecasts from the COSMO LM model, meteorological situations and historical pollution concentrations is computationally expensive. That is why introduction of visualization is important in the forecasting process and helps to estimate the forecast effectiveness at early forecasting stages.

In the paper we present a method of multidimensional data visualization based on fuzzy numbers. This kind of algorithm enables not only for effective data visualization, but also its analysis. The algorithm of changing a sequence into a fuzzy number (SFN) [5] is very useful because it allows for visualization of huge sets of data, in a clear way, on a single image.

The paper is organized in the following way. In Section 2 we explain the notion of explorative forecast of multidimensional data. Next, in Section 3 we present multidimensional data. Then, in Section 4 we describe multidimensional data analysis. Section 5 presents discussion about the proposed visualization technique and shows some examples. In final section, Section 6, we give some concluding remarks.

2   Explorative Forecast of Multidimensional Data

Explorative forecast is a method based on one of the types of forecasting analogies [1]. For explorative forecast of some phenomena we need the knowledge about this phenomena from the past and present. Additionally, we need the knowledge about some correlated phenomenon with the forecast phenomenon in the future. Using this knowledge we can forecast what will happen with this phenomena for a chosen day in the future. For example, in our model (used to forecast pollution concentrations) we use a knowledge about numerical weather forecasts from the past to the future, meteorological situations and pollution concentrations from the past to present. The element which joins this knowledge is the similarity between phenomena. The graphical representation of this dependency is presented in a diagram (Fig. 1).

We choose a day from the set of weather forecasts in the future. Then, we use the knowledge about similarities between phenomena from the past to present. Finally, we receive forecast of pollution concentrations for a chosen day [4].

3   Multidimensional Data

The input data for the algorithms in the explorative forecast are huge sets of multidimensional data. In particular data could be arranged both in a chronological way, as e.g. for meteorological situations and in an unordered way, as e.g. for medical data. Let us denote the set of multidimensional data (data

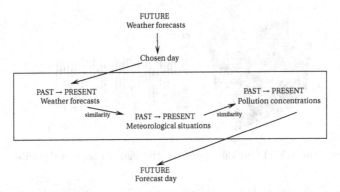

Fig. 1. Explorative forecast of pollution concentrations

cubes) as MS. Each data cube consists of matrices. For $s \in MS$ we have $s = \{s_1, s_2, \ldots, s_n\}, n \in \mathbb{N}$, where $s_i \in \mathbb{R}^{t \times m}$ for $i \in \{1, \ldots, n\}$. So then, computations are performed on data cubes of dimensions $n \times t \times m$. Matrices could be arbitrary ones with one of parameters not necessarily being a time. Also the method do not require that the data is ordered. Rows in matrices from s could have different lengths, i.e. the data is jagged. The left part of Fig. 2 presents example cube filled with data forming a slice of this cube – for n we have a vector of dimension m. Example data, which fill that slice is visible in a graph in the right part of Fig. 2. Parts of the data on the graph lie on each other what causes that the image becomes unreadable.

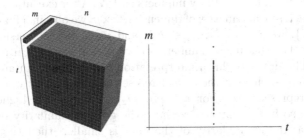

Fig. 2. Data cube (left) and the data from the marked slice of the cube (right)

The left part in Fig. 3 also presents example cube filled with data forming a larger slice of the cube – to fixed n corresponds a matrix of dimensions $t \times m$. Example data which fill that slice is visible in a graph in the right part of Fig. 3. The amount of the data in this graph is larger as in the graph from Fig. 2. That causes that the image is more unreadable. The huge amount of data which we need to visualize and analyse is strongly unclear.

In the further part of the paper we will present a new way of visualization of multidimensional data. The aim of the visualization is for first to see the data in a clear way. For second, determination of the data concentration. For third,

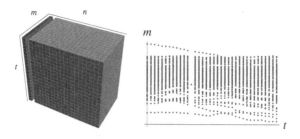

Fig. 3. Data cube (left) and the data from the marked slice of the cube (right)

compare clustered data to the chosen representative what will allow to eliminate points, which similarity to the representative is small.

4   Multidimensional Data Analysis

Basing on experiments we proposed a fuzzy number whose membership function is of the form:

$$\mu(x) = \begin{cases} \exp(\frac{-(x-m_1)^2}{2\cdot\sigma_1^2}) & \text{if } x \le m_1, \\ 1 & \text{if } x \in (m_1, m_2), \\ \exp(\frac{-(x-m_2)^2}{2\cdot\sigma_2^2}) & \text{if } x \ge m_2, \end{cases} \tag{1}$$

where $m_1 \le m_2, \sigma_1 > 0, \sigma_2 > 0$ and $m_1, m_2, \sigma_1, \sigma_2 \in \mathbb{R}$.

Let us denote the family of fuzzy numbers as FN. After execution of the SFN algorithm for each row in a matrix of dimensions $t \times m$ we obtain a fuzzy numbers set $\{A_1, \ldots, A_t\}$, where $t \in \mathbb{N}$, $A_i \in FN$ and μ_i is its membership function for $i = 1, \ldots, t$. For this fuzzy numbers set we perform graphical presentation and analysis. The data graphical interpretation can also contain an additional information. We can check if the considered set of data is a set of data similar to the chosen representative. For $x \in [m_1, m_2]$ we obtain the highest degrees of membership, so in this interval we have the greatest similarity between the considered data. If the similarity of the data is smaller, then the degrees of membership are smaller. So the presentation of the data using fuzzy numbers allows for the elimination of the data which is not similar to oneself. To determine the data concentration around the representative we can use known methods, e.g. k-nearest neighbours with fractional distance [4]. To the determination of the data clustering around the representative we will use the properties of the fuzzy numbers and equation (2). Thanks to that we will be able to determine the fuzziness of a fuzzy number.

$$F_i = \int_{-\infty}^{\infty} \mu_i(x)\mathrm{d}x = \frac{\sqrt{2\Pi}}{2}(\sigma_1^i + \sigma_2^i) + m_2^i - m_1^i, \tag{2}$$

where $i \in \{1, \ldots, n\}$, and $\sigma_1^i, \sigma_2^i, m_1^i, m_2^i \in \mathbb{R}$ are the parameters of the membership function μ_i. For the fuzzy numbers set $\{A_1, \ldots, A_n\}$ using (2) we determine set $F = \{F_1, \ldots, F_n\}$. The fuzziness of the fuzzy numbers tells us if the clustering is good or not. If the fuzziness is small (near to 0) the clustering is good. So we define a threshold value of the fuzziness for which we say that the clustering is good. If the value of the fuzziness is greater than the threshold we calculate new clustering of the data.

5   Experiments and Visualizations

Experiments and visualizations were carried out on a real meteorological data from IMGW. Base of the meteorological situations consists of 5056 measurements, where one measurement corresponds to one day. Measurements are characterized by the hour time step and attributes such as: temperature, pressure, wind speed. In the visualization system we choose parameters which we want to visualize, measurement and the number of hours. Having the chosen measurement in the base we search for group of similar meteorological situations to it. The similarity is characterized by chosen distance ([4]). Next, to verify the similarity of the chosen situations to the measurement we use SFN algorithms, and then we visualize the results. Let t – number of hours ($t = 36$), m – number of measured meteorological situations, n – number of attributes. For the chosen matrices of dimensions $t \times m$, which we want to visualize, we calculate a set of fuzzy numbers with the parameters $m_1, m_2, \sigma_1, \sigma_2$ using the SFN algorithm.

5.1   Graphical Representations of the Obtained Fuzzy Numbers in 3D

From the meteorological data we can obtain only n fuzzy numbers. So there is a need to use interpolation. Example visualizations for the chosen meteorological data parameters are presented in Fig. 4. In these examples we have used Hermite interpolation.

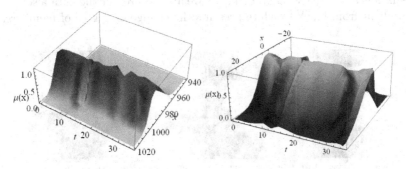

Fig. 4. The results of the visualization method for the: pressure (left), temperature (right) at 15 January 2006

5.2 Graphical Representations of the Similarity of Fuzzy Numbers to the Representative and Their Representative in 3D

To analyse grouped data we add to the visualization a real data plot for the considered day. Thanks to this we will be able to determine the concentration of the presented data to the chosen representative (day). In Fig. 5 we have added representatives in a form of real data plots for the chosen attributes and days.

In Fig. 5 (left) we see large span of the data. The degree of membership $\mu(x)$ is in $(0, 1]$ for $x \in [942, 1020]$ and $\mu(x) = 1$ for $x \in [968, 992]$. Similar situation is in Fig. 5 (center): $\mu(x) \in (0, 1]$ for $x \in [-25, 25]$ and $\mu(x) = 1$ for $x \in [-6, 4]$. In Fig. 5 (right) we see that the data is bounded in the left side. For the majority of hours (except 5) $\mu(x) \in (0, 1]$ if $x \in [-1, 2]$, in particular $\mu(x) = 1$ if $x \in [-1, -0.5]$.

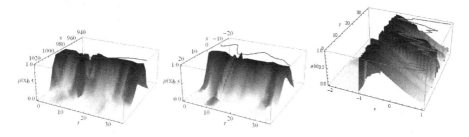

Fig. 5. The results of the visualization method for the: pressure (left), temperature (center) at 17 January 2006, humidity (right) at 29 January 2006 and a real data at this date

5.3 Data Visualization in 2D

Because of the algorithm specification we are able to decide if the chosen data is certain similar to our representative. Taking into account that the presentation of the data is as images with gradient we are able to present the data also in 2D. The gradient from black to white presents the change of degree of membership

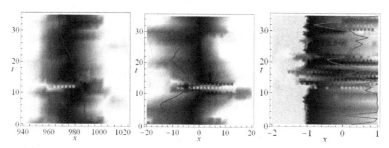

Fig. 6. The similarities for the (fuzzy number): pressure (left), temperature (center) at 17 January 2006, humidity (right) at 29 January 2006 and a real data (curve) at this date

from 1 to 0 for all the data. Fig. 6 present similarities of the chosen data to the representative. Taking into account the used fuzzy number (1) we are able to determine data concentration around the representative. The best data concentration is obtained when the difference between m_1 and m_2 is small. The best if $m_1 = m_2$. The values of σ_1 and σ_2 should be as small as possible. In Fig. 6 we see the representative and data clustering relatively to the representative. The representative in all visualizations holds in the fuzzy numbers scope. The best if the representative overlap with the fuzzy number when $\mu(x) = 1$. In Fig. 6 (left) and (center) we see better similarity of the data to the representative than in Fig. 6 (right).

5.4   Additional Information in the Data Fuzziness Measure Form

Fig. 7 presents the values F_i (fuzziness of a fuzzy number) joined with lines. Thanks to the usage of fuzzy numbers, Hermite interpolation and the fuzziness of a fuzzy number we are also able to see and analyse the similarity of particular elements from the real data group which we visualize. In Fig. 7 (left) we see that the fuzziness is in $[25, 35]$, only one point $t = 12$ has a value equal to 0. The same situation is in Fig. 7 (right). We see that the fuzziness is in $[12, 17]$ and $t = 12$ has value equal to 0. From this data we can infer that the grouping of data is good and the best grouping is for $t = 12$.

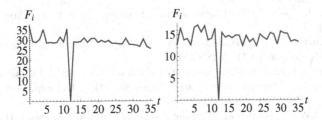

Fig. 7. The fuzziness for the: pressure (left), temperature (right) at 17 January 2006

6   Conclusions

We have presented a meteorological visual analysis. The visualizations are used in system to forecast pollution concentrations. Using fuzzy numbers we are able to present multidimensional data in a 3D, 2D image in a friendly way. Additionally, thanks to the extra information in form of representative we can analyse the visualization and determine data concentration. The use of fuzzy numbers to the visualization and analysis of the data similarity allows us for wide freedom and selection in determination of data concentration around representative.

Using fuzzy numbers to visualize multidimensional data is an interesting approach in graphical presentation. Additionally, we can analyse data and describe fuzziness of the grouped data. This approach can be applied in models to analyse and visualize chaotically disordered data and the fuzziness can decide about the degree of membership of the data to the representative.

The approach presented in this paper can be applied to visualization of any multidimensional data e.g. medical, economical.

References

1. Armstrong, J.S.: Principles of Forecasting, pp. 1–12. Kluwer Academic Publishers, Norwell (2002) ISBN 0-306-47630-4
2. Beyer, K.S., Goldstein, J., Ramakrishnan, R., Shaft, U.: When is "Nearest Neighbour" meaningful? In: Proc. of the 7th Int. Conf. on Database Theory, pp. 217–235 (1999)
3. Bloch, I., Maitre, H.: Fuzzy Mathematical Morphologies: a Comparative Study. Pattern Recognition 28(9), 1341–1387 (1995)
4. Domańska, D., Wojtylak, M.: Application of Fuzzy Time Series Models for Forecasting Pollution Concentrations. Expert Systems with Applications 39(9), 7673–7679 (2012)
5. Domańska, D., Wojtylak, M.: Change a Sequence into a Fuzzy Number. In: Cao, L., Zhong, J., Feng, Y. (eds.) ADMA 2010, Part II. LNCS, vol. 6441, pp. 55–62. Springer, Heidelberg (2010)
6. Domańska, D., Wojtylak, M.: Fuzzy Weather Forecast in Forecasting Pollution Concentrations. In: Proc. of Chaotic Modeling and Simulation International Conference, CD Version (2010)
7. Johnson, R.A., Wichern, D.W.: Applied Multivariate Statistical Analysis. Prentice-Hall, Englewood Cliffs (1992)
8. Koronacki, J., Ćwik, J.: Statistical Learning Systems. Ed. 2, Exit, Warszawa (2008) (in Polish)
9. Ou, G., Murphey, Y.L.: Multi-class Pattern Classification using Neural Networks. Pattern Recognition 40(1), 4–18 (2007)
10. Papageorgiou, E.I.: A New Methodology for Decisions in Medical Informatics using Fuzzy Cognitive Maps Based on Fuzzy Rule-extraction Techniques. Applied Soft Computing 11(1), 500–513 (2011)
11. Sammon, J.W.: A Nonlinear Mapping for Data Structure Analysis. IEEE Transactions on Computers 18(5), 401–409 (1969)
12. Sanyal, J., Dyer, S.Z., Mercer, J., Amburn, A., Moorhead, P., Noodles, R.J.: Noodles: A Tool for Visualization of Numerical Weather Model Ensemble Uncertainty. IEEE Transactions on Visualization and Computer Graphics 16(6), 1421–1430 (2010)
13. Shepard, R.N., Carroll, J.D.: Parametric Representation of Nonlinear Data Structures. In: Krishnaiah, P.R. (ed.) Proceedings of the International Symposium on Multivariate Analysis, pp. 561–592. Academic, New York (1965)
14. Wu, S., Chow, T.W.S.: PRSOM: a New Visualization Method by Hybridizing Multidimensional Scaling and Self-organizing Map. IEEE Transactions on Neural Networks 16(6), 1362–1380 (2005)
15. Zadeh, L.: Fuzzy Sets. Information and Control 8(3), 338–353 (1965)

Automatic Shape Generation Based on Quadratic Four-Dimensional Fractals

Adam Goiński, Tomasz Zawadzki, and Sławomir Nikiel

University of Zielona Góra, Institute of Control & Computation Engineering
Podgórna 50, 65-246 Zielona Góra, Poland
{A.Goinski,T.Zawadzki}@weit.uz.zgora.pl
S.Nikiel@issi.uz.zgora.pl

Abstract. Amorphous shapes have always been a challenge to CG modelers. Apparently natural in look, their topology is hard to retrieve manually. Scientists from different backgrounds have tried to understand and model such phenomena. Fractals belong to the most representative solutions, but still are rare in 3D domain. Methods for generation of fractal objects use mainly quaternion representations for nonlinear systems in four dimensions. In such a case advanced volumetric graphics methods need to be applied to convey multidimensional information. In the paper, we propose a simple and effective approach to use four-dimensional escape-time fractals as automated shape generator. We extend general quadratic fractal maps to four dimensions. The algorithm results in diverse aesthetically balanced volumetric shapes delivered in real time on a modern PC.

Keywords: volumetric graphics, volume rendering, multi-dimensional fractals, procedural modeling, shape synthesis.

1 Introduction

Automated generation of complex and aesthetically pleasing shapes in computer-generated environments is a central concern of the new information technologies. Three-dimensional representations of data and objects are widely accepted in software- and hardware accelerated applications. An important question is how can we improve the shape modeling process through interactive computer graphics? One of the common approaches is to represent models as a set of primitives and build upon them intricate structure but the final object has visible artifacts. The other way is to (re-)create the object with procedural-iterative tools. Fractals as geometrical objects are iterative at their roots. Moreover, they can be multidimensional and can resemble lots of natural phenomena. Fractal properties make them particularly interesting for experimentation in computer graphics. Simplicity of mathematical notation along with geometrical complexity and iterative process of rendering fits well algorithmic nature of computer simulations. The idea of the automated fractal art (object) generation was described by Sprott and Pickover for two dimensions [1] and extended to 3D [2].

L. Bolc et al. (Eds.): ICCVG 2012, LNCS 7594, pp. 71–78, 2012.

The results were so promising that we decided to extend it further to four dimensions to obtain greater diversity of shapes. Four-dimensional fractals are perfect illustration of the chaos theory in practice. They give intuitive insight into four-dimensional representations. Shape construction, animation and multidimensional data visualization completes the list of possible applications of the method. The paper presents features of the fractal modeling tool discussed on the extended procedural shape generation background.

2   Procedural Modeling of 3D Shapes

Complex structures are necessary elements of visually convincing virtual scenes. Buildings [3], whole urban structures [4, 5], terrains [6], clouds [7-15], plants [16] or caves [17-21] can be modeled with help of systems based on automated shape construction. The algorithms that enable full automation of the modeling process help to achieve large savings in the digital media production time and budget. The cinematography and electronic entertainment are a large area that benefits from procedurally generated objects. We can observe a constant development of new methods i.e. merging technology and dynamical systems [22, 23]. The problem of automated shape modeling constitutes an important area of computer graphics activity and has drawn attention of digital media industry for several years. Digital movies have created constant demand for pleasing visual effects in 3D graphics. Apart from pure entertainment interests, shape modeling has the practical use ranging from CAD engineering applications, through scientific visualization to advanced game programming and Virtual Environments. Amorphous shapes are the most challenging ones.

3   Four Dimensional Quadratic Fractal Maps

3.1   Background

Over 20 years ago A. Norton gave some intuitive and straightforward algorithms for the rendering of 3D fractal shapes [24]. For the first time a digital representation of quaternions was presented [25] only a few years later. The quadratic polynomials representing the quaternionic Mandelbrot set were analyzed [26]. That opened new possibilities for generation of complex n-dimensional fractal sets. Among them, Julia quaternions seem to be the most popular ones, perhaps due to the beauty of their symmetrical shapes, e.g. Fig.1 [27]. Some generalization of the fractal representation was necessary to provide access to more diverse shapes, however. D.Rochon presented an interesting solution based on bicomplex number representation [28].

3.2   Generalized Quadratic Fractal Maps

During our experiments with classical 2D escape time fractals we observed that keeping low the degree of nonlinearity in fractal models results in smooth and

Fig. 1. Sample Julia quaternion rendered in POV-RAY

balanced shapes after rendering. A combination of only linear and quadratic functions can equally well describe fractals both in 2D and in 3D [1, 2]. In case of three-dimensional space, fractal solids shapes range from blobs to dust of small elements.

They are always correlated in spaces and never represent noisy behavior. Following interesting results in 3D we extended the quadratic map set to four dimensions. Equation (1) describes linear and quadratic coefficients of the polynomial that transform points in 4D, namely in X,Y,Z and T, standing for the time line. In a similar manner like for 2D and 3D approach, we start the fractal creation by choosing 52 coefficients of the generalized function, limiting ourselves to the simplest (at most quadratic) nonlinearities. Our goal is to automatically and efficiently produce visually interesting structures. The coefficients axx are chosen randomly over the range -1.2 to 1.2 with increments of 0.1. To simplify our nomenclature and for a quick reference, each number is represented as a letter of the alphabet (A=-1.2, B=-1.1, through Y=1.2).

$$
\begin{aligned}
x_{\text{new}} = {} & a_{00}x^2 + a_{01}y^2 + a_{02}z^2 + a_{03}t^2 + a_{04}xy + a_{05}yt \\
& + a_{06}zx + a_{07}tz + a_{08}x + a_{09}y + a_{10}z + a_{11}t + a_{12}; \\
y_{\text{new}} = {} & a_{13}x^2 + a_{14}y^2 + a_{15}z^2 + a_{16}t^2 + a_{17}xy + a_{18}yt \\
& + a_{19}zx + a_{20}tz + a_{21}x + a_{22}y + a_{23}z + a_{24}t + a_{25}; \\
z_{\text{new}} = {} & a_{26}x^2 + a_{27}y^2 + a_{28}z^2 + a_{29}t^2 + a_{30}xy + a_{31}yt \\
& + a_{32}zx + a_{33}tz + a_{34}x + a_{35}y + a_{36}z + a_{37}t + a_{38}; \\
z_{\text{new}} = {} & a_{39}x^2 + a_{40}y^2 + a_{41}z^2 + a_{42}t^2 + a_{43}xy + a_{44}yt \\
& + a_{45}zx + a_{46}tz + a_{47}x + a_{48}y + a_{49}z + a_{50}t + a_{51};
\end{aligned}
\tag{1}
$$

The function is iterated with initial conditions of x, y, z, t taken from the space R4. The output of the algorithm is a 4D set of points with values corresponding to the escape time at a certain position in four-dimensional space. To visualize such a set of one dimension t is considered to be a timeline. Hence, there is a fast way to render such prepared objects. Every time object can be viewed directly as a set of points or as particles with a volumetric element assigned to each point with a selected escape time. It is possible to apply isosurface generation algorithms to obtain a surface of polygons [8]. Volumetric objects represented straightforwardly by points in space need huge amounts of memory to achieve very fine resolution of rendered images (for instance, a high quality rendering with antialiasing and supersampling would need approximately 8GB of memory - a $1000 \times 1000 \times 1000$ set of 8 point voxels with 1 byte color), not to mention problems of lighting and shadows. However, it is possible to render lower-quality fractal solids in real time on a modern PC. The isosurface extraction algorithm can be applied to cut down on the volumetric resolution to meet the real-time criteria. The Marching Cubes algorithm can extract the isosurfaces where the densities are the same (in our case, the escape times). It divides space into a regularly spaced grid. It then considers each cube in the grid, marching through the space one after another. It evaluates the field at each vertex of the cube. If the isosurface passes through the cube, then it is relatively simple to identify inside and outside vertices and to construct a set of triangles approximating the isosurface [8]. The algorithm is very fast and can handle shapes with caves and holes, which is particularly important in case of fractal objects. However, it generates a huge number of triangles for a given surface regardless of its geometrical complexity. It means almost the same number of triangles for a flat surface and for a very complex surface over the same area. Some relaxation algorithms can be used to optimize such a mesh, but their application results in averaging the shape internal differences.

4   Rendering and Visual Appearance

A test application was written in C++ using Win32 API and DirectX 8.1 interface. It takes advantage of 3D accelerators. The application generates fractal objects and represents them as animations throughout the time line (see the image plates). Furthermore, we take special care about saving and re-creating the objects based on the convenient representation as an n-letter code. For a four-dimensional fractal, only 52 chars are needed to save and reconstruct the object in any final volume resolution, in any form and any time. Nonlinear quadratic escape time fractals are purely deterministic. Sample time-changed results are depicted in Figure 2 and 3[1].

We think that prospective users of the approach may enjoy saving such codes and exchanging them with colleagues for artistic evaluation. As it was mentioned before, the huge diversity of fractals shapes is the main advantage of the presented method. The objects seem to behave in more unpredicted manner than the quaternions and hipercomplex fractals. In most cases, they stay coherent in a form throughout the time line, when the Julia sets tend to minimize their

---

[1] More illustrations and the generator itself are available at:
http://fractals.republika.pl

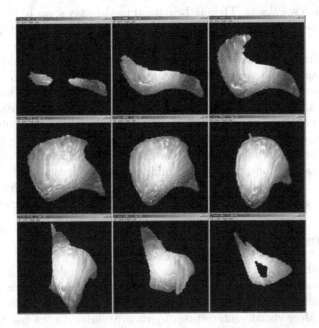

Fig. 2. A sample 3D sections of a 4D quadratic escape time fractal (example A)

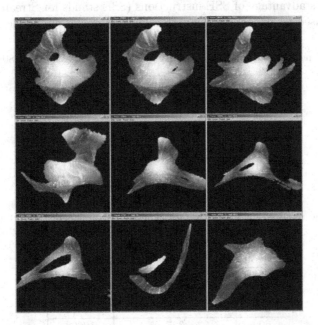

Fig. 3. A sample 3D sections of a 4D quadratic escape time fractal (example B)

structures to a few subsets. The mathematical model may seem to be more convenient because we are accustomed to real numbers rather than to quaternion representation.

Simple nonlinear equations have very complicated solutions. The shapes vary from very balanced and symmetrical to unreal amorphous ones. Some representations look like meteoroids burning up in the Earth atmosphere. Other shapes may be quite similar to those we can obtain in some physical simulations (liquids, evolution of the magnetic field). Finally, more diversity can be obtained by rendering the separated isosurface layers of fractals we create. The layers correspond to different escape times, and outer layers correspond to longer escape times. In high resolutions, the top and middle layers deliver beautiful visual effects and very interesting shapes. We may treat an every layer of a given fractal as a new local generation without change of the global model parameters.

5   Performance

One of our main goals is to achieve close to real-time rendering of 4D fractals. Objects of a reasonable domain (volumetric resolution about: 80x80x80) can be animated smoothly on our test computer (a dual-core processor with hardware acceleration). More visually interesting objects are rendered a few fps (frames per second), what may still be a quite satisfactory performance. The time required to generate a fractal is proportional to the size of a volumetric space. Moreover, the code takes advantage of SSE instructions (SSE stands for Streaming SIMD Extensions, used for enhancing the performance of media applications). In the

Table 1. Time required for fractal frames generation (dimension: 80x80x80x100)

Performance tests		
Frame no.	Time (in milliseconds)	No. of faces
50	513	13276
51	320	12600
56	314	9960
60	307	5564
85	237	8

Table 2. Time required for fractal frames generation (dimension: 100x100x100x100)

Performance tests		
Frame no.	Time (in milliseconds)	No. of faces
50	648	17772
51	343	16576
56	331	13416
60	327	10608
83	208	0

test program, the most time-consuming operation is the generation of fractal points. Hence, the Equation 1 can be easily adapted to such implementation. The following tables represent performance test results obtained for different fractal codes and volume sizes.

6 Conclusions

The method described in the paper brings a fresh idea of the 4D fractal-based shape generation. It is simple yet efficient enough to run in close to real time on a modern PC. From our experiments we can say that general quadratic mappings, when extended to the fourth dimension, behave in the same way as previously observed in 2D and 3D. The most interesting thing of such four-dimensional fractals is that they have well-organized and balanced shapes in all dimensions. The fractal generator can work as an additional tool for modeling complex amorphous shapes. Our future work will focus on efficient isosurface generation algorithms applied along with the triangle mesh optimization and application of various materials and shaders.

References

1. Sprott, J.C., Pickover, C.A.: Automatic generation of general quadratic map basins. Computers & Graphics 19(2), 309–313 (1995)
2. Nikiel, S., Goinski, A.: Generation of volumetric escape time fractals. Computers & Graphics 27(6), 977–982 (2003)
3. Wonka, P., Wimmer, M., Sillion, F., Ribarsky, W.: Instant architecture. ACM Transactions on Graphics 22(3), 669–677 (2003)
4. Parish, Y., Muller, P.: Procedural Modeling of Cities. In: Fiume, E. (ed.) Proceedings (SIGGRAPH 2001), pp. 301–308. ACM Press (2001)
5. Greuter, S., Parker, J., Stewart, N., Leach, G.: Real-time procedural generation of pseudo infinite cities. In: Proceedings (GRAPHITE 2003), pp. 87–95. ACM Press (2003)
6. Peytavie, A., Galin, E., Grosjean, J., Merrilou, S.: Arches: a Framework for Modelling Complex Terrains, Computer Graphics Forum. In: Proceedings EURO-GRAPHICS, vol. 28(2), pp. 457–467 (2009)
7. Bouthors, A., Neyret, F.: Modelling Clouds Shape. In: Proceedings EUROGRAPHICS (2004)
8. Schpok, J., Simons, J., Ebert, D., Hansen, C.: A real-time cloud modeling, rendering, and animation system. In: Symposium on Computer Animation 2003, pp. 160–166 (2003)
9. Dobashi, Y., Kaneda, K., Yamashita, H., Okita, T., Nishita, T.: A simple, efficient method for realistic animation of clouds. In: Proceedings of ACM SIGGRAPH 2000, pp. 19–28 (2000)
10. Ebert, D.: Volumetric procedural implicit functions: A cloud is born. In: Whitted, T. (ed.) SIGGRAPH 97 Technical Sketches Program. ACM SIGGRAPH. Addison Wesley (1997) ISBN 0-89791-896-7
11. Elinas, P., Sturzlinger, W.: Real-time rendering of 3D clouds. Journal of Graphics Tools 5(4), 33–45 (2000)

12. Nishita, T., Nakamae, E., Dobashi, Y.: Display of clouds taking into account multiple anisotropic scattering and sky light. In: Rushmeier, H. (ed.) SIGGRAPH 96 Conference Proceedings, ACM SIGGRAPH, pp. 379–386. Addison Wesley (1996)
13. Harris, M.J., Lastra, A.: Real-time cloud rendering. Computer Graphics Forum 20(3), 76–84 (2001)
14. Gardner, G.Y.: Simulation of natural scenes using textured quadric surfaces. In: Christiansen, H. (ed.) Computer Graphics (SIGGRAPH 1984 Proceedings), vol. 18, pp. 11–20 (1984)
15. Gardner, G.Y.: Visual simulation of clouds. In: Barsky, B.A. (ed.) Computer Graphics (SIGGRAPH 1985 Proceedings), vol. 19, pp. 297–303 (1985)
16. Prusinkiewicz, P., Lindenmayer, A.: The Algorithmic Beauty of Plants, pp. 101–107. Springer (1991) ISBN 978-0387972978
17. Am Ende, B.A.: 3D Mapping of Underwater Caves. IEEE Computer Graphics Applications 21(2), 14–20 (2001)
18. Boggus, M., Crawfis, R.: Procedural Creation of 3D Solution Cave Models. In: Proceedings of the 20th IASTED International Conference on Modelling and Simulation, pp. 180–186 (2009)
19. Boggus, M., Crawfis, R.: Explicit Generation of 3D Models of Solution Caves for Virtual Environments. In: Proceedings of the 2009 International Conference on Computer Graphics and Virtual Reality, pp. 85–90 (2009)
20. Johnson, L., Yannakakis, G.N., Togelius, J.: Cellular Automata for Real-time Generation of Infinite Cave Levels. In: Proceedings of the 2010 Workshop on Procedural Content Generation in Games (PC Games 2010), pp. 1–4 (2010)
21. Schuchardt, P., Bowman, D.A.: The Benefits of Immersion for Spatial Understanding of Complex Underground Cave Systems. In: Proceedings of the 2007 ACM Symposium on Virtual Reality Software and Technology (VRST 2007), pp. 121–124 (2007)
22. Clempner, J.B., Poznyak, A.S.: Convergence method, properties and computational complexity for Lyapunov games. The International Journal of Applied Mathematics and Computer Science 21(2), 349–361 (2011)
23. Di Trapani, L.J., Inanc, T.: NTGsim, A graphical user interface and a 3D simulator for nonlinear trajectory generation methodology. The International Journal of Applied Mathematics and Computer 20(2), 305–316 (2010)
24. Norton, A.: Generation and display of geometric fractals in 3D. Computer Graphics (16), 61–67 (1982)
25. Kantor, I.L.: Hypercomplex Numbers. Springer, New York (1989)
26. Bedding, S., Briggs, K.: Iteration of quaternion maps. Int.Journal Bif. and Chaos, Appl. Sci. Eng. (5), 887–891 (1995)
27. Holbrook, J.A.R.: Quaternionic Fatou-Julia Sets. Annals Sci. Math., Quebcec (11), 79–94 (1987)
28. Rochon, D.: A generalized Mandelbrot set for bicomplex numbers. Fractals 8(2), 355–368 (2000)

Architecture of Algorithmically Optimized MPEG-4 AVC/H.264 Video Encoder

Tomasz Grajek, Damian Karwowski, Adam Łuczak,
Sławomir Maćkowiak, and Marek Domański

Chair of Multimedia Telecommunications and Microelectronics
Poznań University of Technology, Polanka 3, 60-965 Poznań, Poland
{tgrajek,dkarwow,aluczak,smack,domanski}@et.put.poznan.pl

Abstract. Architecture of algorithmically optimized MPEG-4 AVC/
H.264 video encoder is presented in the paper. The paper reveals details
of implementation for the proposed MPEG-4 AVC video encoder. The
presented MPEG-4 AVC encoder was tested with test video sequences
from the point of view of computational performance and coding efficiency. The runtime of the optimized video encoder is 37 to 132 times
smaller relative to runtime of the reference MPEG-4 AVC encoder for
comparable encoder compression performance.

Keywords: Video encoder, MPEG-4 AVC, H.264, fast MPEG-4 AVC.

1 Introduction

Digital video compression is of a great importance in many fields of communication and information technology. A large variety of video compression techniques
were presented in the literature [13]. Nevertheless, hybrid video technology is
mostly used in communication systems and is a cornerstone of all major contemporary video coding standards (MPEG-2, H.263).

Appearance of the high definition television increased requirements for even
higher compression performance. It was the motivation to improve existing video
coding techniques. Intensive research conducted in this area resulted in a new
generation high-performance video encoders like VC-1, AVS, MPEG-4 AVC/
H.264 [1,2,3,9,10]

Among video encoders of a new generation, MPEG-4 AVC/H.264 worldwide
video compression standard is of a great importance due to its superior compression performance in comparison to other technologies [1,2,3,5,7,8]. As a matter
of fact the works are currently in progress on future HEVC technology. Nevertheless, MPEG-4 AVC is currently the most popular solution and is putting into
practice in many areas including limited bandwidth multimedia services, HDTV
television, IPTV and videoconference systems.

2 MPEG-4 AVC Video Compression Technology

The main idea behind MPEG-4 AVC remains unchanged comparing to older video
compression standards (MPEG-2, H.263). MPEG-4 AVC exploits commonly

L. Bolc et al. (Eds.): ICCVG 2012, LNCS 7594, pp. 79–86, 2012.

known hybrid video coding scheme with intra- and inter- frame prediction, transform coding, and entropy coding of residual signal. Nevertheless, relative to older video compression standards each mechanism of a successive video codec was significantly improved. The mechanisms of MPEG-4 AVC exploit the context-based coding paradigm in which, data of an image block is encoded with respect to data of neighboring blocks. Additionally, some new coding tools were also added to MPEG-4 AVC that had not been used in older standards.

Significant improvements were put to intra- prediction mechanism. In order to efficiently represent intra-predicted blocks of an image, 26 prediction modes were de-fined that allow to perform prediction of an image content in 16x16 luma blocks (4 modes), 8x8 luma blocks (9 modes), 4x4 luma blocks (9 modes) and chroma blocks (4 modes). Each predictor realizes idea of context-based coding by the use of data from neighboring blocks. Depending on local content of an image, one of 26 predictors is chosen by encoder.

Mechanism of inter- frame prediction is also much more sophisticated relative to older encoders. In order to adapt to local content of an image, inter- frame prediction is realized in blocks of variable size. MPEG-4 AVC allows partition of a macroblock into 16x16, 16x8, 8x16, 8x8, 8x4, 4x8, 4x4 blocks and perform inter-frame prediction independently in each block. Precision (accuracy) of motion-compensated prediction was additionally increased by the use of many reference frames (up to 16). Each 16x16, 16x8, 8x16 and 8x8 block of a macroblock can use its individual reference frame. Concurrent using of many reference frames is also possible in a weighted prediction mode. Apart from that, MPEG-4 AVC realizes motion-compensated prediction with quarter-pixel accuracy, which reduces energy of residual signal.

Residual signal that is a result of intra-/inter- frame prediction is finally processed with transform coding scheme using an integer, DCT-like transformation and quantization of transform coefficients. In order to extra reduce statistical dependency that exists within data after quantization, entropy coding is used. MPEG-4 AVC exploits two adaptive entropy coding methods: Context-based Adaptive Variable Length Coding (CAVLC) together with Exp-Golomb codes and Context-based Adaptive Binary Arithmetic Coding (CABAC) [4]. These techniques make a major step forward in the field of entropy coding.

Quantization of transform coefficients allows flexible control of the bitrate but also leads to blocking artifacts in reconstructed images. In order to reduce this annoying effect, deblocking filter is used in a prediction loop of both the encoder and the decoder. This is a new tool, that improves subjective quality of the decoded images.

3   Research Problem

Application of the context-based coding methods in MPEG-4 AVC leads to achieving high compression performance of encoder. Nevertheless, the context-based coding scheme makes the algorithms computationally intensive, irregular, and it is extremely difficult to perform computations in parallel in a such case.

Moreover, a great number of different coding modes used in MPEG-4 AVC (26 modes for intra- prediction only, inter prediction performed in blocks of variable size) makes the mechanism of encoder control really complex.

The abovementioned facts cause high computational complexity of MPEG-4 AVC video encoder and great difficulties in realization of real-time compression system even for modern high performance multimedia processors.

An important research problem to solve is the architecture of optimized MPEG-4 AVC video encoder that will be able to perform (near) real-time video compression of standard definition signal when operating on x86 platform. As a matter of fact there already exists fast realizations of MPEG-4 AVC encoder with both the low- and high- level optimizations of encoder program code [14]. Nevertheless, an architecture of the optimized High Profile MPEG-4 AVC encoder with algorithmic optimizations of functional blocks makes the topic of the paper. There is proposed the original structure of such an optimized encoder. Presented MPEG-4 AVC encoder was realized at Chair of Multimedia Telecommunications and Microelectronics as an implementation project.

4   Algorithmically Optimized MPEG-4 AVC Encoder

In order to reduce the number of processor operations when encoding a video, the optimized structure of MPEG-4 AVC video encoder was proposed. The encoder was implemented from scratch in high level C programming language. All computationally complex functional blocks of encoder were algorithmically optimized towards speed. Functional blocks of the encoder were optimized taking into account both the specificity of MPEG-4 AVC technology (hybrid coding scheme, application of context-based coding mechanisms) and general features of x86 target platform (relatively small size of fast cache-memory in a processor and ability to use vector operations). The goal was to propose highly optimized towards speed version of video encoder intended for single processor platforms.

From the encoding time point of view the following parts of MPEG-4 AVC encoder are particularly crucial: access time to context data, the way of motion estimation, the way of encoder mode selection, realization of entropy coding methods. In order to speed up encoding process, all these parts of video encoder were highly optimized in the proposed architecture of MPEG-4 AVC encoder.

4.1   Implementation of Dedicated Data Buffer in Encoder

MPEG-4 AVC exploits context-based coding techniques, in which data of an image block is encoded with respect to information from neighboring blocks (with respect to context data). The location of the neighbors in an image is not fixed. Depending on the coding mode chosen for the current image block (frame mode or field mode) the coordinates of left, upper, upper-left, upper-right neighboring blocks can be different within an image. Therefore, these coordinates must be calculated each time before encoding successive blocks of an image for each syntax element that is encoded using context-based paradigm. Additionally, changing coordinates of neighbors results in copying the context data from different parts of an image. It makes the mechanism of preparing the context information in encoder very irregular and complex.

In order to optimize this process, dedicated data buffers were implemented in encoder for samples of an image as well as for other context information. The structure of dedicated data buffers were presented in Fig. 1

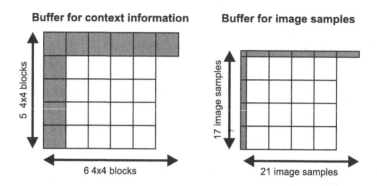

Fig. 1. Dedicated buffers for context data in the proposed optimized video encoder

In Fig. 1 data of a current mackroblock are stored in white blocks whereas context information is stored in grey blocks. Prior to encoding a given mackroblock, the buffers must be filled with context data taken from appropriate parts of an image. This way complex process of calculating the context information is carried out only once per mackroblock and not for individual syntax element separately. Once the buffers are filled in, context data can easily be reached by simple calling within dedicated memory. Besides, due to small size of buffers (data related to one macroblock only) they can be put into processor's cache memory which significantly reduces processing time.

4.2   Fast Motion-Compensated Prediction

Motion estimation is one of the most computationally intensive parts of contemporary video encoders. In MPEG-4 AVC motion-compensated prediction for inter-coded frames can be performed using 1-pel, $\frac{1}{2}$-pel, and $\frac{1}{4}$-pel accuracy. It strongly affects computational complexity of video encoder. In order to speed up the process, fast mechanisms of motion estimation were used in the proposed implementation of encoder [13]. In series of experiments, two such motion estimation methods were chosen: hexagonal motion estimation method for 1-pel accuracy and diamond motion estimation for $\frac{1}{2}$- and $\frac{1}{4}$-pel accuracy. Moreover, interpolation to $\frac{1}{2}$-pel is performed once for a whole image and stored in a memory, whereas interpolation to $\frac{1}{4}$-pel is performed on the fly. Such an approach is a tradeoff between speed, memory requirements, and access time to memory.

4.3 Fast Encoder Control Mechanism

High compression performance of MPEG-4 AVC was obtained by exploiting a huge number of different coding modes that can be adaptively switched depending on local content of an image. Nevertheless, it also strongly affects complexity of video encoder. Optimal solution (from the coding efficiency point of view) is to encode image blocks using each of individual coding mode separately in order to choose the best mode. However, such a solution would result in gigantic complexity of encoder and cannot be used in most applications.

In the proposed architecture of MPEG-4 AVC encoder fast control mechanism was used. This mechanism was worked out during experimental research taking into consideration statistics of selecting the individual coding modes in MPEG-4 AVC for natural video sequences.

In the proposed control mechanism, the idea of 'Early SKIP' mode was used. At the beginning, the encoder tries to encode a block using SKIP coding mode. SKIP mode - mackroblock is encoded with one bit only - there is no residual data for both the transform coefficients and the motion information. If the SKIP mode turns out to be good enough (it does not mean optimal) for the current macroblock, no other coding modes are tested. In the opposite situation, 16x16 and 8x8 coding modes are tested. If 8x8 coding mode does not improve compression (gives higher coding cost than for 16x16 mode), 16x16 coding mode is chosen. In the situation that 8x8 mode gives improvement (relative to 16x16), successive smaller divisions of 8x8 block are checked to test modes that operate on smaller blocks. The criterion for taking a decision is a result of simple filtering of an image using Sobel filter. The Sobel filter masks used to evaluate complexity of a texture were presented in Fig. 2

Fig. 2. Sobel filter masks

If the result of filtering is less than a predefined threshold Th, coding modes for blocks smaller than 8x8 are not tested.

4.4 Optimized Entropy Encoders

In the proposed architecture of encoder both variants of entropy encoder defined by MPEG-4 AVC standard were fully optimized and implemented (i.e. CAVLC+Exp-Golomb and CABAC). For the purpose of the paper, CABAC algorithm is more important.

CABAC algorithm realizes context-based entropy encoding of syntax elements. Previous research of the author on this topic revealed, that data statistics modeling is a bottleneck of contemporary adaptive arithmetic encoders (more than 60% computations in entropy encoder). Therefore, the main optimization technique applied in this part of encoder was reducing the access time to all context data. It was achieved by adapting the implementation of CABAC to exploit the dedicated buffers of context information that were presented in section 4.1. As a result, the procedure of calculating the context data was accelerated several times. Other parts of CABAC (binarizarion and arithmetic encoder core) were implemented on the basis of C pseudo-code presented in the MPEG-4 AVC standard recommendation [1].

5   Methodology of Experiments

Computational complexity of the optimized MPEG-4 AVC encoder was thoroughly investigated with set of test video sequences. The goal was to explore the influence of algorithmic optimizations that were made in the video encoder on its encoding speed. For that reason, commonly available JM reference software of the MPEG-4 AVC standard with no algorithmic optimizations of encoder functional blocks was used as the anchor (version JM 13.2 of the software) [12]. Average encoding times of a frame were measured for both the optimized and the reference encoders. In order to obtain reliable experimental results, equivalent coding tools were activated in both versions of encoders. Experiments were done according to the following encoding scenario:

- Full HD test video sequences were used: BasketballDrive, BQTerrace, Cactus, Kimono1, ParkScene. The sequences were recommended by groups of experts ISO/IEC MPEG and ITU VCEG as a test material for research on new video compression technologies [6].
- Structure of group of pictures (GOP) was set to IBBPBBPBBPBBPBBP
- Experiments were done for a wide range of bitrates using different values of quantization parameter ($QP = 22, 27, 32, 37$). This results in the quality of a reconstructed video from excellent (QP=22) to very poor ($QP = 37$).
- CABAC entropy encoder was used.
- Threshold Th for fast control mechanism was set to 20000 for macroblocks on image border and 25000 for macroblocks on inside the image.
- The following platform was used: Intel(R) Core(TM) i7 CPU 950@3.07 GHz, 12 GB RAM, Windows 7 64-bit.

The two encoders produce two slightly different bitstreams (from the viewpoint of their size and quality of reconstructed videos). The degree of bitstreams variation was measured with Bjøntegaard metric [11]. The metric allows to compare the RD curves of two encoders in terms of bitrate reduction and PSNR gain based on 4 RD points (for $QP = 22, 27, 32, 37$ in experiments). Such tests were done for luma (Y) component.

6   Experimental Results

Experiments revealed, that it is possible to significantly speed-up computations in encoder using algorithmic optimizations of methods. Detailed results of encod-

Table 1. Average encoding times of a frame for the reference and the optimized MPEG-4 AVC encoders in a function of QP value. The factor ratio is a ratio of run times of the reference and the optimized encoders respectively. **BD-Rate** represents average percentage difference of bitstream sizes for optimized and reference encoders respectively. **BD-PSNR Y** represents average difference for PSNR measure for sequences decoded with optimized and reference encoders respectively.

Sequence	BD-Rate [%]	BD-PSNR Y [dB]	QP	Avg. encoding time [ms/frame] Ref	Fast AVC	Ratio
BasketballDrive	1.07	-0.02	22	18 029	406	44.41
			27	16 869	277	60.90
			32	16 489	203	81.23
			37	16 314	158	103.25
BQTerrace	1.63	-0.05	22	17 619	475	37.09
			27	16 427	293	56.06
			32	15 866	176	90.15
			37	15 779	119	132.60
Cactus	2.30	-0.05	22	17 143	401	42.75
			27	15 923	242	65.80
			32	15 592	169	92.26
			37	15 414	129	119.49
Kimono1	-1.70	0.05	22	16 911	346	48.88
			27	16 359	252	64.92
			32	16 094	185	86.99
			37	15 895	140	113.54
ParkScene	-2.01	0.07	22	16 760	386	43.42
			27	16 266	272	59.80
			32	15 989	183	87.37
			37	15 657	129	121.37
					Average	77.61

ing times for none-optimized (reference) and optimized encoders were presented in Table 1.

Results show extraordinary computational performance of the optimized encoder relative to the reference version. The optimized encoder is 37 to 132 times faster relative to the reference version. Higher run time ratios were noticed for higher value of QP (lower bitrate cases) due to smaller contribution of CABAC entropy encoder run time in total encoding time. The optimized software decreases the encoder run time 77 times on average in comparison to the reference encoder. What is very important, encoder speed-up was achieved with no quality degradation of the encoded sequence and with no essential increase of the bitstream size. For *BasketballDrive*, *BQTerrace* and *Cactus* relatively small increase of bitrate (1.07% - 2.3%) was observed for optimized encoder - this is equivalent to really small decrease of PSNR measure (0.02dB - 0.05dB) relative to the reference encoder. In the case of *Kimono1* and *ParkScene* sequences the optimized encoder produced bitstream of a size smaller by 1.7% - 2.01%

for equivalent video quality (which corresponds to 0.05db - 0.07dB increase of PSNR for equivalent bitrate).

7   Conclusions

Computational performance of MPEG-4 AVC video encoder can be significantly improved when applying algorithmic optimizations for encoder functional blocks. Optimization of encoding mechanisms allows to speed up encoder runtime by a factor of 37 to 132, depending on encoding scenario. On average, the throughput of optimized encoder is 77 times higher comparing to performance of an none-optimized version of encoder. What is very important, the optimized encoder has virtually the same compression performance as the reference encoder. Authors see the possibilities of further improving the computational performance of encoder when doing low-level optimizations of encoder program code together with multi-thread programming techniques.

References

1. ISO/IEC 14496-10 (MPEG-4 AVC) / ITU-T Rec. H.264: Advanced Video Coding for Generic Audiovisual Services (2010)
2. Special issue on H.264/AVC video coding standard. IEEE Trans. on Circuits and Systems for Video Technology 13 (July 2003)
3. Richardson, I.E.G.: H.264 and MPEG-4 Video Compression. In: Video Coding for Next-generation Multimedia. Wiley (2003)
4. Marpe, D., Schwarz, H., Wiegand, T.: Context-based Adaptive Binary Arithmetic Coding in the H.264/AVC Video Compression Standard. IEEE Trans. on Circuit and Systems for Video Technology 13(7), 620–636 (2003)
5. Golston, J., Rao, A.R.: Video Compression: System Trade-Offs with H.264, VC-1 and Other Advanced CODECs. Texas Instruments (2006)
6. ISO/IEC JTC1/SC29/WG11 and ITU-T SG16 Q.6: Joint Call for Proposals on Video Compression Technology. MPEG doc. N11113, Kyoto, Japan (2010)
7. Kamaci, N., Altunbasak, Y.: Performance Comparison of the Emerging H.264 Video Coding Standard with the Existing Standards. In: IEEE Int. Conference on Multimedia and Expo (ICME), Baltimore, USA, vol. 1(6-9), pp. 345–348 (2003)
8. Sullivan, G., Wiegand, T.: Video Compression - From Concepts to the H.264/AVC Standard. Proceedings of the IEEE, Special Issue on Advances in Video Coding and Delivery 93(1), 18–31 (2005)
9. Society of Motion Picture and Television Engineers: VC-1 Compressed Video Bit-stream Format and Decoding Proces. SMPTE 421M-2006 (2006)
10. Audio Video Coding Standard Workgroup of China (AVS): The Standards of People's Republic of China GB/T 20090.2-2006, Information Technology - Advanced Coding of Audio and Video - Part 2:Video (2006)
11. Bjøntegaard, G.: Calculation of Average PSNR Differences between RD curves. ITU-T SG16/Q6, 13th VCEG Meeting, Doc. VCEG-M33, Austin, USA (2001)
12. H.264/AVC software coordination site, http://iphome.hhi.de/suehring/tml
13. Woods, J.W.: Multidimensional Signal, Image, and Video Processing and Coding. Academic Press (2012)
14. x264 video codec, http://www.videolan.org/developers/x264.html

A Prototype of Unmanned Aerial Vehicle for Image Acquisition

Paweł Iwaneczko, Karol Jędrasiak, Krzysztof Daniec, and Aleksander Nawrat

Institute of Automatic Control, Silesian University of Technology
Akademicka 16, 44-100, Gliwice, Poland
jedrasiak.karol@gmail.com

Abstract. We present the prototype of unmanned aerial vehicle (UAV) as a platform for multispectral acquisition. We are connecting the real-world simulation environment and control software to perform flight tests in SIL simulation. The full control system is based on the cascade of PI controllers with Anti-Windup mechanism, which stabilize the aircraft in the virtual reality. Stabilization of angular speed reduces problems connected with video disruptions. In this article we are presenting all implemented autonomous algorithms, which are based on ENU coordinate system (commonly used in aviation). Simulations are performed in Prepar3D® from Lockheed Martin which also allows to perform visual and thermal images processing. The prototype successfully completed all the test flights and is ready for various applications.

1 Introduction

Unmanned flying objects are at the moment gaining a lot of interest in both the military and civil organizations. One of the most widespread application of these objects is patrolling and monitoring of the specific areas. The scale of diversity in this case is very large. Starting from searching for injured or missing persons in areas inaccessible to humans (An example could be the organization of Polish GOPR - Mountain Rescue). Another possible application is patrolling the borders in the search for illegal immigrants or illegal road transport. It also possible to patrol military bases or various types of factories. A very interesting application is monitoring stadiums and sport facilities where mass events are held. Finally, it is obvious that unmanned objects are ideal for tracking ground, water and sometimes even the air targets.

Unmanned objects of type "DELTA" are far less expensive and has significantly less complex structure than the those of airplanes, the quad-copter or helicopters. They are also (of course taking into account the scale), lighter and more economical in terms of used energy, so they can fly longer and farther than other types of flying objects. Flying wing objects appear to be very stable in the air, and therefore can be used for the vision acquisition and processing. Despite the above mentioned advantages, prototyping autonomous and flight control algorithms for micro aircraft is still too expensive, time consuming and requires

L. Bolc et al. (Eds.): ICCVG 2012, LNCS 7594, pp. 87–94, 2012.

many assumptions a priori. For this reason, to prototype these algorithms and also to perform tests in the SIL simulation (*Software-In-the-Loop*) we use the simulation environment Prepar3D® from Lockheed Martin. Simulator precisely mapped physics, it allows the creation and configuration of the object models, provides a reading of existing sensory variables and allows you to remote control of these objects in virtual space. It is important that this environment has a very detailed visualization. Visualization includes the real terrain and randomly distributed buildings, vegetation and roads. On these roads is randomly generated road traffic, and in the air is simulated air traffic. The above mentioned elements are sufficient to perform studies with the use of cameras to detect, identify and avoid obstacles in unfamiliar areas.

2   Literature Review

prototyping the control algorithms for unmanned objects using a simulation in the SIL-loop (Software-In-the-Loop) and in the HIL loop (Hardware-In-the-Loop) is widely used among the many institutions from the area of aviation and beyond. To explain, the SIL-loop control is to control a physical process model (simulator) using the software, which is a model of the regulator, which was run on the same hardware platform. In the process in HIL-loop simulation takes part a real controller, which communicates with the simulator through the appropriate interfaces. In the „American Institute of Aeronautics and Astronautics" [1] introduces the HIL-loop simulation. LQR regulator controlled the aircraft mathematical model in Matlab/Simulink® environment. Another important example is the work of Eric N. Johnson and Sumit'a Mishra [2], which uses the SIL and HIL-loop control and flight simulator with visualization. With mathematical model implemented in Matlab / Simulink ® we can also be meet in articles [3] and [4]. Used there simulator „6-DOF" is characterized by highly realistic, because it includes the basic atmospheric model, gravity and Earth's magnetic field. Authors in order to highlight their research, visualize their results in „FlightGear Flight Simulator". Another institution, which deal with unmanned objects is the Procerus Technologies company [5],which has developed its own electronic system (Kestrel Autopilot), which allows to control a real object and perform tests in a HIL-loop. Control is based on a PID controllers cascade, and the autopilot can be used to control objects of flying wing type. Autopilot Kestrel is used by many important organizations. One of them is University of Bialystok [6], who designed the system of robust optimal control based on method H-infinity and μ-Synthesis. Unmanned objects, in order to move fully autonomous, they must have appropriate sensory systems and algorithms, allowing to avoid obstacles in unfamiliar areas. A very good solution proves to be the real images processing from on-board cameras. Such studies were performed and might be found in the work of Bialystok Technical University [7],and as well at the University of Berkeley [8,9]. It is essential to design robust control algorithms and prototype them using the virtual reality in order for future application in UAVs capable of image processing [10] and visual surveillance [11].

3   Prototyping the Algorithms in the Prepar3D®

All algorithms for autonomous flight and controllers cascade have been designed and tested using a simulation environment Prepar3D ® from Lockheed Martin. Flying object model was parameterized in such a way, to reflect the real object by its physical, geometrical and (most importantly) dynamic properties. Using real-world simulations greatly speeds up the testing of any algorithms and reduces the costs associated with the failed tests on real objects. This simulator also allows us to create and test all the video processing algorithms, from video and thermal cameras and use of augmented reality. These algorithms could be used for targets tracking, avoiding obstacles, and collision avoidance.

3.1   Model Description

Flying wing aircrafts structure is different from common aircraft constructions. They have no tail, and specified fuselage, and the whole bearing surface is the only wing. As the wing is an indispensable and necessary part of any aircraft, eliminating all other components, theoretically results the maximum reduction of air resistance. In this type of objects significant difference also plays a control. In the aircraft of type „DELTA" controls are so called elevons. It's a 2 independent ailerons on the left and right wings, which, depending on the settings can be regarded as a rudder or ailerons as in normal airplane. Importantly, the most common seen structures have the engine located on the back and to move wing into motion, it produce a pushing power. In the following figure (Fig. 1) you can see the input-output model of the flying wing unmanned object.

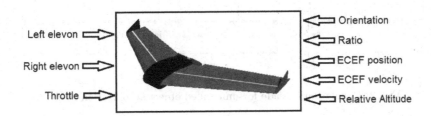

Fig. 1. Input-output model of the flying wing unmanned object

For purposes of autonomous control in the SIL simulation we use the following sensory variables:

- geographical position in ECEF form [12] (Earth-Centered, Earth-Fixed), that is position in Cartesian coordinates connected at the midpoint of the Earth. It is showed in the *(x,y,z)*,
- velocity vector in ECEF form (v_x, v_y, v_z),
- altitude relative to airport (h),
- orientation (3 Euler angles α, β, γ),
- rates (3 angular velocities $\omega_\alpha, \omega_\beta, \omega_\gamma$).

3.2   Regulators System

Object control and stabilization is based on the PI controllers. [13] The following formula describes the control dependence of the controller error:

$$u_i = k_p(e_i + \frac{h}{T_i} \sum_i e_i), \qquad (1)$$

where: u_i – controller output at the moment i, e_i – error, controller input at the moment i, k_p – controller proportional gain, T_I – controller integrator gain, h – delay time. Stabilization algorithm uses seven controllers, of which three are basic, which calculates the direct control for the actuators, and four are master, which calculates the set points for other controllers. In following figure (Fig. 2) you can analyze the full regulation cascade.

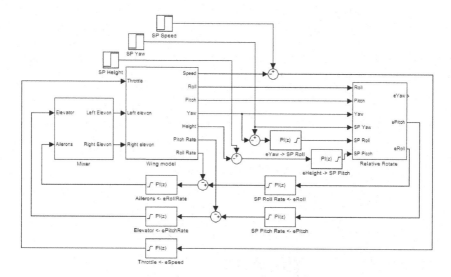

Fig. 2. Regulation cascade for unmanned object stabilization mode

4   Autonomous Flight

Fully autonomous flight is one that must take place without operator intervention. Such a flight often consists of a sequence of geographical position that the object should reach while avoiding collisions with the environment. The avoidance route is constructed by a conversion of geodetic position (ECEF) to ENU coordinates (*East, North, Up*) [14,15]. This transformation determines vector (connecting the reference and destination position) on the tangent plane to the Earth's surface. This is illustrated in (Fig. 3). Obstacle and collision avoidance can be achieved by modifying the object route by processing the images from on-board cameras. There are three additional algorithms for the most crucial operations: circling, landing and taking-off.

4.1 Circling Algorithm

Because of manoeuvrability and stability of the "DELTA" object, circling command is used in the take-off and landing algorithms. The algorithm determines the destination ENU coordinates from the tangent to the circle of object's movement. The algorithm also determines the required turn direction and remaining distance in the circle. The algorithm is described in below listed formulas, while in Fig.3 is shown its graphical interpretation.

$$
\begin{aligned}
T &= sign(mod(\beta - \alpha + \pi, 2\pi) - \pi), & n_{MA} &= n_{CA} - TRsin(\alpha), \\
e_{MA} &= e_{CA} + TRcos(\alpha), & \beta_1 &= atan2(e_{MA}, n_{MA}) - T\alpha_1, \\
n_{BA} &= |AM|cos(\alpha_1)cos(\beta_1), & e_{BA} &= |AM|cos(\alpha_1)sin(\beta_1), \\
d &= mod(atan2(e_{MB}, n_{MB}) - atan2(e_{MC}, n_{MC}), 2\pi)R,
\end{aligned}
\tag{2}
$$

where: n - north axis, e - east axis, A - object actual position, R - circle radius, T - turn direction, α - setpoint outlet direction value, β - direction to the circle end point (C), β_1 - direction to the circle start point (B), M - center of the circle, α_1 - angle between $\overrightarrow{AM}$ and $\overrightarrow{AB}$, d - the remaining distance in the circle.

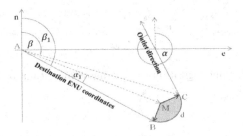

Fig. 3. Circling algorithm graphical interpretation

4.2 Take-off and Landing Algorithms

The landing algorithm is based on the landing in the chimney. This is very useful in the high forests urban and mountain areas. This command consists of moving around a circle with a simultaneous decreasing the height. At the beginning the object must appear over the airport at the desired height. When this happens, it moves in a circle, and the height is calculated on the basis of the remaining distance d. This is illustrated in Fig. 4. When the plane will be at a height below 5m it begins the approach to landing, which is determined by the exponential function.

Before starting the take-off a checklist should be performed, in which among oth-ers: is to run the power, connect the object to the base station, calibration of gyro and a pressure sensors. This applies only to the real object, while for the SIL-loop simula-tion this is provided by the Prepar3D® simulator. After preparing the object for flight operator throws the wing from the hand, and then the object starts the rising sequence in the chimney, what means it is circling

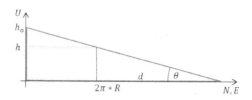

Fig. 4. Determining the height in landing algorithm

around a circle with increasing the height. When the plane reaches the height which was set by the operator, the take-off com-mand is considered as finished. In brief, the take-off procedure is the opposite of landing command. In the figure below have been illustrated the take-off and landing algorithms.

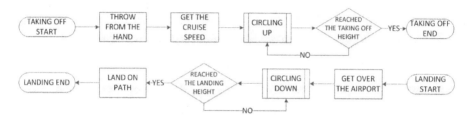

Fig. 5. Take-off and landing algorithms: a) taking-off algorithm, b) Landing algorithm

5   Tests

The presented prototype was build and tested during flight tests. In the screen-shot below (Fig. 6a) is presented an control application. In the chart in part „A" are plotted: the current roll angle (α), current roll rate (ω_α), and their set point values: α_{sp} and $\omega_{\alpha_{sp}}$. The object was performing the route made up of 4 waypoints, as is illustrated on the map in the part „B". In the chart around 138 second may be noticed a large change of the set point roll angle, which took place after the first waypoint. Then we see the aircraft return to the horizontal position and around 160 seconds, we see the situation of turn forcing after passing second waypoint.

The base station application was implemented in C# using the WPF graphics engine. Telemetry data can be presented on diagnostic charts, in the map object context menu on the map module and on gauges.

After the SIL-loop simulation was successfully completed the presented algorithms were implemented in the hardware and the prototype was tuned during flight tests. The same base station was used for both simulation and real flights. All test flights (fig. 6b-c) were successfully ended and the results are very promising.

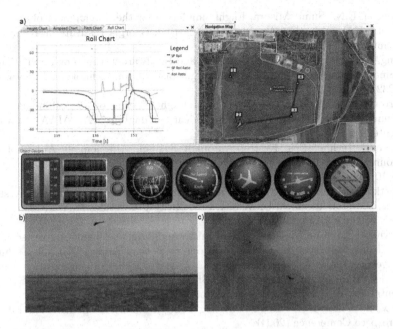

Fig. 6. a) Base station, A – Chart ($\alpha_{sp}, \alpha, \omega_{\alpha_{sp}}, \omega_\alpha$, B – map module „Google Maps",
C – gauges and controls of selected object. The photographs of the object during flight
tests. b) after taking-off, c) during circling.

6   Conclusions

In the article a prototype unmanned aerial vehicle for image acquisition was presented. It is a wing type aerial vehicle. It can be controlled both manually and
auton-omously using the ground base station. The UAV was tested using two
different types of loopbacks: SIL (software in the loop) and HIL (hardware in
the loop). The auton-omous algorithm for controlling the prototype is described
in detail. After prototyping in virtual reality the UAV was tested during real
flight tests. All tests were passed successfully therefore we can announce that
it is possible to acquire aerial videos in real time by the wing type unmanned
flying vehicle described in the article.

In the future we plan to mount to the UAV various gimbals and test image
stabilization algorithms.

Acknowledgements. This work was supported by the National Centre of Research and Development (NCBiR) project with registration number 178438.

References

1. Mueller, E.R.: Hardware-in-the-loop Simulation Design for Evaluation of Unmanned Aerial Vehicle Control Systems, NASA Ames Research Center, Moffett
   Field, CA, 94035

2. Johnson, E.N.: Sumit Mishra, Flight simulation for the development of an experimental UAV, School of Aerospace Engineering, Georgia Institute of Technology, Atlanta, GA 30332-015
3. Jung, D.: Panagiotis Tsiotras, Modeling and Hardware-in-the-Loop Simulation for a Small Unmanned Aerial Vehicle, Georgia Institute of Technology, Atlanta, GA, 30332-0150
4. Sorton, E.F., Hammaker, S.: Simulated Flight Testing of an Autonomous Unmanned Aerial Vehicle Using Flight-Gear, Arlington, VA, AIAA 2005-7083 (September 2005)
5. Procerus Technologies, Kestrel Autopilot System, Autonomous Autopilot and Ground Control for Small Unmanned Aerial Vehicles, UAV Flight Guide, Version 1.8 10/27/08
6. Mystkowski, A.: Robust control of unmanned aerial vehicle - simulation investigations, Biaystok Technical University, Prace Instytutu Lotnictwa, Warszawa (2011) ISSN 0509-6669 216, 82-102
7. Kownacki, C.: Control algorithm of micro aerial vehicle flight in streetsćanyons based on vision system, Faculty of Mechanical Engineering, Biaystok Technical University, Biaystok
8. McGee, T.G.: Obstacle Detection for Small Autonomous Aircraft Using Sky Segmentation. In: Robotics and Automation, ICRA 2005 (2005)
9. Frew, E.: Vision-Based Road Following Using a Small Autonomous Aircraft. In: Aerospace Conference (2004),
10. Jędrasiak, K., Nawrat, A.: Image Recognition Technique for Unmanned Aerial Vehicles. In: Bolc, L., Kulikowski, J.L., Wojciechowski, K. (eds.) ICCVG 2008. LNCS, vol. 5337, pp. 391–399. Springer, Heidelberg (2009)
11. Jedrasiak, K., Nawrat, A.: SETh System Spation-Temporal Object Tracking Using Combined Color And Motion Features. Electrical And Computer Engineering Series, pp. 67–72 (2009)
12. Zhou, Y.: Sensor alignment with Earth-centered Earth-fixed (ECEF) coordinate system. IEEE Transactions on Aerospace and Electronic Systems (1999)
13. Ruszewski, A.: Stabilization of discrete-time systems by PID controllers, Zeszyty Naukowe, Silesian University of Technical, Institute of Automation, 171-176 (2006)
14. Drake, S.P.: Converting GPS Coordinates ($\phi\lambda h$) to Navigation Coordinates (ENU), Surveillance Systems Division Electronics and Surveillance Research Laboratory
15. Meyer, T.H.: Grid, ground, and globe: distances in the GPS ERA, Surveying and Land Information Science (2002)

Application of a Hybrid Algorithm for Non–humanoid Skeleton Model Estimation from Motion Capture Data

Łukasz Janik[1], Karol Jędrasiak[2], Konrad Wojciechowski[1,3], and Andrzej Polański[1,3]

[1] Institute of Computer Science, Silesian University of Technology
Akademicka 16, 44-100, Gliwice, Poland
[2] Institute of Automatic Control, Silesian University of Technology
Akademicka 16, 44-100, Gliwice, Poland
[3] Polish-Japanese Institute of Information Technology
Aleja Legionów 2, 41-902 Bytom, Poland

Abstract. Currently, when Motion Capture being commonly used in gaming and movie industry there is a need of robust, easy and flexible solution to capture motion of non-humanoid characters in order to animate virtual characters in a game or movie. To fill this gap we developed an algorithm which estimates model of skeleton structure of both humanoid and non-humanoid characters. Quality and the possibility of real-life applications of the presented algorithm were experimentally evaluated. During the experiment we estimated the skeleton structure from the markers attached to a dog's skin. Quality of the resulting model is very promising.

1 Introduction

Optical Motion Capture is a widely used technique for recording motion of a character. It enables quick and accurate acquisition of multiple actions, which can be later used for animation, advertisement, medicine, rehabilitation and many more. However this technique suffers a major drawback – its usefulness is highly dependent on the quality of the estimated skeleton model. Nowadays, humanoid skeleton model estimation is an active research field. There are multiple methods of human motion acquisition using optical Motion Capture. End user can freely choose from a variety of techniques in order to satisfy own needs for application. However estimation of model of a non–humanoid skeleton model is left aside. Here we present a developed a robust technique which enables estimation of both humanoid and non–humanoid characters. We assume that recorded actors are composed of many rigid parts (bone segments), and each part may behave different. We distinguished three major bone segment types: spine, limbs, and end of kinematic chain. Pipeline of our algorithm depending on the type of the bone segment selects an appropriate estimation technique. Most of algorithms described widely in the literature use only single method to estimate the skeleton

L. Bolc et al. (Eds.): ICCVG 2012, LNCS 7594, pp. 95–104, 2012.

structure model. Such approach may not be able to reflect subtle character of the bone segment underlying muscle-skeletal mechanics. However here, we present a hybrid algorithm that selects an appropriate estimation method and its parameters depending on the type of the bone segment. The algorithm is experimentally evaluated and it is proved that is possible to use it in order to estimate skeleton model of non-humanoid characters. The algorithm results are compared with the skeleton model computed by Vicon Blade software.

2   Literature Review

There are plenty of algorithms for skeleton model estimation of humans. Those algo-rithms can be assigned to group depending of assumptions which they use for estima-tion. Primordial estimation techniques uses direct methods for markers location, and then estimated skeleton model using rigid body assumption. More advanced algo-rithms consider relocation of surface markers in relation to underlying bones. Such relocation is always present in Motion Capture, due to soft tissue artifacts or complex joints which movement is composed of rotation and translation. Physical constrained model and controller of skeleton model estimation has been proposed by Victor B. Zordan et al. [1]. Authors have not used marker positions directly, but mapped them to the virtual springs corresponding to anatomical landmarks. To find instantaneous pose is assessed all joints are modeled, then pose is retrieved basing on joints model and external forces. Finally bone segments are optimized to constant length for whole capture sequence. [2] contains description of two separate approach local and global, where one can be used to initialize another. Local technique utilizes semi − automa-tion segmentation, where markers are grouped into bone segments based on variation of vectors length connecting them over all captured sequence. Markers for which mentioned variation is lower than threshold defined by user are assigned to the same rigid bone segment. Then user creates skeleton topology by connecting rigid bone segments containing markers by lines which represent bones. Skeleton is estimated locally where child markers are represented in parental frame and position of connecting joint is sought using least squares quadratic optimization. Center of mass of all obtained possible joint locations for all markers belonging to adjacent bone segments serve to estimated final joint position by LSQ. James F. O'Brien et al. in [3] has estimated skeleton using fitting approach from magnetic Motion Capture. Magnetic Motion Capture provides additional information about orientation, thus F. O'Brien reduced estimation to linear solving system of linear equations for each pair of underlying bones. Another group of works base on spherical assumption, where estimation model assume that markers on bone segments linked to joint moves on sphere curves. Works [4] and [5] use mentioned assumption. In [5] authors has proposed energy function in least square sense which enables to estimate ball and hinge joints between connected bone segments. [4] demonstrates a way to automatically build skeleton hierarchy using minimal spanning tree and to estimate skeleton base on spherical assumption. Variation of functional methods for skeleton estimation can be also found in [6] and [7]. Commercial algorithms like those implemented in by Vicon or Biovision also use some variation of functional methods. According to [1] Vicon uses heuristic and strong left – right symmetry to fit statically defined model markers to temporal markers displacement.

Most works focus on capturing human motion from Motion Capture. Application of Motion Capture for non-humanoid characters can be found in [8] and [9]. In [8] proposed technique to use data captured from human motion session to animate non-humanoid character. In [9] authors focused on reproduction of complex dog spine from surface markers. However after correct estimation the temporal change of angles between segments can be used for simulation [10] or poses and movement classification [11].

3   The Algorithm

The designed algorithm for estimating skeleton structure of both humanoids and non-humanoids is based on spatial trajectories of body markers stored in C3D files. The method in order to estimate non-humanoids skeleton structure combines and refines several ideas previously used for humans. A block diagram of the algorithm is pre-sented in Fig. 1.

First step is to read the marker trajectories stored in C3D files. The C3D is the Na-tional Institute of Health standard for storing Motion Capture binary data. One of the main features is capability of storing at the same time synchronized marker trajectories and various analog data e.g. EMG (electromyography) or GRF (ground reaction forces). We have developed our own tool for extracting data from C3D file and a by-product it is also possible to transform C3D binary files into text format, which can be useful for some applications.

The information about the markers coordinates is supplied by kinematic chain relations between the parts of the skeleton defined and written in an XML based format. Those parts are commonly called bones or bone segments. Each bone segment in the kinematic chain is a parent and child to another. The only exceptions are the root of all bones and the bones at the end of the chain which have no children.

We have created the following attributes, which define bone segment type - possible to associate with the bone segments: limb, spine beginning (root), spine end, spine and kinematic end. We apply suitable estimation procedure as shown on Fig. 1 depending on bone segment type. Limb type segment are estimated using minimization of energy function described below, while bone segments of remaining types are computed using suitable geometric calculation. Each attribute is described by a developed heuristic. For instance bone segments attributed as limbs should have at least three non-collinear markers associated to them however more than three markers usually introduces unwanted noise. Concluding, for 53 Vicon Blade marker set we have defined 18 bone segments. A dog presented in the Fig. 2 is composed of 21 bone segments using 31 markers.

We assume that bone segments are rigid and connected by joints therefore attached markers satisfy the assumptions of the three degree of freedom socket

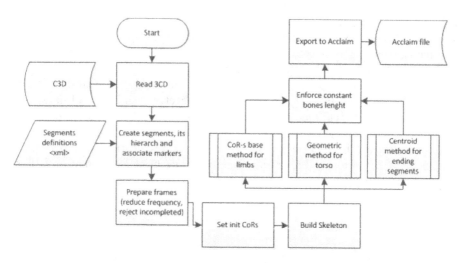

Fig. 1. The algorithm used for both non-humanoids and humanoids skeleton structure estimation

joint model. In this model bone segment ends coincide at exactly one common point called the center of rotation (CoR) or joint. Translations of one bone segment relatively to its parent or child are not allowed, the only possible changes are rotations around CoRs. This assumption is a base for a wide family of algorithms for skeleton structure estimation including the presented algorithm.

During movement of the actor all body segments move constantly according to transformations of elements of the kinematic chain. Bone segments change their positions and orientations at the same time. Let's define local coordinate systems of each bone segment s in the data frame k by position (X_k,Y_k,Z_k) and orientation $(a_{1_k},a_{2_k},a_{3_k})$. It is assumed that the position of the bone segment is computed as a position centroid of the markers attached to it. The basic idea of the algorithm for estimating position of the CoR in the frame k is to divide all bone segments in the kinematic chain into adjacent pairs of bone segments (parent and child) and compute transformation ϕ_k of the parent bone segment such that its position (and therefore the markers attached to it) becomes fixed in a selected frame, which we call a reference frame. Transformation $\phi_k, k \in \{1,\ldots,K\}$ from the k frame to the reference frame of the parent bone segment is defined as follows:

$$\phi_k = [\frac{Q_k}{T_k}], \tag{1}$$

where Q_k is a unit quaternion defining rotation and T_k is a 3D vector defining translation required to transform the bone segment from state k to reference state. Any frame where all the markers from both bone segments are visible can be used as a reference frame. In our procedure we select the first frame where all markers from both segments are visible as the reference frame. The algorithm used to find transformation ϕ_k is based on well-known methods for estimating rigid body displacements and orientation changes based on quaternion algebra. We denote the spatial coordinates of markers attached to the bone segment s by x_k^s, y_k^s, z_k^s. The steps of the algorithm for computing parameters of the transformation ϕ_k are listed below.

1. Let's define a set P_k composed of N markers attached to the parent p bone segment and R set containing N markers associated with parent bone segment p. We put into each set marker coordinates from all k frames of the calibration sequence.

2. Next step is to transform the marker coordinates in the P_k and R sets from global coordinates to local coordinates placed in the centroids of the clouds and write it as quaternion with zero scalar.

$$V_{ik} = \begin{bmatrix} x_{ik} \\ y_{ik} \\ z_{ik} \\ 0 \end{bmatrix}, \; Z_{iR} = \begin{bmatrix} x_{iR} \\ y_{iR} \\ z_{iR} \\ 0 \end{bmatrix} \tag{2}$$

$$V_{ik} = \begin{bmatrix} x_{ik} \\ y_{ik} \\ z_{ik} \end{bmatrix} - \tfrac{1}{N}\sum_y \begin{bmatrix} x_{yk} \\ y_{yk} \\ z_{yk} \end{bmatrix}, \; Z_{iR} = \begin{bmatrix} x_{iR} \\ y_{iR} \\ z_{iR} \end{bmatrix} - \tfrac{1}{N}\sum_y \begin{bmatrix} x_{yR} \\ y_{yR} \\ z_{yR} \end{bmatrix} \tag{3}$$

3. Compute left quaternion multiplication matrices for V and right quaternion multiplication matrices for Z according to below formulas:
Let's define:

$$H = [(x \; y \; z) \; w] = [(v \; w)] \tag{4}$$

where H is a quaternion

$$v_{x-} = \begin{bmatrix} 0 & -z & y \\ z & 0 & -x \\ -y & x & 0 \end{bmatrix} \tag{5}$$

where v_x is 3×3 matrix expressing the cross product of v with an arbitrary vector
then

$$H^+ = \begin{bmatrix} wI + v_{x-} & v \\ -v^T & w \end{bmatrix}, \; H^- = \begin{bmatrix} wI - v_{x-} & v \\ -v^T & w \end{bmatrix} \tag{6}$$

where I is 3×3 identity matrix, H^+ is left multiplication matrix of quaternion H, H^- is right multiplication matrix of quaternion H then using above formulas calculate correct V_{ik}^+ and Z_{iR}^- matrices for quaternions V_{ik} and Z_{iR} form set V and set Z

4. Compute matrix A_k using the following expression:

$$A_k = \sum_{i=1}^{N}(V_{ik}^+ - Z_{iR}^-)(V_{ik}^+ - Z_{iR}^-)^T, \tag{7}$$

5. We define Q_k as an eigenvector of the matrix A_k corresponding to the eigen-value of the lowest absolute value.
6. We compute the transformed center of mass vector $V_k^x t$ defines as V_k^x rotated by Q_k.
7. We compute translation vector $T_k = V_k^x - V_k^x t$.

When the parameters of the transformation are computed we can apply trans-formations ϕ_1 to ϕ_k to both parent and its child bone segment. A cloud of child bone segment points around the fixed parent points are obtained. The cloud can be used in order to estimate the real joint position. We estimate joints locations by minimization an energy function $F(j)$ where j is an approximate initial 3D location of the joint e.g. center of the line bone segment connecting markers placed at the joint. We need to perform such optimization for each pair of adja-cent bone segments. Minimization is performed using Nelder-Mead minimization procedure. Below we define notation for sets of spatial positions of body mark-ers. For simplification we do not introduce additional indexes for distinguishing bone segments:

$$
S_{m,o} = \left\{ \begin{bmatrix} x_{11} \\ y_{11} \\ z_{11} \end{bmatrix}, \begin{bmatrix} x_{12} \\ y_{12} \\ z_{12} \end{bmatrix}, \cdots, \begin{bmatrix} x_{1N} \\ y_{1N} \\ z_{1N} \end{bmatrix}, \begin{bmatrix} x_{21} \\ y_{21} \\ z_{21} \end{bmatrix}, \begin{bmatrix} x_{22} \\ y_{22} \\ z_{22} \end{bmatrix}, \cdots, \begin{bmatrix} x_{2N} \\ y_{2N} \\ z_{2N} \end{bmatrix}, \cdots, \begin{bmatrix} x_{MN} \\ y_{MN} \\ z_{MN} \end{bmatrix} \right\}, \quad (8)
$$

where $S_{(m,o)}$ is the set of markers positions belonging to particular bone segment over all frames; m is marker number, o is frame number. In order to simplify the notation of the $F(j)$ the following notation is introduced:

$$
l_{(e,m,S)} = \frac{\sum\limits_{o=2}^{N} e - S_{m,o}}{N}, \quad k_{(e,m,S)} = \frac{\sum\limits_{o=2}^{N} (\|e - S_{i,o}\| - l_{(e,m,S)})^2}{N}, \quad (9)
$$

where $e = [x, y, x]$ is the joint position to be estimated, $l_{(c,m,S)}$ is average distance for particular marker for parameter e, and $k_{(e,m,S)}$ is the indicator of distance change between joint and marker over all frames. Using the introduced notation we define F_e - the cost function for minimization over parameter e.

$$
F_{(e)} = 0.5 \sum\limits_{i=0}^{A} (k_{(e,i,P)} + \phi l_{(e,i,P)}) + 0.5 \sum\limits_{i=0}^{B} (k_{(e,i,D)} + \phi l_{(e,i,D)}), \quad (10)
$$

where ϕ is a scaling factor aimed at balancing influences of distances $l_{e,m,S}$ and $k_{e,m,S}$ on the cost function. The procedure is performed for each pair of adjacent bone segments. After executing the minimization procedure for each pair of adjacent bone segments the estimated center of rotation (CoR) of their joint j is obtained as the value of argument at the minimal value of the cost function and error residual is returned as the minimal value of the cost function. After estimation of the joint locations we can define bone length as a distance between two adjacent CoRs. However such defined value can vary among the frames, and real bones have constant length. In order to solve the problem we use another cost function F_l (8). The aim of the second optimization is to find optimal constant lengths of the bone segments l and keep the location of the CoR as close as possible to the original position at the same time. Proposed function takes all estimated joints as input. Equalization of bones length is performed globally on the whole skeleton.

$$F_{(l)} = \sum_{f=0}^{N} ||(D_f^I - (P_f + V_f l))||, \qquad (11)$$

where $D_f^C = P_f + V_f \times l$, P_f is set of parent constant (equalized) joint locations over all frames in global coordinates system, D_f^I is set of child inconstant (not equalized) joint locations over all frames in global coordinates system, D_f^C is set of child constant (equalized) joint locations over all frames in global coordinates system, V_f is set of a unit vectors indicating direction from parent to child over all frames in global coordinates system. As initial value of the bone length parameter l we use its value from first frame. We perform estimation for all pairwise adjacent bone segments. Estimation is performed from top to bottom over the skeleton hierarchy, so that parent joint location is used for child joint location estimation. First element is hierarchy (pelvis) does not need to be equalized, because it indicating a point which is a subject location in global coordinates frame and not has length.

In order to apply the algorithm for the real data which contains gaps due to markers occlusion an additional filtering step is required. It is assumed that marker coordinates in the adjacent τ frames to the gap are often erroneous. Hence, they should be removed from the processing to avoid deterioration of the quality of skeleton structure estimation. The τ parameter was experimentally set as 100.

Time of exact CoRs estimation computation can be reduced by a priori setting initial positions of CoRs close to the guessed joints. For instance for knee joint initial guessed CoR could be placed in the center of the line bone segment connecting two knee markers.

4   Experiment

Laboratory where the research was performed [12] is equipped with 10 Vicon NIR MX-T40 cameras which can work in the range of 30 to 2000 frames per second. Cameras are mounted near the ceiling around the laboratory stage allowing acquisition of both humanoid and non-humanoid presence. Cameras are equipped with 4 MP sensor. The reference HD 1080 cameras are Basler Pilot piA 1920-32gc. There are four such devices mounted in pairs on tripods. All 4 types of values: Motion Capture, reference videos, GRF and EMG are possible to acquire synchronously. However during the experiment only Motion Capture and reference videos were used.

We attached a marker set consisting of 31 markers on the skin surface of a dog and started markers position acquisition. A dog was walking around lab and per-formed simple tasks like sitting. After session we prepared suitable skeleton XML definition file and merged it together with markers trajectories to our algorithm. Re-sultant skeleton is shown on Fig. 2. For comparison purposes we prepared similar bone segments definition and generated skeleton using Vicon Blade.

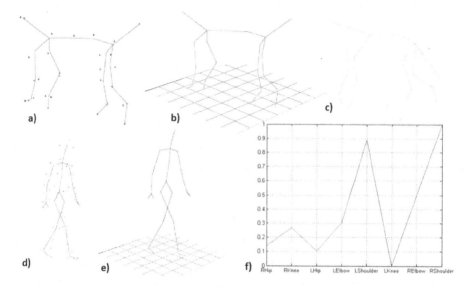

Fig. 2. Pictures a), b), present skeleton structure model of a dog with a tail high obtained by our hybrid algorithm, c) is a skeleton obtained from Vicon Blade. d-e) presents skeleton structure model of a human estimated by our algorithm, f) contains chart which features values of energy function obtained during estimation of dog bone segments in a-b).

We applied a noise with a uniform distribution over all markers from the whole set of movies captured within a single capture session. It was done in order to simulate soft tissue artifact behavior. Noise was applied to each marker position in each frame. Finally, we obtained five different c3d files. The skeleton structure (fig. 3) was estimated from data from each c3d file. Algorithm performed well regardless the noise in data. It proves that algorithm is resistant to soft tissue artifact and other temporal distortion of markers position (*e.g. caused by clothes movement*).

The energy functions accompanying the estimated skeleton structures from the five noisy files is presented in the fig. 4. It can be seen that the original estimation scores the best result. However the deterioration of the quality of the final result is insignificant for animation purposes because it is mostly beyond human perception.

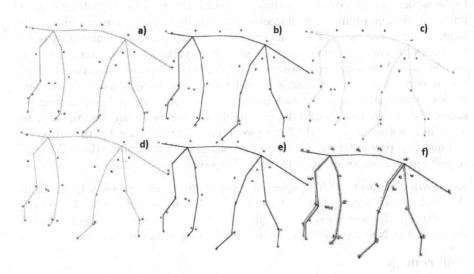

Fig. 3. Figure illustrates skeleton and markers positions obtained from selected frames from five noisy c3d files. Section a) to e) features markers and skeletons from each file separately. Section f) contains cumulated images where all body segments and markers were transformed to the origin of the global coordinate system.

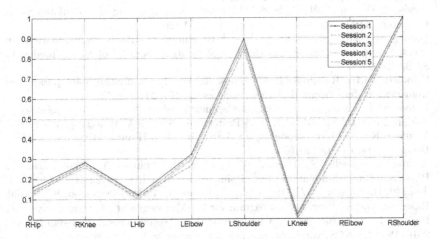

Fig. 4. The chart representing the impact of the soft tissue on the quality of the skeleton structure model estimation. No significant impact was noticed.

5 Conclusions and Future Work

In this work we proposed a novel technique which is able to estimate skeleton of both humanoid and non-humanoid characters. Proposed algorithm uses suitable technique to estimated part of skeleton depending on features of particular body part. It enables to generate good quality skeleton of characters with different anatomy than humans. Nowadays most works in Motion Capture focuses on human skeleton, thus research in area of non-humanoid skeleton is required to fill a gap. During our work we captured a session of walking dog and estimated its skeleton. Estimated skeleton structure model proved good quality and can be firmly used to animate a dog in movie or game. In the future we intend to further develop the proposed technique, in particular to capture motion of various breeds of the dogs. We tend to perform more experiments using hybrid algorithm in the future.

Acknowledgements. This paper was supported by the European Union from the European Social Fund (UDA-POKL.04.01.01-00-106/09-00 Ł. Janik, M.Stawarz). This work was supported by the National Centre of Science (NCN) grant number NN516475740 (K. Jędrasiak, K. Wojciechowski, A. Polański).

References

1. Zordan, V.B., Horst, N.C.V.D.: Mapping optical motion capture data to skeletal motion using a physical model. Work (2003)
2. Silaghi, M.-C., Plänkers R., Boulic R., Fua P.: Local and Global Skeleton Fitting Techniques for Optical Motion Capture Skeleton Fitting (1998)
3. Brien, J.F.O., Hodgins, J.K.: Automatic Joint Parameter Estimation from Magnetic Motion Capture Data. Interface, 1–8
4. Aguiar, E.D., Theobalt, C., Seidel H.P.: Automatic Learning of Articulated Skeletons from 3D Marker Trajectories, pp. 485–494 (2006)
5. Gamage, S.S.H.U., Lasenby, J.: New least squares solutions for estimating the average centre of rotation and the axis of rotation. Journal of Biomechanics 35, 87–93 (2002)
6. Schwartz, M.H., Rozumalski, A.: A new method for estimating joint parameters from motion data. Journal of Biomechanics 38, 107–116 (2005)
7. Cameron, J., Lasenby, J.: A real-time sequential algorithm for human joint localization. In: ACM SIGGRAPH 2005 Posters on - SIGGRAPH 2005, p. 107 (2005)
8. Yamane, K., Ariki, Y., Hodgins, J.: Animating Non-Humanoid Characters with Human Motion Data (2010)
9. Aleotti, J., Caselli, S., Bracchi, P.G., Gosi, S., Animali, P., Veterinarie, B.: Physically-Based Simulation of the Spine in Dog Walking, pp. 22–26 (2008)
10. Josiński, H., Świtoński, A., Jędrasiak, K., Polański, A., Wojciechowski, K.: Matlab Based Interactive Simulation Program for 2D Multisegment Mechanical Systems. In: Bolc, L., Tadeusiewicz, R., Chmielewski, L.J., Wojciechowski, K. (eds.) ICCVG 2010, Part I. LNCS, vol. 6374, pp. 131–138. Springer, Heidelberg (2010)
11. Świtoński, A., Josiński, H., Jędrasiak, K., Polański, A., Wojciechowski, K.: Classification of Poses and Movement Phases. In: Bolc, L., Tadeusiewicz, R., Chmielewski, L.J., Wojciechowski, K. (eds.) ICCVG 2010, Part I. LNCS, vol. 6374, pp. 193–200. Springer, Heidelberg (2010)
12. Human Motion Lab, Bytom, http://hml.pjwstk.edu.pl/en/ (visited March 1, 2012)

A New Method to Segment X-Ray Microtomography Images of Lamellar Titanium Alloy Based on Directional Filter Banks and Gray Level Gradient

Łukasz Jopek[1], Laurent Babout[1], and Marcin Janaszewski[1,2]

[1] Institute of Applied Computer Science, Lodz University of Technology, Poland
{ljopek,lbabout,janasz}@kis.p.lodz.pl
[2] Division of Expert Systems & Artificial Intelligence,
The College of Computer Science, Poland

Abstract. This paper presents a method for segmentation of 2D texture images of titanium alloys. The procedure is fully automated and is able to find and recognize so-called α-colonies from the image. The algorithm combines nonsubsampled directional filter banks (NSDFB) from the contourlet transform and gradient gray-level value to recognize directional orientations of α-colony.

1 Introduction

Titanium alloys are widely used in many industrial applications such as in power generation, aeronautical, and biomedical industry because of excellent mechanical and corrosion properties combined with a relatively low density. The mechanical properties of these alloys are strongly dependent on variations in the microstructure. One important aspect is the understanding of how crack grows in the material and correlate this to the microstructure, because the crack propagation direction is mainly governed by spacial organization of two types of microstructural features in such alloy when the microstructure if fully lamellar [1]: β-grain Boundary and α-lamellae. α-lamellar colonies can be described as group of lines (or parallel planes in 3D), which have a directional orientation. The presence of β-grain boundary is revealed by the growth of so-called α-layer along the previous mentioned boundary and is revealed in X-ray microtomography images within single, large, dark surfaces (see Fig. 1). Material scientists can manually segment microtomography images, but it is very difficult, and time consuming. This is important when one needs to make surveys, and the number of images is large. Therefore, an automatic image analysis seems to be an important alternative. From an image processing point of view, the task to segment the different lamellar colonies in X-ray microtomography images is preferably based on local statistical properties of pixel intensities, because this type of lamellar microstructure is a good example of textured image. Methods should be focused on probing the local orientation of directional structures contained

L. Bolc et al. (Eds.): ICCVG 2012, LNCS 7594, pp. 105–112, 2012.
© Springer-Verlag Berlin Heidelberg 2012

in the image. Previous attempts to segment these images have concentrated on two types of methods: wavelet decomposition [9], co-occurrence matrix [4]. Despite being completely different methods, they have shown similar limitations: low sensitivity and low directional resolution. Low sensitivity is the inability to detect low-contrast structures. The current microtomographic images of titanium alloys present low contrast, despite the use of so-called phase contrast to reveal the α-phase among β-phase and very high levels of noise mainly because of the spatial resolution (0.7 μm), which is of the same order of magnitude as α-colony size and interspace (1-2 μm). Directional low resolution means the ability to split an image for only a few directions. Moreover, directional orientation of colonies on each image may vary. However, the difference between the direction of individual α-colonies may be small, e.g. $10 - 15°$ (see Fig. 1).

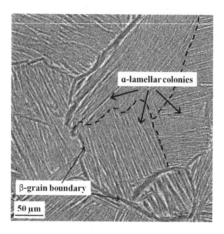

Fig. 1. Example of microstructure of fully lamellar titanium alloys obtained from X-ray microtomography. Boundaries between 3 α-colonies are manually drawn.

A minimum of 6-8 different directions should be considered for the classification which limits the use of methods based on wavelet and co-occurence matrix. In the recent years, new approaches which circumvent the lack of directionality from wavelet transform have been developed, such as the contourlet method [8],[7]. The second group of methods used to detect local directional orientation are those based on the gradient from grey-level value. In the method proposed by Jeulin and Moreaud [5],[6] they have used the gradient to detect local orientation structures similar to α-lamellae. In this work we propose a new method which combines both above mentioned approaches to discreminate α-colonies in microtomography images.

The paper is organised as follows. Section 2 shortly presents the nonsubsampled contourlet transform (NSCT) and the method proposed by Jeulin and Moreaud. Section 3 concerns the algorithm of the presented method. In section 4, results are presented and discussed, before conclusion is drawn in section 5.

2   Methods for the Detection of Local Direction Orientation in 2D Titanium Texture Images

2.1   Contourlet Transform and Directional Filter Bank

The nonsubsampled contourlet transform is a new image decomposition scheme introduced by Cunha et al. [8]. The NSCT is fully shift invariant, multi scale and multi direction. Contourlet transform can be divided into two main steps: Laplacian pyramid (LP) decomposing the input signal in lowpass and bandpass images and directional filter banks (DFB). Each bandpass image is further decomposed by DFB. In the case of NSCT there is no use a signal decimation, so that each element of the decomposition has the same size as the input image.

The nonsubsampled directional filter bank (NSDFB) [8] is constructed from the combination of a critically-sampled two-channel fan filter banks and resampling operations. The outcome is a tree-structured filter bank splitting the 2-D frequency plane into wedges with a fan angle of $180/2^3 = 22.5°$ as shown in Fig. 2 left-top for a 3-level decomposition used in this study. This decomposition is done by solving the upsampled filtered image obtained at level 2 of the LP with a parallelogram filter bank. This is obtained by applying a *shearing* operation [7] on quincunx filter banks with fan filters, as illustrated in Fig. 2 right-down.

2.2   Gradient

Jeulin and Moreaud [5] recently proposed a method based on the detection of orientation discontinuities using PCA to analyse 2D and 3D textured images. This has been further coupled with a semi-automatic watershed-based method to separate α-colonies in microtomographic images of titanium alloy [6]. In the present method is only retained the methodology to estimate local orientation map I_{or}, i.e.:

- computation of the gradient I_{gr} of the input image, I_{in}
- for each pixel p of I_{gr}:
  - calculate the co-variance matrix, using pixels from neighborhood defined in a $w \times w$ window centered on p
  - calculate the eigen vectors and values from the co-variance matrix
  - The local orientation for the pixel p of the output image I_{or} is given by the angle between the eigenvector corresponding to the largest eigenvalue and a reference vector [5], usually the y-axis.

3   Algorithm

The task of the segmentation algorithm is carried out on two-dimensional X-ray microtomography images of $(\alpha + \beta)$ titanium alloys, where the main criterion for classification of a pixel to a particular class is the directional orientation of its environment. The elements forming the structure of the material with respect to the segmentation are: the β-grains boundaries and the $\alpha - lamellar$ colonies (see Fig. 1). In the present paper, the segmentation focuses on the α-lamellar colonies.

The algorithm is applied to 2D images before future extension to the 3D case. The phantom image, shown in Fig. 2a and used to illustrate the different steps of the approach detailed below, is based on a sequence of the same real portion of α-colony, which has been rotated by $10°$ nine times, then flipped horisontally and vertically. This aims at generating both smooth and sharp texture transitions between twenty different regions.

3.1   Use NSDFB to Extract Texture Features from Images

The first step of the algorithm considers filtering of the input image using the NSDFB decomposition. In the present study a 3-level decomposition was considered, resulting in $2^3 = 8$ filtered images $E_l \; for \; l = 1, 2 \ldots, 8$ of the same size $N \times M$ as I_{in}. In the general case for a k-level decomposition, an output image $I_{NSDFB}^k = \{(i, j, P(i, j)) : i = 1, \ldots, N, j = 1, \ldots, M, P(i, j) \in \{1, 2, \ldots, 2^k\}\}$ is created based on the following rule:

$$P(i, j) = \arg \max_l (E_l(i, j)) \tag{1}$$

The number of components (or the label of the components) in equation (1) gives information about the dominant local orientation in the image. Because a FIR filter is used in the NSDFB, the value of this pixel is also a signature of its neighborhood, as well as the size of the kernel fan filter. Results of features extraction using NSDFB and equation (1) are shown in Fig. 2b.

3.2   Denoising

As one can see in Fig. 2a, the input image shows a relatively good contrast between the relatively thin α-phase (bright lines) and β-phase (dark grey). Because filters in NSDFB are sensitive to contrast and show higher response to brighter areas in the image, the local directionality of α-phase is well defined especially for thin curves, while the determination of the β-phase local orientation is more prone to noise (see Fig. 2b). To circumvent the problem, our solution considers segmenting the α-phase using a binarisation algorithm such as the Otsu method [10] (see Fig. 2c) and multiplying I_{Otsu} with I_{NSDFB}^k. The coresponding result is shown in Fig. 2d where all pixels of zero value (dark blue) are background pixels mainly corresponding to the β-phase. Then their classification to the class object is explained in section 3.4.

3.3   Class Object Denoising

The main purpose of the previous step is to classify pixels with no preferential direction to the background class, filtered by the Otsu-based image. Most of the remaining pixels which correspond to the object class are correctly assigned, but some pixels are not (see Fig. 2d). These pixels, neighboring those correctly assigned, are the result of the Otsu-based image, which is grey level dependent and may overestimate the regions defined by the $\alpha - lamellae$. Let for all pixels x from I_{Otsu} such that $I_{Otsu}(x) = 1$ denote $H(i, x)$ the number of pixels from class i, in the window of size $w \times w$ centered in x, and divided by w^2. Then for each x the normalised values $H(i, x), i = 1, 2, \ldots k$ are sorted in descending order, the most represented class is in first place. In this way a new list $H(i_1, x), H(i_2, x), \ldots, H(i_k, x)$ is created. The pixel x is assigned to the class i_1 when the sum of the 2 most represented classes is larger than 50%, i.e.:

$$H(i_1, x) + H(i_2, x) > 0.5 \tag{2}$$

If this condition is not satisified, we consider, in a first step, that there is no preferential orientation at that point. In this case, the pixel is assigned to the 'no direction (ND)' class and its value is set to $k+1$. The result of such denoising approach is presented in Fig. 2e where one can see that pixels at the vicinity of boundaries between 4 objects are assigned to the ND class. In that case w was set to 25.

3.4   I Level Classification

The image after denoising (Section 3.3) contains the different class objects and the background. The I-level classification applies to the background. In the output image I_{cl1}, each background pixel x is assigned to the class which is the most represented among all classes in a window of size $w \times w$ centered in x. The exemplary result of the I level of classification is presented in Fig. 2f. One can see that most of the original regions in Fig. 2a are well retrieved with respect to the fan angle defined by the 3-level decomposition, i.e. 22.5° (see for instance the regions '30°-40°' or '50°-60°' regrouped within 1 class, respectively) and correctly delimited, especially for regions with large misorientation (i.e. between top and botton region layers). However, apart the presence pixels classified to the ND class, some regions in the left and right parts of the image containing more than 1 class (e.g. regions '0°-10°-20°'). This aspect is treated in the next classification step.

3.5   II Level Classifcation

The image obtained after the previous classification step may still contain pixels that have been wrongly classified or can be considered as noise. In the latter case, single pixels incorrectly classified can be assigned to the correct object class using a median filter. However, in the case of larger objects, the problem may be more complex to treat as it can be the cause of two opposite problems. The first problem is associated with the occurrence is the image of areas with no prefentional directionality (class $k+1$, i.e. 9) . Indeed, the lack of directionality in some parts of the image due to lower phase contrast may result in classification problems and the presence of classes embedded in others. The second problem which connected with interweaving of paths of different lamellar colonies, also called Widmanstatten α-laths [11] results in the possible visual effect of having colonies located within others, therefore the same result as in the low contrast-induced classification. In order to treat both problems, the proposed solution

---

Algorithm 1. II level classification(**Input** Image I_{cl1}, Image I_{in}, Resolution R,**Output** I_{cl2})

---

01. Calculation of local orientation map I_{or} based on the algorithm presented in section 2.2
02. Let C=$\{A_1, \ldots, A_n\}$, be a list of n objects in the image I_{cl1}
03. $i = 1$
04. **while** $i \leq \#C$
05.   Ascending sort of the list C using an object size criterion
06.   Define a set $CC_i = \{A_j \in C : A_j$ is connected to $A_i\}$
07.   **for each** element in CC_i
08.   Calculate the average orientation D_j from I_{or}
09. $k = \arg\min_{j} |D_i - D_j|$
10.   **if** $|D_i - D_j| \leq R$
11. $C = C\backslash\{A_i, A_j\}; C = C \cup \{A_i \cup A_k\}$
12.   **if** $k < i$ **then** $i = i - 1$
13.   **else** $i = i + 1$
14. $I_{cl2} = \bigcup_{i=1}^{\#C} A_i$

---

considers the direction of the different objects representing colonies,their location and direction of the neighboring objects in the following algorithm.

Fig. 2g depicts this last stage of the proposed method. The resolution R was set to 15. One can see that objects of similar orientations calculated using the gradient method have been merged, which results in a better segmentation of the original regions (e.g. regions '0°-10°-20°' in Fig. 2a and g).

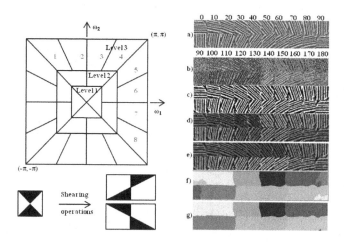

Fig. 2. Results of features segmentation following authors methodology, (a) input image, artificial texture, (b) results of features direction extraction. (c) lamellae segmentation based on Otsu method. (d) background classification, (e) class object denoising, (f) I level classification, (g) II level classification - output image .

4   Results and Discussion

Fig. 3 presents the classification results on a large 2D microtomography image of size $501x500$ pixels similar to Fig. 1. One can see that objects $A - D$ and J in Fig. 3b correspond well to α-colonies $1 - 4$ and 11 in Fig. 3a. Moreover, a small amount of pixels associated to the 'ND' class are present, mainly located at the wide β-grain boundary between α-colonies 1 and 2. This proves the potential of the method to correctly delimit the boundaries of the objects of large mis-orientation. However, it can occur that α-colonies are regrouped within only one object (e.g. colonies $5 - 6$ in object E). The major problem of the presented method is associated with the inability to generally detect β-grain boundary, as it is the case between α-colonies 5 and 6. Indeed, its local orientation is similar to the two colonies. The situation is similar for the colonies $8 - 10$ associated to the object G.

The algorithm was implemented in MATLAB 9. A MATLAB toolbox that implements the NSDFB has been used and can be downloaded from MATLAB Central (http://www.mathworks.com/matlabcentral/) [8]. The execution time was approximately $510s$ on a PC with the following specifications: Intel i7 2.9 GHz, 12GB RAM, Windows XP 64bit.

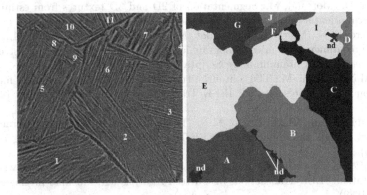

Fig. 3. Segmentation result of a 2D microtomography image of lamellar titanium alloy. (a) input image, (b)result of segmentation after II level classifcation. The resolution parameter R is $15°$.

5   Conclusion

The presented method, which combines directional filter banks and gradient from gray-level value, has proven its capabilities to distinguish low-contrasted texture objects such as the structure of α-lamellae colony, and relatively high sensitivity to misorientation. Boundaries between objects are consistent with those between α-colonies, especially between areas with large misorientation. The method has been developped for 2D images, but can be modified for the 3D case. This will mainly involve the replacement of the 2D contourlet transform by another method such as the 3D surfacelet transform [12]. Extending the algorithm to the 3D space, which is under progress, will enable a full classification of α-colonies in microtomography images of lamellar titanium alloys.

Acknowledgments. The work is supported by the Polish Ministry of Science and Higher Education (grant no: 6522/B/T02/2011/40).

References

1. Birosca, S., Buffiere, J.-Y., Garcia-Pastor, F.A., Karadge, M., Babout, L., Preuss, M.: Three-dimensional characterization of fatigue cracks in Ti-6246 using X-ray tomography and electron backscatter diffraction. Acta Materialia 57, 5834 (2009)
2. Babout, L., Jopek, L., Janaszewski, M., Preuss, M., Buffiere, J.Y.: Towards The Texture Segmentation Of X-Ray Tomography Images Of Lamellar Microstructure In Titanium Based Alloys. In: Babout, L., Nowakowski, J. (eds.) 5th International Symposium on Process Tomography, Zakopane, p. 168 (2008)
3. Theodoridis, S., Koutroumbas, K.: Pattern recognition, 4th edn. Academic Press (2009)
4. Haralick, R.M., Shanmuga, K., Dinstein, I.: Textural features for image classification. IEEE Transactions on Systems Man and Cybernetics SMC3, 610 (1973)
5. Jeulin, D., Moreaud, M.: Segmentation of 2D and 3D textures from estimates of the local orientation. Image Analysis and Stereology 27, 183 (2008)
6. Vanderesse, N., Maire, E., Darrieulat, M., Montheillet, F., Moreaud, M., Jeulin, D.: Three-dimensional microtomographic study of Widmanstatten microstructures in an alpha/beta titanium alloy. Scripta Materialia 58, 512 (2008)
7. Do, M.N., Vetterli, M.: The contourlet transform: An efficient directional multiresolution image representation. IEEE Transactions on Image Processing 14, 2091 (2005)
8. Da Cunha, A.L., Zhou, J., Do, M.N.: The nonsubsampled contourlet transform: Theory, design, and applications. IEEE Transactions on Image Processing 15, 3089 (2006)
9. Mallat, S.G.: A theory for multiresolution signal decomposition: the wavelet representation. IEEE Transactions on Pattern Analysis and Machine Intelligence 11, 674 (1989)
10. Otsu, A.: Threshold selection method from gray-level histogram. IEEE Transactions on Systems, Man, and Cybernetics 9, 62 (1979)
11. Lutjering G.: Influence of processing on microstructure and mechanical properties of $(\alpha + \beta)$ titanium alloys. Materials Science and Engineering A 1998;243:32.
12. Lu, Y.M., Do, M.N.: Multidimensional directional filter banks and surfacelets. IEEE Transactions on Image Processing 16, 918 (2007)

Intelligent 3D Graph Exploration with Time-Travel Features

Peter Kapec[1], Michal Paprčka[1], and Adam Pažitnaj[1]

Faculty of Informatics and Information Technologies,
Slovak University of Technology STU in Bratislava, Slovakia
kapec@fiit.stuba.sk, michal.paprcka@ynet.sk, librus44@gmail.com

Abstract. Graph visualization is an ongoing research area with many open problems. Graphs are often visualized in 2D space, but recently also 3D visualizations emerged. However the added third dimension add additional problems. In this paper we focus on navigating and exploring 3D graph visualizations. We present our approach for the automation of virtual camera movement for better graph exploration that also allows to play-back the exploration and fork other exploration paths at any time.

Keywords: graph visualization, exploration, playback.

1 Introduction

Graphs have found many applications in various domains containing not only informatics. Graph visualizations have recently been in main focus of many research projects, because various information can be effectively modeled by graphs. However pure mathematical analysis of graphs is often not very useful due to graph complexity and/or graph size and density. Graph visualizations aim to help with graph comprehension by providing graphical views that may reveal hidden structures and other interesting topological features.

Exploring graphs involves examining graph nodes and their content. However, the relations between nodes that are represented trough edges are often more important. Navigation between nodes can be done either freely or by inspecting edges from the starting node and following edges of interest. Often such edge following leads to other interesting nodes and this process is repeated. During the exploration process the users may ask what information could we obtain if we explored the graph in another way.

In this paper we present our approach for 3D graph exploration that uses a virtual camera that intelligently calculates it's motion path so that all nodes the user is interested in are always visible, thus preserving contextual information. We enhance this approach by providing exploration history that can be played back. The user can fork other exploration paths from the stored exploration history.

Section 2 presents our algorithm for intelligent camera movement with illustrations and evaluation for several graphs. The section 3 mentions the time-traveling features of our graph visualization system. The next section mentions related work and is followed by conclusions.

L. Bolc et al. (Eds.): ICCVG 2012, LNCS 7594, pp. 113–120, 2012.

2   Intelligent Camera Movement

The simplest approach for exploring 3D visualizations of graphs is to move the virtual camera along a straight line between camera's current position and camera's target position. The camera's target position should be near the graph's node the user selected. This simple approach has however several open problems: a) what is a suitable camera position and orientation near the selected node? b) where should be the camera facing during movement?

These questions are fundamental to the user, because when the movement and final position of the camera is not clear, the user may loose orientation and become confused. To preserve user's mental model it is suitable that the virtual camera at the final position also shows the starting position. During camera movement the user is often interested not only in the node's final position, but is also interested in several other graph nodes. Therefore it is also suitable that the camera also shows graph nodes of user interest during movement.

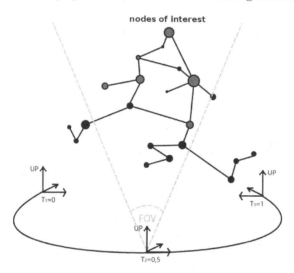

Fig. 1. Illustration of camera movement

2.1   Camera Path Algorithm

Our approach for camera movement addresses the above mentioned situation and is illustrated in Figure 1: the virtual camera starts at position at time $T_1 = 0$ and is oriented towards some graph node. The user then selects another graph node and the camera starts moving towards the target node, which is reached at time $T_3 = 1$. However the user is interested in several nodes from the graph, highlighted as red nodes, and these nodes should be visible during camera movement (shown at $T_2 = 0.5$) and also from camera's final position. The view from camera's final position should also cover camera's starting position, so the user can easily identify the position where he/she came from.

The points of interest our algorithm takes into account are therefore: the initial *starting node*, the *target node* and a cluster of *relevant nodes* [1]. These points form the control points a of Bezier curve that will be used for camera movement. Similarly we define the control points for the camera's target position that lies along camera's view axis. The Algorithm 1 summarizes our approach showing how camera's *CameraPositions* and *CameraTarget* positions are interpolated during motion. The Figure 2 shows in the two top images a blue curve – the calculated camera trajectory for two different graphs. The following six images in Figure 2 show the first graph from camera's viewpoint during camera movement: the camera starts with red node in focus and ends it's movement focusing a green node.

Require: *CameraPosition, CameraTarget, TargetCameraPos, NodesOfInterest, Speed*
1: $t_1 \leftarrow 0$, $t_2 \leftarrow 0$ {comment: interpolation steps}
2: *PointOfInterest* $\leftarrow$ *GetCenter(NodesOfInterest)*
3: *center* $\leftarrow$ *GetCenter(EyePosition, TargetCameraPos, PointOfInterest)*
4: *CameraPositions* $\leftarrow$ {*CameraPosition, PointOfInterest, TargetCameraPos*}
5: *CameraTargets* $\leftarrow$ {*CameraTarget, PointOfInterest, center*}
6: $w_1 \leftarrow \{1, -0.1, 1\}$ {comment: weights for camera's positions}
7: $w_2 \leftarrow \{1, 0.5, 1\}$ {comment: weights for camera's target positions}
8: $a \leftarrow$ *TargetCameraPos* – *center*
9: **while**
    NOT IsVisible(CameraPosition) AND NOT IsVisible(PointOfInterest) **do**
10:      Move *TargetCameraPos* along vector a
11: **end while**
12: **while** *NOT IsVisible(PointsOfInterest)* **do**
13:      Increase trajectory curvature
14: **end while**
15: **while** $t_1 \leq 1$ *OR* $t_2 \leq 1$ **do**
16:      **if** $t_1 \leq 1$ **then**
17:          *NewPos* $\leftarrow$ *GetPointOnBezierCurve(t_1, CameraPositions, w_1)*
18:          $t_1 + =$ *Speed*
19:      **end if**
20:      **if** $t_2 \leq 1$ **then**
21:          *NewTarget* $\leftarrow$ *GetPointOnBezierCurve(t_2, CameraTargets, w_2)*
22:          $t_2 + =$ *Speed*
23:      **end if**
24:      *SetCameraPosition(NewPos, NewTarget)*
25: **end while**

Algorithm 1. Algorithm to calculate camera's motion path

2.2 Evaluating Camera Movement

We have tested our approach on two graphs called Veolia (containing 639 nodes and 917 edges) and Genealogy (containing 515 nodes and 1072 edges).

---

[1] We use the geometric center of these nodes and apply it with a negative weight.

For selecting nodes of user's interest we used two approaches. The first was to let the user manually select nodes and the second was based on graph metrics. We used following four graph metrics [7]: 1. matching node's content 2. the degree of nodes 3. the summation of length of shortest paths 4. distance between nodes. These graph metrics together with user selected nodes can be combined using weights to form various complex node selections.

To verify that our algorithm displays all nodes of interest, we have measured the number of nodes visible on screen during camera movement. The Figure 3 shows the number of visible nodes during camera movement for movement interpolation steps. The total number of nodes of interest was up to 50. The Figure 3 shows that the algorithm was able to display all nodes of interest. These three runs for different starting and ending camera positions also reveal that the time all nodes of interest are visible vary – especially at the beginning and at the end of camera movement not all nodes of interest are visible. Therefore it is important to evaluate not only if all nodes of interest are visible but also the amount of time they are visible.

The Table 1 shows the results for the mentioned two graphs for various metrics and for a selected number of nodes of interest. The number of camera movement interpolation steps was set to 2000. The first column shows the total number of camera movement steps in which the nodes of interest were visible. As can be seen the percentage ranges from 48,8% to 99% of time the nodes were visible. The best results were obtained for user selected nodes and worse for metrics-based selections. The explanation of these results can be seen in the fact, that the user usually selects nodes that are placed very near to each other and the nodes picked by metrics-based selections are usually spread over the whole graph. Other graph metrics may lead to other results.

Table 1. Number of interpolation steps in which all nodes of interest were visible

Steps with visible nodes of interest	Interpolation steps	Percentage	Nodes	Nodes of interest	Metrics	Graph
1467	2000	73,35 %	515	50	combined	Genealogy
1352	2000	67,6 %	639	50	combined	Veolia
1663	2000	83,15 %	515	20	combined	Genealogy
1634	2000	81,7 %	639	20	combined	Veolia
1516	2000	75,8 %	515	50	node degree	Genealogy
976	2000	48,8 %	639	50	node degree	Veolia
1973	2000	98,65 %	515	40	user selected nodes	Genealogy
1980	2000	99 %	639	30	user selected nodes	Veolia

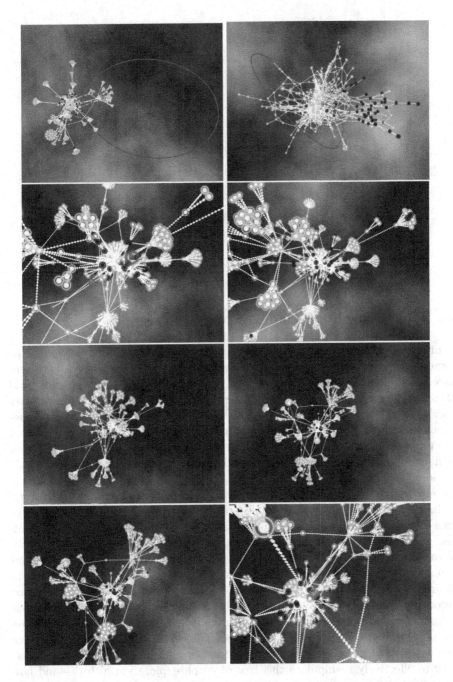

Fig. 2. The blue and red curves displays the calculated trajectories for two different graphs. The bottom six images (left to right and top to bottom) show the first graph from camera's viewpoint during camera movement.

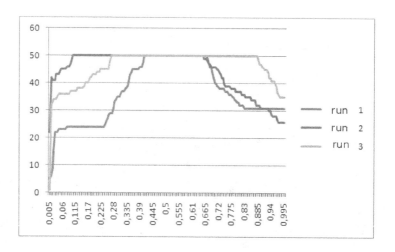

Fig. 3. The number of visible nodes depending on time

3   Time-Traveling Graph Exploration

It often happens that the user is interrupted at work by random noise and he forgets where he stopped working. A possible solution to this problem is to provide a feature that allows to record his work in the form of a recording and then to replay this recording. The exploration of graph structures often involves user's navigation decisions depending on user's current interests. However sometimes the user would like to return to previous graph nodes and start exploring the graph in new ways. Exploring the graph in new ways may lead to different understandings of different graph parts. It would be beneficial if the user could explore the graph in a way, then return back to some point in his exploration history, and to start exploration again changing the previous exploration history.

In our graph visualization system we provide even more complex recording of user's exploration allowing sci-fi like time-travel exploration. The user explores the graph by navigating the virtual camera in the scene containing the visualized graph. This exploration is recorded and the user can return to previous camera positions, either playing back the exploration history or by jumping to desired time. After returning to the desired time position, the user can start recording his exploration again. The most important feature is however that the new exploration recording creates actually a new time-fork from the previous recording, thus preserving the previous recording. This way the user can create a tree of graph exploration histories. Several interesting questions arise: how to effectively manipulate this tree of graph exploration histories and how to present these recorded histories. For manipulating and playback of the three containing recordings of graph explorations we have developed a custom user interface widget.

Fig. 4. Widget to control the tree of exploration histories

The Figure 4 shows this widget with an exploration tree containing four recordings for four exploration forks. These four exploration forks are controlled by four individual sliders. Below these four exploration forks is a slider covering the whole exploration time. To visually compare different graph exploration recordings, our graph visualization system can open a separate window for each graph exploration fork. The Figure 5 shows this situation for four selected graph exploration forks – each window is highlighted with a different frame color. Using sliders the user can playback or jump to specific time for each exploration recording individually. The bottom slider controls all exploration recordings and allows to playback them simultaneously.

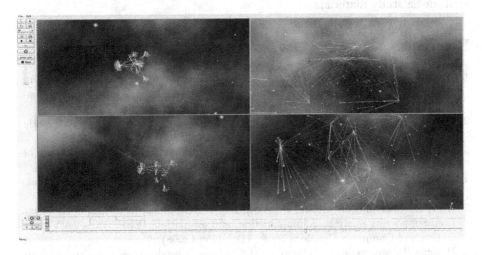

Fig. 5. Four views showing a graph in four different exploration histories

4   Related Work

Graph visualization is a large problem area [6] and we have used the force-directed graph layout proposed in [4]. The presented algorithm for camera movement is related to finding the best viewpoints problematics [2,8,9]. A similar approach to our has been proposed in [1]. However our approach considers also additional points of interests that may not be visible from initial camera viewpoint as opposed to [1], which tries to maximally preserve the initial visible area. Many research projects focus on time-series data visualization, or displaying and managing histories of actions done during data visualization [5]. Several time-line interfaces for visualizing undo, browsing and time travel functionality have been discussed in [3]. However our method for 3D graph exploration with time-traveling features can be considered as a new and unique approach, especially in the graph visualization field.

5 Conclusions

In this paper we have presented our approach for virtual camera movement that considers user's points of interest when moving between two positions. The evaluation of the proposed algorithm for camera movement shows that it is capable to show points of interest most of the time the camera moves. We enriched this virtual camera for graph exploration with time-travel functionality, which allows to play back exploration time-lines and start new graph exploration paths.

Acknowledgement. This work was supported by the KEGA grant 068UK-4/2011: Integration of visual information studies and creation of comprehensive multimedia study materials.

References

1. Ahmed, A., Eades, P.: Automatic camera path generation for graph navigation in 3D. In: Proc. of the 2005 Asia-Pacific Symposium on Information Visualization, vol. 45, pp. 27–32. Australian Computer Society, Inc. (2005)
2. Barral, P., Dorme, G., Plemenos, D.: Visual understanding of a scene by automatic movement of a camera. Limoges (France) (March 2000)
3. Derthick, M., Roth, S.F.: Enhancing data exploration with a branching history of user operations. Knowledge-Based Systems 14(1), 65–74 (2001)
4. Fruchterman, T.M.J., Reingold, E.M.: Graph drawing by force-directed placement. Software–Practice & Experience 21(11), 1129–1164 (1991)
5. Heer, J., Mackinlay, J., Stolte, C., Agrawala, M.: Graphical histories for visualization: Supporting analysis, communication, and evaluation. IEEE Trans. on Visualization and Computer Graphics 14(6), 1189–1196 (2008)
6. Herman, I., Melançon, G., Marshall, M.S.: Graph Visualization and Navigation in Information Visualization: a Survey. IEEE Trans. on Visualization and Computer Graphics 6(1), 24–43 (2000)
7. Huang, X., Lai, W.: On the structural algorithm of filtering graphs for layout. In: Proc. of the Pan-Sydney Area Workshop on Visual Information Processing, VIP 2005, pp. 33–42. Australian Computer Society, Inc, Darlinghurst (2004)
8. Kamada, T., Kawai, S.: A simple method for computing general position in displaying three-dimensional objects. Comput. Vision Graph. Image Process. 14(1), 43–56 (1988)
9. Mackute-Varoneckiene, A., Zilinskas, A., Varoneckas, A.: Multidimensional scaling: multi-objective optimization approach. In: Proc. of the Int. Conference on Computer Systems and Technologies, pp. 1–6. ACM, Ruse (2009)

Improved Adaptive Arithmetic Coding for HEVC Video Compression Technology*

Damian Karwowski

Chair of Multimedia Telecommunications and Microelectronics,
Poznań University of Technology,
Polanka 3, 60-965 Poznań, Poland
dkarwow@multimedia.edu.pl

Abstract. The paper presents Improved Adaptive Arithmetic Coding algorithm for application in forthcoming HEVC video compression technology. The proposed solution is based on standard CABAC algorithm and uses author's new mechanism of data statistics modeling that is based on CTW technique. The improved CABAC algorithm is characterized with better compression performance relative to standard CABAC. In the framework of HEVC encoder 1.6% - 4.5% bitrate reduction was obtained when using improved CABAC instead of the original algorithm.

Keywords: Adaptive arithmetic coding, improved CABAC, HEVC.

1 Introduction

Entropy coding technique is an essential part of contemporary video encoders [4,5,11]. It plays significant role, because it further increases efficiency of encoder by reducing statistical redundancy of residual data. It made up the motivation for researchers to find solutions for more and more efficient entropy coding of data that lead to elaborating many new entropy coding techniques [1,11,12].

The state-of-the-art entropy coding technique used in video compression is the Context-based Adaptive Binary Arithmetic Coding (CABAC) [1,5] that became a part of international video coding standard MPEG-4 AVC/H.264 [4]. Due to application in CABAC of advanced mechanisms of data statistics estimation, it was well experimentally proved, that CABAC algorithm outperforms other entropy encoders in terms of coding efficiency [1].

Currently, the works are in progress towards next, more efficient video compression technology High Efficiency Video Coding (HEVC) that are carried out under auspices of ISO/IEC MPEG and ITU VCEG [6,9]. The works are in a final phase. General architecture of HEVC is already fixed and it is certain now that entropy coding of HEVC will be based on CABAC algorithm.

It was experimentally proved that compression performance of HEVC encoder is superior relative to efficiency of MPEG-4 AVC encoder (up to 20%-40% reduction of bitrate [13] for comparable quality of images). The question arises whether

* The work was supported by a public funds as a research project in years 2010-2012

L. Bolc et al. (Eds.): ICCVG 2012, LNCS 7594, pp. 121–128, 2012.

it is possible to further improve compression performance of HEVC technology by application of even more sophisticated entropy coding methods. Author proposes improved version of CABAC algorithm within HEVC and presents experimental results of its coding efficiency in reference to efficiency of the original HEVC with unmodified CABAC. Detailed methodology of experiments, results and important conclusions are also presented in the paper.

2   HEVC Video Compression Technology - Overview

The HEVC technology, like previous standards [4,11], is based on hybrid coding scheme with motion-compensated prediction, transform coding and entropy coding of residual data. Nevertheless, there are many improvements and new coding tools that distinguishes the HEVC from other existing solutions and lead to extraordinary compression performance of video encoder.

The HEVC uses new coding structure by introducing the coding unit (CU), prediction unit (PU) and transform unit (TU) to perform prediction and adaptive coding of data in blocks of multiple sizes. In general, CU (the basic unit of image splitting) can have the size of 64x64 to 8x8. The PU (contains information related to prediction process) is sub-element of CU and can have its dimensions or can be as small as 8x4 or 4x8. The TU (unit used for transform and quantization processes) can be a square shape with sizes from 4x4 up to 32x32, or can be non-square shape with sizes 32x8, 8x32, 16x4, 4x16 when the PU is also non-square. The new coding structure allows choosing the size of block for prediction and transform in an adaptive manner exploiting local features of an image. Additionally, HEVC uses numerous intra- predictors and inter prediction of high precision within PU units when forming the residual data. In this way, transform coding approach is efficiently realized on highly correlated residual data.

Hybrid coding scheme introduces some artifacts into images, especially for high compression scenario. Therefore, reconstructed images are processed with in-loop filters (deblocking filter, sample-adaptive offset filter and adaptive loop filter) in order to improve subjective quality of decoded images [6]. The filters increases efficiency of inter-frame encoder also, due to the reference frames are more similar to the predicted frame.

Compression techniques described above lead to low-energy residual data. This data is efficiently coded using Context-based Adaptive Binary Arithmetic Coding (CABAC) as an entropy encoder. The CABAC algorithm used in HEVC is discussed in the next section in more details.

3   Entropy Coding in HEVC - CABAC Algorithm

The HEVC video compression technology uses Context-based Adaptive Binary Arithmetic Coding (CABAC) entropy encoder, which is a modified version of CABAC encoder that is used in MPEG-4 AVC/H.264 video compression standard. In order to limit computational complexity of HEVC CABAC codec, the

number of statistical models was significantly reduced relative to version of
CABAC used in MPEG-4 AVC. Nevertheless, general idea of entropy codec
remains the same and it was already described in details in the literature [1,5].
Therefore, only main features of CABAC will be presented in the paper that are
important from the point of view of improvements made by the author. CABAC
realizes entropy coding of data with the use of adaptive arithmetic encoder that
allows to efficiently represent input symbols by exploiting statistics of coded
data. The general block diagram of CABAC encoder was presented in Fig. 1.

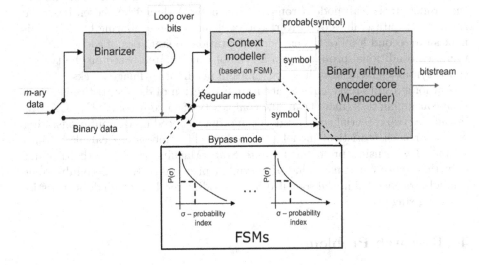

Fig. 1. General block diagram of CABAC encoder

The distinctive feature of CABAC algorithm is application the binary
arithmetic codec core that is able to encode binary symbols from two elements
alphabet only $A=\{0, 1\}$. Such an approach reduces complexity of entropy codec
significantly - there exists fast realizations of binary arithmetic codec cores [5]. Application the binary arithmetic codec core in CABAC put requirement to translate
all m-ary data symbols into string of binary symbols. This task is done by binarizer at the first stage of entropy coding. The way in which the binarizer works significantly affects the number of resulted binary symbols - it determines both the
compression efficiency and the computational complexity of entropy codec. Therefore, the binarizer of CABAC uses several different binarization schemes that are
adapted to specific statistics of individual syntax elements [1,5]. This step can be
understood as adaptive variable-length coding (VLC).

Binary symbols in a binarized word still exhibit some statistical redundancy.
Therefore CABAC, in contrary to traditional VLC, additionally encodes binary symbols using arithmetic encoder core with taking into consideration the
statistics of symbols. The way in which these statistics are calculated significantly influences compression performance of the whole entropy encoder and its

complexity. In order to trade off the two aspects, total number of 225^1 different statistical models were defined in CABAC within HEVC [14] (in HM 3.2 version of the software) to efficiently represent transform coefficients, motion and control data. In general, individual syntax elements of HEVC are characterized with different probability distribution - it is worth to track these statistics independently in entropy encoder for individual data types. To take above mentioned into consideration, CABAC assigns independent sets of statistical models to individual syntax elements. It makes the first level of CABAC adaptation to current signal statistics. Additionally, statistics of coded data locally changes within an image - the proper statistical model (from a set of models) should be chosen based on the context data (values of a given syntax element in neighboring blocks). This makes the second level of the encoder adaptation to statistics of coded data. In this way, conditional probability of a symbol is calculated based on the type of coded syntax element as well as its values in neighboring image blocks.

Author's results revealed that accurate estimation of data statistics is a very time-consuming task (more than 60% complexity of entropy codec [15]). CABAC introduces two essential simplifications in order to speed up computations. First of all, for each statistical model, probabilities of symbols are calculated in a simplified way using pre-defined Finite State Machine (FSM) with 64 states only that represent some value of a symbol probability [1,5]. Secondly, some symbols are encoded in the so-called bypass coding mode with no data statistics modeling stage.

4   Research Problem

Simplifications that were made in the CABAC's context modeler block significantly reduces accuracy of symbols' probabilities. It obviously negatively affects compression performance of CABAC.

In the past, it was the motivation for author to propose improved version of CABAC algorithm with more accurate data statistics estimation based on Context-Tree Weighting (CTW) method [2,3]. Previous versions of improved CABAC were activated in the framework of MPEG-4 AVC video codec and tested in depth. Detailed experimental results revealed the possibility of reducing the bitrate by 2-8% when using improved version of CABAC instead of the original algorithm [7,8].

The question arises to what extent more accurate mechanism of data statistics estimation in CABAC will lead to reduce the bitrate in the state-of-the-art HEVC technology. This paper answers this question. It presents tuned version of the improved CABAC (also based on CTW) with better algorithm of statistical models initialization and mechanism of its selection adapted to character of data coded in currently working out HEVC video compression technology.

---

[1] The number of statistical models is not fixed yet. There are still new proposals toward limiting the number of necessary models in CABAC within HEVC.

5   Improved Version of CABAC Algorithm in HEVC

The main idea of the improved CABAC is using more accurate mechanism of data statistics estimation, relative to the original algorithm. The motivation for such an approach is to calculate conditional probabilities of symbols more precisely in the context modeler block. Previous author's results obtained in the context of MPEG-4 AVC revealed, that it can be successfully done when using well-known in compression the Context-Tree Weighting (CTW) method [7,8].

Starting point to research was the version of CABAC algorithm used in the framework of HEVC encoder (HM 3.2 version of the software). Simplified mechanism of probabilities estimation used in original CABAC (based on FSMs) was replaced by more sophisticated one exploiting CTW technique. Other functional blocks of CABAC (binarizer and binary arithmetic encoder core) were left unchanged. General block diagram of the improved CABAC was presented in Fig. 2.

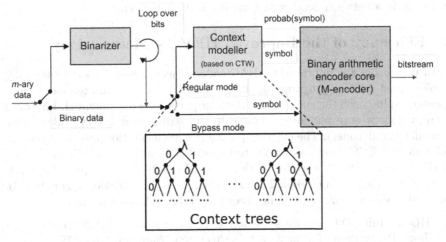

Fig. 2. Block diagram of the improved CABAC with more advanced context modeler

In improved CABAC, the CTW method is used by every statistical model to calculate conditional probabilities of symbols more exactly. In this way, improved CABAC uses 225 different context trees. The probabilities are calculated with respect to symbols that have been coded earlier - it means with respect to context information. The CTW algorithm uses binary context tree of depth D to store information on statistics of previously coded data that appeared in a given context. The general idea behind CTW is to calculate conditional probability of a current symbol with respect to context data of lengths from 0 to D. In the case of non-stationary data it is unknown which context length is the best to calculate probability of a symbol. Therefore, the CTW method appropriately weights probabilities calculated in different context lengths to produce final conditional probability that is used by arithmetic encoder core. More detailed description of CTW algorithm can be found in [2,3,11].

Depth D of context trees influences precision of calculated probabilities. In general, the higher value of D the better efficiency of CTW technique. Thorough research made by author in the framework of MPEG-4 AVC revealed, that $D=8$ makes good compromise between efficiency and complexity of entropy codec. Such a depth of context trees was also assumed in presented version of the improved CABAC.

Two different versions of the improved CABAC were elaborated: first, with smaller number of statistical models for transform coefficients and binarization scheme based on concatenation of truncated unary code, truncated Golomb-Rice code and 0th order Exp-Golomb code [12], and second, with bigger number of statistical models for transform coefficients and binarization scheme based on concatenation of truncated unary code and 0th order Exp-Golomb code [1]. In both versions of the improved CABAC new mechanism of statistical models initialization was used. The mechanism exploits the idea of extended frame slice (slice that contains more than one image frame) that allows carrying statistics of coded data between neighboring frames of the same type.

6   Efficiency of the Improved HEVC - Methodology

Both versions of the improved CABAC codec (encoder and decoder) were fully implemented in C++ programming language. In order to obtain reliable experimental results, both the encoder and decoder parts were implemented. Improved entropy codecs were put and activated in the structure of HEVC video codec (encoder and decoder). The starting point for implementation was the reference software of HEVC known as HEVC test model (HM 3.2) [14]. Coding efficiency of the improved HEVC encoder (with improved CABAC) was explored and referenced to efficiency of original HEVC with standard CABAC algorithm. In particular, experiments were done according to the following scenario:

- HD and full HD test video sequences were used: *Station2* (1920x1080), *River Bed* (1920x1080), *Pozna Street* (1920x1088), *Balloons* (1024x768), *China Speed* (1024x768), *Slice Editing* (1280x720). Two of them (*China Speed* and *Slice Editing*) are synthetic and screen content sequences.
- The IBBBB structure of group of pictures (GOP) was used.
- Tests were done for a wide range of bitrates using values of quantization parameters (QP) equal to 22, 27, 32, 37. In this way experiments were done for quality of reconstructed videos from excellent to poor.
- Rate-distortion control mechanism was based on adaptive VLC codes.
- Other settings used: motion estimation based on Enhanced Predictive Zonal Search (EPZS) method, search range equal to 64, loop filters enabled.

With reference to the original HEVC, efficiency of the improved encoder was measured using known in video compression Bjøntegaard metric [10]. Bjøntegaard metric enables comparison of rate-distortion (RD) curves of two encoders in terms of average bitrate reduction based on several RD points. In the paper, average bitrate reduction was calculated based on 4 RD points (for QP=22, 27, 32, 37) for luma component.

7   Efficiency of the Improved HEVC - Results

Experimental results proved that application of the improved CABAC within HEVC increases compression performance of video encoder. Average bitrate reduction calculated for different test sequences using Bjøntegaard metric were presented in Table 1 for both the first and the second version of the improved CABAC.

Table 1. Average bitrate reduction due to application of the improved HEVC (**version 1** and **version 2**) relative to the original HEVC. Individual versions of the improved CABAC differs from number of statistical models and methods of binarizations.

Test sequence	Average bitrate reduction (1st ver. of improved HEVC)	Average bitrate reduction (2nd ver. of improved HEVC)
Station2	1.78%	1.77%
River Bed	2.90%	3.02%
Poznan Street	2.21%	1.62%
Balloons	2.15%	1.64%
China Speed	4.50%	2.91%
Slice Editing	3.39%	3.57%
Average	**2.82%**	**2.42%**

On average, 2.6% bitrate reduction was obtained for used video sequences. Content and character of a video sequence significantly affects compression results. Better results were observed in the case of sequences containing computer graphics and screen content (*China Speed* and *Slice Editing*) with up to 4.5% and 3.6% bitrate reduction respectively. It results from the fact, that CABAC algorithm was adapted to efficiently encode images that represent natural scenes - it is characterized with limited level of adaptation to real statistics of data. Improved CABAC algorithm is featured with higher level of adaptation to current signal statistics. Therefore, the gap between the improved and the original CABAC is bigger in such cases. Smaller gain was observed in the case of natural scene sequences with bitrate reduction between 1.6% and 3%.

Application of more advanced entropy codec within HEVC affects its computational and memory complexity. The use of the improved CABAC increases complexity of HEVC decoder by a factor of 1.34 (for 3 Mbps scenario) and 1.1 (for 0.5 Mbps scenario) in comparison to the original HEVC with standard CABAC. Improved CABAC also increases memory requirements - memory space needed to store all context trees is about 0.5 MB.

8   Conclusions and Final Remarks

Compression performance of forthcoming HEVC technology can be further increased when using improved entropy encoder. Better mechanism of data statistics estimation in CABAC leads to 1.6% - 4.5% reduction of HEVC bitstream. This compression gain is occupied with higher complexity of the video codec.

Obtained results indicate that it is more and more difficult to increase efficiency of successive generations' video encoders by tuning the entropy encoders. In adequate research performed by author in the framework of AVC, higher gains were achieved [7,8]. Successive generations of video encoders exploits more efficient mechanisms of signal prediction which, in general, leads to residual signal of a smaller energy. Accurate estimation of statistics for such signal is a real problem that limits possibilities of efficient entropy coding the data.

References

1. Marpe, D., Schwarz, H., Wiegand, T.: Context-Based Adaptive Binary Arithmetic Coding in the H.264/AVC Video Compression Standard. IEEE Trans. on Circuits and Systems for Video Technology 13(7), 620–636 (2003)
2. Willems, F.M.J., Shtarkov, Y.M., Tjalkens, T.J.: The Context-Tree Weighting Method: Basic Properties. IEEE Trans. on Information Theory 41(3), 653–664 (1995)
3. Willems, F.M.J.: The Context-Tree Weighting Method: Extensions. IEEE Trans. on Information Theory 44(2), 792–797 (1998)
4. Special issue on H.264/AVC video coding standard. IEEE Trans. on Circuits and Systems for Video Technology, 13 (July 2003)
5. Tian, X., Le, T.M., Lian, Y.: Entropy Coders of the H.264/AVC Standard. Springer (2011)
6. McCann, K., Bross, B., Kim, I.K., Sekiguchi, S., Han, W.J.: HM5: High Efficiency Video Coding (HEVC) Test Model 5 Encoder Description. JCTVC- G1102, JCT-VC Meeting, Geneva (November 2011)
7. Karwowski, D., Domański, M.: Improved Context-Based Adaptive Binary Arithmetic Coding in MPEG-4 AVC/H.264 Video Codec. In: Bolc, L., Tadeusiewicz, R., Chmielewski, L.J., Wojciechowski, K. (eds.) ICCVG 2010, Part II. LNCS, vol. 6375, pp. 25–32. Springer, Heidelberg (2010)
8. Karwowski, D., Domański, M.: Improved Context-Adaptive Arithmetic Coding in H.264/AVC. In: European Signal Processing Conference, EUSIPCO 2009, Glasgow, Scotland (August 2009)
9. ITU-T Q6/16 and ISO/IEC JTC1/SC29/WG11: Joint call for proposals on video compression technology. MPEG Document N11113, Kyoto, Japan (January 2010)
10. Bjøntegaard, G.: Calculation of Average PSNR Differences between RD curves. ITU-T SG16/Q6. In: 13th VCEG Meeting, Austin, Texas, USA, Doc. VCEG-M33 (April 2001)
11. Salomon, D., Motta, G.: Handbook of data compression. Springer (2010)
12. Nguyen, T., Winken, M., Marpe, D., Schwarz, H., Wiegand, T.: Reduced-complexity entropy coding of transform coefficient levels using a combination of VLC and PIPE. JCTVC- D336, JCT-VC Meeting, Daegu (January 2011)
13. Li, B., Sullivan, G., Xu, J.: Comparison of Compression Performance of HEVC Working Draft 5 with AVC High Profile. JCTVC- H0360, JCT-VC Meeting, San Jose (February 2012)
14. Bossen, F., Flynn, D., Suhring, K.: AHG Report - Software development and HM software technical evaluation. JCTVC-G003, JCT-VC Meeting, Geneva (November 2011)
15. Karwowski, D., Domański, M.: Optimized architectures of CABAC codec for IA-32-, DSP- and FPGA-based platforms. Image Processing and Communications (Institute of Telecommunications, Bydgoszcz) 14(2-3), s.5–s.12 (2009)

Extrinsic Camera Calibration Method and Its Performance Evaluation

Jacek Komorowski[1] and Przemysław Rokita[2]

[1] Maria Curie Sklodowska University,
Lublin, Poland
jacek.komorowski@gmail.com
[2] Warsaw University of Technology, Institute of Computer Science,
Warszawa, Poland
p.rokita@ii.pw.edu.pl

Abstract. This paper presents a method for extrinsic camera calibration (estimation of camera rotation and translation matrices) from a sequence of images. It is assumed camera intrinsic matrix and distortion coefficients are known and fixed during the entire sequence. Performance of the presented method is evaluated on a number of multi-view stereo test datasets. Presented algorithm can be used as a first stage in a dense stereo reconstruction system.

1 Introduction

Motivation for development of the method described in this paper was our prior research on human face reconstruction from a sequence of images from a monocular camera. Classical multi-view stereo reconstruction algorithms (as surveyed in [10]) assume fully calibrated setup, where both intrinsic and extrinsic camera parameters are known for each frame. Such algorithms cannot be used when an object moves or rotates freely in front of the camera or if a camera is moved to different positions (in uncontrolled manner) and a number of images of the static object is taken. Even if camera intrinsic parameters are known and fixed during the entire sequence, extrinsic parameters (rotation matrix and translation vector relating camera reference frame with the world reference frame) are not known. So before a multi-view stereo reconstruction algorithm can be used, a prior step to estimate camera pose for each image in the sequence is required.

Our approach is based on ideas used in modern structure from motion products such as Bundler [8] or Microsoft PhotoSynth. These solutions work by finding geometric relationship (encoded by a fundamental matrix) between 2 images of the scene taken from different viewpoints. This is usually done by running a robust parameter estimation method (e.g. RANSAC) combined with 7-point or 8-point fundamental matrix estimation algorithm using putative pairs of corresponding features from 2 images.

In contrast to aforementioned solutions, we assume fixed and known camera intrinsic parameters. Making such assumptions is beneficial for 2 reasons. First, less pairs of corresponding points are required to recover 2-view scene geometry.

L. Bolc et al. (Eds.): ICCVG 2012, LNCS 7594, pp. 129–138, 2012.

Second, fundamental matrix estimation algorithms do not work for planar surfaces (so called planar degeneracy) [2]. When intrinsic matrix is known essential matrix can be estimated instead of fundamental matrix. So assuming known intrinsic parameters is advantageous when processing sequences of images of low texture (e.g. depicting a rotating human face) or planar objects.

Unfortunately known algorithms for essential matrix estimation from 5 pairs of corresponding points are very complex and implementations is not freely available. E.g. Nister 5-point algorithm [5] requires SVD, partial Gauss-Jordan elimination with pivoting of a system of of polynomial equations of the third degree and finally finding roots of a 10th degree polynomial. Such complexity can potentially lead to significant numerical errors and make such methods inapplicable in practice.

The aim of this paper is twofold: first to present a solution for estimation of extrinsic parameters from a sequence of images taken by a calibrated camera, and second, to asses the accuracy of the presented method on various datasets.

2   Extrinsic Camera Calibration Method Details

An input to our extrinsic camera calibration method is a sequence of images from a monocular camera, such as depicted on Fig. 3. It is assumed camera intrinsic matrix $\mathbf{K}$ and distortion coefficients are known and fixed for the entire sequence. The following steps are done to recover camera extrinsic parameters for each image in the input sequence:

1. Initial processing: geometric distortions removal and (when required) object segmentation from the background. In scenarios where camera is moving (such as a sequence depicted on Fig. 3(b)) segmentation is not necessary. When camera is fixed and an object is moving (e.g. placed on a rotating turnstile, such as Fig. 3(a)), the object should be segmented from the background. Further processing is done on undistorted and segmented images.
2. Detection of SIFT features on all images in the sequence.
3. Estimation of the relative pose between 2 initial images in the sequence:
   (a) Finding pairs of putative matches between SIFT features on both images.
   (b) Computation of essential matrix E_{12} relating two images using RANSAC [1] with Nister [5] solution to 5-point relative pose problem. The relative pose (translation vector T_2 and rotation matrix R_2) is recovered from E_{12} as described in [5].
   (c) Construction of a sparse 3D model (as a point cloud $\{X_i\}$) by metric triangulation of pairs of consistent features from two images.
   (d) 3D points and camera pose refinement using bundle adjustment method [9] to minimize reprojection error.
4. Iterative estimation of an absolute pose of each subsequent image I_n with respect to 3D model built so far:
   (a) Finding putative matches between features on the image I_n and 3D points already in the model.

(b) Computation of an absolute pose (translation vector T_k and rotation matrix R_k) of the image I_k with respect to the 3D model. This is done using RANSAC [1] with Finsterwalder 3-point perspective pose estimation algorithm [3].

(c) Guided matching of features from currently processed image I_k and images processed in the previous steps. New 3D points are generated and added to 3D model (and support of existing 3D points is extended) by metric triangulation of matching features.

(d) 3D points and camera pose refinement using bundle adjustment method [9] to minimize reprojection error.

(e) Removal of 3D points with the worst support

Additional notes on algorithm steps:

Step 2. SIFT features [7] are a common choice in modern structure from motion solutions. This is dictated by their invariance to scaling, rotation and, to some extent, lighting variance and small affine image transformations. These properties are important when finding corresponding features on images taken from different viewpoints. At this step SIFT features are found and feature descriptors (represented as vectors from $\mathbb{R}^{128}$) are computed for each image in the sequence. Threshold of SIFT feature detector is dynamically tuned to ensure there's a sufficient number of keypoints found on each image. In our implementation if there's less than 500 keypoints found the detector is re-run with decreased threshold.

As camera intrinsic matrix $\mathbf{K}$ is known and fixed during entire sequence, coordinates of detected features are *normalized*, that is multiplied by $\mathbf{K}^{-1}$. This is equivalent to assuming that camera intrinsic matrix is identity. All further processing is done using *normalized* coordinates and assuming camera intrinsic matrix is identity.

Step 3a. For each keypoint from the first image the closest (in the feature descriptor space) keypoint from the second image is found. Only pairs fulfilling nearest neighbour ratio criterion (that is ratio of a distance to the corresponding keypoint to the distance to the second-closest keypoint on the other image is below given threshold $\Theta = 1.25$) are kept as putative matches. See Fig. 1(a).

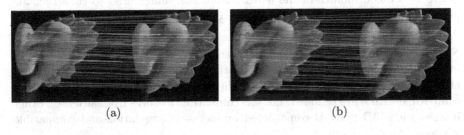

(a)   (b)

Fig. 1. Pairs of matches between 2 images (a) putative matches (b) matches consistent with epipolar geometry encoded by estimated essential matrix E

Step 3b. RANSAC [1] robust parameter estimation is used with our implementation of Nister 5-point algorithm [5] to estimate relative pose between 2 cameras. In each RANSAC iteration 5 pairs (the minimum number of correspondences needed to estimate relative pose between 2 cameras) of potentially matching keypoints are sampled at random from a set of putative correspondences and an essential matrix E is estimated using the chosen sample. The estimation that produces the biggest number of inliers (that is putative matches consistent with epipolar geometry induced by an estimated essential matrix E) is kept. Results of this step are: essential matrix E_{12} describing stereo geometry between first 2 images, rotation matrix $\mathbf{R}_2$ and translation vector T_2 describing the relative pose of the second image with respect to the first image and RANSAC consensus set consisting of pairs of matching features consistent with epipolar geometry (see Fig. 1(b))

Step 3c. 3D model is constructed by metric triangulation of pairs of compatible features from two images. Two criteria are taken into account: *visual compatibility* (Euclidean distance between descriptors of corresponding features is below a threshold) and *geometric compatibility* (reprojection error is below a threshold). First all points from RANSAC consensus set are used to construct 3D points by metric triangulation. Then additional matches between 2 images are sought with a guided matching.

Step 3d. Bundle adjustment method [9] minimizes total reprojection error by joint optimization of camera poses and 3D points position using Levenberg-Marquardt nonlinear optimization algorithm. [1] It is assumed world coordinate frame aligns with the first camera coordinate frame, so first camera pose is fixed ($R_1 = \mathbf{I}, T_1 = \mathbf{0}$) and only second camera pose and 3D points coordinates are optimized by minimizing:

$$\min_{R_2, T_2, \{X_i\}} \sum_{i=1}^{2} \sum_{j=1}^{N} \left\| R_i \left(X_j - T_i \right) - x_j^i \right\| \tag{1}$$

where x_j^i are coordinates of the feature from i-th image used to construct 3D point X_j and $R_i \left(X_j - T_i \right)$ is a projection of a 3D point X_j onto i-th image.

Step 4c. For each keypoint k from a currently processed image I_n a number (20 in our implementation) of closest (in feature descriptor space) keypoints from already processed, nearby images is sought. Features visually and geometrically compatible with k are retained. If k has compatible features from at least 2 other images a new 3D point is constructed by metric triangulation and compatible keypoints form its support.

---

[1] sba sparse bundle adjustment library [6] available at http://www.ics.forth.gr/~lourakis/sba/ is used in our implementation

Step 4e. Support of all 3D points is verified and features which are not geometrically compatible (e.g. due to cameras pose or 3D points position refinement) are removed. Then 3D points not having a support from at least 3 images are removed.

Final results are depicted on Fig. 2, where black crosses represent recovered camera poses for Dino input sequence (Fig. 3(a)).

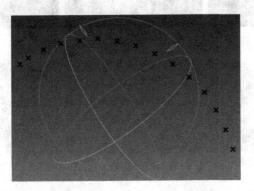

Fig. 2. Estimated camera poses (black crosses) and a sparse object model (dots) recovered from a Dino dataset (Fig. 3(a)

3 Experiments

An accuracy of the proposed method was evaluated quantitatively using five multi-view stereo datasets with given camera intrinsic and extrinsic parameters. The following multi-view stereo datasets were used:

- Dataset [10] [2] (Fig. 3(a)) containing sequences of images (640x480 pixels) of a plaster dinosaur sampled every 7.5 degree on a ring around it. This seems a very demanding dataset for automatic recovery of camera pose as an object is almost textureless and relatively few distinctive keypoints can be found on each image.
- Dataset [11] [3] (Fig. 3(b), 3(c), 3(d), 3(e)) containing sequences of high resolution (3072x2048 pixels) images of architectural objects. Number of images in each sequence vary from 8 to 19.

Error measures. Rotation error R_{err} is measured as the rotation angle needed to align ground truth rotation matrix R_i and estimated rotation matrix $\hat{R}_i$ for i-th image in the sequence.

$$R_{err} = \cos^{-1} \frac{\mathrm{Tr}\,(\Delta R_i) - 1}{2},$$

---

[2] Available at http://vision.middlebury.edu/mview/data/
[3] Available at http://cvlab.epfl.ch/~Strecha/multiview/denseMVS.html

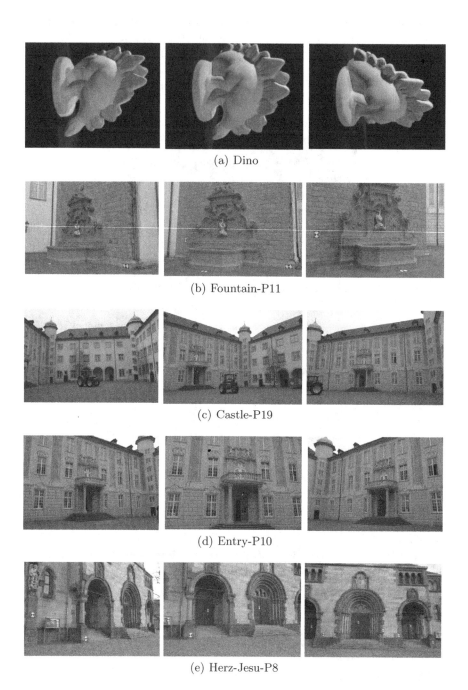

(a) Dino

(b) Fountain-P11

(c) Castle-P19

(d) Entry-P10

(e) Herz-Jesu-P8

Fig. 3. Exemplary images from datasets used in experiments

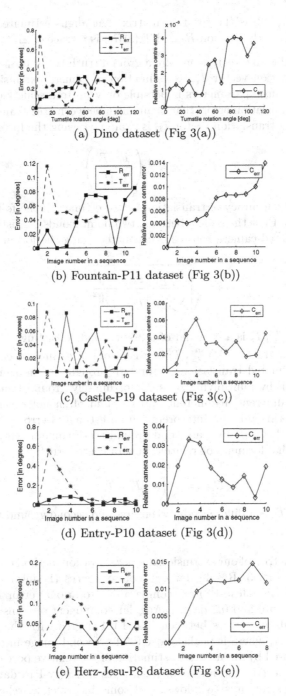

(a) Dino dataset (Fig 3(a))

(b) Fountain-P11 dataset (Fig 3(b))

(c) Castle-P19 dataset (Fig 3(c))

(d) Entry-P10 dataset (Fig 3(d))

(e) Herz-Jesu-P8 dataset (Fig 3(e))

Fig. 4. Performance of extrinsic camera calibration method on test datasets. Left column: rotation error R_{err} and translation error (angular component) T_{err}, right column: relative camera center error C_{err}.

where $\Delta R_i = R_i^{-1}\hat{R}_i$ is the rotation matrix that aligns estimated rotation $\hat{R}_i$ with the ground truth rotation R_i and $\mathrm{Tr}(\Delta R_i)$ is a trace of ΔR_i.

It is not possible to directly compare a ground truth translation vector T_i and estimated translation vector $\hat{T}_i$, as estimation of camera extrinsic parameters given known intrinsic parameters is possible only up to a scale factor. Angular component of translation error, that is an angle between true translation vector T_i and estimated translation vector $\hat{T}_i$, is examined using the formula:

$$T_{err} = \cos^{-1}\left(\frac{\hat{T}_i \cdot T_i}{|\hat{T}_i||T_i|}\right)$$

In order to verify accuracy of translation vector estimation the following procedure is deployed. First the scale s between two point clouds consisting of ground truth and estimated camera centres is calculated using the formula taken from [4]:

$$s = \sqrt{\frac{\sum_{i=1}^{n}\|T_i - T'\|^2}{\sum_{i=1}^{n}\left\|\hat{T}_i - \hat{T}'\right\|^2}} \quad,$$

where $T' = \frac{1}{n}\sum_{i=1}^{n}T_i$ is a centroid of a point cloud consisting of ground truth camera centres and $\hat{T}' = \frac{1}{n}\sum_{i=1}^{n}\hat{T}_i$ is a centroid of estimated camera centres cloud. Then estimated translation vectors are brought to the same scale with the ground truth by multiplying by s. Unfortunately ground truth coordinate system scale is different in different datasets and often not given in physical units. To allow a meaningful interpretation an estimated error is renormalized using a distance between first a second ground truth camera centres as a unit. This gives the final formula for relative camera centre error:

$$C_{err} = \frac{1}{\alpha}\left(s * \hat{T}_i - T_i\right) \quad,$$

where $\alpha = T_0 - T_1$ is a difference between first and second ground truth camera centres.

Results. Error metrics of our extrinsic camera calibration method on test datasets are depicted on Fig. 3. Results for outdoor sequences (Fountain-P11, Castle-P19, Entry-P10, Herz-Jesu-P8) are comparable. Rotational error R_{err} is small and varies between 0 and 0.1 degree. Angular component of translational error T_{err} is also small and varies between 0 and 0.1 degree with the exception of Entry-P10 dataset, where it peaks above 0.5 for second image in the sequence. This is likely caused by an incorrect estimation of the relative pose of the second camera with respect to the first camera. Images in Entry-P10 dataset contain many repetitive structures (windows) and some incorrect matches must have been established between keypoints from first two images.

Relative camera center error C_{err} shows two different characteristics. For Dino, Fountain-P11, Herz-Jesu-P8 datasets it increases for further images in the sequence, whereas for Castle-P19 and Entry-P10 no trend can be noticed and the error doesn't grow. Castle-P19 and Entry-P10 datasets contain a lot of highly distinctive keypoints (e.g. window corners) which are matched across multiple distant images. In each case relative camera centre error C_{err} is below 0.06 which means that if distance between first and second camera is 1m then each camera is positioned with 6 cm accuracy. In all test datasets distance between cameras associated with the first and last image in the sequence is about 10 times bigger than the distance between 2 first cameras. So distant cameras, 10 m apart, are localized with 6 cm accuracy.

Algorithm also performs quite well for the most demanding dataset: Dino. Even for distant frames (where object was rotated over 100 degrees from its initial position) rotation error R_{err} is below 0.4 degree.

4   Conclusions and Future Work

Conducted experiments proved that the presented method can be used to recover camera extrinsic parameters from a sequence of images quite accurately. On all but one datasets relative camera center error C_{err} was below 0.06 which means that if distance between first and second camera is 1m all other cameras are located within 6 cm accuracy. For some sequences results are significantly better, e.g. for Fountain-P11 and Herz-Jesu-P8 C_{err} is below 0.015 which means cameras are located with 1.5 cm accuracy (assuming 1 m distance between first and second camera).

The algorithm performed very well on an objects with relatively little texture (Dino sequence). Errors in subsequent images were increasing (as there were very few keypoints visible from a wide angle) but even when an object rotated almost 120 degrees rotation matrix estimation error R_{err} was below 0.4 degree.

In the future it is planned to use the presented method as a first stage in a dense stereo reconstruction system. After camera pose is estimated for each image in the sequence multi-view stereo reconstruction method will be used to generate a dense point cloud representing an object.

References

1. Fischler, M., Bolles, R.: Random Sample Consensus: A Paradigm for Model Fitting with Applications to Image Analysis and Automated Cartography. Communications of the ACM (1981)
2. Hartley, R., Zisserman, A.: Multiple View Geometry in Computer Vision. Cambridge University Press (2004)
3. Haralick, R., Lee, C., Ottenberg, K., Nolle, M.: Review and analysis of solutions of the three point perspective pose estimation problem. International Journal of Computer Vision (1994)
4. Horn, B.: Closed-form solution of absolute orientation using unit quaternions. Journal of the Optical Society of America 4 (1987)
5. Nister, D.: An efficient solution to the five-point relative pose problem. IEEE Transactions on Pattern Analysis and Machine Intelligence (2004)

6. Lourakis, M., Argyros, A.: SBA: A Software Package for Generic Sparse Bundle Adjustment. ACM Trans. Math. Software 36 (2009)
7. Lowe, D.: Object recognition from local scale-invariant features. In: Proceedings of the International Conference on Computer Vision (1999)
8. Snavely, N., et al.: Modelling the World from Internet Photo Collections. International Journal of Computer Vision (2007)
9. Triggs, B., McLauchlan, P., Hartley, R., Fitzgibbon, A.: Bundle Adjustment — A Modern Synthesis. In: Proceedings of the IWVA (1999)
10. Seitz, S., et al.: A Comparison and Evaluation of Multi-View Stereo Reconstruction Algorithms. In: CVPR 2006, vol. 1 (2006)
11. Strecha, C., von Hansen, W., Van Gool, L., Fua, P., Thoennessen, U.: On Benchmarking Camera Calibration and Multi-View Stereo for High Resolution Imagery. In: CVPR (2008)

Length Estimation for the Adjusted Exponential Parameterization

Ryszard Kozera[1], Lyle Noakes[2], and Mariusz Rasiński[3]

[1] Faculty of Mathematics and Information Science, Warsaw University of Technology,
Pl. Politechniki 1, 00-661 Warsaw, Poland, or
Warsaw University of Life Sciences - SGGW,
Faculty of Applied Informatics and Mathematics,
Nowoursynowska 159, 02-776 Warsaw, Poland
[2] Department of Mathematics and Statistics, The University of Western Australia,
35 Stirling Highway, Crawley W.A. 6009, Perth, Australia
[3] Faculty of Mathematics and Natural Sciences,
University of Cardinal Stefan Wyszyński,
Dewajtis 5, 01-815 Warsaw, Poland
r.kozera@mini.pw.edu.pl, lyle.noakes@maths.uwa.edu.au,
rmario@interia.pl

Abstract. In this paper we discuss the problem of interpolating the so-called reduced data $Q_m = \{q_i\}_{i=0}^m$ to estimate the length $d(\gamma)$ of the unknown curve γ sampled in accordance with $\gamma(t_i) = q_i$. The main issue for such non-parametric data fitting (given a fixed interpolation scheme) is to complement the unknown knots $\{t_i\}_{i=0}^m$ with $\{\hat{t}_i\}_{i=0}^m$, so that the respective convergence prevails and yields possibly fast orders. We invoke here the so-called *exponential parameterizations (including centripetal)* combined with piecewise-quadratics (and -cubics). Such family of guessed knots $\{\hat{t}_i^\lambda\}_{i=0}^m$ (with $0 \leq \lambda \leq 1$) comprises well-known cases. Indeed, for $\lambda = 0$ a *blind uniform guess* is selected. When $\lambda = 1/2$ the so-called *centripetal parameterization* is invoked. On the other hand, if $\lambda = 1$ *cumulative chords* are applied. The first case yields a bad length estimation (with possible divergence). In opposite, cumulative chords match the convergence orders established for the non-reduced data i.e. for $(\{t_i\}_{i=0}^m, Q_m)$. In this paper we show that, for exponential parameterization, while λ ranges from one to zero, diminishing convergence rates in length approximation occur. In addition, we discuss and verify a method of possible improvement for such decreased rates based on iterative knot adjustment.

1 Introduction

Suppose that we deal with the sampled data points $\gamma(t_i) = q_i$, where the pair $(\{t_i\}_{i=0}^m, Q_m)$ constitutes the so-called *non-reduced data*. Here the inequality $t_i < t_{i+1}$ holds. We assume that $\gamma : [0, T] \to \mathbb{R}^n$ (with $T < \infty$) is sufficiently smooth and defines a regular curve (i.e. $\dot{\gamma}(t) \neq \mathbf{0}$). In order to approximate the length of γ reading as $d(\gamma) = \int_0^T \|\dot{\gamma}(t)\| dt = \int_0^T \sqrt{\sum_{j=1}^n \dot{\gamma}_j^2(t)} dt$, with an arbitrary

L. Bolc et al. (Eds.): ICCVG 2012, LNCS 7594, pp. 139–147, 2012.
© Springer-Verlag Berlin Heidelberg 2012

interpolant $\bar{\gamma} : [0,T] \to \mathbb{R}^n$ it is necessary to stipulate that $\{t_i\}_{i=0}^m$ satisfy the the so-called *admissibility condition*:

$$\lim_{m \to \infty} \delta_m = 0, \quad where \quad \delta_m = \max_{0 \le i \le m-1} (t_{i+1} - t_i).$$

Such class of admissible samplings is denoted from now on as V_G^m. We consider in this paper one important subfamily $V_\varepsilon^m \subset V_G^m$, i.e. the so-called *ε-uniform samplings* (see e.g. [9]):

$$t_i = \phi(\frac{iT}{m}) + O(\frac{1}{m^{1+\varepsilon}}), \tag{1}$$

where $\varepsilon \geqslant 0$, $\phi : [0,T] \to [0,T]$ is smooth and $\dot\phi > 0$ (so that $t_i < t_{i+1}$). Such samplings represent the distortion of the uniform distribution (iT/m) by mapping ϕ and by the additional term $O(m^{-(1+\varepsilon)})$. In the latter, the smaller ε gets, the bigger distortion of uniform distribution occurs.

1.1 Parametric Interpolation

We recall now a standard result within the field of parametric interpolation applicable to the *non-reduced data* $(\{t_i\}_{i=0}^m, Q_m)$. Let the interpolant $\bar{\gamma} = \tilde{\gamma}_r$, based on $\{t_i\}_{i=0}^m$, denote a piecewise r-degree polynomial (see [1]). The following result holds (see e.g. [5]):

Theorem 1. *Let $\gamma \in C^{r+1}$ be a regular curve $\gamma : [0,T] \to \mathbb{R}^n$. Assume that the knot parameters $\{t_i\}_{i=0}^m \in V_G^m$ are known. Then a piecewise r-degree Lagrange polynomial interpolation $\tilde{\gamma}_r$ used with $\{t_i\}_{i=0}^m$ known, yields sharp estimates:*

$$\tilde{\gamma}_r = \gamma + O(\delta^{r+1}) \quad and \quad d(\tilde{\gamma}_r) = d(\gamma) + O(\delta^{r+1}). \tag{2}$$

For length of γ estimation the additional assumption is needed i.e. $m\delta = O(1)$.

Visibly, by (2), when $r = 2,3$, a piecewise-quadratic or a piecewise-cubic $\tilde{\gamma}_r$ renders, for both length and trajectory estimation, *cubic* or *quartic* orders of convergence, respectively. This in practice is sufficiently fast as even for the sparse data one obtains satisfactory estimates for γ and $d(\gamma)$. Remarkably, for some subfamilies of admissible samplings, an extra acceleration in convergence rates for $d(\gamma)$ is possible once non-reduced data $(\{t_i\}_{i=0}^m, Q_m)$ are input - e.g. for samplings (1) we obtain $d(\tilde{\gamma}_r) = d(\gamma) + O(\delta^{r+1+\min\{1,\varepsilon\}})$, for r even (see [5]).

1.2 Nonparametric Interpolation

In various applications in computer graphics and computer vision, engineering or physics a common situation is to deal exclusively with the so-called *reduced data* Q_m (see e.g. [4], [7], or [10]), where the corresponding knots $\{t_i\}_{i=0}^m$ remain unknown. Before choosing some interpolation scheme $\hat{\gamma}$ we need here first to find some estimate $\{\hat{t}_i\}_{i=0}^m \approx \{t_i\}_{i=0}^m$. In particular, for curve modeling a well-known *exponential parameterization* (including *centripetal*) $\{\hat{t}_i\}_{i=0}^m$ complementing the unknown knots $\{t_i\}_{i=0}^m$ is often invoked (see e.g. [2] or [7]):

$$\hat{t}_0 = 0, \qquad \hat{t}_{i+1} = \hat{t}_i + \|q_{i+1} - q_i\|^\lambda, \tag{3}$$

where $0 \leq \lambda \leq 1$ and $i = 0, 1, \ldots, m - 1$. We denote a piecewise r-degree polynomial based on (3) as $\hat{\gamma} = \hat{\gamma}_r : [0, \hat{T}] \to \mathbb{R}^n$. Note that for trajectory estimation of γ by $\hat{\gamma}_r$, for each m one needs also to find *a re-parameterization* $\psi : [0, T] \to [0, \hat{T}]$, which synchronizes both domains of γ and $\hat{\gamma}_r$.

The case when $\lambda = 0$, reduces (3) to blind *uniform* guesses:

$$\hat{t}_i = i. \tag{4}$$

This approach, however does not incorporate the geometrical distribution of sampled reduced data Q_m and as such offers poor approximation. Indeed, for $r = 2$ we have the following (see [9]):

Theorem 2. *Let the unknown* $\{t_i\}_{i=0}^m$ *be sampled ε-uniformly, where* $\varepsilon > 0$ *and* $\gamma \in C^4$. *Then there is a uniform piecewise-quadratic Lagrange interpolant* $\hat{\gamma}_2 : [0, \hat{T} = m] \to \mathbb{R}^n$, *calculable in terms of* Q_m *(with (4)) and piecewise C^∞ re-parameterization* $\psi : [0, T] \to [0, \hat{T} = m]$ *such that:*

$$\hat{\gamma}_2 \circ \psi = \gamma + O(\delta^{\min\{3, 1+2\varepsilon\}}) \quad and \quad d(\hat{\gamma}_2) = d(\gamma) + O(\delta^{4\varepsilon}). \tag{5}$$

Note that for $\varepsilon = 0$ the asymptotic $O(1)$ yields a potential loss of convergence - for pertinent examples see [5] or [9].

On the other hand, the choice of $\lambda = 1$ in (3) renders the so-called *cumulative chords* (see e.g. [7] or [10]):

$$\hat{t}_0 = 0, \quad \hat{t}_{i+1} = \hat{t}_i + \|q_{i+1} - q_i\|, \tag{6}$$

for $i = 0, 1, \ldots, m - 1$. This parameterization accounts for the geometrical distribution of reduced data Q_m and as such yields much better approximation properties in comparison to (4). Indeed, the following holds (see [8]):

Theorem 3. *Suppose* γ *is a regular C^k curve in* $\mathbb{R}^n$, *where* $k \geq r + 1$ *and* $r = 2, 3$. *Let* $\hat{\gamma}_r : [0, \hat{T}] \to \mathbb{R}^n$ *be the cumulative chord piecewise-degree-r approximation defined by* Q_m *and (6). Then there is a piecewise-C^r re-parameterization* $\psi : [0, T] \to [0, \hat{T}]$, *with*

$$\hat{\gamma}_r \circ \psi = \gamma + O(\delta^{r+1}) \quad and \quad d(\hat{\gamma}_r) = d(\gamma) + O(\delta^{r+1}). \tag{7}$$

Also, if $k \geq 4, r = 2$, *and if, for some* $\varepsilon \geq 0$, *we have the general uniformity condition:*

$$t_{i+2} - 2t_{i+1} + t_i = O(\delta^{\min\{2, 1+\varepsilon\}}) \quad for \quad i = 0, 3, 5, \ldots, m - 2, \tag{8}$$

then

$$d(\hat{\gamma}_r) = d(\gamma) + O(\delta^{\min\{4, 3+\varepsilon\}}). \tag{9}$$

Note that both results concerning length estimation require an additional assumption, namely $m\delta = O(1)$.

It should be noted that condition (8) is satisfied by (1) and the estimates from Th. 3 are sharp - see [5] and [8]. The orders (7) (and (9)) not only outperform (5) but also match (or exceed) those established for non-reduced data in (2) (for $r = 2, 3$). In the next subsection we pose the questions dealt later in this paper.

1.3   Open Problems and Adjusted Exponentials

A natural consequence of comparing Th. 2 and Th. 3 is to expect, once $\lambda \in [0, 1]$ varies, that the orders $\alpha(\lambda)$ for $d(\gamma) - d(\hat{\gamma}_r) = O(\delta^{\alpha(\lambda)})$ fall within the interval $[\alpha(0), \alpha(1)]$. In particular, for $r = 2$, we expect $\alpha(\lambda) \in [0, 3]$ for arbitrary admissible samplings $\{t_i\}_{i=0}^m \in V_G^m$ and $\alpha(\lambda) \in [4\varepsilon, \min\{4, 3 + \varepsilon\}]$ for any ε-uniform sampling (with fixed ε and $\lambda \in [0, 1]$ varying). Recall that $\alpha(0) = 0$ results in possible divergence of $d(\gamma)$ estimation ($O(m^{-4\varepsilon}) = O(1)$ with $\varepsilon = 0$).

We expect a similar effect of decreased convergence orders to occur also possibly for $r = 3$. In this paper:

- C1: We verify experimentally the above *conjecture* for $r = 2, 3$.
- C2: In addition, we propose *an adjustment scheme* for exponential parameterization (3) (including centripetal one) so that the above effect of diminishing convergence rates with λ getting shrunk to 0 is possibly alleviated. In doing so, for a given $\{t_i\}_{i=0}^m$, let $\hat{\gamma}_r$ be a sum-track of r-degree Lagrange polynomials $\{\hat{\gamma}_{r,j}\}_{j=0}^p$ (with $m = pr$).

1. For a j-th $r + 1$-tuple of points $\{q_{i+j}\}_{i=0}^r$ (here $j \in \{0, r, 2r, \ldots, p\}$) pass $\hat{\gamma}_{r,j}^{(0)} = \hat{\gamma}_{r,j}$ based on exponential knots (3).
2. Next update the knots $\{\hat{t}_i^{(0)}\}_{i=0}^r$ with $\{\hat{t}_i^{(1)}\}_{i=0}^r$ according to:

$$\hat{t}_0^{(1)} = 0, \quad and \quad \hat{t}_{i+1}^{(1)} = \hat{t}_i^{(1)} + (d_i(\hat{\gamma}_{r,j}^{(0)}))^\lambda, \tag{10}$$

where

$$d_i(\hat{\gamma}_{r,j}^{(0)}) = \int_{\hat{t}_i^{(0)}}^{\hat{t}_{i+1}^{(0)}} \|\dot{\hat{\gamma}}_{r,j}^{(0)}(\hat{t})\| d\hat{t}.$$

3. Update the interpolant $\hat{\gamma}_{r,j}^{(0)}$ to $\hat{\gamma}_{r,j}^{(1)} = \hat{\gamma}_{r,j} : [0, \hat{t}_r^{(1)}] \to \mathbb{R}^n$ based on recomputed knots (10).
4. Estimate the length of $d(\gamma)$ with the quantity $d(\hat{\gamma}_r^{(1)}) = \sum_{j=0}^p d(\hat{\gamma}_{r,j}^{(1)})$.
5. Note that the above procedure can be extended to the *iterative one*. Namely, in Step 3 one replaces 0 with $k - 1$ and 1 with k, respectively.

In Fig. 1(a) the difference between quadratics $\hat{\gamma}_2^{(0)}$ and $\hat{\gamma}_2^{(1)}$ based on three points $Q_2 = \{(0, 0), (0, 0.05), (1, 0)\}$ with $\lambda = 1/4$ is shown. Similar comparison between two quadratics $\hat{\gamma}_2^{(0)}$ and $\hat{\gamma}_2^{(1)}$ with $\lambda = 1$ is made in Fig. 1(b). Both pictures demonstrate the difference between two parameterizations upon each iteration as well as the evolution of the interpolant with $k = 0, 1$ for each fixed λ (with $\lambda = 1/4$ it is marginal).

We introduce now *curves* and *samplings* used later in our experiments.

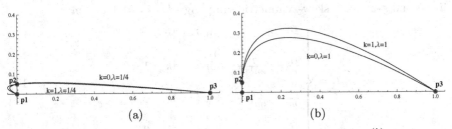

Fig. 1. Interpolating three points $Q_2 = \{(0,0), (0,0.05), (1,0)\}$ with $\hat{\gamma}_2^{(k)}$, for $k = 0, 1$: (a) here $\lambda = 1/4$. (b) here $\lambda = 1$

2   Curves and Samplings

The problems *C1* and *C2* listed in the previous section are tested in this paper with the aid of the following curves:

a) The *cubic curve* $\gamma_{c1}(t) \in \mathbb{R}^2$ with an inflection point and $d(\gamma_{c1}) = 1.548$:

$$\gamma_{c1}(t) = ((t - 0.5), (4(t - 0.5)^3)), \quad for \quad t \in\, <0, 1>. \tag{11}$$

b) The *spiral* $\gamma_s(t) \in \mathbb{R}^2$ with $d(\gamma_s) = 173.608$:

$$\gamma_s(t) = ((6\pi - t) \cdot \cos(t), (6\pi - t) \cdot \sin(t)), \quad for \quad t \in\, <0, 5\pi>. \tag{12}$$

c) The *elliptical helix* $\gamma_h \in \mathbb{R}^3$ with $d(\gamma_h) = 8.090$:

$$\gamma_h(t) = (1.5 \cdot \cos(t), \sin(t), t/4), \quad for \quad t \in\, <0, 2\pi>. \tag{13}$$

d) The *cubic curve* $\gamma_{c2}(t) \in \mathbb{R}^2$ with no inflection point and $d(\gamma_{c2}) = 3.3452$:

$$\gamma_{c2}(t) = (\pi t, (\frac{\pi t + 1}{\pi + 1})^3), \quad for \quad t \in\, <0, 1>. \tag{14}$$

In addition, in our experiments we use special samplings (with $\varepsilon \in [0, 1]$):
(i) ε-uniform sampling - for $i = 0, 1, \ldots, m$:

$$t_i = \frac{iT}{m} + \frac{(-1)^{i+1}}{3m^{1+\varepsilon}}. \tag{15}$$

(ii) First ε-uniform skew-symmetric sampling - for $i = 0, 1, \ldots, m$:

$$t_i = \begin{cases} \frac{iT}{m} & \text{for } i = 3k, \\[2mm] \frac{iT}{m} - \frac{T}{4m^{1+\varepsilon}} & \text{for } i = 3k + 1, \\[2mm] \frac{iT}{m} & \text{for } i = 3k + 2. \end{cases} \tag{16}$$

(iii) Second ε-uniform skew-symmetric sampling - for $i = 0, 1, \ldots, m$:

$$t_i = \begin{cases} \frac{iT}{m} & \text{for } i = 4k, \\[2mm] \frac{iT}{m} - \frac{T}{4m^{1+\epsilon}} & \text{for } i = 4k + 1, \\[2mm] \frac{iT}{m} - \frac{T}{2m^{1+\epsilon}} & \text{for } i = 4k + 2, \\[2mm] \frac{iT}{m} & \text{for } i = 4k + 3. \end{cases} \tag{17}$$

We pass now to the experimental part of this paper.

3   Experiments

All tests are implemented in Mathematica 8.0 using the processor AMD Phenom II X4 955 3, 21GHz and RAM 4096MB. The coefficient $\alpha(\lambda)$ is estimated upon applying *a linear regression* to the collection of points $(\log(m), -\log E_m)$ with $m_0 \leq m \leq m_1$, where $E_m = |d(\gamma_l) - d(\hat{\gamma}_r^{(k)})|$, for $r = 2, 3$, $k = 0, 1$ and $l = 1, 2, 3, 4$. Both m_0 and m_1 are adjusted, in each test accordingly. The latter is the consequence of the following. On one hand, convergence holds for sufficiently big $m = m_0$. On the other hand, $m = m_1$ cannot be too large as machine errors need to be avoided.

The unknown knots $\{t_i\}_{i=0}^m$ are replaced by exponential parameterization (3) with $\lambda \in [0, 1/5, 1/2, 5/6, 1]$. All ε-uniform samplings satisfy: $\varepsilon \in \{0, 1/2, 1\}$.

Test 1: γ_{c1} from (11) is sampled according to (15). The results for asymptotics in $d(\gamma_{c1}) - d(\hat{\gamma}_2^{(k)}) = O(\delta^{\alpha(\lambda)})$ (with piecewise-quadratics $\hat{\gamma}_2^{(k)}$, where $k = 0, 1$) are collated in Tab. 1. Here $m_0 = 150$ and $m_1 = 170$.

Test 2: γ_h from (13) is sampled as defined in (16). The results for asymptotics in $d(\gamma_h) - d(\hat{\gamma}_2^{(k)}) = O(\delta^{\alpha(\lambda)})$ (with piecewise-quadratics $\hat{\gamma}_2^{(k)}$, where $k = 0, 1$), are listed in Tab. 2. Here, again $m_0 = 150$ and $m_1 = 170$.

Test 3: γ_s from (12) is sampled as (17). The results for asymptotics $d(\gamma_s) - d(\hat{\gamma}_3^{(k)}) = O(\delta^{\alpha(\lambda)})$ (with piecewise-cubics $\hat{\gamma}_3^{(k)}$, where $k = 0, 1$), are presented in Tab. 3. Here $m_0 = 99$ and $m_1 = 129$.

Visibly, the results from Tables 1, 2 and 3 *confirm the conjecture C1*. Another transparent feature is that generically, orders of convergence for $k = 0$ are similar as compared to these obtained with $k = 1$.

We test now whether consecutive iterations of our *adjusted exponential scheme* improve approximation orders.

Test 4: We sample now γ_{c1} from (11) with (15) for $\varepsilon = 0$ and $\lambda = 1/2$ (or $\varepsilon = 1/4$ and $\lambda = 1/5$). The results for asymptotics $d(\gamma_{c1}) - d(\hat{\gamma}_2^{(k)}) = O(\delta^{\alpha(\lambda)})$ (with piecewise-quadratics $\hat{\gamma}_2^{(k)}$, where $k = 0, 1, 2, 3, 4, 5$) are listed in Tab. 4. Analogous tests are conducted for γ_{c2} with different values of (λ, ε) - see Tab. 5.

Similar results for multiple iterations follow for $\hat{\gamma}_3$ (i.e. for piecewise-cubic interpolation) coupled with different ε-uniform samplings, curves γ and parameters λ. Hence, as the above experiments show, the conjecture *C2* cannot be confirmed in affirmative.

Table 1. Interpolation of γ_{c1} sampled with (15), by $\hat{\gamma}_2^{(0)}$ and $\hat{\gamma}_2^{(1)}$, for $150 \leq m \leq 170$

λ	ε	$\alpha(\lambda)$ for $\hat{\gamma}_2^{(0)}$	$\alpha(\lambda)$ for $\hat{\gamma}_2^{(1)}$
0	0	-0.03666	-0.03666
1/5	0	0.18170	0.17681
1/2	0	1.99477	1.99477
5/6	0	1.99485	1.99476
1	0	4.04042	4.11680
0	1/2	3.07697	3.07679
1/5	1/2	2.98805	2.98789
1/2	1/2	3.01175	3.01174
5/6	1/2	3.00335	3.00322
1	1/2	3.97626	3.98771
0	1	4.00009	4.00009
1/5	1	3.99126	3.99019
1/2	1	3.99813	3.99812
5/6	1	3.99706	3.99675
1	1	3.99958	4.00028

Table 2. Interpolation of γ_h sampled with (16), by $\hat{\gamma}_2^{(0)}$ and $\hat{\gamma}_2^{(1)}$, for $150 \leq m \leq 170$

λ	ε	$\alpha(\lambda)$ for $\hat{\gamma}_2^{(0)}$	$\alpha(\lambda)$ for $\hat{\gamma}_2^{(1)}$
0	0	1.98236	1.98236
1/5	0	2.02331	2.02226
1/2	0	2.00652	2.00649
5/6	0	2.01108	2.01047
1	0	3.99817	3.99879
0	1/2	-18.6471	-18.6471
1/5	1/2	3.53866	3.53839
1/2	1/2	3.35076	3.35074
5/6	1/2	3.45732	3.34702
1	1/2	4.00081	3.99901
0	1	3.99916	3.99912
1/5	1	3.99869	3.99864
1/2	1	3.99838	3.99837
5/6	1	3.99842	3.99836
1	1	3.99861	3.99836

Table 3. Interpolation of γ_s sampled with (17), by $\hat{\gamma}_3^{(0)}$ and $\hat{\gamma}_3^{(1)}$, for $99 \le m \le 129$

λ	ε	$\alpha(\lambda)$ for $\hat{\gamma}_3^{(0)}$	$\alpha(\lambda)$ for $\hat{\gamma}_3^{(1)}$
0	0	2.03681	2.03681
1/5	0	2.00018	2.00039
1/2	0	1.98394	1.98478
5/6	0	1.94995	1.93961
1	0	3.90493	3.95209
0	1/2	2.35332	2.35322
1/5	1/2	2.33635	2.33768
1/2	1/2	2.26045	2.26216
5/6	1/2	1.51275	1.47892
1	1/2	3.99538	4.02266
0	1	-0.25042	-0.250424
1/5	1	-3.98475	-3.93412
1/2	1	6.05858	6.06158
5/6	1	4.28379	4.29675
1	1	3.99041	4.00620

Table 4. Interpolation of γ_{c1} sampled as in (15) by $\hat{\gamma}_2^{(k)}$, with $k \in \{0, 1, 2, 3, 4, 5\}$, for $150 \le m \le 170$. Here $(\lambda, \varepsilon) = (1/2, 0)$ or $(\lambda, \varepsilon) = (1/5, 1/4)$.

iteration	$\alpha(0.5)$; $\hat{\gamma}_2^{(k)}$; $\varepsilon = 0$	$\alpha(0.2)$; $\hat{\gamma}_2^{(k)}$; $\varepsilon = 0.25$
$k = 0$	1.99477	2.45836
$k = 1$	1.99477	2.45816
$k = 2$	1.99477	2.45816
$k = 3$	1.99477	2.45816
$k = 4$	1.99477	2.45816
$k = 5$	1.99477	2.45816

Table 5. Interpolation of γ_{c2} sampled as in (15) by $\hat{\gamma}_2^{(k)}$, with $k \in \{0, 1, 2, 3, 4, 5\}$, for $150 \le m \le 170$. Here $(\lambda, \varepsilon) = (1/5, 1/4)$ or $(\lambda, \varepsilon) = (1/5, 1/2)$.

iteration	$\alpha(0.2)$; $\hat{\gamma}_2^{(k)}$; $\varepsilon = 0.25$	$\alpha(0, 2)$; $\hat{\gamma}_2^{(k)}$; $\varepsilon = 0.5$
$k = 0$	2.43345	2.93170
$k = 1$	2.43345	2.93169
$k = 2$	2.43345	2.93169
$k = 3$	2.43345	2.93169
$k = 4$	2.43345	2.93169
$k = 5$	2.43345	2.93169

4   Conclusions

We verify in *affirmative* the conjecture raised in *C1*. The *first open problem* is thus, how to extend, for $\hat{\gamma}_r^{(0)}$ ($r = 2, 3$), the theoretical results on convergence orders already established for cumulative chords (with $\alpha(1)$) and uniform one (with $\alpha(0)$) to arbitrary exponential parameterization i.e. for all $\lambda \in [0, 1]$ and $\varepsilon \in [0, 1]$ varying.

Our tests hint that generically, on dense reduced data Q_m next iterations of adjusted exponential parameterizations do not improve $d(\gamma)$ estimation - thus conjecture *C2* is not confirmed. *The second open question* remains however, how to accelerate the convergence orders (for $\lambda \in [0, 1]$) via some kind of iterative scheme as presented in our paper.

Certain clues may be given in [3], where complete C^2 splines are dealt with, to obtain the fourth orders of convergence in length estimation. An iterative scheme to increase convergence orders is also proposed in this paper. The analysis of C^1 interpolation for reduced data with cumulative chords can additionally be found in [6].

Some applications of non-parametric interpolation can be found e.g. in [4] or [7].

References

1. de Boor, C.: A Practical Guide to Splines. Springer, Heidelberg (2001)
2. Lee, E.T.Y.: Choosing nodes in parametric curve interpolation. Computer-Aided Design 21(6), 363–370 (1989)
3. Floater, M.S.: Chordal cubic spline interpolation is fourth order accurate. IMA Journal of Numerical Analysis 26, 25–33 (2006)
4. Janik, M., Kozera, R., Kozioł, P.: Reduced data for curve modeling - applications in graphics. Computer Vision and Physics (submitted)
5. Kozera, R.: Curve modeling via interpolation based on multidimensional reduced data. Studia Informatica 25(4B(61)), 1–140 (2004)
6. Kozera, R., Noakes, L.: C^1 interpolation with cumulative chord cubics. Fundamenta Informaticae 61(3-4), 285–301 (2004)
7. Kvasov, B.I.: Methods of Shape-Preserving Spline Approximation. World Scientific Publishing Company, Singapore (2000)
8. Noakes, L., Kozera, R.: Cumulative chords piecewise-quadratics and piecewise-cubics. In: Klette, R., Kozera, R., Noakes, L., Weickert, J. (eds.) Geometric Properties of Incomplete Data. Computational Imaging and Vision, vol. 31, pp. 59–75. Kluver Academic Publishers, The Netherlands (2006)
9. Noakes, L., Kozera, R., Klette, R.: Length Estimation for Curves with Different Samplings. In: Bertrand, G., Imiya, A., Klette, R. (eds.) Digital and Image Geometry. LNCS, vol. 2243, pp. 339–351. Springer, Heidelberg (2002)
10. Piegl, L., Tiller, W.: The NURBS Book. Springer, Heidelberg (1997)

Sharpness in Trajectory Estimation
by Piecewise-quadratics(-cubics) and Cumulative Chords

Ryszard Kozera and Mateusz Śmietanka

Faculty of Mathematics and Information Science, Warsaw University of Technology,
Pl. Politechniki 1, 00-661 Warsaw, Poland
r.kozera@mini.pw.edu.pl, mateusz.smietanka@gmail.com

Abstract. In this paper we verify sharpness of the theoretical results concerning the asymptotic orders of trajectory approximation of the unknown parametric curve γ in arbitrary Euclidean space. The pertinent interpolation schemes (based on piecewise-quadratics and piecewise-cubics) are here considered for the so-called reduced data. The latter forms an ordered collection of points without provision of the associated interpolation knots. To complement such data i.e. to determine the missing knots, cumulative chord parameterization is invoked. Sharpness of cubic and quartic orders of convergence are demonstrated for piecewise-quadratics and piecewise-cubics, respectively. This topic has its ramification in computer vision (e.g. image segmentation), computer graphics (e.g. trajectory modeling) or in engineering (e.g. robotics).

1 Introduction

In this section we first introduce basic notions concerning the so-called parametric and non-parametric interpolation. In sequel, we invoke the pertinent theoretical approximation results established within the above fields. Finally, we pose the problem, ultimately addressed in the last sections of this paper which forms its novel contribution.

1.1 Preliminaries

Let $\gamma : [0,T] \to \mathbb{R}^n$ be a smooth regular parametric curve of class C^k where $k \geq 1$, $T \in (0, \infty)$ and $\forall t \in [0,T]$ with $\dot{\gamma}(t) \neq \vec{0}$. Our task is to estimate via interpolation the trajectory of γ based on ordered $m+1$-tuple $Q_m = \{q_i\}_{i=0}^m$ data points in $\mathbb{R}^n$ such that $q_i = \gamma(t_i)$. Here the corresponding knot parameter $\{t_i\}_{i=0}^m$ (called also tabular parameters) are assumed to be *unknown*. It is important to underline that $\{t_i\}_{i=0}^m \in [0,T]^{m+1}$ and $0 = t_0 < ... < t_m = T$.

In general, one discerns two interpolation schemes: *parametric interpolation* which is a classical approach based on *non-reduced data* $(\{t_i\}_{i=0}^m, Q_m)$ and *non-parametric interpolation* derived for *reduced data* Q_m (as introduced above). Any interpolation scheme invoked (see e.g. [1], [9] or [10]), including Lagrange polynomial, requires provision of both data points Q_m and the respective knots. Of course, non-reduced data $(\{t_i\}_{i=0}^m, Q_m)$ satisfy such requirement. However, in case of reduced data Q_m, all missing knots need to be first somehow estimated $t_i \approx \hat{t}_i$, yielding *a complemented reduced data* $(\{\hat{t}_i\}_{i=0}^m, Q_m)$. Here $\hat{t}_i \in [0, \hat{T}]$ and $\hat{t}_i < \hat{t}_{i+1}$. The issue of proper knots' estimation

L. Bolc et al. (Eds.): ICCVG 2012, LNCS 7594, pp. 148–155, 2012.
© Springer-Verlag Berlin Heidelberg 2012

and its impact on approximation quality forms an important issue within the field of non-parametric interpolation (see e.g. [3], [4], [5], [7] or [9]).

There are numerous examples, where reduced data occur. E.g. in *computer vision* (image segmentation), *computer graphics* (light-source path estimation) or in *engineering and physics* (robotics or high-speed particle trajectory estimation) - see e.g. [6].

Recall that m-degree Lagrange interpolation, used to the non-reduced data ($\{t_i\}_{i=0}^m$, Q_m), with m getting large, yields bad approximation properties (see Runge effect [1]). The remedy is to invoke *piecewise r-degree polynomial interpolation* for which the order of polynomial is constant and preferably low (usually $r = 2,3$).

Definition 1. *For a given $r + 1$-tuple points $Q_m^{i,r} = (q_i, q_{i+1}, ..., q_{i+r})$ one can define uniquely r-degree Lagrange polynomial $\tilde{\gamma}_{i,r}$ (or $\hat{\gamma}_{i,r}$) based on either $(\{t_i\}_{i=0}^m, Q_m)$ or $(\{\hat{t}_i\}_{i=0}^m, Q_m)$, respectively. Then piecewise r-degree Lagrange polynomial $\tilde{\gamma}_r : [0,T] \rightarrow \mathbb{R}^n$ (or $\hat{\gamma}_r : [0,\hat{T}] \rightarrow \mathbb{R}^n$) interpolating Q_m is defined as a truck-sum of $\{\tilde{\gamma}_{i,r}\}_{i=0}^{\frac{m}{r}-1}$ or $\{\hat{\gamma}_{i,r}\}_{i=0}^{\frac{m}{r}-1}$, accordingly.*

Of course, the data points $q_i = \gamma(t_i)$ used to estimate the trajectory of the unknown curve γ by either $\tilde{\gamma}_r$ or $\hat{\gamma}_r$, should fall within the so-called *admissible class of samplings*.

Definition 2. *The collection of data $\{\gamma(t_i)\}_{i=0}^m$ is said to form admissible class of samplings if the corresponding tabular parameters $\{t_i\}_{i=0}^m$ satisfy:*

$$\lim_{m \to \infty} \delta_m \to 0^+, \quad for \quad \delta_m = \max_{1 \leq i \leq m} \{t_i - t_{i-1} : i = 1, 2, ..., m\}. \tag{1}$$

The class of admissible samplings $\{t_i\}_{i=0}^m$ satisfying (1) is denoted onward by V_G^m. Recall now the definition of *approximation orders*.

Definition 3. *A family $\{f_\delta, \delta \geq 0\}$ of functions $f_\delta : [0,T] \rightarrow \mathbb{R}^n$ is said to be of order $O(\delta^p)$ when there is a constant $K \geq 0$ such that, for some $\delta_0 \geq 0$, $|f_\delta(t)| \leq K\delta^p$ for all $\delta \in (0, \delta_0)$ and, for all $t \in [0,T]$. In such case we write $f_\delta = O(\delta^p)$. For a family of vector-valued functions $F_\delta : [0,T] \rightarrow \mathbb{R}^n$, we write $F_\delta = O(\delta^p)$ when $\|F_\delta\| = O(\delta^p)$, where $\| \cdot \|$ denotes the Euclidean norm.*

In particular, any $\bar{\gamma} : [0,T] \rightarrow \mathbb{R}^n$ (e.g. for $\bar{\gamma} = \tilde{\gamma}_r$) has approximation order p of γ if:

$$\bar{\gamma} - \gamma = O(\delta^p). \tag{2}$$

Note that (2) requires both γ and $\bar{\gamma}$ be defined over the same domain $[0,T]$. The latter is automatically fulfilled when parametric Lagrange interpolation is invoked for $\gamma, \tilde{\gamma}_r : [0,T] \rightarrow \mathbb{R}^n$. On the other hand, for non-parametric interpolation the so-called *knot synchronization* is first required. To achieve this, a re-parametrization of $\hat{\gamma}_r$ to $\hat{\gamma}_r \circ \psi$, for some $\psi : [0,T] \rightarrow [0,\hat{T}]$ is needed (here $\dot{\psi} > 0$ and $\psi(t_i) = \hat{t}_i$). Upon *knot synchronization* step is applied, formula (2) can also be used with non-parametric interpolation. Namely, the approximation $\hat{\gamma}_r : [0,\hat{T}] \rightarrow \mathbb{R}^n$ of curve $\gamma : [0,T] \rightarrow \mathbb{R}^n$, determined by Q_m and chosen $\psi : [0,T] \rightarrow [0,\hat{T}]$ is said to be of order p if:

$$\hat{\gamma}_r \circ \psi - \gamma = O(\delta^p). \tag{3}$$

The problem of finding *a proper re-parametrization $\psi : [0,T] \rightarrow [0,\hat{T}]$* forms an additional task, once the unknown tabular parameters $\{t_i\}_{i=0}^m$ are somehow first *replaced*

with $\{\hat{t}_i\}_{i=0}^m$. These both matters, if properly tackled, should render the trajectory estimation with possibly fast convergence rate. Achieving high orders of convergence, for
dense data (i.e. for m large), usually guarantees equally good approximation properties
for the corresponding *sparse data* (i.e. for m small). The latter is of particular importance in most practical applications. As it turns out (see e.g. [3], [5], [7] or [9]), given
reduced data Q_m, the so-called *cumulative chord parameterization*

$$\hat{t}_0 = 0, \quad \hat{t}_{i+1} = \hat{t}_i + \|q_{i+1} - q_i\|, \tag{4}$$

where $1 \le i \le m-1$, provides an excellent guess for $\{\hat{t}_i\}_{i=0}^m$. Note that here $\hat{T} = \sum_{i=0}^{m-1} \|q_{i+1} - q_i\|$. In the next subsection, pertinent theoretical results concerning (4)
and $\hat{\gamma}_r$ (for $r = 2,3$) are invoked, which in turn permits to raise the question, subse-
quently addressed in this paper.

1.2 Main Theoretical Results

This subsection invokes main theoretical results (see [5] or [7]) on orders of *trajec-
tory* (and *length* $d(\gamma) = \int_0^T \|\dot{\gamma}(t)\| dt$) approximations for non-parametric piecewise La-
grange polynomial interpolation $\hat{\gamma}_{r=2,3}$ (piecewise parabolic and piecewise cubic). The
cumulative chord parametrization (4) is chosen for guessed $\{\hat{t}_i\}_{i=0}^m$ to estimate the missing knots $\{t_i\}_{i=0}^m$.

In order to compare parametric versus non-parametric interpolation we recall now
the basic result establishing the relationship between γ and $\tilde{\gamma}_r$ for a given non-reduced
data $(\{t_i\}_{i=0}^m, Q_m)$ (see e.g. [1] or [5]):

Theorem 1. *Let* $\gamma \in C^{r+1}$ *be a regular curve* $\gamma : [0,T] \to \mathbb{R}^n$. *Assume that knots are
given and are admissible i.e.* $\{t_i\}_{i=0}^m \in V_G^m$. *Then a piecewise-r-degree Lagrange polynomial interpolation* $\tilde{\gamma}_r$ *used with* $\{t_i\}_{i=0}^m$ *known, yields the following:*

$$\tilde{\gamma}_r = \gamma + O(\delta^{r+1}) \quad and \quad d(\tilde{\gamma}_r) = d(\gamma) + O(\delta^{r+1}). \tag{5}$$

The estimates in (5) are *sharp*. The latter means that there exists at least one admissible
sampling $\{t_i\}_{i=0}^m \in V_G^m$ and one curve γ within an a priori specified class of functions
(here $\gamma \in C^{r+1}$) such that (5) is exact i.e. there is no faster convergence rate.

Th. 1 used with $r = 2,3$, yields piecewise-quadratic and piecewise-cubic Lagrange
parametric interpolation rendering cubic and quartic rates of convergence, respectively,
for both trajectory and length estimation.

*Q1) A fundamental question arises here, whether a similar result can also be ex-
tended to the non-parametric interpolation.*

A naïve method of guessing the knots according to the *uniform fashion* i.e. with
$\hat{t}_i = (i/m)$ (where $\hat{T} = 1$) yields a negative answer to above question *Q1* (see e.g. [5] or
[8]). Namely, the following holds:

Theorem 2. *Let the unknown* $\{t_i\}_{i=0}^m$ *be a ε-uniform sampling (9), where* $\varepsilon > 0$, *and
suppose that* $\gamma \in C^4$. *Then, there is a uniform (i.e.* $\hat{t}_i = i/m$) *piecewise-quadratic Lagrange interpolant* $\hat{\gamma}_2 : [0,\hat{T}] \to \mathbb{R}^n$ *calculable in terms of* Q_m *and a piecewise - C^∞
re-parametrization* $\psi : [0,T] \to [0,\hat{T}]$ *such that*

$$\hat{\gamma}_2 \circ \psi = \gamma + O(\delta^{min\{3, 1+2\varepsilon\}}) \quad and \quad d(\hat{\gamma}_2) = d(\gamma) + O(\delta^{min\{4, 4\varepsilon\}}). \tag{6}$$

Note that (6) with $\varepsilon \to 0$ renders linear convergence rate for trajectory estimation and divergence for length estimation, respectively (see [8]). The latter contrasts with the cubic convergence orders to estimate γ and $d(\gamma)$ claimed by Th. 1. The *negative result* stemming from Th. 2 is somehow expected. A blind uniform parameterization takes no account into geometrical distribution of a given reduced data Q_m. This, however is clearly achieved by cumulative chord parameterization (4), which happens to provide *a positive answer* to the question *Q1*. Namely, the following holds (see [5] or [7]):

Theorem 3. *Let $\gamma : [0, T] \to \mathbb{R}^n$ be a regular curve of class C^l, where $l \geq r + 1$ and let r be either 2 or 3. Assume that $\hat{\gamma}_r : [0, \hat{T}] \to \mathbb{R}^n$ defines piecewise-r-degree interpolant based on reduced data Q_m and cumulative chords (4). Then there is a piecewise-C^l re-parametrization $\psi : [0, T] \to [0, \hat{T}]$, with*

$$\hat{\gamma}_r \circ \psi = \gamma + O(\delta^{r+1}) \quad and \quad d(\hat{\gamma}_r) = d(\gamma) + O(\delta^{r+1}). \qquad (7)$$

Evidently, both convergence rates in (7) coincide with those claimed in (5). Thus cumulative chords successfully complement reduced data Q_m and yield analogous convergence rates as these claimed for the non-reduced data $(\{t_i\}_{i=0}^m, Q_m)$ in Th. 1. The latter provides a positive answer to question *Q1*, at least for $r = 2, 3$. In addition, as shown experimentally in [5] or [7] the estimate for length approximation in (7) is *sharp*.

Q2) The question which remains still to be answered concerns the sharpness of the trajectory estimation rendered by (7). Such an issue is discussed in affirmative in the subsequent sections of this paper. More precisely, a series of experimental verifications is conducted to demonstrate the sharpness of the trajectory estimation appearing in (7).

We remark here that our interpolant $\hat{\gamma}_r$ is only of class C^0 at the junction points. In a search of global C^1 or C^2 interpolation scheme on reduced data coupled with cumulative chords see [4] or [3], respectively - quartic rates follow for respective *splines* (see [1]).

2   Curves and Samplings

In this section, we first introduce different curves in $\mathbb{R}^2$ and $\mathbb{R}^3$, used subsequently in our experiments. In the next step, various samplings of admissible samplings V_G^m (see Definition 2) are also briefly discussed (i.e. ε-uniform samplings).

2.1   Experimental Curves

For the experiments conducted in this paper, we consider the following regular curves $\gamma_i : [0, 1] \to \mathbb{R}^n$ (where $n = 2, 3$ and $i \in \{1, 2, 3, 4, 5\}$):

$$\gamma_1(t) = \begin{cases} x(t) = t\sin(2\pi t), \\ y(t) = t\cos(2\pi t), \\ z(t) = 2t, \end{cases} \quad \gamma_2(t) = \begin{cases} x(t) = e^t, \\ y(t) = \cos(\pi t), \\ z(t) = 3t^2, \end{cases} \quad \gamma_3(t) = \begin{cases} x(t) = 0.5\sin(2\pi t), \\ y(t) = 3t^2 + 2t + 3, \end{cases}$$

$$\gamma_4(t) = \begin{cases} x(t) = \cos(\pi(1-t)), \\ y(t) = \sin(\pi(1-t)), \end{cases} \quad \gamma_5(t) = \begin{cases} x(t) = 1.5\cos(t), \\ y(t) = \sin(t), \\ z(t) = \frac{t}{4}. \end{cases}$$

In the next subsection we introduce different samplings used to test sharpness of (7).

2.2   Uniform and ε - Uniform Samplings

The natural extension of the *uniform sampling*:

$$t_i = \frac{iT}{m}, \qquad where\ 0 \le i \le m \tag{8}$$

is the so-called ε-*uniform sampling* forming a vast subfamily $V_\varepsilon^m \subset V_G^m$ and defined as:

Definition 4. *For $\varepsilon \ge 0$, the knots $\{t_i\}_{i=0}^m$ are said to be ε-uniformly sampled when there is an order-preserving C^∞ re-parametrization $\phi : [0,T] \to [0,T]$, i.e $\dot\phi > 0$, such that*

$$t_i = \phi\left(\frac{iT}{m}\right) + O\left(\frac{1}{m^{1+\varepsilon}}\right). \tag{9}$$

Of course, if the quantity $O(m^{-(1+\varepsilon)})$ vanishes and $\phi \equiv id$ then (9) reduces to the uniform sampling (8). Note that if $\varepsilon = 0$ then the distortion of $\phi(iT/m)$ by the second term in (9) is the biggest - again here one needs to assure that $t_i < t_{i+1}$. Clearly, samplings V_ε^m represent a rich subclass of admissible samplings V_G^m and therefore pose a good testing platform to verify experimentally the sharpness of (7).

In our experiments the following ε-uniform samplings are used (with $T = 1$):

- ε-uniform random sampling (I)

$$t_i = \frac{i}{m} + k(Random(0,1) - 0,5)\frac{1}{m^{1+\varepsilon}}.$$

- ε-uniform random sampling (II)

$$t_i = \frac{t(\pi t + 1)}{\pi + 1} + k(Random(0,1) - 0,5)\frac{1}{m^{1+\varepsilon}}.$$

- ε-uniform random sampling (III)

$$t_i = \frac{e^{\pi t} - 1}{e^\pi - 1} + k(Random(0,1) - 0,5)\frac{1}{m^{1+\varepsilon}},$$

where $Random(0,1)$ is a pseudo random, scalar value drawn from a uniform distribution on the unit interval $[0,1]$ and k is a scaling factor decreasing the distortion term - introduced during implementation process in order to improve approximation performance. In addition, two more ε-*uniform samplings* are considered (again with $T = 1$):

- skew-symmetric sampling (IV)

$$t_i = \frac{i}{m} + \frac{(-1)^{i+1}}{3m^{1+\varepsilon}}.$$

- skew-symmetric sampling (V)

$$t_i = \begin{cases} \frac{i}{m} & \text{if } i \text{ even,} \\ \frac{i}{m} + \frac{1}{2m^{1+\varepsilon}} & \text{if } i = 4k+1, \\ \frac{i}{m} - \frac{1}{2m^{1+\varepsilon}} & \text{if } i = 4k+3. \end{cases}$$

The experiments in this paper are conducted for ε-uniform samplings with varying values of $\varepsilon \in \{0.0, 0.2, 0.4\}$. We present now the experimental results testing the sharpness of (7), first for piecewise-quadratics and then for piecewise-cubics.

3 Parabolic Piecewise Lagrange Non-parametric Interpolation

We verify now Th. 3, for $r = 2$ and cumulative chords (4). By (7), the convergence rates of $\hat{\gamma}_2 \to \gamma$ should be no less than 3, once $m \to \infty$. Note that, on one hand, by definition of $O(1/m^\alpha)$, $m = m_0$ cannot be too small as (7) holds for m big. On the other hand, if $m = m_1$ is too large, machine errors distort computing α. For each γ one has to adjust m_0 and m_1. For α, *a linear regression* $y(x) = Ax + B$ to $\mathscr{D} = (log(m), -log(E_m))$ applies, where

$$E_m = \|\hat{\gamma}_2 \circ \psi - \gamma\|_\infty = \sup_{[0,T]} \sqrt{\sum_{j=1}^{n} ((\hat{\gamma}_2 \circ \psi - \gamma)_j(t))^2} = \max_{[0,T]} \lambda(t) \qquad (10)$$

and $m_0 \leq m \leq m_1$ with ψ as in Th 3. The estimated $\alpha = A$ (for more see [5]). To solve a global optimization task (10) Newton's and Monte Carlo methods are invoked [2]. Namely, for a given m, 20 random values $t \in [0,T]$ are drawn first. Next, $t = t_s$ with maximal $\{\lambda(t_j)\}_{j=1}^{20}$ is passed to Newton's scheme as initial guess. 4000 iterations are run to yield λ^{max}. This is repeated 40 times with maximal of $\{\lambda_k^{max}\}_{k=1}^{40}$ set to E_m. The whole procedure is analogous for m increasing. The results are shown in Tab. 1.

Table 1. Approximation orders for piecewise-parabolic Lagrange interpolation with cumulative chords and ε-uniform samplings

curves	samplings	$\varepsilon = 0.0$	$\varepsilon = 0.2$	$\varepsilon = 0.4$	$k_0 \leq k \leq k_1$
	ε-uniform sampling I	2.9942	2.9772	2.9884	120-240
	ε-uniform sampling II	2.9923	2.9930	2.9925	120-240
γ_1	ε-uniform sampling III	2.8973	2.9769	2.9766	120-240
	skew-symmetric sampling IV	2.9940	2.9902	2.9946	120-240
	skew-symmetric sampling V	2.9919	2.9913	2.99075	30-80
	ε-uniform sampling I	3.3552	3.3832	3.3836	120-240
	ε-uniform sampling II	2.9786	2.9772	2.9350	120-240
γ_2	ε-uniform sampling III	2.94688	2.9472	2.9474	120-240
	skew-symmetric sampling IV	2.9938	3.3694	3.3765	120-240
	skew-symmetric sampling IV	2.9968	2.9962	2.9956	120-240
	ε-uniform sampling I	3.00319	3.004	3.0037	120-240
	ε-uniform sampling II	2.9996	3.0015	3.0016	120-240
γ_3	ε-uniform sampling III	2.9943	2.9939	2.9935	120-240
	skew-symmetric sampling IV	3.00403	2.9946	2.9988	120-240
	skew-symmetric sampling V	3.0023	3.0018	3.0015	120-240
	ε-uniform sampling I	3.0013	2.9994	3.0001	120-240
	ε-uniform sampling II	2.9922	2.98939	2.9944	120-240
γ_4	ε-uniform sampling III	2.9789	2.9807	2.9907	120-240
	skew-symmetric sampling IV	2.9802	2.99053	2.9948	120-240
	skew-symmetric sampling V	2.9999	3.0001	3.0002	120-240
	ε-uniform sampling I	3.0026	3.0004	3.0004	120-240
	ε-uniform sampling II	2.9956	2.9936	2.9953	120-240
γ_5	ε-uniform sampling III	2.9844	2.9852	2.9851	120-240
	skew-symmetric sampling IV	2.9989	2.9912	2.9956	120-240
	skew-symmetric sampling V	2.9959	2.9959	2.9958	120-240

The results listed in Tab. 1 demonstrate *sharp cubic estimates* for approximation of the trajectory γ by the interpolant $\hat{\gamma}_2$ based on cumulative chords (4). This matches, at least for $r = 2$, convergence rates (7) claimed by Th. 2 (and by Th 1). Hence, the experiments in this subsection provide a positive answer to our question *Q2* in case of $r = 2$.

Recall that the Def. 1, for the construction of a piecewise-quadratic interpolant $\hat{\gamma}_2$ from the reduced data Q_m, stipulates m to be even, i.e. $m = 2k$. Consequently, for a given m, our k determines the number of parabolic arcs $\{\hat{\gamma}_{2i,2}\}_{i=0}^{k-1}$ defining the entire spline $\hat{\gamma}_2$. Hence in testing our asymptotic the regression is applied to $(log(m), -log(E_m))$ with m set as even, satisfying the following inequalities $m_0 = 2k_0 \leq m \leq m_1 = 2k_1$.

4   Cubic Piecewise Lagrange Non-parametric Interpolation

Similarly, we verify now the sharpness of Th. 3, for $r = 3$ and cumulative chords (4). By (7), the convergence rates of $\hat{\gamma}_3 \to \gamma$ should be no less than 4, once $m \to \infty$. The coefficient α is calculated by substituting $\hat{\gamma}_3$ in (10). The results are shown in Tab. 2.

Again, the experiments presented in Tab. 2 confirm *sharp quartic estimates* for the approximation of γ by piecewise-cubic interpolant $\hat{\gamma}_3$ based on cumulative chords (4).

Table 2. Approximation orders for piecewise-cubic Lagrange interpolation with cumulative chords and ε-uniform samplings

curves	samplings	$\varepsilon = 0.0$	$\varepsilon = 0.2$	$\varepsilon = 0.4$	$k_0 \leq k \leq k_1$
γ_1	ε-uniform sampling I	3.9784	3.9765	3.9769	10 - 65
	ε-uniform sampling II	3.9603	3.9596	3.9591	10 - 65
	ε-uniform sampling III	3.9740	3.97360	3.963	90 - 200
	skew-symmetric sampling IV	3.9916	3.9859	3.9883	20 - 80
	skew-symmetric sampling V	3.9504	3.954	3.9625	20 - 80
γ_2	ε-uniform sampling I	3.8967	3.9059	3.9268	10 - 100
	ε-uniform sampling II	3.9808	3.9687	3.9401	10 - 90
	ε-uniform sampling III	4.0375	4.0404	4.0358	10 - 120
	skew-symmetric sampling IV	3.9515	4.2022	4.3103	10 - 19
	skew-symmetric sampling V	3.8077	3.7891	3.8134	70 - 120
γ_3	ε-uniform sampling I	4.0493	4.0283	4.0229	10 - 90
	ε-uniform sampling II	3.9522	3.9564	3.9515	10 - 115
	ε-uniform sampling III	3.9740	3.9810	3.9485	10 - 115
	skew-symmetric sampling IV	3.9060	3.9742	3.9830	40 - 85
	skew-symmetric sampling V	3.9343	3.9993	3.9518	45 - 85
γ_4	ε-uniform sampling I	3.9439	3.9572	3.9682	10 - 75
	ε-uniform sampling II	3.9549	3.9578	3.9529	10 - 75
	ε-uniform sampling III	3.9344	3.9315	3.9343	30 - 140
	skew-symmetric sampling IV	3.9641	4.0243	4.0251	10 - 70
	skew-symmetric sampling V	3.9991	3.9990	3.9968	10 - 70
γ_5	ε-uniform sampling I	3.9808	3.9840	3.9831	10 - 60
	ε-uniform sampling II	3.9117	3.9408	3.9209	10 - 60
	ε-uniform sampling III	3.9188	3.9128	3.9104	10 - 110
	skew-symmetric sampling IV	3.9544	3.9825	3.9849	10 - 55
	skew-symmetric sampling V	3.9774	3.9800	3.9597	10 - 60

The latter, at least for $r = 3$, coincides with the convergence rate (7) proved in Th. 3 (which also matches (5) established in Th. 1). Consequently, this group of experiments yield also a positive answer to the question $Q2$ with respect to $r = 3$.

Similarly to the previous section, a piecewise-cubic interpolant $\hat{\gamma}_3$ based on reduced data Q_m can be applied for m satisfying $m = 3k$. Thus, the tests conducted to approximate pertinent convergence rates α are run for $m_0 = 3k_0 \leq m \leq m_1 = 3k_1$ and m divisible by 3. As previously, given $m = 3k$ the number of local cubics equals to $\{\hat{\gamma}_{3i,3}\}_{i=0}^{k-1}$.

4.1 Summary

The experimental results presented in Sections 3 and 4 *confirm sharpness* of the convergence rates (7) established in Th. 3 concerning the trajectory estimation. The sharpness of length approximation was already verified in [5] and [7].

Our experiments coupled with Th. 3 show that *cumulative chords* (4) for piecewise--quadratic or piecewise-cubic interpolation based on reduced data Q_m compensate the loss of real *tabular parameters* $\{t_i\}_{i=0}^{m}$. In particular, such parameterization yields the same convergence rates, i.e. cubic (or quartic, respectively) as compared with those established for the non-reduced data $(\{t_i\}_{i=0}^{m}, Q_m)$ - see here Th. 1 with $r = 2, 3$.

The comparison of Th. 2 and Th. 3 indicates also that cumulative chords (4) outperform significantly the *blind uniform guess* $\{\hat{t}_i = i/m\}_{i=0}^{m}$ of the real unknown knots.

We complete this paper with raising an open problem. It addresses the issue of how big the subclass of admissible samplings is, for which the sharp cubic or quartic orders prevail, once piecewise-quadratics (or -cubic) based on (4) are applied. The tests conducted herein (see Tab. 1, 2) suggest that almost if not the entire space of admissible samplings V_G^m satisfies such condition. A justification of such claim would be a bonus.

References

1. de Boor, C.: A Practical Guide to Splines. Springer, Berlin (2001)
2. Ferziger, J.H.: Numerical Methods for Engineering Application. John Wiley & Sons, New York (1998)
3. Floater, M.S.: Chordal cubic spline interpolation is fourth order accurate. IMA Journal of Numerical Analysis 26, 25–33 (2006)
4. Kozera, R., Noakes, L.: C^1 interpolation with cumulative chord cubics. Fundamenta Informaticae 31(3-4), 285–301 (2004)
5. Kozera, R.: Curve modeling via interpolation based on multidimensional reduced data. Studia Informatica 25(4B(61)), 1–140 (2004)
6. Janik, M., Kozera, R., Kozioł, P.: Reduced data for curve modeling - applications in graphics. Computer Vision and Physics (submitted)
7. Noakes, L., Kozera, R.: Cumulative chords and piecewise-quadratics and piecewise-cubics. In: Klette, R., Kozera, R., Noakes, L., Weickert, J. (eds.) Geometric Properties of Incomplete Data. Computational Imaging and Vision, The Netherlands, vol. 31, pp. 59–75 (2006)
8. Noakes, L., Kozera, R., Klette, R.: Length Estimation for Curves with Different Samplings. In: Bertrand, G., Imiya, A., Klette, R. (eds.) Digital and Image Geometry. LNCS, vol. 2243, pp. 339–351. Springer, Heidelberg (2002)
9. Kvasov, B.: Methods of Shape-Preserving Spline Approximation. World Scientific, Singapore (2000)
10. Piegl, L., Tiller, W.: The NURBS Book. Springer, Berlin (1995)

Estimation of Electrooculography and Blinking Signals Based on Filter Banks

Robert Krupiński and Przemysław Mazurek

West Pomeranian University of Technology, Szczecin,
Department of Signal Processing and Multimedia Engineering,
26 Kwietnia 10, 71–126 Szczecin, Poland
{robert.krupinski,przemyslaw.mazurek}@zut.edu.pl
http://www.media.zut.edu.pl

Abstract. Estimation of electrooculography (EOG) and blinking signals are important for medical applications and non–medical, like computer animation. Both signals are measured together using set of electrodes and the separation of them is necessary. Filter banks based technique for the estimation of EOG and blinking signals is considered. The gradient search allows estimation of the height and width of blinking pulses and the slopes between saccades. Improved detection related to the time domain of saccades is proposed too.

1 Introduction

The electrooculography (EOG) and blinking biosignals are measured using a set of skin placed electrodes on the human face. The retina–cornea voltage have about 1 mV value [29] and is dependent on many factors [7, 12, 1] and during controlled conditions is quite stable. The eye movement changes voltage between two electrodes that are placed on the skin (non intrusive measurements) around eye ball. The Ag/Ag–Cl electrodes are used typically. The angle of the eye (the eye orientation) is measured using differential bioamplifier and converted to the digital signal using analog–to–digital converter. Two orthogonally placed pairs of electrodes allow measurement in both orientations. Application of the reduced number is of electrodes is possible also and three electrodes are sufficient also, because both of channels shares a one electrode.

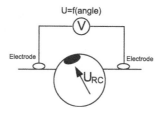

Fig. 1. EOG measurement technique – single channel

L. Bolc et al. (Eds.): ICCVG 2012, LNCS 7594, pp. 156–163, 2012.

There are many of possible placements of the electrodes on the face [5]. The 7/8 configuration [31] uses 7 measurement electrodes and a reference (REF) one. This is advanced configuration that allows the measurements of both eyes independently, what is desired for medical application. The reduced set of electrode in 3/4 configuration [14] allows the placement of electrodes far from eyes and use them for the non–medical applications too.

The eye tracking application based on the biosignal uses EOG (electrooculography) signals that are also related to the eyes orientation and blinking signal. The blinking signal is measured, depending on the configuration, as a peak related to the eyelid movement. The blinking signal disturbs EOG measurements, but is important for the applications, as an additional degree of freedom. In the 3/4 configuration both signal are additive and separation is necessary.

The eye movement consists a few signal features [8, 9]. The rapid movement of the eye is step like features of the signal and is named as saccade. The smooth pursuit movements are observed in the case of tracking of slowly movement of the object's of interest. Smooth pursuits are observed as slow changes (linear typically) of the EOG values. Other features [8, 9], like microsaccades, are less important for the applications and are omitted in this paper. There are many applications of the EOG: the ergonomics, the advertisement analysis [27], the Human–Computer Interaction (HCI) systems (e.g. a virtual keyboard [32], the vehicle control [4], the wearable computers [6]), and the video compression driven by eye–interest [11]. One of the interesting applications of the EOG and blinking biosignals are computer animation purposes [8, 33, 30]. This is kind of the motion capture system that is related to the eye and eyelids. The tracking of the eyes is especially important for the realistic play of the virtual avatars. Computer generated avatars needs very realistic eye movements, because the eyes are on of the most important part of the human face. The realism of the eye movements is necessary for the acceptance of the virtual avatar by human observer.

Alternative techniques for eye tracking applications are also available [8]. There are a few types of such systems: the Infra–Red OcculoGraphy (IROG) based on the reflection of IR light, the VideoOcculoGraphy (VOG) based on video tracking of eye.

2 Techniques for the Estimation of Electrooculography Signals

There are many techniques for the estimation of EOG and blinking signals. The estimation means that both signals are separated.

The EOG and blinking signals are disturbed by the power line (50/60 Hz) interferences, HF interferences from incandescent light sources and many sources of noise. The biological related noise and measurement system noise are observed. Electrical shielding, differential analog measurements and filtering are necessary for high quality EOG signals. This is one of the reasons why in many HCI applications the VOG approach is preferred.

Separation of EOG and blinking signal is possible using median filters and derivative filters that are used for the removal of the blinking pulses

[3, 10, 23, 26, 13, 16]. Median filters are very good if the blinking pulses are well separated in the time and far from saccades. The HCI applications may fulfill such conditions, because they are driven by the human operator, that may be informed and trained. The motion capture application for the animation purposes cannot be limited in such way. The actor's performance may be very expressive and rare patterns of the EOG and blinking signals will occurs.

Another technique based on the estimation by synthesis using EOG and blinking signal model is proposed in [15]. As was show in [15] this approach is well suited for the separation, but the computation cost is large, so real–time processing is very hard to obtain [17, 18, 19, 20]. The non–gradient (evolutionary) and local gradient optimizations algorithms are used together for improving of the convergence. Another solution that is less computationally demanding is necessary.

3 Filter Banks Based Estimation of EOG and Blinking Signals

The wavelets are usefully for the processing of biosignals. The selection of the proper wavelet function is important for the transform results and the capabilities of the filtering [22, 21, 2, 28].

In [14] the algorithm for detection of saccades and blinking in time domain is proposed. The idea is based on the analysis of singularities. In this paper a novel technique for the estimation of EOG and blinking signals based on the filter banks is proposed. This is extension of the technique discussed in [14], which is based on the continuous wavelet transform for the detection of saccades and blinks. The proposed estimation based on the iterative search using gradient approach allows the estimation of the EOG and blinking signal parameters. The height and width of a saccade, the EOG constant level and slope (responsible for smooth pursuit) are estimated.

The filter banks (Fig. 2) consist of 15 digital FIR Gaussian filters.

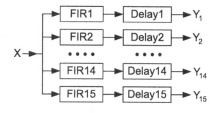

Fig. 2. Filter banks and the delay lines for the delay correction of filter banks outputs

The order of filters ($j = 1 \ldots 15$) is defined by the following formula:

$$N_j = 31 + j \cdot 10 \tag{1}$$

and the filtering equation is:

$$y_k(n) = \sum_{i=1}^{N_k} b_{i,k} \cdot x(n-i) \tag{2}$$

where $y_k(n)$ is the output of k filter bank for n time step, $b_{i,k}$ denotes the k filter bank coefficients.

The response of the filter banks need a time domain correction (shifting) due to different orders of filters. It is obtained by the application of delay lines with different lengths (Fig. 3).

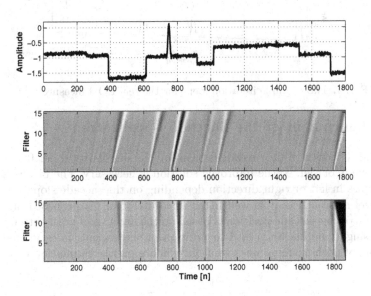

Fig. 3. Example synthetic EOG signal (top), filter banks result (middle), the correction of delay (bottom)

The detection of blink pulses is obtained by the analysis of the extrema analysis of the cone of the output of bank filters. The extrema points are tracked from the low order filter to highest order. The vertical direction of the track of the extrema is related to the blink. The sloping line is obtained for the saccade, and the slope direction depends on the saccade edge. The spatio–temporal track–before–detect algorithm is used for the accumulation of values [25, 24, 14]. The analysis of the track allows finding the position of events (saccades or blink pulses).

The obtained positions allow the segmentation of the signal. The gradient algorithm fits reconstructed signal to the original one for every segmentation range separately. A few gradient steps are sufficient for the reconstruction (Fig. 4).

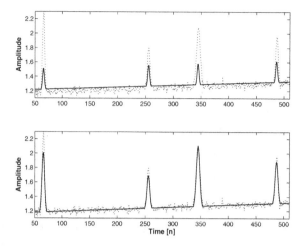

Fig. 4. Two example iteration steps for the real EOG measurements

4   Enhancement of the Saccade Localization

In [14] the detection of the saccade is based on the singularity cone. The position of the cone is biased, so the improved solution is necessary. The bias is about a few samples in left or right direction depending on the saccade slope.

A novel approach that is well fitted into filter bank is proposed, also. The estimation of the saccade position is based on the analysis of both extrema cones instead single one like in [14]. The position of the saccade is estimated using beginning of both extrema lines what gives more precise estimation (Fig. 5).

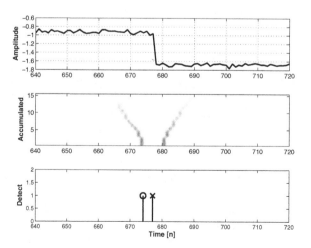

Fig. 5. Example saccade (top), extrema of singularity (middle), detected position (bottom): circle [14], cross – proposed in this paper

5   Conclusions

Proposed technique based on the filter banks has simple software implementations. The tracking of the extrema needs 15 iteration steps, because it is equal to the number of filters. The gradient search is started after estimation of the event type and positions what is also simple, because optimization is local one, related to the area between two neighborhood saccades. The estimation of blinks is also fast, because blinks do not overlaps. Estimation of the position of blinks using median filter is much complicated because width of median filter is fitted to the blink pulses from some range. Filter bank technique is much more reliable, because different widths of blinks are supported.

In further works the real–time implementation will be considered. Proposed algorithm process signal between two neighborhood saccades and intentional forced segmentation is necessary for the limiting latency of the system.

Acknowledgment. This work is supported by the UE EFRR ZPORR project Z/2.32/I/1.3.1/267/05 "Szczecin University of Technology – Research and Education Center of Modern Multimedia Technologies" (Poland).

References

1. Augustyniak, P.: Przetwarzanie sygnałów elektrodiagnostycznych (textbook in Polish), Uczelniane Wydawnictwa Naukowo–Dydaktyczne AGH, Kraków (2001) ISBN 8388408372
2. Augustyniak, P.: Transformacje falkowe w zastosowanich elektrodiagnostycznych (textbook in Polish), Uczelniane Wydawnictwa Naukowo–Dydaktyczne AGH, Kraków (2003) ISBN 8389388103
3. Bankman, I.N., Thakor, N.V.: Noise reduction in biological step signals: application to saccadic EOG. Med. Biol. Eng. Comput. 28(6), 544–549 (1990) ISSN 0140–0118
4. Barea, R., Boquete, L., Mazo, M., López, E.: Wheelchair Guidance Strategies Using EOG. Journal of Intelligent and Robotic Systems 34, 279–299 (2002) ISSN 1573-0409
5. Brown, M., Marmor, M., Vaegan, Zrenner, E., Brigell, M., Bach, M.: ISCEV Standard for Clinical Electro–oculography (EOG). Doc. Ophthalmol. 113, 205–212 (2006) ISSN 1573–2622
6. Bulling, A., Roggen, D., Tröster, G.: Wearable EOG goggles: Seamless sensing and context–awareness in everyday environments. Journal of Ambient Intelligence and Smart Environments (JAISE) 1(2), 157–171 (2009), doi:10.3929/ethz-a-005783740, ISSN 1876–1364
7. Denney, D., Denney, C.: The eye blink electro–oculogram. British Journal of Ophthalmology 68, 225–228 (1984) ISSN 1468–2079
8. Duchowski, A.: Eye Tracking Methodology: Theory and Practice. Springer (2007) ISBN 1846286085
9. Gu, E., Lee, S.P., Badler, J.B., Badler, N.I.: Eye Movements, Saccades, and Multiparty Conversations. In: Deng, Z., Neumann, U. (eds.) Data–Driven 3D Facial Animation, pp. 79–97. Springer (2008) ISBN 1846289068

10. Juhola, M.: Median filtering is appropriate to signals of saccadic eye movements. Computers in Biology and Medicine 21, 43–49 (1991), doi: 10.1016/0010-4825(91)90034-7, ISSN 0010-4825
11. Khan, J.I., Komogortsev, O.: Perceptual video compression with combined scene analysis and eye–gaze tracking. In: Duchowski, A.T., Vertegaal, R. (eds.) ETRA 2004 – Proceedings of the Eye Tracking Research and Application Symposium, p. 57. ACM Press (2004) ISBN 1581138253
12. Krogh, E.: Normal values in clinical electrooculography. 1. Material, method, methodological investigations and distribution of the potential and time parameters. Acta Ophthalmol. (Copenh) 53(4), 563–575 (1975) ISSN 0001-639X
13. Krupiński, R., Mazurek, P.: Estimation of Eye Blinking using Biopotentials Measurements for Computer Animation Applications. In: Bolc, L., Kulikowski, J.L., Wojciechowski, K. (eds.) ICCVG 2008. LNCS, vol. 5337, pp. 302–310. Springer, Heidelberg (2009)
14. Krupiński, R., Mazurek, P.: Real–Time Low-Latency Estimation of the Blinking and EOG Signals. In: Babamir, S.M. (ed.) Real–Time Systems, Architecture, Scheduling, and Application, pp. 313–334. InTech (2012), doi:10.5772/2344, ISBN 9789535105107
15. Krupiński, R., Mazurek, P.: Optimization–based Technique for Separation and Detection of Saccadic Movements and Eye–blinking in Electrooculography Biosignals. In: Arabnia, H.R., Tran, Q.-N. (eds.) Software Tools and Algorithms for Biological Systems, Advances in Experimental Medicine and Biology, vol. 696, pp. 537–545. Springer (2010), doi: 10.1007/978-1-4419-7046-6_54, ISBN 9781441970459
16. Krupiński, R., Mazurek, P.: Median Filters Optimization for Electrooculography and Blinking Signal Separation using Synthetic Model. In: 14th IEEE/IFAC International Conference on Methods and Models in Automation and Robotics MMAR 2009, Miedzyzdroje, Poland (2010), doi:10.3182/20090819-3-PL-3002.00057
17. Krupiński, R., Mazurek, P.: Convergence Improving in Evolution–Based Technique for Estimation and Separation of Electrooculography and Blinking Signals. In: Piętka, E., Kawa, J. (eds.) Information Technologies in Biomedicine. AISC, vol. 69, pp. 293–302. Springer, Heidelberg (2010)
18. Krupiński, R., Mazurek, P.: Towards to Real–Time System with Optimization Based Approach for EOG and Blinking Signals Separation for Human Computer Interaction. In: Miesenberger, K., Klaus, J., Zagler, W., Karshmer, A. (eds.) ICCHP 2010, Part 1. LNCS, vol. 6179, pp. 154–161. Springer, Heidelberg (2010)
19. Krupiński, R., Mazurek, P.: Electrooculography Signal Estimation by Using Evolution–Based Technique for Computer Animation Applications. In: Bolc, L., Tadeusiewicz, R., Chmielewski, L.J., Wojciechowski, K. (eds.) ICCVG 2010, Part I. LNCS, vol. 6374, pp. 139–146. Springer, Heidelberg (2010)
20. Krupiński, R., Mazurek, P.: Sensitivity analysis of eye blinking detection using evolutionary approach. In: Procedings – International Conference on Signals and Electronic Systems, ICSES 2010, Gliwice, Poland, pp. 81–84 (2010) ISBN 142445307
21. Mallat, S.: A wavelet tour of signal processing. Academic Press (1999) , ISBN 012466606x
22. Mallat, S.G., Zhang, Z.: Matching Pursuits with Time–Frequency Dictionaries. IEEE Transactions on Signal Processing, 3397–3415 (1993) ISSN 1053-587X
23. Martinez, M., Soria, E., Magdalena, R., Serrano, A.J., Martin, J.D., Vila, J.: Comparative study of several Fir Median Hybrid Filters for blink noise removal in Electrooculograms. WSEAS Transactions on Signal Processing 4, 53–59 (2008) ISSN 2224-3488

24. Mazurek, P.: Hierarchical Track–Before–Detect Algorithm for Tracking of Amplitude Modulated Signals. In: Choraś, R.S. (ed.) Image Processing and Communications Challenges 3. AISC, vol. 102, pp. 511–518. Springer, Heidelberg (2011)
25. Mazurek, P.: Optimization of bayesian Track–Before–Detect algorithms for GPGPUs implementations. Electrical Review 86(7), 187–189 (2010) ISSN 0033–2097
26. Niemenlehto, P.H.: Constant false alarm rate detection of saccadic eye movements in electro–oculography. Computer Methods and Programs in Biomedicine 96(2), 158–171 (2009), doi:10.1016/j.cmpb.2009.04.011, ISSN 0169–2607
27. Poole, A., Ball, L.J.: Eye Tracking in Human–Computer Interaction and Usability Research: Current Status and Future Prospects. In: Ghaoui, C. (ed.) Encyclopedia of Human Computer Interaction, pp. 211–219. Idea Group (2005) ISBN 1591405629
28. Reddy, M.S., Narasimha, B., Suresh, E., Rao, K.S.: Analysis of EOG signals using wavelet transform for detecting eye blinks. In: 2010 International Conference on Wireless Communications and Signal Processing (WCSP), pp. 1–4 (2010), doi:10.1109/WCSP.2010.5633797, ISBN 1424475568
29. Schlgöl, A., Keinrath, C., Zimmermann, D., Scherer, R., Leeb, R., Pfurtscheller, G.: A fully automated correction method of EOG artifacts in EEG recordings. Clinical Neurophysiology 118, 98–104 (2007), doi:10.1016/j.clinph.2006.09.003, ISSN 1744–4144
30. Sony Pictures Entertainment, Sony Corporation, Sagar, M., Remington, S.: System and method for tracking facial muscle and eye motion for computer graphics animation, Patent US., International Publication Number WO/2006/039497 A2, April 13 (2006)
31. Thakor, N.V.: Biopotentials and Electrophysiology Measurement. In: Webster, J.G. (ed.) The Measurement, Instrumentation, and Sensors Handbook, vol. 74, CRC Press (1999) ISBN 0849383471
32. Usakli, A.B., Gurkan, S., Aloise, F., Vecchiato, G., Babiloni, F.: On the Use of Electrooculogram for Efficient Human Computer Interfaces. Computational Intelligence and Neuroscience 2010, Article ID 135629, 5 pages (2010), doi: 10.1155/2010/135629, ISSN 1687–5273
33. Warner Brothers: E.O.G Beowulf DVD 2'nd disc, Warner Brothers (2008)

A Large Barrel Distortion in an Acquisition System for Multifocal Images Extraction

Adam Łuczak, Sławomir Maákowiak, Damian Karwowski, and Tomasz Grajek

Chair of Multimedia Telecommunication and Microelectronics,
Poznań University of Technology, Polanka St. 3, 61-131 Poznań, Poland
{aluczak,smack,tgrajek,dkarwow}@multimedia.edu.pl
http://www.multimedia.edu.pl

Abstract. This paper presents a new way to use the well-known distortions introduced by the fisheye lens (ultra-wide-angle lenses) and a well-known algorithms for the correction of distortion in order to obtain completely new functionality in supervision and monitoring of video. The suggested way to use the barrel distortion will result in a smoother zooming and allows to achieve the multiple images simultaneously with the same resolution but with a different viewing angle. This feature may vary greatly increase the effectiveness of surveillance application by providing a greater amount of visual data from one camera.

Keywords: barrel distortion, fisheye, surveillance systems, multiresolution.

1 Introduction

The systems of intelligent image analysis automatize CCTV solutions hence simplifying the operation. Real time image processing in the end device enables identification of emergency conditions by providing security personnel with information required to react and take appropriate action quickly.

Particularly interesting solutions are employed in the area of automatic detection and tracking of moving objects in video sequences. A CCTV system makes a perfect solution if one wants certain areas or premises to be surveilled on regular basis, especially when safety of people is at risk. Classification of the type of incident, detection and identification of people, motion detection as well as image and sound registration imply rapid danger warning. If needed, CCTV system recordings constitute reliable evidence for the police or courts. Modern surveillance systems are not only cameras and video recorders. Currently, two types of solutions are being employed in video surveillance systems: those using rotating cameras (speed dome) equipped with varifocal lenses and those offering megapixel cameras with fixed focal lenses [1,2]. Neither of them is free from drawbacks.

(i) *A megapixel camera with a fixed focal lens*

This solution is frequently used when recording a wide surveillance field. Several megapixel resolution cameras and high quality fixed focal lenses are used

L. Bolc et al. (Eds.): ICCVG 2012, LNCS 7594, pp. 164–171, 2012.

and requires transferring of a very large data stream (with no frame compression).Therefore, a connection of approximately 1 Gbit is needed. If the object tracking is necessary, cropping process may be performed. However, the image obtained after the cropping should be with adequate quality, i.e. it should enable identification or tracking and the image must not be compressed. For cameras offering a resolution of up to several megapixels and even 1 Gbit connection this would signify a low framerate of $5 \div 15$ frames/sec. This, in turn, has a negative impact on time resolution which is a critical factor for the algorithms of tracking and may cause their faulty operation.

(ii) *A rotating camera with a zoom lens*

Another possibility is to used a recording system with constant low target resolution and varifocal lens. To zoom, in the selected part of the field of vision, the focal length of lens is changed. High resolution of objects under surveillance is thus obtained as well as high time resolution (with a low spatial resolution). Unfortunately, in this case, the surveilled object sometimes is lost from the frame when it is suddenly quickly moving or it disappears when obstacles that block it out are being passed by. Therefore, increasing of the surveilled field requires changing of the focal length of lens. In this type of a system this would mean changing of both the camera position and focal length [3]. While in manual systems it might be a hindrance, in automatic tracking systems such an approach is ruled out.

An attempt has been made to solve the a foresaid problem by combining the advantages of both the approaches and eliminating or attenuating their drawbacks. Another solution might be to use a relatively cost-effective vision system equipped with a camera of moderate, 1-4 megapixel resolution and a fisheye-type fixed focal lens or a fixed focal lens and a mirror (a reflector).

The proposed system enables recording of a wide field of vision and simultaneously offers the possibility of zooming in the image located in the middle of a scene. This solution supports algorithms of object tracking, since, by offering both images with narrow and wide angle of view, the system prevents situations where the object is lost from the recorded image following its rapid movement.

2 Optical System

The proposed solution exploits an optical system equipped with a wide-angle lens. Such lenses are characterised by different properties of distortion of the recorded field of vision. In the proposed solution it is possible to use a lens with a large barrel distortion (e.g. fisheye) (Fig.1). To make further analysis, the authors used a 'fisheye' lens. In the case of such lenses, with a large barrel distortion (Fig.2), the reconstructed image is obtained by applying a given mapping function [6], e.g.:

- linear mapping (equidistant) $r = f(k\alpha)$,
- stereographic $r = 2f\tan(\frac{k\alpha}{2})$,

Fig. 1. Original image (left) and 'fisheye' lens-recorded image (right)

- orthographic, $r = f \sin(k\alpha)$,
- equisolid angle $r = 2f \sin(\frac{k\alpha}{2})$ or other,

where k is a physical feature of the lens associated with the maximum angle of view. Orthographic or equisolid angle mapping are optimal in terms of use for the proposed solution, as they compress the edges of the frame quite considerably, as a consequence a higher resolution in the centre of the frame is obtained.

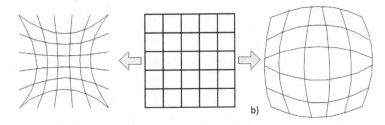

Fig. 2. Spherical distortion effect

3   Analysis

A lens that does not distort space (all image lines are straight) maps points viewed at an angle α onto the position of points on the matrix in the way that is described with the below formula:

$$r_0 = f_0 \tan(k_0 \alpha) \ (1)$$

where r_0 is the distance of matrix point from the matrix center and parameters k_0 and focal length f_0 describe the mapping function and the distance of the focus from the matrix and are typical for a given lens. Distance f_0 has an impact on the size of the image that will be produced on the matrix.

For a lens with a considerable compression of frame edges that was selected as the basis for the analyses, the distortion is described with the following formula:

$$r_1 = f_1 \sin(k_1 \alpha) \ (2)$$

The variables have the same meaning as in formula (1). To obtain a correct non-distorted image, an operation of transformation using a function being a compound of functions (1) and (2) is made, assuming that positions of points are searched for a given angle α. The result is as follows:

$$r_0 = f_0 \tan(\tfrac{k_0}{k_1} sin^{-1}(\tfrac{r_1}{f_1})) \ (3)$$

By performing the transformation of an image using the function (1), a correct image with parallel lines is obtained. This image has a different size in points and its resolution decreases when the distance from the image center grows. Two or three images with different angles of view and different resolutions may be obtained from such an image (Fig. 5).

For analytical purposes, acquisition of the image using a fisheye lens with high image edge compression has been assumed. The next assumption is, that algorithm produces 3 images for 3 different angles of view with similar sampling density (Fig. 6).

To obtain an image with the highest zoom, data of zone A will be used (Figs. 5a and 5c). According to the inverse formula a new image is produced by re-sampling the original image. It has statistically more than one sample per frame pixel in the center of the frame. Whereas at the edge, it is necessary to perform interpolation of the missing samples. In the proposed solution it is sufficient to employ a CCD/CMOS matrix of approximately 1 megapixel together with a

168   A. Łuczak et al.

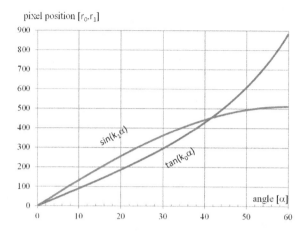

Fig. 3. Functions transforming the surveilled field of vision. In red – a function that does not distort the space; in blue – an example of a function for lenses with considerable frame edge compression.

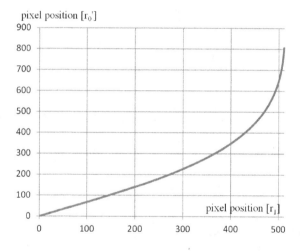

Fig. 4. Conversion of point positions using an inverse function f(x)

distorting lens, e.g. a fisheye. The proposed solution requires a lens with a high compression of image domain at the edges of the frame. A similar approach is made as regards the other two images (Figs. 5b and 5d); with the angles of view growing wider. Also one output image may be produced but with any focal length that will be effective to a certain extent (the result will be similar to a zoom lens). The fragments of a frame responsible for a given angle of view which are compressed are shown in Figure 6. The greater distance from the centre of the frame, the higher the compression, thus the lower the resolution.

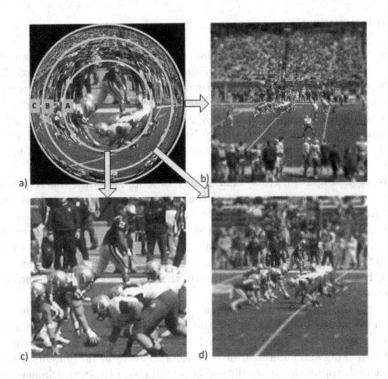

Fig. 5. An example of obtaining of 3 images with similar resolution and different angle of scene capturing (effectively different focal length)

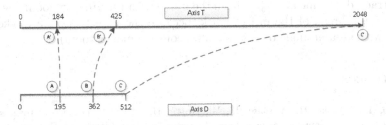

Fig. 6. Correction of a distortion for an example of a fisheye lens. Axis D mapping with distortion (one line from point $(0,0)$ to $(0,511)$) onto the T axis (one line from point $(0,0)$ to $(0,2047)$). Points: (A) – angle of view $40°$, (B) – angle of view $80°$ and (C) – angle of view $160°$.

We can also generate a single output image with a fixed resolution but also with unrestricted (to some extent) the effective focal length. Then we get a similar effect as in the lens with zoom.

Please note, if the portion of the image is located further from the center of the frame, the greater compression of samples and a lower of the output resolution. This results in some loss of resolution is reflected in a blur at the corners of the image.

4   Conclusions

This paper presents the idea of employing a barrel distortion to obtain an effect similar to focal length modification in vision systems equipped with fixed focal lenses. It requires applying a dedicated mapping function. A general computational complexity of such mapping function is very low [4,5].

For instance, if 1 megapixel matrix (512 x 512 pixels) and a lens with a large barrel distortion is used, an image may be obtained with the angle of view of 160° and a segment from the centre of matrix (zoom) with the angle of 40° and resolution (184 x 184 pixels).

According to Figure 6, three images may be obtained with different angles of view and resolution. However, to obtain the same resolution of an image segment (in this case 184 x 184 pixels) from a lens without distortion with the same total angle of view (160°), one would have to use a matrix whose resolution would be approximately 16 times greater, i.e. 16 megapixels. This also means that a framerate as high as the one offered by 1 megapixel matrix would not be obtained. High framerate is an advantage in the case of algorithms of automatic detection or object tracking.

Therefore, the proposed solution may be used to construct a system that would enable fluent modifications of the focal length with a fixed focal lens ('fisheye'). Nevertheless, application of the presented solution in the systems of automatic tracking and identification of objects seems to be far more interesting. The presented approach allows obtaining simultaneously several images with different angles of view and similar resolution based on one source image. As a result of that, it is possible to analyse and track an object in several image planes at the same time which efficiently prevents losing of the object that is being tracked. Escape an object from the frame with the greatest zoom does not result in the break of the object track, because the object may be tracked in planes with greater angle of view simultaneously (smaller zoom).

References

1. Seko, Y., Miyake, H., Yamaguchi, Y., Hotta, H.: Optical 3D sensing by a single camera with a lens of large spherical aberration. In: Intelligent Sensors, Sensor Networks and Information Processing Conference, pp. 179–182 (2004)
2. Pan, Y., Cheng, H.: Hyper-field of view monitoring optical system. In: 2011 10th International Conference on Electronic Measurement and Instruments (ICEMI), vol. 4, pp. 107–109 (2011)
3. Seko, Y., Saguchi, Y., Hotta, H., Miyazaki, J., Koshimizu, H.: Firefly capturing method: Motion capturing by monocular camera with large spherical aberration of lens and Hough-transform-based image processing. In: 18th International Conference on Pattern Recognition, ICPR 2006, vol. 4, pp. 821–824 (2006)

4. Pei-Yin, C., Chien-Chuan, H., Yeu-Horng, S., Yao-Tung, C.: A VLSI Implementation of Barrel Distortion Correction for Wide-Angle Camera Images. IEEE Transactions on Circuits and Systems II: Express Briefs 56(1), 51–55 (2009)
5. Fernandes, J.C.A., Ferreira, M.J.O., Neves, J.A.B.C., Couto, C.A.C.: Fast correction of lens distortion for image applications. In: Proceedings of the IEEE International Symposium on Industrial Electronics, ISIE 1997, vol. 2, pp. 708–712 (July 1997)
6. Bangadkar, S., Dhane, P., Nair, S., Kutty, K.: Mapping matrix for perspective correction from fish eye distorted images. In: International Conference on Recent Trends in Information Technology (ICRTIT), pp. 1288–1292 (2011)

Diamond Scanning Order of Image Blocks for Massively Parallel HEVC Compression

Adam Łuczak, Damian Karwowski, Sławomir Maćkowiak, and Tomasz Grajek

Chair of Multimedia Telecommunication and Microelectronics,
Poznań University of Technology,
Polanka St. 3, 61-131 Poznań, Poland
{aluczak,dkarwow,smack,tgrajek}@multimedia.edu.pl

Abstract. In all hybrid video coders the raster scanning order of macroblock has been used. Such order scheme make parallel processing of macroblock very difficult. or even impossible The paper presents alternative method of macroblock ordering called "diamond scan". This scheme of macroblock ordering allows for strong parallelization of macroblock processing and to have benefit from multicore processors (GP and GPU). Applying presented scheme leads to create a more efficient software and hardware implementations, in terms of energy consumption and efficient use of available equipment.

1 Introduction

Dynamic development of multimedia services led to elaborating numerous video compression techniques [1]. Greatest popularity was gained by technology of hybrid compression of a video that found practical applications in many international and commercial video compression standards [1,2].

The main idea of hybrid video coding is dividing images into non-overlapping rectangular blocks, and coding data of individual blocks by the use of intra prediction, motion-compensated prediction, transform coding and entropy coding of residual data. This approach was extensively improving in video encoders of successive generations. Compression efficiency of encoders was gradually increasing by the application of more and more sophisticated context-based coding mechanisms, in which information from neighboring blocks is used when encoding data of the current block.

The context-based coding paradigm improves compression performance of encoder, but also increases its complexity significantly. Additionally, it makes performing computations in parallel in a video codec extremely difficult. From that reason, the commonly used solution in contemporary video encoders is processing image blocks sequentially one by one in the so-called raster scanning order, i. e. from left to right and from top to bottom of an image. This imposes severe limitations to structure of video encoder that can not be efficiently realized on available multi-processor and hardware-based platforms (ASIC, FPGA) with parallel processing of data.

L. Bolc et al. (Eds.): ICCVG 2012, LNCS 7594, pp. 172–179, 2012.
© Springer-Verlag Berlin Heidelberg 2012

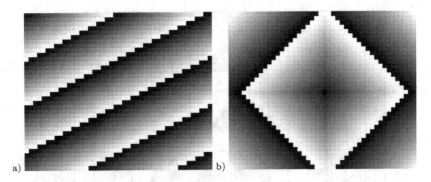

Fig. 1. CU's scanning order for a) WaveFront and b) Diamond

The above mentioned features of context-based coding together with fact of continuous increasing the spatial and temporal resolution of a video material make real-time video coding extremely difficult. From that reason, alternative order of coding image blocks is additionally investigated in new forthcoming technology of High Efficiency Video Coding (HEVC) (known as wavefront processing) with possibility of parallel processing of image data [2,4,6]. Nevertheless, abilities of performing calculations in parallel are still limited for wavefront scheme within HEVC.

The question arises, whether it is possible to modify existing technologies of hybrid video compression to perform computations in a massively parallel way. The authors propose new mechanism of image blocks ordering in encoder that increases degree of computations parallelism with still high compression performance of a video encoder. The proposed mechanism was explored in context of coding tools of forthcoming HEVC video compression technology. Description of the proposed method, detailed methodology of experiments and results were presented in the paper.

2 Proposed Diamond Mechanism of Image Blocks Ordering

Currently available context-based solutions for hybrid video compression technology put the requirement to process image blocks sequentially (for raster scanning order) [1, 7] or enable relatively moderate level of computations parallelism in encoder (in the case of wavefront processing) [2, 3]. Authors proposed new mechanism of image blocks ordering called the diamond scanning scheme, in order to enable massive parallelism of computations in a video codec. What is very important, the idea of context-based coding that is essential from the compression performance viewpoint is still in use for the proposed image block scanning scheme.

The main idea of the diamond scanning scheme is to group image blocks into separate coding zones (marked with successive numbers), with the first coding zone located in the center of an image as presented in figure 2.

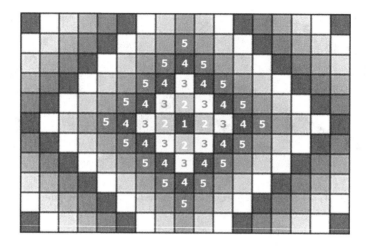

Fig. 2. Diamond scanning order

The size of an image block can be arbitrary determine depending on the compression technology used and desired level of computations parallelism. In this proposal, the image block is a coding unit (CU) of HEVC video compression technology [6], with fixed size of 16x16 luma samples. The coding zone is of diamond shape and collects image blocks that can be processed simultaneously on multi-processors. In turn, in order to take advantage of context-based coding, individual coding zones are processed sequentially, one by one, beginning from the center of an image and going towards the image margins. In this way, when processing a coding zone, data of previously processed coding zones can be used as a context information for more efficient video compression.

In general, the level of computations parallelism increases for successive coding zones for the proposed mechanism. Number of blocks that can be processed simultaneously is not fixed, but is higher than in the case of wavefront processing. Detailed numbers for individual zones were presented in figure 3. What is extremely important, significant percentage of blocks have access to 3 context blocks, which ensures high compression performance of a video encoder. This and other aspects of the proposed mechanism will be investigated in depth in later sections of the paper.

3   Diamond Scanning - Experimental Results

In order to explore the impact of the diamond blocks ordering on various aspects of video compression, the own software of video encoder was elaborated. The encoder was implemented from scratch in C programming language with the use of coding tools taken from HEVC video compression technology (intra-frame prediction, transform and quantization) together with the proposed mechanism of diamond blocks ordering. The proposed method of image blocks ordering was investigated in terms of three aspects that are extremely important in video compression. First of all, what is the number of neighboring blocks that is available for context-based coding mechanism? Secondly, what level of computations parallelism is possible for the proposed method? And finally, to what extent the proposed method affects compression performance of a video encoder?

Methodology. The level of computations parallelism and the number of neighboring blocks, which are available for context-based coding can be easily calculated for a given method of blocks scanning. Nevertheless, The impact of image blocks ordering on compression performance of encoder can be tested only experimentally. In order to conduct such experiments, the mentioned software of video encoder was additionally equipped with two alternative methods of image blocks ordering, i. e. raster scanning scheme and wavefront scanning scheme (besides the default diamond scanning scheme).

The preliminary analysis revealed that in the case of inter-coded frames the influece of the method of image blocks ordering on compression performance is negligible. Motion estimation and compensation is realized in time and not in space, thus the location of a block within an image is not important in the process of motion vector calculation.

Different situation takes place for intra-coded frames. In this case, an image block is coded with reference to data of neighboring image blocks that were already coded. It means that the way of blocks ordering can play significant role in encoder. This aspect was explored by testing the efficiency of HEVC intra prediction mechanism (plane predictor, DC predictor and set of 17 angular predictors) for those three methods of image blocks ordering: raster, wavefront and diamond. For every methods, the quality of prediction was tested by calculating the known in compression PSNR measure between the original and predicted (or reconstructed) frames. Experiments were done for two scenarios: 1) without quantization and without residual signal and 2) with quantization and with adding the residual data. In the first scenario, the prediction is performed on the basis of original image samples, and PSNR is calculated between original and predicted frames. The second scenario refers to standard encoding procedure, i.e. the PSNR is calculated between the original and reconstructed frames.

Due to no signal quantization in the first scenario of experiments (refer to table 3), it allows to determine the boundary (the best) case, because it answers the question what is the best prediction of an image that can be achieved with a given prediction tools and a method of blocks ordering. The second scenario shows the performance of a video encoder working in a lossy compression mode.

In general, in the case of raster and wavefront scanning schemes, the context data (neighboring CUs) is located to the left and above the currently coded CU. For the diamond ordering method, the location of context data is not fixed. Depending on the location of the CU within an image the location of context data changes. From that reason, the prediction tools had to be modified in order to be able to perform prediction from arbitrary direction.

Analysis of computations parallelism: The known solutions described in a literature are oriented for the entropy coding parallelization. This is achieved by

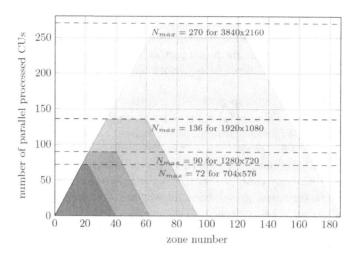

Fig. 3. Number of parallelly processed CU's for given zone

splitting an image into entropy slices. Each entropy slice is composed from one to several CU rows. Mostly, it is possible to process only a few units of CU at a time.

A better solution seems to be the wavefront [5], which introduces the new way of the CU scanning order (figure 1). This scanning mode provides the same number of contexts, as traditional raster scanning.

Unfortunately, the disadvantage of this scanning method is slow increase of the number of CU units processed in parallel. For example, in the theoretical case of an image with the 2:1 aspect ratio, the maximum number of CU (N_{max}) which can be processed simultanously is equal to the vertical size (V_{CU}) of an image counted in CUs. During encoding, the number of parallelly processed CU is increasing from 1 to N_{max} and decreasing to 1. In the real case when the image has an aspect ratio 16:9, the N_{max} is never reached.

Authors' proposal was designed to achieve a massive parallelization of CU encoding. In addition, high level of parallelism is being quickly achieved during image encoding process. These capabilities are particularly important in the phase of encoding. In contrast to the decoder, the encoder must review all combinations of coding methods in order to find the best of them.

Proposed method of scanning order has two main features: 1) the starting point is placed in the center of an image, 2) the CUs have maximum of 3 possible contexts. In result, the number of CU units processed in parallel grows rapidly. Its number is increasing more then 4 times faster than for wavefront method, quickly achieving high value (see figure 3).

Analysis of context availability Changing the way of CU scanning order cause the change of availability and location of the contexts. While in the practice, the position of the context is only a technical problem, whereas a change in the number of available contexts may affect the efficiency of compression. Histogram of contexts number for all three scanning modes (raster, wavefront, diamond)

Table 1. Histogram of available contexts for various scanning schemes.

Sequence resolution	Scanning mode	Number of CU's with N contexts					Total number of CU's
		N=0	N=1	N=2	N=3	N=4	
704x576	Raster	1	43	35	35	1470	1584
	WaveFront	1	43	35	35	1470	1584
	Diamond	1	78	0	1505	0	1584
1280x720	Raster	1	79	44	44	3432	3600
	WaveFront	1	79	44	44	3432	3600
	Diamond	1	123	0	3476	0	3600
1920x1080	Raster	1	119	67	67	7906	8160
	WaveFront	1	119	67	67	7906	8160
	Diamond	1	186	0	7973	0	8160

has been shown in table 1. As has been said, in the wavefront scanning mode availability of contexts is the same as for raster scanning mode. While in the proposed method of CU ordering, there are only 1 or 3 available contexts, which suggests that the quality of intra prediction can be poorer. However, this is the cost of a strong parallelization of calculations. The question is, if such cost is acceptable?

Analysis of coding efficiency In order to estimate the impact of the proposed block scanning order on the coding efficiency, the large set of test sequences has been encoded using various values of quantization parameter (Q) and for three scanning orders. The results of average PSNR (for 250 frames per test) are shown in tables 3 and 3.

How one can see the differences between PSNR for raster and diamond scanning order are very small (see table 3). What is noteworthy, although proposed scheme reduces the maximum number of available contexts from 4 to 3, often gives a better average PSNR than raster scanning mode.

This phenomenon has been investigated by the authors. It was shown that the starting point in the center of the image and growth of the coded area

Table 2. Average PSNR difference between sequences processed with different kind of scanning methods

Test sequence	Sequence resolution	$\Delta PSNR(PSNR_{DIAMON} - PSNR_{RASTER})[dB]$		
		No quant	Q=28	Q=48
Blue Sky	1080p	−0.031	+0.010	0.000
Pedestrian Area	1080p	−0.115	+0.021	+0.002
Sun Flower	1080p	+0.227	+0.223	+0.185
Spin calendar	720p	+0.002	−0.021	−0.025
Crew	720p	+0.003	+0.520	+0.039
Raven	720p	−0.049	+0.044	+0.024
Harbour	720p	+0.009	−0.007	+0.007
Matrix	576p	+0.831	+0.769	+0.724

Table 3. Average PSNR for *Crew* sequence processed with different kind of scanning order

Results for Crew.yuv 1280x720					
	$Q = 8$	$Q = 16$	$Q = 24$	$Q = 32$	$Q = 40$
$PSNR_{RASTER}$	51.220	42.861	36.854	32.515	30.440
$PSNR_{WAVEFRONT}$	51.220	42.861	36.854	32.515	30.440
$PSNR_{DIAMOND}$	51.215	42.841	36.857	32.569	30.338

in the direction of image sides cause improvement the efficiency of intra-frame prediction. This gain compensates the loss associated with reduced amounts of CU contexts. The matrix sequence is a good example of this phenomenon (see table 3), which contains a scene with tunnel. The scene is characterized by the prospect of converging in the center of the picture, which is also the starting point of encoding process. In this case, as it was turned out, intra-frame predictions worked the best. The obtained PSNR gain was about 0.8 dB.

The results obtained for the set of test sequences show that the proposed method of scanning does not affect both the quality of the intra-frame prediction and the compression efficiency. In some cases it may even increase prediction quality and give a substantial profit in PSNR.

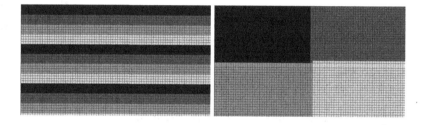

Fig. 4. Exemplary arrangements of entropy slices

4   Scanning Method and the Entropy Coding

It should be noted that the proposed method of parallelism introduction refers only to the coding/processing units but does not include entropy coding. This topic is out of the scope of this paper, but authors have also a concept of parallel entropy coding and i few words will be drafted. In general entropy encoding requires a different approach. In the case of a raster scan mode of CU, we have only one bitstream, the wavefront scanning mode requires as many bitstreams as there are CU rows in a video image. This two solutions have some drawbacks. For raster scanning the entropy coding is a bottleneck of encoder and decoder but for wavefront with a lot bitstreams (e.g. 17 for FullHD) the problem of inter-slice synchronization arises. For diamond scanning mode authors proposes a star scanning mode with 4 entropy slices, one for each quarter of an image, which is a compromise between one and large number of bitstreams.

5   Conclusions

The new method of image blocks ordering has been proposed. The method introduces strong parallelism of computations of encoder and decoder. The analysis prooved that application of the new scanning order does not impair the efficiency of video encoding. The proposed metod was explored in the context of HEVC video compression technology. Nevertheless, the method can also be used for any hybrid video coding technique (i.e. AVC, VC-1, AVS)[2,8,9].

Thanks this, in real-time software and hardware implementations, more complex and accurate compression algorithms can be used. As result it is possible to achieve better coding efficiency. In the future proposed scheme of CU scanning should let to compose a natively multi-threaded coding algorithms or even standards.

References

1. Woods, J.W.: Multidimensional Signal, Image, and Video Processing and Coding. Academic Press (2012)
2. ISO/IEC 14496-10:2010, Coding of Audio-Visual Objects, Part 10: Advanced Video Coding (December 2010)
3. ITU-T Q6/16 and ISO/IEC JTC1/SC29/WG11: Joint call for proposals on video compression technology. MPEG Document N11113, Kyoto, Japan (January 2010)
4. Mesa, M.A., Ramirez, A., Azevedo, A., Meenderinck, C., Juurlink, B., Valero, M.: Scalability of Macroblock-level Parallelism for H.264 Decoding. In: 2009 15th International Conference on Parallel and Distributed Systems (ICPADS), December 8-11, pp. 236–243 (2009)
5. Clare, G., Henry, F., Pateux, S.: Wavefront Parallel Processing for HEVC Encoding and Decoding, JCTVC-F274 / m20694, 6th Meeting: Torino, IT, July 14-22 (2011)
6. Blaszak, L., Domanski, M.: Spiral coding order of macroblocks with applications to SNR-scalable video compression. In: IEEE International Conference on Image Processing, ICIP 2005, September 11-14, vol. 3, pp. III-688–III-691 (2005)
7. McCann, K., Bross, B., Kim, I.K., Sekiguchi, S., Han, W.J.: HM5: High Efficiency Video Coding (HEVC) Test Model 5 Encoder Description. JCTVC- G1102, JCT-VC Meeting, Geneva (November 2011)
8. Society of Motion Picture and Television Engineers: VC-1 Compressed Video Bitstream Format and Decoding Process. SMPTE 421M-2006 (2006)
9. Audio Video Coding Standard Workgroup of China (AVS): The Standards of People's Republic of China GB/T 20090.2-2006, Information Technology Advanced Coding of Audio and Video Part 2:Video (2006)

Edge Preserving Smoothing by Self-quotient Referring ε-filter for Images under Varying Lighting Conditions

Mitsuharu Matsumoto

The Education and Research Center for Frontier Science,
The University of Electro-Communications,
1-5-1, Chofugaoka, Chofu-shi, Tokyo, 182-8585, Japan
mitsuharu.matsumoto@ieee.org

Abstract. This paper describes self-quotient referring ε-filter for images under varying lighting conditions. Edge preserving smoothing is a fundamental feature extraction from the image for multimedia applications. ε-filter is a nonlinear filter, which can smooth the image while preserving edge information. The filter design is simple and it can effectively smooth the image. However, when we handle the image under light variation, the contrast of edge part is low in low contrast area, while it is high in high contrast area. Hence, the existing edge-preserving filters cannot preserve the edge information around low contrast area. Our method solves this problem by combining self-quotient filter and ε-filter. To confirm the effectiveness of the proposed method, we conducted some comparison experiments on face beautification.

Keywords: Self quotient filter, ε-filter, Self-quotient-referring ε-filter, Edge-preserving smoothing.

1 Introduction

Filtering plays an important role in signal and image processing. In the broadest sense of the term "filtering," the value of the filtered image at a given location is a function of the values of the input image in a small neighborhood of the same location. For example, Gaussian low-pass filtering computes a weighted average of pixel values in the neighborhood, in which, the weights decrease with distance from the neighborhood center. However, edge is blurred by low-pass filtering. ε-filter is a nonlinear filter, which can reduce the noise while preserving the edge [1,2]. Although many studies have been reported to reduce the small amplitude noise while preserving the edge [3,4,5], it is considered that ε-filter is a promising approach due to its simple design. It does not need to have the signal and noise models in advance. It is easy to be designed and the calculation cost is small because it requires only switching and linear operation. However, when photographs are taken under lighting variation, they have not only high contrast area but also low contrast area. As ε-filter basically uses the information of local intensity to preserve edge information, it is difficult to handle these types

L. Bolc et al. (Eds.): ICCVG 2012, LNCS 7594, pp. 180–187, 2012.

of images. Although there are some approaches combining flash and non-flash images to handle these types of images, it requires two images [6].

To solve the problems, we pay attention to self-quotient filter (SQF) [7]. SQF aims to differentiate between extrinsic and intrinsic factors in imaging process and analyze their influence on object recognition. SQF is defined as the ratio of the input image and its smooth versions. By referring SQF output instead of the original image in ε-filter, we can distinguish the edge from the other parts not only in high contrast area but also in low contrast area, and can preserve edge information not only in high contrast area but also in low contrast area.

The rests of this paper are organized as follows. In Sec. 2, we describe the algorithm of the conventional ε-filter and its problems. The algorithm and the features of the proposed method are also described in Sec. 2. In Sec. 3, we show our experimental results to confirm the effectiveness on smoothing image while preserving edge information for images under varying lighting conditions. Conclusions follow in Sec. 4.

2   Proposed Algorithm

We explain the algorithm of ε-filter to clarify the feature of ε-filter. To ease the understanding, we first describe the one dimensional case. Let us define $x(i)$ as the input signal (For instance, the signal including speech signal with noise) at time i. Let us also define $y(i)$ as output signal of ε-filter at time i as follows:

$$y(i) = \Phi_\varepsilon[x(i)]$$
$$= x(i) + \sum_{j=-M}^{M} a(j)F(x(i+j) - x(i)), \tag{1}$$

where $a(j)$ represents the filter coefficient. $a(j)$ is usually constrained as follows:

$$\sum_{j=-M}^{M} a(j) = 1. \tag{2}$$

The window size of ε-filter is $2M + 1$. $F(x)$ is the nonlinear function described as follows:

$$|F(x)| \le \varepsilon : -\infty \le x \le \infty, \tag{3}$$

where ε is the constant number. This method can reduce small amplitude noise while preserving the signal. For example, we can set the nonlinear function $F(x)$ as follows:

$$F(x) = \begin{cases} x & (-\varepsilon \le x \le \varepsilon) \\ 0 & (else) \end{cases} . \tag{4}$$

When we employed $F(x)$ in Eq.4, we can rewrite ε-filter as follows:

$$y(i) = \Phi_\varepsilon[x(i)] = \sum_{j=-M}^{M} a(j)x'(i+j) \tag{5}$$

where $x'(i)$ is described as

$$x'(i) = \begin{cases} x(i) & (|x(i) - x(i+j)| > \varepsilon) \\ x(i+j) & (|x(i) - x(i+j)| \le \varepsilon) \end{cases} \tag{6}$$

Figure 1 shows the basic concept of ε-filter when we utilize Eq.4 as $F(x)$. Fig.1(a) shows the waveform of the input signal. Executing ε-filter at the point A in Fig.1(a), we replace all the points where the distance from A is more than ε by the value of the point A. We then summate the signals in the same window. Fig.1(b) shows the basic concept of this procedure. In Fig.1(b), the dashed line represents the points where the distance from A is more than ε. In Fig.1(b), the solid line represents the values replaced through this procedure. As a result, if the points are far from A, the points are ignored. On the other hand, if the points are close to A, the points are smoothed. Because of this procedure, ε-filter reduces the noise while preserving the precipitous attack and decay of the speech signal. In the same way, executing ε-filter at the point B in Fig.1(a), we replace all the points where the distance from B is more than ε by the value of the point B. The points are ignored if they are far from B, while the points are smoothed if the points are close to B. Consequently, we can reduce the small amplitude noise near by the processed point while preserving the speech signal. To simplify the explanation, we use the above ε-filter.

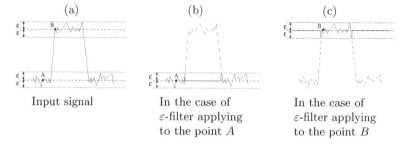

| (a) | (b) | (c) |
| Input signal | In the case of ε-filter applying to the point A | In the case of ε-filter applying to the point B |

Fig. 1. Basic concept of ε-filter

ε-filter can easily be improved not only for one dimension but also for two dimension. Let us define $x(i_1, i_2)$ as the two dimensional image data at $\mathbf{i} = (i_1, i_2)$. Let us define $y(i_1, i_2)$ as the output of two dimensional ε-filter. When we apply ε-filter to two dimensional data such as image, ε-filter is designed as follows:

$$y(i_1, i_2) = \Phi_\varepsilon[x(i_1, i_2)] = \sum_{j_1=-M}^{M} \sum_{j_2=-M}^{M} a(j_1, j_2) x'(i_1 + j_1, i_2 + j_2) \tag{7}$$

where $x'(i)$ is described as

$$x'(i_1, i_2) = \begin{cases} x(i_1, i_2) & (|x(i_1, i_2) - x(i_1 + j_1, i_2 + j_2)| > \varepsilon) \\ x(i_1 + j_1, i_2 + j_2) & (|x(i_1, i_2) - x(i_1 + j_1, i_2 + j_2)| \le \varepsilon) \end{cases} \tag{8}$$

The feature of two dimensional ε-filter is similar to that of one dimensional ε-filter. We can smooth the small amplitude noise near by the processed point while preserving the edge. It requires less calculation when it is compared to bilateral filter because it requires only switching and linear operation.

ε-filter uses the difference between the intensity of the processed pixel and the intensity of the neighbor pixels. Hence, if an image is taken under varying lighting conditions, the edge is preserved, while smoothing in high contrast area. However, the edge is blurred in low contrast area.

To solve the problems, we pay attention to self-quotient filter (SQF). SQF aims to differentiate between extrinsic and intrinsic factors in imaging process and analyze their influence on object recognition. SQF is defined as the ratio of the input image and its smooth versions.

Let us consider $x(i_1, i_2)$ as the image intensity at the point $\mathbf{i} = (i_1, i_2)$ in the image. In self-quotient filter, we restrict our consideration to objects with a Lambertian model, i.e., the image is described by the product of the albedo (texture) and the cosine angle between a point light source and the surface normal. Under the above situation, $x(i_1, i_2)$ can be described as follows:

$$x(i_1, i_2) = \rho(i_1, i_2)l(i_1, i_2)^T s, \tag{9}$$

where $\rho(i_1, i_2)$ is the surface reflectance (gray-level) associated with the point (i_1, i_2) in the image. It is constrained as follows:

$$0 \le \rho(i_1, i_2) \le 1. \tag{10}$$

$l(i_1, i_2)$ is the surface normal direction associated with point (i_1, i_2) in the image. s is the light source direction. Its magnitude is the light source intensity. T represents the transpose. The aim of self-quotient filter is to separate the intrinsic property and the extrinsic factor, and to remove the extrinsic factor. The analytical solutions of $\rho(i_1, i_2)$ and $l(i_1, i_2)$ can not be obtained from a single image. To solve the problem, self-quotient filter assumes that a smoothed version of an image has approximately the same illumination as the original one. In self-quotient filter, we calculate the following equation:

$$y(i_1, i_2) = \frac{x(i_1, i_2)}{\Psi[x(i_1, i_2)]}, \tag{11}$$

where $x(i_1, i_2)$ is the original image and Ψ is the smoothing function. Due to the process of Eq.11, the texture and edge can be extracted because the original image is divided by the smoothed image.

Based on the above prospects about the feature of SQF, we improve ε-filter as follows:

$$z(i_1, i_2) = \Phi_\varepsilon[x(i_1, i_2)] = \sum_{j=-M}^{M} a(j_1, j_2)x'(i_1 + j_1, i_2 + j_2) \tag{12}$$

where $x'(i_1, i_2)$ is described as

$$x'(i_1, i_2) = \begin{cases} x(i_1, i_2) & (|y(i_1, i_2) - y(i_1 + j_1, i_2 + j_2)| > \varepsilon) \\ x(i_1 + j_1, i_2 + j_2) & (|y(i_1, i_2) - y(i_1 + j_1, i_2 + j_2)| \le \varepsilon) \end{cases} \tag{13}$$

where $y(i_1, i_2)$ is the filter output of self-quotient filter defined as follows:

$$y(i_1, i_2) = \frac{x(i_1, i_2)}{\Psi[x(i_1, i_2)]}, \tag{14}$$

As described above, we used the filter output of self-quotient filter to select $x(i_1, i_2)$ and $x(i_1 + j_1, i_2 + j_2)$ instead of the original image. By using the filter output of self-quotient filter, we can smooth the image while preserving the edge information not only around high contrast but also around low contrast. Let us test our method experimentally.

3   Experiments

To clarify the effectiveness of our approach, we conducted some experiments. We selected some images from Yale image database. Fig. 2 shows an example of the input image from Yale face image database (file name: yaleB02_P01A-110E+65.pgm) [8]. The image size is 256 pixels × 256 pixels.

We used a computer with an Intel Core 2 Duo 2.40GHz CPU. The programs were implemented by MATLAB R2007b.

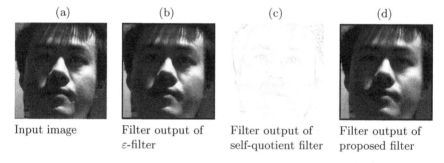

(a)	(b)	(c)	(d)
Input image	Filter output of ε-filter	Filter output of self-quotient filter	Filter output of proposed filter

Fig. 2. Filter output of ε-filter, self-quotient filter and proposed filter (The image is cut from yaleB02_P01A-110E+65.pgm)

Fig. 2(b) and Fig. 2(d) show the filter outputs of ε-filter and the proposed method, respectively. As shown in Fig.2, when we employed a conventional ε-filter, although edge is preserved while smoothing in high contrast area, edge is blurred in low contrast area. On the other hand, the image is smoothed, while preserving edge information not only around high contrast area but also around low contrast when we employed our method as shown in Fig. 2(d). As shown in Fig.2. wrinkle and roughness on the face are smoothed. To clarify the effect of the self-quotient filter, we also show the filter output of self-quotient filter as shown in Fig.2(c). As shown in Fig.2(c), SQF can reduce extrinsic factors from the images, and extract the feature of the face from the image clearly.

To clarify the difference between the ε-filter and the proposed filter, we also show the closeup image around the left eye as shown in Fig.3. As shown in

(a)   (b)   (c)

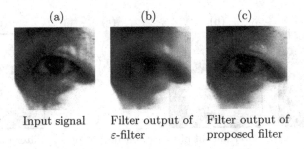

Input signal   Filter output of   Filter output of
                  ε-filter   proposed filter

Fig. 3. Filter output of ε- filter and proposed filter (Closeup around eye area. The image is cut from yaleB02_P01A-110E+65.pgm).

Fig.3, the edge around eye is blurred in the filter output of the ε-filter, while it is preserved in the filter output of the proposed filter.

Figs.4 and 6 show other examples of the input images from Yale face image database (file name: yaleB10_P00A-095E+00.pgm and yaleB01_P01A+035E+65.pgm), respectively. Figs. 5 and 7 show the closeup images around the left eye from the images (file name: yaleB10_P00A-095E+00.pgm and yaleB01_P01A+035E+65.pgm), respectively. As shown in Figs.4 and 6, ε-filter cannot preserve

(a)   (b)   (c)   (d)

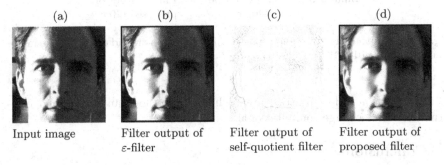

Input image   Filter output of   Filter output of   Filter output of
                ε-filter   self-quotient filter   proposed filter

Fig. 4. Filter output of ε-filter, self-quotient filter and proposed filter (The image is cut from yaleB10_P00A+095E+00.pgm.)

(a)   (b)   (c)

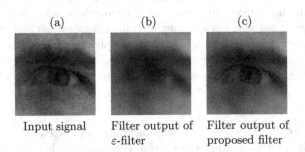

Input signal   Filter output of   Filter output of
                  ε-filter   proposed filter

Fig. 5. Filter output of ε-filter and proposed filter (Closeup around eye area. The image is cut from yaleB10_P00A+095E+00.pgm)

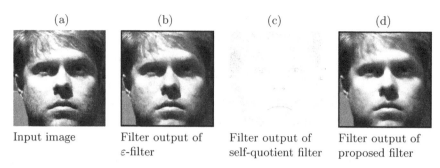

(a)	(b)	(c)	(d)
Input image	Filter output of ε-filter	Filter output of self-quotient filter	Filter output of proposed filter

Fig. 6. Filter output of ε-filter, self-quotient filter and proposed filter (The image is cut from yaleB01_P01A+035E+65.pgm.)

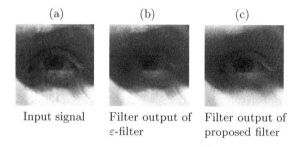

(a)	(b)	(c)
Input signal	Filter output of ε-filter	Filter output of proposed filter

Fig. 7. Filter output of ε-filter and proposed filter (Closeup around eye area. The image is cut from yaleB01_P01A+035E+65.pgm)

edge information in low contrast area, while our method can preserve edge information. The average computational cost is 0.27 sec.

4   Conclusion

In this paper, we proposed edge-preserving smoothing by self-quotient referring ε-filter for images under varying lighting conditions. Unlike the typical ε-filter, we can smooth the image while preserving edge information not only around high contrast area but also low contrast area by using our method. Although we did not handle color images, we would like to apply our method to color images by handling them in LUV image space in the near future. We also would like to implement our method to real-time processing for video such as TV programs and streaming movies.

Acknowledgment. This research was partially supported by Special Coordination Funds for Promoting Science and Technology. This research was also supported by Japan Prize Foundation, NS promotion foundation for science of perception and Foundation for the Fusion Of Science and Technology.

References

1. Arakawa, K., Matsuura, K., Watabe, H., Arakawa, Y.: A method of noise reduction for speech signals using component separating ε-filters. IEICE Trans. on Fundamentals J85-A(10), 1059–1069 (2002)
2. Arakawa, K., Okada, T.: ε-separating nonlinear filter bank and its application to face image beautification. IEICE Trans. on Fundamentals J90-A(4), 52–62 (2005)
3. Boult, T., Melter, R.A., Skorina, F., Stojmenovic, I.: G-neighbors. In: Proc. of SPIE Conf. on Vision Geometry II, pp. 96–109 (1993)
4. Himayat, N., Kassam, S.A.: Approximate performance analysis of edge preserving filters. IEEE Trans. on Signal Processing 41(9), 2764–2777 (1993)
5. Tomasi, C., Manduchi, R.: Bilateral filtering for gray and color images. In: Int'l Conf. on Computer Vision, pp. 839–846 (1998)
6. Eisemann, E., Durand, F.: Flash Photography Enhancement via Intrinsic Relighting. ACM Trans. on Graphics, 673–678 (2004)
7. Wang, H., Li, S.Z., Wang, Y.: Face recognition under varying lighting conditions using self quotient image. In: Proc. of Int'l Conf. on Automation Face and Gesture Recognition, pp. 819–824 (2004)
8. Georghiades, A.S., Belhumeur, P.N., Kriegman, D.J.: From Few to Many: Illumination Cone Models for Face Recognition under Variable Lighting and Pose. IEEE Trans. on Pattern Anal. Mach. Intelligence 23(6), 643–660 (2001)

SPREAD: On Spherical Part Recognition by Axial Discretization in 4D Hough Space

Radhika Mittal and Partha Bhowmick

Department of Computer Science and Engineering,
Indian Institute of Technology, Kharagpur, India
{radhikamittal.iitkgp,bhowmick}@gmail.com

Abstract. A novel algorithm is proposed to locate the sets of adjacent co-spherical triangles for a given object, which enables us to detect spheres and spherical parts constituting the object. An extension of the idea of Hough transform has been used, aided by axial discretization and restricted searching, along with the geometric data structure of doubly connected edge list. The algorithm has been analyzed and shown to achieve significant efficiency in space and run-time. On testing the algorithm with various 3D objects, it is found to produce the desired result. Effects of different input parameters have been explained and the robustness of the algorithm has been shown for rough/noisy surfaces.

1   Introduction

Recognition and analysis of 3D shapes in general, and spherical components in particular, have gained a significant research perspective for several important applications, e.g., detection of pulmonary nodules [19], medical analysis of brains [15], etc. Among different geometric approaches for 3D shape analysis [9,11], the most commonly used is Generalized Hough Transform (GHT) [1,6], as it can easily be adapted based on specific needs of the application, e.g., [3,7,16–18].

We propose here an extension of Hough transform to detect spherical components, using a more space- and time-efficient technique of restricted discretization and localized searching instead of processing a 4D array containing the 3D coordinates of the center and the radius. To work with a significantly large range with a high accuracy, we use the novel idea of *axial discretization*. We take discrete points along the *circum-normal* (axis) of a face (triangle) and use restricted Hough transform to locate the parameters of the sphere it potentially belongs to, with respect to the given object. The restricted HT is based on the observation that if a face belongs to a particular sphere in the given object, then with a very high probability, its adjacent faces would also belong to the same sphere. The geometric data structure of DCEL has been used extensively to achieve an attractive run-time, as shown in this paper.

2   Proposed Algorithm

One of the novel principles while designing the algorithm SPREAD lies in the concept of *axial discretization*. Such a discretization has been resorted to in

L. Bolc et al. (Eds.): ICCVG 2012, LNCS 7594, pp. 188–195, 2012.
© Springer-Verlag Berlin Heidelberg 2012

order to reduce the computational burden of $O(n^4)$ for the conventional Hough transform (HT) [10, 14]. This technique has not been used so far for recognizing spherical parts in 3D objects, although proposed to detect circular arcs in 2D images for several applications [4, 5, 8, 12].

2.1 Principle of SPREAD

We use the following observation: If a (triangular) face f belongs to a particular spherical part in the given 3D object, then with a very high probability, the three faces adjacent to f would also be co-spheric with f. Based on this observation, we estimate the parameters, i.e., center and radius of the sphere, which all the adjacent faces potentially belong to. The algorithm SPREAD considers the discrete points along the *circum-normals* of these faces as input, and finds the approximate center. (The circum-normal of a face f is the normal to f that passes through its circum-center.) The first face f is selected at random. Although there exists a unique circle passing through the three vertices of any triangle, there exists an infinitude of spheres passing through them. The centers of all these spheres are collinear in 3D space. Hence, for a given face f with a center point taken on its circum-normal, the sphere parameters are first obtained, and then we build the initial spherical part on it by considering its three adjacent triangles to obtain the common solution space of these four triangles. The larger spherical part is built from this by doing a breadth-first search iteratively on the set of faces adjacent to each other whose corresponding ε-*balls* in the parameter space have all pair-wise intersection, as explained next.

The parameter space has four dimensions, the first three being corresponding to the three coordinates of the object space and the fourth to the radius. The distance metric used by us in this parameter space is based on L_2-norm. If p_i be the point in the 4D parameter space corresponding to a sphere S_i passing through the vertices of a face f, then the ε-ball corresponding to S_i is denoted by $\phi(p_i, \varepsilon)$ and defined as the 4D hyper-sphere with center at p_i and radius ε. Note that, if S_i has center $c_i = (x_i, y_i, z_i)$ and radius r_i, then it is uniquely represented in the parameter space by the point $p_i = (c_i, r_i) = (x_i, y_i, z_i, r_i)$. Hence, two faces f_i (with circum-normal $\mathbf{N}_i$) and f_j (with circum-normal $\mathbf{N}_j$) are said to be *co-spheric* with each other if and only if there exist two points $p_i(a_i, r_i)$ and $p_j(a_j, r_j)$ in the parameter space such that $a_i \in \mathbf{N}_i$, $a_j \in \mathbf{N}_j$, and there exists a non-empty intersection between $\phi(p_i, \varepsilon)$ and $\phi(p_j, \varepsilon)$. Evidently, two ε-balls are said to intersect each other if and only if the distance between their centers does not exceed 2ε. In general, a set of faces are mutually co-spheric if the two ε-balls corresponding to some axial point of one and some axial point of the other in each pair from the set have a non-empty intersection in the 4D parameter space.

The proposed algorithm SPREAD is made flexible to suit the needs of different objects by providing the hyper-ball radius, ε. The value of ε is specified w.r.t. the normalized scale, and varies from 0.01 to 0.04, as shown in Sec. 3. Smaller the value of ε, tighter is the detection of spherical parts, and larger the value of ε, looser is the detection. The speed and precision of the algorithm is decided by another parameter, namely N, which indicates the number of discrete points to be considered along the circum-normal of each triangle while detecting a spherical part. And lastly, the minimum number of constituent faces of a co-spheric part, namely F, is considered to decide whether the concerned part can be reported as a practically spherical part. The exact usage of these parameters is described in detail later in this section and also in Sec. 3.

To maintain uniformity across different sizes of objects, we apply an isotropic scaling on the object by normalizing the coordinates of all the vertices of the triangulated object surface such that the maximum over the distances for all pairs of vertices is a constant (taken as 10 in our experimentation). We maintain a *Doubly Connected Edge List* (DCEL) [2] which helps in finding the adjacent faces. In this list, we store, for each edge, its source vertex, destination vertex, incident face, and twin edge. The twin $twin[e]$ of an edge e is the edge whose incident face is adjacent to the face incident on e. Note that, for each face, each of its incident (directed) edges is defined in a manner so that the face lies left of the edge. Thus, the source vertex of e coincides with the destination vertex of $twin[e]$, and vice versa (Fig. 1).

For each triangle, we find its circum-center coordinates (x_c, y_c, z_c) as follows.

$$x_c = \frac{\sum_{i=0}^{2} x_i \left(l_i^2 \left(l_{(i+1) \bmod 3}^2 + l_{(i+2) \bmod 3}^2 - l_i^2 \right) \right)}{2 \sum_{i=0}^{2} \left(l_i^2 l_{(i+1) \bmod 3}^2 \right) - \sum_{i=0}^{2} l_i^4}$$

where $l_i (i = 0, 1, 2)$ denotes the length of the side opposite to the ith vertex having coordinates (x_i, y_i, z_i). The corresponding formulas for finding y_c or z_c are similar, and obtained simply by replacing x_i with y_i or z_i, as applicable. The unit circum-normal of each triangle is found by normalizing the cross product of two of its edges, and then by translating it to the circum-center.

We start the process of detecting co-spherical sets of faces with all faces as initially 'unmarked'. Then a face f is picked at random. We find the three faces adjacent to f using the DCEL in constant time (Fig. 1). For each such adjacent face f_i, we uniformly discretize a finite segment of the circum-normal $\mathbf{N}$ passing through its circum-center. The discretization procedure samples $2N + 1$ points on each circum-normal: N points on either side of the plane of the face and one lying on it. They are sampled in a manner such that the distance between the farthest pair of sample points along the concerned circum-normal is a constant (taken to be 100 times the size of the normalized object, in our experimentation). If there exists a sample point $a \in \mathbf{N}$ for f and a sample point $a_i \in \mathbf{N}_i$ for a face f_i with $p = (a, r)$ and $p_i = (a_i, r_i)$, where r is the distance of the point a from a vertex of f (all vertices of f being equidistant from a) and r_i is that of a_i from a vertex of f_i, such that $\phi(p, \varepsilon) \cap \phi(p_i, \varepsilon) \neq \emptyset$, then there exists a solution for the common sphere of f and f_i (see Fig. 1). The parameters corresponding to this solution are obtained from $\phi(p, \varepsilon) \cap \phi(p_i, \varepsilon)$.

We maintain a queue Q to store all the faces that are co-spheric with f. Thus, all the adjacent faces which have been taken into consideration are enqueued in Q

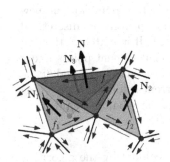

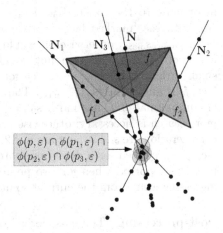

Fig. 1. Left: Information in DCEL. The red triangle denotes a face f having three (directed) edges, shown in blue. Each of of three edges is defined by a pair of vertices (blue), and has a twin edge in its adjacent face (orange). The unit normals are computed from the edges corresponding to the faces. **Right:** Finding the center of the sphere built by a face f (shown in red) and its three adjacent faces $\{f_1, f_2, f_3\}$ (orange), using *axial discretization* of their circum-normals $(\mathbf{N}, \mathbf{N}_1, \mathbf{N}_2, \mathbf{N}_3)$.

along with the face f; these faces are marked ON before being enqueued. We calculate the mean of all satisfying points on the discretized circum-normals to estimate the effective center and radius of the sphere S built by the face f and its surrounding faces. If the estimated radius is larger than a sufficiently large constant (taken to be twice the normalized size of the object in our experimentation), then Q is emptied, indicating that no sphere is formed by f. This is done because a very large radius implies a planar segment instead of a spherical patch.

We build a spherical part S using breadth-first-search. For each face in Q, we find the adjacent faces using the DCEL. If an adjacent face f_i, thus found, is not marked ON, then we check whether there exists a point a_i in the discretized circum-normal of f_i such that $\phi(p_i, \varepsilon)$ has a non-empty intersection with the existing parameter space corresponding to S. If it has a non-empty intersection, then the face f_i is marked ON and enqueued in Q. We continue expansion on each face in Q, until Q stops growing or all faces in Q have been considered.

Speeding up the algorithm. To speed up the procedure of searching the matching points of discretization, if any, while verifying the intersection of one ε-ball with the solution space of the current sphere S, we use the range of indices of the discrete points that correspond to the current solution. Note that, the index varies from $-N$ to N, 0 inclusive. Let $[s_{\min}, s_{\max}]$ be the range of indices that have produced the current solution. Here, $s_{\min}$ is the lowest index of one or more discrete points of some of the circum-normals corresponding to S, and $s_{\max}$ is the highest. If a new face f_i belongs to S, then it is expected that the index of the discrete point a_i from the circum-normal of f_i would lie in or close to the range $[s_{\min}, s_{\max}]$. In fact, if the face f_i is comparable in size with the 'marked faces' corresponding to S, then the index of a_i would lie in $[s_{\min}, s_{\max}]$; otherwise, a_i would lie outside but close to $[s_{\min}, s_{\max}]$. The length of $[s_{\min}, s_{\max}]$ is also quite small if the sizes of the 'marked faces' have a small variation. Hence, the search for the matching discrete point for the new face f_i is guided by $[s_{\min}, s_{\max}]$. The first point picked up from the discretized circum-normal of f_i has index $s_0 = \frac{1}{2} \lfloor s_{\min} + s_{\max} + 1 \rfloor$. If it matches, then no more search is necessary; otherwise the indices of two subsequent points under consideration are $s_0 \pm 1$, next are $s_0 \pm 2$, and so on, until the match is found or the face f_i is rejected for a diverging match with the current solution. A diverging match is reported when for two points in succession, the ε-ball is found to be digressing away from the current solution.

Post-processing. The co-spherical components are colored by the algorithm SPREAD using distinct colors. The coloring is constrained by the condition that each spherical part must have a minimum number of faces. This is to avoid detection of small undesired spherical components and also to avoid detection of cylindrical or similar shapes whose faces may be misinterpreted to be forming a spherical part. Hence, an important restriction is that a spherical component will be colored only if its area is greater than $F \cdot A_{\max}$, where F is the tuning parameter lying in $(0, 1)$ and $A_{\max}$ denotes the area of the largest spherical component found. Post-processing is done by SPREAD using the color information in order to fill up the gaps created by the undetected faces in the detected spherical parts. If a set A of adjacent faces is uncolored and all the faces adjacent to the boundary faces of this set have the same color (i.e., belong to the same sphere, S), then we check whether the area formed by the set A is less than a threshold (taken as 0.1 times the area of the corresponding sphere). If so, the set A is considered to be 'falsely undetected', an hence the color of each face of A is set to the color of the sphere S.

2.2   Complexity Analysis

Let the number of vertices be v, the number of faces be n, and the number of edges be e. Then the DCEL takes $O(v + n + e) = O(n)$ space, since $v = O(n)$ and $e = O(n)$. Apart from the conventional information as mentioned earlier, the DCEL also stores the details of faces, vertices, face areas, normal equations, and circum-centers, taking $O(n)$ space. The queue Q stores all the faces that are currently co-spherical. The *best case* occurs when there is no overlap between two co-spherical sets, resulting in a space complexity of $O(n)$. In the *worst case*, there can be many overlaps among these co-spherical sets. An instance of the queue may contain as many as $O(n)$ faces and there can be $O(n)$ such instances of the queue. However, when a particular instance of Q is processed, other instances do not occupy any space, since they either have been processed earlier or would be processed later. This gives us a space complexity of $O(n)$ for Q.

It takes $O(v + n)$ time to read the object, $O(v^2)$ time to normalize the vertices by computing the maximum distance, and $O(n^2)$ time to prepare the DCEL.

The algorithm checks no more faces adjacent to a face f_{ki} when f_{ki} is found to be not matching with the spherical part S_k currently under consideration. For each spherical part, the first two faces are obtained in $O(N)$ time by index searching. Let the number of faces of S_k be n_k. All these n_k faces can have $O(n_k)$ adjacent faces which are not part of S_k; and each of these faces will be tested, resulting to no positive result. Hence, the time complexity to report S_k is given by the sum of time complexity to report the faces of S_k and that to check the mismatching faces. The *best-case* time complexity is, therefore, given by $O(N)+(n_k-2)O(1)+O(n_k)O(1) = O(n_k+N)$; summing up over all spherical parts and observing that n_k is bounded by $O(n)$ for this sum, we get $O(n+mN)$, where m is the number of spherical parts reported by SPREAD. For the *worst case*, we sum up $O(N) + (n_k - 2)O(N) + O(n_k)O(N) = O(n_kN)$ over all parts, hence getting $O(nN)$.

3   Experiment and Results

We have implemented the algorithm SPREAD in C using OpenGL on an Intel(R) Core(TM)2 Duo CPU E4500 2.20 GHz machine, the OS being Ubuntu Release 10.10. Table 1 shows its results on some objects having one or more spherical parts. The object Sphere is completely covered with $\varepsilon = 0.03$; note that 759 out of 840 triangles are initially detected, and the remaining 81 triangles get included during post-processing (Sec. 2.1).

We take N in the range of 1000–2000; for a low value, the points on the normal are largely separated from each other, thereby giving a bad estimate (Fig. 2). The specified value of ε determines the accuracy with which spheres are detected (Fig. 2). Changing ε by even 0.02 units (in normalized object scale of unity) significantly affects the number of co-spherical triangles. A high value of ε would encompass unwanted triangles in a spherical component, whereas a low value would discard many desired triangles, thereby hindering the formation of

Table 1. Summary of results for running SPREAD on different objects ($\varepsilon - 0.03, F = 0.10, N = 1000$). n = number of faces; m = number of spheres detected; n_k = number(s) of faces for each sphere (shown comma-separated).

Parameter	Sphere	Globe	Balloon	Elk
n	840	7618	2080	6518
m	1	2	2	4
n_k	759	3968, 927	1384, 134	513, 492, 483, 476
CPU time (sec.)	0.596	2.610	0.759	3.542

(a) $(0.04, 0.10, 200)$ (b) $(0.04, 0.08, 2000)$ (c) $(0.06, 0.08, 2000)$ (d) $(0.04, 0.3, 1000)$.

Fig. 2. Output instances showing effect of user paramester (ε, F, N): (a) too small value of N; (b, c) change in ε; (d) large value of F. (For proper results, see Table 1.)

a larger spherical part. For F, a high value may not correctly report a spherical part (Fig. 2); when $F = 0.3$ (see correct result in Table 1), base part of the `globe` is not reported as spherical as its area is appreciably less than the red one.

Post-processing takes care of missing triangles in a spherical part, possibly due to staggering circum-normals. Figure 3(a) shows the result of running SPREAD on `elk`, without post-processing. For testing SPREAD against noisy or rough surface, we have prepared some rough surfaces by introducing Gaussian noise. Figure 3(b) shows that on introducing Gaussian noise with a peak of 1% of the maximum distance (0.05), fairly good results are obtained without post-processing. However, for a Gaussian noise of 2%, we get better results on doing post-processing (Fig. 3(c, d)).

Fig. 3. Role of post-processing: (a) Result on `elk` without post-processing (see Table 1 for result after post-processing. (b-d) Results for rough surfaces, with and without 2nd stage processing. (b) 1% noise, no post-processing; (c) 2% noise, no post-processing; (d) 2% noise, after post-processing ($N = 1000, \varepsilon = 0.06, F = 0.1$ for all three cases).

4   Conclusion

The proposed algorithm SPREAD can detect the adjacent co-spherical triangles for a given object using axial discretization based on the contemporary idea of restricted Hough transform, resulting in usage of less space as compared to the generalized Hough transform. We have tested the algorithm on various 3D objects, have analyzed the effects of different input parameters, and have tested its robustness rough or noisy surfaces. All these results exhibit that the algorithm is quite resistant to noise and can generate fairly accurate results with a space- and time-efficient manner. As a future work, the algorithm can be extended to detect other 3D shapes like ellipsoids and paraboloids by properly applying the concept of axial discretization.

Acknowledgement. A part of this work has been sponsored by the NSF project: NEBULA (CNS-1038695).

References

1. Ballard, D.H.: Readings in computer vision: Issues, problems, principles, and paradigms (1987)
2. Berg, M.D., et al.: Computational Geometry Algorithms and Applications (2000)
3. Cao, M.Y., et al.: Spherical parameter detection based on hierarchical Hough transform. PRL 27, 980–986 (2006)
4. Chiu, S.H., Liaw, J.J.: An effective voting method for circle detection. PRL 26(2), 121–133 (2005)
5. Davies, E.R.: A high speed algorithm for circular object detection. PRL 6, 323–333 (1987)
6. Duda, R.O., Hart, P.E.: Use of the Hough transformation to detect lines and curves in pictures. Commun. ACM 15, 11–15 (1972)
7. Ecabert, O., Thiran, J.P.: Adaptive Hough transform for the detection of natural shapes under weak affine transformations. PRL 25(12), 1411–1419 (2004)
8. Foresti, G.L., et al.: Circular arc extraction by direct clustering in a 3D Hough parameter space. Signal Processing 41, 203–224 (1995)
9. Gelfand, N., Guibas, L.J.: Shape segmentation using local slippage analysis. In: Proc. SGP 2004, pp. 214–223 (2004)
10. Gonzalez, R.C., Woods, R.E.: Digital Image Processing. Addison-Wesley, California (1993)
11. Hofer, M., et al.: 3d shape recognition and reconstruction based on line element geometry. In: Proc. ICCV 2005, pp. 1532–1538 (2005)
12. Ioannoua, D., et al.: Circle recognition through a 2D Hough transform and radius histogramming. IVC 17, 15–26 (1999)
13. Kim, H.S., Kim, J.H.: A two-step circle detection algorithm from the intersecting chords. PRL 22(6-7), 787–798 (2001)
14. Leavers, V.: Survey: Which Hough transform? CVGIP 58, 250–264 (1993)
15. Nain, D., et al.: Statistical shape analysis of brain structures using spherical wavelets. In: Proc. ISBI 2007, pp. 209–212 (2007)
16. Ogundana, O.O., et al.: Fast Hough transform for automated detection of spheres in three-dimensional point clouds. Opt. Eng. 46 (2007)
17. Rong, F., et al.: A novel Hough transform algorithm for multi-objective detection. In: Proc. IITA 2009, pp. 705–708 (2009)
18. Yang, M.C.K., et al.: Hough transform modified by line connectivity and line thickness. IEEE Trans. PAMI 19, 905–910 (1997)
19. Zhang, X., Stockel, J., Wolf, M., Cathier, P., McLennan, G., Hoffman, E.A., Sonka, M.: A New Method for Spherical Object Detection and Its Application to Computer Aided Detection of Pulmonary Nodules in CT Images. In: Ayache, N., Ourselin, S., Maeder, A. (eds.) MICCAI 2007, Part I. LNCS, vol. 4791, pp. 842–849. Springer, Heidelberg (2007)

Multimedia Objects Conversion
for a Digital Repository – A Case Study

Julian Myrcha and Przemysław Rokita

Institute of Computer Science, Warsaw Uniwersity of Technology
Nowowiejska 15/19, 00-665 Warsaw, Poland
P.Rokita@ii.pw.edu.pl
http://www.ii.pw.edu.pl/~pro

Abstract. Here we are presenting a solution we developed for multimedia objects conversion in the digital repository that is being built under SYNAT/PASSIM project [1]. Our aim was to create tools for online format conversion of multimedia objects in a most simple way. We have studied available open source libraries and tools, and proposed an efficient way of integrating them into digital repository conversion module. Open structure of the formats supported by the constructed repository lead us to a plug-in based architecture. Here we are presenting the outline of our solution.

1 Introduction

Repository which is built upon SYNAT/PASSIM project uses web-based client application to work on. Server side is build using Spring MVC framework with multimedia files stored on external file servers. As conversion tool should be visible from the user point of view as a part of the client, it should be installed on the server side. This causes following problems:

- Open source conversion libraries are coded in C or C++ language
- Conversions may require computation power which may influence server availability

Implemented upon SYNAT/PASSIM repository differs from existing or projected library solutions [10] [18] [11] [21] [9] in such way, that allows storage any type of digital objects. This allows storage of wide variety of digital object - also in proprietary formats used in narrow group of users. It will also easily adopt to the changing world and newly developed formats. Common approach, however, is to provide closed list of well selected storage formats [15] [6] [16]. This has many advantages, as it will easily adopt to the rich spectrum of the stored data. Although libraries still concentrate on different text formats [7] there are emerging need for other type of digital objects.

From the implementation point of view it has one major drawback - such structure prevents us from closed implementation of the system. The only, widely used solution is such situation is to hire plug-in based architecture, which filters provided digital objects and provide needed functionality for recognized ones.

L. Bolc et al. (Eds.): ICCVG 2012, LNCS 7594, pp. 196–203, 2012.

Described solution, based on dynamically configured plug-ins solves presentation needs. The second area of interest - searching - is not addressed. It should be solved independently, using additional meta-data attached to the digital objects [17] [22] [8].

1.1 Licensing

Selection of the Open Source libraries to implement plug-ins require strict relationship to their licensing agreements. Each library is provided with one or more licence. We have following licenses to use:

- GNU Affero General Public License [2]
- GNU General Public License version 2 [3]
- GNU General Public License version 3 [4]
- GNU Lesser General Public License [5]

Depending on selected module there must be provided responsible notes in plug-in description or plug-in source code should be provided.

2 Algorithm

2.1 Process

Multimedia files, associated with different digital objects will be stored separately in the external file storage. Using the web application the user will get access to the selected files (see fig Fig. 1). After selection of the interested file, system will use registered plug-ins to establish list of allowed operation on the file:

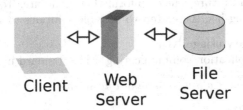

Fig. 1. Architecture overview

- get exact copy of the file - it will be always possible
- get subset of the file - subset of pages or selected part of the stream
- get transformed version in the same format
- get the same data but in different format

It will be possible to get concatenation of the above options - e.g transformed data in different format. To speed-up the process it is possible to store results of investigation of the operations available on the object - the first stage of the process (checking the object type) could be omitted (see Fig. 2).

If the selected operation require file conversion, user will be informed about starting of the process. System will create temporary file containing processed file, which will be presented for the user after refreshing the page.

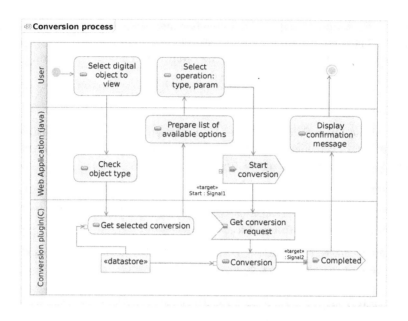

Fig. 2. Conversion process

2.2   Plug-ins

Design of the plug-in structure is a basis for their extensibility:

On the figure 3 we have inheritance structure of the plug-in module. Each plug-ins (current and future) such conform that structure. To further simplify developing of the plug-ins, there are two possible solutions to write them:

− link c/c++ library using JNDI
− call external application communicating using standard input/output

Sample app for testing Calling command line script

```
package passim.b21;

import java.io.File;
import java.io.IOException;
import java.lang.ProcessBuilder.Redirect;

/**
 *
 * @author jmy
 */
public class SampleMain {

    /**
     * @param args the command line arguments
```

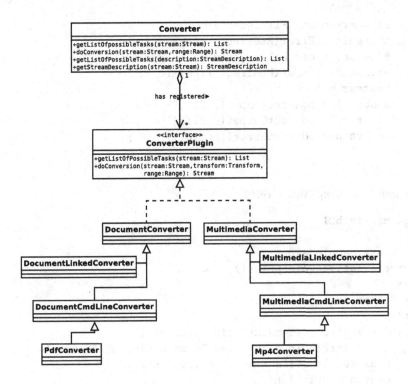

Fig. 3. Methods of converter plug-in

```
*/
public static void main(String[] args) {
    try {
        ConverterPlugin conv = new PdfConverter();
        PassimUtils utils = new PassimUtils(args);
        builder(conv.getCommand(),utils.getSource(),
        utils.getTarget());
        // check errors - if file "err" is not empty
        // ....
    } catch(IOException e1) {
        // check errors - if operation was not possible
    }
}

public static void builder(
        String cmd,
        String srcName,
        String dstName) throws IOException {
    ProcessBuilder pb = new ProcessBuilder(cmd);
    File dst = new File(dstName);
    pb.redirectOutput(Redirect.appendTo(dst));
```

```
        File err = new File("err");
        pb.redirectError(Redirect.to(err));
        File src = new File(srcName);
        pb.redirectInput(Redirect.from(src));
        Process p = pb.start();
        assert 1pb.redirectInput().file() == src;
        assert pb.redirectOutput().file() == dst;
        assert pb.redirectError().file() == err;
    }
}
```

Sample app for testing Native call

```
package passim.b21;

public class SampleMain {
    private native void print();
    /**
     * @param args
     */
    public static void main(String[] args) {
        ConverterPlugin conv = new DocumentLinkedPdfConverter();
        PassimUtils utils = new PassimUtils(args);
        conv.doConversion(
            utils.getSourceStream(),
            utils.getTransform(),
            utils.getRange());
    }
    static {
      System.loadLibrary("DocumentConverter");
    }
}
```

3   Libraries Used in Sample Plug-Ins

3.1   PdfConverter

One of the main format which should be supported is PDF. According with proposed architecture, following operations will be required:

− getting whole document
− getting selected pages of the document

Although more fine-grained selection may be possible (e.g. selected chapter) for the first version of the plug-in it will be not considered.

As far as possible, stored PDF files should be converted into PDF/A format, according to ISO 19005-1:2005 (Document Management – Electronic document file format for long term preservation – Part 1: Use of PDF 1.4 (PDF/A-1)). Files stored in this format are bigger than source ones, but contains full set of data (e.g. font definitions), required to render document exactly the same on any device. Not all other version of the PDF are equally supported by each of the below mentioned tools.

ghostscript. This is PostScript and PDF interpreter. We could convert files to other formats, including pdf. Current version is 9.04, dated August 2011. Distributed under GNU GPL v2[3].

pstoedit. We could convert from PostScript (easily available from PDF) into many other formats, including PDF. Could be used to cut portion of the file Distributed under GNU GPL v2[3].

pdftk. Pdftk (**pdf** toolkit) - widest toolkit to manipulate pdf files. Based on the iText library.

iText. It is library written in C# and Java, widely used by other libraries, among others by pdftk. Distributed under GNU Affero General Public License [2].

Poppler. Poppler (libpoppler) is a library used to rendering and displaying pdf files. It is a successor of the Xpdf tool set. Although this functionality is outside scope of our interest, there are tools in the set (like pdftops) which will be used.

3.2   VideoConverter

Second considered formats are related to motion pictures. Building of the plug-is is similar to those of PdfConverter, although there are more options considered specifying target range and formats:

– selection of specified frames range
– selection of specified time range
– require specified format

There are several formats which must be supported with leading standards first [12] [22] [20] [19] [13]. As the digital objects are considered contain video parts (instead being them) searching and other content-related operations are considered on the upper level of the system, using attached meta-data [14]. Although there are wide spectrum of available options, the libav library was selected as a background for implementation of the plug-in.

libav/ffmpeg. Libav project is a fork of the popular ffmpeg project. Both libraries are almost the same, but libav has faster development speed so it looks more promising. Because of the simplicity of the testing, first version of the plug-in is implemented using calling external command line program.

4 Summary

Here we have presented a plugin-based solution for multimedia objects conversion in a digital repository. Our approach proved to be simple and efficient. In our solution each plug-in is supplying information on available operations, provides input data type recognition and the appropriate processing procedure. Our approach enables: 1) easy testing without requirement of the full application environment, 2) easy way of integrating and using external tools, 3) capability of parallel processing.

Acknowledgements. Presented project is a part of the research task SYNAT: "Establishment of the universal, open, hosting and communication, repository platform for network resources of knowledge to be used by science, education and open knowledge society" and the strategic scientific research and experimental development program: "Interdisciplinary System for Interactive Scientific and Scientific-Technical Information". Presented work was supported by the National Centre for Research and Development (NCBiR) under Grant No. SP/I/1/77065/10.

References

1. SYNAT project home page, http://www.synat.pl/weiti-pw
2. Gnu affero general public license,
   http://www.gnu.org/licenses/agpl-3.0.html (as on January 1, 2012)
3. Gnu general public license version 2 (June 1991),
   http://www.gnu.org/licenses/old-licenses/gpl-2.0.txt (as on January 1, 2012)
4. Gnu general public license version 3, June 29 (2007),
   http://www.gnu.org/licenses/gpl-3.0.txt (as on January 1, 2012)
5. Gnu lesser general public license,
   http://www.gnu.org/licenses/lgpl.html (as on January 1, 2012)
6. Digital future, the library in the information age (Cyfrowa przyszłość, czyli biblioteki w erze informacji). Technical University of Lodz, 2006. Library of the XXI century. Can we survive? II Conference of the Library Technical University of Lodz (Poland), June 19-21 (2006)
7. Where it goes information (Dokąd zmierza informacja). Technical University of Lodz, 2006. Library of the XXI century. Can we survive? II Conference of the Library Technical University of Lodz (Poland), June 19-21 (2006)
8. The role of domain based hypertext systems in science information management (Rola dziedzinowych systemów hipertekstowych w zarządzaniu informacją w nauce), 2006. Knowledge managements in the science, Katowice (Poland), November 24-26 (2006)
9. 9 Digital Libraries and Archives: 7th Italian Research Conference, IRCDL 2011, Pisa, Italy, January 20-21, 2011. Revised Papers (Communications in Computer and Information Science). Springer (2011)
10. Passim B21.Report 1 (November 2011)
11. Bednarek-Michalska, B.: Polish network of digital libraries(2008)

12. Bovik, A.C.: The Essential Guide to Video Processing. Academic Press (2009)
13. Ghanbari, M.: Standard Codecs (Iet Telecommunications Series), 3rd edn. Institution of Engineering and Technology (2011)
14. Gibbon, D.C., Liu, Z.: Introduction to Video Search Engines. Springer (2008)
15. Marek Kolasa, W.: Formats of documents in digital libraries (Formaty dokument w w bibliotekach cyfrowych). E-LIS. E-prints in Library and Information Science (2011)
16. Maciejewska, U.: What are the expectations of academic library users in the era of electronic information (Czego oczekują użytkownicy biblioteki akademickiej w dobie informacji elektronicznej?), pp. 42 – 52. E-LIS. E-prints in Library and Information Science (2008)
17. Moskwa, K., Rossa, P.: The development of digital libraries and electronic repositories in Lower Silesia in 2004-2008 (Rozwój bibliotek cyfrowych i repozytoriów elektronicznych na Dolnym Śląsku w latach 2004-2008), pp. 15 – 26 (2009)
18. Nahotko, M.: Digital Librarians in environment of digital science, libraries and publications (Bibliotekarze cyfrowi w środowisku cyfrowej nauki, biblioteki i cyfrowych publikacji). Biuletyn EBIB (10/80) (2006)
19. Richardson, I.E.: The H.264 Advanced Video Compression Standard. Wiley (2010)
20. Richardson, I.E., Richardson, I.E.G.: H.264 and MPEG-4 Video Compression: Video Coding for Next Generation Multimedia. Wiley (2003)
21. Witten, I.H., Bainbridge, D., Nichols, D.M.: How to Build a Digital Library, 2nd edn. Morgan Kaufmann Series in Multimedia Information and Systems. Morgan Kaufmann (2009)
22. Xiong, Z.: A Unified Framework for Video Summarization, Browsing & Retrieval: with Applications to Consumer and Surveillance Video. Academic Press (2005)

Towards User-Guided Quantitative Evaluation of Wrist Fractures in CT Images

Johan Nysjö[1], Albert Christersson[2], Filip Malmberg[1],
Ida-Maria Sintorn[1], and Ingela Nyström[1]

[1] Centre for Image Analysis, Uppsala University and SLU, Sweden
johan.nysjo@cb.uu.se
[2] Dept. of Orthopedics, Uppsala University Hospital, Sweden

Abstract. The wrist is the most common location for long-bone fractures in humans. To evaluate the healing process of such fractures, it is of interest to measure the fracture displacement, particularly the angle between the joint line and the long axis of the fractured long bone. We propose to measure this angle in 3D computed tomography (CT) images of fractured wrists. As a first step towards this goal, we here present a fast and precise semi-automatic method for determining the long axis of the radius bone in CT images. To facilitate user interaction in 3D, we utilize stereo graphics, head tracking, 3D input, and haptic feedback.

1 Introduction

The standard method for examining the human skeleton after an extremity injury is conventional plain X-ray. This method has the disadvantage of being a two-dimensional (2D) image representation of a three-dimensional (3D) structure. The problem is partially overcome by acquiring images in more than one projection, and since conventional X-ray is partially transparent, it is often possible to detect fractures in the extremities. To be able to decide the correct treatment of a fracture, for example, whether a fracture needs to be operated or not, it is important to assess the fracture displacement. When a fracture is located close to a joint, for example, in the wrist, which is the most common location for fractures in humans, the angulation of the joint surface in relation to the long axis of the long bone needs to be measured [2,7]. This is illustrated in Figure 1a. Since the joint surface in the wrist is highly irregular, and since it is difficult to take X-rays of the wrist in exactly the same projections from time to time, conventional X-ray is not an optimal method for this purpose [3]. In most clinical cases, conventional X-ray is satisfactory for making a correct decision about the treatment, but when comparing two different methods of treatment, e.g., two different operation techniques, the accuracy of the angulation of the fractures before and after the treatment needs to be higher.

To overcome the limitations associated with measuring a 3D angle in a 2D projection, we propose to perform all measurements in 3D computed tomography (CT) images of the wrist (see Figure 1b). To measure the desired angle, we must

L. Bolc et al. (Eds.): ICCVG 2012, LNCS 7594, pp. 204–211, 2012.

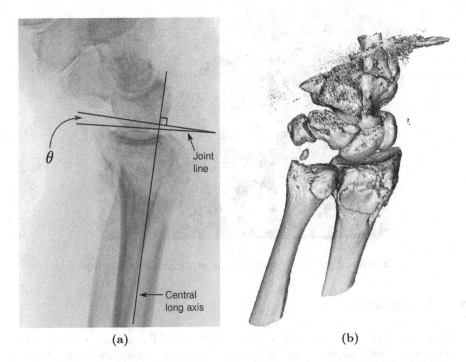

(a)   (b)

Fig. 1. (a) A lateral X-ray image of the wrist with a set of conventional 2D annotations used to measure the dorsal angle θ between the joint line and a line orthogonal to the long axis of the radius bone. (b) A 3D CT image of the same wrist, rendered as a shaded isosurface.

perform two tasks: (1) identify the long axis of the radius bone; and (2) identify the plane of the joint surface.

Here, we present a method for solving the first of these tasks. The proposed method is semi-automatic; the user is required to provide a bounding box for the part of the radius bone that should be used to determine the long axis. This information is subsequently used as input to an automatic algorithm that identifies the long axis with high precision. To facilitate user interaction in 3D, we use a system that supports stereo graphics, head tracking, 3D input, and haptic feedback.

2   User Interface

To provide accurate input to the automatic method, and to assess the accuracy of the results, it is vital that the user can visualize and interact with the 3D image data in an efficient way. In this section, we describe the components of the proposed user interface.

Fig. 2. An orthopedic surgeon working at the visuo-haptic display

2.1 Visualization

During user interaction, the bone regions within the CT image are displayed as shaded isosurfaces, as shown in Figure 1b. To achieve interactive frame rates, those surfaces are rendered using GPU-accelerated raycasting [6].

To enhance the user's ability to judge depth and distances when performing the interactive axis measurements, we run our system on a stereoscopic mirror display coupled with head tracking. See Figure 2.

2.2 Haptic Interaction

Haptic interaction with 3D objects is most commonly performed with haptic devices that have one interaction point and three or six degrees of freedom (DOF). In our work, we use a PHANToM Omni device from Sensable[1]. The PHANToM Omni is designed as a stylus, and the haptic feedback is given at the stylus tip, the haptic probe. The device has 6-DOF for input and 3-DOF for output: it takes a position and an orientation as input; and generates a force vector as output. The device can be used with an ordinary workstation, but in our work, we have used it in combination with a specialized haptic display from SenseGraphics[2] that allows for co-localized haptics and stereo graphics. This setup is shown in Figure 2.

For the task of determining the long axis of the radius bone, the haptic device serves as a 6-DOF input device that enables the user to perform precise positioning, scaling, and rotation of objects in the 3D scene.

---

[1] http://www.sensable.com

[2] http://www.sensegraphics.com

2.3   Implementation Details

We have implemented the various components of the system in C++ and Python, using an open-source software toolkit called WISH. This toolkit is intended for rapid prototyping of haptic-enabled applications (see [5] for an example) and contains implementations of various algorithms for image analysis, volume visualization, and volume haptics. For more information about WISH, please, refer to the project web page[3] or to [8].

3   Identifying the Long Axis of the Radius Bone

To determine the long axis of the radius bone, the user starts by placing a scalable bounding box around the part of the bone located beneath the joint, as shown in Figure 3. The position and orientation of the box is controlled via the haptic device, so that the user can pick up the box and place it in the desired location. The placement of the box does not need to be very precise, as the automatic axis computation method we will use in the next step is robust to variations in box placement.

Once the user is satisfied with the placement of the bounding box, we select all the enclosed voxels. We then use surface normal information and an adapted version of the RANSAC-based method by Chaperon and Goulette [1] to compute an accurate estimate of the long axis. The method consists of the following steps:

1. Use the marching cubes algorithm [4] to extract the surface of the selected part of the radius bone (Figure 4a).
2. Compute interpolated per-vertex normals for the extracted surface.
3. Map the surface normals to points on a unit sphere (Figure 4b). The points corresponding to surface normals that are orthogonal or near orthogonal to the long axis of the bone will form a distinct circle on the sphere.
4. Use RANSAC to iteratively fit a plane to the circle (Figure 4c). At each iteration, RANSAC will first construct a plane by randomly selecting three points from the point cloud, and then extract and count the number of points that are located within a given distance threshold from this plane. The objective here is to find the plane that maximizes the number of inliers. The normal of that plane will correspond to the direction of the long axis.
5. As a refinement step, use principal component analysis (PCA) to fit a plane to the inliers obtained in step 4. The normal of this plane will replace the normal obtained in step 4 and be selected as a candidate axis.
6. Repeat step 4–5 N times to generate a set of candidate axes.
7. Average the N candidate axes to obtain the final axis estimate (Figure 4d).

The method depends on the following parameters: the isovalue t_{iso} used for surface extraction; the distance threshold $t_{dist} \in [0, 1]$ used for outlier removal; the number of iterations K performed by RANSAC; and the number of repetitions N. The value of t_{iso} should be based on the Hounsfield unit (HU) value for bone

---

[3] http://www.cb.uu.se/research/haptics/

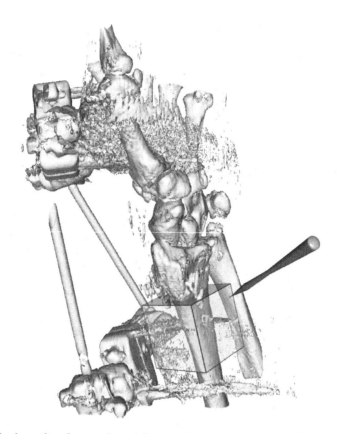

Fig. 3. The bounding box tool used for selecting a part of the radius bone. The box can be translated, rotated, and scaled with the haptic device.

tissue. The value of t_{dist} translates into an angle and can be estimated using a priori shape information about the bone. K should be set to a high value to ensure, with a reasonable high probability, that at least one plane with a good fit to the circle is selected. Experimentally, we have found $K = 1000$ to be sufficient for our datasets. Finally, the value of N should also be set high, e.g., $N = 100$. Axes produced by single runs of RANSAC tend to be slightly misaligned, but by running RANSAC several times and averaging the results, we can obtain an accurate estimate of the desired axis.

A similar method was presented by Winkelbach et al. [9], who used surface normal information and a Hough-transform voting scheme to measure the axes of cylindrical bone fragments. That method, however, can only be used for cylindrical surfaces. In Figures 3 and 4, we can see that the part of the radius bone that we are interested in performing axis measurements on is conical rather than cylindrical. Hence, the method of [9] would not be able to find the desired axis in our case.

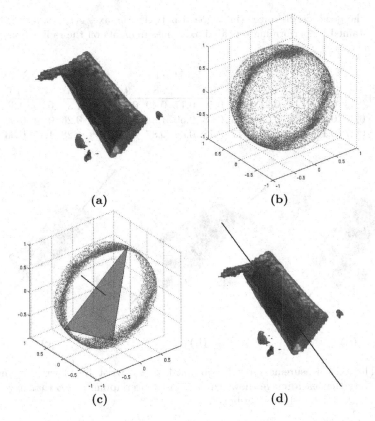

Fig. 4. RANSAC-based axis estimation: (a) extracted isosurface; (b) surface normals mapped on a unit sphere; (c) RANSAC plane fitting; (d) estimated axis

4   Experiment and Results

For this experiment, we used 14 CT images of fractured wrists. The images have the dimensions $512 \times 512 \times N_z$, where the number of slices N_z ranges from 92 to 243. The pixel resolution is between 0.2 and 0.4 mm and the slice thickness ranges from 0.8 to 1.0 mm. Before loading the CT images into our system, we converted them from stacks of DICOM images to 8-bit VTK volume images with graylevel values between 0 and 255.

One user (an orthopedic surgeon) performed repeated axis measurements on the 14 CT images using the proposed system. A short training session allowed the user to become familiar with the system before the measurements started. The user repeated the measurements three times for each image, and was, to reduce learning bias, instructed to change image after each measurement. The axes were computed using the method described in Section 3, with the fixed parameters $t_{\text{iso}} = 90$ (which corresponds to 1084 HU), $t_{\text{dist}} = 0.25$ (which corresponds to a 14 degree angle), $K = 1000$, and $N = 100$. In total, 42 axes were measured.

Table 1. The geodesic distances (in degrees) between the axes $A1$, $A2$, and $A3$ that one user obtained by performing repeated axis measurements on the radius bone in 14 CT wrist images

| | \multicolumn{14}{c}{Wrist image} |
Axis pair	1	2	3	4	5	6	7	8	9	10	11	12	13	14
A1A2	0.43	0.23	0.14	0.21	0.95	0.56	0.17	0.49	0.86	0.82	1.23	0.35	0.36	0.24
A1A3	0.37	0.29	0.18	0.23	1.03	0.68	0.50	1.33	0.10	0.23	0.26	0.83	0.62	0.18
A2A3	0.27	0.11	0.17	0.19	1.77	0.18	0.32	0.87	0.78	0.59	1.28	1.15	0.36	0.32

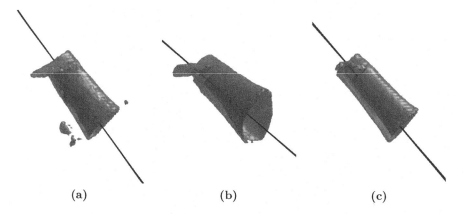

(a)   (b)   (c)

Fig. 5. The axis measurement results obtained for (a) wrist 1, (b) wrist 7, and (c) wrist 12. Note that each image shows three (mostly overlapping) axes that have been computed with different bounding boxes.

The 42 axis measurements required, on average, an interaction time of ~ 20 seconds and a computational time of 20 ± 5 seconds. To assess intra-user precision, we represented the obtained axes as points on a unit sphere and computed, for each axis triplet $\{A1, A2, A3\}$, the geodesic distances between the points. Table 1 shows the resulting distance values expressed in degrees. The overall small distance values achieved indicate that our method has a high repeatability and is robust to variations in the placement of the bounding box. Figure 5 illustrates the axis measurement results. Shifting the parameter values $\pm15\%$ caused only slight (on average, less than 0.5 degrees) differences in the measurement results, indicating that the method is fairly robust to the choice of parameter values. Since we have performed the measurements on real data, there is no ground truth available to verify the obtained axes against. The axes have, however, been visually inspected and deemed acceptable for their intended usage.

5   Conclusions

As stated in the introduction, our goal in this project is to develop a robust and accurate method for measuring the angulation of the joint surface in relation to the long axis of the radius bone in CT images of fractured wrists. Here, we have presented a method for solving the first part of this task: to determine the long axis of the radius bone. In an empirical study, we have demonstrated that the proposed method allows the long axis to be determined with high precision, with only limited user input. The overall measurement procedure takes less than 1 minute to perform, making the method suitable for interactive use.

To facilitate user interaction in 3D, we have implemented the proposed method in a system that utilizes stereo graphics, head tracking, and haptic feedback. In addition to enabling precise quantitative measurements, we believe that this user interface is of great value for qualitative assessment of wrist fractures. Initial response from orthopedic surgeons who have tested the system has been very positive. Next, we plan to complete the system with a method for determining the orientation of the joint surface.

References

1. Chaperon, T., Goulette, F.: Extracting Cylinders in Full 3D Data Using a Random Sampling Method and the Gaussian Image. In: Proceedings of the Vision Modeling and Visualization Conference, VMV 2001, pp. 35–42. AKA-Verlag (2001)
2. Friberg, S., Lundström, B.: Radiographic measurements of the radio-carpal joint in normal adults. Acta Radiologica Diagnosis 17(2), 249–256 (1976)
3. Kreder, H.J., Hanel, D.P., McKee, M., Jupiter, J., McGillivary, G., Swiontkowski, M.F.: X-ray Film Measurements for Healed Distal Radius Fractures. The Journal of Hand Surgery 21(1), 31–39 (1996)
4. Lorensen, W.E., Cline, H.E.: Marching cubes: A high resolution 3D surface construction algorithm. SIGGRAPH Computer Graphics 21(4), 163–169 (1987)
5. Nyström, I., Nysjö, J., Malmberg, F.: Visualization and Haptics for Interactive Medical Image Analysis: Image Segmentation in Cranio-Maxillofacial Surgery Planning. In: Badioze Zaman, H., Robinson, P., Petrou, M., Olivier, P., Shih, T.K., Velastin, S., Nyström, I. (eds.) IVIC 2011, Part I. LNCS, vol. 7066, pp. 1–12. Springer, Heidelberg (2011)
6. Stegmaier, S., Strengert, M., Klein, T., Ertl, T.: A Simple and Flexible Volume Rendering Framework for Graphics-Hardware-based Raycasting. In: Fourth International Workshop on Volume Graphics, vol. 5, pp. 187–241 (2005)
7. Van Der Linden, W., Ericson, R.: Colles fracture. How should its displacement be measured and how should it be immobilized? The Journal of Bone and Joint Surgery 63(8), 1285–1288 (1981)
8. Vidholm, E.: Visualization and Haptics for Interactive Medical Image Analysis. Ph.D. thesis, Uppsala University (2008)
9. Winkelbach, S., Westphal, R., Goesling, T.: Pose Estimation of Cylindrical Fragments for Semi-automatic Bone Fracture Reduction. In: Michaelis, B., Krell, G. (eds.) DAGM 2003. LNCS, vol. 2781, pp. 566–573. Springer, Heidelberg (2003)

Hybrid Feature Similarity Approach to Full-Reference Image Quality Assessment

Krzysztof Okarma

West Pomeranian University of Technology, Szczecin,
Faculty of Electrical Engineering,
Department of Signal Processing and Multimedia Engineering,
26. Kwietnia 10, 71-126 Szczecin, Poland
okarma@zut.edu.pl

Abstract. In the paper the Hybrid Feature Similarity metric is proposed based on the combination of two recently proposed objective image quality assessment methods - Riesz transform based Feature Similarity metric and Feature Similarity index. Both of them have good performance in comparison to most "state-of-the-art" quality metrics but highly linear correlation with subjective scores requires an additional nonlinear mapping for tuning to each dataset. In order to overcome this problem and obtain high quality prediction accuracy the nonlinear combination of both metrics is proposed leading to better performance than using each of the metrics separately. The experiments conducted in order to propose the weighting coefficients for both metrics have been performed using TID2008 dataset which is currently the largest and most comprehensive publicly available image quality assessment database, containing 1700 images together with their subjective quality evaluations. The verification of the obtained results has been also conducted using some other relevant benchmark databases.

Keywords: image quality assessment, feature similarity, image analysis.

1 Introduction

One of the most dynamically developing areas of computer vision and image analysis during the last decade has been the image quality assessment together with its natural extension towards video quality assessment algorithms. One of the main reasons of this fact is the necessity of fast and accurate automatic evaluation of images which should be well correlated with subjective perception of typical distortions. Such objective scores can be used for the optimisation of many image and video processing algorithms such as e.g. filtering or lossy compression as well as the additional information corresponding to the reliability of image analysis results. Since the accuracy of many image recognition and classification algorithms e.g. face recognition strongly depends on the quality of the visual input data, such information may be useful also for the evaluation of the results' reliability.

L. Bolc et al. (Eds.): ICCVG 2012, LNCS 7594, pp. 212–219, 2012.

The main direction of research in this area is related to the achievement of a high correlation between the objective and subjective quality scores. Typical measures applied for evaluation of newly proposed image quality metrics are Pearson linear correlation coefficient used to determine the metrics' prediction accuracy, Spearman Rank Order Correlation Coefficient (SROCC) and Kendall Rank Order Correlation Coefficient (KROCC) related to the prediction monotonicity. Each newly developed objective metric should be tested using several benchmarking databases (briefly described in the further part of the paper) containing numerous images with typical distortions together with Mean Opinion Scores (MOS) or Differential MOS (DMOS) values obtained as the result of many perceptual experiments.

Many new metrics have been developed during the last several years, significantly better than traditionally used pixel-based Mean Squared Error (MSE) or Peak Signal to Noise Ratio (PSNR) in terms of correlation with human perception of various distortions. Most of them belong to the group of full-reference metrics which require the exact knowledge of the reference image without any distortions. A contradictory group of algorithms, known as "blind" or no-reference metrics can determine the quality of an image without any reference information, but such algorithms are usually less universal and sensitive to strongly limited number of distortion types. There is also another group of image quality assessment methods, known as the reduced-reference metrics, which partially utilise the data from the reference image.

Nevertheless, the common problem of objective image quality metrics is the nonlinear relation between their raw scores and subjective results expressed as MOS or DMOS values. In order to compensate it some nonlinear mapping functions can be applied, such as logistic function, increasing the Pearson correlation coefficient's values. Unfortunately the parameters of the mapping function strongly depend on the dataset used in the experiments so different values are obtained for each database as the result of their tuning. Hence, the universality of such metrics is strongly limited, because the result of quality assessment of a single arbitrarily chosen image should not be dependent on any dataset specific parameters. One of the possible solutions, recommended in this paper, is the inclusion of the nonlinearity within the metric's calculation procedure in order to overcome this problem. Such approach increases the linear correlation with subjective scores without the necessity of any nonlinear mapping and may also increase the metric's performance in terms of rank order correlation coefficients.

The results of such approach presented in this paper have been obtained using the nonlinear combination of two recently proposed full-reference similarity based metrics - Riesz based Feature Similarity (RFSIM) [1] and Feature Similarity (FSIM) index [2]. Since the FSIM metric has been also proposed in colour version, the corresponding colour hybrid metric is discussed as well. Nevertheless, a reliable colour image quality assessment is still far from perfection and can be considered as an open field of research [3,4]. A quite similar situation takes place for the video quality assessment.

2   Modern Similarity Based Image Quality Metrics

The first modern approach to the image quality assessment based on the similarity of an original image and its contaminated version is the idea of the Universal Image Quality Index [5] further extended into well-known Structural Similarity (SSIM) [6]. Both metrics are based on the similar assumptions of calculation of the local mean values, variances and covariances within the sliding window in order to determine the local similarity index, further averaged leading to the overall quality score. One of their advantages is the sensitivity to three common types of image distortions: loss of contrast, luminance distortions and the most important structural changes. In recent years some further modifications of the SSIM metric have been proposed e.g. Multi-Scale SSIM [7], gradient based SSIM (G-SSIM), Three-Component Weighted SSIM or CW-SSIM [8] based on the use of steerable complex wavelet transform.

2.1   Riesz Based Feature Similarity

Another interesting idea has been proposed in 2010 in the paper [1] based on the assumption that the most relevant image regions are located near the edges which can be detected e.g. using well-known Canny filter. Considering a strong influence of low level features at key locations, such as edges, lines, corners or zero-crossings on the perceived quality, the Riesz transform has been proposed for applying to the nearest neighbourhood of the detected edges. Using the first and second order Riesz transform coefficients as five masked image features, the comparison of such feature maps for the reference and assessed image (denoted ad f and g respectively) can be conducted locally according to

$$d_i(x,y) = \frac{2 \cdot f_i(x,y) \cdot g_i(x,y) + C}{f_i^2(x,y) + g_i^2(x,y) + C} \tag{1}$$

where $i = 1..5$ and C is a small stabilizing constant value. The overall RFSIM index can be then computed as

$$\text{RFSIM} = \prod_{i=1}^{5} \frac{\sum_x \sum_y d_i(x,y) \cdot M(x,y)}{\sum_x \sum_y M(x,y)} \tag{2}$$

where M is the binary mask obtained as the result of the edge filtering.

2.2   Feature Similarity Index

The Feature Similarity (FSIM) metric has been proposed [2] as the combination of the the phase congruency (PC) and gradient magnitude (G) information calculated locally in order to determine a local similarity index. The overall quality index for greyscale images can be obtained by averaging as

$$\text{FSIM} = \frac{\sum_x \sum_y S(x,y) \cdot PC_m(x,y)}{\sum_x \sum_y PC_m(x,y)} \tag{3}$$

where $PC_m(x,y) = max(PC_1(x,y), PC_2(x,y))$ stands for the higher of the two local phase congruency values obtained for the original and distorted image respectively. The local similarity index $S(x,y)$ can be calculated according to the following formula

$$S(x,y) = \left(\frac{2 \cdot PC_1(x,y) \cdot PC_2(x,y) + T_{PC}}{PC_1^2(x,y) + PC_2^2(x,y) + T_{PC}}\right)^{\alpha} \cdot \left(\frac{2 \cdot G_1(x,y) \cdot G_2(x,y) + T_G}{G_1^2(x,y) + G_2^2(x,y) + T_G}\right)^{\beta} \tag{4}$$

where T_{PC} and T_G are small stabilizing constants and the importance exponents for both elements are set to $\alpha = \beta = 1$ for simplicity. The gradient values can be computed using gradient convolution filters e.g. Prewitt, Sobel or Scharr masks (the last one is recommended by the authors of the FSIM index) and the detailed analysis of the phase congruency measurement can be found in the paper [9]. Additionally, the colour version of the metric (FSIMc) can be computed which is based on the modification of the local similarity value in the equation (3) as

$$S_c(x,y) = S(x,y) \cdot \left[\frac{2 \cdot I_1(x,y) \cdot I_2(x,y) + T_{IQ}}{I_1^2(x,y) + I_2^2(x,y) + T_{IQ}} \cdot \frac{2 \cdot Q_1(x,y) \cdot Q_2(x,y) + T_{IQ}}{Q_1^2(x,y) + Q_2^2(x,y) + T_{IQ}}\right]^{\gamma} \tag{5}$$

where I and Q are the chrominance values in the YIQ colour space with the default value of the parameter $\gamma = 0.03$. The results obtained for the colour version of the metric are slightly better than using greyscale FSIM metric for the most relevant publicly available colour image datasets.

3   Overview of Image Quality Benchmarking Databases

A reliable comparison of the properties of the objective metrics requires the access to numerous subjective scores obtained for images with various distortions (differing both in types and the amount of quality degradation). Some time-consuming experiments resulting in several publicly available image quality assessment databases containing reference and distorted images with their MOS or DMOS values have been successfully conducted by some groups of researchers during last several years. The first such dataset, known as the MICT Image Quality Evaluation Database, has been provided in 2000 by researchers from Toyama University [10] and contains 14 colour reference images and 196 test images, lossy compressed using JPEG and JPEG2000 algorithms assessed by 16 students.

A much more useful dataset has been provided in 2005 by the Laboratory for Image and Video Engineering (LIVE) from Texas University at Austin [11], which contains 779 test images with 5 types of distortions: JPEG and JPEG2000 compression, white noise, Gaussian blue and transmission errors obtained in the simulated fast fading Rayleigh channel (in the Release 2 of the database). This database is currently one of three most relevant ones together with Tampere Image Database (TID2008) [12] and Categorical Subjective Image Quality (CSIQ) database [13]. The TID2008 database contains 1700 distorted colour images with 17 types of distortions (applied for 25 reference images) assessed by 838 observers from three countries using the pairwise sorting. The CSIQ dataset proposed in 2009 is based on 30 reference images and 866 distorted ones assessed by 35 subjects but it contains only 6 types of distortions.

Some other, less important datasets are: Wireless Image Quality (WIQ) database [14] containing 80 greyscale images corrupted by the wireless transmission errors, IRCCyN/IVC [15] containing 160 colour images with 4 distortion types and A57 dataset [16] developed in 2006 at Cornell University based on only three greyscale reference images.

Unfortunately the impact of the benchmark dataset on the performance of image quality metrics may be significant, so the universality of each metric should be confirmed using at least three major or preferably all available databases [17].

4   Proposed Hybrid Approach and Discussion of Results

Since both similarity metrics discussed above utilise different kinds of information present in the images, their correlation with subjective scores differs for various datasets. Considering this, the hybrid metric is proposed as their nonlinear combination, allowing convenient optimization of parameters, defined as

$$\text{HFSIM} = (\text{RFSIM})^a \cdot (\text{FSIM})^b \tag{6}$$

together with its colour version with FSIM replaced with FSIMc. The values of the coefficients a and b can be obtained as the results of the optimisation utilising the TID2008 database, chosen as the most comprehensive of currently available datasets. The obtained sub-optimal values of both exponents are $a = 0.4$ and $b = 3.5$ assuming that there is a little sense in the "exact" optimisation of the exponents, since even the scores of 1700 images present in the Tampere Image Database do not fully correspond to the Human Visual System and perception of various distortions. A similar approach for some other metrics, proposed earlier, has been applied in the paper [18], also leading to the increase of the Pearson linear correlation coefficient with subjective scores.

The scatter plots obtained for three most relevant datasets: TID2008, CSIQ and LIVE using three greyscale metrics are shown in Fig. 1 where the most linear character of the plots obtained for the proposed metric can also be observed, especially for TID2008 and LIVE databases. A strongly nonlinear relation between subjective scores and FSIM metric can be easily noticed as well. The comparison of the correlation coefficients obtained for seven major datasets is presented in Table 1, where not only the increase of the Pearson linear correlation coefficient

Table 1. Obtained results of the correlation coefficients for 7 databases discussed in section 3 in comparison to the use of the standard FSIM and RFSIM metrics

Database	RFSIM	FSIM	FSIMc	**HFSIM**	**HFSIMc**
Pearson linear correlation coefficients					
TID2008	0.8596	0.8300	0.8341	**0.8853**	**0.8861**
CSIQ	0.9130	0.8048	0.8208	**0.9158**	**0.9197**
LIVE	0.9352	0.8586	0.8595	**0.9538**	**0.9532**
IVC	0.7927	0.8563	0.8606	**0.8711**	**0.8721**
WIQ	0.7589	0.7371	– – –	**0.7876**	– – –
A57	0.8419	0.9252	– – –	**0.9319**	– – –
MICT	0.7523	0.8002	0.8049	0.7977	0.7992
Spearman Rank Order Correlation Coefficients (SROCC)					
TID2008	0.8680	0.8805	0.8840	**0.8911**	**0.8925**
CSIQ	0.9295	0.9242	0.9310	**0.9406**	**0.9422**
LIVE	0.9401	0.9634	0.9645	0.9605	0.9604
IVC	0.8192	0.9262	0.9293	0.8898	0.8908
WIQ	0.7368	0.8006	– – –	0.7858	– – –
A57	0.8215	0.9181	– – –	**0.9250**	– – –
MICT	0.7731	0.9059	0.9067	0.8430	0.8437
Kendall Rank Order Correlation Coefficients (KROCC)					
TID2008	0.6780	0.6946	0.6991	**0.7108**	**0.7125**
CSIQ	0.7645	0.7567	0.7690	**0.7900**	**0.7931**
LIVE	0.7816	0.8337	0.8363	0.8254	0.8248
IVC	0.6452	0.7564	0.7636	0.7162	0.7192
WIQ	0.5493	0.6215	– – –	0.6038	– – –
A57	0.6324	0.7639	– – –	**0.7667**	– – –
MICT	0.5752	0.7302	0.7303	0.6479	0.6485

can be observed but also the noticeably higher values of the rank order correlation coefficients, especially for TID2008 and CSIQ databases (better results are indicated by bold numbers).

5   Conclusions and Future Work

Analysing the presented results, the advantage of strong linear correlation of the proposed hybrid metric with the subjective quality evaluation can be observed for major datasets. Obtained results are superior even in comparison to some most recent metrics e.g. proposed in the paper [19], where Pearson's correlation is 0.8462 for TID2008 dataset (SROCC=0.8554, KROCC=0.6651). It proves a significant increase of the proposed metric's consistency with human perception of various distortion types. The application of the hybrid metrics utilising various kinds of information present in the images seems to be an interesting direction of further research, especially towards reliable colour image assessment.

The application of YIQ colour model in the Feature Similarity index should also be verified during further research leading to the choice of a probably more

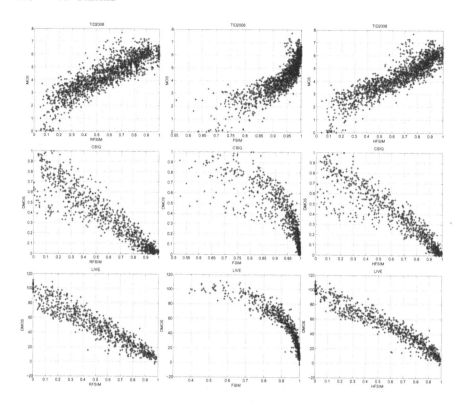

Fig. 1. Scatter plots of the RFSIM, FSIM and HFSIM metrics for three major datasets used in the experiments

appropriate colour space in the colour version of the proposed hybrid metric leading to even better consistency with subjective quality scores. Nevertheless, such research should be based on the image databases containing more colour specific distortion types and TID2008 dataset is currently the only database containing images with such type of distortions.

Another promising direction of further research is the verification of usefulness of the the Hybrid Feature Similarity approach for the video quality assessment purposes.

References

1. Zhang, L., Zhang, L., Mou, X.: RFSIM: A feature based image quality assessment metric using Riesz transforms. In: Proc. 17th IEEE Int. Conf. Image Processing, Hong Kong, China, pp. 321–324 (2010)
2. Zhang, L., Zhang, L., Mou, X., Zhang, D.: FSIM: A Feature Similarity index for image quality assessment. IEEE Trans. Image Processing 20(8), 2378–2386 (2011)
3. Okarma, K.: Colour Image Quality Assessment Using Structural Similarity Index and Singular Value Decomposition. In: Bolc, L., Kulikowski, J.L., Wojciechowski, K. (eds.) ICCVG 2008. LNCS, vol. 5337, pp. 55–65. Springer, Heidelberg (2009)

4. Okarma, K.: Colour Image Quality Assessment Using the Combined Full-reference Metric. In: Burduk, R., Kurzynski, M., Wozniak, M., Zolnierek, A. (eds.) Computer Recognition Systems 4. AISC, vol. 95, pp. 287–296. Springer, Heidelberg (2011)
5. Wang, Z., Bovik, A.: A universal image quality index. IEEE Signal Processing Letters 9(3), 81–84 (2002)
6. Wang, Z., Bovik, A., Sheikh, H., Simoncelli, E.: Image quality assessment: From error measurement to Structural Similarity. IEEE Trans. Image Processing 13(4), 600–612 (2004)
7. Wang, Z., Simoncelli, E., Bovik, A.: Multi-Scale Structural Similarity for image quality assessment. In: Proc. 37th IEEE Asilomar Conf. Signals, Systems and Computers, Pacific Grove, California (2003)
8. Sampat, M., Wang, Z., Gupta, S., Bovik, A., Markey, M.: Complex wavelet structural similarity: A new image similarity index. IEEE Trans. Image Processing 18(11), 2385–2401 (2009)
9. Liu, Z., Laganière, R.: Phase congruence measurement for image similarity assessment. Pattern Recognition Letters 28(1), 166–172 (2007)
10. Parvez Sazzad, Z., Kawayoke, Y., Horita, Y.: MICT/Toyama image quality evaluation database (2000), http://mict.eng.u-toyama.ac.jp/mictdb.html
11. Sheikh, H., Wang, Z., Cormack, L., Bovik, A.: LIVE Image Quality Assessment Database Release 2 (2005), http://live.ece.utexas.edu/research/quality
12. Ponomarenko, N., Lukin, V., Zelensky, A., Egiazarian, K., Carli, M., Battisti, F.: TID 2008 - a database for evaluation of full-reference visual quality assessment metrics. Advances of Modern Radioelectronics 10, 30–45 (2009)
13. Larson, E.C., Chandler, D.M.: Most apparent distortion: full-reference image quality assessment and the role of strategy. Journal of Electronic Imaging 19(1), 011006 (2010)
14. Engelke, U., Zepernick, H.-J., Kusuma, T.: Subjective quality assessment for wireless image communication: The Wireless Imaging Quality database. In: Proc. 5th Int. Workshop Video Processing and Quality Metrics for Consumer Electronics, Scottsdale, Arizona (2010)
15. Le Callet, P., Autrusseau, F.: Subjective quality assessment IRCCyN/IVC database (2005), http://www.irccyn.ec-nantes.fr/ivcdb/
16. Chandler, D., Hemami, S.: VSNR: A wavelet-based visual signal-to-noise ratio for natural images. IEEE Trans. Image Processing 16(9), 2284–2298 (2007)
17. Tourancheau, S., Autrusseau, F., Sazzad, Z., Horita, Y.: Impact of subjective dataset on the performance of image quality metrics. In: Proc. 15th IEEE Int. Conf. Image Processing, San Diego, California, pp. 365–368 (2008)
18. Okarma, K.: Combined Full-Reference Image Quality Metric Linearly Correlated with Subjective Assessment. In: Rutkowski, L., Scherer, R., Tadeusiewicz, R., Zadeh, L.A., Zurada, J.M. (eds.) ICAISC 2010, Part I. LNCS, vol. 6113, pp. 539–546. Springer, Heidelberg (2010)
19. Liu, A., Lin, W., Narwaria, M.: Image quality assessment based on gradient similarity. IEEE Transactions on Image Processing 21(4), 1500–1512 (2012)

Haptic Visualization of Material on TIN-Based Surfaces

Václav Purchart, Tomáš Pašek, Ivana Kolingerová, and Petr Vaněček

Department of Computer Science and Engineering,
University of West Bohemia,
Univerzitni 8, 306 14 Pilsen, Czech Republic
{vpurch,kolinger,pvanecek}@kiv.zcu.cz, prasek@students.zcu.cz

Abstract. Haptic devices are nowadays often used in non-hitech applications due to their increasing availability. These special input/output
devices provide native 3D manipulation and, additionally, unlike mouse
or keyboard, a control with a force. We present a low-level haptic visualization method which is able to simulate material on a surface and which
works natively with the triangulated irregular network terrain models
(TIN). Our method allows to model and visualize several materials, such
as sand, concrete, wood, etc. New materials could be created by setting
five parameters and, optionally, by the creation of a material relief. In our
framework we use the TIN terrain model together with real-time erosion
and interactive haptic editing using a set of virtual tools. We have performed a user study which is also included in the paper. Unlike existing
methods, we use a general shape of the tool; our solution is capable of
geometric editing of the TIN model, and it allows a simulation of several
materials.

1 Introduction

As haptic devices are changing from prototypes to the serial production models,
they are becoming cheaper and affordable for general public. Professional devices
are still priced at about a hundred thousands dollars. We use the low-end haptic
device Phantom Omni® which is priced at $2,400 (April 2012), but there are
even cheaper alternatives such as a Falcon Novint ($250). Thus, existing appli-
cations such as GIS, games, movies creation, or 3D editing in general could be
supplemented by a sense of touch.

Existing approaches usually use a grid or volumetric data structures, which
have high memory consumption. There were some attempts with compression of
these structures, but they have problems with irregular shapes. This problem is
eliminated by using irregular structures, but such methods usually do not allow
geometric editing (a change of the topology) of the model. Furthermore, if the
user wants to simulate more than one material, there is no method to handle it.

We present an easy to use, low-level haptic visualization method which could
be used for haptic visualization of a triangulated irregular network (TIN) terrain
surface models by point-based haptic devices. Our method allows to map forces

L. Bolc et al. (Eds.): ICCVG 2012, LNCS 7594, pp. 220–227, 2012.
© Springer-Verlag Berlin Heidelberg 2012

for the tool with arbitrary shape into a single point which represents a haptic cursor. Unlike grid or volumetric representation, our solution requires less memory and provides better scalability. Moreover, it deals with deformable meshes which are able to perform geometry updates during a computation of haptic frames. The goal of our haptic visualization is to be realistic, easy to use and reasonably fast to be usable. Our method can handle several materials and it is described in this paper together with a user study.

We use the Delaunay triangulation (DT) for the surface mesh representation and Constrained Delaunay triangulation (CDT) for editing. Our framework contains a set of editing tools with various shapes (rectangle, circle, sphere, ellipsoid, and man foot print). The graphics and haptic visualizations are split to separate threads, because haptic visualization requires a high framerate. Each haptic material has five parameters and an additional heightmap which stores the relief of the material.

The paper is structured as follows. The following section will briefly introduce the existing work. Next, our method is described. Next section summarizes our experiments and the last section concludes the paper.

2   Related Work

Haptic editing of non-volumetric 3D objects is very complicated due to a numerical stability of algorithms. Therefore, most authors focus on the editing of surface meshes. Such a representation does not consider material below the surface, but it is sufficient for most applications (e.g., for terrain editing).

Corso at al. [2] presented a haptic visualization method of elastic surface based on B-Splines. They use a medial axis transform where the material is modeled as a set of spheres. Each sphere contains a spring-damper to model elasticity.

Benes at al. [1] presented the method for haptic visualization of the deformable sand. The terrain model is represented as a heightfield stored in a regular grid. This data structure makes both graphics and haptic visualization simpler, but due to its fixed resolution it cannot hold a terrain data for close-ups. For a higher resolution the memory requirements significantly grow up.

Tiest and Kappers [4] published an analysis of 124 different material samples of real materials. Each material was cut to a square $10 \times 10cm$. They focus on a measurement of roughness and compressibility of each material. The roughness has been measured by a sampling of a height change during dragging of a pen of the "Universal surface tester" by Innowed GmpH. This pen acts with the constant force, speed, and angle against the surface. The compressibility has been measured by a special device with a rod on which the force has been applied. The displacement of the rod has been measured.

Purchart at al. [3] published a simple haptic visualization method which works with TIN, but it is not capable to simulate different materials than the sand and it uses a virtual tool border to compute a force feedback.

Basically, there are grid/voxel-based haptic methods, which have a problem with which have high memory consumption. Then there are methods which work with surface meshes or even tetrahedra meshes, but they do not allow change the mesh by changing its geometry.

3   Proposed Method

Our method consists of three main parts – geometric core (TIN), physical simulation (thermal erosion), and haptic interaction. We will focus on the haptic interaction in this paper.

Our framework contains a set of virtual tools which are handled by the user and allow an interactive editing of the model. Each tool consists of at least two parts – the set of outer edges (which form the tool contour), and the set of inner points (which define the tool imprint shape). For enforcing of a tool shape into the model we use the Constrained Delaunay triangulation (CDT).

3.1   Virtual Tools

A TIN model (triangulation) is formed by a set of triangles, a set vertices, a set of edges, and information about neighbors of triangles. A simple tool imprint is achieved by (i) interpolating the terrain height in the current position of vertices which forms the outer part of the tool, (ii) enforcing of a set of outer edges as constrained edges into the triangulation, and (iii) adding vertices of the tool's inner part into the mesh. Because vertices of the outer part of the tool have the same height as the terrain, the area around the imprint is protected from deformations inside the tool. This fact is used in a haptic visualization. The situation is depicted in Figure 1.

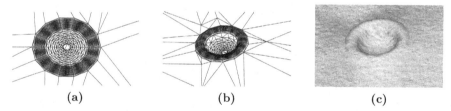

(a)	(b)	(c)

Fig. 1. An example of a tool imprint. (a) Footprint view in a vertical projection. Wireframe model with thick lines indicating constrained edges. The dense area around the imprint is an extruded material. (b) Same as (a) in an isometric view. (c) Textured model.

3.2   Haptic Visualization

Unlike the graphics visualization where 60 FPS is enough for smooth rendering, the haptic visualization has to have about 1,000 FPS. The force feedback feels runny for low framerates. We put haptic visualization into a separate thread but there is a problem with the geometry. Both virtual tools and erosion can cause geometry updates and the mesh is not a valid triangulation most of the time of graphics visualization loop. The only stable state of the mesh is in the end of a graphics loop (all mesh updates have been done and mesh has been repaired). To solve this problem, we have to store area around the tool in the cache to avoid geometry errors.

The haptic device we use is the Phantom Omni® made by SensAble (see Figure 2). It is a point-based haptic device which returns a position of the haptic cursor as a vector $p = [X, Y, Z]$. The correct force feedback has to be set as a vector $F_{out} = [X, Y, Z]$ at least 1,000 times per second in newtons $[N]$. The device then acts in the direction of F_{out} with the given force amount. The maximum force allowed by this device is 10N.

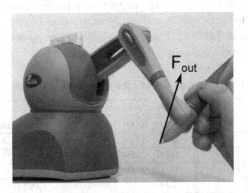

Fig. 2. Phantom Omni® haptic device used in our lab

3.3   Force and Material Computation

When the tool has to be imprinted into the terrain, we enforce the set of outer edges in the way that they do not affect the terrain height as it is mentioned in Section 3.1. Then *before* deforming of the inner part of the tool, we browse all the inner triangles and store their copies in a haptic cache. Browsing can be efficiently implemented, e.g., as a breath-first search because each triangle knows its neighbors and the search is constrained by outer edges of the imprint. For non-continuous tool imprints we perform the search for each part of imprint. After that we can process all the mesh updates without concern about the mesh state in a haptic thread.

When the cache update has been performed, we compute force feedback direction using normals of incident triangles (which are stored in cache). Because all triangles are counter-clockwise oriented, it is guaranteed that all normals direct above the surface. The resulting direction is computed as a weighted-average of normalized normals where the weight is the area of each triangle ABC. Let us first define the edges a, b, c of each triangle as Eq. 1.

$$a_i = C - B, \quad b_i = A - C, \quad c_i = B - A. \qquad (1)$$

Then we compute the normal n_i and area T_i of each triangle using the Heron's formula:

$$
\begin{aligned}
n_i &= -c_i \times a_i, \\
s_i &= \frac{|a_i| + |b_i| + |c_i|}{2}, \\
T_i &= \sqrt{s_i(s_i - |a_i|)(s_i - |b_i|)(s_i - |c_i|)}.
\end{aligned}
\qquad (2)
$$

The direction of the force vector F_{dir} is then computed according to Eq. 3.

$$n = \sum_{i=1}^{t_{num}} \frac{n_i}{|n_i|} \cdot T_i,$$
$$F_{dir} = \frac{n}{|n|},$$

(3)

where t_{num} is the number of browsed triangles.

When the direction of force feedback is known, we can incorporate the material properties as it is described below. In our test we have each material described by its stiffness S, elasticity E, static and dynamic friction (F_S, F_D), and roughness R (all properties are in Table 1). Each material also has its own heightmap which holds its relief for haptic close-ups. Used materials are in Figure 3.

Table 1. Coefficients for our set of materials

	asphalt	cloth	wood	wool	glass	sand	concrete	tiles
stiffness (S [N])	10.0	6.00	10.0	1.50	10.0	6.00	10.0	10.0
elasticity (E [N])	0.70	3.00	1.00	2.00	1.00	2.00	1.00	1.00
static friction (F_S [N])	0.05	0.07	0.08	0.08	$5 \cdot 10^{-4}$	0.06	0.07	0.02
dynamic friction (F_D [N])	0.02	0.03	0.03	0.04	$2 \cdot 10^{-4}$	0.02	0.03	0.01
roughness (R [%])	1.00	0.40	1.00	0.50	1.00	0.60	1.00	0.90

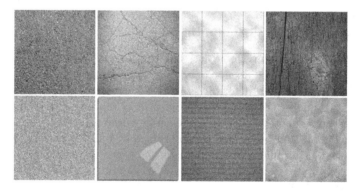

Fig. 3. Modeled materials starting at top-left with asphalt followed by concrete, tiles, wood, sand, glass, cloth, and wool

The force starts to act when the tool comes to contact with the terrain surface. We store the previous depth of the terrain as z_E for elasticity modeling. The friction force depends on the velocity of the tool, therefore we store both current tool position $p = [p_x, p_y, p_z]$ and the old tool position p_{old}. The friction coefficient C_{fr} switches the friction F_r from static to dynamic when the tool velocity is greater than C_{fr} as it is in Eq. 4.

$$F_r = \begin{cases} F_S, & when\ |p_{old} - p| < C_{fr}, \\ F_D, & otherwise, \end{cases}$$

(4)

where F_S and F_D are already mentioned static and dynamic friction.

Let the material relief given by the material heightfield in current tool position be m. Then we can compute force components as in Eq. 5.

$$
\begin{aligned}
F_E &= E \cdot (p_z - z_E), \\
F_z &= (S + F_E) \cdot m \cdot R, \\
F_{xy} &= F_r \cdot (1 - m) \cdot R,
\end{aligned} \tag{5}
$$

where the expression $1 - m$ means that the friction force is increased as the user touches deeper in the material relief. F_{xy} are F_x and F_y components of force F. Now we can incorporate the direction of the force previously computed from normals of incident triangles as in Eq. 6.

$$
F = [F_x \cdot F_{dir\ x}, F_y \cdot F_{dir\ y}, F_z \cdot F_{dir\ z}] \tag{6}
$$

where $F_{dir} = [F_{dir\ x}, F_{dir\ y}, F_{dir\ z}]$. The resulting force F can be greater than 10N which is the maximal force allowed by our device. Therefore, we define a maximum force step ΔF which is the maximum force change between haptic frames. The haptic thread stores the current force F and the desired target force F_T (which is automatically limited to 10N). Then the force F_{out} which is set on the device will be computed as Eq. 7 as long as it is reach the target force F_T.

$$
F_{out} = F + sgn(F_T - F) \cdot \Delta F \tag{7}
$$

The force F_{out} is set on the device.

4   Experiments and Results

We have implemented our algorithm in C++ with the help of OpenGL and GLSL. For haptic visualization we are using the OpenHaptics library. The application runs on Windows 7 and Linux. All data has been measured on a desktop running Windows 7, with 12GB RAM, Intel Core i7 clocked at 3.2GHz, and NVIDIA GeForce GTX 580, with 1.5GB of memory.

We have tested our approach in the user experiment to verify fidelity and usability of material simulation and editing. The number of test participants was 24, a suitable number as described by Tiest and Kappers [4]. The characteristics of the age Ag of participants are: $\overline{Ag} = 31.32\ years$, $med(Ag) = 25$, $mod(Ag) = 24$, $\sigma_{Ag} = 14.52$, $min(Ag) = 20\ years$, and $max(Ag) = 72\ years$.

Our experiment consists of four parts (A, B, C, and D) and each part has some number of questions (A and B have eight questions, C two questions and D has one question). In the part A the user is a kind of "blind". He cannot see the material he is touching and he has to choose a correct answer from the list of available materials. Results of this experiment are in Table 2 as a percentual correctness (Co). The best result had the glass followed by wool and tiles. It shows that the materials with low friction have better correctness.

The part B contains both graphics and haptic visualization of materials and the user has to evaluate his satisfaction with the force feedback E from 1 to 5, where $E = 1$ means the best and $E = 5$ the worst sense. There were also eight

Table 2. Relative ratios of recognition of all tested materials. Correct answers are in bold. The row *eval.* contains satisfaction evaluation of the users (1 – means the best, 5 – means the worst). Rows *A1-A8* corresponds to part *A*.

	asphalt	cloth	wood	wool	glass	sand	concrete	tiles
eval.	1.83	1.88	1.42	2.92	2.50	1.33	2.38	2.33
A1	**45.83%**	4.17%	8.33%	0.00%	0.00%	0.00%	29.17	0.00%
A2	4.17%	**29.17%**	25.00%	0.00%	0.00%	16.67%	12.50%	0.00%
A3	4.17%	16.67%	**25.00%**	0.00%	0.00%	12.50%	16.67%	12.50%
A4	4.17%	0.00%	0.00%	**66.67%**	16.67%	0.00%	0.00%	0.00%
A5	4.17%	8.33%	0.00%	4.17%	**70.83%**	0.00%	0.00%	0.00%
A6	16.67%	8.33%	4.17%	0.00%	0.00%	**41.67%**	12.50%	4.17%
A7	25.00%	4.17%	16.67%	4.17%	0.00%	8.33%	**20.83%**	8.33
A8	0.00%	8.33%	4.17%	4.17%	8.33%	0.00%	0.00%	**62.50%**

questions. The results are also in Table 2 in the row "*eval.*". Surprisingly, the best marks were collected for sand, wood, and asphalt – materials with higher friction.

In the part *C* the user has to guess which continent outline, covered by some of available materials, is touched. There were two questions *C*1 and *C*2. The experiment *C*1 has correctness 83.33% (Africa), *C*2 has 54.17% (Australia).

The part *D* contains a sense evaluation of deformable terrain mesh model. User has to edit the model in some way and to evaluate the editing. Available shapes are @, □, and ○. There was only one question *D*1. The average sense evaluation of the experiment *D*1 was 2.75.

We have measured random variables such as the age and the sex of participants and we have found interesting correlations. Let the Ag be the random variable of age, Co the vector of response correctness of all participants, E the mean evaluation vector for all materials, and S the sex of participants. Then the correlation $\rho_{Ag,Co} = -0.33$ means that the participants with higher age performed more wrong answers than younger ones. $\rho_{E,Co} = 0.50$ means that materials which had better evaluation had worse correctness, and finally $\rho_{S,Co} = 0.02$ shows that the correctness of the answers does not depend on the sex of participants.

Subjectively, the most entertaining questions for the participants were those to guess something (parts *A*, and *C*). Most of the test participants were students, so they took this quiz as a funny competition. The question which was also favored was *D*1, where participants had to create something.

5   Conclusion

Because we use a point-based haptic device, the force feedback is not physically accurate. For this purpose it would be better to use a haptic glove. But as the haptic devices are becoming more available to the general public, the presented method can be useful to the reader.

The presented user study brings some interesting results as that the younger people can more easily adapt to the force feedback and they are able to guess the correct material. Materials with better sense evaluation have been those with higher friction, but in contrast, materials with low friction were more often correctly guessed.

We want to extend our algorithm to model multiple materials at once (it can be probably computed as the weighted-average of the material responses), but it is necessary to modify graphics and erosion pipelines and it would require some additional afford. Another useful extension would be using deformable tetrahedra meshes instead of a surface model.

Acknowledgments. This work has been supported by the Ministry of Education, Youth and Sports under the research project LH11006, and project SGS-2010-028.

References

1. Beneš, B., Dorjgotov, E., Arns, L., Bertoline, G.: Granular material interactive manipulation: Touching sand with haptic feedback. In: Proceedings of the 14th International Conference in Central Europe on Computer Graphics, Visualization and Computer Vision, pp. 295–304 (2006)
2. Corso, J.J., Chhugani, J., Okamura, A.M.: Interactive haptic rendering of deformable surfaces based on the medial axis transform. In: Proc. EUROHAPTICS, pp. 92–98 (2002)
3. Purchart, V., Kolingerová, I., Benes, B.: Interactive sand-covered terrain surface model with haptic feedback. In: GIS Ostrava 2012 - Surface Models for Geosciences. pp. 215–223 (2012)
4. Tiest, W.M.B., Kappers, A.M.: Analysis of haptic perception of materials by multidimensional scaling and physical measurements of roughness and compressibility. Acta Psychologica 121(1), 1–20 (2006)

Some Ways of Distribution Viewing Points for Generating Viewing Representation

Andrzej Salamonczyk[1] and Wojciech Mokrzycki[2]

[1] University of Natural Sciences and Humanities, Siedlce, Poland
andrzej.salamonczyk@ii.uph.edu.pl
[2] University of Warmia and Mazury, Olsztyn, Poland
mokrzycki@matman.uwm.edu.pl

Abstract. The paper presents some ways of distribution viewing points for generating viewing representation on viewing sphere with perspective, including methods using regular polyhedra and spiral path on sphere. The number of viewpoints follows from the required scanning resolution.

Keywords: view representation of polyhedra, view sphere with perspective projection, viewing points on view sphere.

1 Introduction

Methods of generating 3D multiview representation of polyhedron for object visual identification are described in several papers, including informative views [1], iterative (e.g. [3]) and noninterative (e.g. [4]) algorithms.

In this paper we consider non transparent polyhedron without holes or pits. Let its faces be feature areas used as a foundation for accurate multiview 3D model determination. This model is a set of accurate views, acquired through central projection from viewing sphere according to the model from [3], fig. 1.

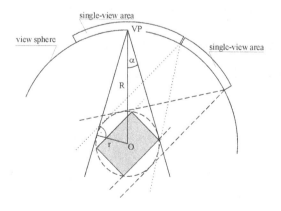

Fig. 1. Idea of viewing sphere with perspective

L. Bolc et al. (Eds.): ICCVG 2012, LNCS 7594, pp. 228–235, 2012.

The generation space model is constructed as follows: First circumscribe a sphere on a polyhedron. The small sphere (radius r) and its center is the same as the polyhedron center. On this sphere place a space view cone with angle of flare 2α . This is the *viewing cone*. The vertex of this cone is a model *viewing point* VP. Unconstrained movement of the cone vertex, where the cone is tangent to the small sphere creates a large sphere with radius R. This sphere is called *view sphere*. Each object has its own viewing sphere, the same for all views of this particular object. Views are obtained, taking into account only object features selected for identification i.e. faces.

The dependency between r and polyhedron vertices coordinates (X_{vi}, Y_{vi}, Z_{vi}) and: R, α, r and angle of view cone vc flare are:

$$r = max_{i=1,\cdots,k}\sqrt{X_{vi}^2 + Y_{vi}^2 + Z_{vi}^2}, \ R \geq \frac{r}{\sin\alpha}, \ \angle(vc) = 2\alpha.$$

Changing one view to the other is a *visual event*. This event occurs as a result of point VP movement and is manifested by appearance of a new feature in a view, disappearance of a feature or both.

Main emphasis in the described methods has been placed on the arrangement of viewpoints on view sphere and includes distribution of viewpoints using regular polyhedra and spiral path. This work provide a new more accurate formula for the number of viewpoints in spiral method and this algorithm is compared with another methods. The first group are methods using the icosahedron.

2 Distribution of Viewpoints Using Regular Polyhedra

The main idea in these methods of generating views is approximately uniform distribution of viewing points on the viewing sphere. The problem of uniform distribution of points on the sphere is widely described in literature, some solutions including using of regular polyhedra (putting view point in vertices of polyhedra). Chen, [2], use dodecahedron to generate Light Field Descriptors, Lindstrom and Turk, [5], also obtain views from vertices of dodecahedron. Icosahedron is also widely used in uniform point distribution on sphere, due to large number of faces and triangular shape of face (which can be easily divided into smaller triangular shapes).

2.1 The Method Based on the Division of the Icosahedron

In the first step of this method view points is putted in vertices of icosahedron inscribed in view sphere. Next, each of icosahedron face id divided into four

Fig. 2. Subsequent iterations in division of icosahedron face

smaller triangles, as shown in fig. 2, by putting new vertices in the middle of each edge (and scale its coordinates, to ensure the distance between view point and the origin was R). Newly established vertices also becomes view points. This process is repeated (in iterative way) until the number of vertices will provide the required minimum distance between viewing points. Some modifications of this method also can be met, e.g. division of edge on n parts, ensuring suitably dense distribution of viewing points. On fig. 3 is shown how shape of sphere is approximated in subsequent iterations of division of triangle face.

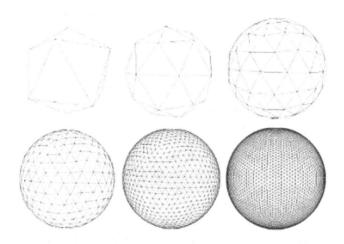

Fig. 3. Creating new viewing points by iterative division of icosahedron

The main advantage of this method is the simplicity of the algorithm and the relatively even distribution of points on the sphere.

2.2 A Method Uses the Convexity of One-View Area

In this method, a way to generate viewing points is the same as the previously described manner. However, here we use the fact, that one-view area is convex (we ignore edge-edge-egde events for simplicity). When the three vertices of the triangle yield the same view, the process of iterative subdivision is stopped. Continuing division and placing viewing points at the vertices we would get already obtained view (fig. 4), but we are focused on looking for new views.

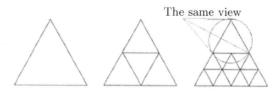

Fig. 4. The face division of icosahedron having regard convexity of one-view area

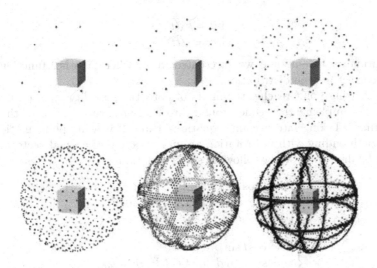

Fig. 5. Viewpoints in subsequent iterations of icosahedron having regard one-view areas

On fig. 5 is shown, how in subsequent iterations new viewing points occur close to boundaries of one-view areas. Boundaries in this case are established by edge-vertex events.

3   Distribution of Viewpoints Using Spiral Methods

3.1   Scanning Visibility Area of Face in Spiral Way

The main idea of this method is designation of all possible views with a given face of polyhedron . Repeating this operation for all faces gives a set of all possible views of objects. Complete set of all views of a single face is obtained by scanning potential visibility area of a face. This region looks like a bowl cut-off from the sphere. We move on this area in a spiral way with the additional requirement that viewpoints should be evenly distributed (approximately). This is achieved by requiring that the angle between successive paths of the spiral was constant.

The equation of a spiral on a sphere, satisfying this assumption, can be write:

$$\begin{cases} x = R \cos \theta \sin \phi \\ y = R \sin \theta \sin \phi \\ z = R \cos \phi, \end{cases} \qquad (1)$$

and angles θ i ϕ are linear dependent $\theta = k \cdot \phi$. For simplicity, the equation is written as a spiral motion around the z axis, angle $\phi \in [0, \pi]$, and number of full rotations around z axis is equal to $2k$.

In spiral described by eq. 1 angle between successive paths of the spiral equals $\frac{2\pi}{k}$. However, points determined by this equation are not uniformly distributed, definitely more densely at the "poles", see fig. 7. To avoid this inconvenience parameter t is nonlinearly mapped as follows:

$$\begin{cases} \theta = k\sqrt{t} \\ \phi = \sqrt{t}. \end{cases} \tag{2}$$

Basic outline of the method was presented in [6] where another function was used to correct uneven distribution.

If the viewing point reaches the limits of potential visibility area, than a full rotation of complementary cone around direction of normal vector of the face is performed. Taking into account equations 1 and 2 viewing point motion on a spiral path ending with full rotation around direction of normal vector of the face can be described by the following set of equations:

$$\begin{cases} x = \cos k\sqrt{t} \sin \sqrt{t} \\ y = \sin k\sqrt{t} \sin \sqrt{t} \ \text{ for } t \in \left[0, \beta^2\right] \\ z = \cos \sqrt{t}. \end{cases} \tag{3}$$

$$\begin{cases} x = \cos t \sin \beta \\ y = \sin t \sin \beta \ \text{ for } t \in \left(\beta^2, \beta^2 + 2\pi\right] \\ z = \cos \beta. \end{cases} \tag{4}$$

Potential Visibility Area (PVA) of face on viewing sphere looks like a bowl cut-off from the sphere. The apex of this area is the intersection of a straight line coinciding with the normal vector of face with the viewing sphere, the base is a circle which is the intersection of the viewing sphere with the plane containing the face (fig. 6a).

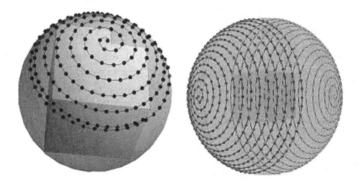

Fig. 6. (a) Sample scanning trajectory over the visibility area of face, described by equations (3 and 4) (b) multiple scanning of the same area on the viewing sphere

During movement of viewpoint on path from each newly generated viewing point we obtain view, if this view is not present in the views database then it is added to the set of view in a database. Thus we obtain a complete set of views included given face. Repeating the described scanning for each face we obtain a set of views for the polyhedron.

The tests of this algorithm have shown that complete set (with an accuracy to the desired resolution) of views were generated. Main idea of this method (scanning PVA of each face) leads to the principal drawback of this method, which is multiple scanning of the same area. Indeed, each area is scanned as many times as potentially visible faces are in this area (see fig. 6b). The method presented in the next section is free from this disadvantage.

3.2   Spiral Scanning of Whole Viewing Sphere

In this method (idea introduced in [7]), spiral trajectory is located not only in an area of potential visibility but on the whole viewing sphere. We demand that the viewpoints should be arranged on a spiral as evenly as possible.

We use equation 1 for spiral path on viewing sphere, but we use another function for correction of uneven distribution of viewpoints, $f(s) : [0, 2] \rightarrow [0, 2\pi]$:

$$\begin{cases} t = \arccos(1 - s); \ \text{dla} \ s \in [0, 1] \\ t = \pi - \arccos(s - 1); \ \text{for} \ s \in (1, 2]. \end{cases} \tag{5}$$

Putting $\theta = kt, \phi = t$ in equation 1 and parameter t defined by 5 we get much more even distribution (see fig. 7).

Before correction   After correction

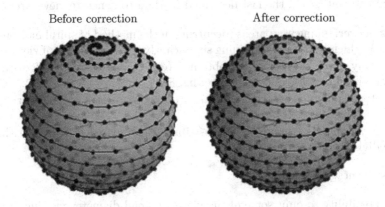

Fig. 7. View points before and after correction funtion

Demanding that the angle between successive turns of the spiral is equal to the desired scan resolution (denote by σ), we obtain the formula for k:

$$k = \tfrac{2\pi}{\sigma}.$$

Taking into account this formula and considering that the length of the spiral path defined by equation 1 is less than $2k + 1$, the formula for the number of viewpoints n on spiral path, sufficient to achieve the desired resolution σ, can be written as $n = \tfrac{2\pi + \sigma}{(\sigma)^2}$. Thus, the greatest distance between successive points is σ and the angle between successive turns of the spiral is equal to σ.

The most disadvantageous position of the viewpoint is in the middle of a square with side σ, therefore to ensure minimal resolution σ we can multiply it by $\sqrt{2}$. In [7] presents a less detailed model were presented taking into account only the distance between the viewpoints.

Having regard to those estimates we obtain the following formula for the number of viewpoints N in the method of spiral scanning of viewing sphere:

$$N = \frac{4\pi + \sqrt{2}\sigma}{2\left(\sigma\right)^2}. \tag{6}$$

The number of viewpoints is inversely proportional to the square of the scan resolution. Sample distribution of points on the trajectory obtained by this method is shown in fig. 7. Resolution in this case does not follow from a geometric features of solid, but from technical parameter of acquisition machine.

Proceeding in the manner described above complete set of views is obtained with an accuracy to the desired resolution.

4   Conclusions

The main advantages of the last described method to generate views are:

1. lack of overlapping scan areas (occurring in the method of spiral motion over faces), which leads to determining significantly smaller number of viewpoints;
2. generally fewer viewpoints are obtained (e.g. compared to the algorithm of the division of the icosahedron, see. fig. 8)
3. set of viewpoints is ordered (convenience in construction of other structures e.g. to generate aspect graphs)
4. set of viewpoints is more evenly distributed (compared to the algorithm of the division of the icosahedron).

The disadvantages include:

1. the possibility to omit some of the views of small diameter viewing area,
2. number of generated views may depend on the starting point of the path.

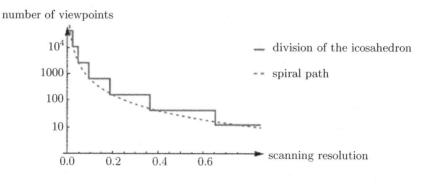

Fig. 8. Comparison of the number of viewpoints, depending on the desired resolution

The areas of non determined views on viewing sphere is relatively small, therefore there is small probability to receive such a view in the process of data acquisition and it is not necessary to determine all possible views (by calculating the intersection of the *edge-edge-edge* and *edge-vertex* event surfaces, which leads to huge number of viewpoints).In practice, the number of views in the database can be further reduced, e.g. by introducing the probability of a view.

References

1. Arbel, T., Ferrie, F.P.: Informative Views and Sequential Recognition. In: Buxton, B.F., Cipolla, R. (eds.) ECCV 1996. LNCS, vol. 1064, pp. 469–481. Springer, Heidelberg (1996)
2. Chen, D.-Y., Tian, X.-P., Shen, Y.-T., Ouhyoung, M.: On Visual Similarity Based 3D Model Retrieval. Computer Graphics Forum 22, 223–232 (2003)
3. Dabkowska, M., Mokrzycki, W.S.: Multi-view models of convex polyhedron. MG&V 6(4), 419–450 (1997)
4. Kowalczyk, M., Mokrzycki, W.S.: Obtaining complete 2 1/2D view representation of polyhedron using concept of seedling single-view area. CV&IU 91, 208–301 (2003)
5. Lindstrom, P., Turk, G.: Image-Driven Simplification. ACM Trans. Graph. 287, 204–241 (2000)
6. Mokrzycki, W.S., Salamonczyk, A.: Spiral Scanning of Faces to Obtain Complete 3D View Representation of Monotonous Polyhedra. In: Kurzynski, M., et al. (eds.) Computer Recognition Systems 2. AISC, vol. 45, pp. 71–178. Springer, Heidelberg (2007)
7. Salamończyk, A., Mokrzycki, W.: Generation of View Representation from View Points on Spiral Trajectory. In: Choraś, R.S. (ed.) Image Processing and Communications Challenges 2. AISC, vol. 84, pp. 67–74. Springer, Heidelberg (2010)

Interactive Browsing of Image Repositories

(Invited Paper)

Gerald Schaefer

Department of Computer Science, Loughborough University, Loughborough, UK
`gerald.schaefer@ieee.org`

Abstract. Image collections, both personal and commercial, are growing very rapidly. Consequently, methods for managing large image databases are highly sought after. In this paper, we look at various ways to visualise and interactively browse image collections. In general, we can divide image database visualisation approaches into three categories: mapping-based techniques which typically employ dimensionality reduction algorithms, clustered visualisations which group, often in a hierarchical manner, similar images, and graph-based approaches where links between images are exploited to arrive at an intuitive display of the dataset.

Once displayed, the user should be able to browse through the collection in an interactive, intuitive and efficient manner. Such browsing can be achieved in several ways. Horizontal browsing navigates through images of the same visualisation plane, and includes operations such as panning, zooming, magnification and scaling. In contrast, vertical browsing allows navigation to a different level of a hierarchically organised visualisation.

Keywords: Image databases, image database navigation, image browsing.

1 Introduction

Image collections are growing at an exponential rate and solutions to manage vast databases of images are hence highly sought after. Content-based image retrieval (CBIR) techniques [1] have shown great potential, yet commonly employed approaches like query-by-example are only of limited usefulness. An interesting alternative is provided by systems that allow visual exploration of an image dataset through a browsing interface. In this paper, we provide an overview of these approaches. We divide this challenging problem into two tasks: visualisation and display of the image collection, presented in Section 2, and browsing of a visualised collection which is covered in Section 3. In Section 4 we briefly introduce a particular system namely the Hue Sphere Image browser, while Section 5 concludes the paper.

L. Bolc et al. (Eds.): ICCVG 2012, LNCS 7594, pp. 236–244, 2012.

2 Visualisation of Image Databases

One of the main challenges of image database navigation systems is the limited screen size which is in stark contrast to both the number and the size of the images in the collection. Consequently, images are typically displayed as thumbnails arranged in such a way that the user can intuitively understand what kind of images are contained in the dataset. We can in general distinguish three main approaches to visualise image databases: mapping-based techniques, clustered visualisations, and graph-based approaches.

Mapping-based visualisations aim to represent the relationships between images in the high-dimensional feature space in a reduced dimensionality, usually confined to the two dimensions of a computer monitor. This way, the human mind can more readily perceive the relationships between the images in the database. To that effect, various dimensionality reduction techniques can be employed. Principal component analysis (PCA) is the simplest approach, where the positions of image thumbnails can be extracted by projecting their high-dimensional feature vectors to a low-dimensional space spanned by the first two or three principal components. PCA has been used in [2, 3] for image database visualisation. In contrast to PCA, multi-dimensional scaling (MDS) [4] attempts to preserve the original relationships (i.e. distances) of the high-dimensional space as best possible in the low-dimensional projection, and has been applied for image database navigation in [5–7]. An example of an MDS visualisation is shown in Figure 1.

Fig. 1. MDS visualisation of the UCID [8] image database

FastMap [9], a dimensionality reduction technique that is computationally less complex, can also be employed as shown in [10]. Alternative techniques, such as ISOMAP (isometric mapping), SNE (stochastic neighbour embedding) and LLE (local linear embedding), have also been applied [11]. Self-organising maps (SOMs) are neural networks that are trained to perform feature extraction and visualisation from the input data. SOMs have been used for image browsing in [12–14].

Clustered visualisations attempt to reduce the number of images that are required to be displayed at any one time by grouping similar images together. This similarity can be defined in various ways. Content-based clustering uses extracted feature vectors in order to group perceptually similar images together. Systems that apply content-based clustering include [15–19]. If image meta-data such as keywords are available, they can also be employed for clustering, as performed in [20, 21]. Time-based clustering uses time stamp information associated with images in order to group images within a collection, and is used in the systems described in [22, 23] where the latter also allows clustering based on a combination of time and content concepts. A user can usually navigate through clustered visualisations, which are often arranged hierarchically [7, 18, 23–25], by selecting a representative image of a cluster in order to bring up images of that particular group.

Graph-based visualisations utilise links between images to construct a graph where the nodes of the graph are the images and the edges link related images. Links can be established through a variety of means including visual similarity between images as in [26, 27], or shared keyword annotations as used in [28, 29]. Image database graphs can be displayed using mass spring models [28, 29], Pathfinder networks [26], or nearest neighbour graphs [27].

More details on visualising image collections can be found in [30, 31].

3   Browsing of Image Databases

Of course, visualisation of a dataset is only useful for obtaining an overview of the image collection. The true potential of image database navigation systems however is only unlocked through the actual interaction with the system by the user. For this, the user must have the ability to actively browse the dataset.

Horizontal browsing can be defined as navigation within a single plane of visualised images. This type of browsing is often useful when an image database has been visualised through a mapping or graph-based scheme, or for a visualisation of a single cluster of images. Several tools have been developed in order to support this browsing experience. If the entire visualised image collection cannot be displayed simultaneously on screen, a panning function is required in order to move around the visualisation [26, 32]. When presenting many images on a single 2D plane, the thumbnail representations of images have to be reduced to small rectangles which are difficult to distinguish. A zooming function as implemented in [5, 10, 17, 24, 33] is therefore often useful. Although similar to zooming, magnification usually occurs when a cursor is placed over an image. This maintains the overall structure of the visualisation by rendering only small thumbnails for each image in the database at first, with higher resolution images being loaded only when required. Magnification as a browsing tool is used in [14, 34–36]. Some browsing systems such as [3, 37] use scaling rather than zooming, to allow users to view a particular image in more detail.

In visualisation approaches that are based on a hierarchical structure, the contained images can also be navigated using vertical browsing methods. Clusters of images are typically visualised through use of representative images. These images are crucial for vertical browsing as these are typically the reason for which a vertical browsing step into the next level of the hierarchy is initiated. Systems that allow vertical browsing include [14, 17, 18, 35]. An example is shown in Figure 2.

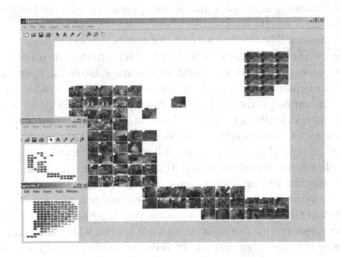

Fig. 2. Example of the system introduced in [7] which allows vertical browsing on an MDS grid

Operations such as panning and zooming can also be applied to graph-based visualisations [26]. The structure of the graph itself however also allows for different methods of browsing between images, in particular follwing edges to browse to connected similar images [27, 29].

As mentioned, time stamp information attached to images can be used to cluster and visualise image collections. Clearly, if a collection is visualised based on temporal concepts, browsing should also be possible in a time-based manner. Time-based browsing is supported in the systems introduced in [3, 22, 23, 38, 39].

More information on browsing image databases can be found in [31, 40].

4   Hue Sphere Image Browser

In the Hue Sphere Image Browser [7, 41–44], a spherical visualisation space is employed. As features for expressing similarity, very simple colour descriptors are employed, namely the median colour expressed in HSV colour space. This has the advantage that it greatly reduces the overall computational complexity, as on the one hand the features themselves can be calculated extremely fast, while on the other hand no computationally intensive dimensionality reduction technique is necessary. Rather, the location of each image is derived directly from the hue and value (brightness) co-ordinates to define longitude and latitude of the position of the image on the sphere.

The visualisation space is then divided using a regular lattice. This means that images cannot overlap nor occlude each other, which in turn has been shown to lead to an improved browsing experience [45]. Each image in the database will fall into exactly one cell on the lattice, and it is hence possible to make use of the advantages of clustering-based methods without actually having to employ a clustering technique, which again makes the approach decisively less demanding in terms of computational load.

Since most users will be familiar with the concept of the earth globe, this provides an immediately intuitive visualisation and browsing interface as users are already aware of how to locate and find something on its surface. Browsing operations at the user's disposal are panning, where the user can rotate the globe to focus on images of a different colour respectively tilt it to bring up darker or brighter images, and optical zooming which allows to narrow down on a specific set of images.

Large databases are handled by employing a hierarchical approach to visualising and browsing images. If multiple images fall into a specific cell, a representative image (that closest to the centre of the cell) will be shown in the browser, while the user has the possibility to open that image cluster and hence navigate to the next level of the browsing hierarchy. Here, the colour space is again divided into (now smaller) cells and the same principles as on the root layer are employed. To ensure more cells are filled, two spreading strategies are applied where the first one moves images from cells to neighbouring empty cells, while the second method spreads out images that are very similar to their surrounding neighbours.

Figure 3 shows a screenshot of the Hue Sphere application, while Figure 4 shows its port to a large multi-touch system [46].

Fig. 3. Hue sphere visualisation of the UCID [8] image database

Fig. 4. Multi-touch Hue Sphere Image Browser

5 Conclusions

Visualisation and browsing of large image databases is a challenging task. Nevertheless many interesting and useful approaches have been presented in recent years. In this paper, we have provided a brief overview of the underlying techniques that these systems employ to provide an intuitive image database navigation experience. A more comprehensive review can be found in [31].

References

1. Smeulders, A., Worring, M., Santini, S., Gupta, A., Jain, R.: Content-based image retrieval at the end of the early years. IEEE Transactions on Pattern Analysis and Machine Intelligence 22(12), 1349–1380 (2000)
2. Keller, I., Meiers, T., Ellerbrock, T., Sikora, T.: Image browsing with PCA-assisted user-interaction. In: IEEE Workshop on Content-Based Access of Image and Video Libraries, pp. 102–108 (2001)
3. Moghaddam, B., Tian, Q., Lesh, N., Shen, C., Huang, T.: Visualization and user-modeling for browsing personal photo libraries. Int. Journal of Computer Vision 56(1/2), 109–130 (2004)
4. Kruskal, J., Wish, M.: Multidimensional Scaling. Sage (1978)
5. Rubner, Y., Guibas, L.J., Tomasi, C.: The earth movers distance, multi-dimensional scaling, and color-based image retrieval. In: APRA Image Understanding Workshop, pp. 661–668 (1997)
6. Rodden, K., Basalaj, W., Sinclair, D., Wood, K.: Evaluating a visualisation of image similarity as a tool for image browsing. In: IEEE Symposium on Information Visualisation, pp. 36–43 (1999)
7. Schaefer, G., Ruszala, S.: Effective and efficient browsing of image databases. Int. Journal of Imaging Systems and Technology 18, 137–145 (2008)

8. Schaefer, G., Stich, M.: UCID - An Uncompressed Colour Image Database. In: Storage and Retrieval Methods and Applications for Multimedia 2004. Proceedings of SPIE, vol. 5307, pp. 472–480 (2004)

9. Faloutsos, C., Lin, K.: FastMap: A fast algorithm for indexing, datamining and visualization of traditional and multimedia datasets. In: SIGMOD International Conference on Management of Data, pp. 163–174 (1995)

10. Nakazato, M., Huang, T.: 3D MARS: Immersive virtual reality for content-based image retrieval. In:.IEEE International Conference on Multimedia and Expo. (2001)

11. Nguyen, G., Worring, M.: Interactive access to large image collections using similarity based visualization. Journal of Visual Languages and Computing 19, 203–224 (2008)

12. Laaksonen, J., Koskela, M., Oja, E.: PicSOM – Self-organizing image retrieval with MPEG-7 content descriptors. IEEE Transactions on Neural Networks 13(4), 841–853 (2002)

13. Deng, D., Zhang, J., Purvis, M.: Visualisation and comparison of image collections based on self-organised maps. In: Australasian Workshop on Data Mining and Web Intelligence, vol. 32, pp. 97–102 (2004)

14. Eidenberger, H.: A video browsing application based on visual MPEG-7 descriptors and self-organising maps. International Journal of Fuzzy Systems 6(3) (2004)

15. Abdel-Mottaleb, M., Krischnamachari, S., Mankovich, N.: Performance evaluation of clustering algorithms for scalable image retrieval. In: IEEE Computer Society Workshop on Empirical Evaluation of Computer Vision Algorithms (1998)

16. Krischnamachari, S., Abdel-Mottaleb, M.: Image browsing using hierarchical clustering. In: IEEE Symposium Computers and Communications, pp. 301–307 (1999)

17. Pecenovic, Z., Do, M., Vetterli, M., Pu, P.: Integrated browsing and searching of large image collections. In: International Conference on Advances in Visual Information Systems, pp. 279–289 (2000)

18. Borth, D., Schulze, C., Ulges, A., Breuel, T.: Navidgator - similarity based browsing for image and video databases. In: 31st Annual German Conference on Advances in Artificial Intelligence, pp. 22–29 (2008)

19. Hilliges, O., Kunath, P., Pryakhin, A., Butz, A., Kriegel, H.: Browsing and sorting digital pictures using automatic image classification and quality analysis. In: International Conference on Human-Computer Interaction, pp. 882–891 (2007)

20. Nakazato, M., Manola, L., Huang, T.: ImageGrouper: A group-oriented user interface for content-based image retrieval and digital image arrangement. Journal of Visual Language and Computing 14(4), 363–386 (2003)

21. Urban, J., Jose, J.: EGO: A personalised multimedia management and retrieval tool. International Journal of Intelligent Systems 21(7), 725–745 (2006)

22. Graham, A., Garcia-Molina, H., Paepcke, A., Winograd, T.: Time as essence for photo browsing through personal digital libraries. In: 2nd ACM/IEEE-CS Joint Conference on Digital Libraries, pp. 326–335. ACM (2002)

23. Platt, J., Czerwinski, M., Field, B.: PhotoTOC: automatic clustering for browsing personal photographs. Technical report, Microsoft Research (2002)

24. Chen, Y., Butz, A.: Photosim: Tightly integrating image analysis into a photo browsing UI. In: International Symposium on Smart Graphics (2008)

25. Gomi, A., Miyazaki, R., Itoh, T., Li, J.: CAT: A hierarchical image browser using a rectangle packing technique. In: 12th International Conference on Information Visualization, pp. 82–87 (2008)

26. Chen, C., Gagaudakis, G., Rosin, P.: Similarity-based image browsing. In: International Conference on Intelligent Information Processing, pp. 206–213 (2000)

27. Heesch, D., Rüger, S.: NN^k Networks for Content-Based Image Retrieval. In: McDonald, S., Tait, J.I. (eds.) ECIR 2004. LNCS, vol. 2997, pp. 253–266. Springer, Heidelberg (2004)

28. Dontcheva, M., Agrawala, M., Cohen, M.: Metadata visualization for image browsing. In: 18th Annual ACM Symposium on User Interface Software and Technology (2005)

29. Worring, M., de Rooij, O., van Rijn, T.: Browsing visual collections using graphs. In: International Workshop on Multimedia Information Retrieval, pp. 307–312 (2007)

30. Plant, W., Schaefer, G.: Visualising image databases. In: IEEE Int. Workshop on Multimedia Signal Processing, pp. 1–6 (2009)

31. Plant, W., Schaefer, G.: Visualisation and Browsing of Image Databases. In: Multimedia Analysis, Processing and Communications. SCI, vol. 346, pp. 3–57. Springer, Heidelberg (2011)

32. Tian, G., Taylor, D.: Colour image retrieval using virtual reality. In: Proceedings of the IEEE International Conference on Information Visualization, pp. 221–225 (2000)

33. van Liere, R., de Leeuw, W.: Exploration of large image collections using virtual reality devices. In: Workshop on New Paradigms in Information Visualization and Manipulation, Held in Conjunction with the Eighth ACM International Conference on Information and Knowledge Management, pp. 83–86. ACM (1999)

34. Rodden, K., Basalaj, W., Sinclair, D., Wood, K.: Does organisation by similarity assist image browsing? In: SIGCHI Conference on Human Factors in Computing Systems, pp. 190–197. ACM (2001)

35. Bederson, B.: Quantum treemaps and bubblemaps for a zoomable image browser. In: Proceedings of the 14th Annual ACM Symposium on User Interface Software and Technology, pp. 71–80 (2001)

36. Liu, H., Xie, X., Tang, X., Li, Z.W., Ma, W.Y.: Effective browsing of web image search results. In: 6th ACM SIGMM International Workshop on Multimedia Information Retrieval, pp. 84–90 (2004)

37. Porta, M.: New visualization modes for effective image presentation. International Journal of Image and Graphics 9(1), 27–49 (2009)

38. Platt, J.: AutoAlbum: Clustering digital photographs using probalistic model mergining. In: IEEE Workshop on Content-Based Access of Image and Video Libraries, pp. 96–100. IEEE (2000)

39. Hilliges, O., Baur, D., Butz, A.: Photohelix: Browsing, sorting and sharing digital photo collections. In: 2nd IEEE Tabletop Workshop on Horizontal Interactive Human-Computer Systems, pp. 87–94 (2007)

40. Plant, W., Schaefer, G.: Navigation and browsing of image databases. In: Int. Conference on Soft Computing and Pattern Recognition, pp. 750–755 (2009)

41. Schaefer, G., Ruszala, S.: Image Database Navigation: A Globe-Al Approach. In: Bebis, G., Boyle, R., Koracin, D., Parvin, B. (eds.) ISVC 2005. LNCS, vol. 3804, pp. 279–286. Springer, Heidelberg (2005)

42. Schaefer, G., Ruszala, S.: Hierarchical Image Database Navigation on a Hue Sphere. In: Bebis, G., Boyle, R., Parvin, B., Koracin, D., Remagnino, P., Nefian, A., Meenakshisundaram, G., Pascucci, V., Zara, J., Molineros, J., Theisel, H., Malzbender, T. (eds.) ISVC 2006. LNCS, vol. 4292, pp. 814–823. Springer, Heidelberg (2006)

43. Schaefer, G.: A next generation browsing environment for large image repositories. Multimedia Tools and Applications 47(1), 105–120 (2010)

44. Schaefer, G., Stuttard, M.: An on-line tool for browsing large image repositories. In: Int. Conference on Information Retrieval and Knowledge Management, pp. 102–106 (2010)
45. Rodden, K., Basalaj, W., Sinclair, D., Wood, K.: Evaluating a visualisation of image similarity as a tool for image browsing. In: IEEE Symposium on Information Visualization, pp. 36–43 (1999)
46. Schaefer, G., Fox, M., Plant, W., Stuttard, M.: Truly interactive approaches to browsing image databases. In: 7th Int. Conference on Signal-Image Technology and Internet-based Systems (2011)

User Study in Non-static HDR Scenes Acquisition

Anna Tomaszewska

West Pomeranian University of Technology, Szczecin,
Faculty of Computer Science and Information Technology,
Zolnierska 49, 71-210, Szczecin, Poland
atomaszewska@wi.zut.edu.pl

Abstract. We present a fast, robust and fully automatic method for high dynamic range (HDR) images acquisition for non-static scenes. To obtain high correctness of the approach, perceptual experiments were conducted. HDR images became popular for realistic scene acquisition, as they register much more information than standard images. The most common approach for their acquisition is a composition of photographs taken with a conventional camera. However, the approach suffers from some limitations caused by even the smallest camera movements as well as by objects in motion in the scene. The last one causes ghost artifacts visible in a final image. The key components of our technique include probability maps calculated on the basis of sequences of hand-held photographs and perceptual experiments. We obtained validation of our results by HDR VDP technique.

1 Introduction

Image composition from input image sequences is a well-known approach. However, overlapping of parts of input images where ghost artifacts may occur is a common problem in the technique. Such an approach is the most frequently used in HDR images acquisition [1]. It is a good alternative to HDR cameras that are still very expensive and unavailable for average users. The technique uses differently exposed photographs to recover the response function of a camera [3]. The main disadvantage of those techniques is a necessity of using a tripod. The second problem is that when the objects in the photographed scenes are in motion, so-called ghost artifacts are caused.

In the paper we focus on HDR image for dynamic scene creation based on a simple hand-held sequence (Figure 1) and we pay particular attention to the correctness of the acquired image. The main problem is proper identification of the areas affected by ghosts during ghosts maps definition. The maps are computed on the basis of input LDR (Low Dynamic Range) images. We solve the problem by using subjective metrics for the quality evaluation of the composed HDR images through perceptual experiments. To provide a convincing evidence that a new method or a set of parameters used in the model is better than the state-of-the-art, image processing projects are often accompanied by user studies,

L. Bolc et al. (Eds.): ICCVG 2012, LNCS 7594, pp. 245–252, 2012.

Fig. 1. Problem: LDR sequence (top row), HDRI: conventional approach (bottom left), our approach (bottom right)

in which a group of observers rank or rate the results of several algorithms. The goal of these experimental procedures is to find a scalar-valued quality correlates that would express the level of overall quality. In our project the interpretation of such a quality in the context of the ghost maps calculation is discussed. To recognize the artifacts that influence the quality of acquired HDR image, the areas of user interest are recorded by eye tracker, which traces the path of the subject's eyes on the screen. Our technique is robust and fast due to GPU-based implementation. The approach validation is performed by HDR VDP algorithm.

The paper is organized as follows. In section 2, previous works are discussed. In section 3, the application of our HDR acquisition technique is presented. Section 4 shows and discusses results achieved. The last section presents conclusions and suggestions for possible future work.

2   Previous Work

There is a growing demand for HDR images of both static and dynamic scenes. As hardware solutions of HDR images acquisition are not easily available, software solutions are needed. A few approaches have been developed in order to remove ghosts artifacts during HDRI acquisition. The first technique is based on non-static objects tracking by matching their key points in a sequence of images [4]. The method does not work with occluded objects or patterns for which it is impossible to find correct matching. Another approach replaces the whole ghost artifact regions with reference ones. The regions can be selected manually [5][8] or detected automatically [6][7]. Unfortunately, the technique works correctly only when the whole dynamic range of a region is registered in a single image exposure. In [13], they proposed a histogram based on ghost removal method, where object motion and background change between two exposures are detected using multi-level thresholding of the intensity histogram. A different solution was presented in [9] where iterative propagation of ghost probability was used. The method requires a large number of images in LDR (Low Dynamic Range) sequence and still background for moving objects. Moreover, it is time consuming and must be computed in many iterations.

While HDR images reflect realistic perception of the scene, and ghosts appearing are visible artifacts, the image acquisition based on user study seems a natural way of receiving high quality and perceptually proper solution. When developing a new imaging or computer graphics algorithm, there is often a need to specify the approach parameters which results in optimal solution. The adjusting of the parameters in trial and error process might be prone to errors and cover only selected amount of objects for which adjusting is suitable. Conducting the perceptual experiments is an effective method, for tuning the parameters in an optimal way. User studies are known as subjective image quality assessment experiments. The subjective image quality assessment methods originate from a wider group of psychometric scaling methods, which were developed to measure psychological attributes [18]. Image quality is an attribute that describes preference for a particular image processing algorithm. Psychometric methods are not new in computer graphics. Recent SIGGRAPH courses, such as [17,20,21,22], demonstrate an increasing interest in them. The interest in image and video quality assessment has been predominantly focused on video compression and transmission applications, which resulted in several recommendations for the design of quality assessment experiments [15,16].

In the paper we propose a pixel-based approach for ghost removing. The key component are the ghost maps calculated using probability of background pixel belonging. The ghost maps are tuned in an experimental way which is based on forced choice metrics.

3   Ghost Removal Algorithm

Generating HDR images of arbitrary static or non-static scene requires introducing a ghost removal component. The approach is modification of our previous algorithm [19]. In order to remove ghosts, a ghost map is generated for each input LDR image. This map shows how much input image pixel color influences result image pixel color. The module is composed of three states: initial map generation, normalization and final smoothing. As input to the ghost maps generation, we provide normalized image sequences for which maps are calculated. In the first stage, corresponding pixel values for every color channel from LDR sequence are compared. The comparison estimates pixel belonging probability either to a still background or to a moving object (ghost). The initial ghost map for each LDR image is computed on a basis of Equation (1).

$$G_i(x,y) = \sum_{j=1, j \neq i}^{k} DCF(P_i, P_j), \tag{1}$$

where: G_i means a ghost map of i-th image, DCF - deghosting comparison function, P_i, P_j - i-th and j-th normalized LDR images respectively , k - number of images.

The deghosting comparison function DCF is based on sigmoid function (Equation (2)). However, the function's shape can influence the results' quality significantly. Therefore to provide correct and stable function to determine acceptable and unacceptable limits in color difference, the subjective experiments should be conducted (see Sect. 4).

For ghost free images values P_i and P_j should be equal. In ghost regions, difference in color is very likely. Function max returns the ratio between brighter and darker value. For each rgb channel such value is transformed by sigmoid function and then summed up to estimate whether the two pixels match or not.

$$DCF(P_i, P_j) = \sum_{c=r,g,b} \frac{1}{1 + \exp\left(-\left(max\left(\frac{P_i c}{P_j c}, \frac{P_j c}{P_i c}\right) - a_1\right) \cdot a_2\right)} \tag{2}$$

where: $P_i c$, $P_j c$ - pixel components c of normalized images i and j respectively. a_1 and a_2 parameters are tuned through perceptual experiments and stabilized to $a_1 = 1.3$ and $a_2 = 20$ respectively (see Sect. 4).

Generation of the HDR image from a sequence of LDR pictures depicting dynamic scene, with calibration and ghost removal taken into account, is similar to traditional approach for static scenes [3]. The novelty is using ghost maps in the final equation, where pixel color is computed according to Equation (3) with weighted function which we tune experimentally (Eq. (4)) in a similar way as DCF in Section 4.

$$H(x,y) = \frac{\sum_{i=1}^{k} \frac{S_i(x,y)_c}{E_i} W_i(x,y) G_i^c(x,y)}{\sum_{i=1}^{k} W_i(x,y) G_i^c(x,y)}, \tag{3}$$

where: $S_i(x,y)$ is pixel of input LDR image i, E_i is exposure value of image i, $G_i^c(x,y)$ is grayscale pixel of ghost map i and $W_i(x,y)$ means pixel weight of image i according to Equation (4).

$$W_i(x,y) = \sum_{c=r,g,b} \min\left(\frac{1}{1 + \exp\left(a_1 - b_1 S_i(x,y)_c\right)}, \frac{1}{1 + \exp\left(a_2 S_i(x,y)_c - b_2\right)}\right) \tag{4}$$

4 Results

Experiment description: To specify the shape of the deghosting comparison function (DCF) (Eq. (2)) we perform the perceptual experiment. Ordering by force-choice pairwise comparison method was used in the experiment. The method is dominant in video quality assessment [15,16]. The observers are shown a pair of images (of the same scene) corresponding to different conditions and asked to indicate the image of higher quality (see Figure 2). Observers are always forced to choose one image, even if they see no difference between them (thus a forced-choice design). There is no time limit or minimum time to make the choice. The method is straightforward and thus expected to be more accurate than rating methods.

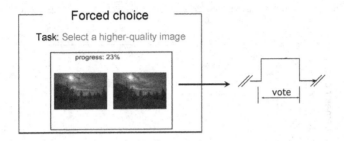

Fig. 2. Overview of the forced choice comparison method. The diagram shows the timeline of the approach and the corresponding screen.

The algorithms were assessed by computer graphics laymen who had normal or corrected to normal vision. The age varied between 20 and 24. There were 4 male and 6 female observers. To estimate the inter-observer variability, the subjects repeated each session three times, but none of the repetitions took place on the same day. The observers were free to adjust the viewing distance to their preference. The illumination in the room was subdued by blackout curtains to minimize the effect of display glare. The images were shown against 50%-gray background. The observers were asked to read a written instruction before every experiment and choose the most realistic image from all the displayed pairs. According to [15] recommendation, the experiment started with a training session in which observers familiarized themselves with the task and interface. After that session, they asked questions or started the main experiment. To ensure that the observers were engaged in the experiment, three random trials were shown at the beginning of the main session without recording the results. The images were displayed in a random order and with a different randomization for each session. Two consecutive trials showing the same scene were avoided if possible. All sessions were preceded by subject calibration.

The measure of the experiment is computed as the number of votes (the number of times one algorithm is preferred to another) assuming that all pairs of algorithms are compared. The result is averaged across the observers and models for every algorithm. The vote count is also equivalent to the position in the ranking. Figure 3 depicts the results. To stabilize results we compute the score by dividing the votes by standard deviation computed per observer.

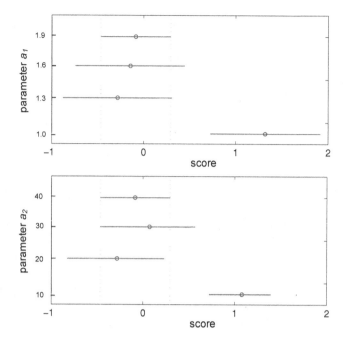

Fig. 3. ANOVA results. Comparison of the quality of the acquired HDR image in relation to the DCF parameters. Top: a_1 parameter and Bottom: a_2 parameter. To stabilize results the quality is denoted by scores, computed as number of votes given to the scene divided by standard deviation computed by observer.

Experiment analysis: The results gained on the basis of the ANOVA statistical test (see Fig. 3) showed an optimal dependence between the HDR image quality and the Deghosting Comparison Function. The observers reported the best HDR image quality for function parameters stabilized on values $a_1 = 1.3$ and $a_2 = 20$ respectively. To stabilize the results between the subjects, the tests were performed on the scores computed according to [14] based on the difference mean opinion score defined as the difference between reference and the test animation. The less difference the better quality.

During the experiment we tracked the region of interest that had influence on the result in quality evaluation. We found that subjects focused on the parts of images affected by ghost which is a proof for the experiment procedure to has been properly designed. The main artifact perceived by observers was the absence of ghosts or their more or less significant presence. The example of the tracked eye path for the test scene is depicted in Figure 4 (Left). To record the gaze points we adopted the experiment application to the eye-tracker which provides the information about the gaze position.

The only visible differences observed by the subjects were connected with the ghost parts. It denotes that the subjects paid attention especially to the parts affected by the ghosts. Therefore, if the scenes were assessed as high quality it means that the image was composed efficiently and is ghosts free.

Fig. 4. Left: An example gaze-point path (white dots) recorded by an eye-tracker during the experiment. Right: Results for HDR-VDP test for image sequences from Figure 1 with static scene.

To test the quality and performance of the HDRI acquisition application we prepared eight different example sequences of images depicting indoor as well as outdoor scenes with different position of objects. The example comparison for image sequences from Figure 1 with static scene via HDR-VDP algorithm [12] is depicted in Figure 4 (Right). The best results were achieved for exposure difference less or equal to two F-stop. It is compatible with exposure bracketing functionality in typical cameras which allows such an exposure change.

5   Conclusions and Future Work

In the paper, we present the ghost removal technique based on user-study and its GPU based implementation for HDRI images of static and dynamic scenes creation. Our approach was applied for HDR image acquisition and validated via HDR-VDP [12] algorithm. To provide the acquisition correctness perceptual experiments were conducted. We noticed that some ghost removal errors could occur for images with many high dynamic range ghost regions like reflections on a waving water.

Acknowledgements. This work was supported by the Polish Ministry of Science and Higher Education through the grant no. N N516 193537.

References

1. Reinhard, E., Ward, G., Pattanaik, S., Debevec, P.: High Dynamic Range Imaging: Acquisition, Display and Image-Based Lighting. Morgan Kaufmann Publishers (2005)
2. Akyüz, A.O., Fleming, R.W., Riecke, B.E., Reinhard, E., Bülthoff, H.: Do HDR displays support LDR content? A psychophysical evaluation. ACM Trans. Graph 26(3), 38 (2007)
3. Debevec, P.E., Malik, J.: Recovering High Dynamic Range Radiance Maps from Photographs. In: SIGGRAPH 1997, pp. 369–378 (1997)

4. Tomaszewska, A., Mantiuk, R.: Image Registration for Multi-exposure High Dynamic Range Image Acquisition. In: WSCG, Int. Conf. on Central Europe on Computer Graphics, Visualization and Computer Vision, pp. 49–56 (2007)
5. Rota, G.: Qtpfsgui - HDR Imaging Workflow Application (2007), http://qtpfsgui.sourceforge.net
6. Grosch, T.: Fast and Robust High Dynamic Range Image Generation with Camera and Object Movement. In: Vision, Modeling and Visualization, RWTH Aachen, pp. 277–284 (2006)
7. HDRsoft: Photomatix Pro. (2003), http://www.hdrsoft.com
8. Mediachance: Dynamic Photo HDR (2008), http://www.mediachance.com
9. Khan, E.A., Akyüz, A.O., Reinhard, E.: Ghost Removal in High Dynamic Range Images. In: IEEE International Conference on Image Procesing, pp. 2005–2008 (2006)
10. Ward Larson, G.: Fast, Robust Image Registration for Compositing High Dynamic Range Photographs from Handheld Exposures. Exponent - Failure Analysis Assoc. (2003)
11. Selesnick, I., Wagner, C.: Double-Density Wavelet Software. Polytechnic University's Brooklyn (2004)
12. Mantiuk, R., Daly, S., Myszkowski, K., Seidel, H.-P.: Predicting Visible Differences in High Dynamic Range Images - Model and its Calibration. In: Human Vision and Electronic Imaging X, IS&T/SPIE's 17th Annual Symposium on Electronic Imaging, vol. 5666, pp. 204–214 (2005)
13. Min, T.-H., Park, R.-H., Chang, S.-K.: Histogram based ghost removal in high dynamic range images. In: IEEE International Conference on Multimedia and Expo, ICME 2009, pp. 530–533 (2009)
14. Wang, Z., Bovik, A.C., Sheikh, H.R., Simoncelli, E.P.: Image quality assessment: from error visibility to structural similarity. IEEE Trans. on Image Processing 13(4), 600–612 (2004)
15. ITU-R.Rec.BT.500-11: Methodology for the Subjective Assessment of the Quality for Television Pictures (2002)
16. ITU-T.Rec.P.910: Subjective audiovisual quality assessment methods for multimedia applications (2008)
17. Ferwerda, J.A.: Psychophysics 101: how to run perception experiments in computer graphics. In: SIGGRAPH 2008: ACM SIGGRAPH 2008 Classes, pp. 1–60 (2008)
18. Torgerson, W.S.: Theory and methods of scaling. Wiley (1985)
19. Tomaszewska, A., Markowski, M.: Dynamic Scene Acquisition. In: Campilho, A., Kamel, M. (eds.) ICIAR 2010, Part II. LNCS, vol. 6112, pp. 345–354. Springer, Heidelberg (2010)
20. Tomaszewska, A.: Real-time algorithms optimization based on a gaze-point position. In: Bebis, G., et al. (eds.) ISVC 2012, Part II. LNCS, vol. 7432, pp. 746–755. Springer, Heidelberg (2012)
21. Tomaszewska, A.: Blind Noise Level Detection. In: Campilho, A., Kamel, M. (eds.) ICIAR 2012, Part I. LNCS, vol. 7324, pp. 107–114. Springer, Heidelberg (2012)
22. Tomaszewska, A., Stefanowski, K.: Real-Time Spherical Harmonics Based Subsurface Scattering. In: Campilho, A., Kamel, M. (eds.) ICIAR 2012, Part I. LNCS, vol. 7324, pp. 402–409. Springer, Heidelberg (2012)

A Curvature Tensor Distance
for Mesh Visual Quality Assessment

Fakhri Torkhani, Kai Wang, and Jean-Marc Chassery

Gipsa-lab, CNRS UMR 5216, Grenoble, France
firstname.lastname@gipsa-lab.grenoble-inp.fr

Abstract. This paper presents a new objective metric for assessing the visual difference between a reference or 'perfect' mesh and its distorted version. The proposed metric is based on the measurement of a distance between curvature tensors of the two triangle meshes under comparison. Unlike existing methods, our algorithm uses not only eigenvalues but also eigenvectors of the curvature tensor to derive a perceptually-oriented distance. Our metric also accounts for some important properties of the human visual system. Experimental results show good coherence between the proposed objective metric and subjective assessments.

1 Introduction

Three-dimensional (3D) meshes are now used in many multimedia applications such as digital entertainment, medical imaging and computer-aided design. It is common that 3D meshes undergo some lossy operations like simplification, compression and watermarking. Since the end users are often human beings, it is thus important to derive metrics that can faithfully evaluate the perceptual distortions introduced by such operations [1]. Classical metrics of simple geometric distances (e.g. root mean squared error and Hausdorff distance) [2,3] have been demonstrated not relevant to human visual perception and thus fail to predict the visual difference between a pair of reference and deformed meshes [1].

In order to design an accurate mesh visual distance metric, this paper attempts to reconcile several properties of the human visual system (HVS) with differential geometric quantities. Our contributions are summarized as follows:

- Introduction of an effective approach to the assessment of mesh visual quality (MVQ) based on a novel distance measure between mesh curvature tensors.
- Use of not only curvature values, but also surface principal directions (which have been proven perceptually important) to define the curvature tensor distance. This distance measure seems generic enough to be used in the future in other applications such as mesh segmentation and shape matching.
- Integration of some HVS features in the metric: we introduce a roughness-based weighting of local visual distance to simulate the *visual masking* effect, and a processing step similar to *Divisive Normalization Transform* (DNT) to mimic an important neural mechanism known as *adaptive gain control*.

L. Bolc et al. (Eds.): ICCVG 2012, LNCS 7594, pp. 253–263, 2012.

The proposed metric has the potential to be used, for instance, to benchmark a variety of mesh processing algorithms, or to guide the design of new perceptually-oriented algorithms. The rest of this paper is organized as follows: The relevant research is briefly reviewed in Section 2; Section 3 details the pipeline of the proposed MVQ metric; Section 4 presents some experimental results, including the comparison with state-of-the-art metrics; Finally, we conclude in Section 5.

2   Related Work and Motivation

Mesh Visual Quality Assessment. The first perceptually-oriented MVQ metric was introduced by Karni and Gotsman [4] for the evaluation of their mesh compression algorithm. The authors derived a metric by combining errors in both vertex positions and mesh Laplacian coordinates. Corsini et al. [5] developed two perceptual metrics, named respectively $3DWPM_1$ and $3DWPM_2$, for the visual quality assessment of watermarked meshes. The visual distortion is measured as the roughness difference between the original and watermarked meshes. Bian et al. [6] derived a perceptual measure where the visual difference between a pair of meshes is defined as the amount of strain energy required to induce the deformation between them. Lavoué et al. proposed a metric called mesh structural distortion measure ($MSDM$) [7], which can be considered as an extension of the well-known structure similarity index of 2D images [8] to the case of 3D triangle meshes. $MSDM$ relates the visual degradation to the alteration of local statistics (i.e. mean, variance and covariance) of mesh curvature amplitudes. An improved multiscale version $MSDM2$ [9] has been recently proposed, which also integrates a vertex matching preprocessing step to allow the comparison of two meshes with different vertex connectivities.

Motivation. $MSDM2$ exhibits good correlation with subjective scores [9], though by considering only the modification in mesh curvature amplitudes. We argue that the modification in surface *principal directions* (as defined by the *orthogonal* directions of minimum and maximum curvatures) is also important to MVQ assessment, because intuitively these directions imply structural information of the surface and thus should be visually important. Indeed, when drawing a 3D object, one strategy of caricaturists is to draw strokes on these lines of curvatures. In the digital world, surface principal directions have been successfully used for describing [10] and illustrating [11] complex 3D objects, and for guiding a remeshing algorithm [12]. Motivated by the above observation, we introduce a new MVQ metric, named $TPDM$ for Tensor-based Perceptual Distance Measure, that makes use of full information of the mesh curvature tensor, i.e. both curvature amplitudes and principal directions. In the following, we will briefly present a technique for estimating mesh curvature tensors and explain how to obtain curvature amplitudes and principal directions from the tensor.

Curvature Tensor Estimation. The estimation of mesh curvature tensor is a well-researched problem. So far, the most popular estimation technique is the one from Cohen-Steiner and Morvan [13]. Based on the solid foundation of normal cycle theory, they derived an elegant per-vertex curvature tensor estimation. Tensors computed on edges are averaged on a geodesic disk window B of user-defined size to obtain the curvature tensor $\mathcal{T}$ on each vertex v:

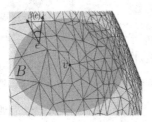

$$\mathcal{T}(v) = \frac{1}{|B|} \sum_{edges\ e} \beta(e)\ |e \cap B|\ \bar{e}\ \bar{e}^t, \tag{1}$$

where $|B|$ is the area of the geodesic disk, $\beta(e)$ is the signed angle between the normals of the two triangles incident to edge e, $|e \cap B|$ is the length of the part of e inside B, and $\bar{e}$ is a unit vector in the direction of e (cf. the inset on right). The minimum and maximum curvature amplitudes (κ_{min} and κ_{max}) are two eigenvalues of tensor $\mathcal{T}$, and the principal directions are two eigenvectors (γ_{min} and γ_{max}). The lines of minimum and maximum curvatures define respectively the directions along which surface normals vary the slowest (e.g. along creases) and the fastest (e.g. across creases), which represent structural features of the surface. In the next section, we will derive a perceptually-oriented distance measure between curvature tensors by incorporating the information from both their eigenvalues and eigenvectors, and use this distance to conduct MVQ assessment.

3 Curvature Tensor Distance Based MVQ Assessment

3.1 Overview of the Pipeline

Figure 1 illustrates the pipeline of our metric $TPDM$. First, in order to compare two meshes with potentially different connectivities, we perform a vertex matching step between the two meshes, based on the AABB tree data structure in the CGAL library [14]. The next step is to compute a curvature tensor distance on each local window centered at a vertex. Afterwards, this local tensor distance is weighted by two roughness-based factors, so as to account for the visual masking effect. Finally, we use a surface-weighted Minkowski pooling of the local distances to obtain a global $TPDM$ value.

3.2 Curvature Tensor Distance

After the vertex matching step, each vertex v in the reference mesh $\mathcal{M}_r$ has a corresponding vertex v' on the surface of the distorted mesh $\mathcal{M}_d$. The curvature tensors on the two vertices are denoted respectively by $\mathcal{T}$ and $\mathcal{T}'$.

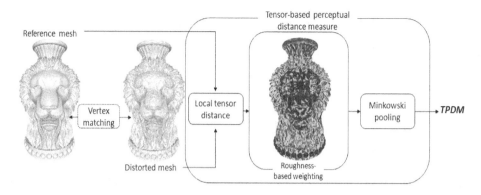

Fig. 1. Block diagram of the pipeline of $TPDM$ (Tensor-based Perceptual Distance Measure). In the roughness map, warmer colors represent larger values.

For the comparison between them, we first establish correspondence relationships between the principal directions and curvature amplitudes of the two tensors. More precisely, for γ_{min} of $\mathcal{T}$, we find the principal direction of $\mathcal{T}'$ that has the smallest *angular distance* to it (this direction is denoted by γ_1'), and relate γ_{min} to γ_1'. Accordingly, κ_{min} of $\mathcal{T}$ is related to the curvature amplitude associated to γ_1' (denoted by κ_1'). Note that κ_1' and γ_1' can be the maximum curvature and its direction of $\mathcal{T}'$. Similarly, the following correspondence relationships are established: $\kappa_{max} \rightarrow \kappa_2'$ and $\gamma_{max} \rightarrow \gamma_2'$. We find that the above correspondence based on the minimum angular distance criterion yields better results of MVQ assessment than the straightforward min→min/max→max correspondence. In particular, it enhances the stability of $TPDM$ under the situations where the principal directions are severely disturbed after strong deformations and where the values of κ_{min} and κ_{max} are very close to each other.

A local tensor distance (LTD) is computed for each pair of v and v' as

$$LTD = \theta_{min}\delta_{\kappa_{min}} + \theta_{max}\delta_{\kappa_{max}}, \qquad (2)$$

where θ_{min} is the angle between γ_{min} and γ_1' (similarly for θ_{max}), and $\delta_{\kappa_{min}}$ is a Michelson-like contrast of the curvature amplitudes κ_{min} and κ_1', i.e. $\delta_{\kappa_{min}} = \left|\frac{\kappa_{min}-\kappa_1'}{\kappa_{min}+\kappa_1'+\varepsilon}\right|$ with ε a stabilization constant fixed as 5% of the avarage mean curvature of $\mathcal{M}_r$ (similarly for $\delta_{K_{max}}$). Both the differences in curvature amplitudes and in principal directions are involved in the derivation of LTD.

3.3   Roughness-Based Weighting of Local Tensor Distance

For the development of an effective MVQ metric, we should take into account some HVS features, in particular the visual masking effect. In the context of MVQ assessment, this effect mainly means that a same distortion is less visible in rough regions of the mesh surface than in smooth regions. In order to account for the visual masking effect, our solution is to modulate the values of $LTD_{i,i=1,2,...,N}$ (evaluated at each vertex v_i of $\mathcal{M}_r$) by two roughness-based weights (the rougher the local surface is, the smaller the weights are). The local tensor-based perceptual distance measure $LTPDM_i$ is computed as:

$$LTPDM_i = RW_i^{(\gamma)}.RW_i^{(\kappa)}.LTD_i, \tag{3}$$

where $RW_i^{(\gamma)}, RW_i^{(\kappa)} \in [0.1, 1.0]$ are respectively the weights derived from principal directions and curvature amplitudes in 1-ring neighborhood of v_i. For $RW_i^{(\gamma)}$, we first project all the principal directions at the 1-ring neighbors on the tangent plane of v_i, and take the sum of the two angular standard deviations of the projected minimum and maximum curvature directions as the local roughness value. This value is then mapped to $[0.1, 1.0]$ to obtain $RW_i^{(\gamma)}$. Similarly, to get $RW_i^{(\kappa)}$, we compute the ratio of the Laplacian of mean curvature in the 1-ring neighborhood and the mean curvature on v_i as the local roughness and map it to $[0.1, 1.0]$. It is worth mentioning that the derivation of the roughness weight $RW_i^{(\kappa)}$ includes a divisive normalization similar to that in the neural mechanism of HVS that partially explains the visual masking effect [15]. Also note that the vertices in isotropic areas, i.e. where κ_{min} and κ_{max} are close to each other, are treated differently. For these vertices, we set $RW_i^{(\gamma)}$ close to 1, and therefore the final weight is dominated by the value of $RW_i^{(\kappa)}$. The reason is that in isotropic areas, principal directions are not well-defined and their estimation is not reliable. A roughness map that combines both weights is shown in Fig. 1.

3.4   Global Perceptual Distance

The global tensor-based perceptual distance measure $TPDM$ from $\mathcal{M}_r$ to $\mathcal{M}_d$ is computed as a *weighted Minkowski sum* of the local distances $LTPDM_i$:

$$TPDM = \left(\sum_{i=1}^{N} w_i |LTPDM_i|^p\right)^{\frac{1}{p}}, \tag{4}$$

where $w_i = s_i / \sum_{i=1}^{N} s_i$ with s_i one third of the total area of all the incident faces of v_i, and we set $p = 2.5$. The surface-based weighting can, to some extent, enhance the stability of the metric to the variation of vertex sampling density over the mesh surface. Compared to the standard mean-squared error in which $p = 2.0$, the choice of $p = 2.5$ can increase the importance of the local distances of high amplitude. This is perceptually relevant since the part of mesh with high-amplitude distortion has experimentally more impact on the result of subjective assessment. Finally, a cumulative Gaussian psychometric function [16] is applied to bring the $TPDM$ value to the $[0, 1]$ interval. More details on the psychometric function will be provided in the next section.

4   Experimental Results

In order to verify its efficacy, the proposed metric $TPDM$ has been extensively tested and compared with existing metrics on three subject-rated databases:

- The LIRIS/EPFL general-purpose database[1] [7]: It contains 4 reference meshes and in total 84 deformed models. The distortion types include noise addition and smoothing, applied either locally or globally on the reference mesh. Subjective evaluations were made by 12 observers.
- The LIRIS masking database[2] [17]: It contains 4 reference meshes and in total 24 deformed models. The local noise addition distortion included in this database was designed specifically for testing the capability of MVQ metrics in capturing the visual masking effect. 11 observers participated in the subjective tests.
- The IEETA simplification database[3] [18]: It contains 5 reference meshes and in total 30 simplified models. 65 observers participated in this study.

$TPDM$ has been compared with five state-of-the-art metrics, i.e. the Hausdorff distance HD [2,3], the root mean squared error RMS [2,3], the two roughness-based metrics $3DWPM_1$ and $3DWPM_2$ from Corsini et al. [5], and $MSDM2$ [9]. The coherence between the distance values produced by the objective metrics and the subjective mean opinion scores (MOS) is measured by using two different kinds of correlation: the Pearson linear correlation coefficient ($PLCC$) that measures the prediction accuracy of the objective metrics, and the Spearman rank-order correlation coefficient ($SROCC$) that measures the prediction monotonicity. Before computing $PLCC$, it is recommended to conduct a psychometric fitting between the objective measures and the MOS values, in order to partially remove the non-linearity between them. In our tests, we apply a cumulative Gaussian psychometric function [16]:

$$g(a, b, R) = \frac{1}{\sqrt{2\pi}} \int_{a+bR}^{\infty} e^{-\left(t^2/2\right)} dt, \tag{5}$$

where R is the raw $TPDM$ value, and the two parameters a and b are obtained through non-linear fitting using the raw $TPDM$ and the corresponding MOS values of the group of Dinosaur models in the general-purpose database. As shown in Fig. 2.(b) and (c), the same psychometric function has been used for the models in the masking and simplification databases.

Tables 1, 2 and 3 present the results on the general-purpose, masking and simplification databases, respectively. In general, $TPDM$ exhibits quite good performance on all the three databases, reflected by its high correlation with subjective scores on most individual models and on the whole repositories. In particular, $TPDM$ has always the highest overall $PLCC$ value (the second last column in the tables), thus the highest prediction accuracy on all the three databases. On the general-purpose database (cf. Table 1), $TPDM$ has the highest $PLCC$ and $SROCC$ for almost every individual model as well as for the whole repository, and there is much improvement in the overall $PLCC$ compared to $MSDM2$, the best metric proposed so far. On the masking database

---

[1] http://liris.cnrs.fr/guillaume.lavoue/data/datasets.html
[2] http://liris.cnrs.fr/guillaume.lavoue/data/datasets.html
[3] http://www.ieeta.pt/~sss/index.php/perceivedquality/repository

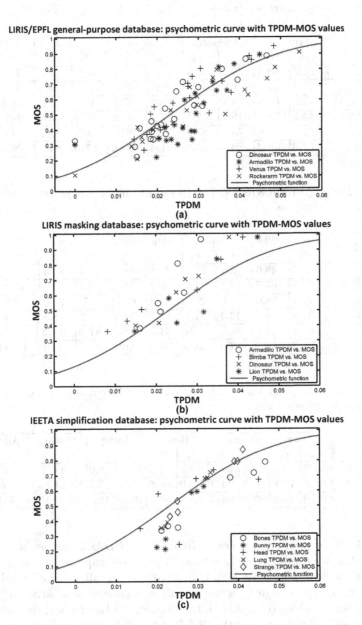

Fig. 2. Psychometric function curve plotted with $TPDM$-MOS values of all the reference/distorted models in: (a) the LIRIS/EPFL general-purpose database; (b) the LIRIS masking database; and (c) the IEETA simplification database

Table 1. $PLCC$ (r_p) and $SROCC$ (r_s) (%) of the different objective metrics on the LIRIS/EPFL general-purpose database

Metric	Armadillo		Dinosaur		Rockerarm		Venus		All models	
	r_p	r_s	r_p	r_s	r_p	r_s	r_p	r_s	r_p	r_s
HD [2,3]	30.2	69.5	22.6	30.9	5.5	18.1	0.8	1.6	1.3	13.8
RMS [2,3]	32.2	62.7	0.0	0.3	3.0	7.3	77.3	**90.1**	7.9	26.8
$3DWPM_1$ [5]	35.7	65.8	35.7	62.7	53.2	87.5	46.6	71.6	38.3	69.3
$3DWPM_2$ [5]	43.1	74.1	19.9	52.4	29.9	37.8	16.4	34.8	24.6	49.0
$MSDM2$ [9]	72.8	81.6	73.5	85.9	76.1	89.6	76.5	89.3	66.2	80.4
$TPDM$	**79.3**	**85.4**	**89.4**	**92.2**	**91.4**	90.6	**87.6**	89.9	**84.9**	**85.2**

Table 2. $PLCC$ (r_p) and $SROCC$ (r_s) (%) of the different objective metrics on the LIRIS masking database

Metric	Armadillo		Bimba		Dinosaur		Lion		All models	
	r_p	r_s	r_p	r_s	r_p	r_s	r_p	r_s	r_p	r_s
HD [2,3]	37.7	48.6	7.5	25.7	31.1	48.6	25.1	71.4	4.1	26.6
RMS [2,3]	44.6	65.7	21.8	71.4	50.3	71.4	23.8	71.4	17.0	48.8
$3DWPM_1$ [5]	41.8	58.0	8.4	20.0	45.3	66.7	9.7	20.0	10.2	29.4
$3DWPM_2$ [5]	37.9	48.6	14.4	37.1	50.1	71.4	22.0	38.3	18.2	37.4
$MSDM2$ [9]	65.8	**88.6**	93.7	**100**	91.5	**100**	**87.5**	**94.3**	76.2	**89.6**
$TPDM$	**91.3**	**88.6**	**97.1**	**100**	**97.1**	**100**	86.7	82.9	**87.1**	87.3

Table 3. $PLCC$ (r_p) and $SROCC$ (r_s) (%) of the different objective metrics on the IEETA simplification database

Metric	Bones		Bunny		Head		Lung		Strange		All models	
	r_p	r_s	r_p	r_s	r_p	r_s	r_p	r_s	r_p	r_s	r_p	r_s
HD [2,3]	84.8	**94.3**	14.3	39.5	53.0	**88.6**	64.9	88.6	27.4	37.1	25.5	49.4
$MSDM2$ [9]	96.7	77.1	96.3	**94.3**	**79.0**	**88.6**	85.3	65.7	98.1	**100**	79.6	**86.7**
$TPDM$	**98.9**	**94.3**	**97.9**	**94.3**	63.1	65.7	**99.9**	**100**	**98.8**	94.3	**86.4**	**86.7**

(cf. Table 2), although the overall $SROCC$ of $TPDM$ is not as high as that of $MSDM2$, we can still conclude that $TPDM$ well captures the visual masking effect, as reflected by the high individual and overall correlation values (all > 80%). $TPDM$ has slightly better overall performance than $MSDM2$ on the simplification database (cf. Table 3). However for the Head model the correlation is rather low, and the reason is that $TPDM$ has difficulties in distinguishing the quality of the simplified Heads generated by different mesh simplification algorithms but with the same vertex reduction ratio.

Figure 3 illustrates the distance maps produced by $TPDM$ and RMS for a noised Bimba model. The map of $TPDM$ is quite consistent with human perception (i.e. the perceived distortion is higher in smooth regions than in

Fig. 3. From left to right: the original Bimba model, the deformed model after uniform noise addition, the distance map of $TPDM$, and the distance map of RMS. In the maps, warmer colors represent higher values.

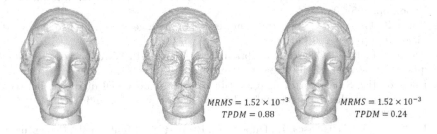

$MRMS = 1.52 \times 10^{-3}$
$TPDM = 0.88$

$MRMS = 1.52 \times 10^{-3}$
$TPDM = 0.24$

Fig. 4. From left to right: the original Venus model, the model watermarked by the method in [19], and the model watermarked by the method in [20].

rough regions), while the map of RMS is purely geometric. Figure 4 shows an application of our metric in the visual quality assessment of watermarked meshes. The two watermarked models have exactly the same geometric maximum root mean squared error ($MRMS$) [3] compared to the original mesh, but their visual quality is quite different. $TPDM$ provides correct MVQ evaluation results that are consistent with a subjective assessment.

5   Conclusions and Future Work

A new curvature-tensor-based approach to the objective evaluation of mesh visual quality has been proposed. We show that it is beneficial to use the full information of the curvature tensor for MVQ assessment. The local curvature distance and the local roughness measures that we propose may be found useful in other mesh applications. Experimental results show that our metric $TPDM$ has high correlation with subjective scores and that it slightly outperforms existing metrics. Future work mainly consists of the integration of more HVS features in the metric (e.g. the contrast sensitivity function), the improvement of the roughness measure which at present appears a little noisy, and the development of a curvature-tensor-based visual quality metric for dynamic meshes.

Acknowledgments. We would like to thank the anonymous reviewers for their helpful and constructive comments. This work has been in part supported by the MOOV3D project of the Minalogic competitive cluster.

References

1. Corsini, M., Larabi, M.C., Lavoué, G., Petřík, O., Váša, L., Wang, K.: Perceptual metrics for static and dynamic triangle meshes. In: Proc. of Eurographics State-of-the-Art Rep., pp. 135–157 (2012)
2. Cignoni, P., Rocchini, C., Scopigno, R.: Metro: measuring error on simplified surfaces. Comput. Graphics Forum 17(2), 167–174 (1998)
3. Aspert, N., Santa-Cruz, D., Ebrahimi, T.: MESH: measuring errors between surfaces using the Hausdorff distance. In: Proc. of IEEE Int. Conf. on Multimedia & Expo., pp. 705–708 (2002)
4. Karni, Z., Gotsman, C.: Spectral compression of mesh geometry. In: Proc. of ACM Siggraph, pp. 279–286 (2000)
5. Corsini, M., Drelie Gelasca, E., Ebrahimi, T., Barni, M.: Watermarked 3-D mesh quality assessment. IEEE Trans. on Multimedia 9(2), 247–256 (2007)
6. Bian, Z., Hu, S.M., Martin, R.R.: Evaluation for small visual difference between conforming meshes on strain field. Journal of Comput. Sci. and Technol. 24(1), 65–75 (2009)
7. Lavoué, G., Drelie Gelasca, E., Dupont, F., Baskurt, A., Ebrahimi, T.: Perceptually driven 3D distance metrics with application to watermarking. In: Proc. of SPIE Electronic Imaging, pp. 63120L.1–63120L.12 (2006)
8. Wang, Z., Bovik, A.C., Sheikh, H.R., Simoncelli, E.P.: Image quality assessment: From error visibility to structural similarity. IEEE Trans. on Image Process 13(4), 600–612 (2004)
9. Lavoué, G.: A multiscale metric for 3D mesh visual quality assessment. Comput. Graphics Forum 30(5), 1427–1437 (2011)
10. Brady, M., Ponce, J., Yuille, A.L., Asada, H.: Describing surfaces. Comput. Vision, Graphics, and Image Process 32(1), 1–28 (1985)
11. Hertzmann, A., Zorin, D.: Illustrating smooth surfaces. In: Proc. of ACM Siggraph, pp. 517–526 (2000)
12. Alliez, P., Cohen-Steiner, D., Devillers, O., Lévy, B., Desbrun, M.: Anisotropic polygonal remeshing. ACM Trans. on Graphics 22(3), 485–493 (2003)
13. Cohen-Steiner, D., Morvan, J.M.: Restricted delaunay triangulations and normal cycle. In: Symp. on Computational Geometry, pp. 312–321 (2003)
14. Alliez, P., Tayeb, S., Wormser, C.: 3D fast intersection and distance computation (AABB tree). In: CGAL User and Reference Manual (2012)
15. Li, Q., Wang, Z.: Reduced-reference image quality assessment using divisive normalization-based image representation. IEEE J. Sel. Topics Signal Process. 3(2), 202–211 (2009)
16. Engeldrum, P.G.: Psychometric Scaling: A Toolkit for Imaging Systems Development. Imcotek Press (2000)
17. Lavoué, G.: A local roughness measure for 3D meshes and its application to visual masking. ACM Trans. on Appl. Perception 5(4), 21:1–21:23 (2009)
18. Silva, S., Santos, B.S., Ferreira, C., Madeira, J.: A perceptual data repository for polygonal meshes. In: Proc. of Int. Conf. In: Visualization, pp. 207–212 (2009)

19. Cho, J.W., Prost, R., Jung, H.Y.: An oblivious watermarking for 3-D polygonal meshes using distribution of vertex norms. IEEE Trans. on Signal Process. 55(1), 142–155 (2007)
20. Wang, K., Lavoué, G., Denis, F., Baskurt, A.: Robust and blind mesh watermarking based on volume moments. Comput. & Graphics 35(1), 1–19 (2011)

A Framework for Combined Recognition of Actions and Objects

Ilktan Ar[1,2] and Yusuf Sinan Akgul[2]

[1] Kadir Has University, Cibali, Istanbul 34083, Turkey
ilktana@khas.edu.tr
[2] Gebze Institute of Technology, Gebze, Kocaeli 41400, Turkey
GIT Vision Lab.
akgul@bilmuh.gyte.edu.tr
http://vision.gyte.edu.tr

Abstract. This paper proposes a novel approach to recognize actions and objects within the context of each other. Assuming that the different actions involve different objects in image sequences and there is one-to-one relation between object and action type, we present a Bayesian network based framework which combines motion patterns and object usage information to recognize actions/objects. More specifically, our approach recognizes high-level actions and the related objects without any body-part segmentation, hand tracking, and temporal segmentation methods. Additionally, we present a novel motion representation, based on 3D Haar-like features, which can be formed by depth, color, or both images. Our approach is also appropriate for object and action recognition where the involved object is partially or fully occluded. Finally, experiments show that our approach improves the accuracy of both action and object recognition significantly.

Keywords: Action and object recognition, Bayesian Network, motion pattern.

1 Introduction

Object recognition is still a challenging problem in Computer Vision. There has been considerable research on object detection and recognition [1,2]. Although most of the object recognition methods are appearance-based (shape, texture, etc.) some of them use contextual information such as text, scene, and human interactions. Carbonetto et al. [3] developed a caption/text guided object detection system which attaches meaningful labels to specific regions of an image and learns spatial relationships between objects. Torralba [4] introduced a framework for object recognition by using the correlation between scenes and the objects.

The idea of using the relationship between actions and objects has been exploited before. Filipovych and Ribeiro [5] recognized primitive actor-object

L. Bolc et al. (Eds.): ICCVG 2012, LNCS 7594, pp. 264–271, 2012.

interactions with the concept of actor-object states. But modeling high-level actions such as taking a picture with a digital camera is more complex than a primitive action such as grasping a spoon. Wu et al. [6] developed a dynamic Bayesian network model which combines RFID and video data to jointly infer the most likely activity and object labels. Kjellstrm et al. [7] investigated object categorization according to its function. They simultaneously segment and classify hand actions with the detection and classification of the involved objects. But their method is dependent on tracking and reconstructing the hand pose.

Human action recognition is one of the most challenging topics in computer vision. The aim of human action recognition frameworks is to recognize human actions from offline/live videos. This task is very difficult because it deals with illumination and view point variations, perspective effects, scene variations, occlusions, individual variations of people due to appearance, clothing, motion, etc [8,9].

In this paper, we examine the role of action understanding in object classification and vice-versa. With the assumption of one-to-one relation between object and action type exists, we propose a novel approach that recognizes actions and objects within the context of each other. Towards this approach, a Bayesian network based framework which combines motion patterns and object usage information is developed. Moreover, the motion patterns which describe motion information in an image sequence are formed by a novel motion representation. This representation is based on 3D Haar-like features and can be created using depth, color, or both image sequences. Finally, using the proposed approach, the accuracy of both action and object recognition are improved.

The rest of this paper is organized as follows. Section 2 presents the dataset. Section 3 describes the proposed framework with related feature representations. Section 4 demonstrates experimental results. Finally, Section 5 concludes the paper.

Table 1. Actions with the related objects

Action	Object
Pour liquid in a cup	Pitcher
Drink	Cup
Use a brush	Brush
Use a remote control	Remote control
Use a roller	Roller
Use a calculator	Calculator
Make a phone call	Phone
Wear headphones	Headphones
Play with a videogame	Gameboy
Take a picture	Camera
Use a pen	Pen

2   Dataset

The public dataset recorded by Gall et al. [10] is modified and used for evaluation. This dataset consists of video sequences acted by 6 different actors. These actors perform 13 different actions. Actions are: 'Pour liquid in a cup', 'Drink with the left hand', 'Drink with the right hand', 'Use a brush', 'Use a remote control', 'Use a roller', 'Use a puncher', 'Use a calculator', 'Make a phone call', 'Wear headphones', 'Play with a videogame', 'Take a picture', and 'Use a pen'. Image sequences are stored as 640x480 RGB images and 144x88 256 gray-level depth images. The sample RGB images are displayed in Fig. 1b.

In this work, we focus on the actions which involve interaction with one object in each image of the image sequences. Therefore, we modify the original dataset in [10]. For example 'Use a puncher' action is discarded because this action involves a paper and a puncher interaction at the same time. 'Drink with the left hand' and 'Drink with the right hand' actions are merged as 'Drink'. The relationship between actions and objects are summarized in Table 1.

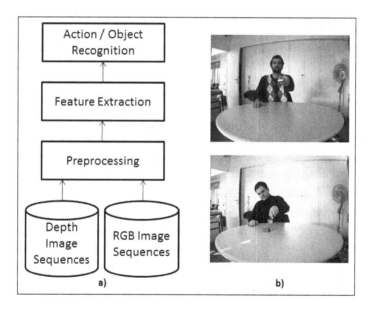

Fig. 1. a) The design of our framework, b) The sample RGB images taken from 'Use a remote control' and 'Use a roller' image sequences.

3   Our Framework

Our framework includes 3 main stages: Preprocessing, Feature extraction, and the Action/Object recognition as shown in Fig. 1a. In the preprocessing stage RGB images are converted to 256 gray-level images (named as G-RGB in this paper). Then a 3x3 median filter is applied to remove noise in G-RGB images.

In the feature extraction stage, object and motion information is obtained by forming the related representations. In the action/object recognition stage, a Bayesian network is built to recognize actions/objects by using object and motion representations which are obtained at feature extraction stage.

3.1 Feature Extraction

Feature extraction in image sequences defines representations of motion and object information. Motion information is built by motion patterns in image sequences. Depth, G-RGB, or both images can be used to extract motion information. Object information represents object availability in still images.

Representation of Motion Information. Motion information in image sequences is the main element of action recognition. To extract motion patterns we propose a novel approach by adopting 3D Haar-like features which are used to detect pedestrians in [11].

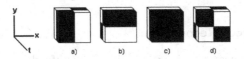

Fig. 2. Cubic filters which are used in the extraction of 3D Haar-Like features (8x8 and 4x4 pixel size in spatial domain, 4 and 8 frames in temporal domain).

In our approach, the motion information contained in the whole image sequence is represented by 16 different cubic filters as shown in Fig. 2. 3D Haar-like features are extracted by applying these cubic filters to depth and/or G-RGB image sequences with a convolution process. 3D Haar-like features are normalized to 0-255 interval for efficiency. Local motion information, LMI, between consecutive images is calculated by the histogram of 3D Haar-like features as

$$LMI_w(t, f) = Histogram[HF_w(x, y, t, f)], \qquad (1)$$

where HF describes 3D Haar-like features, x and y are 2D coordinates, t is the order of image, f is the filter id of our 16 different cubic filters, and w is the image sequence id (it can be either a G-RGB or a depth sequence). To obtain a global motion representation GMR for whole image sequence, variance (var) and mean (μ) are employed as

$$GMR_1(w, f) = \mu(LMI_w(t, f)), \qquad (2)$$

$$GMR_2(w, f) = var(LMI_w(t, f)). \qquad (3)$$

Finally, the motion information MI in a given image sequence w is represented with the concatenation ($||$) process as

$$MI(w) = GMR_1(w, f_1)||...||GMR_2(w, f_n), \qquad (4)$$

where n is the maximum filter id. Representation of motion information can be built for either a G-RGB or depth image sequence separately or combination of them by enlarging the concatenation process defined in (4).

Representation of Object Information. Object information in the image sequences reveals important cues about the type of the action. Although the depth image sequences can be used to detect and classify objects, we prefer using G-RGB image sequences to use state of the art methodologies effectively.

Images are selected at predefined uniform time-intervals (one image out of 20 images) in order to represent object information for a given image sequence. Then the object detection algorithm in [12], which uses bag of words models to detect and classify objects, is adopted to check the availability of the corresponding object in the selected images. The count of images which include the corresponding object are calculated and divided by the total number of selected images. The corresponding objects with related actions are given in Table 1. Note that these ratios, $OI(w, o)$ (where w is the sequence id, o is the object id), represent the object information in the image sequence.

3.2   Action/Object Recognition

In Action/Object recognition stage we aim to classify the action/object in the given image sequence by using the representations obtained at the feature extraction stage. For this classification problem, we need a classifier that assigns an action/object label $a \in A$ to the image sequence. There are two general approaches available to the classification problem as generative or discriminative. Examples of discriminative classifiers are Neural Networks, Additive Models, and Logical Regression. Examples of generative classifiers includes Hidden Markov Models, Fisher Discriminant Analysis, and Bayesian Networks [13]. We prefer to use a Bayesian network structure for this classification problem because of the robustness of Bayesian networks for representing of joint distributions and encoding conditional independence assumptions.

The Bayesian network uses the graphical model in Fig. 3. to represent conditional independence relationships between random variables: action/object type (A), object availability (O), motion information (M), and representation (R). Label assignment process $L(r)$ is defined as

$$L(r) = \underset{a \in A}{argmax} \sum_{M,O} P(A, M, O, R), \tag{5}$$

where r is the representation ($r \in R$) of the given image sequence and $P(A, M, O, R)$ is the joint probability distribution table. $P(A, M, O, R)$ is defined by using the conditional dependencies in the graphical model (Fig. 3.) as

$$P(A, M, O, R) \propto P(A)P(M|A)P(O|A)P(R|M, O), \tag{6}$$

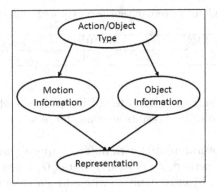

Fig. 3. The graphical model of our framework

where $P(A)$ is constant, and $P(O|A)$ term can be calculated easily by Table 1. For example, $P(O = cup|A = drink)$ is 1 because the drink is done only with cup according to Table 1. $P(R|M, O)$ term needs to be converted by using axioms as

$$P(R|M, O) = \frac{P(M, O|R)P(R)}{P(M, O)}. \tag{7}$$

$P(R)$ and $P(M, O)$ values in (7) are neglected because these are the same for a given image sequence. $P(M, O|R)$ is efficiently represented as

$$P(M, O|R) = P(M|R)P(O|R). \tag{8}$$

Finally, the values of $P(M|R)$ and $P(O|R)$ are needed to obtain label $L(r)$. $P(O|R)$ is equal to the $OI(w_r, o)$ obtained at the end of representation of object information process. $P(M|R)$ is related to MI. For this relation, linear kernel Support Vector Machines (SVMs) are trained by using MIs as inputs. These SVMs assign scores to each MI. The Gibbs distribution is used to translate an SVM score into prediction as

$$P(M|R) = \frac{1}{Z} exp(-Q_m(M, R)), \tag{9}$$

where the potential function $Q_m(M, R)$ carries information about the motion pattern m ($m \in M$) and Z is the normalizing constant (taken as 0.5). Note that the SVMs are used in one-to-all manner with binary fashion.

4   Experimental Results

Evaluation of the framework is conducted with various experiments on the modified [10] dataset. 60 different image sequences (6 for each action/object type)

Table 2. Action/Object recognition accuracy with different approaches

Table 2	[12]	[12] + Action(G-RGB)	[12] + Action(G-RGB+Depth)
Recog. Acc.	61.7%	71.7%	83.3%

are used. The proposed framework is tested in leave-one-actor-out procedure in each experiment. The obtained results are same for object recognition and action recognition.

Table 2 shows the overall results with different approaches. Using only [12] as an object recognition method, we labeled 37 out of 60 image sequences correctly in terms of action and object recognition with a 61.7% recognition accuracy. It is important to mention that the object recognition method suffers from occlusions. Then combination of object availability information with the motion information in the proposed framework improved the recognition accuracy to 71.7%. Note that only G-RGB image sequences are used as a source of motion information in this process. Finally, our framework recognized 50 out of 60 image sequences with an accuracy rate of 83.3% by using depth image sequences along with G-RGB image sequences for motion representation.

Table 3 shows the detailed action/object recognition results with and without using depth image sequences for motion representation. Without depth image sequences, our framework recognizes actions/objects within 3D environment: x-y space and time. The addition of depth image sequences increases this environment to 4D: x-y-z space and time. Recognition accuracy of actions which include hand movements in the z-axis such as using a brush on the table (moving brush towards and away from the camera) and using a remote control (holding and pointing remote control to the camera) improved significantly by addition of depth information. The general misclassified sequence in terms of action and object recognition is 'playing a videogame with gameboy'. In this sequence, gameboy is similar to remote control and cell phone in shape, and the action is similar to using a calculator.

Table 3. Detailed results for each action-object type with/without using depth image sequences. The values on the left side of the / indicates the count of image sequences which are recognized with using depth images and the values on the right side of the / indicates the count of image sequences which are recognized without using depth images.

Table 3	Pour	Drink	Brush	R.Cont.	Calc.	Phone	Headp.	V.game	Pict.	Pen
Pour	5/4	1/1	0/0	0/0	0/0	0/0	0/0	0/0	0/0	0/1
Drink	0/0	6/6	0/0	0/0	0/0	0/0	0/0	0/0	0/0	0/0
Brush	0/0	0/0	6/4	0/0	0/1	0/0	0/0	0/1	0/0	0/0
R.Cont.	0/0	0/0	0/0	5/3	0/0	0/1	0/0	1/1	0/1	0/0
Calc.	0/0	0/0	0/0	0/0	5/4	0/0	0/0	0/1	0/0	1/1
Phone	0/0	0/0	0/0	0/0	0/0	5/5	0/0	1/1	0/0	0/0
Headp.	0/0	0/0	0/0	0/0	0/0	0/0	6/6	0/0	0/0	0/0
V.game	0/0	0/0	0/0	1/2	0/0	1/1	0/0	4/3	0/0	0/0
Pict.	0/0	0/0	0/0	1/1	0/0	1/1	0/0	0/0	4/4	0/0
Pen	0/0	0/0	0/0	0/0	2/2	0/0	0/0	0/0	0/0	4/4

5   Conclusions

In this work, we focused on the role of action understanding in object classification and vice-versa. Then we proposed a framework that recognizes actions and objects within the context of each other. The proposed framework combines information about object availability and motion patterns in image sequences with a Bayesian network. The current framework does not require any temporal segmentation, body-part segmentation, and hand tracking methods. The experimental results demonstrated that the use of action and object context together improved recognition accuracy. Additionaly, we observed that our framework benefited from the depth image sequences efficiently.

References

1. Ullman, S.: High-level vision: object recognition and visual cognition. MIT Press (1996)
2. Fei-Fei, L., Fergus, R., Torralba, A.: Recognizing and learning object categories: short course. In: ICCV (2009)
3. Carbonetto, P., de Freitas, N., Barnard, K.: A Statistical Model for General Contextual Object Recognition. In: Pajdla, T., Matas, J. (eds.) ECCV 2004. LNCS, vol. 3021, pp. 350–362. Springer, Heidelberg (2004)
4. Torralba, A.: Contextual priming for object detection. Int. J. Comput. Vision 53, 169–191 (2003)
5. Filipovych, R., Ribeiro, E.: Recognizing primitive interactions by exploring actor-object states. In: CVPR (2008)
6. Wu, J., Osuntogun, A., Choudhury, T., Philipose, M., Rehg, J.M.: A scalable approach to activity recognition based on object use. In: ICCV, pp. 1–7 (2007)
7. Kjellström, H., Romero, J., Kragić, D.: Visual object-action recognition: interfering object affordances from human demonstration. Comput. Vis. Image Underst. 115, 81–90 (2011)
8. Moeslund, T.B., Hilton, A., Krüger, V.: A survey of advances in vision-based human motion capture and analysis. Comput. Vis. Image Underst. 104, 90–126 (2006)
9. Poppe, R.: A survey on vision-based human action recognition. Image Vision Comput. 28, 976–990 (2010)
10. Gall, J., Fossati, A., Gool, L.J.V.: Functional categorization of objects using real-time markerless motion capture. In: CVPR, pp. 1969–1976 (2011)
11. Ciu, X., Liu, Y., Shan, S., Chen, X., Gao, W.: 3D Haar-like features for pedestrian detection. In: ICME 2007, pp. 1263–1266 (2007)
12. Fei-Fei, L.: Bag of words models: recognizing and learning object categories. In: CVPR 2007 (2007)
13. Rubinstein, Y., Hastie, T.: Discriminative vs. informative learning. In: Proc. of the 3th Int. Conf. on Knowledge Discovery and Data Mining, pp. 49–53 (1997)

A Fast and Robust Feature Set for Cross Individual Facial Expression Recognition

Rodrigo Araujo[1], Yun-Qian Miao[1], Mohamed S. Kamel[1],
and Mohamed Cheriet[2]

[1] University of Waterloo, Center for Pattern Analysis and Machine Intelligence,
Electrical & Computer Engineering
{raraujo,yqmiao,mkamel}@uwaterloo.ca
[2] École de Technologie Supérieure,
Department of Automated Manufacturing Engineering
mohamed.cheriet@etsmtl.ca

Abstract. This paper presents a new simple and robust set of features to classify emotional states in sequences of facial images. The proposed method is derived from simple geometric-based features that deliver a fast, highly discriminative, low-dimensional, and robust classification across individuals. The proposed method was compared to other state-of-the-art methods such as Gabor, LBP and AAM-based features. They were all compared using four different classifiers and experimental results based on these classifiers have shown that the proposed features are more stable in "leave-same-sequence-image-out" (LSSIO) environments, less computational intense and faster when compared to others.

1 Introduction

Facial expression recognition (FER) is a challenging problem in computer vision that involves multidisciplinary knowledge and it is influenced by environmental and cultural aspects to name a few issues [7]. Finding the best set of features has always been one of the main challenges of facial expression recognition and any pattern recognition problem. A good classifier always relies on discriminating and independent features. The goal of this paper is to analyze four of the most established features used in the literature of facial expression classification and compare to a our new proposed features in terms of level of discrimination across individuals and time performance.

The proposed features[1] were the fastest and most robust among the state-of-the-art features for cross-subject performance discrimination when experimented on the extended Cohn-Kanade Dataset (CK+) [5] for basic emotion classification.

2 Literature Review

Several works have been published on face expression recognition and one of the ways publications can be classified is according to feature representation.

---

[1] Source code is available at
https://sites.google.com/site/rodrigoaraujophd/codes

L. Bolc et al. (Eds.): ICCVG 2012, LNCS 7594, pp. 272–279, 2012.
© Springer-Verlag Berlin Heidelberg 2012

Regarding the type of features extracted, two main approaches have been found in the literature. The first one is a geometric-based approach, where features are defined as shapes, specific points or fiducial points [6]. The second category is called appearance-based and the idea of this approach is to treat the image as a whole, some examples are: texture [3], Local Binary Pattern (LBP) [1], Gabor wavelet [10] and moments [4]. Some works have mixed both approaches [10,9].

Appearance-based approaches cope very well with variations of skin pattern or markings but as a downsize it is susceptible to illumination changes. In terms of geometric-based approaches the fact that they only consider some specific points makes them lose information; on the other hand, they are less computational demanding compared to appearance-based features.

3   Geometric Features

In order to capture the face movements of the subjects some features were calculated based on fiducial points provided by the extended Cohn-Kanade Dataset (CK+) database [5]. Each subject is marked with 68 fiducial points in sensitive points of the face like eyes, eyebrows, mouth, etc.

3.1   Active Appearance Models (AAMs)-Based Geometric Features (SPTS)

SPTS is a set of features that was proposed in [5] and is derived from the tracked face estimated by Active Appearance Models (AAMs) [2]. It refers to 68 vertex points x-, and y-coordinates, which result in a raw 136 dimensional feature vector. These points are the vertex locations after all the rigid geometric variation (translation, rotation and scale), relative to the base shape, has been removed. AU0 normalization was used in this work, and it means that the features of the first frame (which was neutral) is subtracted from the apex face. More details on this set of features can be found on the original paper [5].

3.2   Proposed Facial Measure Features (FMF)

The facial measure features are a set of geometric characteristics of the face that are being proposed in this paper as an alternative to more complex and computational demanding features such as Gabor, LBP, etc. This proposed set of features consists of facial measures of three areas: eyes, nose and mouth. Figure 1 shows all the features in a graphical representation.

Eye Region Features. The features of the eye region are defined by Eq. 1, 2, 3, 4, 5, 6, and 7.

$$d_{InnerBrowEye} = d(p_{InnerBrow}, q_{eye}) \tag{1}$$

$$d_{OuterBrowEye} = d(p_{OuterBrow}, q_{eye}) \tag{2}$$

$$A_{Brow} = H_{BBox}(Brow) \times W_{BBox}(Brow) \tag{3}$$

$$m_{Brow} = \frac{\Delta y}{\Delta x} \tag{4}$$

$$d_{Brows} = d(p_{InnerBrow}, p'_{InnerBrow}) \tag{5}$$

$$H_{Eye} = d(p_{eye}, q_{eye}) \tag{6}$$

$$A_{Lid} = H_{BBox}(Lid) \times W_{BBox}(Lid) \tag{7}$$

The first feature for the eye region is the distance $d_{InnerBrowEye}$ from the inner eyebrow $p_{InnerBrow}$ to the eye q_{eye}. $p_{InnerBrow}$ is a point located in the inner corner of the eyebrow and q_{eye} is a point located in the inner corner of the eye. The second feature for the eye region is the distance $d_{OuterBrowEye}$ from the outer eyebrow to the eye. $p_{OuterBrow}$ is a point located in the outer corner of the eyebrow and q_{eye} is a point located in the outer corner of the eye. The third feature, represents the area of the eyebrow region, which is calculated by multiplying the height $H_{BBox}()$ and width $W_{BBox}()$ of the bounding box that encloses the eyebrow image. The bounding box can be defined as the tightest rectangle that includes the image. The fourth feature is the slope of the eyebrow m_{Brow} and it represents the slope of the line that goes diagonally from the outer corner to the inner corner of the eyebrow. The slope is defined by the ratio of Δy and Δx, where Δy is the change in the y coordinate and Δx is the change in the x coordinate. The fifth feature is the distance between the eyebrows d_{Brows} and it represents the distance between the left eyebrow $p_{InnerBrow}$ and the right eyebrow $p'_{InnerBrow}$. $p_{InnerBrow}$ is a point located in the inner corner of the left eyebrow and $p'_{InnerBrow}$ is a point located in the inner corner of the right eyebrow. The sixth is the openness of the eyes H_{eye} and it represents the height of the eye, in other words, the distance between the upper eyelid p_{eye} and the bottom eyelid q_{eye}. The seventh and last geometric feature of the eye region represents the area of the lower eyelid region. The area of the eyelid is calculated by multiplying the height $H_{BBox}()$ and width $W_{BBox}()$ of the bounding box that encloses the lower portion of the eyelid image.

Mouth Region Features. For the mouth region of the face six features were created, mouth openness, mouth width, mouth area, mouth slope, thickness of upper lip and thickness of lower lip. All these features are represented by Eq. 8, 9, 10, 11, 12, and 13.

$$H_{Mouth} = d(p_{upperLip}, q_{lowerLip}) \tag{8}$$

$$W_{Mouth} = d(p_{leftCorner}, q_{rightCorner}) \tag{9}$$

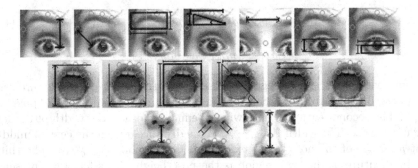

Fig. 1. Eye region features in the first row, mouth region features in the second row, and nose region features in the third row

$$A_{Mouth} = H_{BBox}(Mouth) \times W_{BBox}(Mouth) \tag{10}$$

$$m_{Mouth} = \frac{\Delta y}{\Delta x} \tag{11}$$

$$d_{UpperLip} = d(p_{IntUpLip}, q_{ExtUpLip}) \tag{12}$$

$$d_{LowerLip} = d(p_{IntLowLip}, q_{ExtLowLip}) \tag{13}$$

The first feature of the mouth region is mouth openness. Mouth openness is given by the distance between the middle point of the upper lip $p_{upperLip}$ and the middle point of lower lip $q_{lowerLip}$. The second features of the mouth region is mouth width. Mouth width is given by the distance between the left corner of the mouth $p_{leftCorner}$ and the right corner of the mouth $q_{rightCorner}$. The third feature represents the area of the mouth region. The area of the mouth is calculated by multiplying the height $H_{BBox}(Mouth)$ and width $W_{BBox}(Mouth)$ of the bounding box that encloses the mouth image. The fourth feature is the slope of the mouth. This feature is similar to the slope of the eyebrow. m_{Mouth} is the slope of the line that goes diagonally from the right/left corner to the mouth to the middle of the mouth. The slope is defined by the ratio of Δy and Δx, where Δy is the change in the y coordinate and Δx is the change in the x coordinate. The fifth feature is the thickness of the upper lip. In other words, it is the distance between the internal part of the upper lip $p_{IntUpLip}$ and the external part of the upper lip $q_{ExtUpLip}$. The sixth feature is very similar to the fifth, however taking into account the thickness of the lower lip. In other words, it is the distance between the internal part of the lower lip $p_{IntLowLip}$ and the external part of the lower lip $q_{ExtLowLip}$.

Nose Region Features. For the nose region, three features were created, nose-to-mouth distance, nose wing openness, and nose height. See Eq. 14, 15, and 16.

$$H_{NoseMouth} = d(p_{nose}, q_{mouth}) \tag{14}$$

$$W_{NoseWing} = d(p_{midNose}, q_{wingNose}) \qquad (15)$$

$$H_{Nose} = d(p_{rootNose}, q_{tipNose}) \qquad (16)$$

The first feature of the nose region is nose-to-mouth distance. This feature represents the distance from the base of the nose p_{nose} to the midpoint upper lip q_{mouth}. The second feature is nose wing openness and it is the width of the left wing of the nose. The width $W_{noseWing}$ is the distance d from the central middle point $p_{midNose}$ of the nose to the extreme left wing point $q_{wingNose}$. The third and final feature of the nose region is the nose height. This feature represents the distance from the root of the nose $p_{rootNose}$ to the tip of the nose $q_{tipNose}$.

4   Appearance-Based Features

The second category of features is appearance-based features. The idea of this approach is to treat the image as a whole. For this category three state-of-the-art features were analyzed: Canonical normalized appearance, Gabor descriptors and Local Binary Patterns.

4.1   Canonical Normalized Appearance (CAPP)

One of the appearance-based features used in this paper was also proposed in [5]. CAPP, as called in the referred paper, consists of the canonical normalized appearance where all the non-rigid shape variation are normalized with respect to the base shape. This is accomplished by applying a piece-wise affine warp on each triangle patch appearance in the source image, so that it aligns with the base face shape, as described in the original paper.

4.2   Local Binary Patterns (LBP)

The LBP feature extraction consists of a three-step process based on [8]. First step, the face image normalization, second step, the region division, and third step, the feature extraction itself.

For the normalization, the coordinates of the two eyes (landmark point 39 and 45 of the CK+ AMM points) are identified, then normalization is done by resizing the image with distance between eyes of 55 pixels. Afterwards, the whole face image is cropped to the size of 150 x 110, relative to eyes' position.

After a fixed size normalization, the face image is then divided into 6 x 7 sub-regions. Finally, the LBP descriptors are extracted and then the histograms are mapped into uniform patterns. The final feature vector is of size 2,478 (6 x 7 x 59) for each face.

Table 1. Error rates on six emotions using the 'mixed' setup

Features	dim.	LDA	Naive-Bayes	SVM (linear)	KNN
FMF	16	0.1103 ± 0.004	0.4588 ± 0.004	0.0515 ± 0.002	0.0394 ± 0.004
SPTS	136	0.0425 ± 0.003	0.1497 ± 0.004	0.0104 ± 0.001	0.0557 ± 0.004
CAPP	8,091	0.4093 ± 0.008	0.1609 ± 0.002	0.0028 ± 0.002	0.0058 ± 0.002
Gabor	42,560	0.0474 ± 0.006	0.4423 ± 0.007	0.0138 ± 0.002	0.0121 ± 0.006
LBP	2,478	0.3573 ± 0.024	0.0388 ± 0.007	0.0004 ± 0.001	0.0035 ± 0.003

4.3 Gabor

The Gabor filter features use the same normalization process described for the LBP, leading to 150 x 110 normalized face images [8]. After the normalization, a bank of 2-D Gabor filters is applied to the normalized face using 8 orientations and 5 spatial frequencies. Then, the Gabor magnitude is used to represent the face features (each pixel is represented by 5x8=40 features).

Because in magnitude of Gabor space, features are not changing too much among neighbor points, it is common to down-sample to reduce feature dimensionality. Here, a 4x4 downsampling was adopted, resulting in a Gabor feature vector of 42,560 (40 x 110/4 x 150/4).

5 Experiments

The experiments were run on the CK+ database [5]. From the 593 sequences, a total of 309 sequences that are emotion labeled (anger, disgust, fear, happy, sadness, and surprise) were used in the experiments. In order to increase the samples of apex emotion images, the three last frames of the sequence where considered, resulting in 927 images (135 anger, 177 disgust, 75 fear, 207 happy, 84 sadness, and 249 surprise).

The performance of the methods was evaluated by a 10-fold cross validation scheme and the reported results are based on the average error of the test sets. The experiments were performed using four different classifiers, LDA, Naive Bayes, SVM (linear), and KNN. All the classifiers were trained for six classes. The time performance is based on the average time of the classification phase of all classifiers in a dual core processor and it is given in seconds per sample.

Two different setups were used in order to compare the generalization among the features. The first setup is called "mixed" and it does not prevent images of a subject in a sequence (neutral to apex) to be present in both training and testing set. The second setup is called "leave-same-sequence-image-out" (LSSIO). In this setup a sequence of images is treated as a unit; in other words, images from the same sequence are not allowed to be in both training and test set. In order to have a fair comparison the features were also compared with the same number of dimensions, a total of 16, reduced by PCA.

Table 2. Error rates and processing on six emotions using the LSSIO setup

Feat.	dim.	avg. time (sec)	LDA	Naive-Bayes	SVM (linear)	KNN
FMF	16	0.00015	0.1332 ± 0.005	0.4650 ± 0.004	0.1985 ± 0.014	0.4639 ± 0.006
SPTS	136	0.00021	0.1090 ± 0.003	0.1710 ± 0.010	0.0740 ± 0.002	0.1726 ± 0.005
CAPP	8,091	0.00735	0.6845 ± 0.019	0.4482 ± 0.007	0.1564 ± 0.012	0.4617 ± 0.014
Gabor	42,560	0.02098	0.4757 ± 0.027	0.5054 ± 0.013	0.3328 ± 0.014	0.6793 ± 0.012
LBP	2,478	0.00477	0.6543 ± 0.036	0.2260 ± 0.001	0.1255 ± 0.001	0.7497 ± 0.008

6 Result Discussion and Conclusion

All the features had better results in the mixed setup (Table 1). SPTS, CAPP, Gabor, and LBP showed very low errors between 1.04% and 0.004%. The proposed FMF had 3.6% error. However, in the mixed setup, images from the same sequence can be both in training and testing set, biasing the classifiers. Therefore, LSSIO represents a more realistic setup in terms of real-world applications.

In the LSSIO setup (Table 2), results show that most of the features had great increases in their error rates, except the proposed feature FMF. For example, SPTS, which had 1.04% error on SVM in the mixed setup jumped to 7.40% in the LSSIO, representing an increase of 7.11 times in the error rate compared to 1.2 of FMF. SPTS and LBP had better results than FMF in terms of error rate; however, FMF had a competitive result with 13,32% and a very low standard deviation of 0.005 as well as a better time performance of 40% faster than the second best feature set. It is also very important to notice that differently from SPTS, FMF did not use AU0 normalization in this experiment. Besides, this result was achieved using only 16 features, compared to the other higher-dimensional feature vectors.

A second experiment considered all the features with the same dimensions, a total of 16, and also considered FMF with AU0 normalization, as used in SPTS, and statistical normalization (subtracted by mean and divided by standard deviation) of the landmark coordinates in order to be comparable with of the AAM based features. Table 3 shows the result of the described experiment. The feature dimensionality was reduced using PCA and the results are based on 20 random runs of 10-fold cross validation.

Table 3. Comparison of all features reduced to 16 dimensions and FMF with AU0 face normalization

Features	dim.	LDA	Naive-Bayes	SVM (linear)	KNN
FMF	16	0.0727 ± 0.002	0.0746 ± 0.003	0.0742 ± 0.009	0.0928 ± 0.004
SPTS	16	0.0692 ± 0.004	0.0795 ± 0.007	0.0935 ± 0.011	0.1361 ± 0.007
CAPP	16	0.3814 ± 0.011	0.2871± 0.008	0.2460 ± 0.014	0.4347 ± 0.010
Gabor	16	0.4591 ± 0.009	0.4877 ± 0.010	0.4473 ± 0.009	0.6625 ± 0.007
LBP	16	0.1997 ± 0.007	0.2890 ± 0.011	0.2476 ± 0.021	0.5328 ± 0.008

Note that with the same number of features FMF performed on par with the best features with a result of 7.27% error and standard deviation of 0.002. Besides, the results across the classifiers are much more stable compared with the other features. With AU0 face normalization, FMF achieved 7.27% of error compared to 7.40% of SPTS rate but with only 16 features compared to 136 and 40% faster.

This paper presented a new simple and robust set of features to classify emotional states in sequences of images. The proposed facial features are derived from simple geometric-based features and showed very competitive results compared to state-of-the-art features. It also shows interesting characteristics such as low dimensionality, faster computation, and stable results across individuals and classifiers. For future work, fusing FMF with appearance-based features will be considered.

References

1. Ahonen, T., Hadid, A., Pietikäinen, M.: Face description with local binary patterns: Application to face recognition. IEEE Trans. Pattern Analysis and Machine Intelligence 28(12), 2037–2041 (2006)
2. Cootes, T.F., Edwards, G.J., Taylor, C.J.: Active appearance models. IEEE Trans. Pattern Anal. Mach. Intell. 23(6), 681–685 (2001)
3. Koelstra, S., Pantic, M., Patras, I.: A dynamic texture-based approach to recognition of facial actions and their temporal models. IEEE Trans. Pattern Analysis and Machine Intelligence 32(11), 1940–1954 (2010)
4. Li, P., Phung, S.L., Bouzerdoum, A., Tivive, F.H.C.: Improved facial expression recognition with trainable 2-d filters and support vector machines. In: 20th International Conference on Pattern Recognition, pp. 3732–3735 (August 2010)
5. Lucey, P., Cohn, J., Kanade, T., Saragih, J., Ambadar, Z., Matthews, I.: The extended cohn-kanade dataset (CK+): A complete dataset for action unit and emotion-specified expression. In: 2010 IEEE Computer Society Conference on Computer Vision and Pattern Recognition Workshops (CVPRW), pp. 94–101 (June 2010)
6. Maalej, A., Amor, B.B., Daoudi, M., Srivastava, A., Berretti, S.: Local 3d shape analysis for facial expression recognition. In: 20th International Conference on Pattern Recognition, pp. 4129–4132 (August 2010)
7. Pantic, M., Rothkrantz, L.: Automatic analysis of facial expressions: The state of the art. IEEE Trans. Pattern Analysis and Machine Intelligence 22, 1424–1445 (2000)
8. Shan, C., Gong, S., McOwan, P.W.: Facial expression recognition based on local binary patterns: A comprehensive study. Image Vision Comput. 27(6), 803–816 (2009)
9. Tian, Y.I., Kanade, T., Cohn, J.: Recognizing action units for facial expression analysis. IEEE Trans. Pattern Analysis and Machine Intelligence 23(2), 97–115 (2001)
10. Tian, Y.I., Kanade, T., Cohn, J.: Evaluation of gabor-wavelet-based facial action unit recognition in image sequences of increasing complexity. In: Fifth IEEE International Conference on Automatic Face and Gesture Recognition, pp. 229–234 (May 2002)

Image and Video Saliency Models Improvement by Blur Identification

Yoann Baveye, Fabrice Urban, and Christel Chamaret

Technicolor, 1 av. de belle fontaine
CS 17616 35576 Cesson Sevigne, France
fabrice.urban@technicolor.com

Abstract. Visual saliency models aim at predicting where people look. In free viewing conditions, people look at relevant objects that are in focus. Assuming blurred or out-of-focus objects do not belong to the region of interest, this paper proposes a significant improvement and the validation of a saliency model by taking blur into account. Blur identification is associated to a spatio-temporal saliency model. Bottom-up models are designed to mimic the low-level processing of the human visual system and can thus detect out-of-focus objects as salient. The blur identification allows decreasing saliency values on blurred areas while increasing values on sharp areas. In order to validate our new saliency model we conducted eye-tracking experiments to record ground truth of observer's fixations on images and videos. Blur identification significantly improves fixation prediction for natural images and videos.

Keywords: Visual attention, Saliency, Blur, image processing.

1 Introduction

In image or video content, focal blur or out-of-focus blur occurs when objects in the scene are placed out of the focal range imposed by the focal length of the camera. This limitation is also used as an artistic effect by photographers to reduce the depth of field to emphasize an object in focus. In the human visual system objects need additionally to be projected onto the fovea, the part of the retina that contains most of the visual cells, to appear sharp. Objects that are not fixated appear blurred on the retina. Nevertheless, it has been shown that blurring affects the way an observer will look at an image [1]. People will look at objects in focus, and neglect blurred background.

Visual attention allows the human visual system to understand complex scenes by successively focusing on interesting features or objects. Saliency models [2,3] aim at predicting where an observer will look. They are often based on a frequency analysis of images and extraction of features that contrast with their surroundings. [4,5] experimentally determine functions where contrast sensitivity is measured for an average observer. Those functions perform as band-pass filtering for the contrast identification. Thus visual attention modeling already introduces frequency selection that can be seen as blur differentiation. However, in [6] the authors refine previous assumptions by demonstrating that the

L. Bolc et al. (Eds.): ICCVG 2012, LNCS 7594, pp. 280–287, 2012.

most attractive signal appears in medium frequencies. Consequently, blurred areas can still be salient. An interpretation of this is that the notion of saliency and sharpness might not be processed at the same level in the human brain, sharpness being identified in a second step. Indeed, because of the physiology of the eye, and in particular the small size of the fovea, the observer does not know if the object attended after next saccade is sharp or blurred on the screen. Bottom-up saliency models do not currently detect blurred areas and will mark out-of-focus objects as Region of Interest (RoI). Integrating blur detection to refine the bottom-up saliency map and remove out-of-focus objects from RoI is thus biologically plausible. An attempt of using blur detection to enhance saliency models can be found in [1]. The authors use different state-of-the-art saliency models and a blur identification algorithm based on an edge map, combined with machine learning. They do not provide validation using ground truth eye-tracking data. Besides, they present results for still images only.

This paper proposes two contributions: (i) a new saliency model that integrates blur identification in order to more precisely detect RoI in images and videos and (ii) a validation of such prediction improvement via eye-tracking on a dedicated database with blurred images. One can notice that the blur detection algorithm uses the same frequency analysis stage as the saliency model and thus introduces very little computation cost overhead. The remainder of the paper is organized as follows: section 2 describes the saliency model and the blur identification algorithm, then results are presented in section 3. Finally, conclusions and perspectives are drawn in section 4

2   Visual Attention Model

The saliency model used is a spatio-temporal model of the bottom-up selective visual attention, derived from [7]. In this paper, we present an improvement of an existing spatial saliency model thanks to the identification of blur.

2.1   Bottom-Up Spatial Saliency Model

The spatial saliency model is described in [6]. It is based on the plausible neural architecture of Koch and Ullman [8] and designed to be simple and computationally efficient. Its performances are similar or even higher than state-of-the-art models in terms of prediction.

The visual attention model uses a hierarchical decomposition of the visual signal. Its synoptic is described in Figure 1. The YUV 4:2:0 color space is used. It separates achromatic (Y) and chromatic (U: green-magenta and V: orange-cyan) perceptual signals. This color space has been chosen because it takes the human visual system into consideration and is commonly used in image and video processing.

The first step of the model extracts early visual features from the image. A 9/7 Cohen-Daubechies-Feauveau (CDF) wavelet transform is used to separate frequency bands and orientation ranges. The resulting multi-scale pyramid is

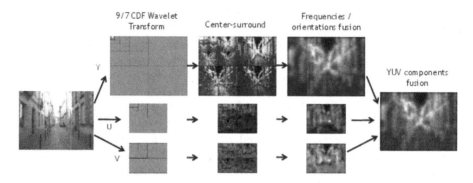

Fig. 1. Bottom-up saliency model

composed of oriented contrast maps with limited frequency range and a low-resolution image.

In the second step of the model, a Difference of Gaussian (DoG) modeling the center-surround response of visual cells is applied on each oriented contrast map (wavelet sub-band). Next, the orientation maps from each level are summed together.

The final step is the fusion of these early feature maps. Two fusions are successively applied: levels fusion and color channels fusion. Levels fusion operation is an across-scale addition using successive bi-linear up-sampling and additions of the per-pixel level maps. YUV components fusion keeps the maximum saliency value between Y, U, and V for each pixel after normalizing with an empirical maximum value taking into account the difference of amplitude between the three channels. The output map is finally mapped in the range of 0 to 1.

2.2   Blur Identification

The implemented blur identification method is a modified version of the method proposed by Tong *et al.* [9] which uses the ability of wavelet transform in both discriminating different types of edges and identifying sharpness from blur. In our implementation, the same wavelet decomposition as the saliency model is used in order to avoid additional computations. Moreover, the CDF wavelet transform leads to a more precise frequency analysis than the Harr wavelets used in [9]. From this decomposition, block-based blur values are computed, leading to a map discriminating blurred from sharp areas (see Figure 2). For each decomposition level, an edge map is computed as:

$$E_{i,l} = \max_{k \in D_i} \left(\sqrt{LH_{k,l}^2 + HL_{k,l}^2 + HH_{k,l}^2} \right), \tag{1}$$

l being the current wavelet level (with the highest resolution level denoted $l = 0$), i the current pixel, LH, HL and HH the wavelet sub-bands and D the squared non-overlapping neighborhood such that it corresponds to a 2×2 block in the smallest resolution level, 4 × 4 in the next, ... Then the final block-based blur value is defined as:

$$
\begin{cases}
0\,(=blurred) & if \min_{l\in[0,L-1]} E_{i,l} < Eblur \\[2ex]
\min\left(255, 4\times\sqrt{\sum_{l\in[0,L-1]}\left(\frac{E_{i,l}^2}{2^l}\right)}\right) & otherwise
\end{cases}
\tag{2}
$$

L is the number of decomposition levels, and $Eblur$ an experimental threshold set to 5 in our implementation. The blur map values are then mapped in the range of 0 (respectively blurred) to 1 (resp. sharp).

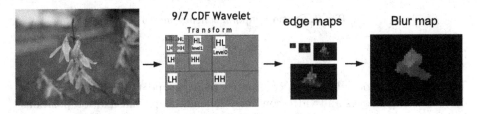

Fig. 2. Wavelet sub-bands decomposition

Blur identification is used to improve RoI detection by removing saliency in blurred areas, as these are considered to be visually unattractive areas. Thus, saliency values of blurred areas need to be reduced, while sharp objects' saliency need to be emphasized. The final spatial saliency map is defined as:

$$
Saliency_{blur} = Saliency \times (.5 + Blur)
\tag{3}
$$

where $Saliency$ is the saliency map as described in section 2.1 and $Blur$ is the blur map as defined in section 2.2. With such a fusion, blur identification has an impact on the final saliency map while the blur map is not totally trusted.

2.3   Spatio-temporal Saliency Model

The temporal model assumes the visual attention is attracted by motion contrast. Such contrast is deduced from the difference between local and global motion. A fast hierarchical block-based motion estimator [10] is used to compute local motion. Then, using a weighted least square optimization approach, the global motion is deduced from block-based vectors with a parametric model. The temporal saliency map highlights blocks that have a different motion relative to the global motion.

The spatio-temporal saliency map is computed as the average of the spatial and the temporal saliency maps. For still images, the saliency map is directly the output of the spatial saliency model as there is no temporal analysis. The global synopsis of the spatio-temporal attention model is depicted in figure 3.

The next section presents results of the application of this algorithm to still images and videos, and its validation on eye-tracking data.

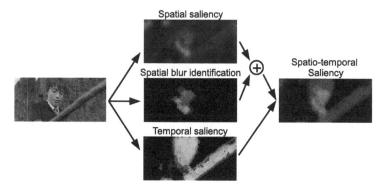

Fig. 3. Spatio-temporal saliency model

3   Results

The presented model has been confronted to a ground truth of eye tracking data with still images and video contents. Saliency maps and fixation positions have been compared using both the NSS (Normalized Scan-path Saliency) metric [11] and the AUC. The AUC (Area Under Curve) is a classification indicator stemming from the ROC (Receiver Operating Characteristic) analysis. An AUC value tending to 1 means a good agreement between the predicted and the experimental saliency maps. The AUC results highly depend on the smoothness of the computed saliency map and the chosen threshold used to compute the binary ground truth. The NSS has the advantage to normalize the salience per scanpath: scanpaths with different number of fixations have the same weight. In other words, every observer has the same impact on salience. Moreover, the NSS gives more weight to areas more often fixated. We use both metrics anyway to show that the results are not metric-biased.

Eye-movements of observers were recorded in free-viewing conditions using an SMI RED 50 IView X eye-tracker with a 50Hz sampling frequency. Two different experiments were conducted, one with still images and one with videos, in order to validate the model in both configurations. Details are given below.

3.1   Still Image Database

25 volunteer subjects (11 females and 14 males) viewed 50 images[1] with a reduced depth of field thus naturally containing blur. All the subjects had normal or corrected-to-normal vision. They were all naive to the purpose of the experiment. Each image was presented during 5 seconds, in a random order, interleaved with a neutral gray image containing a randomly placed black cross to reduce the center bias of the first fixation. The resolution of the images was 800x600 pixels. They have been manually selected on the internet from various topics. Figure 4

---

[1] Part of the photos were by courtesy of Nicolas Le Goff (http://dishio.eu). All rights reserved.

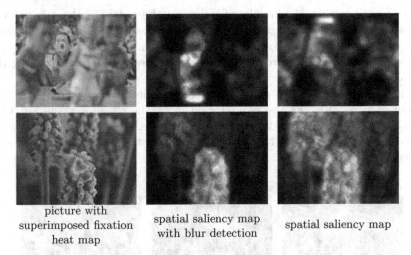

| picture with superimposed fixation heat map | spatial saliency map with blur detection | spatial saliency map |

Fig. 4. Example image stimuli with corresponding fixation heat map and saliency maps

shows example images with fixation positions overlayed as heat map and their corresponding saliency map computed with and without blur detection.

The proposed model improves fixation prediction. An important improvement is seen on highly blurred pictures where the model without blur detection gave too much importance to blurred areas. On pictures containing smooth or homogeneous areas, the improvement is less visible because such areas are detected as blurred. Table 1 presents average NSS and AUC values of the 50 images, for the model without blur identification and the augmented model. Blur identification significantly improves the prediction performances (paired t-test with p<0.001).

Table 1. Average NSS and AUC values comparison of saliency model without and with blur identification for image and video databases

	Average NSS values			Average AUC values		
	no blur	with blur	paired t-test	no blur	with blur	paired t-test
image database	0,83	0,99	4,4E-08 (***)	0.72	0.75	8.3E-08(***)
video database	0,98	1,04	0,005 (**)	0.70	0.71	0.001(**)

**t significant at p<.01   ***t significant at p<.001

3.2 Video Database

The efficiency of the model has also been tested on 21 videos and compared with gaze positions recorded from 30 volunteer subjects during free-viewing task. Selected videos were mainly extracted from movie trailers. They did not contain highly reduced depth-of-field content such as for the experiment with still pictures. The proposed saliency model with blur detection significantly improves fixation prediction in terms of NSS and AUC (paired t-test with p<0.01) (see

Table 1). The impact of blur identification on the video database is reduced compared to the still image database because videos contain less blurred areas than selected pictures. Moreover more significant improvements are averaged in time with other frames where less improvement is obtained, thus reducing the measured improvement.

Blur detection is efficient on close-up scenes where the background is usually out-of-focus. It works also well on wide shots where homogeneous areas are detected as blurred leading to concentrate more salience on the RoI. Screenshots of selected videos with their corresponding fixations and saliency maps are presented on Figure 5.

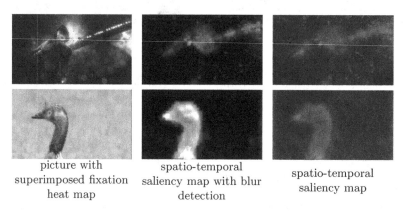

| picture with superimposed fixation heat map | spatio-temporal saliency map with blur detection | spatio-temporal saliency map |

Fig. 5. Video examples with corresponding fixation heat map and spatio-temporal saliency maps

While blur identification improves fixation prediction on images or videos where blurred areas are detected correctly, one must be careful with homogeneous areas. Indeed, those regions have no high frequencies, being detected as blurred areas, but they might be part of RoI where fixations are located (i.e. interior of an object). Detection of homogeneous areas associated with a special treatment is thus necessary to prevent erroneous results.

In this paper, the detection of blur is performed under the assumption of focal blur. Motion blur generates blur in the direction of the motion. This type of blur may not be detected by our blur identification method because it affects only one direction of the wavelet transform coefficients. A motion blur detection taking advantage of already computed wavelet coefficients and motion information in the temporal branch may thus be of interest in a fixation prediction context.

4   Conclusions

In this paper, we presented a new saliency model that uses blur detection to improve fixation predictions. Low-level saliency models can detect blurred areas as salient. This is consistent with the low-level models of the human visual system, but blurred areas are rarely of interest. Identifying sharp from blurred areas and lowering the saliency value on blurred areas improves saliency model performances for images and videos. Eye-tracking experiments have been conducted to create a ground truth of human fixations on images and videos naturally containing blur. A significant improvement has been obtained with the proposed algorithm. As expected, the biggest improvements are obtained for content with a small depth-of-field, where the background is highly blurred. Currently, the blur identification algorithm assumes focal blur only and does not detect motion blur. Further improvement of performances could be achieved with motion blur detection.

References

1. Khan, R.A., Konik, H., Dinet, E.: Enhanced image saliency model based on blur identification. In: 25th International Conference of IVCNZ (December 2010)
2. Le Meur, O., Le Callet, P., Barba, D.: Predicting visual fixations on video based on low-level visual features. Vision Res. 47(19), 2483–2498 (2007)
3. Itti, L., Koch, C., Niebur, E.: Model of saliency-based visual attention for rapid scene analysis. IEEE PAMI 20, 1254–1259 (1998)
4. Daly, S.: The visible differences predictor: An algorithm of image fidelity. In: Digital Images and Human Vision, pp. 179–206 (1993)
5. Mannos, J.L., Sakrison, D.J.: The effects of a visual fidelity criterion on the encoding of images. IEEE TIT 20(4), 525–536 (1974)
6. Urban, F., Follet, B., Chamaret, C., Le Meur, O., Baccino, T.: Medium Spatial Frequencies, a Strong Predictor of Salience. Cogn. Comput. 3, 37–47 (2011)
7. Le Meur, O., Thoreau, D., Le Callet, P., Barba, D.: A spatio-temporal model of the selective human visual attention. In: IEEE ICIP, vol. 3, pp. 1188–1191 (2005)
8. Koch, C., Ullman, S.: Shifts in selective visual attention: towards the underlying neural circuitry. Hum Neurobiol. 4, 219–227 (1985)
9. Tong, H.: Blur detection for digital images using wavelet transform. In: Proceedings of IEEE ICME, pp. 17–20 (2004)
10. Urban, F., Nezan, J.F., Raulet, M.: HDS, a real-time multi-DSP motion estimator for MPEG-4 H.264 AVC high definition video encoding. Springer Journal of Real-Time Image Processing 4, 23–31 (2009)
11. Peters, R., Iyer, A., Itti, L., Koch, C.: Components of bottom-up gaze allocation in natural images. Vision Research 45, 2397–2416 (2005)

Hand Tracking Using Optical-Flow Embedded Particle Filter in Sign Language Scenes

Selma Belgacem[1], Clément Chatelain[1],
Achraf Ben-Hamadou[2], and Thierry Paquet[1]

[1] LITIS EA 4108, University of Rouen,
Saint-Etienne du Rouvray, France
selma.belgacem@etu.univ-rouen.fr
[2] University of Paris-Est, LIGM (UMR CNRS),
Center for Visual Computing, ENPC,
Marne-la-Vallée, France

Abstract. In this paper we present a method dedicated to hand tracking in sign language scenes using particle filtering. A a new penalisation method based on the optical flow mechanism is introduced. Generally, particle filters require the use of a reference model. In this paper we have introduced a new method based on a dictionary of visual references of hand to constitute the reference model. The evaluation of our method is performed on the SignStream-ASLLRP database on which we have provided ground truth annotations for this purpose. The obtained results show the accuracy of our method.

Keywords: hand tracking, particle filtering, optical flow, hand vocabulary, sign language scene.

1 Introduction

In this article we propose a method for hand tracking in sign language scenes. Hand gestures are characterised by frequently changing hand configuration (fingers and palm pose) and random motion [13], thus requiring a robust and accurate tracking method.

Particle filter [3,10] is a state-of-the-art framework based on a probabilistic *predictive* tracking formalism that has shown to be efficient in various applications as sports tracking [6,16], face and hand tracking [1,4,11] and vehicle tracking [5]. Prediction is based on a Markovian motion model, and an iterative Monte Carlo *weighted Sampling* applied on a set of particles. *Particles* are the target region hypotheses, typically points, bounding boxes or more complex geometrical models. Particle filters are based on three essential models: *observation model* which weights particles according to the associated extracted measurements, *reference model* which is a reference representation of the tracked object, and *motion model* according to which particles are propagated. In this paper, we present a contribution to each of these stages which we introduce in the *condensation* implementation [4] of a particle filter.

L. Bolc et al. (Eds.): ICCVG 2012, LNCS 7594, pp. 288–295, 2012.
© Springer-Verlag Berlin Heidelberg 2012

Our main contribution is the integration of estimated and observed motion information in the motion model and the observation model. Indeed, the random aspect of hand gestures in sign language scenes makes it difficult to use predefine motion models. In this respect, Bhandarkar et al. and Yao et al. [1,16] have introduced an optical-flow-based velocity term to the classic equation of the particle filter motion model. Optical-flow technique is known for its robustness against luminosity variations and deformations of the tracked object shape [1]. In the case of multiple objects moving in the same sequence, this observed velocity term becomes ambiguous. We propose to integrate similar information in the motion model based on the estimated position provided by the filter and weighted by a global observation deduced from optical-flow. The dominant hand in sign language has mostly the dominant motion in the scene. Then, a global velocity observation is highly influenced by dominant hand motion. Optical-flow observation can also be exploited locally to enhance the observation model. In fact, particles which move against the observed flow should be penalised. We propose a new method to apply this optical-flow local penalization by *re-weighting* particles.

In the framework of particle filtering, particles *weights* are iteratively computed using the *observation likelihood*. This observation likelihood is generally estimated thanks to a distance between a particle associated observation and the reference model. The reference model can be determined by either an initial detection [15] or an off-line learning process [9]. The first strategy is highly sensitive to deformations of patterns while the second requires an annotated data. We design a new method to automatically build a reference model. It is based on the construction of a vocabulary of the tracked object images thumbnails (figure 1) with different configurations, collected from the sequence in which the object will be tracked afterwards. In addition, our observation model is based on features invariant to deformation.

The outline of our paper consists of three sections. Section 2 introduces our observation and reference models. Section 3 explains our motion model and optical-flow penalisation at the global and local levels. Section 4 presents the experiments conducted and the evaluation results.

2 Particle Filter

In this study, a particle X^i ($i \in \{1, \ldots, \mathcal{N}\}$) is associated to a bounding box defined by $p^i = (x, y)$ the particle position in the image and $s^i = (w, h)$ its width and height. $\mathcal{N}$ is the number of particles. A weight π^i is associated to each particle and is proportional to the observation likelihood $P(Y^i|X^i)$ where Y^i is a *features vector* associated to a particle X^i. Finally, for a given frame t, the *estimated position* $\hat{X}_t$ of the target T is the barycentre of the set of particles. In our case, the target T is the right hand.

Next in this section, we detail our reference and observation models involved in the particle filter.

2.1   Reference Model : Hand Vocabulary

Since the hand is a deformable object, its appearance changes very often in the images. We, therefore, chose to use a *vocabulary* of hand appearances as a reference model (see Figure 1).

Fig. 1. Sample from hand vocabulary automatically extracted from a sequence

This vocabulary is built automatically off-line from the video sequence S as follows. We first use the well-known and robust face detection method of Viola and Jones [14] to localise the face in the first image of S. This allows for extracting a prior information about the colour range (*i.e.,* histogram) of the skin. Then, we extract skin blobs from the whole images using histogram back-projection and CamShift [2] algorithms. Afterwards, using some geometric assumptions, we select the most likely blobs standing for the right hand which is our target object T. It is worth noticing that we do not retain ambiguous configurations such as hand intersections or when the right hand is very close to the face. Finally, we end up with a set of cropped images of the hand to be tracked over the sequence S. Note that this method of skin blob detection is also used to localise the hand in the first image of S and initialize the filter.

The set of cropped images represent our hand vocabulary. We associate a reference feature vector Y^R to this vocabulary. Y^R is the average of the feature vectors of all the cropped images.

2.2   Observation Model

The observation model allows the filter to compare a given particle X^i with the reference model so that a weight π^i is computed according to its similarity to the model.

Selected features. The most important features for hand tracking are colour and shape. The colour is a classic feature used in the observation model of particle filters for tracking. The hand is characterised by a skin colour range. In our case, the *skin colour histogram* is represented in the HSV colour space as is very often used [12].

In sign language scenes, colour features are not sufficient to discriminate between the hand and the face. Therefore, we additionally consider two complementary shape descriptors namely, Hu and Zernike moments. Hu moments are invariant with respect to translation, scaling and symmetry of shapes while Zernike moments are invariant with respect to rotation.

Observation likelihood. Following the Condensation algorithm, $\pi^i = P(Y^i|X^i)$ $\forall\, i \in \{1,\ldots,\mathcal{N}\}$. We compute these weights using equation (1) which has a simple form that we define.

$$P(Y^i|X^i) = \prod_{l=1}^{m} \left(\frac{1}{1 + D_l(Y^i, Y^R)}\right)^{c_l} \tag{1}$$

In equation (1), m is the number of features, $c_l \in \mathbb{R}^+$ is used to give importance to some features, D_l measures a distance for the feature l between the feature vector Y^i of a particle i and the feature vector Y^R of our reference model. There is a specific D_l for each feature l.

We present in the next section our motion model and optical-flow penalisation.

3   Optical Flow Penalisation

Our goal is to integrate in the particle filter information about motion. First, we compute an optical-flow map Ψ_t for each frame t of S using Lucas-Kanade method [7]. Then, the integration is done at two levels: particles weights and particles motion model.

3.1   Velocity and Particles Re-weighting

The idea here is to penalise particles which are moving against the observed flow. To do so, we characterise each particle X_t^i with $\boldsymbol{\nu}_t^i$ which is the median velocity computed from the corresponding X_t^i window in the Ψ_t map. The optical-flow penalisation of particles with $\boldsymbol{\nu}_t^i$ is done via a kind of weighting term ξ_t^i which we define as follows:

$$\xi_t^i = \frac{1}{1 + \lambda_t^i}[cos(\widehat{\rho\boldsymbol{\nu}_t^i, \dot{p}_t^i})]^{\tau_t^i}. \tag{2}$$

In the equation (2), $\dot{p}_t^i$ is the particle displacement vector, $\rho = \delta t$, and λ_t^i and τ_t^i values are defined in the table 1 according to conditions on optical-flow observation $\boldsymbol{\nu}_t^i$ and the associated particle displacement $\dot{p}_t^i$.

In table 1, $|\ |_1$ stands for L_1-norm, $\Lambda \in \mathbb{R}^+$ is an empirical value which should be chosen big enough to make ξ_t^i tends to 0. In the case of condition 1, the particle X^i and the associated observed flow $\boldsymbol{\nu}_t^i$ are stationary, then X^i is not

Table 1. (λ_t^i, τ_t^i) values according to conditions on optical-flow observation and the associated particle displacement

Conditions	condition 1	condition 2	condition 3	condition 4
	$\|\rho\boldsymbol{\nu}_t^i\| = 0$ AND	$\|\rho\boldsymbol{\nu}_t^i\| = 0$ XOR	$\|\rho\boldsymbol{\nu}_t^i\|\|\dot{p}_t^i\| \neq 0$	
	$\|\dot{p}_t^i\| = 0$	$\|\dot{p}_t^i\| = 0$	$cos(\rho\boldsymbol{\nu}_t^i, \dot{p}_t^i) \leq 0$	$cos(\rho\boldsymbol{\nu}_t^i, \dot{p}_t^i) > 0$
(λ_t^i, τ_t^i) values	$(0,0)$	$(\Lambda,0)$	$(\Lambda,0)$	$((\|(\|\rho\boldsymbol{\nu}_t^i\|, \|\dot{p}_t^i\|)\|_1, 1)$

penalized. In the case of conditions 2 and 3, X^i and ν_t^i have opposite states, then X^i is maximally penalized. In the case of condition 4, X^i and ν_t^i have the same orientation, then X^i is only penalized by the velocity value difference $|(\|\rho\nu_t^i\|, \|\dot{p}_t^i\|)|_1$ and the direction difference $cos(\widehat{\rho\nu_t^i, \dot{p}_t^i})$.

ξ_t^i is then used to re-weight particles as follows: $\pi_t'^i = \pi_t^i \xi_t^i$, where $\pi_t'^i$ is the new weight of a particle X_t^i. Afterwards, particles are sampled according to $\pi_t'^i$. This first integration of optical-flow is qualified as local penalisation. Next, we present our motion model with an optical-flow global penalisation.

3.2 Velocity and Particles Motion Model

The classic particle motion prediction equation according to the condensation algorithm is:

$$X_t^i = AX_{t-1}^i + BR_t^i. \tag{3}$$

In the equation (3), A is the transition matrix, R_t^i is a random vector and B is a random walk matrix. In our case, A and B are constant. As explained before, the signing hand motion model should be more elaborated to improve the tracking. Thus, we keep the classic prediction equation (3) and we introduce the velocity and acceleration of the filter estimation $\hat{X}_{t-1}$ as follows:

$$X_t^i = AX_{t-1}^i + BR_t^i + \alpha_t \begin{bmatrix} \dot{p}_{t-1} \\ 0 \\ 0 \end{bmatrix} + \beta_t \begin{bmatrix} \ddot{p}_{t-1} \\ 0 \\ 0 \end{bmatrix} \tag{4}$$

In equation (4), $\dot{p}_{t-1}$ and $\ddot{p}_{t-1}$ are respectively the displacement vector and the acceleration vector computed from the previous estimated positions, α_t and β_t are two 4×4 diagonal matrices gathering coefficients to weight the filter velocity and acceleration respectively. We define them as follows:

$$\alpha_t = \begin{pmatrix} \frac{\bar{\vartheta}(\Psi_t^x)}{\max_j \vartheta^j(S)} & 0 & 0 & 0 \\ 0 & \frac{\bar{\vartheta}(\Psi_t^y)}{\max_j \vartheta^j(S)} & 0 & 0 \\ 0 & 0 & 0 & 0 \\ 0 & 0 & 0 & 0 \end{pmatrix} \quad \beta_t = \begin{pmatrix} \frac{\bar{\gamma}(\Psi_t^x)}{\max_j \gamma^j(S)} & 0 & 0 & 0 \\ 0 & \frac{\bar{\gamma}(\Psi_t^y)}{\max_j \gamma^j(S)} & 0 & 0 \\ 0 & 0 & 0 & 0 \\ 0 & 0 & 0 & 0 \end{pmatrix}$$

where $\vartheta^j(\Psi_t^x)$ is the absolute value of the x-axis velocity component for a pixel j (resp. y-axis), and $\gamma^j(\Psi_t^x)$ is the absolute value of the x-axis acceleration component for a pixel j (resp. y-axis). Taking into account both velocity and acceleration estimations in the motion model allows the generated particles to smoothly follow up T and to handle severe motion variations, respectively. By computing α_t and β_t from the whole velocity and acceleration maps, we handle the global motion in the scene. In fact, if the global motion is important in the scene, those coefficients will have important values, whereas, if the global motion is attenuated, those coefficients will have small values.

4   Experiments and Results

4.1   Experiments

Evaluated systems. In order to assess the robustness of our method and to show the contribution of its components, we propose to compare four configurations of the particle filter, namely, PF, VPF, 2VPF, and 3VPF. PF is the classic particle filter using only the observation model presented in section 2.2. VPF is the PF with the use of a reference vocabulary. 2VPF integrates the estimation velocity and acceleration to VPF. In that case, α_t and β_t have constant values determined experimentally. Finally, 3VPF is the whole approach adding the optical-flow global and local penalisation to 2VPF. The particle filter parameters are the same for the four systems, namely, $\mathcal{N}$ equals 100, A is the identity matrix, and B and c_l are experimentally determined.

Experimental data and evaluation criteria. We performed Hand tracking experiments on the American sign language database SignStream-ASLLRP [8]. It consists of four videos containing between 1310 and 5046 frames acquired in a recording studio. Their capturing rate is between 30 and 32 fps. Frames size is between 288×216 and 320×240. There is no constraints on signers clothes. We tuned our system parameters on S_1, S_2, and S_3 video sequences, and we used S_4 sequence for the evaluation. We build ground-truth data for these four videos by manually drawing a bounding box G on the dominant hand (the object to track) in all frames. From these drawings, we get for each frame, G_p the ground truth position of the hand and G_s its area. Our evaluation criteria are based on two measures: an error measure $\bar{\epsilon}$ (equation (5)) and the Jaccard index which is a ratio $\bar{\varrho}$ indicating the degree of overlap between the filter estimation $\hat{X}$ and the ground truth G (equation (6)). $\bar{\epsilon}$ measures T position tracking accuracy and $\bar{\varrho}$ measures T region tracking accuracy. $|S|$ stands for the number of frames in a sequence S.

$$\bar{\epsilon} = \frac{1}{|S|} \sum_{t=1}^{|S|} ||\hat{p}_t - G_{p,t}|| \tag{5}$$

$$\bar{\varrho} = \frac{1}{|S|} \sum_{t=1}^{|S|} \frac{\hat{X}_t \cap G_t}{\hat{X}_t \cup G_t} \tag{6}$$

4.2   Results

Table 2 shows the results on the same S_4 video according to $\bar{\epsilon}$ and $\bar{\varrho}$ measures. PF $\bar{\varrho}$ value is too small because the filter is totally distracted by the face and sometimes attracted by the hand when it passes closely. However, a clear progress is noticed between PF and VPF. This progress proves the contribution of our reference model. Table 2 shows also the contribution of our complete system 3VPF, particle filter with optical flow penalisation. Clearly, it improves tracking performance. Moreover, figure 2 shows that the integration of velocity and acceleration

Table 2. Filter estimation position average error ($\bar{\epsilon}$) and matching average ratio ($\bar{\varrho}$) for S_4:1310 frames

	PF	VPF	2VPF	3VPF
$\bar{\epsilon}$	54.28	31.82	29.23	21.22
$\bar{\varrho}$	0.004	0.279	0.315	0.369

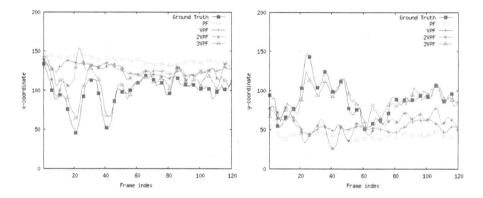

Fig. 2. x-coordinates and y-coordinates of the filter estimation along 120 frames of S_4 (for the sake of clarity) for our four systems

within 2VPF and 3VPF systems enables the filter to follow fast and random variations of T motion compared with classic PF and VPF which seems to generate monotonous motion. Figure 2 shows also that our 3VPF system has the ability to follow even acute motions of the hand. In fact, optical flow prohibits particles from moving on motionless zones and adjust in some way their orientation. Then particles are further concentrated on moving objects. Thus, with adequate observation model and reference model, particles track the right target.

5   Conclusion

We presented in this paper a hand tracking method based on a modified condensation algorithm and optical flow penalisation. The experiments done on an annotated database show the performance of our method compared to classic particle filter schemes. Nevertheless, we still have to improve our method so that it can handle multiple object tracking and occluded object.

References

1. Bhandarkar, S.M., Luo, X.: Integrated detection and tracking of multiple faces using particle filtering and optical flow-based elastic matching. CVIU 113(6), 708–725 (2009)

2. Bradski, G.R.: Computer Vision Face Tracking For Use in a Perceptual User Interface. Intel Technology Journal Q2 (1998)
3. Gordon, N.J., Salmond, D.J., Smith, A.F.M.: Novel approach to nonlinear/nongaussian bayesian state estimation. IEE Proceedings F Radar and Signal Processing 140(2), 107–113 (1993)
4. Isard, M., Blake, A.: Condensation - conditional density propagation for visual tracking. Int. J. Comput Vison 29, 5–28 (1998)
5. Klein, J., Lecomte, C., Miche, P.: Preceding car tracking using belief functions and a particle filter. In: IEEE ICPR - International Conference on Pattern Recognition, pp. 1–4 (2008)
6. Lu, W.-L., Okuma, K., Little, J.J.: Tracking and recognizing actions of multiple hockey players using the boosted particle filter. Image Vision Comput. 27(1-2), 189–205 (2009)
7. Lucas, B.D., Kanade, T.: An iterative image registration technique with an application to stereo vision. In: Int. Joint Conf. Artif. Intel., IJCAI 1981, vol. 2, pp. 674–679. Morgan Kaufmann Publishers Inc., San Francisco (1981)
8. Neidle, C., Sclaroff, S., Athitsos, V.: Signstream: A tool for linguistic and computer vision research on visual-gestural language data. Behav. Res. Meth. Ins. C 33(3), 311–320 (2001)
9. Perez, P., Vermaak, J., Blake, A.: Data fusion for visual tracking with particles. Proceedings of the IEEE, 495–513 (2004)
10. Ristic, B., Arulampalam, S., Gordon, N.: Beyond the Kalman Filter: Particle Filters for Tracking Applications. Artech House (2004)
11. Shan, C., Tan, T., Wei, Y.: Real-time hand tracking using a mean shift embedded particle filter. PR 40(7), 1958–1970 (2007)
12. Sigal, L., Sclaroff, S., Athitsos, V.: Skin color-based video segmentation under time-varying illumination. PAMI 26, 862–877 (2003)
13. Stokoe, W.C.: Sign language structure: An outline of the visual communication systems of the american deaf. Journal of Deaf Studies and Deaf Education 10(1) (2005)
14. Viola, P., Jones, M.J.: Robust Real-Time face detection. Int. J. Comput Vison 57(2), 137–154 (2004)
15. Yang, S., Ge, W., Cheng, Z.: Detecting and tracking moving targets on omnidirectional vision. Transactions of Tianjin University 15(1), 13–18 (2009)
16. Yao, A., Uebersax, D., Gall, J., Van Gool, L.: Tracking People in Broadcast Sports. In: Goesele, M., Roth, S., Kuijper, A., Schiele, B., Schindler, K. (eds.) DAGM 2010. LNCS, vol. 6376, pp. 151–161. Springer, Heidelberg (2010)

Objects Detection and Tracking
in Highly Congested Traffic
Using Compressed Video Sequences

Marcin Bernaś

Faculty of Transport, Silesian University of Technology
Krasińskiego 8, 40-019 Katowice, Poland
marcin.bernas@polsl.pl

Abstract. The paper presents a model to detect and track vehicles in highly congested traffic using low quality (usually compressed) video sequences. Robustness of the model is provided by applying a data fusion for various detection and tracking algorithms. The surveys to find reliable detection algorithms were performed. Basing on the experiments, the model calibration and results were presented. The proposed model provides data, which can be used by traffic engineers in various microscopic traffic simulations.

1 Introduction

Acquiring data for accurate road traffic control or surveillance is a very complex issue. In case of big cities, where ITS systems are implemented, the video detection is a major source of information about the traffic. However, data provided by these systems are not detailed enough and inaccurate to be used in most traffic microscopic simulation models. There can be found several reasons for this state. The traffic cameras are not present at every intersection. Moreover, cameras are installed above selected traffic lanes or some intersection inlets or outlets. Additionally, temporary road closures, which can modify traffic flows are not supported by changes in ITS monitoring infrastructure. Therefore, particular research activities have to be made using temporary camera stations, which are placed on high spots like bridges or nearby buildings.

The paper proposes a video-detection model customized to fulfill following requirements: the model doesn't have to work in real-time, if used for long-term statistical analysis. However, while used for traffic management, real-time processing feature is an essential one. Moreover, calibration process should be semi-automatic (useful to traffic engineers). What is more, input data is a low quality compressed sequence from camera located at non-optimal angles. Additionally, the algorithm should not only detect the presence of vehicles, but also track their movements. Section 2 presents related works concerning the vehicle tracking in congested traffic. Section 3 provides the method definition, which is followed by calibration description and simulations results in Section 4. Finally, Section 5 provides summary and further development guidelines.

L. Bolc et al. (Eds.): ICCVG 2012, LNCS 7594, pp. 296–303, 2012.

2   Related Works

Moving objects, like vehicles, can be detected by their shapes, appearances and actions [1,10]. The most common and developed practice in object tracking is to identify the object first. This task can be achieved by finding the object representation in a separate frame [6,16]. The object can be represented as a set of points, set of geometric figures or a defined silhouette.

To track the features several methods have been proposed: commonly used classical and extended Kalman filter [3,4] as well as the particle filter [5]. Kalman filter are used for linear systems with Gaussian noise, while nonlinear one with non-Gaussian noise distribution, are handled by the extended Kalman filter or the particle filter. The classical particle filters are characterised by high computational complexity and are inadequate for real-time tracking, unless using hardware solutions. There are many particle filter modifications, which are trying to solve the computing complexity issue [7,8].

Additionally, several algorithms was proposed, which are using prior knowledge and moment invariants [9,11]. The Hidden Markov Model (HMM) or selected AI models are also used to learn the object patterns [13,14]. While processing compressed video sequences (MPEG stream) [12], the extraction of features and estimation of motion vector is more difficult, due to blurred edges and corners in the image. The proposed method estimates vehicle motion and its positions based on spatial and temporal changes between separate frames in accordance to selected microscopic traffic model.

3   Model of Object Detection and Tracking

A first step was a pre-selection of detection and tracking algorithms, which could be applied in the proposed model. Based on state of the art analysis [1,2,3] several algorithms were selected for further research. The proposed model, presented in Fig. 1, was divided into four functional blocks.

In a first block data acquisition process is performed. The camera used to verify the model was a standard portable video camera(640x480,20fps) with hardware mpeg2 and mpeg4 compression.

To evaluate fundamental parameters of the traffic flow, the video record have to be several days or even weeks long. Uncompressed data of that length, even in low quality, occupies hundreds of terabytes of the data space per single intersection. In contrast, compressed videos lack precise details and make object tracking more difficult. To reduce the data size the frame rate is lowered in case of congested city traffic.

A second block of the model is used to transform perspective of a picture to an orthogonal view, narrowing it to the detection window at the same time. Additionally, background subtraction is performed. A third block, based on the transformed picture, detects characteristic features of moving objects. Three methods are used to increase the robustness: edges, segments and optic flow detection with and without background subtraction. Finally, detected features are verified using implemented cellular automata creating the microscopic traffic description.

The dash-dot line represents optional blocks in the method, which can be turned off to decrease computational complexity.

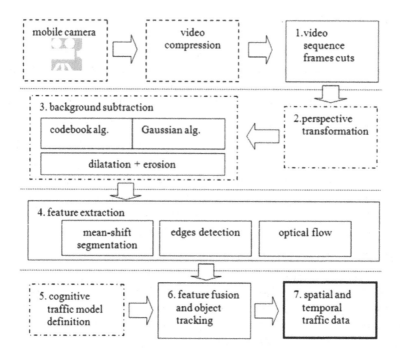

Fig. 1. Object tracking functional block definition

3.1 Data Verification

To transform image data into a format appropriate for microscopic traffic models data unification was proposed. Using Nagel-Schreckenberg cellular automata model as entry point [15] the matrix $P(t)$ was proposed. The matrix contains cells p_i representing current vehicle state vector at time t. Matrix elements represent cell position s_i and are described by velocity $v_i = (v_x, v_y)$ and additionally by segment description from separate classifiers. The vehicle movement follows the traffic rules simulated by the cellular model:

$$v_i(t) = min\{v_i(t-1)+1, g_i(t), vmax\}, \tag{1}$$

$$g_i(t) = x_j(t) - x_i(t) - 1, \xi < p \text{ then } v_i(t) = min\{0, v_i(t) - 1\}, \tag{2}$$

where: i - no of vehicle in t time step, z - probability threshold (usually set to 0,19), j - no of vehicle in front of vehicle at i-th position, j is selected basing on evaluated direction from previous frames and velocity, $s_i(t) = (x_i^c, y_i^c)$ - no of cell occupied by vehicle i at time step t, ξ - statistical variable with uniform distribution (values within range [0, 1]). Vector operation are performed for x and y axis separately.

The model was enhanced to manage various road traffic conditions with average speed of 90-130km/h and urban traffic with uncongested speed equal to 50km/h. If a vehicle state change is in contradiction with the cellular model, change is discarded. To calculate the minimal frame rate, the maximal displacement tracked by algorithm must be defined. The required number of frames per second is defined from the velocity and area per pixel rate in frame image $I(t)$ using following equation:

$$framerate = \frac{(1 + d_v)v_{max} * min(\frac{max(x_i)}{a_w}, \frac{max(y_j)}{a_l})}{min(d_s)} \tag{3}$$

where: v_{max} - maximal allowed vehicle speed, a_w, a_l - area width and length, x_i, y_j - analysed picture $I(t)$ pixels and d_s - maximal pixel distance tracked by separate detector and d_v-tolerance rate. The frame rate value are defined in the calibration process. The cell size in pixels is defined based on vehicle template or as equivalent of 6.5m on processed image.

3.2 Scene Transformation and Background Subtraction

To transform the perspective to the orthogonal cast, corners of the tracked area are defined, using four points: (x_i, y_i), $i = 1..4$. The points, organised in clockwise order, are inputs for a transformation matrix. The matrix is defined according to the equation [2]:

$$\begin{bmatrix} t_i x_i' \\ t_i y_i \\ t_i \end{bmatrix} = \begin{bmatrix} M_{11} & M_{12} & M_{13} \\ M_{21} & M_{22} & M_{23} \\ M_{31} & M_{32} & M_{33} \end{bmatrix} \begin{bmatrix} x_i \\ y_i \\ 1 \end{bmatrix} \tag{4}$$

Using equation 5 the M matrix is estimated and then it is used to perform perspective transformation:

$$I'(x_i, y_i) = (\frac{M_{11}x_i + M_{12}y_i + M_{13}}{M_{31}x_i + M_{32}y_i + M_{33}}, \frac{M_{21}x_i + M_{22}y_i + M_{23}}{M_{31}x_i + M_{32}y_i + M_{33}}) \tag{5}$$

Transformation matrix is evaluated once, while each frame is transformed separately. The operation narrows the area of a frame to the analysed fragment and transform it to the orthogonal view.

The simplification of segmentation process was achieved using background subtraction. Classical averaging over long period of time in compressed video sequences generates additional noise, therefore Gaussian background subtraction and Codebook subtraction method was used [9]. The algorithms parameters are presented in table 1.

Table 1. Background subtraction algorithm comparison

Gaussian transformation	Gaussian transformation
- subtraction from second frame	- long learning time: 200-2000 frames
- long learning time: 200-2000 frames	- minimal registered changes
	- maximal registered changes
	- maximal codebook length
	- number of colour channels: 1..3

The preliminary background subtraction experiments showed that received segments were rigid and inconsistent, therefore the dilatation and erosion procedure was implemented. The number of dilatation and then erosion operations is defined by dil parameter - by default equals 2.

3.3 Features Extraction and Object Tracking

To create robust model three distinct detection algorithms (F) were implemented. To detect segments colour mean-shift segmentation was used [5]. To evaluate the highly compressed sequences the following parameters have to be defined: spatial and colour radius and maximal pyramid segmentation level. The segments are described by their moments.

To detect point features the Haar edge detector was used [7]. In this case the window size, maximal number of features and detection distance between separate features are used. Features are tracked within defined input areas or within detection window. To decrease the computing complexity, a number of added features in each frame is limited and previously detected features are removed within output areas. Additionally, the feature removal mechanism was added. The features are removed when they don't change position within defined time period (lost a tracked object). The feature and segment detection can be performed with or without background subtraction. Finally, the Lucas-Kanade optical flow algorithm were used to track detected objects. A third algorithm uses Farneback optical flow. The algorithm defines a regular mesh and detects displacements within it. Tracked object within image I is cast to the cellular cells by the tracking and detection algorithms:

$$F(I'(t), I'(t-1)) \Rightarrow P'(t) \tag{6}$$

To merge data from separate detection algorithms the cellular model was used. It divides tracked area into cells, according to the size of P' matrixes. Each P' matrix cell contains the vehicle position, its speed and class. If only one of the classifiers are used, the P' matrix is treated as an output (P) matrix. If more than one classifier is used, weighted result is defined according to its weights (w_k):

$$P = \sum_k P'_k w_k \tag{7}$$

The weights w_k can be defined empirically or based on training set, reducing detection error rate.

4 Model Calibration and Experiments

The calibration process sets the parameters of detection algorithms and its weights (w_k). The calibration is performed in six simple steps presented in fig. 2.

First step consists of the evaluation of minimal frame rate. For calculated examples of congested traffic the area a_w, a_l differed from 100m to 1000m. The frame resolution was from 240x170 to 720x520. Basing on equation 1 and the tolerance rate d_v=20% and used methods sensitivity d_s=20, frame rate for a city traffic is equal 6 fps and 14 fps for highway traffic. Next step requires frame transformation. For intersections, only the box junction area is selected (fig. 2b_1), in case of highway (fig. 2b_2) the lanes are chosen. Additionally, input and output areas can be selected as well as the vehicle templates. However, if no templates are defined, the standard vehicle size is used for tracking.

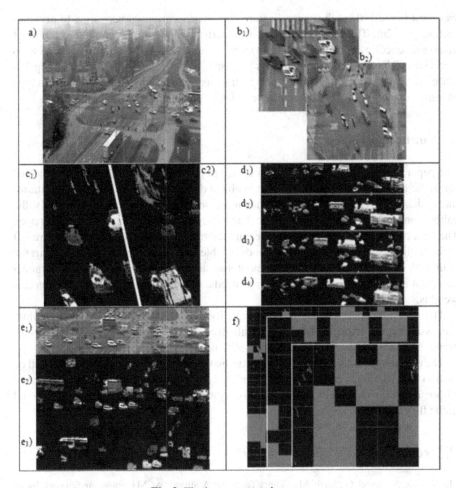

Fig. 2. The image processing steps

The occlusions are managed using moments - mass centres, width and height. The background subtraction is used: codebook subtraction (fig. $2c_1$) with frame learning rate: 2000 for high congested traffic, and Gaussian subtraction (fig. $2c_2$) with learning rate -0,5 for low congested intersections. To improve subtraction, the dilatation and erosion

Table 2. Object detection and tracking summary

	Haar feature + LK optical flow	Farneback optical flow	Segmentation + Moments	Proposed model
LC detection rate	85%	91%	87%	95%
LC false detection rate	2%	3%	1%	2%
HC detection rate	63%	72%	65%	81%
HC false detection rate	3%	5%	3%	5%

was used (fig. 2d: 0,1,2..3 times). Feature classifiers, were used according to pervious section (fig. 2e). The finall calibration was performed using 40 5-minute samples of video sequences of high (*HC*) and low traffic volume (*LC*). The optimised parameters were: size of *P* matrix, detector weights (w_k), spatial and colour radius and tracking distance. Table 2 presents the results for a testing sequences, where user pre-defines type of traffic, detection fields and vehicles templates.

5 Summary

The paper presents the model for vehicle-like object detection and tracking dedicated for traffic engineers. Using several simple object detectors and optical flow algorithms, the model is able to detect objects from compressed video sequences. Additionally, the calibration was divided into two stages. The basic calibration is described in the paper. The final calibration, which consist selecting the traffic type and detection area, are left to the traffic engineer. Moreover, the model is able to detect objects in congested traffic with high accuracy thanks to the segment size analysis and optical flow. The model detection abilities can be adapted to one's needs, while changing the separate detector weights.

The detection rate depends on video quality, however the proposed model, while processing image sequence from commonly used camera (with hardware mpeg2 compression), is able to detect correctly up to 90% of vehicles.

The acquired data can be used to verify traffic microscopic models. The model will be used to obtain data for further reserch. Obtained data, together with data form vehicular ad-hoc networks (VANET) and localisation systems will allow to describe and model traffic flow more precisely.

References

1. Yilmaz, A., Javed, O., Shah, M.: Object Tracking: A Survey. ACM Computing Surveys 38(4), Article 13 (2006)
2. Jeyakar, J., Babu, V., Ramakrishnan, K.R.: Robust object tracking with background-weighted local kernels. Computer Vision and Image Understanding 112, 296–309 (2008)
3. Yun, X.P., Bachmann, E.R.: Design, Implementation, and Experimental Results of a Quaternion-Based Kalman Filter for Human Body Motion Tracking. IEEE Transactions on Robotics 22, 1216–1227 (2006)
4. Jwo, D.J., Wang, S.H.: Adaptive Fuzzy Strong Tracking Extended Kalman Filtering for GPS Navigation. IEEE Sensors Journal 7, 778–789 (2007)
5. Cho, J.U., Jin, S.H., Pham, X.D., Jeon, J.W., Byun, J.E., Kang, H.: A Real-Time Object Tracking System Using a Particle Filter. In: IEEE International Conference on Intelligent Robots and Systems, pp. 2822–2827. IEEE Press, Beijing (2006)
6. Pamula, W.: Determining Feature Points for Classification of Vehicles. In: Burduk, R., Kurzyński, M., Woźniak, M., Żołnierek, A. (eds.) Computer Recognition Systems 4. AISC, vol. 95, pp. 677–684. Springer, Heidelberg (2011)
7. Pamula, W.: Feature Extraction Using Reconfigurable Hardware. In: Bolc, L., Tadeusiewicz, R., Chmielewski, L.J., Wojciechowski, K. (eds.) ICCVG 2010, Part II. LNCS, vol. 6375, pp. 158–165. Springer, Heidelberg (2010)

8. Hesse, C.W., James, C.J.: The Fast ICA Algorithm with Spatial Constraints. IEEE Signal Processing Letters 12, 792–795 (2005)
9. Kyungnam, K., Harwood, D., Davis, L.: Real-time foreground-background segmentation using codebook model. Real-Time Imaging Journal 11(3) (2005)
10. Pan, J.Y., Hu, B., Zhang, J.Q.: Robust and Accurate Object Tracking under Various Types of Occlusions. IEEE Transaction on Circuits and Systems for Video Technology 18, 223–236 (2008)
11. Hyvarinene, A.: Fast and Robust Fixed-point Algorithms for Independent Component Analysis. IEEE Transactions on Neural Networks 10, 626–634 (1999)
12. Jayabalan, E., Krishnan, A.: Detection and Tracking of Moving Object in Compressed Videos. In: Das, V.V., Stephen, J., Chaba, Y. (eds.) CNC 2011. CCIS, vol. 142, pp. 39–43. Springer, Heidelberg (2011)
13. Chen, Y., Rui, Y.: Real Time Object Tracking in Video Sequences. In: Signals and Communication Technology, Part II, pp. 67–88 (2006)
14. Bajaj, P.R., Daigavane, M.B.: Vehicle Detection and Neural Network Application for Vehicle Classification. In: Proc. of Computational Intelligence and Communication Networks (CICN), pp. 758–762 (2011)
15. Placzek, B.: Fuzzy Cellular Model for On-Line Traffic Simulation. In: Wyrzykowski, R., Dongarra, J., Karczewski, K., Wasniewski, J. (eds.) PPAM 2009, Part II. LNCS, vol. 6068, pp. 553–560. Springer, Heidelberg (2010)
16. Płaczek, B.: A Real Time Vehicle Detection Algorithm for Vision-Based Sensors. In: Bolc, L., Tadeusiewicz, R., Chmielewski, L.J., Wojciechowski, K. (eds.) ICCVG 2010, Part II. LNCS, vol. 6375, pp. 211–218. Springer, Heidelberg (2010)

Syntactic Algorithm of Two-Dimensional Scene Analysis for Unmanned Flying Vehicles

Andrzej Bielecki[1], Tomasz Buratowski[2], and Piotr Śmigielski[3]

[1] Institute of Computer Science
Faculty of Mathematics and Computer Science
Jagiellonian University
Łojasiewicza 6, 30-348 Kraków, Poland
[2] Chair of Robotics and Mechatronics
Faculty of Mechanical Engineering and Robotics
AGH University of Science and Technology
Al. Mickiewicza 30, 30-059 Kraków, Poland
[3] Asseco Poland S.A.
Podwale 3, 31-118 Kraków, Poland
bielecki@ii.uj.edu.pl, tburatow@agh.edu.pl, smigielski.piotr@gmail.com

Abstract. In this paper the approach to on-line object recognition for autonomous flying agent is considered. The method is divided into two parts. First the algorithm for scene objects vectorization is introduced. As the second step of the overall method we present the rotation and scale invariant algorithm for vectorized object identification based on syntactic language.

Keywords: autonomous flying agents, vectorization, object recognition, syntactic languages.

1 Introduction

Vision systems play crucial role in various types of robots [9,10] and unmanned vehicles [1,2]. The autonomous flying robots (also referred to as autonomous flying agents) are the class of unmanned mobile robots that operate in the air. They are equipped with sensors that are used to collect information about surrounding environment [5,6]. Beside the need to collect mission-specific data such information enables the robot to find a collision-free path between obstacles. Another typical challenge for the mobile agents is to identify their location in space [2]. Such task is difficult as it has to be solved on-line [10]. During the robot flight it has to process information quickly to operate confidently in complex and sometimes changing environment. In this paper the algorithm of two-dimensional scene analysis is presented. The presented algorithm is the first step in creating a visual-based system for an autonomous flying agent system of scene analysis and understanding in the context of navigation possibilities. It should be stressed that the problem of the image understanding is far more general and abstractive than pattern recognition - see [11,12] in the context of medical images.

L. Bolc et al. (Eds.): ICCVG 2012, LNCS 7594, pp. 304–312, 2012.

2   Problem Formulation

Let us consider an autonomous flying robot equipped with the map which is a preprocessed satellite image of an urban environment. The robot has to be equipped with the camera pointed in the ground to be able to take the pictures of the surface that it flies above. The map that the robot carries presents the buildings extracted from the base satellite image (see Fig.1). The problem of preprocessing which, beside others, consists of object extraction from the image is out of the scope of this paper.

In order to find its location on the map the robot takes successive pictures of the ground below. Then it compares the extracted shape of the building from the picture and locate it in the bigger map. The example of the picture with one building is shown in Fig.2. The method of the objects recognition has to be rotation and scale invariant as the pictures of the ground are taken from different altitudes and various directions of the robot's flight. This problem belongs to the group of tasks consist in recognition and representing polynomial-type object by a robot sensory systems [4].

3   Syntactic Algorithm of an Object Vectorization and Recognition

In this section we present the algorithm based on syntactic methods for raster picture vectorization and object recognition. The tests were run with the use of similar maps to these shown above in Fig.1 and Fig.2. In the big map one building that is supposed to be similar to the one from small map is outlined. In real test data the building was not outlined. To perform the action of objects recognition the new representation of the picture has to be introduced. Every extracted building is turned into a vector representation of its shape.

3.1   Vectorization Algorithm

The vectorization algorithm works on prepared data based on the raster picture. It is a binary matrix in which zero represents the background pixels and value equal to one represents the pixels of the building. This algorithm searches through table until it finds first unmarked building. It processes the shape of the building, turning it into vector representation and marking its space by changing values 1 into other number to avoid running into it while searching again for the next building to be vectorized. It is worth mentioning that each unmarked point that is found while searching through the table is a corner of a building. The process of vectorization of a single building can be divided into following steps

Creating Complex Contour

In this step contour of a building is found and its representation in the form of short vectors is created. Beginning from the first point of the contour (corner

Fig. 1. Preprocessed satellite map with extracted buildings (white vertices)

Fig. 2. Preprocessed picture presenting the small area with only one building

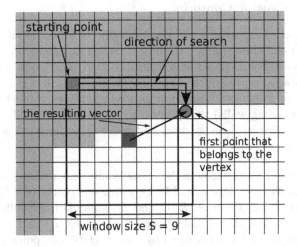

Fig. 3. Search around the window, starting from the point outside the building contour

of a building) the next point is found using the *window*. If starting point of the *window* lies outside the contour of a building the search of the border point is conducted clockwise (see Fig.3). In the other case counter-clockwise (see Fig.4). The search conducted in such manner leads to circling around the building contour clockwise. It is important for the object recognition algorithm to build the list of points in the same direction in all cases. The output of this step is the sequence of points which can be interpreted as a sequence of vectors located around the building contour (a point that is not the first or last in the sequence is the end of the one vector and the beginning of the next one).

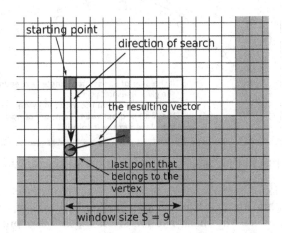

Fig. 4. Search around the window, starting from the point inside the building contour

Smoothing the Vector Contours

After obtaining the long sequence of points in the contour it is vital to simplify
that representation before running the object recognition algorithm. In this part
the new sequence of points based on sequence created in previous step is created.
The points in new list represent the corners of the building. To avoid the situation
in which there are corners with no point located exactly on it (that would result
in the effect of bending walls) the corners are not taken straight from the list of
points but calculated in the way described below. The final list is obtained in
the following two steps:

1. The algorithm iterates through the list of points and searches for those that
   deviate from the line determined by two previous points (see Fig.5). Let us
   have four following points A, B, C and D (point D is actually processed).
   Two angles are calculated. One given by vector (A, B) and point C (with
   apex in point B) and another given by vector (B, C) and point D (with apex
   in point C). If the sum of those angles exceeds the given threshold T the
   following three points are added to the new list (the sequence is important):
   B, q, D. Point B is the apex of the first angle and D is the end point of the
   second angle (B and D belong to two adjacent walls of the building). Point
   q which plays the role of a marker is added to detect the placement of the
   corner in the next step. The output of this step is the list having following
   form $(X_1, X_2, q, X_3, X_4, q, X_5, X_6, ..., X_{n-3}, X_{n-2}, q, X_{n-1}, X_n)$.

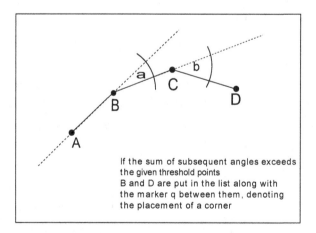

If the sum of subsequent angles exceeds
the given threshold points
B and D are put in the list along with
the marker q between them, denoting
the placement of a corner

Fig. 5. Checking the deviation of the successive points

2. The algorithm iterates through previously obtained list and searches for
   markers q. When the marker is found on the list two preceding and two
   following points are taken for further computations (for the example let
   it be X_1, X_2, X_3, X_4). The lines determined by the vectors (X_1, X_2) and
   (X_3, X_4) are determined. The crossing point C of that lines is taken as the

actual corner of the building. As a result we obtain the list which consists of the starting corner and the rest of the corners that replaces the markers $(X_1, C_2, C_3, ..., C_m)$, where m is the overall number of corners (and walls in the same time) in the building.

There is a special case in which a marker does not have four neighbour points but only one on left or right side. It can happen, when two or more corners are found very close to each other. In that case crossing point can not be calculated and one of the neighbours of marker is taken as the corner point (in tests it was

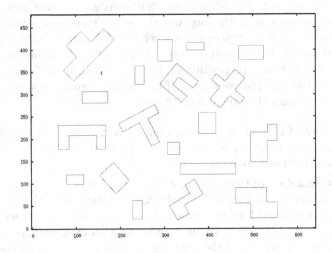

Fig. 6. Vectorized map

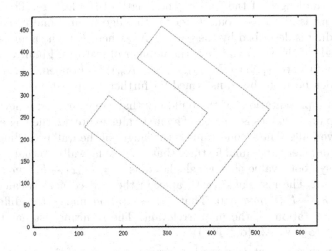

Fig. 7. Vectorized picture of one building

preceding one). The vectorization algorithm was run for the big map and the picture of single building. The results of the algorithm are presented in Fig.6 and Fig.7.

3.2   Object Recognition Algorithm

The aim of the object recognition algorithm is to find the building in the big map that is similar to the one in the small map. The input for this algorithm consists of two vectorized maps. One is the map presenting large area filled with buildings and the other has only one building, similar to one placed in the big map, but scaled and rotated. The algorithm transforms each vector representation of the buildings from both the big and the small map into a more suitable representation. The shape representation which is utilized by this algorithm is based on the notion of the nominal features [13]. After the transformation the algorithm takes each new representation of the building from the big map and compares it to the new representation of the building from the small map. The comparison is conducted in the following way:

1. The number of corners of both buildings is compared. If it is different the buildings are not the same. Process is stopped. If the number is the same the algorithm moves to another step.

2. The representation of the building which is the list of corners is turned into representation which uses angle and length of the walls. This can be considered as a nominal feature representation. To change the corner representation into angle (nominal feature) representation each wall (pair of points determining the vector) of the building is taken and its length and angle is calculated. The nominal feature is described directly by the angle which is calculated with a given accuracy and the number of features is obtained by dividing the length of the wall by the length of the feature. The length of the feature is given as a parameter for the algorithm. Finally each wall of the building is described by the pair (F, N), where F is the nominal feature sign (angle of the wall) and N is the number of features. Finally, as a result the list of form $((F_1, N_1), (F_2, N_2), ..., (F_m, N_m))$ is obtained. This is the first form which needs to be transformed for further computations.

3. For both representations of the buildings that are compared a new list containing pairs of values is created. The first value expresses the angle between successive walls. The second value is the length of the wall preceding the corner (the number of nominal features that creates the wall). Actually the angle has the symbolic value as it is calculated as $\alpha_i = (F_{i+1} - F_i) \bmod 360$; $i \in 1, ..., m - 1$. The last angle (with apex in the first corner) is calculated as $\alpha_m = (F_1 - F_m) \bmod 360$. That representation makes the difference in buildings rotation on the map irrelevant. The resulting list has the form: $((\alpha_1, N_1), (\alpha_2, N_2), ..., (\alpha_m, N_m))$.

4. Having such representation one list (representing one of the compared buildings) is doubled. Then the substring similar to the sequence of nominal

features of the second building is searched in the doubled list (see Fig.8). To make this algorithm less prone to inaccuracies of the process parsing the raw pictures and building the vector representation the matching values do not have to be exactly equal. Instead, they are compared with a given threshold ($\Delta\alpha$). Formally the compared angles are matching if $\left| \alpha_i^1 - \alpha_j^2 \right| < \Delta\alpha$, where α_i^1 is the angle from the first list and α_j^2 is the angle from the second list. If the overall match between angles is found the quotients of matching wall lengths is calculated. If all the quotients are similar (the standard deviation is below the given threshold) the buildings are treated as similar and the algorithm quits. If the quotients differ significantly (the lengths of the paired walls are different with respect to the scale) the search for the matching substring is continued. The maximum number of checks is equal to m.

Representation with nominal features

angle between successive walls (expressed in degrees)

number of nominal features which expresses the length the wall

[[45, 12], [315, 12], [225, 3], [135, 8], [225, 4], [315, 8], [225, 3], [135, 12]]

[[45, 17], [315, 40], [45, 21], [135, 40], [45, 18], [315, 61], [225, 57], [135, 61]]

Representation describing the angles
between following walls
(example of match found between two patterns)

[[270, 12] [270, 12] [270, 3] [90, 8] [90, 4] [270, 8] [270, 3] [270, 12]|[270, 12] [270, 12] [270, 3] [90, 8] [90, 4] [270, 8] [270, 3] [270, 12]]

[[270, 17] [270, 40] [270 21] [270, 40] [270, 18] [270, 61] [270, 57] [270, 61]]

Fig. 8. Representaions used in object recognition

4 Concluding Remarks

The results of the vectorization algorithm show its ability to locate accurately and circle round the object in the picture. The representation requires the minimum amount of memory as it consists only of buildings corners locations. The described method shows the ability to find the match between scaled and rotated objects. Besides that, it can find similarity between not exactly the same buildings as the quotients of wall lengths can vary to the given threshold. Both algorithms are fast and memory efficient. That is important because they are meant to be used in on-line processing of the pictures collected by the autonomous flying agent. The described results are the first step in creating a visual-based system for a flying agent localization based on syntactic scene analysis. It should be mentioned that syntactic methods for scene analysis based on graph approach have been considered [3] also in the context of aid them by probabilistic [7,8] and fuzzy [1] methods. Parallel parsing has been studied as well [1].

References

1. Bielecka, M., Skomorowski, M., Bielecki, A.: Fuzzy syntactic approach to pattern recognition and scene analysis. In: Proceedings of the 4th International Conference on Informatics in Control, Automatics and Robotics ICINCO 2007, ICSO Intelligent Control Systems and Optimization, Robotics and Automation, vol. 1, pp. 29–35 (2007)
2. Filliat, D., Mayer, J.A.: Map-based navigation in mobile robots. A review of localization strategies. Journal of Cognitive Systems Research 4, 243–283 (2003)
3. Flasiński, M.: On the parsing of deterministic graph languages for syntactic pattern recognition. Pattern Recognition 26, 1–16 (1993)
4. Katsev, M., Yershova, A., Tovar, B., Ghrist, R., LaValle, S.M.: Mapping and pursuit-evasion strategies for a simple wall-following robot. IEEE Transactions on Robotics 27, 113–128 (2011)
5. Muratet, L., Doncieux, S., Briere, Y., Meyer, J.A.: A contribution to vision-based autonomous helicopter flight in urban environments. Robotics and Autonomous Systems 50, 195–229 (2005)
6. Sinopoli, B., Micheli, M., Donato, G., Koo, T.J.: Vision based navigation for an unmanned aerial vehicle. In: Proceedings of the International Conference on Robotics and Automation ICRA, vol. 2, pp. 1757–1764 (2001)
7. Skomorowski, M.: Use of random graph parsing for scene labeling by probabilistic relaxation. Pattern Recognition Letters 20, 949–956 (1999)
8. Skomorowski, M.: Syntactic recognition of syntactic patterns by means of random graph parsing. Pattern Recognition Letters 28, 572–581 (2006)
9. Tadeusiewicz, R.: Vision Systems of Industrial Robots. WNT, Warszawa (1992)
10. Tadeusiewicz, R.: A visual navigation system for a mobile robot with limited computational requirements. Problemy Eksploatacji 4, 205–218 (2008)
11. Tadeusiewicz, R.: Medical Image Understanding Technology. Springer, Heidelberg (2004)
12. Tadeusiewicz, R.: Automatic image understanding - a new paradigm for intelligent medical image analysis. Bio-Algorithms and Med-Systems 2(3), 3–9 (2006)
13. Tadeusiewicz, R., Flasiński, M.: Pattern Recognition. Polish Scientific Publishers PWN, Warsaw (1991)

Hough Transform for Opaque Circles Measured from Outside and Fuzzy Voting For and Against

Leszek J. Chmielewski and Marcin Bator

Warsaw University of Life Sciences (SGGW),
Faculty of Applied Informatics and Mathematics
{leszek_chmielewski,marcin_bator}@sggw.pl
http://wzim.sggw.pl

Abstract. Geometrical limitations on the voting process in the classical Hough transform resulting from that the detected objects are opaque to the applied means of measurement are considered. It is assumed that the measurements are made from one point, like in LIDAR scanning. The detected object is a circle and the two point elementary voting set forming its chord is considered. The first type of conditions are those which can be used during the accumulation process. The *side condition* says that the circle lies at the opposite side of the chord than the laser source. The *magnitude condition* requires that points in the elementary set must not be occluded with respect to the source by any circle hypothesised in voting. The second type of conditions can be checked after after the detection. They require that points are neither inside the object not in its shadow. Departures from this rule are admitted, so fuzzy voting between positive and negative evidence for the object is considered.

Keywords: Hough transform, opaque circles, negative evidence, LIDAR.

1 Introduction

Hough transform (HT) is one of the oldest methods of robust detection of objects [2]. Although a lot has been said on occlusions in images (e.g. [6]), it seems that little or no attention has been paid to the geometrical limitations on the evidence accumulation process coming from that the detected object can be opaque to the means which forms the measuring points. Special cases are radar and LIDAR detectors. Without losing generality, let us concentrate on LIDAR (LIght Detection And Ranging) measurements. One of the applications of LIDAR are measurements of forest and trees being the subject of intensive investigations (cf. [5]). Similar measurements are made for example on architectural objects.

The result of LIDAR measurements is a cloud of points being a sparse image in which direct differentiation is impossible. Therefore, from the many versions of HT we chose that with the elementary voting set formed by two points (see e.g. [4], Section 5.4.5.2).

In this paper our target is to present the conditions which constitute a theoretical result rather than their influence on the quality of specific measurements belonging to some chosen class. However, selected real-world results will be shown to exemplify the considerations.

L. Bolc et al. (Eds.): ICCVG 2012, LNCS 7594, pp. 313–320, 2012.

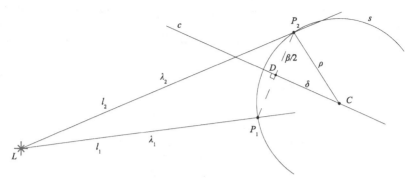

Fig. 1. Geometry for the circle detection with the Hough transform with a pair of points as an elementary set. See text.

2 Basic Geometry

The points will be denoted by uppercase Roman letters; lines, line segments, circles and arcs – by lowercase Roman letters, and distances – by Greek letters.

The laser light source or the viewpoint is L, as shown in Fig. 1. To form one vote two measuring points are taken into account: P_1 and P_2, where P_2 is the farther from the source L. A point P_j has its intensity I_j. As the intensity of the pair to be used in the accumulation the intensity of the weaker point will be taken. Let us call $\overline{P_1P_2}$ the base. The lines connecting the source with the measuring points are l_1 and l_2, and the respective distances are λ_1 and λ_2. The distance between points is β (base distance). The circles for which these two points can vote have to pass through them, so their centres must lie on c which is the midperpendicular of $\overline{P_1P_2}$. Let D be the middle of $\overline{P_1P_2}$.

In Fig. 1 a possible circle s is shown with the centre C lying at the distance δ from D, and with radius ρ. Usually in HT a range of possible radii is assumed, $\rho \in [\rho_{m'}, \rho_x]$. Subscripts m' and x denote minimum and maximum, respectively. As the locus of possible circle centres the points on c at the distance $\delta \in [\delta_{m'}, \delta_x]$ to D should be considered:

$$\delta_{m'}^2 + (\beta/2)^2 = \rho_{m'}^2 , \quad \delta_x^2 + (\beta/2)^2 = \rho_x^2 . \tag{1}$$

In the classical HT this is basically all what is done to limit the range of locations of centres on the line c. Now we shall pass on to the new conditions which result from that the circular object is opaque and the measurement points are all visible from the source of measuring rays.

3 Conditions

The conditions which follow from the geometry of the problem can be divided into two types. The first type are those conditions which can be checked using only the knowledge on the viewpoint and the currently considered measuring points. These conditions can be checked during the accumulation. They influence

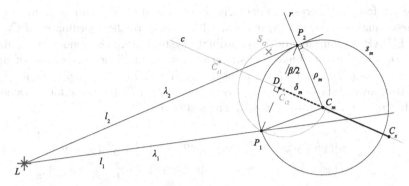

Fig. 2. Geometry for conditions checked during accumulation. Minimum possible circle $s_m(C_m, \rho_m)$ (black) and impossible circle s_{i2} (grey). See text.

the accumulator contents and in this way they improve the quality of detection results during the process of their formation. The second type are the conditions for which it is necessary to have the information on the detected circles and on some or all the measuring points. These conditions can be used to check the consistence and possibly to correct the results after they have been received.

3.1 During the Accumulation

Condition of side. We shall use some more notations shown in Fig. 2.

The first, basic observation is that the circle must be behind rather than in front of the base $\overline{P_1 P_2}$ with respect to the source L:

$$\overrightarrow{LD} \circ \overrightarrow{DC} > 0 . \tag{2}$$

The centre C_{i1} is on the wrong side of the base and hence it is impossible. To visualise this condition the part of c at the left from D has been marked grey.

This simple observation eliminates the false detection of concave objects as circles (see Fig. 4a1-b2, Section 4).

Condition of magnitude. It can be seen in Fig. 2 that the circle s_{i2} which satisfies the condition of shades the point P_2 from the light source L. The circle segment which protrudes above l_2 marked with a grey slanted cross is impossible, so the whole circle is impossible due to that it is too small. There exists a minimum radius ρ_m for which the shading phenomenon does not take place. The minimum circle $s_m(C_m, \rho_m)$ is tangent to l_2 going from L to the farther measuring point P_2, so r passing through P_2 and C_m is normal to l_2. Note that the location of C_m and the lengths ρ_m, δ_m are different from those marked with m' in (1). Finally, the more restrictive values should be taken. The locus of impossible circle centres at the right-hand side of D, has been marked with a thick broken line.

Now, the equations are

$$2\,\overrightarrow{P_1 D} = \overrightarrow{P_1 P_2} , \quad \overrightarrow{LP_2} \circ \overrightarrow{P_2 C_m} = 0 , \quad \overrightarrow{P_1 P_2} \circ \overrightarrow{DC_m} = 0 . \tag{3}$$

There are four unknowns: the coordinates of D and C_m. D can be found from the first equation. The set (3) is linear with respect to the coordinates of C_m.

In LIDAR measurements the coordinate system origin is frequently located in L. Denote the coordinates x and y of any point T or projections of any distance τ as x_T, y_T and x_τ, y_τ, respectively. Then, $x_{\lambda_j} = x_{P_j}$, $y_{\lambda_j} = y_{P_j}$, $j = 1, 2$. Also, always $x_\beta = x_{P_2} - x_{P_1}$, $x_D = (x_{P_2} + x_{P_1})/2$, the same for y. Denote plainly $x_{P_j} = x_j$, $y_{P_j} = y_j$, $j = 1, 2$. The solution is

$$T = x_2 y_1 - y_2 x_1 ,$$
$$T_{x_{C_m}} = [(x_2^2 + y_2^2) - (x_1^2 + y_1^2)] \, y_2/2 \;-\; (x_2^2 + y_2^2)(y_2 - y_1) , \qquad (4)$$
$$T_{y_{C_m}} = (x_2^2 + y_2^2)(x_2 - x_1) \;-\; [(x_2^2 + y_2^2) - (x_1^2 + y_1^2)] \, x_2/2 .$$

$$x_{C_m} = T_{x_{C_m}}/T , \quad y_{C_m} = T_{y_{C_m}}/T . \qquad (5)$$

The main determinant T is not zero as long as P_1 does not belong to l_2, which is compatible with the visibility condition. Now it is easy to find the minimum distance $\delta_m = |\overrightarrow{DC_m}|$ and radius $\rho_m = |\overrightarrow{P_2 C_m}|$.

The locus of possible circle centres is marked in Fig. 2 with a thick black line from C_m just found to C_x at the distance δ_x from D in the direction out from L, found as previously from (1).

An example of a positive influence of the condition of magnitude on the detection result can be seen in Fig. 4a and c in Section 4.

Both conditions are relatively simple to calculate and their complexity is linear with respect to the calculations routinely made in the Hough transform.

3.2 After the Detection

The measurement points should be on the surface S of the detected object. They can also be outside, but neither inside the object nor in its shadow, with respect to L. The points on the surface which gave rise to a maximum in the Hough accumulator pertaining to the object constitute the positive evidence for its existence E_+. The points inside and in the shadow constitute negative evidence E_-. Both $E. \leq 0$. Due to practical reasons some negative evidence can be admitted as long as it is much smaller than the positive one. What this means should be defined according to the domain at hand. A reasonable simple condition could be linear:

$$\kappa E_+ > E_- , \quad \kappa \in (0, 1) . \qquad (6)$$

If a point can be inside the object to some extent, then it should be acceptable for it to be in the shadow to the corresponding extent. A definition of a fuzzy membership function μ_j for evidence carried by a single point j is necessary. It can be assumed that any of the evidences E^+, E^- is an algebraic sum of evidences of points that constitute it, weighted by their intensities:

$$E^\pm = \sum_j I_j \, \mu_{P_j^\pm} , \quad \mu_j \in [0, 1] . \qquad (7)$$

It is reasonable to assign the membership 1 to any point which constituted a maximum corresponding to the object in the Hough accumulator. To find such points it may be necessary to use the HT with reverse addressing.

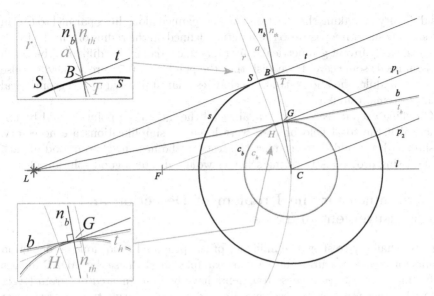

Fig. 3. Geometry for the conditions to be checked after the detection. Grey circle c_H has half radius of the object surface circle s. Its tangent passing through L and normal to tangent passing through C drawn in grey. Objects related to the bisector b of angle CLB and its tangent circle c_b marked in black. Details in the lower part of the image, symmetrical around l, are omitted. See text.

Now let us consider the membership function for the points of negative evidence P_j^-. Let us span the membership function along the radius, from the surface s of the object down to its centre C, so that it is zero at s and one in C (Fig. 3). Assume we wish this function to be liberal towards negative evidence so assign it the value 0.5 at half radius. An example of such a function is

$$\mu(P) = \frac{1}{2}\left(\cos\frac{\pi|\overline{CP}|}{|\overline{CS}|} + 1\right). \tag{8}$$

This function will hold in the frontal part of the circle, that is, in front of r (and downward, symmetrically). It can be extended to the shadow part in two ways. The first way is to draw lines parallel to the tangent t, first p_1 tangent to circle c_h (with half radius) and second p_2 passing through C. The function (8) can be spanned between t and p_2 with p_1 in the middle, forming a continuation to the right of r of the frontal part of s with c_h in the middle. So, the admissible zone for shadowed points has constant width and is parallel to the tangent t. The second way is related to a postulate that the width of the admissible zone should grow together with the distance from L. A good idea would be to construct it around the bisector b of $\angle CLB$. However, B is tangent to a circle c_b different from c_h. This can be seen by investigating the details of Fig. 3: b divides $\angle CLB$ into halves and it is tangent to c_b, while c_h divides $\overline{CB}$ into halves and is tangent to t_h. T is near but never equal to B (they both lie on arc a). What links c_h to b is a short fragment of p_1 from r to n_b. It is tangent to c_b but forms an angle with b, so the link is only C^0 smooth. Hence, there is a difficulty in making the function like (8) spanned along lines parallel to CB in the shadow smoothly pass into the function defined on the radius of s in the front. One can easily invent geometrical constructs to overcome this difficulty, but each of them needs some care. If we wish that the point $\mu = 0.5$ were somewhere else than the middle, the above structure changes quantitatively but the geometrical relations remain similar.

Checking each detected circle against all the measuring points would be impractical if the total field of view were large, so simplifications are necessary. A simple idea would be to restrict the tests to the near neighbourhood of each circle. Using probabilistic voting schemes would also be a good solution [3].

4   Examples for the Problem of Detection and Measurement of Trees

Here we shall try to show the influence of the proposed conditions on detection results for actual measurements. As the examples we shall use the LIDAR images of fragments of a forest. These fragments have been segmented out from larger data with the intention to receive a cross-section of a single tree at the breast height in one image, as described in our previous work [1]. However, due to small diameters of some trees and the presence of clutter (leaves and thin branches), some images contain multiple tree trunks. The classic HT can fail to find only the trunks. The conditions introduced above improve some of the erroneous results.

Conditions checked during accumulation. The functioning of these conditions is shown in Fig. 4. The contents of the accumulator shown in image $b1$ is irrational. Moreover, there is a local maximum pertaining to the lower right object, which is concave. The global result $a2$ is still erroneous, but the maximum coming from the concave object is now cancelled. The condition of side makes the accumulator contents more realistic for the case. After applying the magnitude condition a large number of false votes are dismissed so the largest maximum in image $b3$ and the result in image $a3$ are correct.

The parameters used in the accumulation process were: 500 pix/m, minimum circle radius 0, maximum 0.3 m, accumulator fuzzified with the inverted parabolic function in a 5×5 pix window. The layer containing about 700 measurement points projected on the image plane extended for ± 2 cm around the breast height equal to 130 cm above the ground. Data used in this paper can be made available at request.

Conditions checked after the detection. In Fig. 5a, a typical example of data points ie inside a circle but are acceptable is shown. In this case a detected tree had a natural hollow or was partly broken. The spurious points are less numerous than those at the surface, so their negative evidence can be considered as weak with respect to the positive evidence. Such images were the rationale for designing the membership function which accepts seemingly false points relatively deep under the front surface of the object. Another cue for accepting some points inside the objects and in their shadows was the dynamic character of a tree which

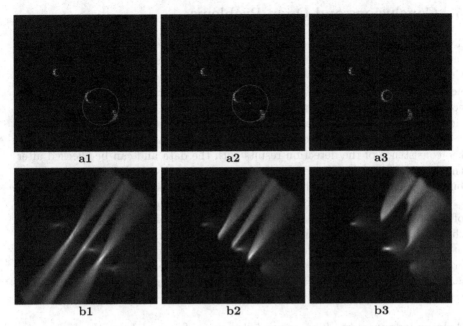

Fig. 4. Example of the influence of conditions checked during accumulation (Section 3.1) on the accumulator and the detection result. (**a**) Data points and the detected strongest circle; (**b**) accumulator. (**1**) Classical HT, no conditions; (**2**) condition of side checked; (**3**) condition of magnitude checked. The laser was at the west, at a relatively large distance with respect to the image size.

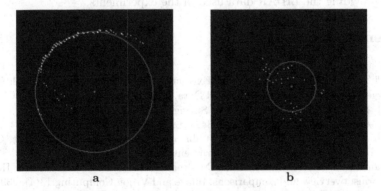

Fig. 5. Example for the conditions checked after the detection (Section 3.2) on the accumulator and the detection result. (**a**) good; (**b**) bad. Laser was far at north-west.

can wave in the wind. This is not the case for architectural objects. The example of unacceptable points is in Fig. 5b, where there are less points on the surface than inside the tree.

5 Conclusions and Open Problems

Two types of conditions necessary in the detection of opaque objects have been proposed. The conditions are implied by that the measuring points indicating the surface of the object have to be visible from the viewpoint of the measuring device. The case of detecting circular objects with the Hough transform has been considered. The proposed conditions of the first type, that is, the conditions of side and magnitude are applied during the accumulation process itself and do not require extensive additional calculations. The conditions of the second type verify the consistence of the detection results with the data and can be checked after the detection is made. The results can be used to modify the Hough accumulator, but the accumulation and checking the condition are separate processes.

The presented study opens a number of new problems. Efficient organisation of the processes of verification after detection and of backtracking to correct the inconsistent results is an interesting open question. Extension to the shapes other than circles is possible. Verification of various membership functions for creating the sets of positive and negative evidence seems to be the vital next step which should be made in order to improve the quality of measurements as far as practical applications are considered.

Acknowledgements. The research has been financed from the budget resources for science in the years 2010-2013 as the project of the Ministry of Science and Higher Education no. N N309 139739.

We wish to thank Krzysztof Stereńczak and Michał Zasada from the Faculty of Forestry, Warsaw University of Life Sciences (SGGW), for valuable discussions and for providing the LIDAR data used in the experiments.

References

1. Chmielewski, L.J., Bator, M., Zasada, M., Stereńczak, K., Strzeliński, P.: Fuzzy Hough Transform-Based Methods for Extraction and Measurements of Single Trees in Large-Volume 3D Terrestrial LIDAR Data. In: Bolc, L., et al. (eds.) ICCVG 2010, Part I. LNCS, vol. 6374, pp. 265–274. Springer, Heidelberg (2010), http://dx.doi.org/10.1007/978-3-642-15910-7_30
2. Hough, P.V.C.: Machine analysis of bubble chamber pictures. In: Proc. Int. Conf. on High Energy Accelerators and Instrumentation, CERN (1959)
3. Kälviäinen, H., Hirvonen, P., Erkki, O.: Probabilistic and non-probabilistic Hough transforms: overview and comparisons. Image and Vision Computing 13(4), 239–252 (1995), http://dx.doi.org/10.1016/0262-88569599713-B
4. Nixon, M., Aguado, A.: Feature Extraction & Image Processing. Newnes, Oxford (2002)
5. Rönnholm, P., Hyyppä, H., Hyyppä, J. (eds.): Proc. ISPRS Workshop on Laser Scanning 2007 and SilviLaser 2007, IAPRS, Espoo, Finland, September 12-14, vol. XXXVI (2007)
6. Soukup, D., Bajla, I.: Robust object recognition under partial occlusions using NMF. In: Computational Intelligence and Neuroscience, vol. 2008, Article ID 857453, 14 pages (2008), http://dx.doi.org/10.1155/2008/857453

Adaptive Structuring Elements
Based on Salience Information

Vladimir Ćurić and Cris L. Luengo Hendriks

Centre for Image Analysis
Uppsala University and Swedish University of Agricultural Sciences
Box 337, SE-751 05 Uppsala, Sweden
{vlada,cris}@cb.uu.se

Abstract. Adaptive structuring elements modify their shape and size according to the image content and may outperform fixed structuring elements. Without any restrictions, they suffer from a high computational complexity, which is often higher than linear with respect to the number of pixels in the image. This paper introduces adaptive structuring elements that have predefined shape, but where the size is adjusted to the local image structures. The size of adaptive structuring elements is determined by the salience map that corresponds to the salience of the edges in the image, which can be computed in linear time. We illustrate the difference between the new adaptive structuring elements and morphological amoebas. As an example of its usefulness, we show how the new adaptive morphological operations can isolate the text in historical documents.

Keywords: Adaptive mathematical morphology, adaptive structuring elements, spatial variability, salience distance transform.

1 Introduction

Mathematical morphology [1, 2] is based on structuring elements that are used to probe the image and enhance desirable features in it. When mathematical morphology was developed, the same structuring element was used for each point in the image, i.e., structuring elements do not change their size and shape. Currently, it is a popular and challenging task in mathematical morphology to construct adaptive structuring elements that vary their shape and size according to local image structures.

Several methods for adaptive structuring elements were introduced for binary images. A modified version of the distance transform for the construction of adaptive structuring elements was proposed [3], as well as adaptive structuring elements for edge linking [4]. A number of different methods were presented for the construction of adaptive structuring elements to gray-valued and multi-valued images as well. Morphological amoebas were introduced as adaptive structuring elements that change their shape according to geodesic distances [5]. Similar approaches based on distance measures have been considered by others

L. Bolc et al. (Eds.): ICCVG 2012, LNCS 7594, pp. 321–328, 2012.

as well [6]. Instead of being based on distance measure, the size of the structuring element is linked to the area of the connected components of the image [7], which emphasizes connectivity in the images. A method where adaptive structuring elements depend on average squared gradient fields was presented [8] as well as an interesting connection between bilateral filtering and adaptive structuring functions [9]. An efficient algorithm for adaptive rectangles that can be computed in linear time was proposed [10]. Several papers presented theoretical advances of adaptive structuring elements [11–13]. An overview on adaptive mathematical morphology had also been recently presented [14].

Despite a high flexibility of adaptive structuring elements to the local image structures and consequently their applicability to different image analysis tasks, the aforementioned methods for adaptive structuring elements are highly dependent on several important parameters. Moreover, the time complexity to construct adaptive structuring elements is relatively high (morphological amoebas can be computed in $\mathcal{O}(Nr^2 \log r^2)$, where N is the number of image points and r is the radius of the morphological amoeba). These are probably the main issues why adaptive structuring elements are rarely used on a wider scale.

In this paper, we construct structuring elements that are variable in size, but their shape remains fixed for the whole image and can be a disk, an octagon, or any other predefined shape. To determine the size of structuring elements, we use the salience distance transform [15]. The salience distance transform is a modified version of the distance transform and can be computed in linear time.

2 Background

Let D be a subset of the Euclidean space $\mathbb{Z}^2$ that corresponds to the support of the image, and let $T \subset \mathbb{R}$ be a set that corresponds to the gray level values in the image. Then, a gray level image can be represented by a function $f : D \to T$.

2.1 Morphological Amoebas

Morphological amoebas are adaptive structuring elements that adapt their shape using the amoeba distance, which is similar to the gray-weighted distance transform [16]. Let $\mathcal{P}_{xy} = \{x = x_0, x_1, ..., x_n = y\}$ be a path between points $x, y \in D$. The cost C of the path $\mathcal{P}_{xy}$ is defined as [5]

$$C(\mathcal{P}_{xy}) = \sum_{i=0}^{n-1} \Big(d_s(x_i, x_{i+1}) + \lambda d_t(f(x_i), f(x_{i+1})) \Big),$$

where d_s is a spatial distance between two pixels, while d_t stands for a tonal distance, i.e., a distance between corresponding gray level values. In the original paper on morphological amoebas [5], the following distances were used: $d_s(x_i, x_{i+1}) = 1$ and $d_t(f(x_i), f(x_{i+1})) = |f(x_i) - f(x_{i+1})|$. The amoeba distance between points x and y is defined as

$$d_\lambda(x, y) = \min_{\mathcal{P}_{xy}} C(\mathcal{P}_{xy}).$$

Then, a morphological amoeba with a centre at a point x can be defined as

$$A_\lambda^r(x) = \{y : d_\lambda(x,y) \le r\},$$

where r stands for the radius of the morphological amoeba.

Instead of having fixed spatial distance $d_s(x_i, x_{i+1}) = 1$, other distance measures, such as the Euclidean or a weighted distance, i.e., $\langle 3, 4\rangle$ distance [17], may provide better results. The tonal distance $d_t(f(x_i), f(x_{i+1})) = |f(x_i) - f(x_{i+1})|$ utilizes information about the gradient in the image. Although different combination of gray level values $f(x_i)$ and $f(x_{i+1})$ can be used as well, they can yield completely different properties of the amoeba distance.

Morphological amoebas are derived from a regularized version of the input image, the so called pilot image [5]. For the pilot image, a smoothed version of the input image is often used, usually given by a mean or Gaussian filter, which suppresses the noise in the input image. This procedure is performed since the noise might have a large impact on adaptive structuring elements. Therefore, the use of the pilot image is desirable in order to avoid the issues that might appear when noise had been present in the image.

2.2 Salience Distance Transform

The salience distance transform (SDT) [15] is a modified version of the distance transform (DT), where instead of having binary edges as an input for DT, a property of the edges is incorporated. Edge strength (gradient magnitude) may be used, but any other edge information, such as edge length or curvature, can be considered as well. Several different algorithms for salience distance transform were proposed [15, 18]. In this paper, we use the algorithm that takes the edge image as an input. Here, the edge pixels are initialized with the negative values of their salience and the non-edge pixels are set to infinity [15]. Then, the SDT is computed with the classical two-pass chamfering algorithm [17] using the Euclidean distance. Consequently, such SDT contains the information about the spatial distance between the pixels, but also takes into account the salience of the edges in the image. Moreover, weak edges located close to stronger edges have a small effect on the resulting SDT since they can be overshadowed by distance propagation from the strong ones.

To determine the radii of adaptive structuring elements, we use the salience map SM, a modified version of SDT (see Fig. 1). The edges in the image are determined by using Canny's edge detector [19], where only the estimation of the gradient and non-maximal suppression are used (denoted as NMS(f)), excluding hysteresis thresholding. Hence, the edges with a small response in the gradient image are preserved. The gradient of the input image is computed using Gaussian derivatives, which introduces the same amount of smoothing as the pilot image for morphological amoebas. For the experiments in this paper, the standard deviation of the Gaussian filter is set to $\sigma = 1$ pixel. The salience map SM can be further adjusted by proportionally changing the values of NMS(f). Also, the edges can be detected by any other edge detector.

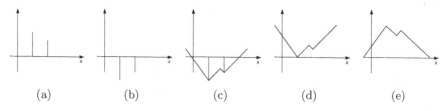

Fig. 1. Computation of the salience map SM. (a) NMS(f); (b) $-$ NMS(f); (c) SDT; (d) SDT$^+$; (e) SM.

3 Method

A desirable property of an adaptive structuring element is to adjust its size according to the neighbouring edges, taking into account the salience of the edges. Hence, an adaptive structuring element at a point x (see Fig. 2(a) for 1D example) should have a radius that is smaller than $|x - \bar{x}|$, where $\bar{x}$ denotes a point that corresponds to the position of the edge in the input image. Since the propagation of the distance is linear (the Euclidean distance is used), $|x - \bar{x}|$ can be approximated by the difference of the salience map SM at the two points, i.e., $|\bar{x} - x| = \mathrm{SM}(\bar{x}) - \mathrm{SM}(x)$. This equation is drawn from the isosceles right angled triangle $\triangle PQR$, where $PQ = QR$ and $\angle PQR = \frac{\pi}{2}$. Consequently, the approximation $d_s(x, \bar{x}) \approx \mathrm{SM}(\bar{x}) - \mathrm{SM}(x)$ is valid for 2D images.

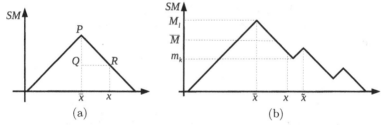

Fig. 2. (a) Linear propagation of the salience map SM; (b) Salience map SM with several local minima and maxima

The salience map SM usually has several local maxima. Ideally, a segmentation of SM can produce disjoint regions of the image, where each region has one and only one local maximum. Due to the construction of the salience map SM, the simple thresholding is not acceptable, while other segmentation techniques have relatively high computational complexity. Moreover, after the segmentation, it may appear that the structuring elements include the point that corresponds to the maximum of the neighbouring region, which is undesirable. For instance, the structuring element at point x is determined by the local maximum at point $\bar{x}$ and also contains the point $\tilde{x}$, where $\mathrm{SM}(\tilde{x}) < \mathrm{SM}(\bar{x})$ (see Fig. 2(b)). Therefore, we propose a procedure, where a segmentation of SM is not required, and the radii of structuring elements can be computed using only two points from the salience map SM.

Let $m_1, ..., m_k$ be local minima and $M_1, ..., M_l$ be local maxima of SM such that $0 < m_1 \leq m_2 \leq ... \leq m_k$ and $0 < M_1 \leq M_2 \leq ... \leq M_l$. In order to preserve the strongest edge(s) in the image, we find the largest local minimum and maximum, i.e., m_k and M_l, respectively (see Fig. 2(b)). We use $|\text{SM}(x) - \overline{M}|$, where $\overline{M} = \frac{M_l + m_k}{2}$, to preserve the stronger edges in the image. Similarly, to preserve the weakest edges in the image, we use $|\text{SM}(x) - \underline{M}|$, where $\underline{M} = \frac{m_1 + M_1}{2}$. Then, for all $x \in D$, we define the radius of the structuring element as

$$r(x) = \begin{cases} |\text{SM}(x) - \overline{M}| \cdot \overline{C}, & \text{to preserve strong edges} \\ |\text{SM}(x) - \underline{M}| \cdot \underline{C}, & \text{to preserve weak edges}. \end{cases}$$

Two positive constants $\overline{C}$ and $\underline{C}$ additionally adjust the size of structuring elements. Instead of computing local minima and maxima for the whole image, it is possible to compute them in a neighbourhood of the each point.

Now, when the radii of structuring elements are determined, any shape for structuring elements can be used. Still, the shape of structuring elements has to be predefined by the user, depending on prior knowledge of the image content. To compute the salience map SM, the time complexity is $\mathcal{O}(N)$ since that is the time complexity for the Canny edge detector and for the distance transform. Therefore, time complexity for the newly proposed adaptive structuring elements remains linear.

4 Experiments and Results

To test the proposed method for adaptive structuring elements, we used images of discrete disks of different sizes and contrasts (the shapes in each row have the same size and different contrast, see Fig. 3(a)). When the radii of adaptive structuring elements were determined, we computed an erosion, ε, and a dilation, δ, of the input image. Erosion and dilation were computed taking the infimum and supremum of the gray-level values over the adaptive structuring elements, respectively [5]. In our tests, a disk defined by the Euclidean distance was used as the shape of structuring elements.

The performance of morphological operators using the new structuring elements for an image of disks is presented in Fig. 3 using two different definitions for the radius. In Fig. 3(b), we present erosion for the radius that preserves strong edges, while Fig. 3(c) depicts erosion for the radius that preserves weak edges. Note that, to shrink the brightest objects in the image $\overline{C} > \underline{C}$ was required. It appears that the shapes were better preserved (without artefacts at the boundary of the objects) with structuring elements that preserve weak edges.

We also illustrate the difference between the newly proposed structuring elements and morphological amoebas (see Fig. 3(d)-(f)). Since these two methods are based on different parameters, it is a difficult task to perform a direct comparison. One of the possible comparisons is by visual inspection, similarly as has been done in the literature [5,7–9]. We used various parameters for morphological amoebas, and for the tests were used the Euclidean distance and $\lambda = 0.25$.

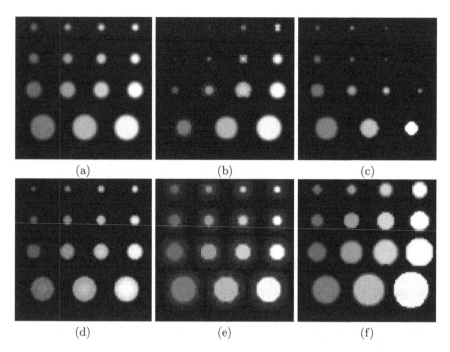

Fig. 3. Erosion using the new structuring elements. (a) Disk image I_d; (b) $\varepsilon(I_d)$ by preserving strong edges for $\overline{C} = 0.2$; (c) $\varepsilon(I_d)$ by preserving weak edges for $\underline{C} = 0.2$; (d) $\varepsilon(I_d)$ using morphological amoebas for radius $r = 5$; (e) $\delta(I_d)$ using morphological amoebas for radius $r = 5$; (f) $\delta(I_d)$ using the proposed structuring elements for $\underline{C} = 0.2$.

One of possible applications of the morphological operators defined with the new adaptive structuring elements is to modify high-contrast objects while leaving low-contrast objects unaffected. Here, we used this property to isolate text on a page of a historical document, see Fig. 4(a). On this page, the text printed on the back side can be seen as lighter text going through the darker text of the front side. Using our new adaptive structuring elements, we defined a morphological

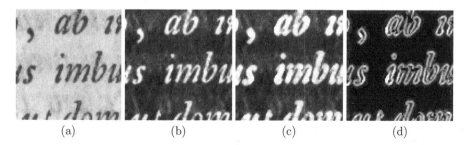

Fig. 4. (a) Colour image of a historical document; (b) Inverted gray-valued image I_g; (c) $\delta(I_g)$ using the proposed structuring elements for $\underline{C} = 0.3$; (d) The difference between $\delta(I_g)$ and $\varepsilon(I_g)$ using the proposed structuring elements for $\underline{C} = 0.3$

edge detector that is only sensitive to the high-contrast edges. The morphological edge operator is the difference between the dilation and the erosion. In this case, the dilation (Fig. 4(c)) and the erosion only affected the high-contrast letters. Their difference (Fig. 4(d)) did not contain any of the low-contrast text. To enhance the salience of the letters, the salience map SM was constructed using $\frac{1}{5}$ NMS(I_g), where I_g is the gray-valued image shown in Fig. 4(b). As before, we used an Euclidean disk as the structuring element.

5   Discussion and Conclusions

We have introduced the method to determine the size of structuring elements that are adaptive to the image content. The size of adaptive structuring elements was computed using salience information from the image. We have also proposed a method for which the user can specify to preserve strong or weak edges in the image.

Morphological erosion and dilation with the newly proposed structuring elements treat differently objects of the same size and different contrast. This is an important advantage over using fixed structuring elements that treat all objects of the same size in the same way. Erosion and dilation preserve the intensity profile of the considered digital objects, while the symmetry of the object may be destroyed. Conversely, due to the high adaptability of morphological amoebas, morphological operators defined with these adaptive structuring elements do not preserve the intensity profile of the boundary of the objects, which is undesirable behaviour. Nevertheless, they preserve the symmetry of the objects.

Additionally, we have presented the applicability of the newly proposed adaptive structuring elements to the problems of text recognition. These initial results are encouraging, and we intend to further investigate the usefulness of adaptive structuring elements for the problems of text recognition as well as for other image analysis tasks.

Acknowledgement. This work is finance by the Graduate School in Mathematics and Computing at Uppsala University, Sweden. Scientific support from Prof. Gunilla Borgefors is highly appreciated. Fig. 4(a) is used courtesy of Per Cullhed, Uppsala University Library and Fredrik Wahlberg, the Handwritten Text Recognition project at Uppsala University.

References

1. Matheron, G.: Random Sets and Integral Geometry. Willey, New York (1975)
2. Serra, J.: Image Analysis and Mathematical Morphology. Academic Press, London (1982)
3. Cuisenaire, O.: Locally adaptable mathematical morphology using distance transform. Pattern Recognition 39(3), 405–416 (2006)
4. Shih, F., Cheng, S.: Adaptive mathematical morphology for edge linking. Information Sciences 167, 9–21 (2004)

5. Lerallut, R., Decencière, E., Meyer, F.: Image processing using morphological amoebas. In: Proc. of International Symposium on Mathematical Morphology, pp. 13–25 (2005)
6. Grazzini, J., Soille, P.: Edge-preserving smoothing using a similarity measure in adaptive geodesic neighbourhoods. Pattern Recognition 42(10), 2306–2316 (2009)
7. Debayle, J., Pinoli, J.: Spatially Adaptive Morphological Image Filtering using Intrinsic Structuring Elements. Image Analysis and Stereology 24(3), 145–158 (2005)
8. Verdú-Monedero, R., Angulo, J., Serra, J.: Anisotropic morphological filters with spatially-variant structuring elements based on image-dependent gradient fields. IEEE Transactions on Image Processing 20(1), 200–212 (2011)
9. Angulo, J.: Morphological Bilateral Filtering and Spatially-Variant Structuring Functions. In: Proc. of International Symposium on Mathematical Morphology, pp. 212–223 (2011)
10. Dokládal, P., Dokládalová, E.: Grey-Scale Morphology with Spatially-Variant Rectangles in Linear Time. In: Blanc-Talon, J., Bourennane, S., Philips, W., Popescu, D., Scheunders, P. (eds.) ACIVS 2008. LNCS, vol. 5259, pp. 674–685. Springer, Heidelberg (2008)
11. Bouaynaya, N., Charif-Chefchaouni, M., Schonfeld, D.: Theoretical Foundation of Spatially-Variant Mathematical Morphology Part I: Binary Images. IEEE Transactions on Pattern Analysis and Machine Intelligence 39(5), 823–836 (2008)
12. Bouaynaya, N., Schonfeld, D.: Theoretical Foundation of Spatially-Variant Mathematical Morphology Part II: Gray-Level Images. IEEE Transactions on Pattern Analysis and Machine Intelligence 39(5), 837–850 (2008)
13. Roerdink, J.: Adaptive and group invariance in mathematical morphology. In: Proc. of IEEE International Conference on Image Processing, pp. 2253–2256 (2009)
14. Maragos, P.A., Vachier, C.: Overview of adaptive morphology: Trends and perspectives. In: Proc. of IEEE Int. Conference on Image Processing, pp. 2241–2244 (2009)
15. Rosin, P., West, G.: Salience distance transforms. CVGIP: Graphical Models and Image Processing 57(6), 483–521 (1995)
16. Ikonen, L.: Distance Transform on Gray Level Surfaces. PhD thesis, Lappeeranta University of Technology, Lappeeranta, Finland (2006)
17. Borgefors, G.: Distance transformations in digital images. Computer Vision, Graphics and Image Processing 34, 344–371 (1986)
18. Rosin, P.: A simple method for detecting salient regions. Pattern Recognition 42(11), 2363–2371 (2009)
19. Canny, J.: A Computational Approach To Edge Detection. IEEE Transactions on Pattern Analysis and Machine Intelligence 8(6), 679–698 (1986)

Directional Votes of Optical Flow Projections for Independent Motion Detection

László Czúni[1] and Mónika Gál[2]

[1] Department of Electrical Engineering and Information Systems
University of Pannonia, Egyetem utca 10, Veszprém H-8200, Hungary
[2] Department of Mathematics
University of Pannonia, Egyetem utca 10, Veszprém H-8200, Hungary
czuni@almos.uni-pannon.hu

Abstract. In our paper we discuss some of the problems of camera independent motion dection and propose the use of a qualitative method based on the projections of the optical flow. By applying several projections of the optical flow and using a voting mechanism we can increase the performance of motion detection: the F-measure, examined on 20 artificial and real-life test videos, was increased with about 10-25% in general compared to the average performance of individual projections.

Keywords: Camera Independent Motion Detection, Detectability, Optical Flow, Motion Analysis, Corner Detection.

1   Introduction

Today there are several applications of camera independent motion detection such as driver assistance systems, pan-tilt-zoom (PTZ) surveillance cameras, and analysis of videos of hand-held cameras. The difficulty of the problem depends on the rigidity, motion, colour, texture of objects, the 3D structure of the scene, and the ego-motion of the camera. In case of uncalibrated cameras and arbitrary motion the F-measure of different methods is quite low and can be easily below 50% [8]. Unfortunately, due to the great variance of applications' environment no general test bed is available to quantitatively compare the different approaches. Our purpose is to improve the use of the so called divergence property which was found promising previously [2]. Unfortunately, often the low number and the nonuniform distribution of feature points and the detectability of motion direction can easily result in very low performance of the original method. In our paper we propose a technique to avoid most of these problems significantly improving the detection performance.

2   Brief Overview of Other Methods

A classical approach is to apply bilinear, affine or pseudo perspective transforms for the motion compensation of consecutive images. If we could find the optimal warping transform then frame differencing applied on the result will show

L. Bolc et al. (Eds.): ICCVG 2012, LNCS 7594, pp. 329–336, 2012.
© Springer-Verlag Berlin Heidelberg 2012

the areas of moving objects. Unfortunately, large difference values can also occur due to occlusions, light changes, nonrigid shapes, etc. In [6] particle filters while in [8] kernel density estimation is used for further analysis to reduce false alarms. In [3] the authors present a surveillance system with a PTZ camera. The proposed method is focused particularly on the determination of a set of well trackable features and on the computation of the displacement vector. It uses a reference image for maintaining information about well trackable features. In [9] the purpose is to track people in crowded pedestrian areas with the help of stereo cameras. Bayesian nets are used to estimate the ground level with objects, Kalman filter and RANSAC is used for the tracking of objects and to create a map of objects. As a result the vehicle can design its path avoiding the collision with moving objects on the ground plane. In [5] Irani and Anandan attack the problem of moving object detection with the categorization of videos into three main classes: in the first group 2D parametric transforms can model the change induced by camera motion; in the second group several scene layers are needed to handle the image motion; while in the third group 3D models are required for motion parallax analysis.

Our aim is to develop an application which can process simple images sequences, without additional information such as camera egomotion, camera calibration parameters, the assumption of plain surfaces or stereo image pairs. In addition the target is to reduce significantly computational costs, so our choice was the optical flow projection method discussed in [2]. It is based on the tracking of feature points and the analysis of two motion constraints as discussed in Section 3.

3   Analysis of the Projections of the Optical Flow

The motion of a camera can be described with translational (U, V, W) and rotational $(\Omega_x, \Omega_y, \Omega_z)$ components in 3D space. We start from the well-know motion equation describing the horizontal and vertical components of the optical flow (u, v) of pixels at position (x, y):

$$u(x, y) = \frac{x - x_0}{Z_0(x, y)} + \Omega_x xy - \Omega_y(1 + x^2) + \Omega_z y \tag{1}$$

$$v(x, y) = \frac{y - y_0}{Z_0(x, y)} + \Omega_x(1 + y^2) - \Omega_y xy + \Omega_z x \tag{2}$$

where $[x_0, y_0] = [\frac{U}{W}, \frac{V}{W}]$ defines the so called Focus of Expansion (FOE) and $Z_0 = \frac{Z}{W}$ is the scaled distance (Z) of points from the camera center. Based on these equations two constraints can be formalized and those points not satisfying the qualitative requirements can be considered as outlier points detected as parts of moving objects.

3.1   Divergence Constraint

To analyse the optical flow vectors we use the concept of [2] where the projections of the optical flow field are analyzed in a qualitative way. For simplification, considering the horizontal projection case of parallel cross sections of motion vectors, we define the projection as:

$$u_y(x) := u(x, y) \ y \ constant. \tag{3}$$

Assuming narrow field of view and non-zero translation we can simplify eq. 1 to

$$u(x, y) = \frac{x - x_0}{Z_0(x, y)} + \Omega_x xy - \Omega_y(1 + x^2) + \Omega_z y \approx \frac{x - x_0}{Z_0(x, y)} - \Omega_y + \Omega_z y \tag{4}$$

This implies the following constrains for the projection:

$$\forall x : \begin{cases} x \leq x_0 : u_y \leq u_y(x_0) \\ x \geq x_0 : u_y \geq u_y(x_0) \end{cases} \tag{5}$$

That is if we know the location of the FOE (x_0) we can check if a given point satisfies eq. 5. Without egomotion estimation we can assume that most points don't belong to the foreground so finding x_0 means finding the position in the (x, u_y) plane where the number of points at the *North West* and at the *South East* region shows minima. Figure 1 shows an example test video and the corresponding projection data (at 150°) in case of a forward translating camera. There are two moving objects: a car in the right and a car far in the front. Red points denote detected points while green ones are the real moving objects. These points can be found at the *South East* region from the FOE, found as the position with the least number of outliers. Please note that the search for the FOE means a simple, but rapid scanning of the (x, u_y) space. In general we apply a small threshold around the candidate FOE point during the search to compensate the inaccuracy in optical flow estimations. The example of Figure 1 is a relatively good result: Only the car in the far front was not detected due to its little motion compared to the motion of the background and the car in the right.

Fig. 1. An example frame taken from the PETS database. Green points are the points belonging to moving points; red points are the detected ones.

3.2 Linearity Constraint

We can also take the orthogonal projections[1] of optical flow along the line going through the FOE. In this case the translational component disappears from eq. 4:

$$u_{x_0}(y) = \Omega_x x_0 y - \Omega_y(1 + x_0^2) + \Omega_z y, \qquad (6)$$

Thus the projection is a linear function of the remaining variables. In general while both constraints can be used for motion detection in our paper we deal only with the improvement of the divergence constraint.

4 Problems with the Divergence Constraint

One advantage of using only projections of the optical flow is the lower computational cost while it also has been demonstrated [10] that several points suffering the aperture problem can still be used successfully for motion estimation by partial motion information. Unfortunately, there are two main limitations for the efficient usage of the divergence constraint. The algorithm described above is based on finding the right position of the FOE in the (x, u_y) plane. Unfortunately, if the number of correctly trackable feature points is low, or the distribution of those points is not uniform in (x, u_y) then the solution is unreliable. Please, see Figure 2 for the illustration of the problem. Naturally, the relation of motion direction and the direction of the projection determines the detectability of independent motion (for more details and explanation please see [2]). This is shown in Figure 3 where the two objects, moving towards each other, can't be detected in the 90 degree projection but in the horizontal direction. To resolve these two limitations, often arising simultaneously making the problem even more difficult to be solved, we propose to combine a set of predictions made from several projection directions.

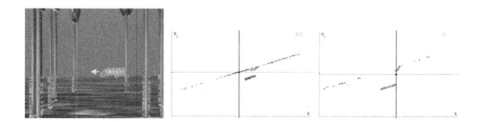

Fig. 2. Illustration of the problem of insufficient number of feature points. While in case of the projection at 60°the points belonging to the moving object (truck) lie in the outlier zone, in case of the projection at 0°they are not detected due to the wrongly recognized FOE.

---

[1] This projection is called orthogonal since the line where the feature points to be considered lie is orthogonal to the direction of the projection.

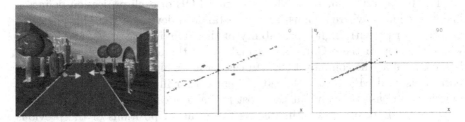

Fig. 3. Illustration of detectability: the two opposing objects can be detected from projection at 0° but not from projection at 90°

5   The Proposed Method

5.1   Preprocessing

The latest methods for feature point selection are SIFT [11] and SURF [12] select size and rotation invariant points in the image. The SIFT method has rather high computational cost, so its application was rejected. SURF has lower complexity and it is considered to be applied in the next phase of our research as future work. In this application, the Harris corner detector [4] was used to detect feature points. For the calculation of the optical flow the algorithm of Lucas and Kanade with pyramids [1] was applied.

5.2   Estimation of the Common FOE by Several Projections

The basic method for finding the FOE relies on eq. 5. As explained above we should not count only on individual projections to denote the position of the FOE and to detect the outliers. Instead we use 8 projection directions (at degrees 0,

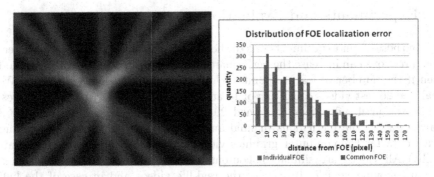

Fig. 4. Left: Gauss weighted FOE estimations. Yellow colour points denote the highest probability locations of the common FOE. Right: the distribution of the error of FOE position in case of the individual projections and in case of the globally estimated common FOE.

30, 45, 60, 90, 120, 135, 150). The estimated FOE of each projection defines a line in the image where a Gaussian (with standard deviation 15.65) is placed to denote a stripe with higher probability of the FOE in the ridge. The location where the sum of these Gaussians is highest, as the most probable coordinate, is considered as the common FOE. (In case of more highest points their average position is used.) Please see the left of Figure 4 for illustration of the Gaussian functions. In case the value at the most probable location is below a threshold then the FOE position is estimated as the mean of positions of the previous and succeeding frames. Using the globally determined FOE now we return to the individual projections and find the outliers as those points located *North West* and *South East* of this common FOE. The right of Figure 4 shows the distribution of FOE position errors for 230 frames of 8 different test videos. As it can be seen in case of the common FOE the error is smaller than in case of the average of the individual projections.

5.3   Voting for Outlier Detection

As illustrated in the left of Figure 4 it is general that most of the Gaussian stripes, denoting the possible position of the FOE, overlap each other but it often happens that some of them run far from the real FOE position. To evaluate the confidence of the motion detection results of individual projections we can use the distance from the common FOE. Each projection will give votes for feature points weighted with $w_{i,p} = \max\{1 - \frac{d_{i,p}}{d_t}, 0\}$, where $d_{i,p}$ is the distance of the line from the common FOE for frame i and projection p while d_t is a parameter set to the sum of the average distances of the two least successful projection (with the highest average distance in the video). Each feature point gets weighted votes if detected as outlier according to a given projection. If the sum of votes for a given point reaches a limit (T) the point is classified as a moving object point. In our experiments T was set between 1 and 1.5.

6   Experiments and Evaluations

The purpose of our experiments was to show that the utilization of several projection directions can increase the performance of the divergence constraint method even if the number of feature points is low or they are evenly distributed. We analyzed 20 test videos consisting of 16 artificial and 4 real-life image sequences. While the artificial videos contained 29 frames the natural ones had only 8 frames due to the meticulous manual annotation work required. (The ground truth data for the computer graphics video files could be generated automatically.) All videos are similar in content: the videos were *"recorded"* from a forward moving vehicle. In case of the real-life videos and in case of the half of the artificial sequences the camera also showed some horizontal and vertical translation. The number, size, and motion of foreground objects greatly varied in the test sequences. We ran several tests with different number of feature points and found that the improvement due to our method is greater if the number of feature points is relatively low (this conforms the first kind of problem given in 4). The performance of the methods was evaluated by F-measure, recall and precision. Figure 5 shows the average results for all 20 videos. The graph compares four types of classification methods: A) Individual FOEs: the average of 8 directions (the original algorithm). B) Common FOE: The common FOE, found by the method given in Section 5.2, is used for the evaluation of feature points in each projection. No weighting is applied but the results of the 8 directions are averaged. C) Individual FOEs with weighting: Each projection uses its own FOE but votes are weighted to sum up the votes for each feature point. D) Common FOE with weighting: The common FOE is used for each projection and projection votes are weighted as given above. As we expected the recall increased with about 20-30% (depending in the number of points) when comparing the average of the 8 projections with individual FOE and the distance weighted method with the common FOE. The precision basically remained the same that is the F-measure showed significant improvements from 10% to 25%. If the number of feature points is large then the F-measure benefit melted away due to the poorer advantage in recall and a slight decreasing of precision. The right side of Figure 5 illustrates the performance of the 8 projections for 200 points in case of their own FOE detection mechanism and using the globally detected common FOE. There is only one direction (at 90°) when the performance decreased a little. The shape of the graph (decreasing performance towards 90°) can be explained by the forward translating camera.

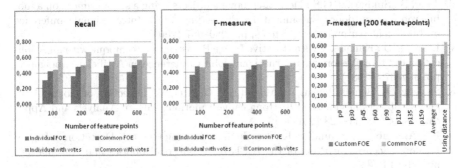

Fig. 5. Left: average recall values. Center: average F-measure values. Right: average F-measure for the different projection directions for 200 feature points.

7 Summary

The detectability of independent motion greatly depends on the direction of motion of objects relative to the motion of the camera, on the rigidity of objects, on the 3D structure of the scene, and on the intensity distribution of patterns being observed. In our paper we investigated the use of the so called divergence constraint and found that the original method can be significantly improved if several projections are used to generate weighted votes for the classification of feature points. The gain in F-measure was between 10% and 25% for the tested 20 videos. We believe that the utilization of time domain filtering and applying the linearity constraint in future will produce enhanced results.

Acknowledgement. The work and publication of results have been supported by the Hungarian Research Fund, grant OTKA CNK 80368 and by TÁMOP-4.2.2/B-10/1-2010-0025.

References

1. Bouguet, J.Y.: Pyramidal Implementation of the Lucas Kanade Feature Tracker Description of the algorithm. Intel Corporation Microprocessor Research Labs (2000)
2. Fejes, S., Davis, L.S.: Detection of independent motion using directional motion estimation. Computer Vision and Image Understanding 78, 101–120 (1999)
3. Foresti, G.L., Micheloni, C.: A robust feature tracker for active surveillance of outdoor scenes. Electronic Letters on Computer Vision and Image Analysis, 21–34 (2003)
4. Harris, C., Stephens, M.: A combined corner and edge detector. In: Proc. Alvey Vision Conf., pp. 147–151 (1988)
5. Irani, M., Anandan, P.: A unified approach to moving object detection in 2D and 3D scenes. IEEE Transactions on Pattern Analysis and Machine Intelligence, 577–588 (1998)
6. Jung, B., Sukhatme, G.S.: Detecting moving objects using a single camera on a mobile robot an outdoor environment. In: Proceedings of the International Conference on Intelligent Autonomous Systems, pp. 980–987 (2004)
7. Lucas, B.D., Kanade, T.: An Iterative Image Registration Technique with an Application to Stereo Vision. In: International Joint Conference on Artificial Intelligence, pp. 674–679 (1981)
8. Szolgay, D., Benois-Pineau, J., Megret, R., Gaestel, Y.: Detection of moving foreground objects in videos with strong camera motion. Pattern Analysis and Applications 14(3), 311–328 (2011)
9. Ess, A., Leibe, B., Schindler, K., van Gool, L.: Moving Obstacle Detection in Highly Dynamic Scenes. In: Proc. of the IEEE Int. Conf. on Robotics and Automation, pp. 56–63 (2009)
10. Czúni, L., Gál, M.: Independent Motion Detection in the Light of the Aperture Problem. Research Report, University of Pannonia (2012)
11. Lowe, D.G.: Object recognition from local scale-invariant features. In: Proc. 7th International Conference on Computer Vision, pp. 1150–1157 (1999)
12. Bay, H., Ess, A., Tuytelaars, T., Van Gool, L.: SURF: Speeded Up Robust Features. Computer Vision and Image Understanding 110(3), 346–359 (2008)

Recognition of Hand-Written Archive Text Documents

László Czúni[1], Tamás Szöke[1], and Mónika Gál[2]

[1] Department of Electrical Engineering and Information Systems,
University of Pannonia, Egyetem utca 10, Veszprém H-8200, Hungary
[2] Department of Mathematics,
University of Pannonia, Egyetem utca 10, Veszprém H-8200, Hungary
czuni@almos.uni-pannon.hu

Abstract. The processing of the large amount of hand-written archive documents is an unsolved problem. We propose a semi-automatic text recognition approach for those documents containing a limited size of vocabulary. Our approach is word based and uses the Scale Invariant Feature Transform for finding and describing saliency points of hand-written words. For testing we used a book of a Central-European city census of the year 1771 containing mainly Christian and family names. At reasonable database size we could achieve about 80% recognition rate.

Keywords: Optical character recognition, Hand-written text recognition, Feature extraction, SIFT, Archive document processing.

1 Introduction

The manual processing of hand-written documents of archives is a very time demanding and costly process. Our purpose is to help this procedure with a semi-automatic pattern recognition method reducing the requirement for manual work.

The recognition of continuous hand-written text is the least solved task in automatic document processing. While printed hand-written text contains relatively regular characters, continuously written text can have a wide variety of appearance. The segmentation of characters of such text can be a very difficult task due to overlapping, slant, thin and/or broken lines, excessive curves (see Fig. 3) causing even word segmentation complicated. Although, the word separation and the segmentation of the page of documents is outside the scope of our paper, in the special case of our documents the layout of words in tables would ease the task of word segmentation anyway (see Fig. 1). Fortunately, the look of the writing of a person can be considered uniform but it is easy to find cases when the same character is written differently (first example of Fig. 4) or when similar look belongs to different letters (the second example of Fig. 4).

Since we are targeting archive documents there are several factors increasing the obscureness of the scripts: fading, dirt, missing areas, crease, smear, blur.

L. Bolc et al. (Eds.): ICCVG 2012, LNCS 7594, pp. 337–344, 2012.

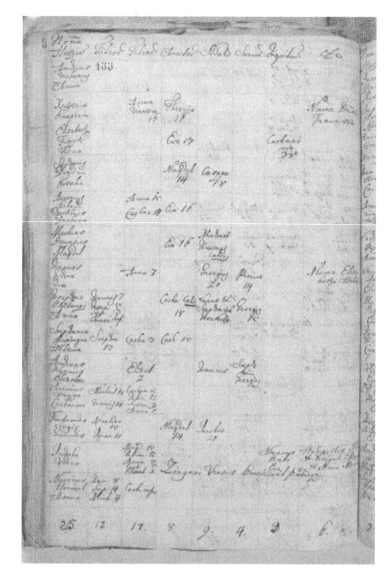

Fig. 1. The look of a typical page of the archive document from 1771

In our paper we propose a semi-automatic recognition procedure where the users can make annotations in an archive book then, based on these inputs, the algorithm learns the local features of already trained words thus can advise text to unknown words. We report that the Scale Invariant Feature Transform (SIFT), often used in image retrieval, can be quite successful in the recognition of archive scripts thus can lower the amount of manual annotation to only 20% of its original.

2 Short Overview of Recent Methods

Since the separation of characters of hand-written text is very difficult most modern methods are based on word-level recognition.

In [3] first the manually separated words are pre-processed to remove parts of overlapping words. Then the slant of words and skew of rows are estimated and compensated. As a third step the background colour of the word is normalized and the baseline of the word is positioned. Two types of features are used to generate Hidden Markov Models of the text:

- scalar features (e.g. number of descenders and ascenders, width, height, etc.)
- Discrete Fourier Transform coefficients of profile features (projection profiles, upper word and lower word profiles)

This method could achieve 65% accuracy on some historical documents.

Paper [5] describes the word based recognition of archive documents with the clustering of word images where the similarity of images is calculated by the application of Dynamic Time Warping. The skew of rows and slant of words are compensated during pre-processing. The similarity, to create clusters, is based on the comparison of upper and lower profiles and the number of foreground-background transitions. The best minimal error rate was around 31.5% on archive documents.

Based on these papers we implemented a feature based approach and tested several classifiers to recognize the word images of archive documents of census. Unfortunately, the average recognition rate was only about 50% below our expectations. The SIFT is popular in image retrieval tasks even in case of words. [2] uses SIFT for the recognition of words in real-life scenes by head-mounted camera. The recall of experiments was around 70% depending on viewing conditions.

3 The Description of the Problem

In our research we target archive documents containing a limited size of vocabulary. For example a book of census of a medium size city has a few thousand expressions with a few hundred class of expressions, family and Christian names almost.

Fig. 2 illustrates the number of new words (new classes) as a function of new pages of a book of census of a Central-European city from 1771. Since the probability of new words is increasing only logarithmically, the grounds of a continuously learning systems seems to be reasonable.

The full length of the book is 175 pages with about 50-100 words per page. The test database created from the book and used in our experiments contains 1638 manually segmented and annotated words of 177 different names from the first 22 pages of the book. The average occurrence of a name is 9.25 (ranging from 1 to 111).

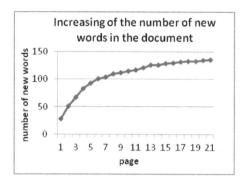

Fig. 2. The number of new words appearing from page-to-page. From about the 20th page the number of new words is increasing very slowly.

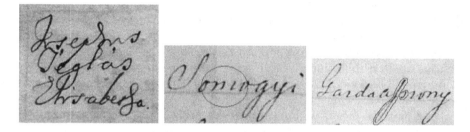

Fig. 3. Left: overlapping of words; Middle: broken line transforms "m" into "n" and "r"; Right: misspelling of the 7th letter which should look like the 8th letter

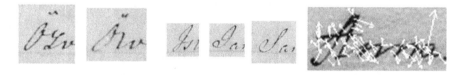

Fig. 4. Left: difference of the same letter "z" in the same hand-writing (beginning of "Özvegy"); Middle: similarities of different letters in the same hand-writing (beginning of "István", "János", "Sámuel"); Right: SIFT points, arrows sign the orientation of feature points

4   The Proposed Method

Traditional OCR software products, such as Onlineocr.net, Abby Finereader, and SimpleOCR, were tested without any success. On the other hand we experimented with several classifiers such as k-NN, Random Tree, Random Forest, Naive Bayes, BFTree, J48, and SMO [6] to carry out the recognition based on descriptors of length 329. These descriptors contained information about the image of words, such as: horizontal and vertical size and their ratio; minimum, maximum, and average intensity; average intensity derivatives; upper profile; lower profile; right profile; left profile; center of gravity; black-white transitions; black-white ratio; black count; black density; image moments.

Without going into details the average performance of these classifiers were around 50% and even the application of Principal Component Analysis, to reduce the dimension from 329 to 90, could not increase the efficiency. To solve the problem we propose to use the so called Scale Invariant Feature Transform (SIFT) in an image retrieval framework as described in the following subsections.

4.1 The SIFT Descriptors

The algorithm published by David Lowe [4] is widely used to detect and describe local feature points in images. First saliency points are selected as local maxima and minima values of the output of difference of Gaussian functions applied to a series of smoothed and resampled images. Points with low contrast and at straight edges are discarded. To achieve invariance to rotation each feature point is assigned an orientation based on local gradients. Besides gradient direction (Θ) the gradient magnitude (m) is calculated on the low-passed version of images (L):

$$m(x, y) = \sqrt{(L(x + 1, y) - L(x - 1, y))^2 + (L(x, y + 1) - L(x, y - 1))^2} \quad (1)$$

$$\Theta(x, y) = \tan^{-1}\left(\frac{L(x, y + 1) - L(x, y - 1)}{L(x + 1, y) - L(x - 1, y)}\right) \quad (2)$$

The orientation of a feature point is decided by orientation histograms made on neighbouring points. The orientations corresponding to the highest peak and local peaks that are within 80% of the highest peaks are assigned to the keypoint. In the case of multiple orientations being assigned, an additional keypoint is created having the same location and scale as the original keypoint for each additional orientation.

Feature points are described with a magnitude weighted and normalized 128 element orientation histogram vector describing the neighbourhood of the points at their selected scale. For more details of the algorithm please see [4].

4.2 The Application of SIFT to Continuous Hand-Writing Recognition

The right of Fig. 4 shows the SIFT points of a hand-written word illustrating the local orientations, where the magnitude of the arrow is set to approximately the radius of the region used to compute the descriptor. As given above, for each feature point we have a descriptor vector of length 128, with its orientation, scale, and location parameters. Although the size of letters through the book shows little variance, we normalized the position by the physical size of the words.

The recognition problem can be considered as a classical information retrieval task where the objects to be found are specified with a number of SIFT descriptors. The question is how to find the proper evaluation criteria for the comparison of query and candidate objects. For this reason first we compare pairs of feature points and based on these comparisons we evaluate the similarity of whole words.

The comparison of two SIFT points (q: query and c: candidate) is made by the following similarity function:

$$sv = \sum_{i=1}^{128}(255 - |q_i - c_i|)^2 \qquad (3)$$

For the first feature point of the query image we look for the most similar point of the candidate (one of the already annotated words). Then two constraints are investigated related to the orientation and relative position of the points, otherwise too many similarities could be found on hand-written scripts. Only 30 degree difference in orientation and 0.1 difference in relative position is allowed. The point-pair, found with the lowest sv value, not satisfying these constraints are disregarded from the following steps. For all remaining points in the query image we summarize the value of sv and select the candidate c where this summed sv is minimal. As common in information retrieval we create a limited list of the results typically containing the best 10 candidates. In our experiments we found that if the database of already annotated words is large enough (above 1000 images of words) then it is 90% that the list of the best 10 words contains the sought word. That is in a semi-automatic application the operator could choose from a roll-down list of 10 elements to translate the image of a word into text.

5   Experimental Results

The first 22 pages of the 177 have been manually annotated with 1638 word images. There are 68 words with only 1 occurrence meaning that the maximum recognition rate could not go above 96%. While the rows of script were almost horizontal the image of individual names showed strong slant in many cases. We tested the removal of slant by the method of [7] but this type of pre-processing did not increase the accuracy of retrieval.

In the numerical evaluations we selected a random query and compared it to the remaining 1637 images. The following results are based on the average of such 103 queries. Five types of evaluation criteria were investigated:

- The result with the highest sv (correct recognition).
- The modus of the best 5 candidates.
- The modus of the best 10 candidates.
- The probability that the list of the best 5 includes the query.
- The probability that the list of the best 10 includes the query.

First we tested the effects of the orientation and position constraints described above. We found that it is much more worthy to first find the best match for the query feature point and then apply the constraints than vice versa. This and the effect of the distance threshold are shown in Fig. 5 (while the threshold for orientation was always 30 degree).

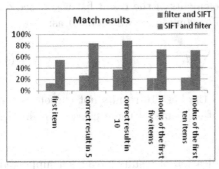
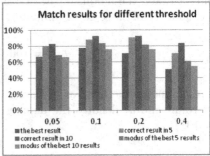

Fig. 5. Left: results in the case of different order of filtering steps; Right: results for different distance thresholds

Analyzing the results in the right of Fig. 5 we see that the modus of the best 5 results ends in the best recognition at 81.5%. The modus of the 10 and the first item of the result list is always outperformed. Fig 6 illustrates the recognition rate as a function of word frequency. The probability of correct recognition goes logarithmically with the number of occurrences of the same word.

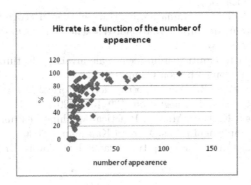

Fig. 6. Hit rate as a function of word appearance

6   Summary

The task of hand-writing recognition of archive documents is an important problem. By analyzing traditional word-based image features we could not achieve results above 50% even with 7 different classification methods and using more than 300 image features per word.

In our paper we propose to use an image retrieval approach based on the SIFT. With testing over 1600 word images of noisy scripts we could achieve 81.5% hit rate. In future we plan to increase the efficiency by assigning confidence values to possible results. In our initial experiments we could achieve a further 1% increase in performance when the final decision between the first item of the results list, and the modus of the first 5 elements of the result list was based on the confidence of these two candidates. The confidence was defined as:

$$C = 100 - \sum_{i=1}^{n} d_i{}^2, \tag{4}$$

where n denotes the number of classes in the best 10 results not chosen as the final result and d_i denotes the number of elements of these classes within the best 10.

Acknowledgement. The work and publication of results have been supported by the Hungarian Research Fund, grant OTKA CNK 80368 and by TÁMOP-4.2.2/B-10/1-2010-0025.

References

1. Forney, G.D.: The Viterbi Algorithm. Proc. of the IEEE 61, 268–278 (1973)
2. Kobayashi, T., Toyama, T., Shafait, F.L., Dengel, A., Iwamura, M., Kise, K.: Recognizing Words in Scenes with a Head-Mounted Eye-Tracker. In: 10th IAPR Workshop on Document Analysis Systems, DAS 2012, Gold Coast, Australia (2012) (Accepted for Publication)
3. Lavrenko, V., Rath, T.M., Manmatha, R.: Holistic Word Recognition for Handwritten Historical Documents. In: International Workshop on Document Image Analysis for Libraries, pp. 278–287 (2004)
4. Lowe, D.G.: Object recognition from local scale-invariant features. In: Proceedings of the International Conference on Computer Vision, vol. 2, pp. 1150–1157 (1999)
5. Rath, T.M., Manmatha, R.: Word Spotting for Historical Documents. Int. Journal on Document Analysis and Recognition, 139–152 (2007)
6. Witten, I.H., Frank, E.: Data Mining: Practical Machine Learning Tools and Techniques with Java Implementations. Morgan Kaufmann (2000)
7. de Zeeuw, F.: Slant Correction using Histograms, BSc Thesis, University of Groningen (2006)

Comparison of Tensor Unfolding Variants for 2DPCA-Based Color Facial Portraits Recognition

Paweł Forczmański

West Pomeranian University of Technology, Szczecin
Faculty of Computer Science and Information Technology
Żołnierska 49, 71–210 Szczecin, Poland
pforczmanski@wi.zut.edu.pl

Abstract. The paper presents a problem of recognition of color facial images in the aspect of dimensionality reduction performed by means of Principal Component Analysis employing different variants of input data organization. Here, input images are represented by tensors of 3rd order and the PCA is applied for matrices derived from such tensors. Its main advantage is associated with efficient representation of images leading to the accurate recognition. The paper describes practical aspects of the algorithm and its implementation for three variants of tensor unfolding. Furthermore the impact of the number of training/testing images, the reduction ratio and the color model on the recognition accuracy is investigated. The experiments performed on Essex facial image databases showed that face recognition using this type of feature space dimensionality reduction is particularly convenient and efficient, giving high recognition performance.

1 Introduction

Principal Component Analysis (PCA) / Karhunen Loeve Transform (KLT) has been a popular method in the field of pattern recognition for many recent years [1,2]. It is mainly used for reduction of data dimensionality, however, it is possible to use it to perform both the dimensionality reduction as well as the clustering. However, using PCA for such tasks as image recognition, compression or retrieval, can be challenging because it treats data as one-dimensional, when in fact they are two-dimensional. That is why almost all known algorithms involve some sort of dimensionality pre-reduction (from 2D into 1D). For an image of size $M \times N$ pixels they form vectors of $MN \times 1$ elements. It is practically impossible to implement classical PCA on such data in a straightforward way, since the covariance matrix has a very large dimensions. The problem is even more complex, when data are representing color images, since the dimensionality of a single object in the set is equal to $M \times N \times D$, where D is responsible for the number of bands (or channels).

One of the possible solutions of this problem is a two-stage processing, where the first stage is used for preliminary dimensionality reduction of input data.

L. Bolc et al. (Eds.): ICCVG 2012, LNCS 7594, pp. 345–353, 2012.

There are many methods used at this stage, and they include specific features selection, downsampling or transformation into different domains, i.e. FFT or DCT [3]. In case of color images (e.g. RGB), simple transformation into luminosity or hue subspace is employed. Such an approach is easy to apply, yet it suffers from one important limitation, since preliminary reduction can lead to loss of particular (maybe important) information, what can influence the classification in undesirable way. The other way of solving above problem employs two-dimensional transformation based on PCA/KLT. There has been many scientific works published in the recent years that are related to the data dimensionality reduction by means of PCA, as well as their application to one of the most popular tasks, namely face recognition problem, taking into account the two-dimensional nature of images. Such algorithms have got different names e.g. 2DPCA [4], MatPCA [5], etc. Most of them are associated with the processing of two-dimensional data by means of data reduction algorithms performed along one dimension of image matrix only or by dividing an image into smaller parts and reducing them with help of classical PCA. On the other hand, the clear and handy algorithms of 'true' two-dimensional reduction are also available. The first algorithm from this group was presented by Tsapatsoulis et al. in [6]. It is a novel, two-dimensional version of KLT for face recognition task. A continuation of this method (as PCArc — for row and column representation) was presented in [7].

Above methods manage to process grayscale images in a very efficient way, however they can not cope with color images, since they are represented by 3D structures, which can be expressed as tensors. There are several solutions to this problem, and they include Horizontal Vertical Discriminant Analysis [8], Multilinear PCA, Color PCA [9]. For the first time, 3D Principal Component Analysis was introduced in [10] in the problem of three-way data analysis. A generalized method based on above approach was presented in [11], which shows the mathematical principles of the Higher Order Singular Value Decomposition (HOSVD). In the field of face recognition, the first successful application of HOSVD was presented by the authors of [12] who developed a framework to handle multidimensional image data and called it *Tensorfaces*. However, according to those authors, the main problem in practical implementation of HOSVD is related to its high computational complexity.

The main goal of this paper is to present much more simple method which performs PCA/KLT in a two-dimensional manner for a certain representations of color images, namely for different types of unfolding the tensors that capture the spatial properties of color images. The classification is performed using minimum-distance classifiers working in a specific subspace, responsible for different unfolding variants.

The most important properties of the presented method are simplicity and low computational cost, coming from low-dimensional representation of objects in the database. In the paper we show that such strategy of joining 2DPCA and conversion into a proper color-space can be applied to facial images database and fulfils clustering requirement, improving recognition efficiency. Additionally, we find the minimal number of samples in the training database which are responsible for a acceptable recognition accuracy.

2   Tensor Representation of Color Image

The idea of tensors was introduced to describe linear relations between vectors, scalars, and other tensors. Typically, a tensor can be represented as a multi-dimensional array of numerical values. Vectors and scalars themselves are also tensors, thus a vector can be represented as a one-dimensional array and is a 1st-order tensor, while a scalar is a single number and is thus a zeroth-order tensor. There are several approaches to defining tensors. The origin of the approach used in this paper is multilinear algebra [11,12]. From the general point of view, tensors are used to denote multidimensional objects, the elements of which are addressed by more than two indices [11]. The number of indices used in the description defines the order of the tensor and each index defines one of the so-called *modes*. Many still image and video data can be described by tensors. For example, color images are three-dimensional (3rd order tensor) objects with column, row and band dimensions. Gray-scale video sequences can also be viewed as 3rd order tensors with column, row and time dimensions. In the most promising area of biometrics, namely face recognition, face detection and recognition using 3D information described by tensors can be seen as an important research direction. Beyond a biometric signal analysis, many other computer vision and pattern recognition tasks can be also viewed as problems defined in the tensor domain. Such tasks exist in machine vision, medical image analysis, content-based image/video retrieval, human-computer interaction, etc. This wide range of applications and the importance of the whole idea justifies a large number of current works and strong authors interest.

Since a typical tensor object in pattern recognition or machine vision applications is commonly specified in a high-dimensional tensor space, recognition methods operating directly on this space suffer from the so called curse of dimensionality, namely handling high-dimensional samples is computationally inefficient and many classifiers perform poorly in high-dimensional spaces if there is a small number of training samples. However, since single elements in a tensor object are often highly correlated with their surroundings, it is quite favourably to assume that the tensor objects encountered in most applications are highly constrained and thus the tensors can be projected into a subspace with intrinsically low dimension.

3   Method Description

3.1   Initial Assumptions

Let us assume that each input color image X of $M \times N$ 3-component pixels is represented by a tensor of 3rd order. The assumption of three-component representation of color is valid for most of the color-spaces, e.g. RGB, HSV, YIQ,

YCbCr, etc. Let us also assume, that the image recognition system works on a set of images divided into classes. Parameters of the system are: $\{M, N, D, K, Q, L\}$, where M, N and D are dimensions of image (D is responsible for the number of color channels, or bands and in most cases is equal to 3), $K-$ number of classes, Q – number of class members, L – number of training images in a single class ($Q - L$ - the number of testing images). Hence, the training set consists of KL images, while the testing set contains $K(Q - L)$ images.

3.2   Data Preparation

In order to employ classical linear algebra methods, each i-th color image X_i has to be unfolded, thus stored as a matrix. In further parts of this paper we use three independent representations: $X^{(1)}_{MN \times D}, X^{(2)}_{M \times ND}$ and $X^{(3)}_{MD \times N}$ for variant-1, variant-2 and variant-3, respectively. In each representation we perform a concatenation of pixel triples (variant-1), image rows across all bands in an interleaved manner (variant-2) and image rows across bands in band-wise manner (variant-3) – see Fig. 1 for a graphical explanation. Further processing is performed on each of these representations in an independent way, hence for the comparison purposes we create three independent subspaces and perform three independent classification procedures. Compared to the two variants presented in [9], we perform three variants of unfolding. In the experimental part of the paper we show the results of classification in each of these subspaces. All processing steps are common. The only difference is the unfolding variant and the dimensionality of respective data objects.

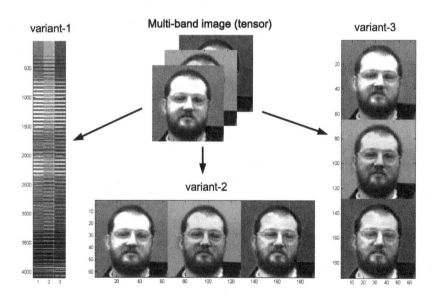

Fig. 1. Three variants of unfolding a color (multiband) image into 2D matrices

Here we employ a simplified 2DPCA method, such as described in [4], which is different from a 'true' two-dimensional PCA described in [7]. We do it in order to make computations less complicated, yet with acceptable performance degradation. First, we calculate mean matrices for the whole training set:

$$\bar{X}^{(1)} = \frac{1}{KL} \sum_i^{KL} X_i^{(1)}, \ \bar{X}^{(2)} = \frac{1}{KL} \sum_i^{KL} X_i^{(2)} \ \text{and} \ \bar{X}^{(3)} = \frac{1}{KL} \sum_i^{KL} X_i^{(3)}.$$

Then we center all images by removing the mean value and calculate respective covariance matrices: $C^{(1)} = \frac{1}{KL} \sum_i^{KL} (X_i^{(1)} - \bar{X}^{(1)})(X_i^{(1)} - \bar{X}^{(1)})^T$ $C^{(2)} = \frac{1}{KL} \sum_i^{KL} (X_i^{(2)} - \bar{X}^{(2)})(X_i^{(2)} - \bar{X}^{(2)})^T$ and $C^{(3)} = \frac{1}{KL} \sum_i^{KL} (X_i^{(3)} - \bar{X}^{(3)})(X_i^{(3)} - \bar{X}^{(3)})^T$ Thus, we have covariance matrices of size: $MN \times MN$, $M \times M$ and $MD \times MD$ elements, respectively. Then, we solve the three individual eigenproblems, through the decomposition of $C^{(1)}$, $C^{(2)}$ and $C^{(3)}$. Hence, we obtain three sets of eigenvalues and eigenvectors, from which we select a limited number of components (p_1, p_2, p_3, respectively), according to the usual energetic manner. In this way, we get three transform matrices: $F_{MN \times p_1}^{(1)}$, $F_{M \times p_2}^{(2)}$, and $F_{MD \times p_3}^{(3)}$. For each i-th image X from the training subset we calculate its reduced representations Y in each subspace by standard two-dimensional KLT transform:

$$Y_{p_1 \times D}^{(1)} = F^{(1)T}_{MN \times p_1} X_i^{(1)}, \ Y_{p_2 \times ND}^{(2)} = F^{(2)T}_{D \times p_2} X_i^{(2)}, \ Y_{p_3 \times MD}^{(3)} = F^{(3)T}_{D \times p_3} X_i^{(3)},$$

and store in a training database. The sizes of all data involved in the recognition process are presented in Tab. 1.

Table 1. Dimensionality of data structures in 2DPCA-based recognition

Unfolding variant	variant-1	variant-2	variant-3
Input object (face image) dim.	$MN \times D$	$M \times ND$	$MD \times N$
Covariance matrix dim.	$MN \times MN$	$M \times M$	$MD \times MD$
Transformation matrix dim.	$MN \times p_1$	$M \times p_2$	$MD \times p_3$
Output object dim.	$p_1 \times D$	$p_2 \times ND$	$p_3 \times N$
Training database dim.	$p_1 D \times (Q - L)$	$p_2 ND \times (Q - L)$	$p_3 N \times (Q - L)$

3.3 Reduction and Classification Stage

For each j-th image X from testing subset we create its 'unfolded' representation, subtract mean matrix calculated at the data preparation stage and calculate its reduced representation. The processing is performed in each subspace in the same manner, as it was described above. The classification is performed using simple Euclidean distance calculation to either all reduced training images or centres of all classes. The minimum distance points to a class of origin of the testing sample. Class center means here the average reduced feature vector for all images that belong to the particular class. Such an approach is less computationally expensive and generally faster, yet it fails when classes are not-well distributed and overlap each other. In general, the second approach gives slightly worse accuracy, however from the practical point of view, it is much faster and requires less memory.

4   Experiments

4.1   Datasets

All algorithms were tested on publicly available datasets containing facial portraits: Faces95 and Faces96 [13]. There is another dataset of this kind - Faces94, however it contains images taken in a very well controlled conditions and the results of the experiments performed on this set are not representative. All these datasets are provided by University of Essex, Department of Electronic Systems Engineering. Above datasets were chosen, first of all because they contain a large number of full-color images (large number of classes with high number of elements), then because they contain portraits with most of the distortions spotted in real-life applications. The images in datasets (24-bit RGB color JPEGs) present isolated faces with different expression, and variable shot orientation divided into classes related to the depicted subjects, 20 images each. Images contain portraits of male and female subjects, people of various racial origins, different age. Some of subjects wear glasses and have beards. Lighting is artificial, mixture of tungsten and fluorescent overhead. People in Faces95 are photographed over a uniform background (see first row of Fig. 2), while portraits from Faces96 are taken in front of some changing complex background (see third row of Fig. 2). Each face occupy most of the picture, but its size changes (since the distance to the camera changes over time). Detailed descriptions of both databases are given in Table 2. The experiments were performed on images taken directly from each set, as well as on cropped images, containing face-area only (see second and fourth row in Fig. 2). The crop procedure was performed in a semi-automatic way, using the distance between eyes (marked by human

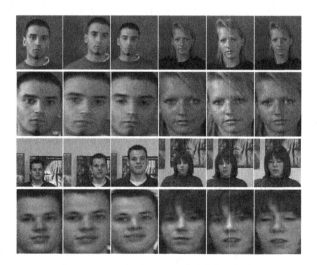

Fig. 2. Exemplary images from Faces95 (first row), cropped Faces95 (second row), Faces96 (third row) and cropped Faces96 (fourth row) used in the experiments

operator) as the reference dimension. Hence the total number of testing datasets were virtually increased to four.

Each input dataset was used to build two databases, which are independent from each other: one for training and one for testing purpose. In order to make the results more objective we employ cross-validation technique, since it is a very handy tool to protect against testing hypotheses suggested by the data. We performed 20 rounds of cross-validation, which involved random selection of training and testing images in each class. The final results are calculated as an average of all these rounds. In our experimental scenario, the number of training images was increased from 1 to 19, while the number of testing images was decreased from 19 to 1, respectively. The tests were performed across different sizes of images and dimensionality of features after reduction in order to find the most optimal parameters for each algorithm. Additionally, we investigated the influence of the number of training images vs. the number of testing images in order to find the minimum number of images that give acceptable recognition accuracy. This problem is very important for a traditional PCA approach in case of high-dimensional feature vectors which should be supported by large number of samples in the database [7].

Table 2. Characteristics of databases used in the experiments

Dataset	Faces95	Faces96
Number of classes (K)	72	151
Number of images in class (Q)	20	20
Total number of images (KQ)	1440	3020
Image dimensions ($M \times N$) [px]	180×200	196×196
Acquisition conditions	uniform background, changes in scale and lighting	variable background, changes in scale and lighting
Cropped facial area size [px]	120×160	120×160
Facial area after downsampling [px]	48×48	48×48

4.2   Results

The plots in Figure 3 present the results of experiments for all databases mentioned above, with input images downsampled to 48×48 pixels, and the reduction parameters $p_1 = 48$, $p_2 = 1$, and $p_3 = 3$, so that the output dimensionality of each feature-space was equal to 48, which makes the accuracy comparison objective. The distance was calculated according to the nearest-neighbour rule (the nearest object in the feature space points at the class of origin). The accuracy is presented as a function of learning samples number $L = 1,\ldots,19$. As it was written above, the final (average) results were obtained as an effect of 20 rounds of cross-validation. The plots present the results for different color-spaces (grayscale, RGB, HSV, YCbCr, YIQ) and different unfolding variants (as introduced in Section 3.2). In contrast to the work [9], we observed the superiority of HSV color space over the other color spaces, as well as the generally higher accuracy for first variant of tensor unfolding (HSV_1, YIQ_1, RGB_1). On the other hand, the worst recognition accuracy is obtained for second variant of unfolding (Gray_2, RGB_2, YCbCr_2), which is probably related to the dimensions of co-variance matrix (the smallest dimensions among all methods - see Tab 1). As a comparison, typical approach involving one-dimensional PCA on color and gray-scale images was also analysed. The results of those experiments show that the maximal recognition accuracy of one-dimensional PCA applied for color images (in a HSV representation, which gives the highest recognition rate) is lower than for the 2DPCA and varies from 0.7 (for full-frame images) to 0.9 (for cropped faces) in case of Essex Faces95 dataset and from 0.8 to 0.85 in case of Essex Faces96, respectively.

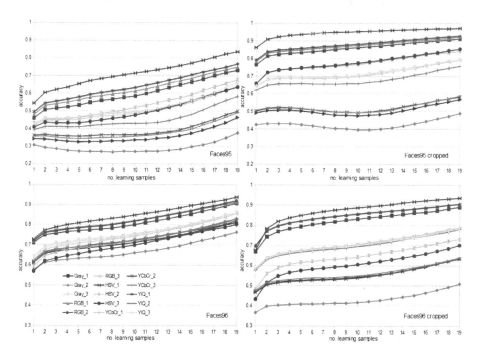

Fig. 3. The results of recognition for Essex Faces datasets

5   Summary

The experiments presented in this paper confirms the fact that employing full color representation of images improves the accuracy of a face recognition algorithm based on two-dimensional Principal Component Analysis. It is consistent with the results presented in [9], however an unanimous superiority of only one color space was observed. Performed experiments showed, that in case of face recognition, the HSV color space is superior to the grayscale representation and other investigated color models (RGB, YCbCr and YIQ). Another important observation is that the size of the covariance matrix is a determining factor, when it comes to recognition accuracy. For the pixel-wise unfolding (variant-1) of the color image tensor we obtain the largest covariance matrix which dramatically improves the recognition accuracy. On the other hand, the smaller covariance matrices associated with vertical and horizontal line-based unfolding (variant-2 and variant-3, respectively) lead to lower recognition accuracy with much lower memory requirements. Moreover, computing only a partial unfolding of the original image tensor and performing the simplified 2DPCA on the resultant two-dimensional matrix leads to a much less computationally expensive problem, than in case of full HOSVD, which from the practical point of view is very important.

References

1. Turk, M., Pentland, A.: Eigenfaces for Recognition. Journal of Cognitive Neuroscience 3(1), 71–86 (1991)
2. Li Stan, Z., Jain, A.K.: Handbook of Face Recognition, vol. 395. Springer (2005)
3. Forczmański, P., Kukharev, G.: Comparative analysis of simple facial features extractors. J. of Real-Time Image Processing 1(4), 239–255 (2007)
4. Yang, J., Zhang, D., Frangi, A.F., Yang, J.-Y.: Two-Dimensional PCA: A New Approach to Appearance-Based Face Representation and Recognition. IEEE Trans. Pattern Anal. Mach. Intell. 26(1), 131–137 (2004)
5. Chen, S., Zhu, Y., Zhang, D., Yang, J.-Y.: Feature extraction approaches based on matrix pattern: MatPCA and MatFLDA. Pattern Recognition Letters 26, 1157–1167 (2005)
6. Tsapatsoulis, N., Alexopoulos, V., Kollias, S.: A Vector Based Approximation of KLT and Its Application to Face Recognition. In: Proceedings of The IX European Signal Processing Conference EUSIPCO 1998, Island of Rhodes, Greece (1998)
7. Kukharev, G., Forczmański, P.: Data Dimensionality Reduction for Face Recognition. Machine Graphics and Vision 13(1/2), 99–122 (2004)
8. Yang, J., Liu, C.: Horizontal and Vertical 2DPCA Based Discriminant Analysis for Face Verification Using the FRGC Version 2 Database. In: Lee, S.-W., Li, S.Z. (eds.) ICB 2007. LNCS, vol. 4642, pp. 838–847. Springer, Heidelberg (2007)
9. Thomas, M., Kumar, S., Kambhamettu, C.: Face Recognition Using a Color PCA Framework. In: Gasteratos, A., Vincze, M., Tsotsos, J.K. (eds.) ICVS 2008. LNCS, vol. 5008, pp. 373–382. Springer, Heidelberg (2008)
10. Tucker, R.L.: Some mathematical notes on the three-mode factor analysis. Psychometrika 31, 279–331 (1966)
11. De Lathauwer, L., De Moor, B., Vandewalle, J.: A multilinear Singular Value Decomposition. SIAM 21(4), 1253–1278 (2000)
12. Vasilescu, M.A.O., Terzopoulos, D.: Multilinear Analysis of Image Ensembles: TensorFaces. In: Heyden, A., Sparr, G., Nielsen, M., Johansen, P. (eds.) ECCV 2002, Part I. LNCS, vol. 2350, pp. 447–460. Springer, Heidelberg (2002)
13. University of Essex, Department of Computer Science. Essex Faces - facial images collection, http://cswww.essex.ac.uk/mv/allfaces (accessed April 01, 2012)

Comparative Analysis of Benchmark Datasets for Face Recognition Algorithms Verification

Paweł Forczmański and Magdalena Furman

West Pomeranian University of Technology, Szczecin
Faculty of Computer Science and Information Technology
Żołnierska Str. 52, 71–210 Szczecin, Poland
{pforczmanski,mfurman}@wi.zut.edu.pl

Abstract. The paper presents a problem of recognition of facial portraits in the aspect of benchmark database quality. The aim of the work presented here was to analyse the potential of datasets published over the Internet and the predicted applicability of such data for the task of face recognition performance verification. We gathered 41 datasets created and published by various academic and commercial bodies. In the paper we focus on both pure data characteristics, including the number of images, their spatial resolution, quality, content and usability, as well as more high-level properties, e.g. face orientation, expression, background, lighting, and attributes like hats, glasses and beards. We have chosen several datasets on which we performed more detailed experiments related to face recognition. We employed several database preparation algorithms (cross-validation based on different schemes) to make the results as much objective as possible. Here, Principal Component Analysis was employed, as a standard tool for dimensionality reduction. The classification was performed using simple Euclidean metrics. Performed experiments showed a true potential of selected databases.

1 Introduction and Motivation

Let us assume that automatic human authentication and identification based on facial portraits is performed by a Face Recognition System (FaReS). Typical FaReS consists of several modules, i.e. initial processing, face detection, user registration and database creation/update, feature extraction, classification or comparison stage. The most complicated stages are face detection, feature extraction and classification, which is related to the often unstable conditions of enrolling the input data, the large number of individuals with small number of template images, sophisticated methods of processing and ambiguous interpretation. Because of the non-rigid characteristics and complex three-dimensional form, the appearance of a face is influenced by a number of factors including face pose, illumination, facial expression, age, occlusion, and hair. Many algorithms robust to these variations have been developed so far, however most of them have been tested on very limited number of benchmark datasets, sometimes with very

L. Bolc et al. (Eds.): ICCVG 2012, LNCS 7594, pp. 354–362, 2012.
© Springer-Verlag Berlin Heidelberg 2012

limited number of samples. It should be remembered, that every recognition algorithm requires databases of sufficient size that include carefully controlled variations of these factors. Moreover, such databases are necessary to comparatively evaluate algorithms. Of course, collecting a high quality database is a resource- and time-intensive task. Hence, the availability of public face databases is important for the advancement of the field. In this paper we review 41 publicly available benchmark databases used for face recognition, face detection, and facial expression analysis. It is an obvious improvement over the previous work on this topic presented in [1], where only 27 datasets were presented.

There are three main areas of applicability of face databases, namely algorithms mainly associated with: (i) face detection, (ii) face identification or verification, and (iii) expression recognition. Typical benchmark database is used at the stages of algorithm development and testing. Hence, it is so important for the database to contain images representing as many real-world situations as possible. Face detection algorithms typically have to be trained on face and non-face images to build up an internal representation of the human face as a set of general rules. On the other hand, face identification/verification algorithms, have to extract original features of each face in order to create individual representations of an enrolled person. Finally, expression recognition algorithms are oriented at detecting specific features of every face, i.e. localize and describe interesting landmarks (eyes, nose, mouth, etc.), so in such case, it is important to create a database with many faces presenting specific expressions. Our survey shows that there is no universal database oriented at all above problems. Further in the paper we present several databases with their basic characteristics and show an example application related to human face recognition investigated on 24 of 41 presented datasets.

2   Benchmark Datasets

All face databases included in this comparison have been obtained from the Internet. Most of the data describing basic features of those datasets had been collected from their web sites at the stage of writing this text (see Tab. 1). However, not all authors provide detailed descriptions, so the remaining data had been collected by a dedicated Matlab script or individually investigated.

2.1   Databases Characteristics

Almost all of the databases contain images in RGB colour system, stored in typical file formats (i.e. jpeg, png), with resolution between $86 \times 86 - 2048 \times 1536$. The number of classes in all databases is not lower than 10. More detailed characteristics of files , the number of classes and images in each class are presented in Tab. 1. Several databases are not divided into classes or contain variable number of images in each class, which makes further classification (using ground-truth) a little bit complicated.

The basic characteristics related to image resolution or the number of images is sufficient, when we deal with algorithms of face detection. However, in case

Table 1. Basic face databases properties

No.	Src.	Name	Fmt.	No. of clas.	Total img.	Avg. img. / class	Min-Max img. / class	Width [px]	Height [px]	R G B	M	F
1	[5]	PICS Aberdeen	jpeg	90	687	8	1 - 18	336-624	480-544	Y	61	29
2	[5]	PICS Iranian	jpeg	34	369	11	2 - 21	1200	900	Y	0	34
3	[5]	PICS Stirling	jpeg	35	312	9	3 - 9	269	369	N	17	18
4	[5]	PICS Pain	jpeg	23	599	26	25-28	720	576	Y	10	13
5	[5]	PICS Paincrop	jpeg	12	84	7	7	181	241	N	0	12
6	[5]	PICS Utrecht	jpeg	69	131	2	1 - 3	900	1200	Y	49	20
7	[6]	FEI Face DB	jpeg	200	2800	14	14	640	480	Y	100	100
8	[7]	CVL Face DB	jpeg	114	797	7	7-10	640	480	Y	108	6
9	[8]	Faces in Wild	ppm	1680	13000	8	NA	86	86	Y	NA	NA
10	[9]	Indian Face DB	jpeg	61	677	11	6 - 22	640	480	Y	39	22
11	[10]	Color FERET	jpeg	1199	14126	12	NA	256	384	Y	NA	NA
12	[11]	PIE DB, CMU	jpeg	68	41368	608	NA	640	486	Y	50	18
13	[12]	BioID Face DB	pgm	23	1521	66	NA	384	286	N	16	7
14	[13]	MUCT Face DB	jpeg	276	3755	14	10-15	480	640	Y	135	141
15	[14]	IMM Face DB	bmp	40	240	6	6	640	480	Y	33	7
16	[15]	Faces94	jpeg	153	3059	20	20-38	180	200	Y	134	19
17	[15]	Faces95	jpeg	72	1440	20	20	180	200	Y	60	12
18	[15]	Faces96	jpeg	152	3016	20	20	196	196	Y	130	22
19	[15]	Grimaces	jpeg	18	360	20	20	180	200	Y	16	2
20	[16]	AT&T (ORL)	pgm	40	400	10	10	92	112	N	36	4
21	[17]	MIT CBCL orig.	jpeg	10	59	6	5 - 8	768	576	Y	7	3
22	[17]	MIT CBCL synth.	pgm	10	3240	324	324	200	200	N	7	3
23	[17]	MIT CBCL test	jpeg	10	2000	200	200	115	115	N	7	3
24	[18]	CalTech Faces	jpeg	25	450	18	5 - 29	896	592	Y	15	10
25	[19]	GeorgiaTech Faces	jpeg	50	750	15	15-16	640	480	Y	43	7
26	[20]	Pointing Head DB	jpeg	15	2790	186	186	384	288	Y	13	2
27	[21]	UM CVL FD	bmp	576	1142	2	NA	640	480	Y	219	357
28	[22]	FPT asian	jpeg	53	1284	24	NA	250	250	Y	19	34
29	[22]	FPT caucasian	jpeg	106	3362	32	NA	250	250	Y	49	57
30	[22]	FPT black	jpeg	34	937	28	NA	250	250	Y	16	18
31	[22]	FPT multiracial	jpeg	23	497	22	NA	250	250	Y	6	17
32	[22]	FPT hispanic	jpeg	19	494	26	NA	250	250	Y	2	17
33	[23]	JAFFE DB	tiff	10	213	21	20-41	256	256	N	0	10
34	[24]	Sheffield/UMIST	pgm	20	564	28	24-84	220	220	N	16	4
35	[25]	XM2VTS DB	ppm	295	1180	4	NA	720	576	Y	157	138
36	[26]	BANCA	png	208	6240	30	NA	720	576	Y	104	104
37	[27]	PUT Face DB	jpeg	100	9971	100	NA	2048	1536	Y	178	22
38	[28]	AR Face DB	raw	126	4000	32	NA	768	576	Y	70	56
39	[29]	Yale Face	gif	15	165	11	NA	640	480	N	NA	NA
40	[30]	Yale Face B	pgm	10	5850	585	NA	640	480	N	NA	NA
41	[30]	Yale Face B+	pgm	28	16128	576	NA	640	480	N	NA	NA

of more sophisticated algorithms of face classification or expression recognition, we have to chose a database which fits our needs in a much better way. Table 2 presents database features, which are useful while choosing the dataset for further computations and algorithms verification. It includes information about background in images, face position and orientation. Most of the images have been taken in front of uniform background, have various face orientation, the background is the same inside and outside classes. Faces are usually not cropped and occupy fixed place. Analysed databases contain portraits of male and female subjects, people of various racial origins, and different age. Some of the subjects wear glasses and have beards. Lighting is, in most cases, artificial - mixture of tungsten and fluorescent overhead, however, sometimes it is natural.

Most of the analysed databases contain images enrolled during a short period of time with similar environmental conditions. This is an obvious advantage for face recognition algorithms. However, in our comparison we also include databases with special properties, which are especially desirable in case of face detection and expression recognition, i.e. (No. 33 in Tab. 1). Vital longevity database (No. 27) contains photos of people divided according to gender, race and age. This same rule, related to race only, is used in case of FPT (No. 18). There are several landmarked databases (No. 8, 9, 10, 23, 24), which contain text files describing position of face feature points such as eyes, eyebrows, lips and nose, which are useful for gesture recognition and facial analysis. FERET (No. 11) and Face Place Tarrlab (No. 28—32) contain images of people with or without special attributes, such as glasses, hats, scarves, etc. There are four databases (No. 9, 11, 12 and 40) that contain more than 10000 images. Special column about race of people has been provided in case that result can depend on races of people included in dataset. Only few of them have been categorized as containing only Caucasian race, other are multiracial.

3   Sample Application

There is a variety of algorithms employed in the facial portrait recognition. One of the most popular, yet very efficient, is the whole family of subspace methods (i.e. Principal Component Analysis [2], Independent Component Analysis [3], Linear Discriminant Analysis [4] etc.). In order to show the applicability of presented databases for the purpose of face recognition, we have developed a dedicated software framework in Matlab. For the purpose of this work, this framework employs one-dimensional PCA approach, since it shows database properties and their potential in the aspect of recognition. The PCA is also a *de facto* standard which serves as a base algorithm in testing more sophisticated methods.

In the processing we focused on the proper preparation of data in order to make the results of recognition very accurate and reliable. That is why we divided the dataset into training and testing subsets according to several cross-validation modes. We employed the following configurations: (i) Leave-one-out, (ii) Holdout with 0.1, 0.5, and 0.9, and (iii) K-fold with 2, $0.5 * K$, and $K - 1$ (where K is a number of class members). This strategy allows to see the distribution of the results (in case of different K value).

Table 2. Detailed characteristic of databases (Columns `Race` means Caucasian (1) or Multiracial (2), `Grimace` : none (1), normal+smile (2), light (3), strong (4))

No.	Race (*)	Backgr. color	Var. backgr. in class	Var. face orient.	Var. light-ing	Face pro-file	Var. backgr. out class	Uniform backgr.	Grim. (**)	Var. face loc.	Crop.
1	2	white	N	N	Y	N	N	Y	1	N	N
2	2	white	N	Y	N	Y	N	Y	2	N	N
3	1	black	N	Y	N	Y	N	Y	2	N	Y
4	1	white	N	N	N	Y	N	Y	4	N	Y
5	1	white	N	N	N	N	N	N	4	N	Y
6	2	blue	N	N	N	N	N	Y	4	N	N
7	2	white	N	Y	Y	Y	N	Y	2	N	N
8	1	white	N	Y	N	Y	N	Y	2	N	N
9	2	various	Y	Y	Y	N	Y	N	4	N	Y
10	2	white	N	Y	N	Y	N	Y	2	N	N
11	2	white	N	N	N	N	N	Y	3	N	Y
12	2	lab	Y	Y	Y	Y	N	N	3	Y	N
13	2	office	Y	Y	Y	N	Y	N	4	Y	N
14	2	blue	N	Y	Y	N	N	Y	2	N	N
15	1	green	N	Y	N	N	N	Y	2	N	N
16	2	green	N	N	N	N	N	Y	1	N	Y
17	2	red	N	N	Y	N	N	Y	1	Y	N
18	2	various	N	N	Y	N	Y	N	1	Y	N
19	2	white	N	N	N	N	N	Y	4	N	Y
20	1	grey	N	Y	N	N	N	Y	2	N	Y
21	2	white	N	Y	N	Y	N	Y	1	Y	N
22	2	grey	N	Y	Y	N	N	Y	1	N	N
23	2	black	Y	Y	Y	N	Y	N	1	Y	N
24	2	various	Y	N	Y	N	Y	N	2	Y	N
25	2	lab	Y	Y	N	N	N	N	2	Y	N
26	2	white	N	Y	N	Y	N	Y	1	Y	N
27	2	white	N	N	N	Y	N	Y	4	N	N
28	2	white	N	Y	N	Y	N	Y	2	N	N
29	1	white	N	Y	N	Y	N	Y	2	N	N
30	2	white	N	Y	N	Y	N	Y	2	N	N
31	2	white	N	Y	N	Y	N	Y	2	N	N
32	2	white	N	Y	N	Y	N	Y	2	N	N
33	2	grey	N	N	N	N	N	Y	3	N	N
34	2	grey	N	Y	N	Y	N	Y	1	N	Y
35	2	blue	N	N	N	N	N	Y	1	N	N
36	2	various	Y	N	N	N	Y	N	3	Y	N
37	NA	white	N	Y	N	Y	N	Y	1	N	N
38	2	white	N	N	Y	N	N	Y	4	N	N
39	NA	white	N	N	Y	N	N	Y	4	N	Y
40	2	various	Y	N	Y	N	Y	N	4	N	N
41	2	lab	N	Y	Y	N	N	N	1	N	N

Using a classical PCA approach for such tasks as image recognition can be challenging because it treats the data as one-dimensional, when in fact they are two-dimensional. Hence, we employed a down-scaling and image rows concatenation as the first stage of preprocessing. Employed datasets contain both grayscale and full-color images, thus all images have been converted to grayscale.

3.1 Applied Recognition Algorithm

According to the PCA-framework, each face image had been substituted by a combination of the eigenfaces corresponding to the largest eigenvalues. In order to make computations faster, images had been downscaled to 25×35 pixels each. The algorithm of recognition contains the following steps:

1. Obtain the data set of face images, divide into training and test set.
2. Calculate the eigenfaces of training set.
3. Project each image from a test set onto a reduced PCA representation.
4. Classify each element from test set into the closest classes.

We applied three variants of feature vector length, as it shows the variability of the results: first 10 components (PC10), first 50 comp. (PC50), and first 100 comp. (PC100). Such numbers are a result of testing on a small dataset, which showed, that a classification with more than 15 principal components representation performs with similar efficiency as 50 or 100.

3.2 Experimental Results

The results of three experiments are presented in Fig. 1, Fig. 2, and Fig. 3. As it can be seen, the lowest performance give databases: No. 2, No. 8, No. 24 and No. 28-32, while the highest - No. 16 and No. 19. Databases No. 16 and No. 19 have the same values in Tab. 2 hence it is probably the most efficient configuration of database properties for a face recognition. Performance of those databases did not change significantly while changing the representation of an image (10 — 100 element vector), such that 10-element representation is enough to perform face recognition in an effective way. Common characteristic of databases with the lowest PCA performance (No. 2, 8, 28-32) are: variable face orientations (face profile and frontal views in different configurations) and not cropped images. The CalTech DB (No. 24) is an exception having 8 out of 10 characteristics different. Databases No. 28-32 are the most problematic datasets, where faces are presented with various combination of attributes such as hats, glasses and wigs.

Based on our observations we divide the analysed databases into three classes, according to the suggested application area (numbers refer to Tab. 1):

1. face detection: 12, 13, 17, 18, 21, 23, 24, 25, 26, 36 (with variable face location);
2. expression recognition: 4, 5, 6, 9, 11, 12, 13, 19, 27, 33, 36, 38, 39, 40 (with grimaces);
3. face recognition: 1, 5, 6, 9, 11, 14, 15, 16, 17, 18, 19, 20, 22, 23, 24, 25, 33, 35, 36, 38, 39, 40, 41.

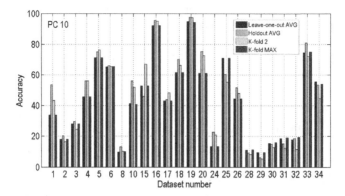

Fig. 1. The accuracy of classification with 10 principal components

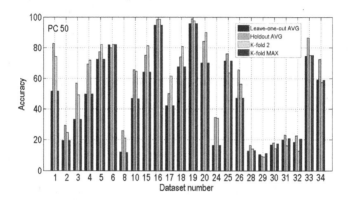

Fig. 2. The accuracy of classification with 50 principal components

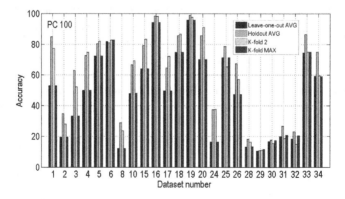

Fig. 3. The accuracy of classification with 100 principal components

4 Summary

In the paper we presented a survey on benchmark databases that can be applied in the field of face recognition algorithms, including face detection, face classification and expression recognition. In opposition to the other similar projects our work contains very large number of publicly available datasets and it presents some experiments that indicate the potential of some of the databases. Our observations are related to appearance-based PCA recognition algorithms, as such algorithms are the most popular in the scientific community. The most important observations coming from our experiments are as follows. When a database contains cropped face images, it is important to have a normalized view, such that the eyes are in the same position. Databases with various position of face in the image, should be cropped before classification to get better results. Databases that contain classes with a single item are not useful in PCA-based classification at all. By including a profile view we may increase the classification error rate. The most desirable database features are: (i) Uniform background (the same in whole dataset), (ii) Only frontal view of faces, (iii) Fixed location of faces, and (iv) Cropped portraits.

References

1. Gross, R.: Face Database. In: Li, S., Jain, A. (eds.) Handbook of Face Recognition, p. 395. Springer (2005)
2. Turk, M., Pentland, A.: Eigenfaces for Recognition. Journal of Cognitive Neuroscience 3(1), 71–86 (1991)
3. Bartlett, M.S., Movellan, J.R., Sejnowski, T.J.: Face recognition by independent component analysis. IEEE Trans. on Neural Networks 13(6), 1450–1464 (2002)
4. Swets, D., Weng, J.: Using Discriminant Eigenfeatures for Image Retrieval. IEEE Trans. on Pattern Analysis and Machine Intelligence 18(8), 831–836 (1996)
5. Hancock, P.: Psychological Image Collection at Stirling, PICS (2011), http://pics.psych.stir.ac.uk/2D_face_sets.htm
6. Thomaz, C.E., Giraldi, G.A.: A new ranking method for Principal Components Analysis and its application to face image analysis. Image and Vision Comp. 28(6), 902–913 (2010)
7. Solina, F., Peer, P., Batagelj, B., Juvan, S., Kovac, J.: Color-based face detection in the "15 seconds of fame" art installation. In: Mirage 2003, Conference on Computer Vision / Computer Graphics Collaboration for Model-based Imaging, Rendering, image Analysis and Graphical special Effects, INRIA Rocquencourt, France, Wilfried Philips, Rocquencourt, INRIA, pp. 38–47 (2003)
8. Huang, G.B., Ramesh, M., Berg, T., Learned-Miller, E.: Labeled Faces in the Wild: A Database for Studying Face Recognition in Unconstrained Environments. University of Massachusetts, Amherst, Tech. Rep. 07-49 (2007)
9. Jain, V., Mukherjee, A.: The Indian Face Database (2002), http://vis-www.cs.umass.edu/~vidit/IndianFaceDatabase
10. Phillips, P., Wechsler, H., Huang, J., Rauss, P.: The FERET database and evaluation procedure for face recognition algorithms. Image and Vision Comp. 16/5, 295–306 (1999)

11. Sim, T., Baker, S., Bsat, M.: The CMU Pose, Illumination, and Expression Database. IEEE TPAMI 25(12) (2003)
12. BioID-Technology Research. The BioID Face Database. (2001), http://www.bioid.com/downloads/software/bioid-face-database.html
13. Milborrow, S., Morkel, J., Nicolls, F.: The MUCT Landmarked Face Database, Pattern Recognition Association of South Africa (2010), http://www.milbo.org/muct
14. Nordstrøm, M.M., Larsen, M., Sierakowski, J., Stegmann, M.B.: The IMM Face Database - An Annotated Dataset of 240 Face Images, Informatics and Mathematical Modelling, Technical University of Denmark, DTU (2004), http://www2.imm.dtu.dk/pubdb/p.php?3160
15. Spacek, L.: Collection of facial Images. Computer Vision Science Research Projects, University of Essex, Department of Computer Science, Essex (2008), http://cswww.essex.ac.uk/mv/allfaces
16. AT&T Laboratories Cambridge. Database of Faces (1994), http://www.cl.cam.ac.uk/research/dtg/attarchive/facedatabase.html
17. Weyrauch, B., Huang, J., Heisele, B., Blanz, V.: Component-based Face Recognition with 3D Morphable Models. In: First IEEE Workshop on Face Processing in Video, Washington, D.C. (2004)
18. Weber, M.: Frontal face dataset. California Institute of Technology (1999), http://www.vision.caltech.edu/html-files/archive.html
19. Georgia Tech Face Database (2011), http://ftp.ee.gatech.edu/pub/users/hayes/facedb/
20. Gourier, N., Hall, D., Crowley, J.L.: Estimating Face Orientation from Robust Detection of Salient Facial Features Proceedings of Pointing. In: ICPR, International Workshop on Visual Observation of Deictic Gestures, Cambridge, UK (2004)
21. Minear, M., Park, D.C.: A lifespan database of adult facial stimuli. Behavior Research Methods, Instruments, & Computers 36, 630–633 (2004)
22. Tarr, M.J.: Face-Place, Center for the Neural Basis of Cognition, Carnegie Mellon University (2008), http://www.tarrlab.org/
23. Lyons, M.J., Akamatsu, S., Kamachi, M., Gyoba, J.: Coding Facial Expressions with Gabor Wavelets Proceedings. In: Third IEEE Internat. Conference on Automatic Face and Gesture Recognition, pp. 200–205. IEEE Comp. Society, Nara Japan (1998)
24. Graham, D.B., Allinson, N.M.: Characterizing Virtual Eigensignatures for General Purpose Face Recognition. In: Wechsler, H., Phillips, P.J., Bruce, V., Fogelman-Soulie, F., Huang, T.S. (eds.) Face Recognition: From Theory to Applications, NATO ASI Series F, Computer and Systems Sciences, vol. 163, pp. 446–456 (1998)
25. Messer, K., Matas, J., Kittler, J., Luettin, J., Maitre, G.: Xm2vtsdb: The extended m2vts database. In: Second Inter. Conf. of Audio and Video-based Biometric Person Authentication (1999)
26. The BANCA Database (2004), http://www.ee.surrey.ac.uk/CVSSP/banca/
27. Kasiński, A., Florek, A., Schmidt, A.: The PUT Face Database. Image Processing & Communications 13(3-4), 59–64 (2008)
28. Martinez, A.M., Benavente, R.: The AR Face Database. CVC Tech. Rep. #24 (1998)
29. Bellhumer, P.N., Hespanha, J., Kriegman, D.: Eigenfaces vs. fisherfaces: Recognition using class specific linear projection. IEEE TPAMI, Special Issue on Face Recognition 17(7), 711–720 (1997)
30. Georghiades, A.S., Belhumeur, P.N., Kriegman, D.J.: From Few to Many: Illumination Cone Models for Face Recognition under Variable Lighting and Pose. IEEE Trans. Pattern Anal. Mach. Intelligence 23(6), 643–660 (2001)

An Experimental Evaluation of the Polar-Fourier Greyscale Descriptor in the Recognition of Objects with Similar Silhouettes

Dariusz Frejlichowski

West Pomeranian University of Technology, Szczecin
Faculty of Computer Science and Information Technology
Żołnierska 52, 71-210, Szczecin, Poland
dfrejlichowski@wi.zut.edu.pl

Abstract. The use of the Polar-Fourier Greyscale Desicrptor in the recognition of objects, which are very similar in shape is evaluated in the paper. For this purpose, a benchmark image database consisting of six butterflies species was applied. The investigated descriptor, which was designed for the representation of objects extracted from digital images, is based on the combination of polar and Fourier transforms applied for objects in greyscale. Some other operations are applied in order to improve the efficiency of the algorithm as a whole. The method was tested using 120 images of butterflies, 20 for 6 species, and has obtained 90% of efficiency.

1 Introduction and Motivation

The automatic analysis of digital image content can be based on the recognition of particular objects visible within an image. The complete approach would be based on several crucial stages, e.g. pre-processing, image enhancement, segmentation, extraction of objects and finally — their classification. This paper is devoted to the last of these stages, i.e., the recognition of objects extracted from a digital image. For this purpose, these objects have to be properly described using particular representation algorithms, which employ such properties as shape, texture, colour, luminance, context of the information, movement, etc. ([1]). Each of the enumerated features has its advantages and drawbacks. Hence, for each application it is important to carefully select the appropriate features. Usually only one feature is considered, but sometimes, in order to improve the effectiveness, a combination of two or more descriptors is proposed.

The shape is often considered as the most distinguishable feature. This assumption is usually correct, especially in the case of technical objects. A majority of computer vision systems work with shapes that may be clearly differentiated for various classes, but sometimes the application enforces the recognition of very similar silhouettes. An example is the recognition of airplanes, in which different classes can contain very similar instances. Nevertheless, there exist algorithms that can handle this difficult task and obtain sufficient efficiency ([2,3]).

L. Bolc et al. (Eds.): ICCVG 2012, LNCS 7594, pp. 363–370, 2012.

However, there are some applications, in which the distinction between different classes is not that obvious. An example is considered in this paper — the recognition of particular butterfly species. In this case the shape is not sufficient for the reliable identification, since butterflies of different species can have the same shape of wings and the body. Hence, for their identification some other features have to be used, e.g. dominant wing pattern element ([4]), local characteristics of wings ([5]) or information about colors ([6]).

In this paper a different approach for solving this difficult problem is investigated. Taking into consideration the peculiar character of the butterfly objects extracted from digital images, a method combining information about the shape and other features of an object is studied, namely the Polar-Fourier Greyscale Descriptor. Until now, this algorithm was utilized only in two applications — the recognition of erythrocytes for the automatic (or semi-automatic) diagnosis of some diseases ([7]), and the identification of persons based on ear images ([8]).

The descriptor has several advantages. It is invariant to translation, scaling and rotation. It is also robust to some level of noise, thanks to the application of the Fourier transform. It works on objects in greyscale, hence it contains more information than in those cases in which only a shape is used.

The remaining part of the paper is organised as follows. The second section presents a detailed description of the Polar-Fourier Greyscale Descriptor, as well as its former application results. The third section describes the experimental methodology and the results. Finally, the last section concludes this paper.

2   The Polar-Fourier Greyscale Descriptor

The Polar-Fourier Greyscale Descriptor has some useful properties. As opposed to shape descriptors, this algorithm works on objects represented in greyscale. The advantage here results from the fact that the most important problem concerning algorithms based on a shape is the influence of the shape extraction process and noise on its final description. It is assumed that the use of a greyscale area with an object instead of an extracted shape will be more efficient thanks to the limited number of essential stages in the algorithm which can hamper the later feature representation. Moreover, in some applications (as in the problem of butterfly species identification investigated in this paper) the silhouette of an object can be insufficient. In the mentioned case, the specific pattern visible on wings has also to be taken into consideration. The usage of greyscale information in the investigated descriptor will be very helpful in the distinction between objects belonging to different classes.

The Polar-Fourier Greyscale Descriptor was proposed in [7] and applied in the recognition of erythrocytes extracted from digital microscopic images, stained using the May-Grunwald-Giemsa method. For this purpose, 55 images converted into greyscale were applied. Since there may be hundreds of cells within a single image, the number of objects for processing was close to ten thousand in the experiment. Every cell was automatically localised and extracted using the approach described in [9]. Next, it was represented using the Polar-Fourier

Greyscale Descriptor and matched with the templates. Having in mind the variety of appearances of the erythrocytes, five templates were stored and used for each of the twelve classes. They were also represented using the mentioned descriptor. The total average recognition result was close to 86%. It can be considered a very promising result when taking into account two aspects. Firstly, the ideal identification of cells is not possible, because of the poor quality of microscopic images. Secondly, for the automatic (or semi-automatic) diagnosis the results do not have to be ideal. In most cases even the presence of one abnormal red blood cell is sufficient to indicate a possibility of a disease ([7]).

In [8] the descriptor was applied in the identification of persons based on ear images. There were no pre-assumed limitations for the images which have been used in the experiments. They were distorted by the weather or light conditions, influenced by the acquisition process, or they were the result of the lossy compression. And above all, the presence of some other objects (e.g. earrings) hampered the proper identification. The initial experiments gave an average 84% efficiency of recognition.

The described approach is a combination of polar and Fourier transforms. Firstly, the transformation from Cartesian to polar co-ordinates is applied, then the two-dimensional Fourier transform of the achieved polar image. In the final stage, a small subspectrum is extracted which represents the described object. Owing to these two transforms the descriptor is invariant to rotation and translation of the object within the image plane. The usage of the Fourier transform, as well as the selection of the spectrum subpart, results in the robustness to noise and a property of generalisation.

In order to solve several other problems, few operations were added to the described algorithm. In order to reduce the influence of image quality on the recognition results firstly the subimage covering an object is pre-processed using the median and low-pass filters. Because the size of the input subimage is not known it needs to be expanded according to the maximal distance from the centre of the object (calculated by means of the moment theory). The resulting new areas have to be filled with the constant greyscale value. Later, the polar transform can be applied. Another problem is the varying size of the represented object. It was solved by resizing it to the constant size (128×128 pixels). The resultant image is subjected to 2D Fourier transform. Finally, the square subpart from the absolute spectrum with the size of 10×10 is extracted, concatenated, and stored as a vector representing the object.

Below, the algorithm for the object representation using Polar-Fourier Greyscale Descriptor is provided:

Step 1. Modify the input subimage I by means of the median filter with the kernel size equal to 3, i.e. the mask with size 3×3 pixels.

Step 2. Smooth the subimage I using the low-pass convolution filter, with size of the mask 3×3 pixels, with ones, and normalisation parameter equal to 9.

Step 3. Calculate the centroid O by means of the simple moment theory:

Step 3a. Calculate moment values m_{00}, m_{10}, m_{01} by means of the general formula ([10]):

$$m_{pq} = \sum_x \sum_y x^p y^q I(x, y). \tag{1}$$

Step 3b. Calculate the centroid O with coordinates x_c, y_c using the formulas ([10]):

$$x_c = \frac{m_{10}}{m_{00}}, \qquad y_c = \frac{m_{01}}{m_{00}}. \tag{2}$$

Step 4. Derive d_{maxX}, d_{maxY} — the maximal distances from the centroid O to the boundaries of the subimage I:

Step 4a. Calculate the distances from O to particular boundaries of the subimage I:

$$d_1 = x_c, \qquad d_2 = M - x_c, \qquad d_3 = y_c, \qquad d_4 = N - y_c, \tag{3}$$

where: M, N — the height and width of the subimage I.

Step 4b. Select the highest values of (d_1, d_2, d_3, d_4) for particular axes:

$$d_{maxX} = max(d_1, d_2), \qquad d_{maxY} = max(d_3, d_4). \tag{4}$$

Step 5. Expand I into X direction by $d_{maxX} - x_c$ pixels, and into Y direction by $d_{maxY} - y_c$ pixels. Fill in the new parts of I with the constant greyscale level (equal to 127).

Step 6. Transform I into polar co-ordinates (into new image P), using the formulas:

$$\rho_i = \sqrt{(x_i - x_c)^2 + (y_i - y_c)^2}, \qquad \theta_i = atan\left(\frac{y_i - y_c}{x_i - x_c}\right). \tag{5}$$

Step 7. Resize the P image into the constant rectangular size, e.g. 128×128.

Step 8. Derive the absolute spectrum of the 2D Fourier transform ([13]):

$$C(k, l) = \frac{1}{HW} \left| \sum_{h=1}^{H} \sum_{w=1}^{W} P(h, w) \cdot e^{(-i\frac{2\pi}{H}(k-1)(h-1))} \cdot e^{(-i\frac{2\pi}{W}(l-1)(w-1))} \right|, \tag{6}$$

where: H, W — height and width of the polar image P; k — sampling rate in vertical direction ($k \geq 1$ and $k \leq H$); l — sampling rate in horizontal direction ($l \geq 1$ and $l \leq W$); $C(k, l)$ — value of the coefficient of discrete Fourier transform in the coefficient matrix in k row and l column; $P(h, w)$ — value in the image plane with coordinates h, w.

Step 9. Extract the square subpart of the obtained absolute spectrum with the indices $1, \ldots, 10$ for both axes, concatenate it and finally put into the vector V that represents an input object.

3   Methodology and Results of the Experiment

The main goal of the experiment described in this paper was the investigation of the efficiency of the Polar-Fourier Greyscale Descriptor in the recognition of very similar objects, even if they belong to different classes, what is a very specific and rather unusual problem. For this purpose, the images of six species of butterflies were experimentally investigated. The shape in this case is usually very similar for objects from different classes. Hence, other information should be additionally applied. In the mentioned descriptor, the information about the pattern visible on wings will be included, since the algorithm calculates the polar co-ordinates for all pixels belonging to the object in greyscale.

During the experiment data from the benchmark database, introduced in [11], was used. It consists of the images of six species — admiral, black swallowtail, machaon, monarch, peacock and zebra. Some examples of the tested images are provided in Fig. 1.

Fig. 1. Exemplary images of butterflies (introduced in [11]) used in the experiment

For each of the six classes twenty test objects were used. On the other hand, only one template for each class was applied. Hence, there were 120 test objects and 6 templates. Obviously, the images used as the templates were not considered during the constructions of the test data.

All butterfly objects (both test and template ones) were represented using the algorithm described in the previous section. Some examples of the test objects, as well as the descriptions obtained for them, are presented in Fig. 2.

The recognition was performed according to the classical template matching approach. It means that a test object was matched with all the templates, and the

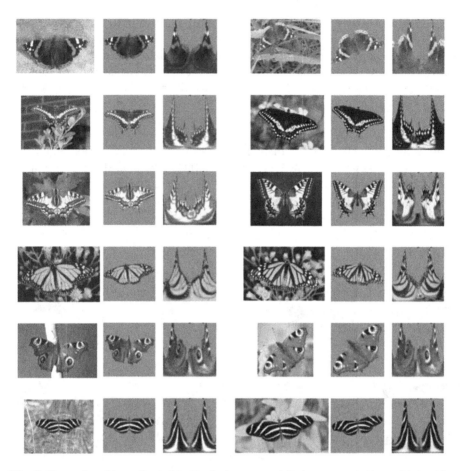

Fig. 2. Examples of investigated butterfly images and their representations obtained by means of the investigated algorithm. The normalised polar-transformed images, before the 2D Fourier transform, are presented.

smallest dissimilarity measure indicated the recognised class. Because after the Fourier transform and concatenation a vector of numbers representing an object is obtained, the simple approach for the dissimilarity measure calculation was sufficient — the Euclidean distance. If a greyscale object in polar co-ordinates is used one can apply some other methods. Calculation of a correlation coefficient would be a good selection, since it is robust to mean luminance levels of images.

The problem concerning the localisation of an object of interest within an image is beyond the scope of this paper. Hence, it was assumed that it was firstly localised and the subpart of an image containing it could be treated as the input for the description method. However, for this purpose any localisation algorithm can be applied, e.g. the active contours as described in [12].

The obtained recognition results for particular classes, as well as the average overall efficiency, were provided in Table 1.

Table 1. Average recognition rates achieved by means of the Polar-Fourier Greyscale Descriptor for particular classes of butterflies

Class	Correct results	Wrong results	Efficiency
'admiral'	19	1	95%
'black_swallowtail'	15	5	75%
'machaon'	19	1	95%
'monarch'	16	4	80%
'peacock'	20	0	100%
'zebra'	19	1	95%
TOTAL	**108**	**12**	**90%**

As can be seen in Table 1, the overall recognition result for tests performed on 120 objects was equal to 90%. The best result was obtained for the 'peacock' class. In this case all the test objects were recognized properly. Only one object out of half of investigated classes was wrongly named — 'admiral', 'machaon' and 'zebra'. For the last two classes the result was worse. The 'black_swallowtail' class obtained 75% efficiency, while the 'monarch' class — 80%.

4 Conclusions

In this paper the Polar-Fourier Greyscale Descriptor was applied to a very specific problem, in which objects under automatic recognition are very similar in shape, hence additionally another feature for their representation has to be used. The descriptor applied for this purpose uses the greyscale values of the object and the pattern that can be seen on it. However, owing to the method of deriving the representation, the object's silhouette is also taken into consideration. The most important property of the descriptor investigated in this paper is the combination of the polar and Fourier transforms. Firstly, for the earlier extracted object the transformation from Cartesian to polar co-ordinates is performed, and the two-dimensional Fourier transform for it is used. Then, the sub-spectrum is extracted and concatenated in order to obtain the description of an object. It is matched with all stored templates (one for a class), represented by means of the same algorithm. The smallest dissimilarity measure indicates the recognised class.

The described approach was tested using 120 images of butterflies belonging to six different species, 20 for each class. The benchmark data for experiments was taken from [11]. The average recognition rate was equal to 90% and only for two classes the number of wrongly recognized test objects was higher than one. In the future, the described algorithm will be developed in order to obtain even better properties and results.

References

1. Frejlichowski, D.: An Algorithm for Binary Contour Objects Representation and Recognition. In: Campilho, A., Kamel, M. (eds.) ICIAR 2008. LNCS, vol. 5112, pp. 537–546. Springer, Heidelberg (2008)

2. Osowski, S., Nghia, D.D.: Fourier and Wavelet Descriptors for Shape Recognition Using Neural Network — a Comparative Study. Pattern Recognition 35(9), 1949–1957 (2002)
3. Glendinning, R.H., Herbert, R.A.: Shape Classification, Using Smooth Principal Components. Pattern Recognition Letters 24(12), 2021–2030 (2003)
4. Silveira, M., Monteiro, A.: Automatic Recognition and Measurement of Butterfly Eyespot Patterns. Biosystems 95(2), 130–136 (2009)
5. Schmid, C., Dorko, G., Lazebnik, S., Mikolajczyk, K., Ponce, L.: Pattern Recognition with Local Invariant Features. In: Chen, C.H., Wang, P.S.P. (eds.) Handbook of Pattern Recognition and Computer Vision, 3rd edn., pp. 71–92. World Scientific Publishing Co. (2005)
6. Lee, C., Chen, C.: Color Pattern Recognition using Image Encoding Joint Transform Correlator. Microwave and Optical Technology Letters 49(7), 1665–1669 (2007)
7. Frejlichowski, D.: Identification of Erythrocyte Types in Greyscale MGG Images for Computer-Assisted Diagnosis. In: Vitrià, J., Sanches, J.M., Hernández, M. (eds.) IbPRIA 2011. LNCS, vol. 6669, pp. 636–643. Springer, Heidelberg (2011)
8. Frejlichowski, D.: Application of the Polar-Fourier Greyscale Descriptor to the Problem of Identification of Persons Based on Ear Images. In: Choraś, R.S. (ed.) Image Processing and Communications Challenges 3. AISC, vol. 102, pp. 5–12. Springer, Heidelberg (2011)
9. Frejlichowski, D.: Pre-processing, Extraction and Recognition of Binary Erythrocyte Shapes for Computer-Assisted Diagnosis Based on MGG Images. In: Bolc, L., Tadeusiewicz, R., Chmielewski, L.J., Wojciechowski, K. (eds.) ICCVG 2010, Part I. LNCS, vol. 6374, pp. 368–375. Springer, Heidelberg (2010)
10. Hupkens, T.M., de Clippeleir, J.: Noise and Intensity Invariant Moments. Pattern Recognition Letters 16(4), 371–376 (1995)
11. Lazebnik, S., Schmid, C., Ponce, J.: Semi-Local Affine Parts for Object Recognition. In: Proc. of the British Machine Vision Conference, vol. 2, pp. 959–968 (September 2004)
12. Ngoi, K.P., Jia, J.C.: An Active Contour Model for Colour Region Extraction in Natural Scenes. Image and Vision Computing 17(13), 955–966 (1999)
13. Kukharev, G.: Digital Image Processing and Analysis. Szczecin University of Technology Press (1998) (in Polish)

Application of 2D Fourier Descriptors and Similarity Measures to the General Shape Analysis Problem

Dariusz Frejlichowski and Katarzyna Gościewska

West Pomeranian University of Technology, Szczecin
Faculty of Computer Science and Information Technology
Żołnierska 52, 71-210, Szczecin, Poland
dfrejlichowski@wi.zut.edu.pl, katarzyna.gosciewska@smartmonitor.pl

Abstract. The General Shape Analysis (GSA) is a problem of finding the most similar basic shape to the test one. It is close to traditional recognition or retrieval of shapes. Main difference is that GSA does not aim at the identification of an exact object shape but at the indication of one or few most similar to it general templates – simple shape figures, e.g. rectangle, circle or triangle. By comparing more complicated shapes with simple ones it is possible to determine the most general information about a particular object. In order to perform the comparison using the template matching approach it is necessary to define methods for the representation and similarity estimation of shapes. In this paper the attention is paid to two-dimensional Fourier Descriptor applied for the representation of a shape and two matching methods, namely Euclidean distance and correlation. The effectiveness of the shape descriptor is estimated as a convergence between the experimental results and results provided by humans through the inquiry forms concerning the same GSA task. Performed experiments allowed us to determine the influence of the matching method on the final effectiveness of the approach applying Fourier Descriptors. Selection of the absolute spectrum subpart size is also discussed.

1 Introduction

In the General Shape Analysis problem the group of templates consists of small number of simple geometric objects such as rectangle, triangle or circle. Test objects form larger group of more complicated shapes that are under analysis and do not belong to the previous group. The analysis of general shape is similar to traditional recognition or retrieval, however it does not aim at identifying exact class of a shape but on the determination of only basic information about it. For each of the test objects one or few most similar, general templates are indicated and that allows the conclusion about a shape – how rectangular, triangular or circular the processed shape is ([1]). Discussed problem is depicted in Fig. 1. For an airplane the most similar templates are for example triangle, pentagon or five-pointed star.

L. Bolc et al. (Eds.): ICCVG 2012, LNCS 7594, pp. 371–378, 2012.

Fig. 1. Illustration of the General Shape Analysis problem – which general shape is the most similar to the tested one?

The problem of General Shape Analysis has been described in the literature and some experimental results exploring effectiveness of various shape descriptors have been discussed, e.g. in [1,2]. The similarity between obtained shape representations has been usually estimated by means of the Euclidean distance.

One can also find completely another way of exploring shape characteristics. It was introduced by Paul Rosin and concerns shape measurements ([3,4,5]). Author describes a group of shape descriptors designated to determine a particular shape feature, e.g. rectangularity, triangularity or ellipticity. Traditional algorithms as well as some new approaches were reviewed and tested by him.

The rest of the paper is organized as follows. The second section presents two-dimensional Fourier Descriptor and its application to the GSA problem. The third one contains a definition of two measures that were applied for the estimation of the similarity between representations, i.e. Euclidean distance and correlation coefficient. Some experiments were carried out to investigate which measure allows for higher percentage of the effectiveness. Experimental conditions and results are provided and discussed in Section 4. The last section concludes the paper.

2   Two-Dimensional Fourier Descriptor

Two-dimensional Fourier Descriptor (FD) is widely used in pattern recognition (e.g. [6]), mainly thanks to its useful properties, when applied to a region shape. It is able to generalize the processed shape what can be very important in solving the GSA task. Moreover, it is robust to noise and invariant to scale and translation.

FD can be represented as a matrix of complex values, however usually only the absolute spectrum is used. Its values are derived using the following formula ([7]):

$$C(k,l) = \frac{1}{HW} \left| \sum_{h=1}^{H} \sum_{w=1}^{W} P(h,w) \cdot e^{(-i\frac{2\pi}{H}(k-1)(h-1))} \cdot e^{(-i\frac{2\pi}{W}(l-1)(w-1))} \right|, \quad (1)$$

where: H, W — height and width of the polar image P; k — sampling rate in vertical direction ($k \geq 1$ and $k \leq H$); l — sampling rate in horizontal direction ($l \geq 1$ and $l \leq W$); $C(k,l)$ — value of the coefficient of discrete Fourier transform in the coefficient matrix in k row and l column; $P(h,w)$ — value in the image plane with coordinates h, w.

It is known that more general information can be obtained after selecting the part of the Fourier coefficient matrix. That explains the reason of examining various sizes of absolute spectrum subparts, what is discussed in Section 4.

3   Applied Similarity and Dissimilarity Measures

The analysis of general object shape is performed using the template matching approach. Each test object is compared with every template shape in order to estimate the similarity or dissimilarity between them. Having a set of measured values, one value for each template, we can order them in an ascending or descending order. That indicates the degree of similarity (or dissimilarity). The most commonly used metric includes Euclidean distance.

As it is well known, the Euclidean distance between two vectors $V_A(a_1, a_2, , a_N)$ and $V_B(b_1, b_2, , b_N)$, representing object A and object B in N-dimensional features space and denoted as d_2, can be derived as follows ([8]):

$$d_2(V_A, V_B) = \sqrt{\sum_{i=1}^{N}(a_i - b_i)^2}. \tag{2}$$

As it was mentioned, FD has a form of a matrix or a vector with absolute values. That allows us for utilizing another matching method, based on the correlation coefficient, denoted as c. It can be derived using the formula ([9]):

$$c = \frac{\sum_m \sum_n (A_{mn} - \bar{A})(B_{mn} - \bar{B})}{\sqrt{(\sum_m \sum_n (A_{mn} - \bar{A})^2)(\sum_m \sum_n (B_{mn} - \bar{B})^2)}}, \tag{3}$$

where: A_{mn} and B_{mn} — pixel values with coordinates (m, n), respectively in image A and B, $\bar{A}$, $\bar{B}$ — average value of all pixels, respectively for image A and B.

Correlation coefficient gives values between 0 and 1. The higher the measure value the higher the correlation what indicates more similar objects. That method of estimating similarity brings an opportunity for utilizing both matrix and vector form of FD, while Euclidean distance is calculated only for vectors. In opposite to the correlation, if the distance value is 0 then the similarity is the highest.

In the following section the experimental results of employing two-dimensional Fourier Descriptor and both mentioned matching procedures are described. An influence of Euclidean distance and correlation coefficient on final descriptor effectiveness is discussed. Experiments were carried out with the use of various sizes of absolute spectrum subparts what led to some conclusions about its influence on the effectiveness as well.

4   Experimental Conditions and Results

Each experiment was composed of five tests for varying size of extracted absolute spectrum subpart. The problem was explored using the database with 50 objects that were the binary shapes represented as 200×200 pixels size images. Shapes were divided into 10 general templates and 40 test objects, what is depicted in Fig. 2.

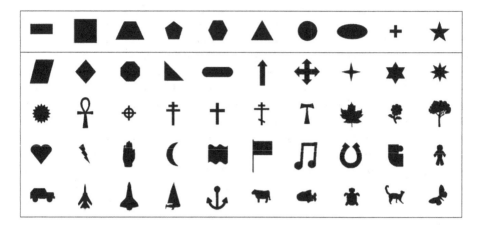

Fig. 2. Shapes used in the experiments – 10 templates and 40 test objects

Both experiments were performed in the same way, only the matching method changed. Firstly, for all shapes, Fourier Descriptors were calculated. Secondly, in each test, various size of absolute spectrum was used. The parameter n, determining $n \times n$ subpart size, was equal to 2, 5, 10, 25 and 50. Each obtained block was transformed into a vector and finally formed the representation of a shape. Templates that were firstly indicated using particular matching method were considered the most similar.

In order to evaluate the experimental results objectively an inquiry form was filled in by more than 200 persons. It concerned the same General Shape Analysis task – the indication of five the most similar templates for each of the test objects. The most often indicated template determined the most similar one. Results provided by humans were utilized as a benchmark, but only three most similar templates were taken into consideration. The final effectiveness was estimated as a percentage convergence between the test results and the shapes selected by humans. Three firstly indicated templates in the experiments were matched with three most often selected in the inquiries. However, in many cases the differences between the most popular and the second human indication were very small. Therefore, both of them were treated equally as the most similar template and compared separately with the first shape indicated in a particular test. That is the second method for estimation of the effectiveness. The first experiment applied the Euclidean distance. The percentage results for each test for one and three most similar templates are provided in Table 1. The results of all tests were very similar but slightly better effectiveness was obtained in the test utilizing the smallest subpart of the absolute spectrum. Pictorial representation of the best result is provided in Fig. 3.

Table 1. Percentage efficiency obtained in the first experiment

Subpart	Three most similar templates			One most similar
size	1st indication	2nd indication	3rd indication	template
2×2	30.0%	20.0%	25.0%	32.5%
5×5	25.0%	17.5%	35.0%	27.5%
10×10	25.0%	17.5%	20.0%	30.0%
25×25	25.0%	17.5%	22.5%	30.0%
50×50	25.0%	17.5%	20.0%	30.0%

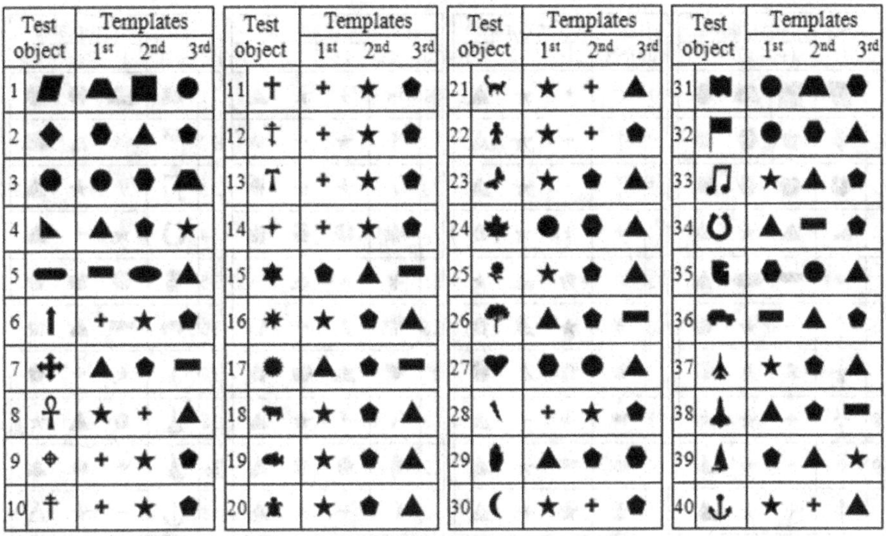

Fig. 3. Results of the first experiment for the test utilizing 2×2 block of the Fourier absolute spectrum and Euclidean distance

In the second experiment the correlation coefficient was applied. That method has not been explored in the GSA problem so far. As can be concluded from the results of all tests provided in Table 2, in opposite to the first experiment, the efficiency for 2×2 block was the worst. For a slightly larger spectrum subpart, i.e. 5×5 block, the efficiency was the highest. Moreover, a tendency became noticeable – the larger the block size the worse the result. That concerns mainly the 1st and the 2nd indication out of three most similar templates and the selection of only one most similar template. The 3rd indication varies differently in both experiments. Pictorial results of the best test are provided in Fig. 4.

The analysis of experimental results brought a significant conclusion that matching method has an important influence on final effectiveness. Conditions of both experiments were the same but the difference lied in applied measure. For the Euclidean distance, obtained test results were very similar while for correlation coefficient the percentage effectiveness was varying and strongly depended on the size of the absolute spectrum subpart. In many cases the effectiveness of the second experiment was higher. Moreover, in both experiments the best

Table 2. Percentage efficiency obtained in the second experiment

Subpart size	Three most similar templates			One most similar template
	1st indication	2nd indication	3rd indication	
2×2	15.0%	15.0%	22.5%	20.0%
5×5	35.0%	25.0%	25.0%	40.0%
10×10	32.5%	22.5%	27.5%	37.5%
25×25	27.5%	17.5%	27.5%	32.5%
50×50	25.0%	15.0%	27.5%	32.5%

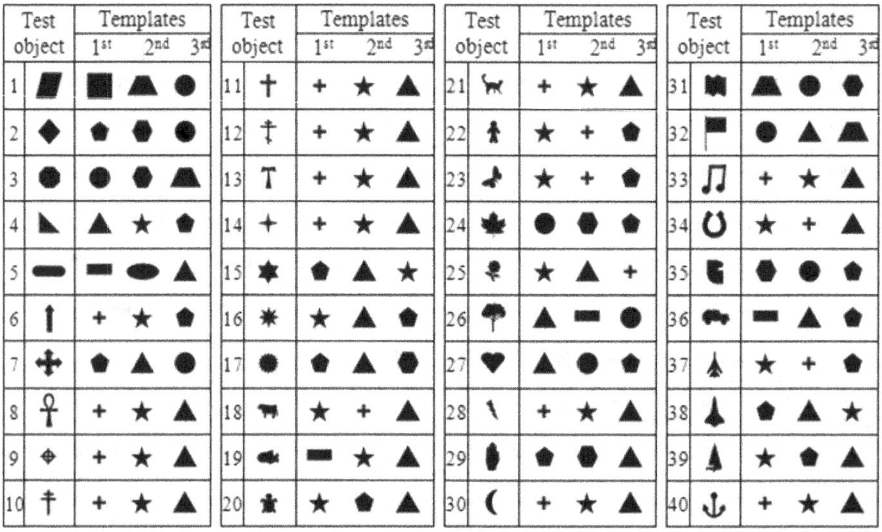

Fig. 4. Results of the second experiment for the test utilizing 5×5 block of the Fourier absolute spectrum and correlation coefficient

results were associated with two smallest absolute spectrum subparts. That proved that only small amount of information is sufficient to deal with the GSA problem.

The second method for the estimation of the efficiency – the first shape selected in each test – brought better results. It means that in some cases the second shape selected by humans turned out to be the most similar template in the experiments. That explains the reason for taking into consideration the incidence of particular templates indicated firstly in the inquiry. Therefore, slight differences could affect the final results as well.

5   Conclusions

In the paper the problem of General Shape Analysis was considered. It is similar to the traditional recognition or retrieval of shapes but does not aim at the exact identification or classification. The main goal is to indicate one or few most similar general templates for a test object. That brings the most basic information about a shape and allows for determining e.g. how triangular, rectangular or circular it is.

The key issue described in the paper concerns the comparison of different similarity and dissimilarity measures that are able to match Fourier Descriptors. In order to explore the influence of Euclidean distance and correlation coefficient on final effectiveness, two experiments consisting of five tests were performed. All test results were compared with human benchmark results. The percentage convergence between them defined the effectiveness of Fourier Descriptor and utilized matching method.

The most important conclusion is that matching method has a strong influence on the efficiency of the General Shape Analysis. Better results were obtained using correlation coefficient. Additionally, the results depended on utilized size of absolute spectrum subpart, i.e. the size of the shape representation derived using Fourier transform. The best efficiency was obtained for 5 × 5 block — 35% for 1st, 25% for 2nd and 25% for 3rd indication out of three most similar templates. If taking into account only the first template indicated in the test with first or second template selected by humans, the effectiveness turns out to be higher and equal to 40%. The results are similar to the best obtained so far using Zernike Moments ([10]). An experiment performed with the same conditions and Zernike Moments descriptor resulted in efficiency equal to 37.5%, 25.0% and 17.5% for the 1st, 2nd and 3rd indication respectively and 40% for one most similar template. For the 2nd indication and for the one most similar template the results on utilizing Zernike Moments and Fourier Descriptor with correlation coefficient were identical. For the 1st indication Zernike Moments achieved better results, but for the 3rd one they were much worse. Summarizing, the most important conclusion is that the effectiveness of Fourier Descriptor depends on the size of absolute spectrum subpart and is strongly influenced by applied similarity or dissimilarity measure. For discussed General Shape Analysis task, the best results were obtained using correlation coefficient and 5 × 5 block of the representation. Nevertheless, some future work on exploring other shape descriptors should be done. Additionally, another approach to GSA problem can be introduced. As it was described by Rosin, each descriptor has an ability to determine a particular information about a shape. Therefore, in General Shape Analysis each template could be represented using one shape descriptor and then every test object would be described by a set of descriptors. In order to compare obtained representations their values must be on the same scale. The best representation indicates the most similar general shape to the test one.

References

1. Frejlichowski, D.: An experimental comparison of seven shape descriptors in the general shape analysis problem. In: Campilho, A., Kamel, M. (eds.) ICIAR 2010, Part I. LNCS, vol. 6111, pp. 294–305. Springer, Heidelberg (2010)

2. Frejlichowski, D., Forczmański, P.: General Shape Analysis Applied to Stamps Retrieval from Scanned Documents. In: Dicheva, D., Dochev, D. (eds.) AIMSA 2010. LNCS, vol. 6304, pp. 251–260. Springer, Heidelberg (2010)
3. Rosin, P.L.: Measuring Rectangularity. Machine Vision and Applications 11, 191–196 (1999)
4. Rosin, P.L.: Measuring Shape: Ellipticity, Rectangularity and Triangularity. Machine Vision and Applications 14, 172–184 (2003)
5. Rosin, P.L.: Computing Global Shape Measures. In: Chen, C.H., Wang, P.S.P. (eds.) Handbook of Pattern Recognition and Computer Vision, 3rd edn., pp. 177–196 (2005)
6. Osowski, S., Nghia, D.D.: Fourier and Wavelet Descriptors for Shape Recognition Using Neural Network — a Comparative Study. Pattern Recognition 35(9), 1949–1957 (2002)
7. Kukharev, G.: Digital Image Processing and Analysis. Szczecin University of Technology Press (1998) (in Polish)
8. Kpalma, K., Ronsin, J.: An Overview of Advances of Pattern Recognition Systems in Computer Vision. In: Obinata, G., Dutta, A. (eds.) Vision Systems: Segmentation and Pattern Recognition, pp. 169–194 (2007)
9. Chwastek, T., Mikrut, S.: The Problem of Automatic Measurement of Fiducial Mark on Air Images. Archives of Photogrammetry, Cartography and Remote Sensing 16, 125–133 (2006) (in polish)
10. Frejlichowski, D.: The Application of the Zernike Moments to the Problem of General Shape Analysis. Control and Cybernetics 40(2), 515–526 (2011)

Supervised Texture Classification Using a Novel Compression-Based Similarity Measure

Mehrdad J. Gangeh[1], Ali Ghodsi[2], and Mohamed S. Kamel[1]

[1] Center for Pattern Analysis and Machine Intelligence
Department of Electrical and Computer Engineering
University of Waterloo, Ontario N2L 3G1, Canada
{mgangeh,mkamel}@pami.uwaterloo.ca
[2] Department of Statistics and Actuarial Science
University of Waterloo, Ontario N2L 3G1, Canada
aghodsib@uwaterloo.ca

Abstract. Supervised pixel-based texture classification is usually performed in the feature space. We propose to perform this task in (dis)similarity space by introducing a new compression-based (dis)similarity measure. The proposed measure utilizes two dimensional MPEG-1 encoder, which takes into consideration the spatial locality and connectivity of pixels in the images. The proposed formulation has been carefully designed based on MPEG encoder functionality. To this end, by design, it solely uses P-frame coding to find the (dis)similarity among patches/images. We show that the proposed measure works properly on both small and large patch sizes. Experimental results show that the proposed approach significantly improves the performance of supervised pixel-based texture classification on Brodatz and outdoor images compared to other compression-based dissimilarity measures as well as approaches performed in feature space. It also improves the computation speed by about 40% compared to its rivals.

1 Introduction

Texture images can be divided to two broad types: stationary that contains only one texture type per image and nonstationary that consists of more than one texture type per image [1]. The main application domain on stationary texture images is supervised classification of each texture image into one class; whereas on nonstationary texture images, there are two main application domains [1,2]. First, unsupervised texture segmentation that partitions the texture image into disjoint regions of uniform texture. Second, pixel-based texture classification, which is similar to texture segmentation in the sense that the given texture image is segmented to uniform texture regions. The difference, however, is that in pixel classification, the segmentation is performed using supervised techniques [2]. In this paper, our focus is on supervised pixel classification and hence, we deal with nonstationary texture types.

Common trend in literature on pixel-based texture classification is the computation of some texture features for every pixel using its neighboring pixels

L. Bolc et al. (Eds.): ICCVG 2012, LNCS 7594, pp. 379–386, 2012.

and a particular texture method [2,3,4]. However, as texture is a complicated phenomenon, there is no definition that is agreed upon by the researchers in the field [5,6]. This is one of the reasons that there are various feature-based techniques in the literature, each of which tries to model one or several properties of texture depending on the application in hand. The performance of each of these features depends on the texture type and there is no single feature method that performs well on all different textures [2,3]. To avoid this problem, textures can be represented in (dis)similarity space. In this approach, pairs of texture patches are compared by a (dis)similarity measure reflecting their mutual resemblance.

Among similarity measures in the literature, the metric based on the notion of Kolmogorov complexity, i.e., so called normalized information distance (NID) [7] has attracted the attention of many researchers. However, due to non-computability of Kolmogorov complexity, it has been mainly approximated using real-world compressors introducing normalized compression distance (NCD) [8]. NCD has attractive characteristics, e.g., it is parameter-free, i.e., does not use any feature or background knowledge about the data; and it is quasi-universal, (NID is universal, i.e., it minorizes all other distances, but NCD inherits this from NID to some extent [8]).

NCD was originally defined on binary strings with the explanation that all data types can be converted to binary strings. Many initial applications on which NCD was applied successfully were based on 1D data such as in bioinformatics or plagiarism detection. The extension of NCD application to 2D data such as images, however, does not seem to be straightforward. While some researchers linearize 2D data to represent them using 1D strings [9,10], this causes the loss of the spatial locality and connectivity of neighboring pixels. The effect of linearization on the overall performance of NCD-based system has been empirically investigated in [9] with this important conclusion: "images may not be fully expressible as a string, at least using current compression algorithms". Using 2D compressors such as JPEG and JPEG2000 for NCD on images led to contradictory results in the literature: while [11] shows that using JPEG2000 on 2D satellite images yields better results than converting images to 1D data and using string compressors, it is shown in [9] and [12] that JPEG and JPEG2000 does not work well as compressors for computing NCD-based similarity measure on images.

An alternative approach is using MPEG encoders as 2D compressors in NCD. The main advantage of MPEG compared to JPEG encoder is that while JPEG is designed for compressing one image, MPEG encodes frames of images and hence, by considering two images as two frames, they can be compressed in reference to each other which is desired in NCD. In this paper, we propose a novel formulation based on MPEG encoder for measuring (dis)similarity between images/patches. We will show that this new measure works well on both small and large patch sizes. Introducing this new measure in this paper, we will also show that the results of pixel-based texture classification can be significantly improved compared to other NCD-based approaches in the literature.

2   Compression-Based Dissimilarity Measure

In this section, we first briefly review the concept of NID and NCD and then provide the formulation for our proposed approach. Some illustrative results are then presented to show the effectiveness of the proposed approach on both small and large patch sizes.

2.1   Normalized Compression Distance

The normalized compression distance (NCD) [8] is an approximation for normalized information distance (NID) [7], a universal parameter-free similarity measure based on Kolmogorov complexity that minorizes all other distance measures [7].

To understand the definition of the NID, we need to define two notations: $K(x)$ and $K(x|y)$. The former is the Kolmogorov complexity of string x, which is defined as the length of the shortest binary program to compute x on a universal computer such as universal Turing machine, whereas the latter is the conditional Kolmogorov complexity, which is defined as the length of a shortest program to compute x if y is provided as an auxiliary input for the reference [7]. The NID is defined as

$$NID(x,y) = \frac{\max\{K(x|y), K(y|x)\}}{\max\{K(x), K(y)\}}. \tag{1}$$

Since Kolmogorov complexity is a noncomputable measure, the NID defined in (1) is computed by approximating Kolmogorov complexity using a compressor denoted by C as follows [8]

$$NCD(x,y) = \frac{\min\{C(xy), C(yx)\} - \min\{C(x), C(y)\}}{\max\{C(x), C(y)\}}, \tag{2}$$

where xy means that the strings x and y are concatenated. To have more insight into (2), we consider the case that $C(y) \geq C(x)$[1] and the compressor is symmetric such that $C(xy) = C(yx)$. In this case, we can rewrite (2) as $NCD(x,y) = \frac{C(xy)-C(x)}{C(y)}$, which means that the NCD distance between x and y is improvement on compressing y using x (the numerator, which is also denoted as $C(y|x)$) over compressing y by its own (the denominator) [8]. This interpretation will help to explain our proposed measure later in next subsection.

2.2   Proposed Distance Measure

Since we are using MPEG-1 encoder in our proposed (dis)similarity measure, we first provide some description on how this encoder works. MPEG-1 is a 2D encoder and thus, it takes into account the spatial locality and connectivity of the neighboring pixels in images for compression. MPEG-1 was originally designed

---

[1] The opposite condition can be interpreted similarly as NCD distance defined in (2) is symmetric.

for compressing movies based on three different coding schemes, i.e., intra-frame (I-frame) coding, predictive frame (P-frame) coding (also called inter-frame coding), and bidirectional frame (B-frame) coding [13]. I-frame coding is performed on individual frames without reference to other frames using discrete cosine transform (DCT). P-frame codes a frame in reference to the previous one by using a block matching algorithm for motion estimation and using DCT on the residual. Finally, B-frame coding compresses a frame with reference to its next and previous frames. To utilize MPEG-1 as compressor in compression-based similarity measures, patches/images are considered as two successive frames and compressed using MPEG-1 encoder. This avoids the need to linearize the images that causes the loss of spatial locality as explained in Section 1. Since there are only two frames (two images whose similarity are to be computed), B-frame coding is not utilized.

Now, if we want to use MPEG-1 as compressor for (dis)similarity measure, we need to use proper formulation based on how MPEG-1 works. To this end, based on the description provided above on MPEG-1 encoder and also the explanation provided on (2) at the end of Subsection 2.1, we would like to propose our new dissimilarity measure considering these two points: First, we utilize MPEG-1 for the computation of $C(x|y)$ (the conditional compression of x given y) using only P-frame coding and bypass I-frame coding as it does not provide any information on the similarity of x and y and we denote it using $C_p(x|y)$. Since the P-frame coding indicates the differences between two frames, which is essential in finding the (dis)similarity between them, we encode it with maximum resolution, i.e., minimum quantization scale, which is one in MPEG-1 (quantization scale for I-frame does not have any effect as I-frame coding is bypassed). Second, we notice that because the second image/patch is compressed in reference to the first one, $C_p(x|y)$ (also $C(x|y)$) is not symmetric. However, if both x and y are from the same distribution (class), we expect $C_p(x|y)$ to be close to $C_p(y|x)$ (because x and y are from the same class and it does not make very much difference whether we compress x in respect to y or y in respect to x), while if x and y are from different distributions (classes), $C_p(x|y)$ and $C_p(y|x)$ should be largely different. Hence, we propose our new measure as follows

$$d_N(x,y) = \frac{|C_p(x|y) - C_p(y|x)|}{C(x|x) + C(y|y)}, \tag{3}$$

where the absolute of the difference is taken in the numerator to ensure positive distances. $C(x|x) + C(y|y)$ is used as the normalizing factor. In $C(x|x)$ and $C(y|y)$, since both frames are the same, P-frame coding generates zero (the difference between two frames is zero). Thus, $C(x|x)$ is equivalent to $C(x)$ in (2). However, since in MPEG-1 encoder, there are at least two frames, we use $C(x|x)$ notation instead of $C(x)$. I-frame quantization scale can be maximized in this case. The proposed distance is symmetric and nonnegative.

Although MPEG-1 has been also used in [14] for dissimilarity measure, our proposed measure is different in following aspects. Firstly, our proposed formulation is different from what they have proposed. Their distance measure is defined as follows

$$d_{CK}(x, y) = \frac{C(x|y) + C(y|x)}{C(x|x) + C(y|y)} - 1, \tag{4}$$

where $C(x|y)$ is computed based on both I- and P-frames coding, while in our approach, it is computed solely based on P-frame coding (denoted by $C_p(.|.)$). Secondly, in (4), the compression is maximized by using large quantization scales for both I- and P-frames coding through MPEG-1 external parameters to prefer compressibility over image quality [14]. In our approach, since P-frame is essential in finding the (dis)similarity between two frames, we encode it with maximum resolution. Thirdly, our proposed measure performs properly on both small and large patches while $d_{CK}(x, y)$ cannot represent dissimilarity between small patches properly. This is explained more in next subsection.

2.3   Illustrative Results

To better realize how $d_{CK}(x, y)$ works, we have computed the distances among patches of 17×17, 33×33, 65×65, and 129×129 extracted from two texture images of Brodatz, i.e., D4 (Fig. 1a) and D5 (Fig. 1f) as shown in Fig. 1b-1e. As can be seen, the distances computed (300 patches per class) among patches are normalized to the interval of $[0, 1]$ to ease the comparison and displayed using color code. We expect to see smaller distances among patches extracted from the same class, i.e., in $c_i - c_i, i = 1, 2$ areas and larger distances among the patches extracted from two different classes, i.e., in $c_i - c_j, i, j = 1, 2$ & $i \neq j$ areas (see Fig. 1b as reference). However, except for large patch size of 129×129, this behavior cannot be observed in Fig. 1b-1e. This problem can be also seen for any other texture pair and the main reason is explained next.

The major problem with $d_{CK}(x, y)$ defined in (4) is that it compresses the concatenated patches based on both I- and P-frames. This is while only P-frame coding is based on the (dis)similarity of patches and I-frame coding is performed using DCT solely based on the frequency contents of a patch/image. This causes that for small patch sizes, where the compression based on P-frame is still limited (due to small search region) comparing to I-frame coding, the distances mainly be dominated by I-frame coding, i.e., frequency contents and distributions of the first frame. Hence, the patches from the texture class that have low frequency contents show lower distances (in this case D5; one can investigate this by taking the Fourier transform of both textures and looking at their spectrum). This is while in this example, due to more homogeneity of D4, we expect lower distances among the patches extracted from D4, i.e., in region $c_1 - c_1$.

Fig. 1g-1j shows the distances computed using our proposed measure among the same patches used for d_{CK} to illustrate the effectiveness of the proposed distance on finding the (dis)similarities among texture pairs. It can be seen that the distances are consistently small among the patches of the same class for all patch sizes and also the distances among the patches extracted from D4, which is a more homogeneous texture than D5, are smaller. This behavior is consistent on other texture pairs as our experiments indicate (not shown here due to space limit).

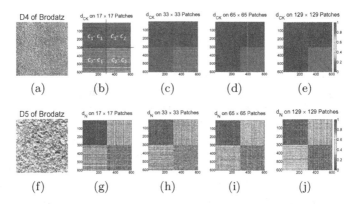

Fig. 1. The distances computed on patches extracted from (a) D4 and (f) D5 of Brodatz album. (b) to (e) distances computed on various patch sizes as indicated in the figures using d_{CK} and (g) to (j) using proposed measure (d_N).

3   Experimental Setup and Results

The effectiveness of the proposed similarity measure is shown in the application of supervised pixel-based classification on nonstationary texture images. In this application, there is a trade-off between the patch sizes at smooth areas and on the borders. While large patch size at the uniform texture areas improves the performance of classification (as more information is included to identify the textures correctly), small patch sizes are more desired on the borders to prevent mixing textures from two different classes.

Here, the distances are first computed on 200 patches per class with the size of 17×17 extracted from the training images. These are used to train a support vector machine (SVM) with linear kernel $k_{\mathrm{tr}} = d_{\mathrm{tr}}.d'_{\mathrm{tr}}$ (d_{tr} is the distance matrix computed on the patches extracted from the training set). This kernel is p.s.d. as it is obtained using an inner product. The optimal cost function (C^*) of the SVM is tuned in a 5-fold cross-validation on the training set. Then the patches of the same size are extracted from the test image and the distances among these patches and the training patches are computed using the proposed approach. A linear kernel is computed subsequently using $k_{\mathrm{ts}} = d_{\mathrm{ts}}.d'_{\mathrm{tr}}$ (d_{ts} is the computed distances from the test to training patches), which is used in the trained SVM.

Data used is the same as what is used in [2]. It is consisting of some texture composites from Brodatz and some outdoor images. The test images are shown on the first column of Fig. 2. The results are compared to two other distance measures using d_{CK} and NCD approach and also to two feature-based approaches published in [2] that yield the best results on these texture images, i.e., local binary pattern ($LBP_{8,1}^{riu2}$) and MeasTex (Gabor, 5NN) (refer to Table 3 of [2]). To get rid of the speckle-noise type in final classification, the same as in [2], a median filter with the same size as the patch sizes (17×17 in this case) is applied to the final classified pixels. The results are shown quantitatively in Table 1 and

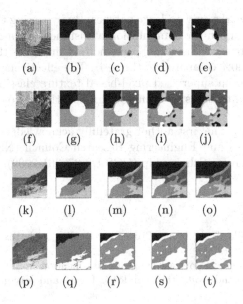

Fig. 2. The results of supervised pixel-based texture classification on Brodatz and outdoor images. (a, f, k, and p) test images; (b, g, l, and q) ground truth; (c, h, m, and r) proposed method; (d, i, n, and s) d_{CK}; (e, j, o, and t) NCD.

Table 1. The classification rate (%) compared among the proposed method and other distance- or feature-based approaches. The results on LBP (local binary pattern) and MeasTex (Gabor, 5NN) methods are based on what is reported in [2] for the same images.

Approach	Test Images			
	Fig. 2a	Fig. 2f	Fig. 2k	Fig. 2p
Proposed	**89.5**	**83.2**	**75.8**	**72.3**
d_{CK}	82.1	74.0	75.0	71.6
d_{NCD}	83.3	73.3	75.3	71.4
$LBP_{8,1}^{riu2}$ [2]	85.4	77.5	69.4	37.9
MeasTex (Gabor, 5NN) [2]	83.7	70.5	68.5	55.1

qualitatively in Fig. 2. As can be seen, our results are significantly better than other distance-based approaches and also compared to what is reported in [2].

4   Discussion and Conclusion

In this paper, we have proposed a new compression-based distance measure using MPEG-1 encoder that takes into account the spatial locality and connectivity of pixels in images. The proposed measure computes distances based on P-frame coding and can properly find the distances on both small and large patch sizes, unlike d_{CK} which works only on large patches. By bypassing the I-frame coding, which is not necessary in the computation of distances anymore (except for the case that the patches are the same), our method improves the performance in terms of speed by 40% compared to the d_{CK}. The effectiveness of the proposed measure was shown on supervised pixel-based texture classification of outdoor images and Brodatz textures resulting in significantly improved performance.

Acknowledgment. The first author gratefully acknowledges the funding from the Natural Sciences and Engineering Research Council (NSERC) of Canada under Canada Graduate Scholarship (CGS D3-378361-2009).

References

1. Petrou, M., Sevilla, P.G.: Image Processing Dealing with Texture. John Wiley & Sons, West Sussex (2006)
2. Garcia, M., Puig, D.: Supervised texture classification by integration of multiple texture methods and evaluation windows. Image and Vision Computing 25(7), 1091–1106 (2007)
3. Randen, T., Husøy, J.: Filtering for texture classification: A comparative study. IEEE Trans. Pattern Analysis and Machine Intelligence 21(4), 291–310 (1999)
4. Melendez, J., Puig, D., Garcia, M.: Multi-level pixel-based texture classification through efficient prototype selection via normalized cut. Pattern Recognition 43(12), 4113–4123 (2010)
5. Mirmehdi, M., Xie, X., Suri, J.: Handbook of Texture Analysis. Imperial Collage Press, London (2008)
6. Ahonen, T., Pietikainen, M.: Image description using joint distribution of filter bank responses. Pattern Recognition Letters 30(4), 368–376 (2009)
7. Li, M., Chen, X., Li, X., Ma, B., Vitányi, P.: The similarity metric. IEEE Trans. Information Theory 50(12), 3250–3264 (2004)
8. Cilibrasi, R., Vitányi, P.: Clustering by compression. IEEE Trans. Information Theory 51(4), 1523–1545 (2005)
9. Mortensen, J., Wu, J.J., Furst, J., Rogers, J., Raicu, D.: Effect of Image Linearization on Normalized Compression Distance. In: Ślęzak, D., Pal, S.K., Kang, B.-H., Gu, J., Kuroda, H., Kim, T.-H. (eds.) SIP 2009. CCIS, vol. 61, pp. 106–116. Springer, Heidelberg (2009)
10. Macedonas, A., Besiris, D., Economou, G., Fotopoulos, S.: Dictionary based color image retrieval. Journal of Visual Communication and Image Representation 19(7), 464–470 (2008)
11. Cerra, D., Mallet, A., Gueguen, L., Datcu, M.: Algorithmic information theory-based analysis of earth observation images: An assessment. IEEE Geoscience and Remote Sensing Letters 7(1), 8–12 (2010)
12. Vázquez, P., Marco, J.: Using normalized compression distance for image similarity measurement: an experimental study. The Visual Computer, 1–22 (2011)
13. Ghanbari, M.: Standard Codecs: Image Compression to Advanced Video Coding. The Institution of Electrical Engineers, London (2003)
14. Campana, B., Keogh, E.: A compression-based distance measure for texture. Statistical Analysis and Data Mining 3(6), 381–398 (2010)

A Real-Time Drivable Road Detection
Algorithm in Urban Traffic Environment

Yuan Gao, Yixu Song, and Zehong Yang

Department of Computer Science and Technology
Tsinghua University, Beijing, 100084, China
faringao@gmail.com, songyixu@163.com, yangzehong@sina.com

Abstract. Road detection plays an important part in intelligent vehicle driving assistance system. In this paper, we present a real-time
vision-based method which can detect drivable road area on unstructured urban roads. It first trains road models based on color cues from
consecutive frames. Then, region growing method is employed on current
frame to extract drivable areas with seeds points selected according to
trained models. This method can adaptively detect drivable lane areas
under normal and complicated road environment where there are shadows, lane markings or unstable lighting conditions. Experimental results
on complex traffic scenes show that the proposed algorithm is effective
and stable for real-time drivable road detection.

Keywords: driving assistance, drivable road detection, color statistics,
region growing.

1   Introduction

Road detection is a crucial part in driving assistance system. Many researchers
have been studying the subject for decades and great development has been
made. Among them, vision-based method research is an important branch. Some
researchers focus on unstructured roads such as contest roads or highways which
usually have clear markings and boundaries. Road detection is thus simplified
to the detection of lines, curves and road markings (see [1] and [2]).

Obviously, these methods are not appropriate in most real-life situations such
as urban roads or other unstructured roads where there are fuzzy edges and no
clear markings. There are basically three approaches proposed on this problem:

1. Feature-based. Such methods employ features such as colors (see [3]), textures (see [4]) or others (see [5]) as visual cues on the road surface to extract
   the road region. These methods are usually sensitive to illumination, shadows
   or marker lines on road surface (see [6]).
2. Model-based. Such methods often assume a road model first and then find
   the fittest model to match road areas by adjusting parameters. A lane model
   presented in [7] is based on geometrical model and Gabor filter. In [8]-[10]
   models with vanishing point are used to assist initial orientation and road

L. Bolc et al. (Eds.): ICCVG 2012, LNCS 7594, pp. 387–396, 2012.

width estimation. These methods extract road regions integrally thus are shadow resistant but may be invalid when road shapes fail to meet the assumptions.

3. Knowledge-based. Such methods train Artificial Neural Networks (*ANN*) based on feature data collected from road images and apply the networks to new environment. They are independent of road markings or edges and can detect road areas adaptively (see [11]-[13]). However, these methods often fail when current road condition differs to that of the training set.

We define *drivable road region* as a connected region in front of the vehicle on the road surface where the vehicle can pass safely taking no account of shadows, markings or traffic regulations. For example, shadows on the road surface should be marked as drivable road region if they are not occupied by other vehicles. A desirable detection algorithm should be able to extract all drivable road regions from a road image regardless of disturbance such as shadows, lane markings or uneven lighting. Feature-based segmentation has been proven to be a good way to solve drivable road detection on unstructured road detection problem, such as region growing method (see [3] and [14]). However, this method often fails to get over obstacles on the road surface such as lane markings due to sudden change of color feature and achieves only partial correct results. Another method is color statistical method adopted by Standford in DARPA contest which achieves good detection result in off-road conditions (see [15]).

In this paper, we propose an efficient real-time road detection algorithm working on urban roads using region growing method with dynamic seeds selection based on color cues statistical road model which can detect most drivable road regions. The proposed method is mainly composed of two modules (as shown in Fig. 1):

1. Road model training module based on color cues and statistics in Part 2.
2. Drivable road detection module based on region growing in Part 3.

Module 1 collects color cues on successive frames to train a probability model which can determine whether a pixel on current frame belongs to drivable road region or not. Module 2 is performed on current frame which firstly generates a series of seed points based on the road model from Module 1. It then detects all possible road areas by region growing method based on Gaussian Mixture Model (*GMM*).

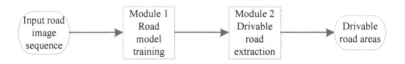

Fig. 1. Procedure of our proposed algorithm

2   Road Model Training Module

For a given road image, we define *region of interest* (*ROI*) to be its lower half part which represents an empirical possible road region (as shown in Fig. 2). The rest of our proposed algorithm is conducted in *ROI* on each frame, so as to reduce unnecessary computation.

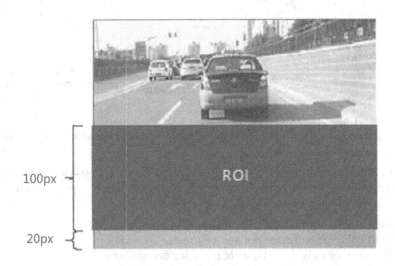

Fig. 2. *ROI* (the blue rectangle) on a 320×240 road image with the size of 320×110 and a 20px margin to the image bottom

Our basic assumption is that, for *ROI*s in n consecutive frames, the more often a color appears, the more likely it belongs to the drivable road region. So our basic idea is to record the count of each color in n frames, calculate its probability of being the road color, form a probability map for each frame and finally extract a probability model indicating possible lane region. The procedure for training road model is shown in Fig. 3.

2.1   Color Cues Statistics in RGB Space

When road conditions are relatively consistent, it is easy to see that there is limited variation between consecutive frames. Color distribution is thus calculated in *ROI* on current frame and former $n-1$ frames. So the assumption that most part of *ROI* belongs to drivable road region is still guaranteed despite of the occasional disturbance of shadows, lane markings or uneven luminance on the road surface. RGB space is used in this module, because we find that RGB space, especially channels R and G can effectively distinguish between road and non-road areas after a lot of experiments. We denote P_{all} to be the set of all pixels appeared in *ROI* of n frames:

$$P_{all} = \{p \mid p \in F_1, ..., F_n, (x_p, y_p) \in ROI\} \tag{1}$$

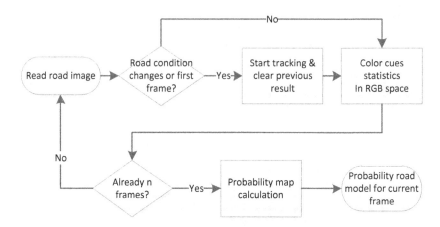

Fig. 3. Procedure of Module 1: road model training based on color cues and statistics

where, p is a certain pixel in ROI from frame F_1 to F_n positioned at (x_p, y_p). We first remove invalid pixels from the set P_{all} according to the priori knowledge which includes (not exclusively):

1. Road colors are mainly gray, white or luminous yellow.
2. Road colors usually are not red or green.
3. We consider only RG channels for color cue statistics.

Eligible pixels P_f are thus filtered using the following rule:

$$P_f = \left\{ p \left| \begin{array}{l} r_p - \max(g_p, b_p) < T_{red} \\ g_p - \max(r_p, b_p) < T_{green} \\ \frac{r_p + g_p + b_p}{3} > T_{gray} \\ p \in P_{all} \end{array} \right. \right\} \tag{2}$$

where, (r_p, g_p, b_p) is the color value of pixel p. $T_{red}, T_{green}, T_{gray}$ are thresholds chosen empirically based on the above priori knowledge to exclude non-road pixels from P_f as many as possible.

Then, we calculate the distribution of each pixel in P_f on RG plane. Count the appearance $time_{(r,g)}$ of each color value (r, g) as:

$$time_{(r,g)} = count((r_p, g_p) \in P_f) \text{ where } r_p = r \text{ and } g_p = g \tag{3}$$

2.2   Probability Map Calculation

The biggest value among all $time_{(r,g)}$ is denoted as $time_{max}$. The closer a color's count is to $time_{max}$, the more likely it stands for the road region. Hence, we regard a pixel p as road point if its $time_{(r_p, g_p)}$ are no less than $k \times time_{max}$ and define its probability of being road region $prob_p$ as 1. For other pixels, $prob_p$ is computed with the following formula:

$$prob_p = \frac{time_{(r_p, g_p)}}{k \times time_{max}} \tag{4}$$

In this way, each pixel p in current frame F is now associated with a $prob_p$ which shows how likely it belongs to the road region. $prob'_p$ is obtained after smoothing and pixels with small $prob'_p$ are omitted to reduce interference and final probability value $prob^*_p$ is acquired:

$$prob'_p = smooth(prob_p) \tag{5}$$

$$prob^*_p = \begin{cases} prob'_p & \text{if } prob'_p \geq T_{prob} \\ 0 & \text{otherwise} \end{cases} \tag{6}$$

where, T_{prob} is the threshold for minimal $prob'_p$. We define the set P_l as follows:

$$P_l = \{p \mid prob^*_p = 1, (x_p, y_p) \in ROI, p \in F\} \tag{7}$$

If pixel p on current frame F is in the set P_l, it is believed to fall in the lane region.

2.3 Tracking Predication

It is reasonable to evaluate $prob^*_p$ of nth frame based on former $n - 1$ frames when road conditions are alike. However, when traffic environment change exceeds certain criteria, the color cues statistics should stop tracking and restart. Previous results such as $time_{(r,g)}$, $prob_p$ and etc. must be cleared. Bhattacharyya Distance (see [16]) between color histograms of two adjacent frames is adopted to detect road conditions change between successive two frames. If the distance exceeds the threshold value, it means that the road environment has changed and color cues tracking should be restarted.

With this, probability road model is obtained and serves as an input for next module of our algorithm.

3   Drivable Road Extraction Module

For road surfaces with shadows or light intervention, Module 1 can learn such scenarios and classify them as drivable road regions due to the fact that the training process is performed on multiple frames. However, it only gives a pile of points which most likely are road points. Module 2 will join isolated road points by growing from seed points and finally expand to intact drivable road regions.

3.1 Seed Points Selection

The trained road model provides us the information that how likely a certain pixel in current frame F is part of the road region. We scatter a series of points $p_i(i = 1, 2, ...)$ evenly in ROI. If $p_i \in P_l$ which is defined in Equation(7), we add it to our seed list $List_{seed}$.

3.2   Region Growing

The basic idea of region growing method is that, for each seed $s_i \in List_{seed}$, we compare it with all of its neighboring points according to certain similarity rules. If a neighbor point p_j meets the requirement, p_j is added to $List_{seed}$. Repeat the above process until all neighboring points of s_i are scanned. The connected region composed by points in $List_{seed}$ is the result of region growing method, namely drivable road regions.

The key for region growing method now comes down to designing similarity rules between two pixels. We adopt *GMM* in *HSI* space to depict characteristics of each pixel on the road image. The intensity I_p of each pixel p is computed as follows:

$$I_p = \frac{r_p + g_p + b_p}{3} \tag{8}$$

Our similarity rules with intensity feature representing likelihood between seed point s and its neighbor $neighbor(s)$ are as follows:

$$\begin{cases} \left| I_s - I_{neighbor(s)} \right| < \gamma \\ \left| I_{neighbor(s)} - \mu_n \right| < \sigma_n \end{cases} \tag{9}$$

where, γ is the threshold for intensity difference between s and $neighbor(s)$, μ_n is the mean intensity value of road area Ω in n^{th} frame while σ_n represents the standard deviation. Road area Ω is estimated as follows:

1. For initial frame, the triangle in *ROI* is regarded as the road region as shown in Fig. 4(a).
2. Due to continuity of video stream, images vary little between two frames. So road region detected in $(n-1)^{th}$ frame can be used as approximate road region in n^{th} frame as shown in Fig. 4(b).

(a) Ω for 1st frame   (b) Ω for n^{th} frame

Fig. 4. Approximate road region Ω

μ_n and σ_n can be obtained by maximum likelihood method as follows:

$$\begin{cases} \mu_n = \frac{1}{m-1} \sum\limits_{p \in \Omega} I_p \\ \sigma_n = \frac{1}{m-2} \sum\limits_{p \in \Omega} (I_p - \mu_n)^2 \end{cases} \tag{10}$$

where, p is a certain pixel in Ω and m is the number of pixels in Ω.

When $I_{neighbor(s)}$ meets the similarity rule in Equation(9), $neighbor(s)$ becomes a new seed point and is added to $List_{seed}$. After all the points in $List_{seed}$ are checked, connected regions of seed points are formed on which final drivable road regions of current frame F can be extracted by employing post-processing such as erosion and dilation.

4   Experimental Results

Several experimental results are displayed and explained in this section. We implemented the proposed algorithm in C++ code and conducted the experiments on a PC with 2.8-GHz CPU. In our experiment, we denote: $k = 0.6$ in Equation(4) and $T_{prob} = 0.3$ in Equation(6). Our algorithm achieves real-time detection under video clips collected form Beijing urban roads with a frame rate of 25 fps under monocular vision. Each image frame is down-sampled to size 320×240 pixels.

We first present the experiment results using our algorithm on three scenarios which are normal straight road, shadowed road and marked road respectively. For comparison, we implemented two previous methods: color statistical method and region growing method. In normal straight road situation, all algorithms performed very well and detected complete drivable areas (see Fig. 5(a)). In cases where there were shadows on the roads, both of the previous methods failed to detect all the drivable areas leaving part of the shadow region undetected (see Fig. 5(b)). In cases where there were markings on the roads, color statistical method could not classify lighted region as drivable roads, while region growing method was not able to grow over two marker lines (see Fig. 5(c)). As a result, our algorithms showed correct detection in all scenarios, while these two earlier methods failed to recognize all the drivable regions.

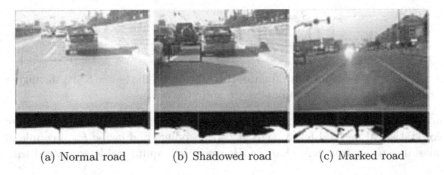

(a) Normal road   (b) Shadowed road   (c) Marked road

Fig. 5. Detection results under different road conditions using the proposed method (lower left), color statistical method (lower middle) and region growing method (lower right)

We then present the experiment results on the same three scenarios but with light intervention. As we can see from Fig. 6, no matter on normal, shadowed or marked roads, color statistical method would fail to detect road areas where lighting changed severely. Region growing method is less sensitive to light intervention, but it had trouble growing outside of the shadow or cross the marker lines so that it could not detect all the drivable road areas. Our algorithm could detect correct and complete drivable road regions in above three scenarios under light intervention. In conclusion, our algorithm can better detect normal, shadowed or marked roads with or without light intervention.

(a) Normal road   (b) Shadowed road   (c) Marked road

Fig. 6. Detection results under different road conditions with light intervention using the proposed method (lower left), color statistical method (lower middle) and region growing method (lower right)

We now evaluate the stability of the three detecting algorithms. Stability criteria is defined as follows:

1. Pixel number in detected drivable road regions on each frame, for our algorithm and region growing method.
2. Sum S^* of $prob_p^*$ of each pixel $p \in ROI$ on each frame, computed using the following formulas:

$$
\begin{cases}
S = \sum\limits_{p \in ROI} prob_p^* \\
S^* = \dfrac{S}{mean\left(\{prob_p^* \mid prob_p^* \neq 0, p \in ROI\}\right)}
\end{cases}
\tag{11}
$$

where, $prob_p^*$ is defined in Equation(6). Obviously, the larger S^* is, the bigger the detected drivable road areas are and vice versa.

The result is depicted in Fig. 7. As we can see, the total road probability S^* of color statistical method fell to zero at certain points and lasted for a couple of frames due to environment changes. However, it is quite stable compared with

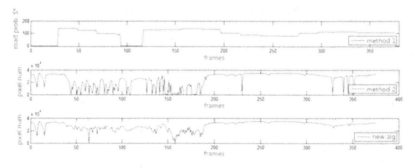

Fig. 7. Stability curves of three algorithms: color statistical method (top), region growing method (middle) and our proposed algorithm (bottom)

region growing method whose result shocked severely due to the limitation of seed point selection. However, our algorithm seldom failed to give any detection and thus is more stable.

5   Conclusion

In this paper, we present a drivable road detection algorithm which works on urban unstructured roads. The method first trains road models based on color cues. Then, seed points are selected according to the models. Finally, drivable road regions are grown from seed points by region growing method. Our algorithm not only works well under normal road condition, but also gets correct result on shadowed or marked roads and even with light intervention. It is also very robust, stable and can quickly adjust to road condition changes.

References

1. Bertozzi, M., Broggi, A.: GOLD: A parallel real-time stereo vision system for generic obstacle and lane detection. IEEE Transactions on Image Processing 7(1) (1998)
2. Kreucher, C., Lakshmanan, S.: A frequency domain approach to lane detection in roadway images. In: Proceedings of the International Conference on Image Processing 1999, vol. 2, pp. 31–35 (1999)
3. He, Y., Wang, H., Zhang, B.: Color-based road detection in urban traffic scenes. IEEE Transactions on Intelligent Transportation Systems 5(4), 309–318 (2004)
4. Zhang, J., Nagel, H.H.: Texture-based segmentation of road images. In: IEEE Symposium on Intelligent Vehicles, Washington, DC, pp. 260–265 (1994)
5. Jian, W., Zhong, J., Yuting, S.: Unstructured road detection using hybrid features. In: International Conference on Machine Learning and Cybernetics, Baoding, China, pp. 482–486 (2009)
6. Wang, Y., Chen, D., Shi, C.: Vision-Based Road Detection by Adaptive Region Segmentation and Edge Constraint. In: Second International Symposium on Intelligent Information Technology Application, pp. 342–346 (2008)
7. Zhou, S., Jiang, Y.: A Novel Lane Detection based on Geometrical Model and Gabor Filter. In: IEEE Intelligent Vehicles Symposium, San Diego, CA, USA, pp. 59–64 (2010)
8. Kong, H., Audibert, J.-Y.: General Road Detection From a Single Image. IEEE Transactions on Image Processing 19(8) (2010)
9. Zhang, G., Zheng, N., Cui, C.: An Efficient Road Detection Method In Noisy Urban Environment. In: IEEE Intelligent Vehicles Symposium, Xi'an, China, pp. 556–561 (2009)
10. Rasmussen, C.: Texture-Based Vanishing Point Voting for Road Shape Estimation. In: British Machine Vision Conference (2004)
11. Conrad, P., Foedisch, M.: Performance Evaluation of Color Based Road Detection Using Neural Nets and Support Vector Machines. In: Proc. Applied Imagery Pattern Recognition Workshop, Washington, DC (2003)
12. Foedisch, M., Takeuchi, A.: Adaptive Real-Time Road Detection Using Neural Networks. In: Proceedings of the 7th International IEEE Conference on Intelligent Transportation Systems, Washington, DC, October 3-6 (2004)

13. Sha, Y., Zhang, G.-Y.: A road detection algorithm by boosting using feature combination. In: 2007 IEEE Intelligent Vehicles Symposium, pp. 364–368 (2007)
14. Álvarez, J.M., López, A.M., Baldrich, R.: Shadow Resistant Road Segmentation from a Mobile Monocular System. In: Martí, J., Benedí, J.M., Mendonça, A.M., Serrat, J. (eds.)' IbPRIA 2007. LNCS, vol. 4478, pp. 9–16. Springer, Heidelberg (2007)
15. Dahlkamp, H., Kaehler, A., Staven, D., et al.: Self-supervised Monocular Road Detection in Desert Terrain. In: Proceedings of Robotics: Science and Systems (2006)
16. Bhattacharyya, A.: On a measure of divergence between two statistical populations defined by their probability distributions. Bulletin of the Calcutta Mathematical Society 35, 99–109 (1943)

Learning-Based Object Segmentation Using Regional Spatial Templates and Visual Features

Iker Gondra and Fahim Irfan Alam

Department of Mathematics, Statistics, and Computer Science
St. Francis Xavier University, Nova Scotia, Canada
{igondra,x2009lij}@stfx.ca

Abstract. Semantically accurate segmentation of an object of interest (OOI) is a critical step in computer vision tasks. In order to bridge the gap between low-level visual features and high-level semantics, a more complete model of the OOI is needed. To this end, we revise the concept of directional spatial templates and introduce *regional* directional spatial templates as a means of including spatial relationships among OOI regions into the model. We present an object segmentation algorithm that learns a model which includes both visual and spatial information. Given a training set of images containing the OOI, each image is over-segmented into visually homogeneous regions. Next, Multiple Instance Learning identifies regions that are likely to be part of the OOI. For each pair of such regions and for each relationship, a regional template is formed. The computational cost of template generation is reduced by sampling the reference region with a pixel set that is descriptive of its shape. Experiments indicate that regional templates are an effective way of including spatial information into the model which in turn results in a very significant improvement in segmentation performance.

1 Introduction

A fundamental task of the human visual system is the ability to find objects in an image, i.e., segmenting an image into semantically meaningful regions. Thus, in computer vision tasks such as object recognition, semantically accurate segmentation of a particular object of interest (OOI) is a critical step.

Homogeneity, which is largely related to local visual information extracted from an image and reflects how uniform a region is, plays a very important role in weak (traditional) segmentation since the result of such segmentation is homogeneous regions. Algorithms that follow such traditional approach (e.g., [1], [2]) perform well in narrow domains, where the variability of low-level visual content is limited. Unfortunately, in broader domains, homogeneous regions do not necessarily correspond to semantically meaningful units. Under these circumstances, a number of learning-based approaches have been proposed. Although these methods incorporate high-level knowledge, the major disadvantage is their lack of flexibility due to the assumption that such knowledge in the form of, e.g., the full object model (e.g., [3]), partial object model information such as its

L. Bolc et al. (Eds.): ICCVG 2012, LNCS 7594, pp. 397–406, 2012.
© Springer-Verlag Berlin Heidelberg 2012

structure or shape of its probability density function (e.g., [4]), hand-specified information (e.g., [5]), is provided in advance.

In [6], this lack of flexibility is addressed by a framework which does not require high-level knowledge to be provided in advance, i.e., it is learned from the training data. They present a relevance feedback-based content-based image retrieval system that uses Multiple Instance Learning (MIL) [7] to perform a semantically guided context adaptation of segmentation parameters for a particular OOI. In [8], an MIL formulation is also used but for the purposes of object recognition. Spatial relationships among the OOI regions are included into the model learned in [9]. The algorithm also uses MIL to learn prototypes of OOI regions and Bayesian networks for learning spatial relationships among regions.

Intrigued by the relative simplicity of directional spatial templates [10] in comparison to e.g., Bayesian Networks, in this paper we adapt them to and study their performance as a means of including spatial relationships among OOI regions into the model. We introduce *regional* directional spatial templates and present an object segmentation algorithm that learns a model of the OOI which includes both visual and spatial information. The algorithm uses MIL to learn prototypical visual representations of each region of the OOI and regional directional spatial templates to learn directional relationships between OOI regions.

2   Background

2.1   Multiple Instance Learning

In multiple instance learning (MIL) [7] each training sample consists of a set of instances which is labeled positive if at least one instance is positive, or negative otherwise. Different from standard supervised learning, we are only given set labels but not instance labels. The goal is to find the prototype(s) responsible for positive labeling. Maximum diverse density (MDD) [11] assumes a unique prototype $\mathbf{t} \in \Re^d$ accounting for the labels. Formally, let $B_i^+ = \{B_{i,1}^+, B_{i,2}^+, \ldots\}$ be the ith positive set with $\mathbf{x}_{i,j}^+ \in \Re^d$ as the jth instance, and similarly defined for negative sets. We can find $\mathbf{t}$ by examining a random vector $\mathbf{x} \in \Re^d$ that has the maximum probability of being $\mathbf{t}$, conditioned on the observations $\{\{B_1^+, B_2^+, \ldots\}, \{B_1^-, B_2^-, \ldots\}\}$ (for details, see [11]). Rooted in the formulation, the performance of MDD depends heavily on prior knowledge about the number of prototypes, which is often unknown in image analysis tasks. To relax this dependency, an adaptive kernel diverse density (AKDDE) estimate [12] uses a localized estimating window to generate estimates close to the prototypes.

2.2   Spatial Templates

In a directional spatial template [10] (a.k.a fuzzy landscapes [13], spatial templates [14], applicability structures [15], potential fields [16]) between a reference region and all other pixels in an image, the value of each pixel indicates the degree to which the pixel satisfies the directional relationship to the reference region. Let an image be defined as a non-empty set of pixels $I_i = \{p_1, p_2, \ldots\}$ where a pixel is represented by its xy coordinates $p = (x, y)$. Let $r_{i,j} \subset I_i$ be the jth region in the image. The *directional spatial template* $T_{I_i}^{d_w, r_{i,j}}$ of I_i in direction $d_w \in \{d_1, d_2, \ldots\} \subset (-\pi, \pi]$ relative to $r_{i,j}$ is defined as [10]

$$\forall p \in I_i \quad T_{I_i}^{d_w, r_{i,j}}(p) = \begin{cases} 1 & \text{if } p \in r_{i,j} \\ \sup_{p' \in r_{i,j}} \mu(\overrightarrow{p'p} - d_w) & \text{otherwise} \end{cases} \quad (1)$$

where $\overrightarrow{p'p} \in (-\pi, \pi]$ and μ is a mapping from $\Re$ into $[0,1]$, periodic with period 2π, even, decreasing on $[0, \pi]$, with $\mu(0) = 1$ and $\mu(\pi/2) = 0$.

We revise this definition and define the *regional* directional spatial template between two regions in an image. The value of each pixel indicates the degree to which each pixel of one region satisfies the directional relationship to the other, i.e., the reference, region. Let $r_{i,j}, r_{i,q} \subset I_i$ be regions in the image. The *regional* directional spatial template $T_{r_{i,q}}^{d_w, r_{i,j}}$ of $r_{i,q}$ in direction d_w relative to $r_{i,j}$ is defined as

$$\forall p \in I_i \quad T_{r_{i,q}}^{d_w, r_{i,j}}(p) = \begin{cases} 0 & \text{if } p \notin r_{i,q} \\ \sup_{p' \in r_{i,j}} \mu(\overrightarrow{p'p} - d_w) & \text{otherwise} \end{cases} \quad (2)$$

3   Segmentation Algorithm

3.1   Learning OOI Model

Let an image be defined as a non-empty set of pixels $I = \{p_1, p_2, \ldots\}$ where a pixel is represented by its xy coordinates and its R, G, B color component values $p_i = (p_i^x, p_i^y, p_i^R, p_i^G, p_i^B)$. Given a training set $T = \{I_1, I_2, \ldots\}$, $I_i \in T$ is segmented into a set of visually homogeneous regions $\{r_{i,1}, r_{i,2}, \ldots\}$ where $r_{i,j} \subset I_i$ and $\mathbf{x}_{i,j} = \frac{1}{|r_{i,j}|} \sum_{p_i \in r_{i,j}} [p_i^R p_i^G p_i^B]$ is the visual feature vector representation of $r_{i,j}$. T is written as a set of labeled tuples $\{(\{\mathbf{x}_{1,1}, \mathbf{x}_{1,2}, \ldots\}, 1), (\{\mathbf{x}_{2,1}, \mathbf{x}_{2,2}, \ldots\}, 1), \ldots\}$ where the positive, i.e., "1", labeling indicates that the image contains OOI instance(s). After AKDDE takes place on this MIL formulation, we obtain a set of prototypes $P = \{\mathbf{t}_1, \mathbf{t}_2, \ldots\}$ where $\mathbf{t}_i \in \Re^3$ represents the average visual appearance of pixels in a common instance. With this visual-only OOI model, Alg. 1 is defined.

For each $r_{i,j}$, $k^* = \arg\min_{k \in \{1,2,\ldots|P|\}} (\|\mathbf{x}_{i,j} - \mathbf{t}_k\|^2)$. If $\|\mathbf{x}_{i,j} - \mathbf{t}_{k^*}\|^2 < \delta$ where $\delta \in \Re$ is a threshold, $r_{i,j}$ is assumed to be an instance of the k^*th part of the OOI and it is denoted by $r_{i,j}^{k^*}$. To learn the spatial relationships, for each pair $(r_{i,j}^k, r_{i,q}^h)$ and for each directional relationship $d_w \in \{d_1, d_2, \ldots\} \subset (-\pi, \pi]$, we find a regional directional spatial template. The computational cost of the template generation is reduced by representing the reference region $r_{i,j}^k$ with a sampling of pixels that, by following the sampling method presented in [17], is descriptive of the region's shape. The sampling of the reference region $r_{i,j}^k$ is

---

Algorithm 1. Visual Segmentation

Inputs: I, $P = \{\mathbf{t}_1, \mathbf{t}_2, \ldots\}$, δ
Output: Segmentation S of I
    for each $p_i \in I$ **do**
      $S(p_i) = p_i$; $k^* = \arg\min_{k \in \{1,2,\ldots |P|\}}(\| [p_i^R p_i^G p_i^B] - \mathbf{t}_k \|^2)$
      if $\| [p_i^R p_i^G p_i^B] - \mathbf{t}_{k^*} \|^2 > \delta$ **then**
        $S(p_i) = (p_i^x, p_i^y, 255, 255, 255)$ /* whiten out pixel */

---

initiated by determining the center of gravity and the maximum radius of $r_{i,j}^k$. The center of gravity $O = (O^x, O^y)$ of $r_{i,j}^k$ is

$$O^x = \frac{1}{|r_{i,j}^k|} \sum_{p_i \in r_{i,j}^k} p_i^x \quad O^y = \frac{1}{|r_{i,j}^k|} \sum_{p_i \in r_{i,j}^k} p_i^y \tag{3}$$

The maximum radius R of $r_{i,j}^k$ is defined as

$$R = \max_{(E^x, E^y)} ((E^x - O^x)^2 + (E^y - O^y)^2) \tag{4}$$

where $E = (E^x, E^y) \in r_{i,j}^k$ is a point on the edge of $r_{i,j}^k$.

Next, the length of OE is divided into $n-1$ equal distances and circles are drawn centered at O and with radii $\frac{R}{(n-1)}, \frac{2R}{(n-1)}, \cdots \frac{(n-1)R}{(n-1)}$. Next, each circle is divided into m equal arcs (with OE being one of the arcs), each arc being $d\theta = 360/m$ degrees. Then the intersecting points $C_{c,a}$ between the circles and the equally spaced arcs where $c \in \{0, 1, \ldots n-1\}$ and $a \in \{0, 1, \ldots m-1\}$ are found. An approximation of (2) is then

$$\forall p \in I_i \quad T_{r_{i,q}^h}^{\widehat{d_w, r_{i,j}^k}}(p) = \begin{cases} 0 & \text{if } p \notin r_{i,q}^h \\ \sup_{C_{c,a} \in r_{i,j}^k} \mu(\overrightarrow{C_{c,a}p} - d_w) & \text{otherwise} \end{cases} \tag{5}$$

where $\overrightarrow{C_{c,a}p} \in (-\pi, \pi]$ (see Fig. 1). The average (over T) of (5) is then

$$\overline{T_h^{d_w, k}}(p) = \frac{\sum_{i=1}^{|T|} T_{r_{i,q}^h}^{\widehat{d_w, r_{i,j}^k}}(p)}{|T|} \tag{6}$$

See Fig. 2. Alg. 2 summarizes this learning process.

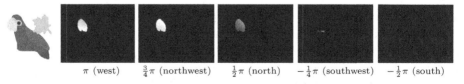

π (west) $\frac{3}{4}\pi$ (northwest) $\frac{1}{2}\pi$ (north) $-\frac{1}{4}\pi$ (southwest) $-\frac{1}{2}\pi$ (south)

Fig. 1. Approximate regional directional spatial templates between yellow (beak) and green (wings) regions. The brighter the pixel, the more it satisfies the relationship.

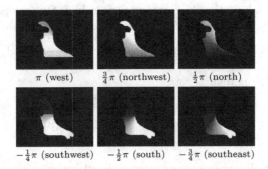

π (west) $\frac{3}{4}\pi$ (northwest) $\frac{1}{2}\pi$ (north)

$-\frac{1}{4}\pi$ (southwest) $-\frac{1}{2}\pi$ (south) $-\frac{3}{4}\pi$ (southeast)

Fig. 2. Average (Eq. (6)) over T in Fig. 3 between the red (body) and green (wings) regions in the OOI. The brighter the pixel, the more it satisfies the relationship.

Algorithm 2. Learning OOI Model

Inputs: $T = \{I_1, I_2, \ldots\}$, $D = \{d_1, d_2, \ldots\}$, n, m, δ

Output: $P = \{\mathbf{t}_1, \mathbf{t}_2, \ldots\}$, $\{\overline{T_h^{d_w,k}}(p), \overline{T_k^{d_w,h}}(p)\}_{h=1,w=1,k=h+1}^{h=|P|,w=|D|,k=|P|}$

  for each $I_i \in T$ **do**

    Oversegment to generate $\{r_{i,1}, r_{i,2}, \ldots\}$

  Run AKDDE on $\{(\{\mathbf{x}_{1,1}, \mathbf{x}_{1,2}, \ldots\}, 1), (\{\mathbf{x}_{2,1}, \mathbf{x}_{2,2}, \ldots\}, 1), \ldots\}$; $P = \{\mathbf{t}_1, \mathbf{t}_2, \ldots\}$

  for each $I_i \in T$ **do**

    for each $r_{i,j}$ **do**

      $k^* = \arg\min_{k \in \{1,2,\ldots|P|\}}(\|\mathbf{x}_{i,j} - \mathbf{t}_k\|^2)$

      if $\|\mathbf{x}_{i,j} - \mathbf{t}_{k^*}\|^2 < \delta$ **then**

        Denote $r_{i,j}$ by $r_{i,j}^{k^*}$

  for each $r_{i,j}^k$, $k = 1 \ldots, |P|$ **do**

    Find sample pixels $C_{c,a}$ using Eqs. (3) and (4)

  for each $r_{i,j}^k$, $k = 1 \ldots, |P|$ **do**

    for each $d_w \in D$ **do**

      for each $r_{i,q}^h$, $h = k+1 \ldots, |P|$ **do**

        Form $T_{r_{i,q}^h}^{\widehat{d_w, r_{i,j}^k}}$ and $T_{r_{i,j}^k}^{\widehat{d_w, r_{i,q}^h}}$ using Eq. (5)

  for each $h = 1 \ldots, |P|$ **do**

    for each $d_w \in D$ **do**

      for each $k = h+1 \ldots, |P|$ **do**

        Compute $\overline{T_h^{d_w,k}}(p)$ and $\overline{T_k^{d_w,h}}(p)$ using Eq. (6)

3.2   Segmenting a New Image

Upon given a new image I, it is segmented into a set of visually homogeneous regions $\{r_1, r_2, \ldots\}$ where $r_i \subset I$ and $\mathbf{x}_i = \frac{1}{|r_i|} \sum_{p_i \in r_i} [p_i^R p_i^G p_i^B]$ is the visual feature vector representation of r_i. Then, for each r_i, $k^* = \arg\min_{k \in \{1,2,\ldots|P|\}}(\|\mathbf{x}_i - \mathbf{t}_k\|^2)$. If $\|\mathbf{x}_i - \mathbf{t}_{k^*}\|^2 < \delta$ where $\delta \in \Re$ is a threshold, r_i is assumed to be an instance of the k^*th part of the OOI and it is denoted by $r_i^{k^*}$.

To find the spatial relationships among regions in I, for each pair (r_i^k, r_j^h) and for each directional relationship $d_w \in \{d_1, d_2, \dots\} \subset (-\pi, \pi]$, we find the corresponding $T_{r_i^h}^{d_w, r_i^k}$. The fuzzy agreement (or fuzzy intersection) $A_h^{d_w, k}(p)$ between $\widehat{T_{r_i^h}^{d_w, r_j^k}}$ and $\overline{T_h^{d_w, k}}(p)$ is then

$$A_h^{d_w, k}(p) = \min \left(\widehat{T_{r_i^h}^{d_w, r_j^k}}(p), \overline{T_h^{d_w, k}}(p) \right) \tag{7}$$

The average (over all agreements or intersections) is then

$$M(p) = \frac{\sum_{h=1, d_w=1, k=h+1}^{h=|P|, d_w=|D|, k=|P|} A_h^{d_w, k}(p) + A_k^{d_w, h}(p)}{(|T| - 1) * |D|} \tag{8}$$

The final *segmentation template* $S(p)$ is then

$$\forall p \in I \quad S(p) = \begin{cases} p & \text{if } M(p) > \gamma \\ (p^x, p^y, 255, 255, 255) & \text{otherwise} \end{cases} \tag{9}$$

where $\gamma \in [0, 1]$ is a segmentation threshold and whitening a pixel means not including it in the segmentation. Algorithm 3 summarizes the segmentation process.

Algorithm 3. Visual+Spatial Segmentation

Inputs: I, $P = \{\mathbf{t}_1, \mathbf{t}_2, \dots\}$, $D = \{d_1, d_2, \dots\}$, $\{\overline{T_h^{d_w, k}}(p), \overline{T_k^{d_w, h}}(p)\}_{h=1, w=1, k=h+1}^{h=|P|, w=|D|, k=|P|}$,
      n, m, δ, γ

Output: $S(p)$

Oversegment I to generate $\{r_1, r_2, \dots\}$
for each r_i **do**
  $k^* = \arg\min_{k \in \{1, 2, \dots |P|\}} (\|\mathbf{x}_i - \mathbf{t}_k\|^2)$
  if $\|\mathbf{x}_i - \mathbf{t}_{k^*}\|^2 < \delta$ **then**
    Denote r_i by $r_i^{k^*}$
for each r_i^k, $k = 1 \dots, |P|$ **do**
  Find sample pixels $C_{c,a}$ using Eqs. (3) and (4)
for each r_i^k, $k = 1 \dots, |P|$ **do**
  for each $d_w \in D$ **do**
    for each r_i^h, $h = k + 1 \dots, |P|$ **do**
      Form $T_{r_i^h}^{d_w, r_j^k}$ and $T_{r_i^k}^{d_w, r_j^h}$ using Eq. (5)
for each $h = 1 \dots, |P|$ **do**
  for each $d_w \in D$ **do**
    for each $k = h + 1 \dots, |P|$ **do**
      Compute $A_h^{d_w, k}(p)$ and $A_k^{d_w, h}(p)$ using Eq. (7)
Compute $M(p)$ using Eq. (8) and $S(p)$ using Eq. (9)

Fig. 3. Images in Training Set

4 Results

We experimented on a dataset of JPEG-format images of a parrot. It consists of the training set (see Fig. 3) and test set (see Fig. 5(a)) which contain 10 and 5 images respectively of the OOI in a variety of settings. Alg. 2 runs with input: the training set; $D = \{-\pi, -\frac{3\pi}{4}, -\frac{\pi}{2}, -\frac{\pi}{4}, 0, \frac{\pi}{4}, \frac{\pi}{2}, \frac{3\pi}{4}\}$; $n = 40$; $m = 30$; $\delta = 0.1$. For the initial oversegmentation done in Algs. 2 and 3, K-means++ [18] is used to cluster the pixels into homogenous regions based on their visual feature vectors. The output of Alg. 2 consists of: $P = \{t_1, t_2, t_3, t_4, t_5, t_6\}$, which correspond to the colors of the 6 fragments of the OOI; $\{\overline{T_h^{d_w,k}}(p), \overline{T_k^{d_w,h}}(p)\}_{h=1,w=1,k=h+1}^{h=6,w=8,k=6}$ (See Fig. 4). For each image in the test set, Alg. 3 runs with input: the image; D; n; $\{\overline{T_h^{d_w,k}}(p), \overline{T_k^{d_w,h}}(p)\}_{h=1,w=1,k=h+1}^{h=6,w=8,k=6}$, m; δ; $\gamma = 0.1$. Alg. 3 generates $\{A_h^{d_w,k}(p), A_k^{d_w,h}(p)\}_{h=1,w=1,k=h+1}^{h=6,w=8,k=6}$ (See Fig. 4). The output of Alg. 3 is $M(p)$ and $S(p)$ (See Fig. 5).

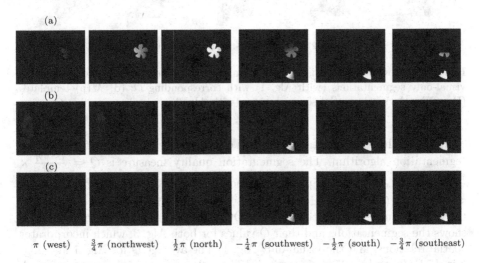

π (west) $\frac{3}{4}\pi$ (northwest) $\frac{1}{2}\pi$ (north) $-\frac{1}{4}\pi$ (southwest) $-\frac{1}{2}\pi$ (south) $-\frac{3}{4}\pi$ (southeast)

Fig. 4. Agreement for first (leftmost) image in Test Set between the blue (tail) and green (wings) regions in the OOI: (a) regional directional templates (Eq. (5)) of the test image; (b) averages (Eq. (6)); (c) agreements (Eq. (7)). Notice how, due to its position in the test image, the blue flower does not appear in the agreement templates.

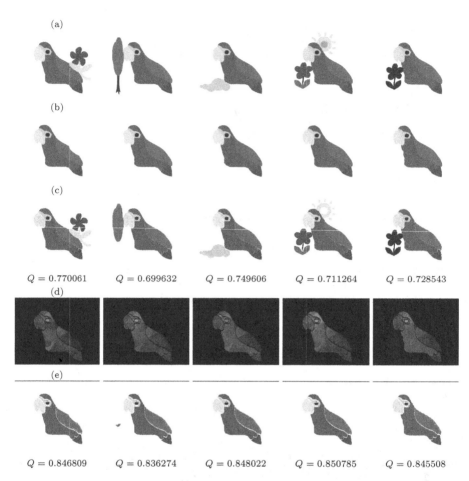

(a)

(b)

(c)

$Q = 0.770061$ $Q = 0.699632$ $Q = 0.749606$ $Q = 0.711264$ $Q = 0.728543$

(d)

(e)

$Q = 0.846809$ $Q = 0.836274$ $Q = 0.848022$ $Q = 0.850785$ $Q = 0.845508$

Fig. 5. Segmentation comparison: (a) test images; (b) ground-truth segmentations; (c) visual-only segmentations (with Alg. 1) with corresponding Q; (d) $M(\mathrm{p})$ templates (Eq. (8)); (e) visual+spatial segmentations (with Alg. 3) with corresponding Q

Let R be the final set of OOI pixels, i.e., non-white pixels, generated by the segmentation algorithm. The segmentation quality measure is $Q = \frac{|R \cap G|}{|G|} \times \frac{|R \cap G|}{|R|}$ where G is the set of pixels corresponding to the OOI in the ground-truth segmentation (See Fig. 5). Hence, Q is the percentage of pixels in agreement with the ground-truth segmentation over the OOI. Thus, Q is to be maximized. Fig. 5 shows the segmentations and their Q values for both Alg. 3, which incorporates spatial relations, and the visual-only Alg. 1. The average Q for Alg. 1 and Alg. 3 is 0.731821 and 0.84548 respectively. Thus, there is a 15.5% improvement. A larger improvement is expected with larger values of n and m, i.e., more accurate sampling. But, the computational cost would also increase.

5   Conclusion

We introduced *regional* directional spatial templates as a means of including spatial relationships among regions into an OOI model. Experiments show that templates are an effective way of including spatial information into the model which in turn results in a significant improvement in segmentation performance. However, the template is not invariant to scaling, rotation and translation and its computational cost (even with the approximation scheme) is high. We will work on those limitations in the future.

Acknowledgments. This work was supported by a Discovery Grant from the Natural Sciences and Engineering Research Council (NSERC) of Canada.

References

1. Carson, C., Belongie, S., Greenspan, H., Malik, J.: Blobworld: color and texture-based image segmentation using EM and its applications to image querying and classification. IEEE Transactions on Pattern Analysis and Machine Intelligence 24(8), 1026–1038 (2002)
2. Vicente, S., Kolmogorov, V., Rother, C.: Graph cut based image segmentation with connectivity priors. In: Proceedings of IEEE Conference on Computer Vision and Pattern Recognition, pp. 1–8 (2008)
3. Peng, J., Bhanu, B.: Closed-loop object recognition using reinforcement learning. IEEE Transactions on Pattern Analysis and Machine Intelligence 20(2), 139–154 (1998)
4. Crandall, D.J., Huttenlocher, D.P.: Weakly Supervised Learning of Part-Based Spatial Models for Visual Object Recognition. In: Leonardis, A., Bischof, H., Pinz, A. (eds.) ECCV 2006. LNCS, vol. 3951, pp. 16–29. Springer, Heidelberg (2006)
5. Viola, P., Platt, J.C., Zhang, C.: Multiple instance boosting for object detection. Advances in Neural Information Processing Systems 18, 1417–1424 (2006)
6. Gondra, I., Xu, T.: A multiple instance learning based framework for semantic image segmentation. Multimedia Tools and Applications 48(2), 339–365 (2010)
7. Dietterich, T., Lathrop, R., Lozano-Perez, T.: Solving the multiple-instance problem with axis-parallel rectangles. Artificial Intelligence 89(1-2), 31–71 (1997)
8. Todorovic, S., Ahuja, N.: Extracting subimages of an unknown category from a set of images. In: Proceedings of IEEE Conference on Computer Vision and Pattern Recognition, pp. 927–934 (2006)
9. Alam, F.I., Gondra, I.: A bayesian network-based tunable image segmentation algorithm for object recognition. In: Proceedings of IEEE International Symposium on Signal Processing and Information Technology, pp. 11–16 (2011)
10. Matsakis, P., Ni, J., Wang, X.: Object localization based on directional information: Case of 2d raster data. In: Proceedings of IAPR International Conference on Pattern Recognition, pp. 142–146 (2006)
11. Maron, O., Lozano-Perez, T.: A framework for multiple instance learning. In: Proceedings of the Conference on Advances in Neural Information Processing Systems, vol. 10, pp. 570–576 (1998)
12. Xu, T., Gondra, I., Chiu, D.: Adaptive kernel diverse density estimate for multiple instance learning. In: Proceedings of 2011 International Conference on Machine Learning and Data Mining, pp. 185–198 (2011)

13. Bloch, I.: Fuzzy relative position between objects in image processing: A morphological approach. IEEE Transactions on Pattern Analysis and Machine Intelligence 106, 657–664 (1999)
14. Logan, G.D., Sadler, D.D.: A computational analysis of the apprehension of spatial relations. In: Language and Space. MIT Press, Cambridge (1996)
15. Gapp, K.P.: Basic meaning of spatial relations: Computation and evaluation in 3d space. In: Proceedings of National Conference on Artificial Intelligence, pp. 1393–1398 (1994)
16. Olivier, P., Tsuji, J.I.: Quantitative perceptual representation of prepositional se-
.   mantics. Artificial Intelligence Review 8, 147–158 (1994)
17. Goshtasby, A.: Description and discrimination of planar shapes using shape matrices. IEEE Transactions on Pattern Analysis and Machine Intelligence 7(6), 738–743 (1985)
18. Arthur, D., Vassilvitskii, S.: K-means++: The advantages of careful seeding. Technical Report 2006-13, Stanford InfoLab (June 2006)

Gesture Based Robot Control⋆

Tomasz Grzejszczak, Michał Mikulski, Tadeusz Szkodny, and Karol Jędrasiak

Silesian University of Technology
Akademicka 2, 44-100 Gliwice, Poland
tomasz.grzejszczak@polsl.pl

Abstract. The paper proposes a method of controlling robotic manipulators with use of human gestures and movement. Experiments were performed with the use of 4 degree-of-freedom AX-12 Robotic Arm manipulator with force gripper and ASUS Xtion depth sensor also called motion controller. Depth and video capture has been done via OpenNI library. The infrastructure is based on Windows Communication Foundation (WCF) for remote access, authorization, multimedia streaming and servo control. Control of robotic manipulator is implemented with use of human computer interaction algorithm basing on depth sensor information.

1 Introduction

Robotic manipulators can work automatically or manually. In manual mode it is important to retain a high level of precision (e.g. for surgical operations or transporting objects in atypical environments). This can be done using joysticks [4], or force feedback devices. However in sterile environments touching the human-machine interface carries a risk of contamination, and disease transmission. In such conditions a different approach is needed. Thus there is a need to improve the communication between human and machine to ensue a touch-free operations and to be more intuitional. This article proposes a natural way of controlling the AX-12 Robotic Arm using gestures and position of hand. The human machine interaction is provided by depth controller. There are two similar low price depth controllers: Asus Xtion and Microsoft Kinect. This article shows the solution using Asus Xtion PRO and a vision system program created with use of OpenNI library.

2 Asus Xtion PRO

Most vision systems use standard RGB camera in order to track objects. The standard image can contain an object that could be described using (x,y) coordinates. This solution however does not give us the information about how far the objet is placed. On contradiction, the depth controller such as Asus Xtion

---

⋆ This work has been supported by the Polish Ministry of Science and Higher Education under research grant no. IP2011 023071 from the Science Budget 2012–2013.

or Microsoft Kinect is able to provide us with standard gray scale image where the value of pixels are proportional to distance of environment to depth sensor.

The solution of proposed problem is solved using Asus Xtion depth sensor. It can work within range between 0.8m and 3.5m with 58ř H, 45ř V, 70ř D (Horizontal, Vertical, Diagonal) angle of view. The output data is represented as a VGA (640x480) or QVGA (320x240) matrix with data proportional to distance from sensor to its field of view. The communication with PC is supported by USB [1].

Asus Xtion is delivered with programming library called OpenNI. OpenNI (Open Natural Interaction) is a multi-language, cross-platform framework that defines APIs for writing applications utilizing Natural Interaction. OpenNI APIs are composed of a set of interfaces for writing NI applications [5].

3   Vision System

In order to control the manipulator, user need to stand in front of depth sensor within the operating range. Vision system has been programmed in such way that it detects the closest object on field of view, thus the user can control the manipulator by reaching and moving hand. Vision system program has been created as a namespace that could be attached to manipulator control program. Its main purpose is to get image from depth sensor, perform the calibration and calculate the displacement of hand.

Fig. 1. Depth map with control command presented as displacement from zero point

The first and main function is image acquisition. This apparently easy task is composed of series of functions. First the depth sensor needs to be initialized, the depth data matrix is acquired, than this matrix needs to be converted into RGB matrix that finally can be interpreted as an image. This image is a colorized depth data, where changes of distance from sensor are represented as different color saturation or lightness level.

The aim of calibration is to get the three dimension (x,y,z) point that can be refereed as zero point. From this point all the displacements of hand would result in manipulator movement. In order to perform the calibration, user needs to stand in front of the depth sensor with his hand outstretched. After calling the calibrate function, program is searching for the closest point on the field of view witch is users hand and remembers this point.

After calling the displacement function, program is searching for the users hand and comparing its closest point to the zero point from calibration. The differences are calculated and the function is returning values of displacement. The examples are shown of Fig. 1.

4   AX-12 Robotic Arm

AX-12 Robotic Arm is a 4 degree-of-freedom serial manipulator with 7 AX-12+ Dynamixel servomechanisms constructed by CrustCrawler Inc. It consists of 4

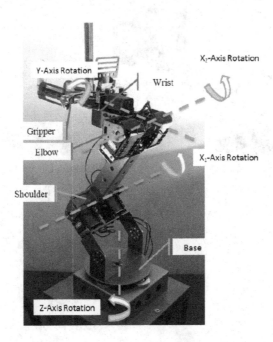

Fig. 2. AX-12 Robotic Arm revolute axes

revolute joints named by the community as: base, shoulder, elbow and wrist, as well as a gripper end effector, presented in Fig. 2.

AX-12 Servomechanisms are controlled with by a UART half-duplex single wire Dynamixel Network [2]. Individual servomechanisms can be addressed by their unique ID. The built in control circuits allow for a precise position control, making AX-12+ servos a popular choice for many mobile robots, UAVs and simple manipulators. Because RS232 PC ports allow for a maximal 115200 or 128000 bps, USB2Dynamixel servo controller was used, which is based on Future Technology Devices International (FTDI) FT232RL USB to UART converter that allows for speeds beyond 1 Mbits [3], required by AX-12+ servos.

5   System Configurations

In the current environments such as the medical sector are reaching towards Internet oriented distributed systems. RIS (Radiology information system), PACS (Picture archiving and communication system) and many other medical information systems are using the Internet as means of data transfer. With the growth of robotics and their integration in Service-oriented architectures (SoA), medical manipulators can perform tasks with the surgeon miles away.

Because of the need to separate the robot environment from the human control environment a distributed, network based system was created. As both the

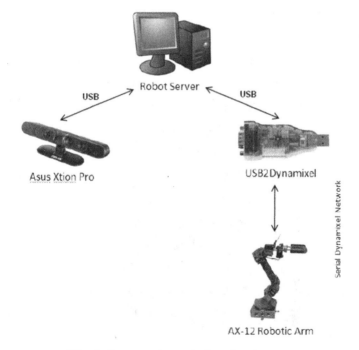

Fig. 3. System schematic for a local system

AX-12 Robotic Arm, as well as Asus Xtion PRO can be programmed using C#, the system has been designed to operate both in a localized environment on a single PC (presented on fig. 3), as well as in a distributed system (presented on fig. 2) using Windows Communication Foundation (WCF). WCF provides a reliable, fast and encrypted framework for distributed systems, and because of it's object orientated architecture, the classes can easily implement remote operations. Furthermore, WCF was chosen for the project because of it's universality, interoperability and security. More detailed description of Windows Communication Foundation for remote robot operations can be found in [4].

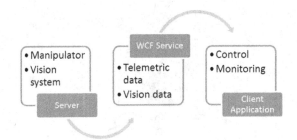

Fig. 4. WCF data flow

The WCF Service is using an interface consisting of the following core functions [4]:

- int GetDataJoint(int index, int property) : Gets the value of a property (CurrentPosition, GoalPosition, MovingSpeed, CurrentLoad) for indexed joint.
- bool SetDataJoint(int index, int property, int value) : Sets the value of a property (CurrentPosition, GoalPosition, MovingSpeed, CurrentLoad) for indexed joint.
- bool StopDataJoint(int index) : Stops any movement of a indexed joint.
- Stream GetImageStream(int divider) : Requests a current image stream, captured from the camera.

Both a localized system, and a distributed one have advantages, as well as disadvantages. A single PC requires the operator to be in the vicinity of the robot, and depth controller. It significantly reduces the control lag, but requires additional processing power, and multithreaded approach. Due to the single application requirement, only a single programming language may be used.

The distributed approach for using a depth sensor allows the control algorithms to be implemented in a different programming language than the robot control. The WCF can be implemented in different languages and for diverse operating systems. It also separates the robot interface from the depth controller, which can be useful for example for synchronous development.

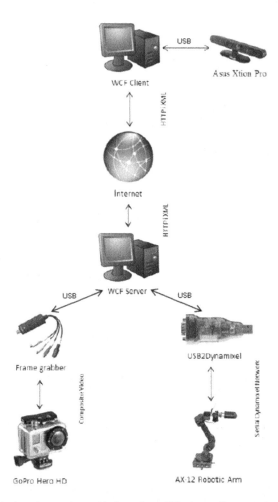

Fig. 5. Distributed system schematic based on Windows Communication Foundation

6   Conclusion and Future Work

The research presented in this paper proves the great potential in human computer interaction algorithms. During tests the presented way of controlling the
manipulator was proven to be intuitional and precise. People testing this solution found it much easier to learn how to control the manipulator using hand
position than using joystick.

The Windows Communication Foundation based distributed system adds a
control delay, dependant from the network configuration, transfer delays and
bandwidth. In order to provide the smoothest operation possible, a network
architecture must be considered.

In future, more research would be done in order to identify not only the
position of hand but the statical and dynamical gestures. User by showing the

specific gesture would be able to give a command to the manipulator to pass one of the objects directly to the hand of user which position would be dynamically detected.

References

1. ASUS: Xtion pro documentation (2012),
   http://www.asus.com/Multimedia/Motion_Sensor/Xtion_PRO/
2. CrustCrawler Inc.: Dynamixel AX-12 User's Manual (2006)
3. Future Technology Devices International Ltd.: FT232RL USB UART IC Datasheet Version 1.9 (2009)
4. Mikulski, M.A., Szkodny, T.: Remote Control and Monitoring of AX-12 Robotic Arm Based on Windows Communication Foundation. In: Czachórski, T., Kozielski, S., Stańczyk, U. (eds.) Man-Machine Interactions 2. AISC, vol. 103, pp. 77–83. Springer, Heidelberg (2011)
5. organization, O.: Openni documentation (2012),
   http://openni.org/Documentation/

Analysis of White Blood Cell Differential Counts Using Dual-Tree Complex Wavelet Transform and Support Vector Machine Classifier

Mehdi Habibzadeh, Adam Krzyżak, and Thomas Fevens

Dept. of Computer Science & Software Engineering
Concordia University, Montréal, Québec
{me_habi,krzyzak,fevens}@encs.concordia.ca

Abstract. A widely used pathological screening test for blood smears is the complete blood count which classifies and counts peripheral particles into their various types. We particularly interested in the classification and counting of the five main types of white blood cells (leukocytes) in a clinical setting where the quality of microscopic imagery may be poor. A critical first step in the medical analysis of cytological images of thin blood smears is the segmentation of individual cells. The quality of the segmentation has a great influence on the cell type identification, but for poor quality, noisy, and/or low resolution images, segmentation is correspondingly less reliable. In this paper, we compensate for less accurate segmentation by extracting features based on wavelets using the Dual-Tree Complex Wavelet Transform (DT-CWT) which is based on multi-resolution characteristics of the image. These features then form the basis of classification of white blood cells into their five primary types with a Support Vector Machine (SVM) that performs classification by constructing hyper-planes in a high multi-dimensional space that separates cases of different classes. This approach was validated with experiments conducted on poor quality, normal blood smear images.

1 Introduction

The complete blood count (CBC) is a capacious pathology screening test, broadly used to detect such abnormalities as infections, allergies, disorders with clotting, and for diagnosing and reporting numerous diseases. It examines different particles of the blood smears and includes the Leukocyte or White Blood Cell (WBC) count, Erythrocyte or Red Blood Cell (RBC) count, WBC differential, evidence of disease, and the number of infected cells. To do this, the blood film is stained (e.g., Wright, Giemsa, or May-Grünwald staining) [11] and then imaged with a transmission light microscope.

The most reliable and complete diagnosis of blood smear infection is done by manually finding disorders and abnormalities in blood samples through microscopic qualitative and quantitative analysis, particularly looking at the shape, nucleus and cytoplasm of the cells, occlusion and degree of contact with each other, and so on, and by counting blood smear particles. Pathologists use such

L. Bolc et al. (Eds.): ICCVG 2012, LNCS 7594, pp. 414–422, 2012.
© Springer-Verlag Berlin Heidelberg 2012

screening tests to understand and interpret the minor and major changes that help identify different abnormalities in the cells.

1.1 Background and Literature Review

An important aspect of the CBC is the WBC count and WBC differential. An increased number of WBC is called leukocytosis, the presence of inflammation, leukemia, trauma, intense exercise, or stress. However, a decreased WBC count called leukopenia, determine chemotherapy, radiation therapy, or diseases of the immune system, pregnancy (final months) and heavy smoking. The leukocyte differential is the total number of WBCs expressed as thousands/μl in a volume of blood.

There are five primary types of WBCs (with typical percentage of occurrence in normal blood): Neutrophil (40- 75%); Lymphocyte (25-35%); Monocyte (3-9%); Eosinophil (<5%); and Basophil (<1%) [11] (see Fig. 1). The counting and classification of each class manually is a tedious, time-consuming, labor-intensive activity in medical laboratories that can be eased by flow cytometry systems or image processing software. These automated counters improve the reproducibility and accuracy of the WBC differential results and relieve the burden of these clinical activities. Flow cytometry is the dominant automated technique for examining microscopic particles such as blood elements and available for the last 25 years in medical laboratories [16]. Flow cytometry is combination of chemical, electrical and software approaches which is not very economical and also restricted to major medical centers.

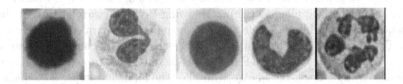

Fig. 1. WBC (typical shapes), left to right: Basophil, Eosinophil, Lymphocyte, Monocyte, Neutrophil

Computerized image and pattern processing allows for the improvement of the reliability and precision of blood examination without additive burden expenses. The history of computerized steps into automated blood examination dates back to Bentley and Lewis [2] in 1975. The first fully automated processing of blood slides was introduced by Rowan [12] in 1986. The background on automatic WBC classification by using computer vision concepts is quite considerable and involves different feature extractors, classifiers and qualitative process, e.g., [11,16,15,10,13,17].

Some recent work, e.g., [16] has introduced how the SVM classifier, by applying a hierarchical tree-based multi-class strategy on a set of morphometrical, textural and colorimetric features, can be employed to segment WBCs. Moreover

[3] has studied the blood cell segmentation problem through using conventional wavelet transformation combined with an morphology operation in order to improve the segmentation of touching or adjacent cells.

This present work aims to improve WBC type recognition and counting for poor quality blood smear images by using wavelet coefficients computed by the Dual-Tree Complex Wavelet Transform (DT-CWT) [14] in combination with a Support Vector Machine (SVM) [1] for WBC type classification. Experimentation indicates that this approach is effective on poor imagery with low magnification.

2   Proposed Approach

Our medical image processing system deals with WBC differential counting. In particular, only normal thin blood smears will be considered. The proposed approach is composed of three general steps: 1. Image acquisition and discrimination of WBCs from RBCs; 2. Feature extraction by DT-CWT; 3. Classification by means of an SVM in the five WBC types. Details of each step are presented in the following sections.

3   Image Acquisition and Leukocyte Separation

The input for our framework are images of thin blood smears saved in BMP format of size 512×512 pixels. Next the WBCs are localized and segmented by the following procedure as introduced in previous work [7,5]. Robust and efficient denoising is applied to the images using Bivariate wavelet thresholding, compensating for its blurring side-effect by using a Kuwahara edge preservation filter. These images are then enhanced by using a combination of Otsu and Niblack binarization algorithms. Finally, WBCs and RBCs are separated into two sub-images using a mask-based algorithm. For the following steps, the separated WBCs are converted into normalized 28×28 pixel images.

4   Feature Extraction

Feature extraction is the effective preprocessing for automated white blood cell classification into five main classes. In previous work [6] we applied two different strategies to extract features: kernel-PCA [18], a statistical technique, over pixel intensity to distinguish characteristic of individual Leukocyte white blood cell to the blood smear was served; and also the CNN (convolution neural network) [9] in first layers topological properties from the gray-scale image is automatically by convolution approach and down-sampling by 2 extracted is applied. In this study, Dual-Tree Complex Wavelet transform (DT-CWT) coefficients, a rich, multi-scale description of local informative structure extractor for better efficiency as a primary step before the SVM classifier is applied.

4.1   Dual-Tree Complex Wavelet

Wavelet analysis provides efficient tools for capturing local structure with powerful analysis performance and multi-resolution properties which is suitable for image analysis although it has several drawbacks. The wavelet transform has *four* unsolved structured problems [14]: *Oscillations* (the coefficients tend to oscillate positive and negative around singular points, thus coefficients is represented as greater than is true or reasonable (exaggerated)), *Shift variance* (a minor shift, rotation of the signal leads to considerable variations in the distribution of energy between coefficients at different scales), *Aliasing* (since wavelet coefficient is quite vast and are computed via down-sampling with non-ideal low-pass and high-pass filters tends to signal aliases of one another and make them to become indistinguishable) and *Lack of directionality* (lack of directional selectivity notably makes difficult processing of geometric image features such as ridges and edges).

To overcome to these *four* Discrete Wavelet Transform (DWT) weak points, the Dual-Tree Complex Wavelet (see [14,8] for more details and theory behind approach) was introduced as an enhanced version to the typical DWT, with efficient additive properties, shift invariance and being directionally selective in two and higher dimensions. DT-CWT is inspired by Fourier transform in wavelet concepts. However, the coefficients of DWT are real-valued while the Fourier transform is based on complex-valued oscillating sinusoids (the real and imaginary parts) forms a Hilbert transform pair with $\pi/2$ phase difference which it performs two different sub-band filtering schemes for real and imaginary parts separately.

We use the Dual-tree Complex Wavelet Transform to provide a multi-scale description of local structure which is also translation, scale, and rotation invariant. It is faster compared with the traditional template matching method [16] and also overcomes using wavelet thresholding [3] by having freedom degrees in variance and directional selectivity. In practice, DT-CWT combines two Digital Wavelet Transforms, using even and odd wavelets to provide complex coefficients. The wavelet analysis is applied in $1 - D$, along rows and columns, and *six* oriented $2 - D$ complex wavelets are constructed from different combinations of the outputs. The outcome of the DT-CWT is thus a set of complex coefficients as a sufficiently rich representation of local structure at each pixel for six different $(\pm\frac{\pi}{12}, \pm\frac{\pi}{4}, \pm\frac{5\pi}{12})$ orientations (sub-bands), (see Fig. 2) and for each of a number of scales by factor 2. Regarding to using the information in the feature vectors for SVM, the complex values (real and imaginary) are converted in polar form (magnitude, phase) to place alternate into feature vector (magnitude$_1$, phase$_1$, magnitude$_2$, phase$_2$ and so on) give the best results in classifier.

For our segmented cell images, DT-CWT is applied at 6 scales, the number of levels of wavelet decomposition and 14-tap Q-shift [14,8] filters to image samples, giving a total of 3204 (6 scales ($14*14, 7*7, 4*4, 2*2, 1*1, 1*1$) × 6 sub-bands $(\pm\frac{\pi}{12}, \pm\frac{\pi}{4}, \pm\frac{5\pi}{12})$ × 2 magnitude, phase components) features for each 28×28 sample.

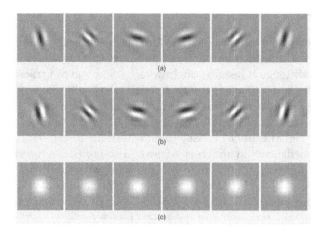

Fig. 2. [14] : 2-D dual-tree CWT. (a) the real part of each complex coefficient; (b) the imaginary part; and (c) illustrates the magnitude.

5 Machine Learning Approach

Some commonly used classifiers are non-parametric techniques like k-Nearest Neighbour, non-metric approaches like Decision Tree, parametric techniques like Bayesian, Artificial Neural Network (ANN) [4], Support Vector Machine (SVM), etc. Below, we will use the SVM.

5.1 Support Vector Machines

We classify White Blood cells pixels into five sub-types based on their dual tree complex wavelet coefficients, using a support vector machine classifier as an approach that is well-suited and robustness to non-linear classification in a high-dimensional space and efficient in modeling diverse sources of data. Given a set of training and testing data consisting of 5×28 samples which is a D (448560)-dimensional ($5 * 28 * 3204 = 5 * 28 * 2 * 1602$) feature vector labeled as belonging to classes (see Fig 1). Training a SVM [1] is finding the large margin hyperplane, where kernel parameters also have effective impacts on the decision boundary. To find the best kernel like most practical problems in machine learning, several kernels (Gaussian and Polynomial) could be tried and typically the lowest degree polynomial, linear kernel is performed and provides a baseline which presents the best performance in our available database such as many other bio-informatics applications when Polynomial and Gaussian kernels frequently leads to over-fitting in high dimensional data sets (DT-CWT coefficients) with a small number of examples (28 samples for each individual class) [1]. SVM implementation can be done by one-2-all (1AA strategy) or one-2-one (AAA strategy).

In this work support vector machines with a linear kernel, soft-margin (by allowing to misclassify some points (slack variables)) and *1AA* strategy [1] with 5-fold validation over DT-CWT outcome is performed. We can efficiently train

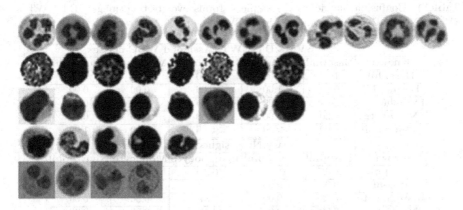

Fig. 3. WBC testing data, top to down: Neutrophil(N), Basophil(B), Lymphocyte(L), Monocyte(M), Eosinophil(E)

and test the into two subsets comprising of 82% = 23 for training and 18% =5 samples for tuning in each class to have a balanced database.

6   Experimentation

Similar to our previous related work [6], we perform test on sets of normal blood slides with different characteristics, magnification, staining, etc. High variability of samples is intended to simulate large variation of real blood samples. The experiments (training & testing) are carried through on low quality images normalized to 28×28 pixels to simulate low quality data and poor sampling (see Fig. 3).

Given a SVM classifier and a set of dual tree complex wavelet transform instances (the test set), a 5×5 confusion matrix (also called a contingency table) representing the known classes of all WBC objects classified to determine the effectiveness and accuracy of classification of proposed framework. In this work we also compare the reliability the use of DT-CWT coefficient with Convolution Neural Networks (CNN) [9], a feed-forward networks which extract topological features in first layers and classify patterns with its last layers; SVM using features extracted by Kernel Principal Component Analysis (K-PCA) [18], a primary statistical technique for transforming data into lower dimensional space from image intensity; and using a simple linear SVM.

For 115 (5 ∗ 23) training images and 25 (5 ∗ 5) testing images, the confusion matrices (with normalized rows) for normal testing WBC images for hybrid DT-CWT & SVM; CNN (recognition rate after 105 epoch); K-PCA (with polynomial D=2) & SVM; and linear SVM are summarized in Table 1.

In particular, for normal WBCs using SVM & DT-CWT 95.2% of known WBCs were classified as such, with this classification rate decreasing to 85% for CNN , 70% for hybrid K-PCA & SVM, and then to 62% for linear SVM. So, based on the confusion matrices with five classes the proposed SVM & DT-CWT

Table 1. Confusion matrices for classifiers, totals over testing images: DT-CWT & SVM; CNN; K-PCA & SVM; and Linear SVM

SVM&DT-CWT: Assigned WBC classes					
Known	**Basophil**	**Eosinophil**	**Lymphocyte**	**Monocyte**	**Neutrophil**
Basophil	1.00	0.00	0.00	0.00	0.00
Eosinophil	0.00	1.00	0.00	0.00	0.00
Lymphocyte	0.04	0.00	0.96	0.00	0.00
Monocyte	0.20	0.00	0.00	0.80	0.00
Neutrophil	0.00	0.00	0.00	0.00	1.00

CNN: Assigned WBC classes					
Known	**Basophil**	**Eosinophil**	**Lymphocyte**	**Monocyte**	**Neutrophil**
Basophil	0.625	0.125	0.250	0.00	0.00
Eosinophil	0.00	0.95	0.05	0.00	0.00
Lymphocyte	0.125	0.00	0.875	0.00	0.00
Monocyte	0.00	0.00	0.00	0.80	0.20
Neutrophil	0.00	0.00	0.00	0.014	0.985

SVM&K-PCA: Assigned WBC classes					
Known	**Basophil**	**Eosinophil**	**Lymphocyte**	**Monocyte**	**Neutrophil**
Basophil	0.50	0.00	0.30	0.20	0.00
Eosinophil	0.00	1.00	0.00	0.00	0.00
Lymphocyte	0.30	0.20	0.50	0.00	0.00
Monocyte	0.00	0.00	0.20	0.80	0.00
Neutrophil	0.10	0.00	0.20	0.00	0.70

Linear SVM: Assigned WBC classes					
Known	**Basophil**	**Eosinophil**	**Lymphocyte**	**Monocyte**	**Neutrophil**
Basophil	0.20	0.00	0.80	0.00	0.00
Eosinophil	0.00	1.00	0.00	0.00	0.00
Lymphocyte	0.40	0.10	0.50	0.00	0.00
Monocyte	0.20	0.00	0.00	0.80	0.00
Neutrophil	0.00	0.00	0.20	0.20	0.60

classifier is much more reliable and precise even in the presence of similarity among classes (specially between Basophil and Lymphocyte cells) in this difficult database yielding acceptable accuracy when compared to SVM (refer to diagonal confusion matrix such as Lymphocyte classification rate of 96% for DT-CWT & SVM versus 50% for linear SVM). The false positive rate (FPR) of the SVM & DT-CWT is also very negligible than the FPR of CNN or a SVM using kernel PCA and it again proves the importance of optimized features by DT-CWT.

7   Conclusions

The method as outlined presents a detailed computerized description of an acceptable visual perception of laboratory task when automated and and semi automated clinical instruments such as used in flow methods initially became dominant to perform WBC classification. WBC differential counts such as manual counting, impedance counters and flow cytometry techniques however, they would be expected to have feasible false-positive rates that is also very trivial in these current computerized image processing solutions even in very low quality. As confusion matrices show even in case of poor samples (messy images, small and faded WBCs) WBC counts are much more accurate when Hybrid DT-CWT & SVM classifier is used rather than CNN, K-PCA & SVM classifier (see confusion matrices given in Table 1). Experimental results indicate that current analysis offers remarkable recognition accuracy even in presence of poor quality samples and multiple classes. Advances in implementation result in the possibility of extending the use of this framework to quantitatively measure the subtypes cells (sub-differentiation) in the entire field of hematology analysis or other similar research.

Acknowledgements. Thanks to Prof Nick Kingsbury from the University of Cambridge, UK for providing his DT-CWT code.

References

1. Ben-Hur, A., Weston, J.: A user's guide to support vector machines. In: Carugo, O., Eisenhaber, F. (eds.) Data Mining Techniques for the Life Sciences. Methods in Molecular Biology, vol. 609, pp. 223–239. Humana Press (2010)
2. Bentley, S., Lewis, S.: The use of an image analyzing computer for the quantification of red cell morphological characteristics. British Journal of Hematology 29, 81–88 (1975)
3. Chan, H., Li-Jun, J., Jiang, B.: Wavelet transform and morphology image segmentation algorism for blood cell. In: 4th IEEE Conference on Industrial Electronics and Applications (ICIEA), pp. 542–545 (May 2009)
4. Duda, R.O., Hart, P.E., Stork, D.G.: Pattern Classification, 2nd edn. Wiley Interscience (November 2001)
5. Habibzadeh, M., Krzyżak, A., Fevens, T.: Application of pattern recognition techniques for the analysis of thin blood smear images. Journal of Medical Informatics & Technologies 18, 29–40 (2011)
6. Habibzadeh, M., Krzyżak, A., Fevens, T.: Comparative Analysis of White Blood Cell Differential Counts using CNN and SVM with K-PCA Classifiers (2012) (manuscript)
7. Habibzadeh, M., Krzyżak, A., Fevens, T., Sadr, A.: Counting of RBCs and WBCs in noisy normal blood smear microscopic images. In: SPIE Medical Imaging, vol. 7963, pp. 79633I-1 – 79633I-11 (February 2011)
8. Kingsbury, N.: Design of q-shift complex wavelets for image processing using frequency domain energy minimization. In: International Conference on Image Processing (ICIP), vol. 1, pp. I – 1013–16 (2003)
9. Lauer, F., Suen, C.Y., Bloch, G.: A trainable feature extractor for handwritten digit recognition. Journal of Pattern Recognition 40(6), 1816–1824 (2007)
10. Montseny, E., Sobrevilla, P., Romani, S.: A fuzzy approach to white blood cells segmentation in color bone marrow images. In: IEEE International Conference on Fuzzy Systems, vol. 1, pp. 173–178 (2004)
11. Ramoser, H., Laurain, V., Bischof, H., Ecker, R.: Leukocyte segmentation and classification in blood-smear images. In: 27th IEEE Annual Conference Engineering in Medicine and Biology, Shanghai, China, pp. 3371–3374 (September 2005)

12. Rowan, R., England, J.M.: Automated examination of the peripheral blood smear. In: Automation and Quality Assurance in Hematology. ch. 5, pp. 129–177. Blackwell Scientific, Oxford (1986)
13. Sabino, D.M.U., Costa, L.F., Rizzatti, E.G., Zago, M.A.: Toward leukocyte recognition using morphometry, texture and color. In: IEEE International Symposium on Biomedical Imaging: Nano to Macro, vol. 1, pp. 121–124 (April 2004)
14. Selesnick, I.W., Baraniuk, R.G., Kingsbury, N.C.: The dual-tree complex wavelet transform. IEEE Signal Processing Magazine 22(6), 123–151 (2005)
15. Theera-Umpon, N., Dhompongsa, S.: Morphological Granulometric Features of Nucleus in Automatic Bone Marrow White Blood Cell Classification. IEEE Transactions on Information Technology in Biomedicine 11(3), 353–359 (2007)
16. Ushizima, D.M., Lorena, A.C., de Carvalho, A.C.P.L.F.: Support Vector Machines Applied to White Blood Cell Recognition. In: International Conference on Hybrid Intelligent Systems, Los Alamitos, CA, USA, pp. 379–384 (2005)
17. Yampri, P., Pintavirooj, C., Daochai, S., Teartulakarn, S.: White Blood Cell Classification based on the Combination of Eigen Cell and Parametric Feature Detection. In: 1st IEEE Conference on Industrial Electronics and Applications, pp. 1–4 (May 2006)
18. Dambreville, S., Rathi, Y., Tannenbaum, A.: Statistical shape analysis using kernel PCA. In: SPIE Electronic Imaging (2006)

A Prototype Device for Concealed
Weapon Detection Using IR and CMOS Cameras
Fast Image Fusion

Karol Jędrasiak, Aleksander Nawrat, Krzysztof Daniec, Roman Koteras,
Michał Mikulski, and Tomasz Grzejszczak

Institute of Automatic Control, Silesian University of Technology
Akademicka 16, 44-100, Gliwice, Poland
karol.jedrasiak@polsl.pl

Abstract. Concealed weapon detection (CWD) is an important part of
everyday law enforcement. There are numerous facilities that are endan-
gered of an terrorist or an fanatic individual attack. Commercially used
weapon detection gates are very expensive and sometimes impossible to
install into already existing security infrastructures. Here we present a
miniature prototype device for concealed weapon detection using two
cameras: IR and visual. The prototype consists of two printed circuit
boards (PCB). First PCB is responsible for analog to digital and digital
to analog conversions of the video stream. The second board is the main
processing unit realizing the presented fast image fusion algorithm. The
relative size of the prototype can be assumed as a miniature in comparison to the current used solutions. Such miniature device could be
mounted under the ceiling or inside 3 DOF gimbals for wider view angle.
Presented device can be considered as an alternative to already existing
man-sized gates traditionally used for CWD.

1   Introduction

It is known that concealed weapon detection (CWD) is gaining attention in the
law enforcement. The terrorism threat is increasing and the danger of an terrorist act becomes real not only in the airports but as well in stadiums, various
sport facilities and shopping malls. Hence, it can be stated that installing CWD
devices in the mentioned facilities is one of the most critical aspects for law
enforcement. Most of existing algorithms for CWD are based on thermal difference between human and weapon, thus IR image processing. There are also
classic approaches using metal detectors. Unfortunately, a person might be holding or wearing multiple metal objects that cannot be named as a weapon like e.g.
watches or shoe elements. Another type of devices possible to use are millimeter
wave imaging systems and an ultra-wide bandwidth terahertz (THz) imaging
radar. Unfortunately those devices are still very expensive and their application
for law enforcements requires more time. Each of mentioned technologies has its
advantages and disadvantages. It is assumed that a combination of various types

L. Bolc et al. (Eds.): ICCVG 2012, LNCS 7594, pp. 423–432, 2012.

of sensors can improve the overall performance of the existing CWD surveillance systems. There are also visual cameras which are not suitable for detection. However, they are essential for a standard human observer in order to fully utilize the device. It is important to develop fast and simple algorithms allowing enhancement of the resulting image using embedded solutions because there are multiple applications for visible light and IR imagery fusion that does not allow using a standard PC computer. There is not much research in the field of fast and easy to implement using hardware image fusion algorithms. One of the main assumptions of fast algorithms for hardware is that fusion based enhancement of the imagery from the infrared and visible light cameras can be achieved without using pyramids. The assumption is done due to the small amount of memory available for embedded solutions. During research we have tested and evaluated the most popular fusion methods and decided that results of much more simple methods by taking into account the context of human observer could be comparable with the results from tested algorithms. In the article we present a hybrid prototype of cheap device utilizing features of IR and visual cameras by performing image fusion. The device's input are two cameras of the mentioned type and the output is a video stream consisting of fused images. All the processing is done in the hardware and the output can be observed using a standard television or monitor with PAL interface.

2   Literature Review

CWD is a topic widely study in the literature. One of the most wide surveys was performed by the National Institute of Justice of the U. S Department of Justice [1]. A wide range of electronic devices capable of CWD was noted. There are devices based on acoustic reflectivity, magnetic fields, x-ray and microwaves, millimeter radars and IR, THz imaging systems. However nowadays mostly IR, THz and millimeter radars are still in use. The accuracy or safety level of the other devices is unfortunately too low for law enforcement applications. Weapons vary in terms of size and materials motivate the using of imaging systems.

The idea of image fusion is to integrate information from multimodality images so that new images are more suitable for the purpose of human visual perception or computer processing or both. Hence, the task is depending on the application and can consist of methods of aiding image processing or the often opposite improving the visual perception. Before the fusion is possible the mandatory step is to synchronize the signals. In case of images it is done by estimating the geometrical transformation between two images. After registration the fusion can be explained as a process of combining two images into one image containing more information.

Most of the fusion methods are operating at the pixel level of the image. The popular fusion algorithms can be classified into four primary categories based on: substitution, mathematical combination, optimization methods and multi-resolution transform domains. Fusion schemes based on substitution are using weighted averaging, color mixed RGB [2] or principal component analysis (PCA)

[3]. PCA fusion is based on statistical method for transform multivariate data set with correlated variables into a new set usually with a significantly lower number of elements. The required for the transform parameters are acquired by minimizing the covariance of error between original and reduced set of components.

As an example of mathematical combination of multispectral bands the application of Brovey Transform was presented in [4]. Main stream of optimization approaches is based on artificial intelligence methods such as neural networks and Bayesian optimization [5]. Using multi-resolution decomposition is an active field of research. For example in the work [6] a Laplacian pyramid was used in order to fuse images. Another approach is based on using wavelets [7] and curvlet [8]. Different approach based on contourlet transform was presented in [9]. Using wavelet based methods in order to perform fusion was also applied in the works [14, 15, 16, 17]. Usually a Discrete Wavelet Transform (DWT) is used. A process of fusion can be divided into two partial stages. First the DWT transform is applied to the both images and the resulting multi-scale representation is acquired. During this step a selection of an optimal coefficients from a set of salient wavelet coefficients is performed. A more simple approach can be based on the maximum of the absolute values or on an area based maximum energy value. The second stage consists of performing an inverse DWT. The described method cannot be applied without flicker to the video sequences due to the lack of shift invariants. A number of corrections were introduced in work [18]. A concept of a discrete wavelet frame (DWF) is presented in [19]. It allows for shift invariant DWT computation in an efficient way. Regardless the fusion method an important element of the mentioned algorithms is using pyramids. An image pyramids is a set of usually lowpass filtered or bandpassed copies of an image where each copy represents the base image at a different scale. It is usually assumed that every level of the pyramid is smaller by a factor two. There are multiple pyramidal approaches used and studied in the literature.

One of the most commonly used is a Gaussian pyramid. It is a sequence of images such as each element is filtered using Gaussian filter [10]. Another pyramidal approach is using Laplacian pyramids [11]. It is a pyramid such that each level is a bandpass copy of its predecessor. Each copy it obtained as the difference between the respective levels of Gaussian pyramid. In Laplacian fusion in order to decide pixel from which source should contribute to the resulting image a strength measure is used. Typically it is a simple local area sum. Another type of pyramid is Ratio of Low Pass Pyramid. It is such a pyramid in which at every level the ratio of the successive levels of the Gaussian pyramid [12]. In the fusion method based on this pyramid a score factor is computed as the maximum value of the largest deviation from unity from both image sources. Another approach is based on Contrast pyramid which is similar to the ratio of Low Pass Pyramid approach. The contrast parameter was defined a ratio of the difference between luminance at a specified pixel (x, y) in the image. Luminance was defined as a quantitative measure of brightness of a surface point in a given direction. In the work [13] a more efficient variation of the Gaussian Pyramid was presented.

It was named Filter-Subtract-decimate (FSD). A challenge of creation a set of pyramid levels that are unaffected by the shape changing morphological filters was addressed in [14] by Burt and Adelson. The introduced filters are a complex filters constructed from a set of partial filtering stages using morphological opening and closing operations. Whether one use a gradient of an image at each level of a pyramid the result is called Gradient Pyramid. Usually the gradient is applied in four directions: horizontal, vertical and two diagonal. However there are also approaches trying to use more directions.

Another approach to image fusion is based on biology. A wide number of biologically-inspired fusion methods were presented in the works [20, 21, 22]. The fusion and some higher-level process for the human and many other higher organisms take place in the retina, the visual cortex, and the brain. Two main approaches can be distinguished in this group. First is trying to apply the mechanisms known from the primates and the monkeys. The second group is trying to reproduce the effect that occurs in a number of neuron classes in the optic tectum of two groups of snake, namely rattlesnake and pythons. During the process of the fusion the images are contrast enhanced in such a way that it is presumed is done in the visual cortex of primates.

3   Image Fusion Algorithm

The aim of the presented fast fusion algorithm is to aid the human visual perception in order to allow CWD. Therefore maximizing the number of salient features in the fused image is not the main task. In contrast the main task is to enhance the color image with the most important areas of the image for the observer. The concealed weapon areas can be defined as pixels in the image that are characterized by significantly higher pixel value in the IR image. In order to perform the color fusion as well it was decided to use the Hue-Saturation-Value color space which was designed as a color space close to the human visual perception (fig. 1).

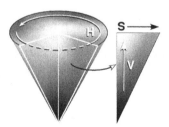

Fig. 1. The Hue-Saturation-Value (HSV) color space model

In the HSV color space each color is derived from a white light. In order to transform from RGB to HSV the following formula is used (1):

$$V = max(R, G, B)$$

$$S = \frac{max(R,G,B) - min(R,G,B)}{max(R,G,B)}$$

$$H = \left\{ \begin{array}{l} \frac{G-B}{max(R,G,B)-min(R,G,B)}, when R = V = max(R, G, B) \\ 2 + \frac{B-R}{max(R,G,B)-min(R,G,B)}, when G = V = max(R, G, B) \\ 4 + \frac{R-G}{max(R,G,B)-min(R,G,B)}, when B = V = max(R, G, B) \end{array} \right\} \quad (1)$$

Due to the microcontroller hardware limitations the fusion has to be as simple as possible therefore it is achieved in three steps which for efficiency reasons can be merged into single iteration. For each pixel is performed:

1. Compute the HSV value from the color image.
2. Compare the V value from the HSV and the value from IR image or with the threshold α. Choose larger.
3. Convert from HSV to RGB where S is equal to parameter β, H is equal to parameter γ and V from point two of the algorithm.

Additional parameters can be introduced. First the start parameter α which decide whether the fusion perform for each pixel or skip some pixels if their IR values are below chosen start parameter threshold. Another variables can be introduced for the resulting H and S values. During all of the experiments the parameter β was equal to value S from HSV and the parameter γ was chosen as 360° (*red hue*). It can be noticed that changing those values would affect the result and make a strong impact on the fused IR values.

An example image pair from set of images used for the test of the fusion algorithm and acquired results using described parameter values are presented in the fig. 2.

Fig. 2. An example images acquired using the proposed algorithm. A) image from a visible light camera, B) image from IR camera, C) resulting fusion image using the proposed fast fusion method. The parameter α was set to 120, β to S value from HSV and γ to 360° (*red hue*).

4 Hardware

The schema of the developed hardware platform performing presented fast IR (*camera 1 in the schema*) and visual camera (*camera 2 in the schema*) fusion is presented in fig. 3. It consists of two printed circuit boards (PCB). PCB2 is responsible for decoding video stream from analog to digital (A/D) and coding digital stream to analog (D/A). The microcontroller (*UC2*) is mainly used for managing the input from the camera 2 and the output from both PCB. Analog visual camera 2 is connected to the PCB2 via video decoder. The UC2 also transmits bidirectional the decoded stream to the main processing unit UC1.

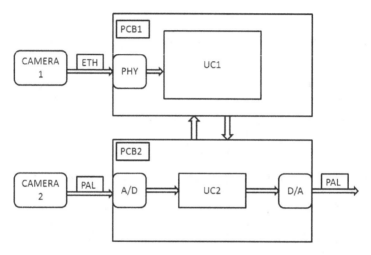

Fig. 3. The operating schema of the prototype device for IR and visual camera image fusion

IR camera is connected via the Ethernet interface to the main processing unit. UC1 performs the described algorithm and transmits the resulting fused video stream back to UC2 which is responsible for generating the output PAL format. The prototype device which implements presented solution is presented in fig. 4.

Fig. 4. The prototype of the IR and visual camera image fusion device

5   Experiments

We have evaluated capabilities of the realized prototype during an experiment. A person was asked to hide various toy weapons under the clothes. Acquired output images were captured from the device using Tv tuner card. During the experiment person was sitting in a chair and asked to perform various tasks. In

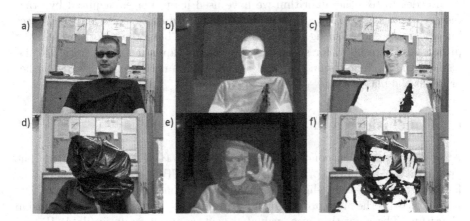

Fig. 5. Sample images from the collected data using the presented prototype for IR and visual camera image fusion. A-D) images from visual camera, B-E) images from IR camera, C-F) images from the prototype device after the fusion.

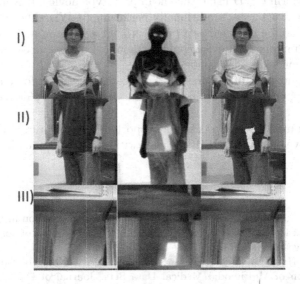

Fig. 6. Results of the tests of the image fusion algorithm using freely available CWD data. Data set is separated into three rows. In each row there is a visible light image, IR image and the resulting fused image by the proposed algorithm with the threshold 220.

the fig. 5 we present some of the images from the collected data set. Three main conclusions were made after the experiment. First, that the realized prototype device worked and can be freely used as a cheap CWD device of a miniature size in comparison to traditionally used human-sized gates. Second, that it is possible to detect concealed weapon under the clothes using the proposed simple algorithm. And finally the last conclusion is that concealed weapons are detected regardless they are clearly visible, hidden under the clothes or in plastic bags.

In order to test the algorithm we have used it on images acquired by other research teams [23] or by our own [24,25]. The acquired results and the source images are presented in fig. 6. It can be seen that both the algorithm and the prototype device allow for successful concealed weapon detection using IR and visual camera image fusion. Regardless the weapon is hidden under the clothes or under the plastic bag.

6   Conclusions and Future Work

A prototype device for concealed weapon detection (CWD) was presented. The prototype consists of two printed circuit boards (PCB). First PCB is responsible for analog to digital and digital to analog conversions of the video stream. The second board is the main processing unit realizing the presented fast image fusion algorithm. The algorithm was evaluated using a set of freely available IR and visual camera images. The results were promising and therefore the algorithm was implemented in the hardware. The completed prototype was tested in the laboratory and the acquired results are presented. It can be stated that it is possible to perform CWD using the cheap prototype device. It is an alternative to a large man-sized gates traditionally performing CWD. The relative size of the prototype can be assumed as a miniature in comparison to the current used solutions. Such miniature device could be mounted under the ceiling or inside 3 DOF gimbals for wider view angle.

Possible applications of the presented device include law enforcement, surveillance, medicine, sports, mining industry and various military applications.

Acknowledgements. This work was supported by the National Centre of Research and Development (NCBiR) project with registration number 178438.

References

1. Paulter, N.G.: Guide to the Technologies of Concealed Weapon and Contraband Imaging and Detection (NIJ Guide 602-00), U. S. Department of Justice, Office of Justice Program, National Institute of Justice (2001),
2. Baum, K., Helguera, M., Krol, A.: Fusion Viewer: A New Tool for Fusion and Visualization of Multimodal Medical Data Sets. Journal of Digital Imaging 21, 59–68 (2008) ISSN 0897-1889

3. Ghassemian, H.: A retina based multi-resolution image-fusion. In: IEEE 2001 International Geoscience and Remote Sensing Symposium, IGARSS 2001, vol. 2, pp. 709–711 (2001) ISBN 0-7803-7031-7
4. Pohl, C., Van Genderen, J.L.: Multisensor image fusion in remote sensing: concepts, methods and applications. International Journal of Remote Sensing 19, 823–854 (1998) ISSN 0143-1161
5. Lai, S.H., Fang, M.: A hierarchical neural network algorithm for robust and automatic windowing of MR images. Artificial Intelligence in Medicine 19, 97–119 (2000) ISSN 0933-3657
6. Burt, P.J.: The pyramid as a structure for efficient computation. In: Rosenfeld, A. (ed.) Multiresolution Image Processing and Analysis, pp. 6–35. Springer (1984) ISBN 0-3871-3006-3
7. Zhang, Y., Hong, G.: An IHS and wavelet integrated approach to improve pan-sharpening visual quality of natural colour IKONOS and QuickBird images. Information Fusion 6, 225–234 (2005) ISSN 1566- 2535
8. Ali, F.E., El-Dokany, I.M., Saad, A.A., Abd El-Samie, F.E.S.: Curvelet fusion of MR and CT images. Progress In Electromagnetics Research C 3, 215–224 (2008) ISSN 1937-8718
9. Zhang, Q., Gui, B.: Multifocus image fusion using the nonsubsampled contourlet transform. Signal Processing 89, 1334–1346 (2009) ISSN 0165-1684
10. Olkkonen, H., Pesola, P.: Gaussian Pyramid Wavelet Transform for Multiresolution Analysis of Images. Graphical Models and Image Processing 58(9), 394–398 (1996) ISSN 1077-3169
11. Burt, P., Adelson, E.: The Laplacian Pyramid as a Compact Image Code. IEEE Transactions on Communications 31, 532–540 (1983) ISSN 0090-6778
12. Toet, A.: Image fusion by a ratio of low-pass pyramid. Pattern Recognition Letters 9, 245–253 (1989) ISSN 0167-8655
13. Anderson, H.: Filter-Subtract-Decimate Hierarchical Pyramid Signal Analyzing And Synthesizing Technique, U.S. Patent, 4-718-104 (1988)
14. Ramac, L.C., Uner, M.K., Varshney, P.K., Alford, M.G., Ferris, D.D.: Morphological filters and wavelet based image fusion for concealed weapon detection. In: Proceedings of SPIE, vol. 3376, pp. 110–119 (1998) ISBN 0-8194-2825-6
15. Mallat, S.: Wavelets for a Vision. Proceedings of the IEEE 84, 604–614 (1996) ISSN 0018-9219
16. Lejune, C.: Wavelet transforms for infrared applications, Infrared Technology XXI. In: Proc. SPIE, vol. 2552, pp. 313–324 (1995)
17. Rockinger, O.: Image Sequence Fusion Using a Shift Invariant Wavelet Transform. In: Proceedings of the International Conference on Image Processing, vol. 3, pp. 288–291 (1997) ISBN 0-8186-8183-7
18. Sévigny, L.: Multisensor Image Fusion for Detection of Targets in the Battlefield of the Future, NATO AC/243, Panel 3, RSG9 38th Meeting Progress Report - Canada, Defense Research Establishment, Valcartier (1996)
19. Waxman, A.M., et al.: Solid-State Color Night Vision: Fusion of Low-Light Visible and Thermal Infrared Imagery. MIT Lincoln Laboratory Journal 11, 41–60 (1999)
20. Schiller, P.A.: The ON and OFF channels of the visual system. Trends in Neuroscience 15, 86–92 (1992) ISSN 0166-2236

21. Xue, Z., Blum, R.S.: Concealed Weapon Detection Using Color Image Fusion, Information fusion. In: Proceedings of the Sixth International Conference of Image Fusion, vol. 1, pp. 622–627 (2003) ISBN 0-9721-8444-9
22. Jędrasiak, K., Nawrat, A.: Image Recognition Technique for Unmanned Aerial Vehicles. In: Bolc, L., Kulikowski, J.L., Wojciechowski, K. (eds.) ICCVG 2008. LNCS, vol. 5337, pp. 391–399. Springer, Heidelberg (2009)
23. Jedrasiak, K., Nawrat, A.: SETh System Spatio-Temporal Object Tracking Using Combined Color And Motion Features. Electrical and Computer Engineering Series, pp. 67–72 (2009) ISBN 978-960-474-078-9

Application of Image Processing Algorithms in Proteomics: Automatic Analysis of 2-D Gel Electrophoresis Images from Western Blot Assay

Katarzyna Jonak[1], Karol Jędrasiak[1,2], Andrzej Polański[1,2], and Krzysztof Puszyński[1]

[1] Institute of Automatic Control, Silesian University of Technology, Akademicka 16, 44-100, Gliwice, Poland
[2] Polish-Japanese Institute of Information Technollogy, Aleja Legionów 2, 41-902 Bytom, Poland

Abstract. Studying changes in the cell after treatment by a potentially genotoxic agent is a very important approach in biological experimental techniques. A researcher in molecular biology can study the structure of cellular pathways related to responses to external agents stress, damage or ionizing radiation by measuring the amount of cellular species, such as certain proteins, RNA or DNA. For this aim the electrophoresis-based tests are widely used. In this paper we will focus on the Western blot assay for estimating the quantity of the proteins. Often such information is obtained by visual analysis of a gel, which is prejudicial and time-consuming. We developed a new, rapid and exact image processing method for automatic detection of the spots in 2-D gels and calculation the quantity of the protein produced by the cell. The proposed method can significantly reduce the time required for analysis. We have obtained very promising results with accuracy more than 96% allowing for automated analyzes of 2-D gel electrophoresis images.

1 Introduction

External factors, like ionizing radiation, can lead to single or double breakages of DNA strands. Such breakages may cause activation or inhibition of proteins production required for many processes occurring in the organismal living cells, for example cell division and growth. Studying concentrations of these protein species in cells provides information on mechanism of cellular resistance and responses to external factors. Therefore, it is important to develop methodologies for quantifying changes of protein species in the cell. A lot of tests based on a 2-D gel electrophoresis are used, like Southern Blot for the detection of DNA fragments [1], Northern blot for RNA [2] and Western blot for proteins [3]. In this paper we focus on the Western blot assay. By knowing the quantity of the protein, which interact with each other, we can predict what happen when we put the cell into a stress and how the cell will response to the damage.

The essence of gel electrophoresis experiments is the separation, under the influence of electric field, of the mixture of chemical compounds into fractions,

L. Bolc et al. (Eds.): ICCVG 2012, LNCS 7594, pp. 433–440, 2012.

called spots, according to their weight or shape. The related problem is the analysis of the images derived from the experiment conducted on an electrophoretic gel. A critical issue is to determine the quantity of the specific proteins produced by the cell after treatment by damaging agents. This kind of information is obtained by visual analysis of the resulting spots on the basis of their size and intensity of illumination. However, that kind of analysis is highly prejudicial and fraught with large errors associated with human perception and environmental influences, such as poor lighting during image analysis. This kind of analysis is inaccurate and time-consuming, so it is important to develop an automated algorithm that can detect the presence of the protein in the electrophoretic gel and determines its quantity.

The main contribution of this paper is presentation of the semi-automatic method for the analysis of the images obtained from the Western blot assay. We propose a new algorithm based on combination of several existing methods related to image processing. As shown by examples we obtain satisfactory results allowing for an automated analysis of electrophoretic gel images.

2   Literature Review

There are several software programs for the analysis of electrophoretic gels which are available commercially, for example, Progenesis MALDI [4]. Unfortunately, these programs are difficult to obtain and very expensive. Also, their algorithms are not publicly available.

The main problem in the automatic analysis of 2-D gel electrophoresis images is image quality. Several aspects of experimental procedures are responsible for that. The quality of image affected by decisions made by human, like during the sample preparation, electrophoretic transfer, protein-gel interactions, duration of gel staining or gel purification and scanning [5]. An important step is the last stage of the experiment: a transfer of the proteins from the membrane to a photographic film. The quality of the spots depend on the exposure time. Short acquisition results in less contaminated images. However, sometimes the protein spots become apparent only with longer exposure time, for example due to low level of protein production. It was observed that the quality of the resulting images also depend on the cameras and scanners used during acquisition [6].

Majority of the algorithms for automatic electrophoretic gel image analysis are mainly focused on spots detection and calculation the distance between them. Fast and accurate detection is very important when analyzing the data [7]. Methods relating to detection of the protein occurrence are usually based on segmentation algorithms, such as the algorithm described in [8] based on counting pixels corresponding to the certain range of density levels. In [9] and [10] the emphasis is on detection and removal of the image background. Also, in order to detect spots the MaxRST algorithm may be used, like in [11]. The authors obtained precision rate about 95-100%, but they were testing only synthetic images. In [12] authors used slice tree algorithm and they got the accuracy equal to 97.29%. A commonly used environment for the implementation of algorithms for biological image processing is Matlab® [13].

In the literature known to the authors of this paper no information about publicly available algorithms for automatic detection and quantification of spots obtained in Western blot assays can be found.

3   Methods

The algorithm was tested on the images obtained from the experiments performed at the Institute of Oncology in Gliwice in the framework of the project grant number N N518 287 540.

3.1   The Algorithm for Scoring Results of Western Blot

This paper presents a new, rapid and exact image processing technique to automatic detection of the spots in 2-D gels and to count its intensity. This algorithm is based on a noise reduction using FISTA (A Fast Iterative Shrinkage Thresholding Algorithm) [14] and Wellner'a adaptive threshold method [15].

An important step required for analysis of electrophoretic gel images is a digitalization of the images of photographic film. For this purpose, the scanner with transmitted light or a CCD-camera-based system is used [16]. Then the image is treated starting with the cropping to the width of the gel used in the experiment. The next steps are performed by the program aided with little user intervention.

The user has to add a number of samples, which means number of columns in electrophoretic gel. In addition, the user can adjust the results by providing the information about the spots distribution in 2-D gel: are they bright or dark, arranged broadly or are they merged in such a way that it is difficult or sometimes impossible to distinguish the boundaries between them. For each value of the provided input parameter the corresponding function of Wellner'a adaptive threshold is adapted. At the output the user receives charts specifying the amount of the protein normalized to the protein detected in the control sample: the brightest spot or the spot specified by the user.

The spots detection and determination of their value consists of several steps shown in figure 1. The first step is to improve the quality of the image. Initially we used the morphological closing operation [17]. The operation consists of the closure of the elements from picture A using structuring element B. It removes small holes, for example the bright elements of the spots, which are hardly detectable. After morphological operations the filtering with Gaussian blur is performed [18].

An important part of the algorithm is to remove noise and artifacts in the image, because the strong noise could disrupt the process of extracting spots. This problem was solved using the FISTA algorithm [14]. The FISTA algorithm is widely used in digital image processing, like it was shown in [19] and [20]. It is an optimal gradient method, in which the combination of the previous pixels are used to designate a new pixel in each subsequent iteration.

The image is segmented into regions of interest (ROI), where the spots may occur. The whole image is divided into n equal parts, where n is the number of columns given by the user. For each column, the following steps are performed: determination of the spots location, specify the number and intensity of the pixels in the region-found belonging to the spot and calculation the quantity of the protein. The spots detection is performed using Wellner's adaptive threshold [15]. Wellner's algorithm traverses the image from left to right and from top to bottom tracking the average color of the last x number of pixels. If the algorithm encounters a pixel above threshold value than his current average, the pixel is colored in black, and the other in white [15].

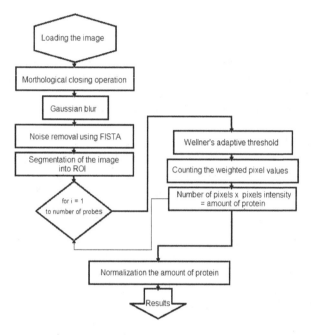

Fig. 1. The new algorithm for automatic computing the Western blot test's score described in this paper. ROI – region of interest.

To determine the quantity of the protein the algorithm counts all the pixels that are detected at earlier stages. It is assumed that in each column there is only one blob indicating one protein. There the number of pixels and their gray-scale intensity from the source image are counted. Assuming that the images have a white background, while the spots are indicated by gray and black, the quantity of protein in one position (pixel) is calculated as the inverse of the pixel intensity values - the lower the value of the spots, the more protein is there. The pixel values of the spots are added. All of them are normalized to the spot with a minimum amount of protein (the smallest and the brightest one) or to the spot indicated by the user. In this way, we can specify the value of a protein production and its level of growth or decline.

4   Experimental Results

The algorithm was tested on 108 images depicting the results of the Western blot experiments. Figures 2-5 show the examples of this results. All of the images can be divided into groups depending on the shape and intensity of the spots. In each of the columns there is always one spot, which mean there is only one protein. The first picture shows the problem of large overlapping spots. The second image presents fold spots line and as a result the differences in column width. The third picture is an example of the image in which the spots are clearly visible. The fourth image shows no spots in one of the column and in one of them a fuzzy trace spot. In all of these cases, the program coped with the diagnosis of protein position in 2-D gel and with determination of quantity of protein.

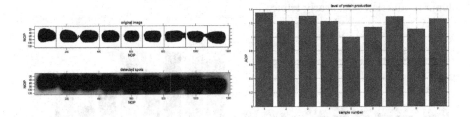

Fig. 2. The result of the first test image. NOP - number of pixels. AOP - amount of protein. The image was divided into 9 columns. The quantities of the proteins was normalized to the brightest spot. The minimum spot (No. 5) has value 1. At this point, the protein production was the weakest. In a picture titled "detected spots" columns are separated by vertical black lines. The graph shows the change in the protein production. The amount of the protein in different experiments does not change much (the maximum change is ± 20%).

In order to describe the quality of the protein species detection we used indexes of accuracy, true positive rate (TPR), precision rate (PR) and F-measure (harmonic mean of precision) defined in expressions (1.1)-(1.4) below:

$$Accuracy = \frac{TP+TN}{TP+TN+FP+FN}100\% \ (1.1) \quad TPR = \frac{TP}{TP+FN}100\% \ (1.2)$$

$$Accuracy = \frac{TP+TN}{TP+TN+FP+FN}100\% \ (1.3) \quad TPR = \frac{TP}{TP+FN}100\% \ (1.4)$$

In the above expressions TP, TN, FP and FN denote respectively rates of true positives, true negatives, false positives and false negatives.

The algorithm was tested on a total of 996 spots. The program correctly identified them or lack of them in 961 cases, giving accuracy (formula 1.1.) in excess of 96.49%. The algorithm obtained a TPR of more than 98.34%, PR of 97.80% and F-mean of 98.07%. The results are satisfactory and show that the program is able to achieve recognition of the spots close to 100% after slight modification. Than the counting the quantity of protein production will be more accurate.

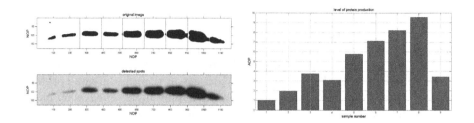

Fig. 3. The result of the second test image. The image was divided into 9 columns. The quantities of the proteins was normalized to the first spot. The amount of the protein increases in the second column and third column twice to the previous. In the fourth column it slightly decreases (20%), than increases twice in the fifth one. In the sixth column it increases by 20%, followed by 15% and 17%. In the ninth column production falls nearly tripled.

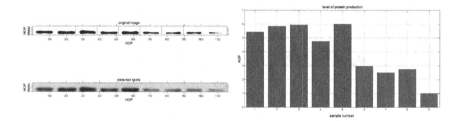

Fig. 4. The result of the third test image. The image was divided into 9 columns. The quantities of the proteins was normalized to the brightest spot (No. 9). Reading the chart from the column 1 to 9 the numerical values of protein productioncan be deduced as follows: in the second column the amount of the protein increases by 7% relative to the first one, in the third by 2% relative to the other, next the number of the protein is reduced by $\frac{1}{4}$ of the previous column. In the fifth column it increases by more than $\frac{1}{4}$, then decreases twice and decreases by 15%. In the eighth increases by a similar amount in the ninth decline has nearly tripled.

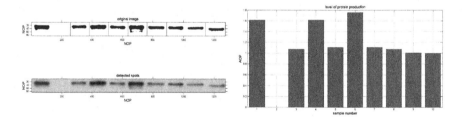

Fig. 5. The result of the fourth test image. The image was divided into 10 columns. The quantities of the proteins was normalized to the brightest spot (No. 10). A high production decrease in column 2 by 1,5 times, next increases twice, increases by more than a half and next decreases also by more than a half. In the sixth column the amount of the protein increases by 70% and next decreases. In subsequent columns, the protein does not undergo major changes.

5   Conclusions and Future Work

A new algorithm for the spots detection in the images obtained by a Western blot was proposed. The algorithm determines the quantity of the protein produced by the cell. In many cases the results obtained by the electrophoretic gels are analyzed visually. The biggest drawback of such analysis is that this method is very time-consuming and subjective. Automating the process of 2-D gel analysis is essential to improve the results and significantly reduce the time required for the analysis. Therefore, we decided to create an algorithm for automatically counting the quantity of the proteins. In the literature that is known to the authors no information about solving this problem in a Western blot experiments has been found.

The algorithm uses morphological closing operations, Gaussian filtering and removal of noise using FISTA. Our method allows the user to enter the number of columns, the number of the control sample and to regulate the degree of removing noise. The image is divided into equal parts according to user-entered number of columns. Then spots are detected by Wellner's adaptive threshold in each column. The number and intensity of the pixels of each spot are counted, then the normalization is performed. The user receives the exact amount of the protein after standardization and prior to normalization. The algorithm was testing on 108 images obtained from the Western blot experiments. The accuracy of our new method is more than 96% and F-measure is 98%. The results are very promising.

The authors plan to improve the algorithm and extend the range of its possible applications not only to the Western blot assay, but also to the other tests performed on the electrophoretic gels. Another possible improvement is removal of artifacts found in images due to too long exposure during handling of experimental data from the membrane to photographic film.

Acknowledgements. This work was supported by the National Centre of Science (NCN) grant number N N518 287540.

References

1. Southern, E.M.: Detection of specific sequences among DNA fragments separated by gel electrophoresis. Journal of Molecular Biology 98(3), 503–517 (1975)
2. Kevil, C.G., Walsh, L., Laroux, F.S., Kalogeris, T., Grisham, M.B., Alexander, J.S.: An Improved, Rapid Northern Protocol. Biochem. and Biophys. Research Comm. 238, 277–279 (1997)
3. Burnette, W.N.: 'Western blotting': electrophoretic transfer of proteins from sodium dodecyl sulfate–polyacrylamide gels to unmodified nitrocellulose and radiographic detection with antibody and radioiodinated protein A. Analytical Biochemistry 112(2), 195–203 (1981)
4. Nonlinear Dynamics, http://www.nonlinear.com/products/progenesis/maldi/overview/ (date of visit: April 27, 2012)

5. Lopez, J.L.: Two-dimensional electrophoresis in proteome expression analysis. Journal of Chromatography. Analytical Technologies in the Biomedical and Life Sciences 849, 190–202 (2007)
6. Wheelock, A.M., Goto, S.: Effects of post-electrophoretic analysis on variance in gel-based proteomics. Expert Review of Proteomics 3, 129–142 (2006)
7. Mahon, P., Dupree, P.: Quantitative and reproducible twodimensional gel analysis using Phoretix 2D full. Electrophoresis 22(10), 2075–2085 (2001)
8. Cutler, P., Heald, G., White, I.R., Ruan, J.: A novel approach to spot detection for two-dimensional gel electrophoresis images using pixel value collection. Proteomics 3(4), 392–401 (2003)
9. Peer, P., Corzo, L.G.: Local Pixel Value Collection Algorithm for Spot Segmentation in Two-Dimensional Gel Electrophoresis Research. Comparative and Functional Genomics (2007)
10. Rye, M., Fargestad, E.M.: Preprocessing of electrophoretic images in 2-DE analysis. Chemometr. Intell. Lab. Syst (2011)
11. Liu, Y.-S., Chen, S.-Y., Liu, R.-S., Duh, D.-J., Chao, Y.-T., Tsai, Y.-C., Hsieh, J.-S.: Spot detection for a 2-DE gel image using a slice tree with confidence evaluation. Mathematical and Computer Modelling 50 (2009)
12. Lin, D.-T.: Autonomous sub-image matching for two-dimensional electrophoresis gels using MaxRST algorithm. Image and Vision Computing 28, 1267–1279 (2010)
13. Daszykowski, M., Færgestad, E.M., Grove, H., Martens, H., Walczak, B.: Matching 2D gel electrophoresis images with Matlab 'Image Processing Toolbox'. Chemometrics and Intelligent Laboratory Systems 96, 188–195 (2009)
14. Beck, A., Teboulle, M.: Fast Gradient-Based Algorithms for Constrained Total Variation Image Denoising and Deblurring Problems (2009)
15. Wellner, P.: Adaptive Thresholding for the DigitalDesk. Xerox Research Center Technical Report n. EPC-1993-110 (1993)
16. Berth, M., Moser, F.M., Kolbe, M., Bernhardt, J.: The state of the art in the analysis of two-dimensional gel electrophoresis images. Applied Microbiology and Biotechnology 76, 1223–1243 (2007)
17. Sternberg, S.R.: Grayscale morphology. Computer Vision Graph 35, 333–355 (1986)
18. Shapiro, L.G., Stockman, G.C.: Computer Vision, pp. 137–150. Prentice Hall (2001)
19. Kamilov, U., Bostan, E., Unser, M.: Wavelet Shrinkage With Consistent Cycle Spinning Generalizes Total Variation Denoising. IEEE Signal Processing Letters 19(4), 187–190 (2012)
20. Vonesch, C., Unser, M.: Fast Iterative Thresholding Algorithm for Wavelet-Regularized Deconvolution (2007)

3D Semantic Map Computation Based on Depth Map and Video Image

Włodzimierz Kasprzak[1] and Maciej Stefańczyk[2]

[1] Industrial Research Institute for Automation and Measurements
Al. Jerozolimskie 202, 02-486 Warszawa, Poland
wkasprzak@piap.pl
http://www.piap.pl/
[2] Institute of Control and Computation Engineering,
Warsaw University of Technology, ul. Nowowiejska 15-19, 00-665 Warsaw, Poland
stefanczyk.maciek@gmail.com
http://www.ia.pw.edu.pl/

Abstract. A model-based object recognition in video and depth images is proposed for the purpose of semantic map creation in mobile robotics. Three types of objects are modeled: a human silhouette, a chair/table and corridor walls. A bi-driven hypothesis generation and verification strategy is outlined. The object model includes a hierarchic semantic nets, combined with a graph of constraints and a Bayesian network for hypothesis generation and evaluation. For the purpose of model-to-image matching we define an incomplete constraint satisfaction problem and solve it. Our CSP-search allows partial assignment solutions and uses a stochastic inference to provide judgments of such solutions. The verification of hypotheses is due to a top-down occlusion propagation process, that explains why some object parts are hidden or occluded.

Keywords: Bayesian net, constraint satisfaction, depth map, object recognition, semantic map.

1 Introduction

Three general paradigms for object classification and recognition in images are most often distinguished: the stochastic Bayesian approach [1], the neuro-computational and biological approach [2], and the rule-based approach [3]. Although of different nature these approaches share the concept of *rationality*, as the recognition and understanding processes in all paradigms need to satisfy some appropriate optimization criteria.

In model-based object recognition fundamental problems are: knowledge representation language (KRL), a search-based control and the evaluation of partial model-to-data matches. Here we follow an object-oriented KRL build around semantic networks, and we integrate it with another three general-purpose tools: (1) a modified search for constraint satisfaction problems ([3]), applied as the

L. Bolc et al. (Eds.): ICCVG 2012, LNCS 7594, pp. 441–448, 2012.

control of partial model-to-data matches [4] (hypothesis generation), (2) the
Bayesian approach to statistical inference [1] (applied for evaluation of hypotheses), and (3) rules of an attributed structure grammar [5] (applied for hypothesis verification). All these abstract tools are of dominating declarative nature and there exists well-known machine learning approaches for them, e.g. inductive inference for the concept learning, and ML- or MAP-estimation for the learning of Bayesian net probability distributions [6].

This object recognition system is applied for labeling of 3D environment maps in mobile robotics, i.e. the creation of 3D semantic maps [7].

2   3D Map Generation

First, a 3D environment map need to be reconstructed from measurements that combine laser scans (if a scan line laser is used) and video images. Initially, the individual scan lines are integrated into a cloud of 3D points (e.g. the ICP (iterated closest point) algorithm [8]. Next, the point set is approximated by triangle faces (e.g. Delaunay triangulation) [9] or by fitting superquadrics surfaces patches [10]. The map texturing steps follow - an addition (or stretching) of the video image content onto the 3D surfaces [11]. Finally, the triangle net is approximated by larger planar of curved surface patches - using incremental growth [9] or point elimination-based algorithms [12].

3   Semantic Labeling Due to Object Recognition

We are interested to recognize objects, like chair, table and wall, and humans in the neighborhood of a service mobile robot. This means - to add semantic labels to the environment map. The person can eventually sit in a chair or stay in front of a wall or behind the table or chair, i.e. the human is fully or only partially visible. The 3D object recognition approach consists of following processes (Fig. 1): hypothesis generation (model-to-data matching), hypothesis evaluation (stochastic inference), object visibility test, hypothesis verification (occlusion propagation).

To accomplish the overall task we have to define four models: the hierarchic structure of concepts and graphs of constraints per concept, a *Bayesian network* for quality judgement of an *instance* or *modified concept*, the mutual object occlusion relations, and the occlusion propagation rules.

The model-to-data matching is seen as a specific constraint satisfaction problem [3], that needs to be satisfied only partially [4]. The judgement (score) of instance is estimated by a stochastic inference in the Bayesian net, linked to given concept. The hypothesis verification process is a bottom-up explanation of possible mutual object occlusions and self-occlusions [5]. The hidden parts are added as evidence and a Bayesian inference for given instance is repeated with additional evidence variables set to synthesized parts.

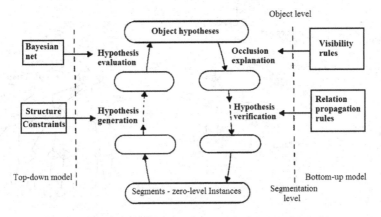

Fig. 1. The 3D object recognition approach

4 Object Hypotheses Generation

4.1 The 3D Object Model

Common to semantic networks is the explicit structuring of domain knowledge along two hierarchies: the decomposition (vertical) hierarchy and the specialization (horizontal) hierarchy of concepts. Starting from the pixel level the vertical hierarchy expresses increasingly abstract representation levels ("part" or "concrete" links). Simple elements are combined into more complex one, being parts of objects and scenes. Specialization links ("spec") represent inheritance relations between elements at the same abstraction level.

Every node (called "concept") represents some object category and it contains a parameter vector (called "attributes"), where every parameter is evaluated by some *term*, and every concept defines a set of constraints, evaluated by *predicates*, among its parts and related concepts.

The generic object types (e.g. human, chair, table), required for 3D map labeling, take the form of wire-frame models (Fig. 2, 3). There are default dimensions of object parts provided - this especially allows to constrain the human object hypotheses.

4.2 Partial CSP

A discrete *Constraint Satisfaction Problem* is defined in terms of states, actions and the goal test. A state set S, where a particular *state*, $\mathbf{s} = (d_1, d_2, ..., d_n)$, is defined by assignments to its variables, $X = x_1, x_2, ..., x_n$, where each $x_i, (i = 1, ..., n)$, can take values from a domain D_i. The *actions*, $a \in A$, mean transitions between states: $a_k : s_i \rightarrow s_j$. The *goal test* checks a set of constraints, $C(X)$, which induces allowed combinations of assignment values for subsets of state variables. A *solution state* is every state that satisfies the goal test. In particular, in our problem: the variables in X correspond to parts of some model concept,

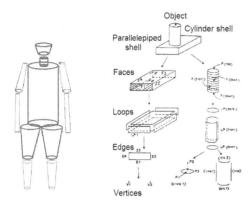

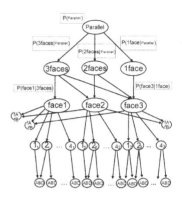

Fig. 2. A human model

Fig. 3. The decomposition of a cylinder and parallelepiped shell onto faces and edge loops

Fig. 4. The Bayesian net for a "parallelepiped" solid

the values in domain D represent the current data entities (instances) and an action is assigning a value to some variable in given state. The variables and the set of constraints, $C(X)$, can be represented as a graph, $G(X, C(X))$ where nodes X represent variables and arcs $C(X)$ represent constraints between particular variables. For example, typical constraints for edges are: A = *edges are connected*; B = *edges are parallel*; D = *edges are of similar length*.

A modified CSP search is proposed that allows partial solutions (some variables may have no assigned value) Table 1. While starting from an empty assignment the goal is to match (assign) eligible image segments (values) with model entities (variables). We introduced two *modifications* to the basic CSP search. The first modification is due to the definition of a *Bayesian network* for every problem. The subfunction *Score* calculates probability value of a partial solution, that consists of eligible assignments to variables. This score is due to a stochastic inference process performed in a dedicated Bayesian net, created for current CSP problem. The second modification of a typical CSP is that now partial paths can be potential solutions. The backtrack step is performed now when currently selected (extended) path does not satisfy the constraints of given problem or its score is lower than the score of predecessor path. In our view this is not a general failure but a situation where the previous state corresponds to a partial solution. The current path is stored as a possible partial solution if it has higher score than the previous best one.

5   Hypothesis Evaluation

A Bayesian network (BN) is a simple, graphical notation for conditional independence assertions and hence for compact specification of full joint distributions. The syntax of a BN: a set of nodes, one per variable; a directed, acyclic graph - incoming links of given node represent a conditional distribution for

Table 1. Partial-solution incremental CSP-search for model-to-data matching

function BacktrackSearch(*csp*) **returns** *Solution*
static *solution* = { } ;
path = { }
solution = RecursiveBacktrack(*solution, path, csp)*
return *solution*

function RecursiveBacktrack(*solution, path, csp)* **returns** *solution*		
IF	*path* is complete (Stop test)	
THEN	**return** *solution*	
var ← SelectUnassignedVariable(*csp.variables, path*)		
valueList ← GetDomainValues(*var, path, csp*)		
FOR	EACH *value* ∈ *valueList*	
	IF	(*path* ∪ {*var* ← *value* }) are consistent with *csp.constraints* AND Score(*path* ∪ { *var* ← *value* })> Score(*path*)
	THEN	add { *var* ← *value* } to *path*
		IF Score(*path*) > Score(*solution*) THEN *solution* = *path*
		result = RecursiveBacktrack(*solution, path, csp*)
		IF *result* ≠ *failure* THEN **return** *result*
		remove { *var* ← *value* } from *path*
return *failure*		

this node given its parents, $P(X_i|Parents(X_i))$. In the simplest discrete case, conditional distribution is represented as a conditional probability table (CPT), giving the distribution over X_i for each combination of parent values. Example: for a parallelepiped concept the structure of a corresponding Bayesian model is automatically generated as shown on (Fig. 4).

A Bayesian network will here represent stochastic dependencies between the solid type "parallel", intermediate-level "views" and "faces", and low-level "edges" (the latter correspond to image segments). The parallelepiped solid has 3 alternative views. The "face" concepts consist of 4 edges. The constraints in CSP model now correspond to additional evidence variables (nodes) in the Bayesian net. There are evidence nodes that represent constraints between faces (fA, fB) and constraints between squares (A, B, D). The rank, to which a particular constraint is satisfied, can be measured after its "parents" (the "edge" variables) have been assigned to image segments.

The score of a partial solution (assignment in terms of CSP), in which some variables X_i have already been assigned to image segments l_k but not all of them, is obtained due to stochastic inference in Bayesian net. For example the computation of posterior probability of a "cube" instance (that is a *cause* in terms of BN) given its parts (that are *evidences* in BN). For example, if segments are assigned to X_0 and X_1 then one needs to compute the probability: $P(cube|X_0 = l_1, X_1 = l_2)$.

This leads to a summation of the pdf-s over all domain values for remaining (non-evidence) variables, $X_2, ..., X_l$. Thus, the scores of partial or complete matches, between image segments and model entities, are naturally obtained by the same evaluation method.

6 Hypothesis Verification

As a result of the hypothesis generation process many competitive object instances exist. In general, to find a best consistent subset one needs a search procedure. In our test implementation we make a simplifying assumption that at most one instance per object type can exist. This allows us to make a systematic check of all the subsets.

The top-down verification process for a selected subset of hypotheses consists of two steps: the initial generation of occlusion relations (between objects) and the propagation of occlusion relations from an upper level L to a lower level $L-1$ (Fig. 5). There are three types of relations used: "potentially hidden", "partially hidden", "hidden". A set of generic propagation rules is used. In general, when an instance is "potentially hidden" then its visibility case has to be resolved at the lower level, with regard to its parts. As a result of such check the relation will be canceled, kept or replaced by "partially hidden" or "hidden". The last two labels induce additional evidence (support) for a hypothesis, as they explain why a given part has not been matched with image data.

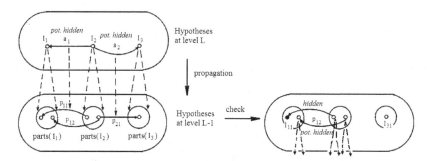

Fig. 5. Illustration of the occlusion propagation and visibility check. The relations a_1 and a_2, specified at level L as "potentially hidden", are resolved among the parts of instances I_1, I_2 and I_3. Assume, the visibility check turned some relations into a "hidden" status (terminate instance I_{11}), some others were rejected (terminal instance I_{31} and remaining relations were propagated to level $L-2$.

7 Results

The first example demonstrates the color image analysis in the absence of a depth map. The number of possible objects is limited to at most one per modeled type (Fig. 6 - 11). An important step is the color-based human skin detection (the implementation is based on a B.Sc. work of A. Wyszomierski, ICCE WUT). Also image regions of small size are eliminated, whereas large regions are eventually split into convex parts. In order to detect faces of a solid, sufficiently strong line segments are set in correspondence (geometrical proximity) with the post-processed regions. If sufficient "face evidence" is available a solid and object hypotheses are generated. Eventually multiple hypotheses of given type are still allowed at this stage. Finally, subsets of hypotheses are eventually verified by considering the visibility relations.

Fig. 6. Example of a room scene

Fig. 7. Region-based image segmentation

Fig. 8. Skin color filtering

Fig. 9. After morphological filtering

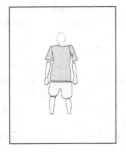

Fig. 10. Regions related to "human" object

Fig. 11. Detected 3 object instances

The second example demonstrates surface generation if corresponding video image and depth map are both available (Fig. 12 - 17). The depth map and surface patches are based on a B.Sc. work of K. Przedniczek, ICCE WUT. The laser scanner SICK LMS 200 acted as the acquisition device. Here, the 3D surface patches are approximated by planar surfaces. Accordingly, strong ling segments in the video image are defined at places with large discontinuity of depth information. Now face hypotheses are generated from four line segments "enclosing" a planar surface. The next processing steps are the same as in the first example.

Fig. 12. "Corridor" scene

Fig. 13. Image regions

Fig. 14. Edge image

Fig. 15. 3D surface patches in depth image

Fig. 16. 3D surfaces

Fig. 17. Wall detection

References

1. Jain, A.K., Duin, R.P.W., Mao, J.: Statistical Pattern Recognition: A Review. IEEE Trans. on Pattern Analysis and Machine Intelligence 22(1), 4–37 (2000)
2. Marr, D.: Vision: A computational investigation into the human representation and processing of visual information. New Freeman, New York (1982)
3. Russel, S., Norvig, P.: Artificial Intelligence. A modern approach, 2nd edn. Prentice Hall (2002)
4. Kasprzak, W., Czajka, Ł., Wilkowski, A.: A Constraint Satisfaction Framework with Bayesian Inference for Model-Based Object Recognition. In: Bolc, L., Tadeusiewicz, R., Chmielewski, L.J., Wojciechowski, K. (eds.) ICCVG 2010, Part II. LNCS, vol. 6375, pp. 1–8. Springer, Heidelberg (2010)
5. Kasprzak, W.: A Linguistic Approach to 3-D Object Recognition. Computers & Graphics 11(4), 427–443 (1987)
6. Duda, R.O., Hart, P.E., Stork, D.G.: Pattern Classification and Scene Analysis, 2nd edn. J. Wiley, New York (2001)
7. Surmann, H., Nuchter, A., Hertzberg, J.: An autonomous mobile robot with a 3d laser range finder for 3d exploration and digitalization of indoor environments. Robotics and Autonomous Systems 45(3-4), 181–198 (2003)
8. Zhang, Z.: Iterative Point Matching for Registration of Free-Form Curves. International Journal of Computer Vision 13, 119–152 (1994)
9. Faugeras, O., Hebert, M., Mussi, P., Boissonnat, J.D.: Polyhedral approximation of 3-D objects without holes. Computer Vision Graphics and Image Processing 25, 169–183 (1984)
10. Jaklic, A., Leonardis, A., Solina, F.: Segmentation and Recovery of Superquadrics. Computational Imaging and Vision, vol. 20. Kluwer, Dordrecht (2000)
11. Dias, P., Sequeira, V., Vaz, F., Gonalves, J.G.M.: Registration and Fusion of Intensity and Range Data for 3D Modeling of Real World Scenes. In: Proc. 4th International Conference on 3-D Digital Imaging and Modeling, pp. 418–425 (2003)
12. Soucy, M., Laurendeau, D.: Multiresolution surface modeling based on hierarchical triangulation. Computer Vision and Image Understanding 63(1), 1–14 (1996)

Skin Detection Using Color and Distance Transform*

Michal Kawulok

Institute of Informatics, Silesian University of Technology
Akademicka 16, 44-100 Gliwice, Poland
michal.kawulok@polsl.pl

Abstract. Skin regions detection has been intensively studied and many methods were proposed which are based on skin color modeling in different color spaces. This makes it possible to transform color images into skin probability maps and extract skin regions. However, in very few cases spatial alignment of the skin pixels is taken into account. In this paper we present how the pixel-wise detectors can be improved using distance transform performed in a combined domain of the skin probability maps and luminance. The proposed method is compared theoretically and experimentally with a well-established controlled diffusion technique for determining skin regions from skin probability maps.

1 Introduction

The skin detection problem, i.e. classification of every pixel in a given digital image as belonging to skin or not, is receiving considerable attention from the computer vision community. Among many applications, skin detection is an important source of information for locating faces and hands for human-computer interaction, indexing images in multimedia databases, for content-based filtering and parental control.

Human skin has been effectively modeled in virtually all of the existing color spaces. However, effectiveness of pixel-wise color-based detectors is limited by two important constraints, namely: 1) high variance of skin color in digital images due to interpersonal differences and lighting conditions changes, and 2) background objects having skin-like color. Undoubtedly, color is the main distinctive skin feature, but without taking into account additional information, skin detection task cannot be improved significantly. Surprisingly, there are very few methods which benefit from textural or spatial features to increase the stability of color-based models.

In the work reported here the distance transform (DT) is applied to extract skin regions from the probability maps obtained using the statistical approach [1]. At first, the skin blob seeds are determined as regions of very high

---

* This work has been supported by the Polish Ministry of Science and Higher Education under research grant no. IP2011 023071 from the Science Budget 2012–2013.

L. Bolc et al. (Eds.): ICCVG 2012, LNCS 7594, pp. 449–456, 2012.

probability, similarly as it has been proposed for the controlled diffusion method [2]. The seeds are later expanded using the propagation scheme based on Dijkstra's algorithm, performed in a combined domain derived from the luminance channel and the probability map. This implements a distance transform which effectively determines the boundaries of the skin regions. This is our key contribution, and as it is later explained and justified, the detection errors can be reduced significantly, which makes the proposed method competitive compared to alternative techniques.

The paper is organized as follows. In Section 2 an overview of existing approaches to skin segmentation is presented. The proposed method is explained in Section 3, and experimental validation results are shown and discussed in Section 4. The paper is concluded in Section 5.

2 Related Work

Existing skin segmentation techniques take advantage of the observation that skin-tone color has common properties which can be defined in various color spaces. In general, skin color detectors are based on parametric or statistical skin modeling. An interesting, thorough survey which compares various color-based skin detection routines was presented in 2007 by Kakumanu et al. [3].

Parametric skin models are based on fixed decision rules defined empirically in various color spaces after skin-tone distribution analysis. These rules are applied after color normalization to determine if a pixel color value belongs to the skin. Kovac et al. [4] proposed a model defined in RGB color space. Skin-tone color was also modeled in HSV by Tsekeridou et al. [5]. An approach proposed by Hsu et al. [6] takes advantage of common skin color properties in nonlinearly transformed YC_bC_r color space, in which elliptical skin color model is defined. Some techniques operate in multiple color spaces to increase the stability, for example a composed skin detector [7] defined in RGB and YC_bC_r color spaces. Recently, Cheddad et al. proposed to reduce the RGB color space to a single dimension, in which the decision rules are defined [8].

Statistical modeling is based on analysis of skin pixel values distribution for a training set of images, in which skin and non-skin areas are already identified and marked. This creates a global model of skin color, which allows determining the probability that a given pixel value belongs to the skin class. Skin color can be modeled using a number of techniques, including Bayes classifier [1], Gaussian mixture model [9] or random forests [10].

There are a number of adaptive models that improve the segmentation accuracy. Lee et al. proposed to extract lighting features from every analyzed image to adjust the skin detector [11]. Phung et al. introduced a method for adapting the segmentation threshold in the probability map [12], and this approach was later extended by Zhang et al. [13]. Also, the global skin model can be adjusted to every face detected in the image [14].

The features helpful for skin segmentation can be extracted using texture analysis performed in grayscale [15, 16] or color domain [17]. When skin segmentation is performed in video sequences, the system may take advantage of dynamic information. Sigal et al. used Markov models to predict illumination changes in subsequent video frames to adjust the skin color model [18]. Furthermore, background extraction techniques and motion detectors may be used to find potential locations of skin pixels.

Spatial alignment of skin-tone pixels can be taken into account to reduce false positives and increase the precision of determined skin regions boundaries. Ruiz-del-Solar [2] proposed the controlled diffusion method, which is given more attention later in this Section. Also, the cellular automata can be used to determine skin regions [16], but this process requires many iterations to achieve satisfactory results.

2.1 Controlled Diffusion

The controlled diffusion [2] consists of two general steps: 1) diffusion seeds extraction, and 2) the proper diffusion process. The seeds are determined from the pixel-wise skin probability map as those pixels which exceed a certain high threshold (P_{seed}). During the second step, the skin regions are built from the seeds by adjoining the neighboring pixels which meet the diffusion criteria, defined either in the probability map or color space domain. These criteria are as follows: 1) distance of the neighboring pixels in the diffusion domain is below a given threshold (Δ_{max}), and 2) skin probability for the pixel which is to be adjoined must be over a certain threshold (P_β).

It is worth to note that this is the hysteresis thresholding with an additional constraint on maximal difference between the neighboring pixels. Hence, this works well if the region boundaries are sharp (diffusion stops due to high local differences), but the method fails when there exists a smooth transition between the pixel values that leads from one region to another (the diffusion will then "leak" outside the region).

3 Distance Transform for Skin Segmentation

The main drawback of the diffusion method [2] lies in observing leakages when the skin region boundaries are not sharp in the diffusion domain. A similar problem was observed and solved for image colorization, where chrominance is propagated from annotated points using various distance metrics [19, 20]. There, the propagation paths are determined using Dijkstra's algorithm, and color is propagated based on the distance integrated along the paths. In the work reported here, this approach was adapted to skin region segmentation, and it is the skin probability that is propagated from the seeds. The "skinness" is integrated along the propagation paths, which allows the region boundaries to be determined even in case of smooth transitions between the regions.

3.1   Optimizing the Propagation Paths

The propagation paths from the seed to every pixel are determined by minimizing a *total path cost*:

$$C(p) = \sum_{i=0}^{l-1} \rho\left\{p(i), p(i+1)\right\}, \tag{1}$$

where ρ is a *local dissimilarity measure* between two neighboring pixels and l is the path length. The minimization is performed using Dijkstra's algorithm [21] in the following way:

1. A priority queue Q is initialized with all seed pixels.
2. Distance array D which covers all image pixels is created. Every pixel $q \in Q$ is assigned a zero distance $(D(q \in Q) = 0)$ and all remaining pixels are initialized with an infinite distance.
3. A pixel q, for which the distance $D(q)$ is minimal in Q, is popped from Q and for each of its 7 neighbors $N_i(q)$ (excluding the source) two actions are performed:
   (a) Local distance $\rho(q, s)$ between q and its neighbor s is calculated to find a total cost of p_s, i.e., $C(p_s) = C(q) + \rho(q, s)$.
   (b) If $C(p_s) < D(s)$, the distance $D(s)$ is updated, s is enqueued in Q, and the pixel s is associated with a new path p_s.
4. If the queue is not empty, step (3) is repeated.

The path route depends mainly on how the local costs are computed, which is addressed later in this Section. Complexity of the optimization is $O(n)$, and the propagation process can be accelerated by imposing the maximal distance constraint (i.e. the update step (3b) is performed only if the new cost $C(p_s)$ is smaller than a maximal distance threshold).

3.2   "Skinness" Propagation

Usually the skin regions contain many pixels with very high skin probability values that are seldom observed in the background. Hence, the propagation seeds can be extracted by applying a high-value threshold in the probability image. The seed value should be high enough to eliminate false positives, but on the other hand it cannot be too high; otherwise some regions will not be detected at all, increasing the post-propagation false negative error. In addition, we erode the seeds to eliminate isolated high-probability pixels that are sometimes observed in the background.

The seeds are propagated over the image taking advantage of two observations: 1) skin regions are generally smooth and present low luminance variance, 2) skin probability is usually high. Therefore, we compute the local cost from pixel x to y $(\rho(x, y))$ as a sum of the luminance (ρ_Y) and probability (ρ_P) costs:

$$\rho(x, y) = \rho_Y(x, y) + \rho_P(x, y), \tag{2}$$

$$\rho_Y(x, y) = 1 - \exp\left(-0.1\left|Y(x) - Y(y)\right|\right), \tag{3}$$

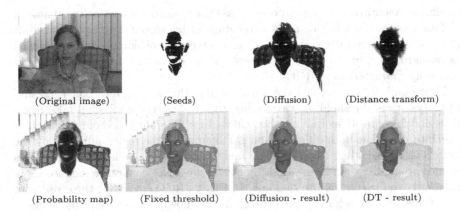

(Original image)   (Seeds)   (Diffusion)   (Distance transform)

(Probability map)   (Fixed threshold)   (Diffusion - result)   (DT - result)

Fig. 1. Skin segmentation based on probability map

$$\rho_P\left(x,y\right) = \begin{cases} 0 & \text{for } P(y) > P_\alpha \\ 0.01\left(P(y) - P_\alpha\right) & \text{for } P_\beta < P(y) \leq P_\alpha \\ \infty & \text{for } P(y) \leq P_\beta \end{cases} \tag{4}$$

where $Y(\cdot)$ is the pixel luminance value, $P(\cdot)$ is the skin probability, and P_α and P_β are the probability thresholds. While P_β has the same practical meaning as the adjoining threshold indicated in Section 2.1, P_α is usually larger than P_{seed}, so for high probabilities the cost depends only on ρ_Y. The total path cost obtained after the optimization is inversely proportional to the "skinness", hence the final skin probability map is obtained by scaling the costs from 0 to P_{seed}. The seed regions remain unmodified, and the pixels which are not adjoined during the propagation process are assigned with zeroes. Finally, skin regions are extracted using a fixed threshold in the distance domain.

An example of the segmentation result is presented in Fig. 1. Here, the original image is transformed into the probability map using Jones and Rehg's method [1] (darker shade indicates higher probability), and the seeds are extracted using $P_{seed} = 0.84$. The controlled diffusion, performed in the probability map, fails because of smooth transitions between the skin and the background. The false positives (indicated by a red shade in the result image) are virtually eliminated using the proposed method.

4   Experimental Validation

The experiments were carried out using 4000 images from the ECU database [12]. They were acquired in uncontrolled lighting conditions, present people of different races, and skin-color objects often appear in the background, which makes the skin regions difficult for segmentation. The images are associated with ground-truth skin binary masks, which makes it possible to train and validate skin detectors. All of the images were split into two equinumerous sets used for training and validation. For generating probability maps, the statistical detector [1] was used.

Skin segmentation performance was assessed based on two errors, namely: a) false positive rate (δ_{FP}), i.e. a percentage of background pixels classified as skin, and b) false negative rate (δ_{FN}), i.e. a percentage of skin pixels misclassified as background. Mutual relation of these two errors is presented using *receiver operating characteristics* (ROC).

First of all, we determined the most suitable threshold values (i.e. P_{seed} and P_β). Hysteresis thresholding was applied to investigate the minimal false negatives and false positives that can be achieved for different threshold values. It is worth to note that both diffusion and DT operate in the region adjoined by the hysteresis thresholding between P_{seed} and P_β thresholds. Hence, false positives cannot be smaller than in the seeds, and false negatives cannot be reduced more than after the hysteresis thresholding. In Fig. 2a ROC curves for three different seed values as well as for the fixed threshold are shown. The subsequent points at each curve indicate the error obtained using different values of P_β. It can be seen from the figure that for $P_{seed} = 0.92$, δ_{FP} equals only 0.98%, but δ_{FN} is high even for large P_β (this is because some skin regions are left without seeds and remain undetected). For lower P_{seed} values, δ_{FP} in the seeds is higher, but false negatives can be reduced more. For further experiments the following values were used: $P_{seed} = 0.84$ ($\delta_{FP} = 2.1\%$, $\delta_{FN} = 46.4\%$) and $P_\beta = 0.29$ ($\delta_{FP} = 16.9\%$, $\delta_{FN} = 9.1\%$).

The proposed method was tested using $P_\alpha = 0.6$. In Fig. 2b DT is compared with a) the fixed threshold, b) with the controlled diffusion in color domain and c) in the probability map domain. Subsequent points on the diffusion curves were obtained using different diffusion thresholds Δ_{max}. Basically, for small Δ_{max} the seeds were not enlarged significantly which keeps δ_{FP} at a low level, but does not reduce δ_{FN} much. For larger Δ_{max}, the diffusion converges to the result obtained using hysteresis thresholding. The proposed DT-based method achieves better results than the diffusion, offering definitely larger error reduction. This can also be observed in several examples presented in Fig. 3. Here, the fixed thresholding (a) of the probability maps (b) delivers high δ_{FP}. For images I. and II. the diffusion (d) performs worse than the proposed DT-based method (e) because of

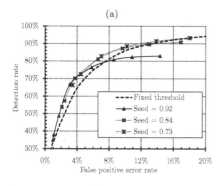
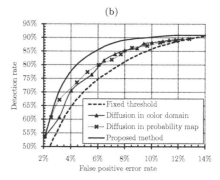

Fig. 2. ROC curves obtained using fixed threshold and: a) hysteresis thresholding with different seed threshold values, b) controlled diffusion and distance transform

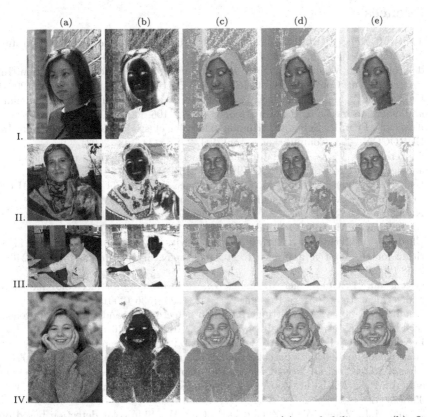

Fig. 3. Examples of obtained results: original image (a), probability map (b), fixed threshold (c), segmentation using diffusion [2] (d) and proposed method (e)

the leakages (there are smooth transitions between skin and non-skin regions in the probability maps). It can be noticed that in case of image II. the seeds are incorrectly detected which leads to false positives, however, they are still smaller using DT. In case of III. and IV. the result obtained using diffusion and DT is similar, and definitely better than using the fixed threshold.

5   Conclusions and Future Work

In this paper a new method for detecting skin regions has been proposed. The method has a strong theoretical advantage over the well-established controlled diffusion, which was confirmed by the obtained experimental results.

Among many possible directions for improving the proposed technique, our efforts will be focused on finding better methods for seed detection. Errors committed at this step are literary propagated and have large impact on the final result. Furthermore, the obtained result depends much on the propagation domain and this also will be a subject of our future investigation.

References

1. Jones, M., Rehg, J.: Statistical color models with application to skin detection. Int. J. of Comp. Vision 46, 81–96 (2002)
2. del Solar, J.R., Verschae, R.: Skin detection using neighborhood information. In: Proc. IEEE Int. Conf. on Automatic Face and Gesture Recogn., pp. 463–468 (2004)
3. Kakumanu, P., Makrogiannis, S., Bourbakis, N.G.: A survey of skin-color modeling and detection methods. Pattern Recogn. 40(3), 1106–1122 (2007)
4. Kovac, J., Peer, P., Solina, F.: Human skin color clustering for face detection. In: EUROCON 2003. Computer as a Tool, vol. 2, pp. 144–148 (2003)
5. Tsekeridou, S., Pitas, I.: Facial feature extraction in frontal views using biometric analogies. In: Proc. of EUSIPCO 1998, pp. 315–318 (1998)
6. Hsu, R.L., Abdel-Mottaleb, M., Jain, A.: Face detection in color images. IEEE Trans. Pattern Anal. and Machine Intell. 24(5), 696–706 (2002)
7. Kukharev, G., Nowosielski, A.: Fast and efficient algorithm for face detection in colour images. Machine Graphics and Vision 13, 377–399 (2004)
8. Cheddad, A., Condell, J., Curran, K., Mc Kevitt, P.: A skin tone detection algorithm for an adaptive approach to steganography. Signal Process. 89(12), 2465–2478 (2009)
9. Greenspan, H., Goldberger, J., Eshet, I.: Mixture model for face-color modeling and segmentation. Pattern Recogn. Lett. 22, 1525–1536 (2001)
10. Khan, R., Hanbury, A., Stöttinger, J.: Skin detection: A random forest approach. In: Proc. IEEE Int. Conf. on Image Process., (ICIP), pp. 4613–4616 (2010)
11. Lee, J.S., Kuo, Y.M., Chung, P.C., Chen, E.L.: Naked image detection based on adaptive and extensible skin color model. Pattern Recogn. 40, 2261–2270 (2007)
12. Phung, S.L., Chai, D., Bouzerdoum, A.: Adaptive skin segmentation in color images. In: Proc. IEEE Int. Conf. on Acoustics, Speech and Signal Process, pp. 353–356 (2003)
13. Zhang, M.J., Wang, W.Q., Zheng, Q.F., Gao, W.: Skin-color detection based on adaptive thresholds. In: Proc. Third Int. Conf. on Image and Graphics, ICIG 2004, pp. 250–253. IEEE (2004)
14. Kawulok, M.: Dynamic Skin Detection in Color Images for Sign Language Recognition. In: Elmoataz, A., Lezoray, O., Nouboud, F., Mammass, D. (eds.) ICISP 2008. LNCS, vol. 5099, pp. 112–119. Springer, Heidelberg (2008)
15. Wang, X., Zhang, X., Yao, J.: Skin color detection under complex background. In: Proc. Int. Conf. on Mechatronic Science, Electric Engineering and Computer, pp. 1985–1988 (2011)
16. Abin, A.A., Fotouhi, M., Kasaei, S.: A new dynamic cellular learning automata-based skin detector. Multimedia Syst. 15(5), 309–323 (2009)
17. Conci, A., Nunes, E., Pantrigo, J.J., Sánchez, Á.: Comparing color and texture-based algorithms for human skin detection. In: ICEIS, vol. 5, pp. 166–173 (2008)
18. Sigal, L., Sclaroff, S., Athitsos, V.: Skin color-based video segmentation under time-varying illumination. IEEE Trans. on Pattern Anal. and Machine Intell. 26, 862–877 (2003)
19. Kawulok, M., Smolka, B.: Competitive image colorization. In: Proc. IEEE Int. Conf. on Image Process., pp. 405–408 (2010)
20. Yatziv, L., Sapiro, G.: Fast image and video colorization using chrominance blending. IEEE Trans. on Image Process. 15(5), 1120–1129 (2006)
21. Ikonen, L., Toivanen, P.: Distance and nearest neighbor transforms on gray-level surfaces. Pattern Recogn. Lett. 28(5), 604–612 (2007)

Human Fall Detection by Mean Shift Combined with Depth Connected Components

Michal Kepski* and Bogdan Kwolek

Rzeszow University of Technology
Al. Powstańców Warszawy 12, 35-959 Rzeszów, Poland
bkwolek@prz.edu.pl

Abstract. Depth is very useful cue to achieve reliable fall detection since humans may not have consistent color and texture but must occupy an integrated region in space. In this work we demonstrate how to accomplish reliable fall detection using depth image sequences. The depth images are extracted by low-cost Kinect device. The person undergoing monitoring is extracted through mean-shift clustering. A depth connected component algorithm is used to delineate he/she in sequence of images. The system permits unobtrusive fall detection as well as preserves privacy of the user. The experimental results indicate high effectiveness of fall detection in indoor environments and low computational overhead of the algorithm.

1 Introduction

Falls are major causes of mortality and morbidity in the elderly. As humans become old, their bodies weaken and the risk of accidental falls increases. Many research findings show that high percentage of injury-related hospitalizations for seniors are the results of falls [8]. Thus, considerable research is devoted to the problem of fall detection, mainly due to the big demand and social values of assistive technologies [14]. Assistive technology or adaptive technology is an umbrella term that encompasses assistive, adaptive, and rehabilitative devices for people with special needs [4]. Among others, the assistive technology can contribute toward independent living of the elderly. Such an assistive device or system should detect the fall occurrence as soon as possible and to generate a warning to caregivers or an alarm to monitoring authorities. However, despite many efforts undertaken to attain reliable fall detection, the offered technology does not meet the requirements of the users [17].

A wide range of methods have been proposed for detecting a fallen person. Most of the proposed methods relies on a wearable device, which monitor the motion of an individual, recognize a fall and trigger alarm. Such methods employ accelerometers or both accelerometers and gyroscopes to separate fall from activities of daily living (ADLs) [14]. However, on the basis of such sensors it is not easy to discriminate real falls from fall-like activities [2]. In this context, it

---

* M. Kępski is currently a student, doing his MSc thesis on fall detection.

L. Bolc et al. (Eds.): ICCVG 2012, LNCS 7594, pp. 457–464, 2012.

is worth noting that quite a lot of ADLs like fast sitting have comparable motion patterns with real falls. In consequence, such methods can generate considerable number of false alarms. Moreover, such fall detectors, which are usually attached to a belt around the hip, are inadequate to be worn during the sleep [6]. In addition, they are not capable of monitoring in critical phases like getting up from the bed. In general, such devices are somewhat intrusive for humans since they require wearing continuously at least one smart sensor or mobile device.

During the last decade, a lot of work has been done on detecting falls using a wide range of sensor types [14][17], including pressure pads [16], single CCD camera [1][15], multiple cameras [5], specialized omni-directional ones [13] and stereo-pair cameras [9]. Video cameras offer several advantages over other sensors including the capability of detection of various activities. The further benefit is low intrusiveness and the possibility of remote verification of fall events. However, the currently available solutions require time for installation, camera calibration and they are not generally cheap. As a rule, CCD-camera based systems require a PC computer or a notebook for image processing. The existing video-based devices for fall detection cannot work in night-light or low light conditions. Additionally, the lack of depth information can lead to lots of false alarms. Moreover, in most of such systems the privacy is not preserved adequately.

Recently, in fall detection systems the time-of-flight cameras (TOF) have become more and more attractive [11]. In systems using such cameras the extrinsic calibration is restricted to the determination of the camera pose, whereas the intrinsic calibration is not required at all. TOF cameras are independent of external light conditions, since they are equipped with an active light source. It is worth noting that the TOF cameras can guarantee the person's privacy.

The existing technology permits reaching quite high performance of fall detection. However, it does not meet the requirements of the users with special needs. To make such human-assistive technology more unobtrusive and preserving privacy we developed a depth-based system for fall detection. Depth is very useful cue to achieve reliable fall detection since humans may not have consistent color and texture but must occupy an integrated region in space.

The Kinect is a revolutionary motion-sensing technology that permits sensing and tracking human position and motion. Unlike 2D cameras, Kinect allows tracking the body movements in 3D. It is the world's first system that combines an RGB camera and depth sensor. In order to achieve reliable and unobtrusive fall detection, our system employs the low-cost Kinect. The algorithm extracts the person in depth images using mean-shift algorithm [7]. Mean-shift is a general non-parametric mode finding/clustering procedure. It was extended to low-level vision problems [3], including, image segmentation and object tracking. In this work we propose to utilize the mean-shift to extract the person in depth image sequences at a low computational cost. The system can reliably distinguish the falls from activities of daily living, and thus the number of false alarms is reduced. An advantage of Kinect is that it can be put in selected places according to the user requirements. Moreover, the system operates on depth images and thus preserves privacy of people being monitored. In this context, it is worth noting that Kinect uses infrared light and therefore it is able to extract depth images in a room that is dark to our eyes. In [10] we demonstrated an embedded system for fall detection in which a wearable motion-sensing device and Kinect complement each other. Due to limited computational power of the PandaBoard, at which the system has been implemented, a simple algorithm relying on reference map-based extraction of the person has been employed. However, after changing the setting of furniture the performance of the person detection drops. In such conditions, the wearable device contributes more to the decision of a fuzzy inference engine. The contribution of this work is an algorithm for person extraction, which delineates of individual even in case of changing the setting of furniture. It has low computational demands and runs in real-time.

2   The System for Fall Detection

At the beginning of this section we discuss usefulness of the Kinect for the detection of human fall. Afterwards, the extraction of the object of interest in depth images is presented. In the last part a proposed low-cost algorithm for person delineation is discussed.

2.1   Depth Images

The hardware employed in this work is Kinect, a motion sensing device developed by PrimeSense company. It is composed of an RGB camera, infrared laser-based IR emitter, an infrared camera, a multi-array microphone and a motorized tilt. The IR camera and the IR projector comprise a stereo pair with a baseline of approximately 75 mm. In this work, only the RGB and depth sensors are utilized to provide the input data. The device simultaneously captures depth and color images at a frame rate of about 30 fps. The resolution of color images is 640×480 pixels with 8 bits for every color channel. The Kinect projects the structured light code with an infrared laser onto the scene. Such a pattern is then read by an infrared camera and the 3D information is reconstructed from the distortions of the pattern. The disparity measurements are supplied in VGA resolution (640×480 pixels) as 11-bit integers, where 1 bit is reserved to mark the pixels for which no disparity is available. Since depth is inversely proportional to disparity, the depth resolution is also inversely related to the disparity. Thus, the depth resolution is not fixed and drops off with the distance growing to the sensor. For example, the depth resolution is about 1 cm at 2 m distance, whereas at 5 m distance one disparity level corresponds to about 7 cm depth resolution. Kinect's field of view is fifty-seven degrees horizontally and forty-three degrees vertically. The minimum range for the Kinect is about 0.6 m and the maximum range is somewhere between 4-5 m. Thanks to the Kinect's capability to extract the depth images in unlit or dark rooms, the fall detection can be performed in the late evening or even in the night.

The depth images can be acquired using OpenNI (Open Natural Interaction) library[1]. The OpenNI framework supplies an application programming interface

---

[1] Available at: http://www.openni.org/

(API) as well as it provides the interface for physical devices and for middle-ware components. The NITE middleware, which is supplied by PrimeSense is a perception component enabling extraction of a person and tracking his/her skeleton. The discussed engine that enables natural human-computer interaction is protected by copyright and does not run on embedded platforms like PandaBoard.

2.2   Extraction of the Object of Interest

In our previous work [10] we presented an embedded system for person fall detection, in which a wearable motion-sensing device and Kinect complemented each other. Due to limited computational power of the PandaBoard, at which the system has been implemented a reference map-based extraction of the person has been employed. The depth reference map was extracted on the basis of several consecutive depth images without the subject to be monitored and then it was stored for the later use in the person detection mode. In the detection mode the foreground objects were extracted through differencing the current image from such a reference depth map.

The procedure responsible for extraction of the object of interest in the depth reference images has low computational cost. However, the disadvantage of such an approach is that in the case of modification of the furniture settings, the furniture will appear in the depth difference images as foreground objects. Therefore, to cope with such an undesirable effect the depth difference images were segmented using mean-shift algorithm. Mean-shift is a nonparametric estimator of probability density [3]. The mean-shift vector always points toward the direction of the maximum increase in the density. The main idea behind mean-shift is to treat the points in the d-dimensional feature space as an empirical probability density function, where dense regions (or clusters) in the feature space correspond to the modes (or local maxima) of the underlying distribution. In contrast to the classic k-means clustering approach, it does not require prior knowledge on the shape of the distribution nor the number of modes or clusters.

Given n data points $\mathbf{x}_k, k = 1, \ldots, n$ on a d-dimensional space R^d the mean-shift is calculated on the basis of the following equation:

$$m(\mathbf{x}) = \frac{\sum_{k=1}^{n} \mathbf{x}_k g(||\frac{\mathbf{x} - \mathbf{x}_k}{h}||^2)}{\sum_{k=1}^{n} g(||\frac{\mathbf{x} - \mathbf{x}_k}{h}||^2)} - \mathbf{x} \tag{1}$$

where g is a kernel function and h denotes bandwidth. The mean-shift algorithm clusters a d-dimensional data set by associating each point with a peak of the data set's probability density. Each pixel is assigned a feature point $\mathbf{x}_k$. To account for the pixel position and depth, 3-d vectors were used. For each image pixel the mean-shift computes its associated peak by first defining a spherical window at the data point and computing the mean of the pixel values that lie within the window. The algorithm then shifts the window to the mean and repeats until convergence, i.e., until the shift is less than a threshold.

In the assumed model the depth of the point k in the object space depends from the observed disparity as follows:

$$Z_k = \frac{Z_o}{1 + \frac{Z_o}{fb}d} \tag{2}$$

where b is the base length, f denotes the focal length of the IR camera, d is the observed disparity in the image space, whereas Z_o is the distance of the reference pattern. The parameters b, f, Z_o can be obtained by calibration of the camera.

Figure 1 illustrates the main steps of the extraction of the object of interest using mean-shift. In the upper row are shown the disparity images, in the middle row are depicted the segmented images, whereas on the bottom row are shown images with the extracted object of the interest. The mean-shift - based segmentation was done on the difference image, which was obtained through differencing the current disparity image with the reference image. The images were then median filtered to remove small artefacts. Afterwards, the foreground object was extracted through determining the largest connected component in the segmented map. A correspondence between the segments was taken into account at this stage. It is also assumed that the depth values on the surface of a human object are continuous and vary only within a specific range. Finally, the center of gravity of the object of interest was calculated. As we can observe in frames #490 - 600 the person opens the door, which then appears as a separate segment in the image. Afterwards, in frames #650 - 670 the person moves the chair, which also appears in the segmented image. As we can see on images depicted on the bottom row, the person was extracted correctly in the considered image sequence despite change of the furniture settings.

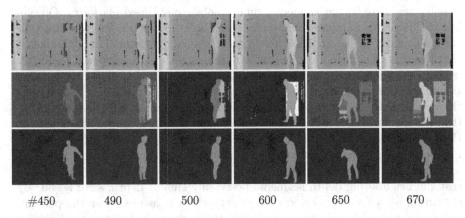

| #450 | 490 | 500 | 600 | 650 | 670 |

Fig. 1. Person detection. Disparity images (upper row), the segmented images (middle row) and the extracted person (bottom row).

Fig. 2. Update of the depth reference image

As one can notice in the above images, the modifications of the furniture settings contribute towards clutter in the segmented image, which in turn can lead to difficulties in extraction of the object of interest, see also images in middle row on Fig. 1. Thus, in our approach we update the depth reference image on the basis of median filtered collection of images. Figure 2 illustrates the depth reference image (left), image on which a chair is moved (middle), and the updated reference image (right). As we can observe, the chair is at new location and no person is present on the extracted depth reference image. The updated depth reference image has been obtained on the basis of 30 depth images. Every 20th depth image was included in the collection of the images.

Using the discussed algorithm, the fall alarm was triggered on the basis of the distance of the person's gravity center to the altitude at which the Kinect was placed. In a more sophisticated approach a height/width ratio of the person's bounding box in k-nearest neighbor classifier can be used to detect the fall [12].

2.3 Low-Cost Algorithm for Person Segmentation in Depth Images

The mean-shift is too slow to be used for image segmentation, where each pixel is a data point. In particular, the computational overhead is too large to make possible real-time image segmentation on mobile/embedded platforms. On mobile platforms the computational cost should be as low as possible to reduce the energy demand. Thus, in order to decrease the computational cost the mean-shift based person extraction was done in images with reduced spatial resolution by factor 5, i.e. on depth images of size 128×96. On Fig. 3 b-c) are shown the images that were segmented using the mean-shift. On the discussed images the ground plane is not shown since it was removed using a method similar to [18]. As one can observe the mean-shift is able to delineate the whole person. However, in some images the person is represented by several components, see Fig. 3c. Thus, in the next stage the segmented images are further refined using a connected components algorithm. Its aim is to connect at a low computational cost the neighboring depth segments possessing similar depth, see Fig. 3d. By starting from a seed connected component, which is located near the person's gravity center in the previous frame and simultaneously has the most similar depth to the depth at the gravity center, and then linking the neighboring components with similar depth the algorithm is able to extract the person in long image sequences, say several hundred of images, see also Fig. 3e.

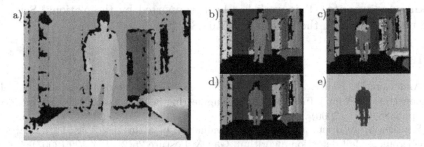

Fig. 3. Person detection. Depth image a), segmented images using mean-shift b), c), refined segmentation using connected components d), extracted person e). For visualization purposes the images b-e were resized to the half of the size of image a.

3   Experimental Results

Five volunteers with age over 26 years attended in evaluation of our developed algorithm and the system. Intentional falls were performed in home by four persons towards a carpet with thickness of about 2 cm. Each individual performed three types of falls, namely forward, backward and lateral at least three times. Figure 4 depicts a person who has fallen and some daily activities that can be distinguished from the fall. All intentional falls were detected correctly.

Fig. 4. A fallen person and some activities of daily living: sitting down, squatting/picking up objects from the floor, bending down, which were shot by Kinect

The system has been implemented in C/C++ and runs at 25 fps on 2 Duo T8100 (2.1 GHz) notebook powered by Linux. The execution time needed for mean-shift segmentation of depth images of size 128×96 is about 35 ms. We are planning to implement the system on the PandaBoard.

4   Conclusions

In this work we demonstrated how to achieve reliable fall detection using Kinect. A mean-shift based algorithm with low computational burden was proposed to extract a person in depth image sequences. A depth connected component algorithm is used to extract the person in sequence of images. A fall alarm is generated on the basis of the gravity center of a connected component representing the extracted person. The system permits unobtrusive fall detection and preserves privacy of the user.

Acknowledgments. This work has been supported by the National Science Centre (NCN) within the project N N516 483240.

References

1. Anderson, D., Keller, J., Skubic, M., Chen, X., He, Z.: Recognizing falls from silhouettes. In: Annual Int. Conf. of the Engineering in Medicine and Biology Society, pp. 6388–6391 (2006)
2. Bourke, A., O'Brien, J., Lyons, G.: Evaluation of a threshold-based tri-axial accelerometer fall detection algorithm. Gait & Posture 26(2), 194–199 (2007)
3. Comaniciu, D., Meer, P.: Mean shift: A robust approach toward feature space analysis. IEEE Trans. Pattern Anal. Mach. Intell. 24(5), 603–619 (2002)
4. Cook, A., Hussey, S.: Assistive Technologies: Principles and Practice, 2nd edn. Mosby (2002)
5. Cucchiara, R., Prati, A., Vezzani, R.: A multi-camera vision system for fall detection and alarm generation. Expert Systems 24(5), 334–345 (2007)
6. Degen, T., Jaeckel, H., Rufer, M., Wyss, S.: Speedy: A fall detector in a wrist watch. In: Proc. of IEEE Int. Symp. on Wearable Computers, pp. 184–187 (2003)
7. Fukunaga, K., Hostetler, L.D.: The estimation of the gradient of a density function, with applications in pattern recognition. IEEE Tr. Inf. Theory 21(1), 32–40 (1975)
8. Heinrich, S., Rapp, K., Rissmann, U., Becker, C., Knig, H.H.: Cost of falls in old age: a systematic review. Osteoporosis International 21, 891–902 (2010)
9. Jansen, B., Deklerck, R.: Context aware inactivity recognition for visual fall detection. In: Proc. IEEE Pervasive Health Conference and Workshops, pp. 1–4 (2006)
10. Kepski, M., Kwolek, B.: Fall Detection on Embedded Platform Using Kinect and Wireless Accelerometer. In: Miesenberger, K., Karshmer, A., Penaz, P., Zagler, W. (eds.) ICCHP 2012, Part II. LNCS, vol. 7383, pp. 407–414. Springer, Heidelberg (2012)
11. Leone, A., Diraco, G., Siciliano, P.: Detecting falls with 3d range camera in ambient assisted living applications: A preliminary study. Medical Engineering & Physics 33(6), 770–781 (2011)
12. Liu, C.L., Lee, C.H., Lin, P.M.: A fall detection system using k-nearest neighbor classifier. Expert Syst. Appl. 37(10), 7174–7181 (2010)
13. Miaou, S.G., Sung, P.H., Huang, C.Y.: A customized human fall detection system using omni-camera images and personal information. Distributed Diagnosis and Home Healthcare, 39–42 (2006)
14. Noury, N., Fleury, A., Rumeau, P., Bourke, A., Laighin, G., Rialle, V., Lundy, J.: Fall detection - principles and methods. In: Annual Int. Conf. of the IEEE Engineering in Medicine and Biology Society, pp. 1663–1666 (2007)
15. Rougier, C., Meunier, J., St-Arnaud, A., Rousseau, J.: Monocular 3D head tracking to detect falls of elderly people. In: Annual Int. Conf. of the IEEE Engineering in Medicine and Biology Society, pp. 6384–6387 (2006)
16. Tzeng, H.W., Chen, M.Y., Chen, J.Y.: Design of fall detection system with floor pressure and infrared image. In: Int. Conf. on System Science and Engineering, pp. 131–135 (July 2010)
17. Yu, X.: Approaches and principles of fall detection for elderly and patient. In: 10th Int. Conf. on e-health Networking, Applications and Services, pp. 42–47 (2008)
18. Zhao, J., Katupitiya, J., Ward, J.: Global correlation based ground plane estimation using v-disparity image. In: IEEE Int. Conf. on Robotics and Automation, pp. 529–534 (2007)

Stability of Dimensionality Reduction Methods Applied on Artificial Hyperspectral Images

Jihan Khoder[1,2], Rafic Younes[1], and Fethi Ben Ouezdou[2]

[1] LISV Laboratory, Université de Versailles Saint-Quentin en-Yvelines, Paris, France
[2] Azm Center for research in biotechnology, Lebanese University, Tripoli, Lebanon

Abstract. Dimensionality reduction is a big challenge in many areas. In this research we address the problem of high-dimensional hyperspectral images in which we are aiming to preserve its information quality. This paper introduces a study stability of the non parametric and unsupervised methods of projection and of bands selection used in dimensionality reduction of different noise levels determined with different numbers of data points. The quality criteria based on the norm and correlation are employed obtaining a good preservation of these artificial data in the reduced dimensions. The added value of these criteria can be illustrated in the evaluation of the reduction's performance, when considering the stability of two categories of bands selection methods and projection methods. The performances of the method are verified on artificial data sets for validation. An hybridization for a better stability is proposed in this paper, Band Clustering (BandClust) with Multidimensional Scaling (MDS) for dimensionality reduction. Examples are given to demonstrate the hybridization originality and relevance(BandClust/MDS) of the analysis carried out in this paper.

Keywords: Dimensionality reduction, manifold learning, stability spectral criteria, hyperspectral data.

1 Introduction

Hyperspectral imaging has become an active research topic in recent years due to its wide-spread applications in areas such as resource management, agriculture, mineral exploration, and environmental monitoring. With the number of channels in the hundreds instead of in the tens, hyperspectral imagery possesses much richer spectral information than multispectral imagery [1]. However, identifying the material reflecting specific spectral signature remains a challenge for realizing the full potential of hyperspectral technology. It is clear that more effective data processing techniques are needed to deal with hyperspectral cubes. Because it is necessary to have a minimum ratio of training pixels to the number of spectral bands [2], dimension reduction has become a significant part of hyperspectral image interpretation. Dimension reduction is the transformation that brings data from a high order dimension to a low one, thus conquering the curse of dimensionality.

L. Bolc et al. (Eds.): ICCVG 2012, LNCS 7594, pp. 465–474, 2012.

Similar to a lossy compression method [3], dimension reduction reduces the size of the data, but unlike compression, dimension reduction is application-driven.

Mathematically, given n points $x_1, \ldots, x_n$ in a high dimensional subspace of R^D the goal of dimensionality reduction is to find a mapping: $F : R^D \rightarrow R^d, y_i = F(x_i), i = 1, \ldots, n$. Where $y_i \in R^d, i = 1 \ldots n$ and d is the dimensionality of the embedding space. Here, in mathematical terms, intrinsic dimensionality means that the points in dataset X are lying on or near a manifold with dimensionality d that is embedded in the D-dimensional space. Dimensionality reduction techniques transform dataset X with dimensionality D into a new dataset Y with dimensionality d, while retaining the geometry of the data as much as possible. Ideally, the reduced representation should have a dimensionality that corresponds to the intrinsic dimensionality of the data. Which is the minimum number of parameters needed to take into account for the observed properties of the data [4]. As a result, dimensionality reduction facilitates, among others methods, classification, visualization, and compression of high-dimensional data.

Several local approaches of dimension reduction methods were used to address this problem. Chang and al. have proposed a robust modification of Locally Linear Embedding (LLE), Robust LLE [5]. They provided an efficient algorithm to detect and remove the large noises, namely, the outliers. However, RLLE would also fail when the data have some small noises. Pan et Ge. have generated a multiple weights LLE, NLLE [6]. This method uses the $(k - d)$ linear independent combination weights to represent the local structure. Chen et al. have also proposed an effective preprocessing procedure for current manifold learning algorithms [7]. They analyzed the imput data statistically and then detected the noises. Ridder et al. have also solved the robustness problem of LLE [8] by introducing a weighted reformulation in the embedding step. Hou and Zhang have been developed a large number of local approaches, stemming from statistics or geometry [9]. In practice, these local approaches are often in lack of robustness, since in contrast to maximum variance unfolding (MVU), which explicitly unfolds the manifold; they merely characterize local geometry structure. Moreover, the eigenproblems encountered are hard to solve. These methods try to tackle this problem through a unified framework that explicitly unfolds the manifold and reformulate local approaches as semi-definite programs instead of the above-mentioned eigenproblems. Three well known local approaches (LLE-LE-LTSA) are interpreted and improved within this framework. These methods proposed several experiments on both synthetic and real datasets. These results have shown that the dimensionality reduction techniques SLLE-SLTSA-SLE also have some troubles are not stable, so sensitive in the presence of noises levels and more stable the parameter k. Tsai studied current linear and nonlinear dimensionality reduction techniques in the context of data visualization [10]. Experiments were conducted on varying the neighborhood, density and needed noise levels of data taken into account. He used the manifold metric based on the correlation coefficient that computes the pair wise geodesic distance vector between the original manifold and the lower-dimensional embedding results used. The calculation of the metric is similar to the correlation used by Geng et al [11], but the pair wise geodesic distance vector is calculated for the original data instead of the Euclidean distance vector. A previous study carried out by Tsai and Chan [12] showed that this metric was more suitable for representing the visualization results if the original data lies on a manifold.

A new approach we used to measure the stability of these linear and nonlinear techniques to reduce the size of a disturbance in the data set is based on the noise variance at different scales. Stability criteria, as defined in section 3 are used. These criteria take into account the intrinsic structure of the original hyperspectral and disturbed images. This comparative study focuses on the influence of noise variance in the data set with respect to the spectral dimension. The outline of the remainder of this paper is as follows. Section 2 describes the methodology of the approaches used. We give a formal definition of linear techniques for dimensionality reduction and subdivide the 15dimensionality reduction techniques into two linear and eleven non-linear techniques [13–22]. Moreover, in Section 3, we define the quality criteria and present the results of the experiments in Section 4. Section 5, discusses the influence of the rate disturbance in the phenomenon of reduction allowing us to conclude about the main contributions of this paper.

2   Methodology Approach

2.1   Stability Test

An unsupervised approach to band reduction in hyperspectral remote sensing imagery [24]. The band selection involves selecting a minimal subset of M bands $S = (S_1, S_2, \ldots, S_M)$ from the original set $F = (F_1, F_2, \ldots, F_N)$, where $(M \ll N)$ and $(S \subseteq F)$. Hyperspectral imaging offers high richness of information which is often necessary to achieve good classification performance at the pixel level. Hyperspectral images generally show a high amount of correlation between adjacent spectral bands. Therefore, removing this redundancy would reduce the amount of data that are relevant to further classification and interpretation stages. This selects an appropriate subset of image bands to fulfill the same applications the full image can, to some extent The BandClust method using mutual information between two bands as selection criterion provides a rather increased stability is presented in [24].

Although, our comparative review study for stability includes the most important nonlinear techniques for dimensionality reduction, our aim is to identify an demonstrate an efficient algorithm to detect and remove the large noises. The approaches of this framework that we propose deal with reduction for high-dimensional noisy signals. The problem of nonlinear dimensionality reduction can be defined as follows. Assume we have dataset represented in $n \times D$ matrix X consisting of n data vectors x_i for $i = \{1, 2 \ldots n\}$ with dimensionality; assume further that this dataset has intrinsic dimensionality d where $d < D$. In practice, the signal-subspace perturbation ξ_i from observed vectors has to satisfy the following general model: $\Xi_i = x_i + z_i$, $i = 1 \ldots n$. Where $x_i \in R^D$ is the observed random vector $z_i \in R^D$ is the data-acquisition or/and model noise; finally, the stability test will be used on a set data and data perturbed. The approached is illustrated in the figure 1.

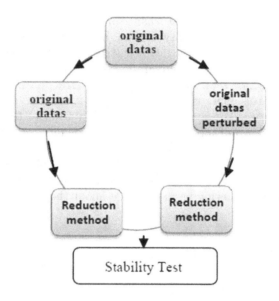

Fig. 1. Proposed Method for Stability Study applied on Hyperspectral Images

3   Description of Quality Criteria

Before beginning the study of the Dimensionality Reduction of images (DR), it is necessary to define several normalized quality criteria derived from classical statistical measures for the reduction. These unsupervised stability criteria will allow comparing and evaluated the performances of reduction and the stability of these methods of reduction in the analysis of image and in particular to measure the different types of degradations (loss of information, etc.) caused by the various methods DR. An approach is then proposed to appreciate the appropriateness of these criteria, to applications of a Hyperspectral images. Every value individually is considered according to the spatial and dimensions spectral. The artificial image is represented as a three-dimensional matrix $I(x, y, \lambda)$, with x is the position of the pixel in the line, y there is the number of the line and λ the spectral considered band. n_x, n_y, n_λ are respectively the number of pixels by line, the number of lines and the number of spectral bands. Note also equally $\sum_{x=1}^{n_x} \sum_{y=1}^{n_y} \sum_{\lambda=1}^{n_\lambda} I(x, y, \lambda)$ by $\sum_{x,y,\lambda} I(x, y, \lambda)$.

3.1   Structural Content (SC)

SC is the ratio of Power Spectral Density (PSD) of the two images (image disturbance reduced $\tilde{I}(x, y, \lambda)$ on the reference image $\tilde{I}(x, y, \lambda)$ presented in [25] and is defined as: $SC = (\sigma_{\tilde{I}}^2 + \mu_{\tilde{I}}^2)/(\sigma_{\tilde{I}}^2 + \mu_{\tilde{I}}^2)$ And hyperspectral images:

$$SC = (\sum\nolimits_{x,y,\lambda} [\tilde{I}(x, y, \lambda)]^2)/(\sum\nolimits_{x,y,\lambda} [\tilde{I}(x, y, \lambda)]^2)$$

3.2   Normalized Cross-Correlation (NCC)

The Normalized Cross-Correlation (NCC) is mentioned in [25] as those proposing to use fidelity. $NCC = (\sum_{x,y,\lambda} I(x, y, \lambda) \tilde{I}g(x, y, \lambda))/(\sum_{x,y,\lambda} [Ix, y, \lambda]^2)$

4   Experiments and Results

In order to evaluate and compare the various techniques, experiments were conducted using dimensionality reduction techniques on three synthetic datasets (S-Curve, helix and twin peaks). The datasets were specifically selected to investigate how the dimensionality reduction techniques deal with: (i) data that lies on a low-dimensional manifold that is isometric to Euclidean space, (ii) data lying on a low-dimensional manifold that is not isometric to Euclidean space, (iii) data that lies on or near a disconnected manifold, and data forming a manifold with a high intrinsic dimensionality. All artificial datasets consist of 5,000 samples [23]. We examined the results of the various dimensionality reduction techniques under different levels of noise.

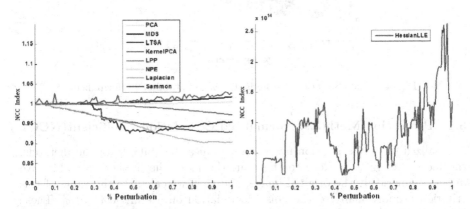

Fig. 2. Projection Methods, 1st and 3rd Category of reduction methods

5   Influence Disturbance

A selection of the curves obtained for the tested criteria of the Normalized Cross Correlation are presented above. In the following, we explain the influence rate of disturbance of a pixel introduced to the data observation in the reduction phenomenon and the results obtained from simulations.

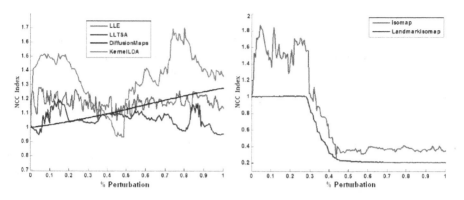

Fig. 3. Projection Methods, 3rd Category of reduction methods

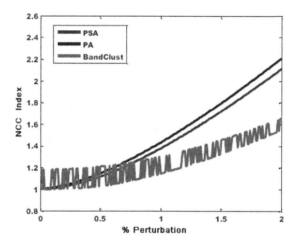

Fig. 4. Bands Selection Methods, Curves of stability performances

5.1   Projection Methods: Normalized Correlation Coefficient(NCC)

Normalized Cross Correlation numerically values the stability of the methods, the more this value is close to the unit, the more the method is stable. We disturb numerically the original image, and then we calculate the value of this criterion proportionally to the noise degradation on a scale [0%; 10%]. These NCC curves tested on 15 reduction methods show the following facts: We notice many similar performances for the methods: *Principal component analysis (PCA)*, Multidimensional scaling (MDS), NPE LTSA, Laplacian, KernelPCA, LPP and Sammon. Also, we notice many similar performances for the other categories of nonlinear techniques like: DiffusionMaps, LLTSA, LLE, and KernelLDA. The NCC criterion tested on NPE, MDS and PCA reflects a good performance compared to other methods in the same category. In reality, the NCC value that varies around the unit [1, 1.025], offers a well increased stability under a noise scale [0%, 10%] followed by a small deformation of the original image. The quantity of information stored in diffusionMaps, LLE, DM and LLTSA is almost equivalent. But not constant according to degradation of noise, bound to a geometrical deformation of increasing NCC value all around the unit proportionally to the variation of noise. This fact reveals the partial performance on the quantities of data stored by this set of methods. The study on Isomap and Landmark Isomap shows bad performances compared to the other reduction methods interpreted above. Some of them present some disturbances also being able to decrease the global potential value of these methods. This is illustrated by the deformation of information bound by a strong fall of degradations compared to the other methods of reduction on a scale of noise [2%; 10%], and NCC value [0.2; 1.8] rather near to the unit. In contrary to all other methods, the study of HessianLLE reveals a large total influence of noise disturbance. In conclusion, the NCC criterion shows a better partial performance on the PCA, MDS followed by NPE method. The variation rate of noise equal to 40 seems to be a best alternative.

In the Table 1, a classification of the methods of projection is ranked of three categories (good, average and bad) presenting the performances of the application in comparison with the similarity criterion NCC and SC observed.

Table 1. The various reduction methods of projection used, in order to categorize, with NCC and SC, on artificial data with different noise variances

Classification derived by projection reduction of methods		
Good	Average	Bad
PCA- MDS- NPE- LTSA- KernelPCA-LPP- Laplacian-Sammon-	Isomap- Landmarkisomap-LLE- Kernel LDA	HessianLLE

5.2 Proposition of Hybrid BandClust/MDS Algorithm

Considering this discussion of the results obtained for the stability tested is presented above. We explain the interpretations that one can pull along with the conclusions obtained from simulation results. It is important to notice that hybridization between the best techniques of projection methods and band selection ones will be able to lead towards better quality of reduction in term of stability and preservation of information. The principle of this hybridization is not recent [24, 26], but the optimization of this process can be an important result of this study.

After several tests of hybridizations, we thus concluded to use BandClust for the classification of the similar bands in term of mutual information, then to use MDS to project each class towards only one band (Figure 5). The curves Figure 6 concerning the values of "Normalized Cross Correlation" and "Structural Content" show the good performances obtained by this hybridization.

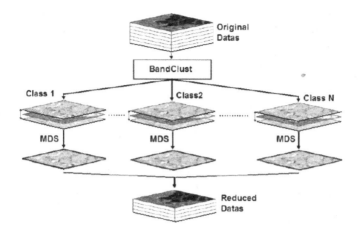

Fig. 5. Hybrid BandClust/MDS Algorithm

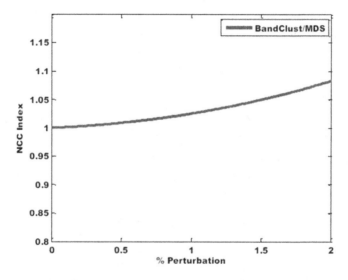

Fig. 6. NCC Index for Hybrid BandClust/MDS Algorithm

6   Conclusion

The paper presents a review and comparative study of techniques for dimensionality reduction. In this comparative study on the stability of non-parametric algorithms, unsupervised by dimension reduction of large images (by projection and by selection of spectral bands) and taking into account the stability evolution criteria presented in section 3. It is revealed that the techniques unsupervised by projection are either limited by their linear character (ACP, MDS), or difficult to use because of their algorithm complexity when working on high dimensional data. Moreover, the majority of them are sensitive to the different undergoing variations as the noise degradation and the information loss. This is the reason making these techniques does not fully meet our two main points of interest: stability and preservation of the rare event. Despite the PCA-MDS algorithms followed by NPE that are quite sensitive to noise degradation in comparison with other reduction techniques of projection, to preserve the geometrical structure local / global of reduced data. It seems more relevant on synthetic data, in comparison with the other techniques of projection. We can conclude from this study on the robustness of the hybrid method BandClust / MDS, which found very encouraging results on the stability of hyperspectral data compared to the influence of noise during the reduction. Several extension of this work can be considered, such as the development of new techniques by band selection for dimensionality reduction, which does not rely on the local properties of various data. In addition, we suspect a change at the point towards the development of techniques for the dimensionality reduction with the hybrid function BandClust/MDS which showed its effectiveness through simulations performed on the stability criteria during the reduction. Indeed, BandClust / MDS could be improved by maximizing the dissimilarity between each two spectral bands, and the use of an information criterion involving several objectives, like storing the statistically rare information and minimize the spectral redundancy.

References

1. Grahn, H., Geladi, P. (eds.): Techniques and Applications of Hyperspectral Image Analysis. Wiley, Chichester (2007)
2. Richards, J.A.: Remote Sensing Digital Image Analysis: An Introduction, 2nd edn. Springer (1993)
3. Gao, Shi, Q., Caetano, T.S.: Dimensionality reduction via compressive sensing. Pattern Recognition Letters 33(9), 1163–1170 (2012)
4. Fukunaga, K.: Introduction to Statistical Pattern Recognition. Academic Press Professional, Inc., San Diego (1990)
5. Álvarez-Meza, A., Valencia-Aguirre, J., Daza-Santacoloma, G., Castellanos-Domínguez, G.: Global and local choice of the number of nearest neighbors in locally linear embedding. Pattern Recognition Letters 32(16), 2171–2177 (2011)
6. Pan, Y., Ge, S.S., Mamun, A.A.: Weighted locally linear embedding for dimension reduction. Pattern Recognition 42(5), 798–811 (2009)
7. Wahba, G.: Spline models for observational data. CBMS-NSF Regional Conference series in applied mathematics. Society for Industrial and Applied Mathematics, Philadelphia (1990)
8. Scholkopf, B., Smola, A., Muller, K.R.: Nonlinear component analysis as a kernel eigenvalue problem. Neural Computation 10, 1299–1319 (1998)
9. Jiao, Y., Wu, Y., Hou, C., Zhang, C.: Stable local dimensionality reduction approaches. Pattern Recognition 42(9), 2054–2066 (2006)
10. Tsai, F.S.: Comparative Study of Dimensionality Reduction Techniques for Data Visualization. Journal of Artificial Intelligence 3(3), 119–134 (2010)
11. Geng, X., Zhan, D.C., Zhou, Z.H.: Supervised nonlinear dimensionality reduction for visualization and classification. IEEE Trans. Syst. Man Cybernetics Part B 35, 1098–1107 (2005)

12. Tsai, F.S., Chan, K.L.: A manifold visualization metric for dimensionality reduction. Nanyang Technological University Technical Report (2009)
13. Hotelling, H.: Analysis of a complex of statistical variables into principal components. Journal of Educational Psychology 24, 417–441 (1933)
14. Pearson, K.: On lines and planes of closest fit to systems of points in space. Philiosophical Magazine 2, 559–572 (1901)
15. Williams, C.K.I., Cand, D.: Barber. Bayesian classification with processes. IEEE Transactions on Pattern Analysis and Machine Intelligence 20(12), 1342–1351 (1998)
16. Vapnik, V.N.: The nature of statistical learning theory. Springer, New York (1995)
17. Zhang, Z., Zha, H.: Principal manifolds and nonlinear dimensionality reduction via local tangent space alignment. SIAM Journal of Scientific Computing 26(1), 313–338 (2004)
18. Nadler, B., Lafon, B., Coifman, R.R., Kevrekidis, I.G.: Diffusion maps, spectral clustering and the reaction coordinate of dynamical systems. Applied and Computational Harmonic Analysis: Special Issue on Diffusion Maps and Wavelets 21, 113–127 (2006)
19. De Backer, S., Naud, A., Scheunders, P.: Non-linear dimensionality reduction techniques for unsupervised feature extraction. Original Research Article Pattern Recognition Letters 19(8), 711–720 (1998)
20. Lee, J.A., Verleysen, M.: Nonlinear dimensionality reduction. Springer, New York (2007)
21. Donoho, D.L., Grimes, C.: Hessian eigenmaps: Locally linear embedding techniques for high-dimensional data. PNAS 100, 5591–5596 (2003)
22. Belkin, M., Niyogi, P.: Laplacian eigenmaps for dimensionality reduction and data representation. Neural Comput. 15, 1373–1396 (2003)
23. vanderMaaten, L.J.P.: An introduction to dimensionality reduction using Matlab. Technical Report 07-06, MICC-IKAT, Maastricht University, Maastricht, The Netherlands (2007)
24. Baofeng, S.R., Gunn, G., Damper, R.I., Nelson, J.D.B.: Band Selection for Hyperspectral Image Classification Using Mutual Information. IEEE Geoscience and Remote Controle Sensing Letters 3(4), 522–526 (2006)
25. Eskicioglu, M., Fisher, P.S.: A survey of quality measures for gray scale image compression. In: 9th Computing in Aerospace Conference, pp. 49–61. AIAA (October 1993)
26. Hongtao, D., Hairong, Q., Wang, X., Ramanath, R., Snyder, W.E.: Band selection using component analysis for hyperspectral image processing. In: 32nd Workshop for Applied Imagery, Pattern Recognition, pp. 93–98 (2003)
27. Yang, J., Frangi, A.F., Yang, J., Jin, Z.: KPCA Plus LDA: A Complete Kernel Fisher Discriminant Framework for Feature Extraction and Recognition. IEEE Trans. Pattern Anal. Mach. Intell. 27(2), 230–244 (2005)
28. Saxena, A., Gupta, A., Mukerjee, A.: Non-linear Dimensionality Reduction by Locally Linear Isomaps. In: Pal, N.R., Kasabov, N., Mudi, R.K., Pal, S., Parui, S.K. (eds.) ICONIP 2004. LNCS, vol. 3316, pp. 1038–1043. Springer, Heidelberg (2004)

Revisiting Component Tree Based Segmentation Using Meaningful Photometric Informations

Michał Kazimierz Kowalczyk[1], Bertrand Kerautret[1], Benoît Naegel[2], and Jonathan Weber[1]

[1] Université de Lorraine, LORIA, UMR 7503, 54506, France
mkk@ekk.pl, {kerautre,jonathan.weber}@loria.fr
[2] Université de Strasbourg, LSIIT, UMR 7005 67412, France
b.naegel@unistra.fr

Abstract. This paper proposes to revisit a recent interactive segmentation algorithm based on an original image representation called the component-tree [1]. This method relies on an optimisation process allowing to choose a segmentation result fitting at best some image markers defined by the user. We propose different solutions to improve the efficiency of the method, in particular by including meaningful photometric informations and by assessing automatically the user parameter α.

1 Introduction

As segmentation is an ill-posed problem, interactive segmentation is considered as an efficient way for obtaining good results according to the user need. Moreover, recent devices with camera and tactile interface offer new perspectives and have shown their relevance for interactive segmentation [2]. Due to their restricted computing and memory capacities, segmentation algorithms implemented on tablets have to be computationally and memory inexpensive. Besides, tactile interface do not provide precise markers and majority of interactive segmentation method based on markers are very sensitive to marker quality. In this context, interactive segmentation based on component tree seems particularly relevant [1] since it is a fast, efficient and robust to rough markers segmentation method. But this algorithm fails to segment some type of object and needs a parameter α which can be tedious to set. So, in this article we propose some image preprocessing to improve object segmentation and introduce an automatic way of setting α based on meaningful scales [3]. Furthermore, we have implemented the proposed method on tactile tablet.

In the next section, we recall the principles of the component-tree based segmentation. We then propose some ways of including image information in component-tree based segmentation and illustrate their relevancy by some experiments.

2 Component-Tree Based Segmentation

In the following, we summarize the segmentation algorithm based on the component-tree structure described in [1].

L. Bolc et al. (Eds.): ICCVG 2012, LNCS 7594, pp. 475–482, 2012.

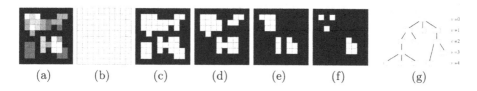

Fig. 1. (a) A grey-level image $I : [0,9]^2 \to [0,4]$ (from 0, in black, to 4, in white). (b–f) Threshold images $X_v(I)$ (white points) for v varying from 0 (b) to 4 (f). (g) The component-tree of I. Its levels correspond to increasing thresholding values v. The root (*i.e.*, the upper node located at the level $v = 0$) corresponds to the support $E = [0,9]^2$ of the image.

2.1   Component-Tree: Definition

A discrete grey-level image can be defined as a function $I : E \to V$, with $E \subseteq \mathbb{Z}^n$ a finite connected set and $V = [V_{min}, V_{max}] \subseteq \mathbb{Z}$ the finite set of values of I.

Let $X \subseteq \mathbb{Z}^n$ be a non-empty set. The set of connected components of X is denoted by $\mathcal{C}[X]$. Let X_v the thresholding function defined for any $v \in V$ by: $X_v(I) = \{p \in E \mid I(p) \geq v\}$. Let $\mathcal{K} = \bigcup_{v \in V} \mathcal{C}[X_v(I)]$ be the set of all the connected components obtained from the different thresholdings of I at values $v \in V$. The *component-tree* of I is the rooted tree $T = (\mathcal{K}, L, R)$ such that:

(i) $\mathcal{K} = \bigcup_{v \in V} \mathcal{C}[X_v(I)]$,
(ii) $L = \{(X,Y) \in \mathcal{K}^2 \mid Y \subset X \wedge \forall Z \in \mathcal{K}, Y \subseteq Z \subset X \Rightarrow Y = Z\}$,
(iii) $R = \sup(\mathcal{K}, \subseteq) = X_{V_{min}}(I) = E$.

The elements of $\mathcal{K}$ (resp. of L) are the *nodes* (resp. the *edges*) of T. The element R is the *root* of T. An example of component-tree is illustrated in Fig. 1.

2.2   Segmentation Based on Component-Tree

Based on this structure, a segmentation of I can be achieved by selecting a subset of nodes $\mathcal{K}' \subseteq \mathcal{K}$ and computing the associated binary image S defined as the set $S = \bigcup_{N \in \mathcal{K}'} N$ (see Fig. 2).

Let $G \subseteq E$ be a binary image: G can be, for example, a marker manually drawn on an original image I. The segmentation procedure consists in selecting automatically the subset $\mathcal{K}'$ of nodes in order to obtain the binary image S which is "closest" to G. More formally, given a similarity criterion d, the segmentation process is an optimisation problem consisting in determining the set:

$$\widehat{\mathcal{K}} = \arg \min_{\mathcal{K}' \subseteq \mathcal{K}} \left\{ d\left(\bigcup_{N \in \mathcal{K}'} N, G \right) \right\}.$$

Given a parameter $\alpha \in [0,1]$, the pseudo-distance d^α taking into account the amount of false-positives/negatives between the marker G and the binary segmentation $S = \bigcup_{N \in \mathcal{K}'} N$ is defined for any $X, Y \subseteq E$ by: $d^\alpha(X,Y) = \alpha.|X \setminus Y| + (1-\alpha).|Y \setminus X|$. The optimisation scheme is based on this pseudo-distance which

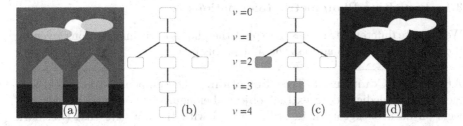

Fig. 2. (a) Example image and (b) its component-tree T. (c) In grey: subset $\mathcal{K}'$ of nodes selected from T. (d) The associated binary image S.

constitutes an efficient similarity measure between two binary images. It can be efficiently solved by using dynamic programming (see [1] for more details).

The segmentation procedure consists in (i) the manual delineation of a rough marker inside the object to segment and (ii) the interactive setting of the α parameter in order to choose the "best" segmentation. Indeed, the quality of the result is highly dependent of the α parameter as illustrated in Fig. 3.

Fig. 3. Illustration of the influence of the α parameter on the segmentation quality (represented in blue). The marker G is superimposed in red.

3   Including Meaningful Image Information in Component Tree

The segmentation method previously described suffers of two main drawbacks which limits its efficiency in real-world image applications. First, the method is devoted to the extraction of objects which are represented by a node of the component-tree: this limits the extraction process to bright objects surrounded by dark background. A second problem is the manual setting of the parameter α which can be tedious and time consuming.

In this paper, we propose to address these drawbacks by: (i) exploiting the contrast information given by the marker in order to automatically compute the most relevant component-tree structure enabling to extract the object and (ii) determining automatically the most relevant α parameter based on gradient information and contour smoothness.

3.1   Exploiting Photometric Informations

We propose different strategies to exploit the photometric informations given by the marker in order to address the first problem.

Automatic Component Tree Selection. The component-tree based segmentation is dedicated to extract objects belonging to nodes, *i.e.* bright objects on dark background. In order to deal with the opposite case (*i.e.* dark objects on bright background) we need to compute the dual component-tree (the component-tree of the negative image). We propose an efficient strategy to determine automatically the nature of the tree.

Let $\mu_I(G)$ be the mean value of the points of the image I belonging to the marker G: $\mu_I(G) = \frac{1}{|G|} \sum_{p \in G} I(p)$.

Let N_G be a neighbourhood region associated to the marker G. Let $c_I(X,Y)$ be the contrast function defined by:

$$c_I(X,Y) = \mu_I(X) - \mu_I(Y),$$

with $X, Y \subseteq E$ and $X \cap Y = \emptyset$. If $c_I(G, N_G) < 0$, it means that the marked object is possibly darker than its neighbourhood: in this case the dual component-tree of source image I is computed. In this paper we consider the neighbourhood defined as the complement of G, *i.e.* $N_G = G^c = E \setminus G$.

Image Values Shifting. In order to deal with objects which corresponds neither to component-tree nor to dual component-tree nodes, we propose to transform the source image. Let $s_o(I)$ the function defined for all $p \in E$ by:

$$s_o(I)(p) = V_{max} - |(I(p) - o)|,$$

where $o \in V$ is a reference colour defined by the marker G (*i.e.* $o = \mu_I(G)$). This function enables (as in [4]) to enhance pixels having a colour close to the marker, therefore favouring the presence of the marked object in a leaf of the associated component-tree.

Exploiting Colour Information. Finally, we propose a way of working with colour images (*i.e.* images having their values in $V \subseteq \mathbb{Z}^k$). Indeed, the component-tree algorithm is devoted to grayscale images: its extension to colour images is not trivial and has been addressed in [4] and [5]. One possibility consists in transforming a colour image in a grayscale one in order to obtain a total ordering on the set of values.

For this purpose, we propose to transform the colour image by taking into account the most significants colour channels with respect to the local contrast between the marker and its background. More formally, let m be the ponderation function defined for each $p \in E$ by:

$$m(I)(p) = \frac{w_1 * I_1(p) + w_2 * I_2(p) + \ldots + w_n * I_k(p)}{w_1 + w_2 + \ldots + w_k},$$

where the $I_{i=0}^{k}$ represent the k colour channels of I and the $w_{i=0}^{k}$ are the weights associated to each channels.

Let r_i be the function giving, for each channel I_i, a contrast measure between the marker and its neighborhood: $r_i(G) = c_{I_i}(G, N_G)^2$.

We take $w_i = r_i(G)$ in order to favour, in the ponderation function, the channels in which the marker has a high contrast with respect to its neighborhood. Our approach allows to use RGB as well as CMYK and HSL/HSV (after translation hue to range $[0, 255]$) colour models. We can also remove channels that are not significant enough (by imposing for example a minimal threshold on the weights). The full preprocessing algorithm includes the three strategies described above and is illustrated in Fig. 4.

Fig. 4. Illustration of the image preprocessing based on image marker photometric informations. Two different markers G_a and G_b were used to experiment the image transformation from the source image (a). The resulting images are shown in (c,d).

3.2 Automatic Setting of the Alpha Parameter

As illustrated in the previous section 2, the quality of the resulting segmentation is very sensitive to the choice of the parameter α. To remove this limitation, we propose to define a criterion allowing to assess automatically the best parameter α. In the same spirit as the deformable model based algorithms, we propose to take into account the image gradient intensity and the smoothness contour quality.

Meaningful Scale Detection on Discrete Contour. To evaluate the degree of contour quality we use the method of the meaningful scale detection which allows to detect automatically what is the relevant scale of a given contour [3]. This method is based on the multiscale analysis of the length of the digital straight segments primitive. Note that this method can also be evaluated online [6]. Fig. 5 illustrates such meaningful scale detection obtained on synthetic and real image.

Note that given a maximal scale S_{max} the meaningful scale detection can be considered as parameter free. In the following we will denote by $\eta(p)$ the amount of noise level given for a contour point p. This noise level values will be include in $[1, S_{max}]$.

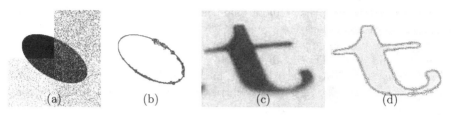

Fig. 5. Illustration of the meaningful scale detection on two images tests (a,c). The resulting meaningful scale is illustrated on images (b,d). For each contour point we display a blue box of size equals to the detected noise level.

Image Gradient Intensity. We also propose to choose, among all the possible segmentations induced by the α parameter, the one whose contour coincides with regions of high gradient intensity.

Let $W \subseteq E$ a segmentation result, and $O \subseteq W$ the set of contour pixels of W. Let $Y = \{O_1, O_2, \ldots, O_n\}$ the set of all connected contours of the result and D the longest contour of Y (*i.e.* $|D|$ is maximal for all $O_i \in Y$). Let $j(O_i)$ be weight function defined for a contour as follows:

$$j(O_i) = \frac{|D|}{(|D| - |O_i| + 1) * N_{MP}(D)},$$

where $N_{MP}(D)$ is the number of meaningful pixels p of D (the number of pixels of D for which $\eta(p) = 1$). We have tested several criteria and obtained the best results by choosing the segmentation minimizing:

$$k = \frac{\sum_{O_i \in Y} |O_i|}{(\sum_{O_i \in Y} g_{max}(O_i) * j(O_i))},$$

where $g_{max}(O_i) = \sum_{p \in O_i}(\max\{g(p')|p \in O_i \wedge max(|x_p - x_{p'}|, |y_p - y_{p'}|) \leq 1\})$ and g is the image gradient. In this work, the gradient of I is approximated using the Sobel operator.

4   Experiments and Comparisons

To evaluate the efficiency of the proposed solutions, we have first experimented the contrast feature improvements in comparison to the initial component tree algorithm. Fig. 6 shows the results obtained on two real images. We can clearly see that the proposed contrast based method really improves the original approach.

The efficiency of the alpha automatic settings was evaluated on four various test images and compared with another segmentation method called *Morphological Snakes* which can also be applied in real time [7] (see Fig. 7). The improved component tree algorithm presents better quality result and has no parameter to tune contrary the morphological snake approach. Note that the source code of an online version working on *Android* and *PC* is available [8].

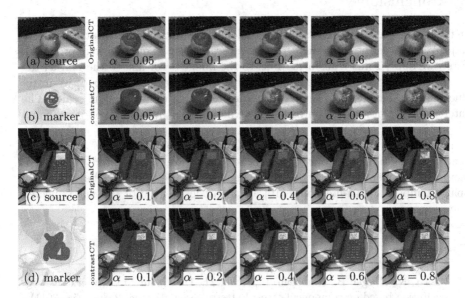

Fig. 6. Comparisons of the original Component Tree Algorithm (originalCT) and the improved algorithm exploiting contrast information (contrastCT) for different values of the parameter α

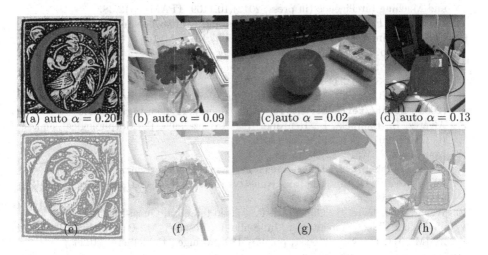

Fig. 7. Experiments of the automatic set of the alpha value (a-d) and comparisons with the *Morphological Snake* algorithm [7] (e-h) with the same markers than experiments (a-d) and with the expansion ballonforce (experimented from the author source code and displayed with the DGtal library [9])

5   Conclusion

In this paper, we have addressed the problem of interactive segmentation. Several improvements to the component-tree based segmentation method were proposed. First, we apply some transformations to the image according to the marker defined in order to adapt the component-tree to the user need. Second, we introduce an automatic way of setting α parameter based on meaningful scales. The interest of the proposed approach was experimented by some experiments and comparisons.

In future works, we will focus on highly-textured objects, which are not currently segmentable with our approach. Moreover, we plan to study the extension of component-tree to video data, one possible solution can be the use of spatio-temporal quasi-flat zones [10] as tree nodes instead of spatial connected components.

References

1. Passat, N., Naegel, B., Rousseau, F., Koob, M., Dietemann, J.L.: Interactive segmentation based on component-trees. Pattern Recognition 44, 2539–2554 (2011)
2. Liu, D., Xiong, Y., Shapiro, L., Pulli, K.: Robust interactive image segmentation with automatic boundary refinement. In: Proc. of ICIP, pp. 225–228 (2010)
3. Kerautret, B., Lachaud, J.O.: Meaningful scales detection along digital contours for unsupervised local noise estimation. IEEE Transactions on Pattern Analysis and Machine Intelligence (in press, 2012),10.1109/TPAMI.2012.38.
4. Naegel, B., Passat, N.: Component-Trees and Multi-value Images: A Comparative Study. In: Wilkinson, M.H.F., Roerdink, J.B.T.M. (eds.) ISMM 2009. LNCS, vol. 5720, pp. 261–271. Springer, Heidelberg (2009)
5. Passat, N., Naegel, B.: An extension of component-trees to partial orders. In: Proc. of ICIP, pp. 3981–3984 (2009)
6. Kerautret, B., Lachaud, J.O.: Meaningful scale detection: online demonstration (2009), http://kerrecherche.iutsd.uhp-nancy.fr/MeaningfulBoxes
7. Alvarez, L., Baumela, L., Henrquez, P., Mrquez-Neila, P.: Morphological snakes. In: CVPR 2010, pp. 2197–2202 (2010)
8. Kowalczyk, M.K: (2012),
   https://github.com/michal-kowalczyk/RealTimeCTSegmentation
9. DGtal team: DGtal: Digital geometry tools and algorithms library (2012), http://liris.cnrs.fr/dgtal.
10. Weber, J., Lefèvre, S., Gançarski, P.: Spatio-temporal Quasi-Flat Zones for Morphological Video Segmentation. In: Soille, P., Pesaresi, M., Ouzounis, G.K. (eds.) ISMM 2011. LNCS, vol. 6671, pp. 178–189. Springer, Heidelberg (2011)

Oversampling Methods for Classification of Imbalanced Breast Cancer Malignancy Data

Bartosz Krawczyk[1], Łukasz Jeleń[2,3], Adam Krzyżak[4], and Thomas Fevens[4]

[1] Department of Systems and Computer Networks, Wrocław University of Technology
Wybrzeże Wyspiańskiego 27, 50-370 Wrocław, Poland
bartosz.krawczyk@pwr.wroc.pl
[2] Wrocław School of Applied Informatics
Wejherowska 28, 54-238 Wrocław Poland
ljelen@horyzont.eu
[3] Institute of Agricultural Engineering
Wrocław University of Environments and Life Science
Chełmońskiego 37-41, 51-630 Wrocław Poland
[4] Department of Computer Science and Software Engineering, Concordia University
1455 de Maisonneuve Blvd. West Montréal, Quebec, Canada
{krzyzak,fevens}@cse.concordia.ca

Abstract. During breast cancer malignancy grading the main problem that has direct influence on the classification is imbalanced number of cases of the malignancy classes. This poses a challenge for pattern recognition algorithms and leads to a significant decrease of the classification accuracy for the minority class. In this paper we present an approach which ameliorates such a problem. We describe and compare several state of the art methods, that are based on the oversampling approach, i.e. introduction of artificial objects into the dataset to eliminate the disproportion among classes. We also describe the automatic thresholding and fuzzy c-means algorithms used for the nuclei segmentation from fine needle aspirates. Based on the segmented images a set of 15 feattures used for classification process was extracted.

Keywords: pattern recognition, image processing, imbalanced classification, oversampling, classifier ensemble, breast cancer, nuclei segmentation.

1 Introduction

Automatic detection of pathologies from medical images is currently a very active and important field of research worldwide. This involves a creation of automated computer frameworks capable of assisting doctors during the diagnostic process. In this paper we concentrate on two parts of such a system: segmentation of nuclei and classification of malignancies based on the features extracted from the segmented images. Determination of cancer malignancy grade is a very important part of the diagnostic process. A fine needle aspiration biopsy (FNA) and mammography are the most common diagnostic tools. FNA is an invasive procedure to extract a small cytological sample of the questionable breast tissue. It is

L. Bolc et al. (Eds.): ICCVG 2012, LNCS 7594, pp. 483–490, 2012.

used to describe the type of the cancer in detail. Using this method pathologists can very adequately describe not only the type of the cancer but also its genealogy and malignancy. The determination of the malignancy is essential when predicting the progression of the cancer and is performed by assigning a malignancy grade to the case. To help in this very difficult task a grading scale was proposed by Bloom and Richardson in 1957 [2]. This system is based on grading cells polymorphy, the ability to reform histoformative structures, and mitotic index. All of these features are described by the Bloom-Richardson scheme as three factors that use a point based scale for assessing each feature. The malignancy of the tumor is assigned a grade that depends on the quantitative values of the above factors and is determined by the summation of all awarded points for each factor. Depending on the value, the tumor is assigned a low, intermediate or high malignancy grade.

2   Nuclei Segmentation

The role of a classification system is to assign an item to a certain category called a class, based on the features describing that item. To be able to extract features, the unwanted data from the image has to be removed. This is where segmentation algorithms are applied. In this study we make use of two segmentation algorithms: automatic thresholding and fuzzy c–means. The choice of the segmentation method depends on the type of the image used for feature calculations. During the fine needle aspiration biopsy examination two images with different magnifications are taken into consideration: low magnification (100x) and high magnification (400x). When low magnification images are used then an automatic thresholding is used to segment nuclear groups and for high magnification images a fuzzy c–means technique is applied.

In this paper we make use of the iterative clustering approach for automatic image thresholding. This method was proposed by Riddler and Calvard [14]. In principle, their method seeks a threshold T, represented by a curve, within an image, that is restricted to have a bimodal histogram and the final threshold level is calculated according to the following equation:

$$T = \frac{\mu_1 + \mu_2}{2}, \tag{1}$$

where μ_1 and μ_2 are the means of the components separated by T.

Due to the staining process of FNA images, the red channel provides best information about nuclear structures out of the three RGB channels. During the staining process, nuclei stain with shades purple and when red channel is extracted all the nuclear features are preserved while the background information is lost. This observation allows us to extract and threshold the image red channel and then to use it for further feature extraction. Fig. 1a shows the obtained segmentation boundaries superimposed on the original image.

To segment nuclei from high magnification images a fuzzy approach of Klir and Yuan [10] is used to partition the image. In general, a set of data $X =$

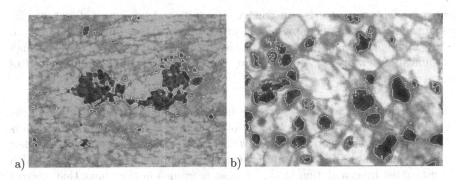

Fig. 1. Segmentation boundaries obtained for images. a) 100x magnification with automatic thresholding, b) 400x magnification with fuzzy c–means

$\{x_1, x_2, ..., x_n\}$ is supposed to be divided into c clusters with assumption that $P = \{A_1, A_2, ..., A_c\}$ is known pseudo–partition where A_i is a vector of all memberships of x_k to cluster i. The memberships are defined by equation 2 below if $\|x_k - v_i\|^2 > 0$ for all $i \in \{1, 2, ..., c\}$. If $\|x_k - v_i\|^2 = 0$ for some $i \in I \subseteq \{1, 2, ..., c\}$ the memberships are defined as a nonnegative real number satisfying equation 3 below for $i \in I$.

$$A_i(x_k) = \left[\sum_{j=1}^{c} \left(\frac{\|x_k - v_i\|^2}{\|x_k - v_j\|^2}\right)^{\frac{1}{m-1}}\right]^{-1} \tag{2}$$

$$\sum_{i \in I} A_i(x_k) = 1 \tag{3}$$

where $m > 1$ is a weight that controls the fuzzy membership.

The clustering algorithm seeks a set P that minimizes the performance index $J_m(P)$ which is defined by equation 4. The example of the segmentation is shown in Fig. 2b.

$$J_m(P) = \sum_{k=1}^{n} \sum_{i=1}^{c} [A_i(x_k)]^m \|x_k - v_i\|^2. \tag{4}$$

The database used in this study consists of 340 images of fine needle aspirates with known malignancy grades collected at the Department of Pathology of Medical University of Wrocław, Poland. All of the images in the database were stained with the Haematoxylin and Eosin technique (HE) which yielded purple and black stain for nuclei, shades of pink for cytoplasm and orange/red for red blood cells. The images had a resolutionesolution of 96 dots per inch (dpi) and a size of 764x572 pixels.

3   Feature Extraction

When the nuclei has been successfully segmented from the image, the features that allow for malignancy classification are calculated. Based on the extracted features a feature vector is constructed. It consists of two types of features depending on the magnification of the input image. These images are used to assess different cellular properties and lead to the calculation of low and high magnification features [9]. In this study we have extracted the following set of features:

a) **100x magnification features** – here we calculate the area of the nuclei groups (A_g) as the average number of nuclei pixels. This feature represents the tendency of cells to form groups. If A_g is large then there is one or few large groups in the image. Another feature is number of groups (NG) which is estimated by calculation of the number of groups in the image that weren't removed during segmentation process. Here, if NG is large then there are numerous groups in the image, which suggests high malignancy. The last low magnification feature extracted for malignancy classifiaction is called dispertion. The dispersion is a statistical variation of cluster areas (A_i). Large values of this feature represent less disperse cells and therefore lower malignancy of the caner [8].

b) **400x magnification features** – the high magnification features include features describing the nuclei polymorphy and orientation as well as features calculated from the image histogram and red channel histogram [8]. The first high malignancy feature used in this study is a perimeter of a nucleus which is the length of the nuclear envelope. Calculated as the length of the polygonal approximation of the boundary (B). To be able to distinguish between healthy and cancerous cells we also need to define a measure that represents the convexity of the nucleus. For this purpose we calulated a feature called convexity (C). It is defined as the ratio of nucleus area and its convex hull [9], which is the minimal area of the convex polygon that contains the nucleus. Another set of features describes the orientation of the nucleus. Here we use the x–centroid of the nucleus, its orientation and vertical projection. These features are calculated based on the binary representation of the nucleus after the segmetnation. Additionally we also calculate one feature based on the image momentum. We call that feature φ_3 momentum feature.

During the malignancy estimation not only the shape information is taken into account but also a variability of color between the healthy and cancerous nuclei. To assess this we have extracted three histogram features such as histogram mean, energy and textural homogeneity. Due to the staining process, the nuclei is stained in shades of purple and when the red channel is extracted the nuclear structures are more visible. This allows us to calculate additional three features from the histogram of the image red channel. These features are: red channel histogram mean, skew and width.

According to the above description, we calculated features for all of the images in the database and constructed a 15 element feature vector that is later used for the determination of the breast cancer malignancy grade.

4   Oversampling Techniques for Imbalanced Classification

A data set is imbalanced if the classification categories are not approximately equally represented. Often real-world data sets are predominately composed of normal examples with only a small percentage of abnormal or interesting examples. The performance of classification algorithms is typically evaluated using predictive accuracy. However, this is not appropriate when the data is imbalanced. Therefore this is a crucial problem in the process of pattern recognition, very often encountered in real-life applications, such as bioinformatics or chemoinformatics [11].

4.1   Artificial Data-Based Oversampling

The most common approach to resolve this problem is the SMOTE algorithm [3]. For a subset $S_{min} \in S$, where S stands for training set and S_{min} for minority class, the *k-nearest neighbors* (kNN) are considered for each one of the examples $x_i \in S_{min}$. The *kNN* are the K elements of S_{min} whose Euclidian distance between themselves and x_i exhibits the smallest magnitude along the n-dimensions of feature space X. To create a synthetic data, one of the *kNN* is randomly selected, its corresponding feature vector difference is multiplied by a random number between [0 - 1] and added to x_i:

$$x_{new} = x_i + (\widehat{x_i} - x_i) \times \delta \tag{5}$$

where x_i is the minority example under consideration, $\widehat{x_i}$ is one of the kNN of x_i (randomly chosen) and δ is a random number between 0 and 1. The resulting synthetic example is some point along the segment joining x_i under consideration and the randomly selected $\widehat{x_i}$.

In recent years several modifications of the SMOTE algorithm have been introduced. In this paper we use two of them. Only short descriptions will be provided, as they are extensions of the original SMOTE algorithm.

First one is the Adaptive Synthetic Sampling (ADASYN) [7]. It uses a weighted distribution, set individually for each of the objects from minority class with respect to their level of 'difficulty' in learning. It means that more synthetic data is generated for minority class objects that are harder to learn than those minority objects that do not contribute to the increase of the classification error. According to its authors, the ADASYN approach improves learning with respect to the data distributions in two ways: it reduces the bias introduced by the class imbalance and adaptively shifts the classification boundary toward the more difficult objects from the minority class.

We also use the Ranked Minority Over-sampling (RAMO) [5], which adaptively ranks minority class objects with respect to a given sampling probability distribution, which should use the underlying data distribution as a base. RAMO can adaptively shift the decision boundary toward objects which cause classification errors by using a hypothesis assessment procedure. It is an extension of the ADASYN algorithm, but instead of specifying the number of artificial instances generated for each minority object, RAMO determines the chance of each minority example for generating the synthetic instances.

4.2 Ensemble-Based Oversampling

An interesting approach for dealing with imbalanced datasets is the use of classifiers ensembles. The idea behind them is to combine several learners together, which may result in better performance than any single committee member could deliver. Yet using canonical ensembles for imbalance class problem is not enough. Therefore in recent years there have been proposed several modifications of ensembles, such as cost-sensitive approach [16], one-class ensembles [12] or committees using preprocessing methods [6]. In this paper we will concentrate on the last group, testing two types of ensembles which use oversampling.

Unlike canonical bagging OverBagging [17]do not use a random sampling of the whole data-set. Instead it conducts an oversampling for each of the bags separately, before training classifiers on them. It increases the number of minority class objects by their replication, but at the same time all majority class objects can be a part of the new bootstrap iteration. In this approach all instances will take part in at least one bag, but each bootstrap iteration will contain more instances than input dataset.

SMOTEBoost introduces synthetic instances just before the assignment of weights in original AdaBoost.M2 algorithm [4]. The weights of the new instances are proportional to the total number of instances in the new, expanded dataset. Therefore the weights of artificial objects are always the same, while the weights of original objects change with respect to the boosting algorithm. After each iteration a new oversampling is applied, which increases the diversity of the ensemble.

5   Experimental Investigations

In the following experiment we used a dataset consisting of 170 objects in total. 144 objects come from the intermediate malignancy class and 26 objects come from the high malignancy class. This means that the imbalance ratio was almost 6:1. Each of the objects is described by a 15 element feature vector.

5.1 Set-Up

As a base classifier we have used a Support Vector Machine (SVM) with the Gaussian kernel and Sequential Minimal Optimization training procedure [15].

All experiments were carried out in R language [13] and computer implementations of used classification and preprocessing methods were taken from the dedicated packages built-in the software mentioned above or were implemented by the authors.

For testing, we used a statistical test to compare the results and judge if their differences were statistically significant. For this purpose, we used a combined 5 x 2 cv F Test [1], where preprocessing procedures were run independently for each of the folds.

5.2 Results

The results of the experiment are presented in the Table 1. They show classifiers sensitivity and specificity. Numbers in the *statistical test* row indicates in comparison with which other tested classification methods there exists a statistically significant differences.

Table 1. Results of the experiment

	SVM[1]	SMOTE[2]	ADASYN[3]	RAMO[4]	OverBagging[5]	SMOTEBoost[6]
Sensitivity	15.38	73.07	76.92	76.92	84.61	**88.46**
Specificity	**92.36**	84.72	85.41	79.86	86.05	88.88
Statistical test	2, 3, 4, 5, 6	1, 5, 6	1, 5, 6	1, 5, 6	1, 2, 3, 4	1, 2, 3, 4

5.3 Discussion

As we can see in Table 1 the increase of recognition rate of minority class always leads to some decrease of the accuracy for majority class objects. This is a trade-off that is worth its cost, as early detection of high malignancy breast cancer is crucial for the health and life of the patients. All the tested methods improved significantly the sensitivity of classification. The ensemble methods outperformed simple preprocessing approaches based on a single classifier. Best results were returned by SMOTEBoost algorithm, yet it is important to note, that statistical test indicates that there is no significant difference between this committee and OverBagging approach.

6 Conclusions

In this paper we described an imbalance data problem, that arises during design of clinical decision support system for automatic breast cancer malignancy grading. We have described the whole process of decision making form image acquisition, through image segmentation and feature extraction, to classification step. It is important to note that segmentation methods used are very precise and allow for extraction of good features. The proposed feature vector allows for high quality classification of breast cancer images.

By using methods based on oversampling we have significantly increased the recognition rate of a minority class. Experimental results showed that hybrid approaches, consisting of oversampling algorithms tuned to the classifier ensembles, return better results than simple data preprocessing, independent from the classifiers at hand.

In our future works we would like to examine the behavior of more ensembles for imbalance class problems, not only those based on oversampling.

References

1. Alpaydin, E.: Combined 5 x 2 cv f test for comparing supervised classification learning algorithms. Neural Computation 11(8), 1885–1892 (1999)
2. Bloom, H.J.G., Richardson, W.W.: Histological Grading and Prognosis in Breast Cancer. British Journal of Cancer 11, 359–377 (1957)
3. Chawla, N.V., Bowyer, K.W., Hall, L.O., Kegelmeyer, W.P.: Smote: Synthetic minority over-sampling technique. Journal of Artificial Intelligence Research 16, 321–357 (2002)
4. Chawla, N.V., Lazarevic, A., Hall, L.O., Bowyer, K.W.: SMOTEBoost: Improving Prediction of the Minority Class in Boosting. In: Lavrač, N., Gamberger, D., Todorovski, L., Blockeel, H. (eds.) PKDD 2003. LNCS (LNAI), vol. 2838, pp. 107–119. Springer, Heidelberg (2003)
5. Chen, S., He, H., Garcia, E.A.: Ramoboost: Ranked minority oversampling in boosting. IEEE Transactions on Neural Networks 21(10), 1624–1642 (2010)
6. Galar, M., Fernandez, A., Barrenechea, E., Bustince, H., Herrera, F.: A review on ensembles for the class imbalance problem: Bagging-, boosting-, and hybrid-based approaches. IEEE Transactions on Systems, Man and Cybernetics Part C: Applications and Reviews (2011) (article in press)
7. He, H., Bai, Y., Garcia, E.A., Li, S.: Adasyn: Adaptive synthetic sampling approach for imbalanced learning. In: Proceedings of the International Joint Conference on Neural Networks, pp. 1322–1328 (2008)
8. Jeleń, L.: Computerized Cancer Malignancy Garding of Fine Needle Aspirates. PhD thesis, Concordia University (2009)
9. Jeleń, L., Krzyżak, A., Fevens, T.: Comparison of Pleomorphic and Structural Features Used for Breast Cancer Malignancy Classification. In: Bergler, S. (ed.) Canadian AI. LNCS (LNAI), vol. 5032, pp. 138–149. Springer, Heidelberg (2008)
10. Klir, G.J., Yuan, B.: Fuzzy Sets and Fuzzy Logic: Theory and Applications. Prentice-Hall, New Jersey (1995)
11. Krawczyk, B.: Pattern recognition approach to classifying cyp 2c19 isoform. Central European Journal of Medicine 7(1), 38–44 (2012)
12. Krawczyk, B., Woźniak, M.: Combining Diverse One-Class Classifiers. In: Corchado, E., Snášel, V., Abraham, A., Woźniak, M., Graña, M., Cho, S.-B. (eds.) HAIS 2012. LNCS (LNAI), vol. 7209, pp. 590–601. Springer, Heidelberg (2012)
13. R Development Core Team. R: A Language and Environment for Statistical Computing. R Foundation for Statistical Computing, Vienna, Austria (2008) ISBN 3-900051-07-0
14. Ridler, T.W., Calvard, S.: Picture thresholding using an iterative selection. IEEE Trans. System, Man and Cybernetics 8, 630–632 (1978)
15. Schölkopf, B., Smola, A.J.: Learning with kernels: support vector machines, regularization, optimization, and beyond. Adaptive Computation and Machine Learning. MIT Press (2002)
16. Sun, Y., Kamel, M.S., Wong, A.K.C., Wang, Y.: Cost-sensitive boosting for classification of imbalanced data. Pattern Recognition 40(12), 3358–3378 (2007)
17. Wang, S., Yao, X.: Diversity analysis on imbalanced data sets by using ensemble models. In: 2009 IEEE Symposium on Computational Intelligence and Data Mining, CIDM 2009 Proceedings, pp. 324–331 (2009)

View Independent Human Gait Recognition Using Markerless 3D Human Motion Capture

Tomasz Krzeszowski[2,1], Bogdan Kwolek[2,1], Agnieszka Michalczuk[1],
Adam Świtoński[1,3], and Henryk Josiński[1,3]

[1] Polish-Japanese Institute of Information Technology
Koszykowa 86, 02-008 Warszawa, Poland
bytom@pjwstk.edu.pl
[2] Rzeszow University of Technology
Al. Powstańców Warszawy 12, 35-959 Rzeszów, Poland
{tkrzeszo,bkwolek}@prz.edu.pl
[3] Silesian University of Technology
Akademicka 16, Gliwice, 44-101 Poland
{Adam.Switonski,Henryk.Josinski}@polsl.pl

Abstract. We present an algorithm for view-independent human gait recognition. The human gait recognition is achieved using data obtained by our markerless 3D motion tracking algorithm. The tensorial gait data were reduced by multilinear principal component analysis and subsequently classified. The performance of the motion tracking algorithm was evaluated using ground-truth data from MoCap. The classification accuracy was determined using video sequences with walking performers. Experiments on multiview video sequences show the promising effectiveness of the proposed algorithm.

1 Introduction

People are able to identify acquaintances on the basis of their walking style, bearing or carriage as one walks. Successful identification can be done even when acquaintance is too far to be recognized by his/her face. Gait arises from coordinated, cyclic combination of movements that lead to individual style or manner of walking. It is the only feature suitable for human identification when the subject is far from the camera. Recently, vision-based gait recognition has attracted increased attention due to possible applications in intelligent biometrics and visual surveillance systems [2].

The seminal work in the area of gait recognition was done in the psychology field [8]. It is commonly believed upon that human visual system is very sensitive to motion stimuli, although the exact mechanism of perception is not fully clear. Johansson's seminal psychophysical experiments [6] demonstrated that humans can recognize biological motion, such as gait on the basis of a small set of points attached to the human body, which are called Moving Light Displays (MLDs). These findings inspired computer vision community to start research on extracting characteristic gait signatures from image sequences for human identification.

L. Bolc et al. (Eds.): ICCVG 2012, LNCS 7594, pp. 491–500, 2012.

In one of the earliest approaches to automatic identification by gait, the gait signature was derived from the spatio-temporal pattern of a walking person [13]. It was assumed that the head and the legs have distinctive signatures in XT (translation and time) dimensions. They first find the bounding contours of the walker, and then fit a five elements stick model on them. On a database of 26 sequences of five different subjects, taken at different times during the day the classification rate varied from nearly 60% to 80% depending on weighting factors.

There are two major approaches to gait recognition, namely appearance based (model free) and model based ones [12]. The majority of the approaches proposed for gait-based identification rely on analysis of image sequences acquired by a single camera. The main drawback of such approaches is that they can perform recognition from a specific viewpoint, usually fronto-parallel. To achieve view-independent motion classification [14], recently, an image-based reconstruction method was proposed [1]. However, in tracking real human movements the 2D models are often unsuitable due to their inability to take into account the self-intersection constraints as well as to encode joint angle limits. Recently, a gait database [5] has been developed to stimulate research on gait recognition in the presence of occlusion.

The major advantage of the model-based approaches is that they can reliably handle self-occlusion, noise, scale and rotation, as opposed to silhouette-based approaches. In general, the methods that are based on holistic space-time features or space-time shapes depend more on the training data in comparison to the model-based approaches. One of the earliest model-based approaches to gait-based human identification was developed by Cunado in 1997 [3]. The gait signature has been derived from the spectra of measurements of the thigh's orientation. A recognition rate of 90% on a database of 10 subjects was achieved.

Model-based gait recognition algorithms are usually based on 2D fronto-parallel body models and model human body structure explicitly, with support of the biomechanics of human gait [18]. Some work has also been done on coarser human body models. For example, in [10] several ellipses are fitted to different parts of the binary silhouettes and the parameters of these ellipses (e.g., location and orientation) are used as gait features. Coarse models are usually employed in 3D approaches to gait recognition. The 3D approaches to gait recognition are far more resistant to view changes in comparison to 2D ones. In [17], an approach relying on matching 3D motion models to images, and then tracking and restoring the motion parameters is proposed. The evaluation was performed on datasets with four people, i.e. 2 women and 2 men walking at 9 different speeds ranging from 3 to 7 km/h by increments of 0.5 km/h. Motion models were constructed using Vicon motion capture system. To overcome the non-frontal pose problem, more recently multi-camera based gait recognition methods have also been developed [4]. In the mentioned work, joint positions of the whole body are employed as a feature for gait recognition.

In this work we present an algorithm for view-independent gait recognition, which is based on 3D articulated body model. The motion parameters are estimated using our algorithm for markerless human motion tracking. The algorithm captures human motion on the basis of video sequences acquired by four calibrated and synchronized cameras. We show the tracking performance of the motion tracking algorithm using ground-truth data from a commercial motion capture (MoCap) system from Vicon Nexus. The captured motion was stored in ASF/AMC data format. Afterwards, a second order tensor was calculated. The tensorial gait data were reduced using Multilinear Principal Components Analysis (MPCA) algorithm and then classified.

2 Markerless System for Articulated Motion Tracking

2.1 3D Human Body Model

The human body can be represented by a 3D articulated model formed by 11 rigid segments representing key parts of the human body. The model of a human body specifies a kinematic chain, where the connections of body parts comprise a parent-child relationship, see Fig. 1. In our approach the pelvis is the root node in the kinematic chain. Then the pelvis is the parent of the upper legs, which are in turn the parents of the lower legs. In consequence, the position of a particular body limb is partially determined by the position of its parent body part and partially by its own pose parameters. In this way, the pose parameters of a body part are described with respect to the local coordinate frame determined by its parent. The 3D geometric model is utilized to simulate the human motion and to recover the current position, orientation and joint angles. Although typical human bodies can be represented by such model, individuals have different body part sizes, limb lengths, and exhibit different ranges of motion. In our approach the individual parameters are pre-specified. For each degree of freedom the model has constraints beyond which movement is not allowed. The model is constructed from truncated cones and is used to generate contours, which are then compared with edge contours. The configuration of the body is parameterized by the position and the orientation of the pelvis in the global coordinate system and the angles between the connected limbs.

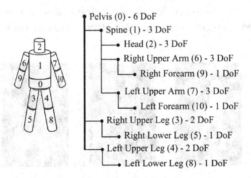

Fig. 1. 3D human body model. Human body consisting of 11 segments (left), hierarchical structure (right).

2.2   Articulated Motion Tracking

Estimating 3D motion can be cast as a non-linear, high-dimensional optimization problem. The degree of similarity between the real and the estimated pose is evaluated using an objective function. Recently, particle swarm optimization (PSO) [7] has been successfully applied to body motion tracking [19][9]. In PSO each particle follows simple position and velocity update equations. Thanks to interaction between particles a collective behavior arises. It leads to the emergence of global and collective search capabilities, which allow the particles to gravitate towards the global extremum. Human motion tracking can be achieved by a sequence of static PSO-based optimizations, followed by re-diversification of the particles to cover the possible poses in the next time step. In this work the tracking of human motion is achieved using the Annealed Particle Swarm Optimization (APSO) [9].

2.3   Fitness Function

The fitness function expresses the degree of similarity between the real and the estimated human pose. It is calculated on the basis of following expression: $f(x) = 1 - (f_1(x)^{w_1} \cdot f_2(x)^{w_2})$, where x stands for the state (pose), whereas w denotes weighting coefficients that were determined experimentally. The function $f_1(x)$ reflects the degree of overlap between the extracted body and the projected model's into 2D image. The function $f_2(x)$ reflects the edge distance-based fitness. Figure 2 illustrates the extraction of the body and calculation of the edge distance. A background subtraction algorithm [9] is employed to extract the binary image of the person, see Figure 2b. The binary image is then utilized as a mask to suppress edges not belonging to the person, see Figure 2d.

The calculation of the objective function is the most consuming operation. Moreover, in multi-view tracking the 3D model is projected and then rendered in each camera's view. Therefore, in our approach the objective function is calculated by OpenMP threads, which communicate via the shared memory. Each core calculates the fitness score for single camera and every PSO thread has access to the shared memory with the objective function values.

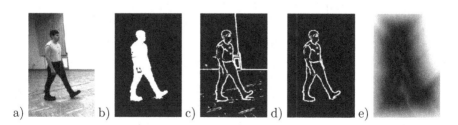

Fig. 2. Person segmentation. Input image a), foreground b), gradient magnitude c), masked gradient image d), edge distance map e).

3   Gait Characterization and Recognition

The markerless motion tracking was achieved using color images of size 960×540, which were acquired at 25 fps by four synchronized and calibrated cameras. Each pair of the cameras is approximately perpendicular to the other camera pair. Figure 3 depicts the location of the cameras in the laboratory.

Fig. 3. Layout of the laboratory with four cameras. The images illustrate the initial model configuration, overlaid on the image in first frame and seen in view 1, 2, 3, 4.

A commercial motion capture system from Vicon Nexus was employed to provide the ground truth data. The system uses reflective markers and sixteen cameras to recover the 3D location of such markers. The data are delivered with rate of 100 Hz and the synchronization between the MoCap and multi-camera system is achieved using hardware from Vicon Giganet Lab.

A set of $M = 39$ markers was attached to main body parts. From the above set of markers, 4 markers were placed on the head, 7 markers on each arm, 12 on the legs, 5 on the torso and 4 markers were attached to the pelvis. Given such a placement of the markers on the human body and the estimated human pose, which has been calculated by our algorithm, the corresponding positions of virtual markers on the body model were determined. Figure 4 illustrates the distances between ankles, which were determined by our markerless motion tracking algorithm and the MoCap system. High overlap between both curves formulates a rationale for the usage of the markerless motion tracking to achieve view-independent gait recognition. In particular, as we can observe, the gait cycle and the stride length can be calculated with sufficient precision.

Figure 5 illustrates components of a typical model-based system for gait recognition. Given a gallery database, consisting of gait patterns from a set of known

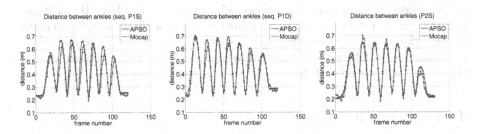

Fig. 4. Distance between ankles during walking in sequences P1 (straight and diagonal) and P2 (straight)

subjects, the objective of the gait recognition system is to determine the identity of the probe samples. In this work we treat each gait cycle as a data sample. Thus, a gait sample is a second-order tensor, and the state space with the time space account for its two modes.

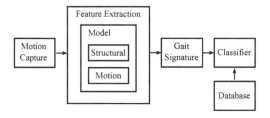

Fig. 5. Components of a typical model-based gait recognition system

The data extracted by markerless motion tracking algorithm were stored in ASF/AMC data format. For a single gait cycle consisting of two strides a second order tensor was calculated. Before feeding the gait samples to MPCA, the tensorial inputs need to be normalized to the same dimension in each mode. The number of frames in each gait sample has some variation and therefore the number of frames in each gait sample was subjected to normalization. The normalized time mode dimension was chosen to be 30, which was roughly the average number of frames in each gait sample. As mentioned in Subsection 2.1, the configuration of the body is parameterized by the position and the orientation of the pelvis in the global coordinate system and the angles between the connected limbs. A set of the state variables plus the distance between ankles and the person's height account for the second mode of the tensor. Among the state variables there is roll angle of the pelvis and the angles between the connected limbs. In consequence, the dimension of the tensor is 30×33, where 30 is the number of frames and the second dimension is equal to the number of bones (excluding pelvis) times three angles plus three (i.e. pelvis roll angle, distance between ankles and the person's height). Such a gait signature was then reduced using Multilinear Principal Components Analysis (MPCA) [11] algorithm. MPCA is a multilinear extension of Principal Component Analysis (PCA) algorithm. There is one orthogonal transformation for each dimension (mode). The MPCA transformation aims to capture as high a variance as possible, accounting for as much of the variability in the data as possible, subject to the constraint of mode-wise orthogonality. It determines a tensor-to-tensor projection that captures most of the signal variation present in the original tensorial representation.

4   Experimental Results

The markerless motion tracking system was evaluated on video sequences with 10 walking individuals. In each image sequence the same actor performed two walks, consisting in following a virtual line joining two opposite cameras and following a virtual line joining two nonconsecutive laboratory corners. The first subsequence is referred to as 'straight', whereas the second one is called 'diagonal'. Given the determined pose estimate, the model was overlaid on the images. Figure 6 depicts some results which were obtained for person 1 in a diagonal walk. The degree of overlap of the projected 3D body model with the performer's silhouette reflects the accuracy of the tracking.

Fig. 6. Articulated 3D human body tracking in sequence P1D. Shown are results in frames #0, 20, 40, 60, 80, 100, 120. The left sub-images are seen from view 1, whereas the right ones are seen from view 2.

In Fig. 7 are shown some motion tracking results that were obtained in the same image sequence, but with the performer following a virtual line connecting two opposite cameras. The body model is overlaid on the images from the right profile view and the frontal view. The discussed results were obtained in 20 iterations per frame using APSO algorithm consisting of 300 particles.

Fig. 7. Articulated 3D human body tracking in sequence P1S. Shown are results in frames #0, 20, 40, 60, 80, 100, 120. Left sub-images are seen from view 1, whereas the right ones are seen from view 2.

The plots in Fig. 8 illustrate the accuracy of motion estimation for some joints. As we can observe, the average tracking error of both legs is about 50 mm and the maximal error does not exceed 110 mm. The discussed results were obtained by APSO algorithm in 20 iterations using 300 particles.

In Tab. 1 are presented some quantitative results that were obtained in the discussed image sequences. The errors were calculated on the basis of 39 markers. For each frame they were computed as average Euclidean distance between individual markers and the recovered 3D joint locations [15]. For each sequence they were then averaged over ten runs with unlike initializations.

Table 2 illustrates the recognition accuracy that was obtained on 10 image sequences, each containing both straight and diagonal walks, which were performed by a sole actor. Each sequence consisted of 2 or 3 full gait cycles.

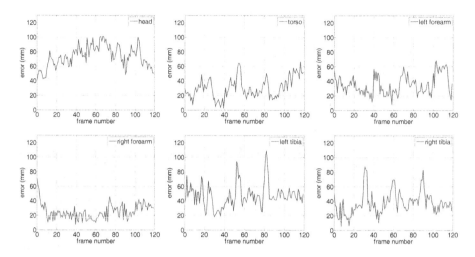

Fig. 8. Tracking errors [mm] versus frame number

Table 1. Average errors for $M = 39$ markers in four image sequences. The images from seq. P1S are shown on Fig. 7, whereas the images from seq. P1D are depicted on Fig. 6.

	#particles	it.	Seq. P1S error [mm]	Seq. P1D error [mm]	Seq. P2S error [mm]	Seq. P2D error [mm]
APSO	100	10	56.4±29.9	61.0±30.4	51.0±28.3	67.7±41.9
	100	20	51.4±28.3	53.6±24.9	47.1±27.1	62.1±40.7
	300	10	51.9±28.5	53.6±24.5	47.9±28.0	62.4±38.3
	300	20	50.0±27.3	48.6±20.5	45.5±25.7	56.5±38.2

Given such a collection of sequences, we obtained a database with 52 gait cycles. 10-fold cross-validation was used to evaluate the performance of the proposed algorithm for gait recognition. In the person identification we employed Naïve Bayes (NB) and multilayer perceptron (MLP) classifiers. The parameter Q denotes the ratio of variations, which should be kept in each mode, whereas A denotes the number of the attributes corresponding to given Q. In practical recognition tasks, Q is commonly set to a large value to capture most of the variation. As one can observe, for $A = 3$ attributes and rank 2 the NB classifier achieves 100% recognition accuracy, whereas the MLP gives 92% recognition accuracy. For Q equal to 0.95 and 17 attributes and rank 2 both classifiers allows us to obtain 90% recognition accuracy. As one can observe, for $Q = 0.99$, 111 attributes and rank 1 the MLP classifier gives somewhat better classification accuracy than 80%.

In [16] a far better gait recognition accuracy using data from maker-based MoCap system has been obtained. The above work demonstrates that given a

Table 2. Identification accuracy [%]

Q	A	Naïve Bayes			MLP		
		Rank 1	Rank 2	Rank 3	Rank 1	Rank 2	Rank 3
0.60	3	88	100	100	83	92	96
0.90	7	85	94	94	75	88	90
0.95	17	81	90	92	81	90	96
0.99	111	38	63	71	81	87	90

sufficiently precise location of the joints it is possible to obtain high recognition accuracy of the gait. Therefore, in order to obtain better recognition accuracy of marker-less based gait recognition the precision of the motion tracking should be improved.

The complete human motion capture system was written in C/C++. The evaluation of the recognition performance was performed using WEKA software. The marker-less motion capture system runs on an ordinary PC. Our implementation of MPCA is based on Jama-1.0 library, supporting matrix operations and eigen decomposition.

5 Conclusions

We have presented a view-independent approach to gait recognition. The recognition is done using gait data obtained by our markerless human motion tracking algorithm. We demonstrated the tracking performance of the algorithm using the MoCap data as ground-truth. High-dimensional tensor data were reduced by the MPCA algorithm and subsequently classified. Experiments on multiview video sequences demonstrated that the algorithm achieves high recognition accuracy.

Acknowledgments. This work has been supported in part by the National Science Centre (NCN) within the research project N N516 483240, the National Centre for Research and Development (NCBiR) within the project OR00002111 and Ministry of Science and Higher Education within the grant U-8604/DS/M.

References

1. Bodor, R., Drenner, A., Fehr, D., Masoud, O., Papanikolopoulos, N.: View-independent human motion classification using image-based reconstruction. Image Vision Comput. 27(8), 1194–1206 (2009)
2. Boulgouris, N.V., Hatzinakos, D., Plataniotis, K.N.: Gait recognition: a challenging signal processing technology for biometric identification. IEEE Signal Processing Magazine 22, 78–90 (2005)

3. Cunado, D., Nixon, M.S., Carter, J.N.: Using gait as a biometric, via phase-weighted magnitude spectra. In: Proc. of the First Int. Conf. on Audio and Video-Based Biometric Person Authentication, pp. 95–102 (1997)
4. Gu, J., Ding, X., Wang, S., Wu, Y.: Action and gait recognition from recovered 3-D human joints. IEEE Trans. Sys. Man Cyber. Part B 40(4), 1021–1033 (2010)
5. Hofmann, M., Sural, S., Rigoll, G.: Gait recognition in the presence of occlusion: A new dataset and baseline algorithms. In: 19th Int. Conf. on Computer Graphics, Visualization and Computer Vision (WSCG) (2011)
6. Johansson, G.: Visual perception of biological motion and a model for its analysis. Perceptron & Psychophysics 14, 201–211 (1973)
7. Kennedy, J., Eberhart, R.: Particle swarm optimization. In: Proc. of IEEE Int. Conf. on Neural Networks, pp. 1942–1948. IEEE Press, Piscataway (1995)
8. Kozlowski, L.T., Cutting, J.E.: Recognizing the sex of a walker from a dynamic point-light display. Perception Psychophysics 21(6), 575–580 (1977)
9. Kwolek, B., Krzeszowski, T., Wojciechowski, K.: Swarm Intelligence Based Searching Schemes for Articulated 3D Body Motion Tracking. In: Blanc-Talon, J., Kleihorst, R., Philips, W., Popescu, D., Scheunders, P. (eds.) ACIVS 2011. LNCS, vol. 6915, pp. 115–126. Springer, Heidelberg (2011)
10. Lee, L., Dalley, G., Tieu, K.: Learning pedestrian models for silhouette refinement. In: Proc. of the Ninth IEEE Int. Conf. on Computer Vision, pp. II:663–II:670 (2003)
11. Lu, H., Plataniotis, K., Venetsanopoulos, A.: MPCA: Multilinear principal component analysis of tensor objects. IEEE Trans. on Neural Networks 19(1), 18–39 (2008)
12. Nixon, M.S., Carter, J.: Automatic recognition by gait. Proc. of the IEEE 94(11), 2013–2024 (2006)
13. Niyogi, S.A., Adelson, E.H.: Analyzing and recognizing walking figures in xyt. In: Proc. of the Int. Conf. on Computer Vision and Pattern Rec., pp. 469–474 (1994)
14. Seely, R., Goffredo, M., Carter, J., Nixon, M.: View invariant gait recognition. In: Handbook of Remote Biometrics: for Surveillance and Security, pp. 61–82. Springer (2009)
15. Sigal, L., Balan, A., Black, M.: HumanEva: Synchronized video and motion capture dataset and baseline algorithm for evaluation of articulated human motion. Int. Journal of Computer Vision 87, 4–27 (2010)
16. Świtoński, A., Polański, A., Wojciechowski, K.: Human identification based on the reduced kinematic data of the gait. In: 7th Int. Symp. on Image and Signal Processing and Analysis, pp. 650–655 (2011)
17. Urtasun, R., Fua, P.: 3D tracking for gait characterization and recognition. In: Proc. of IEEE Int. Conf. on Automatic Face and Gesture Rec., pp. 17–22 (2004)
18. Yam, C., Nixon, M.S., Carter, J.N.: Automated person recognition by walking and running via model-based approaches. Pattern Rec. 37(5), 1057–1072 (2004)
19. Zhang, X., Hu, W., Wang, X., Kong, Y., Xie, N., Wang, H., Ling, H., Maybank, S.: A swarm intelligence based searching strategy for articulated 3D human body tracking. In: IEEE Workshop on 3D Information Extraction for Video Analysis and Mining in Conjuction with CVPR, pp. 45–50. IEEE (2010)

Gender Classification from Pose-Based GEIs*

Raúl Martín-Félez, Ramón A. Mollineda, and J. Salvador Sánchez

Institute of New Imaging Technologies (INIT)
Universitat Jaume I. Av. Sos Baynat s/n, 12071, Castelló de la Plana, Spain
{martinr,mollined,sanchez}@uji.es

Abstract. This paper introduces a new approach for gait-based gender classification in which some key biomechanical poses of a gait pattern are represented by partial Gait Energy Images (GEIs). These pose-based GEIs can more accurately represent the shape of the body parts and some dynamic features with respect to the usually blurred depiction provided by a general GEI comprising all poses. Gait-based gender classification is based on the weighted decision fusion of the pose-based GEIs. Results of experiments on two large gait databases prove that this method performs significantly better than clasiffiers based on the original GEI.

1 Introduction

Gait is a term to describe a particular manner of moving on foot, mainly walking. The main interest in gait analysis comes from conclusions drawn in [1], where the ability of humans to recognize their friends from their unique gait pattern is proved. Therefore, gait can be deemed as a behavioral biometric feature, that allows the estimation of other properties inherent to humans such as gender [2–5] and age [6]. In addition, gait has several important strengths in comparison with other biometric features (face, voice, fingerprint, etc), being the possibility of a reliable perception at a distance without requiring contact with any capturing device the most relevant one. Nevertheless, there are also important factors that hinder the implementation of gait-based systems. For instance, gait analysis is very sensitive to deficient segmentation of silhouettes, but also to variations in clothing, footwear, mood, walking speed, carrying conditions, etc.

One of the main approaches to gait analysis is the so-called model-free techniques [2–4, 7–9]. They attempt to represent the subject appearance changes from a sequence of silhouettes, which implicitly contain dynamic information. The most widely used model-free method is the *Gait Energy Image* (GEI) [8]. It consists of obtaining an average silhouette image to represent both body shape and movements over a gait cycle. However, most of shape regions usually appear blurred in a GEI because of the body movements. Even so, this method has proved to be effective in gait-based gender classification [3, 4, 6].

* This work has partially been supported by projects CSD2007-00018 and CICYT TIN2009-14205-C04-04 from the Spanish Ministry of Innovation and Science, P1-1B2009-04 from Fundació Caixa Castelló-Bancaixa and PREDOC/2008/04 grant from Universitat Jaume I. Portions of this research use the CASIA Gait Database collected by Institute of Automation, Chinese Academy of Sciences.

L. Bolc et al. (Eds.): ICCVG 2012, LNCS 7594, pp. 501–508, 2012.

From a biomechanical viewpoint, some studies [10] assert that several poses successively happen during a gait cycle. A first attempt to pose segmentation consisted of selecting a key frame per pose in each stride [9]. Thereby, a gait sequence was represented by a series of key frames that were used in a distance-based classifier. Consequently, results depended on quality of the chosen frames.

This work goes a step beyond and introduces a pose-based implementation of GEI. In this proposal, four key poses within the gait cycle are considered and represented by partial GEIs, each of which is computed by averaging those frames of the gait sequence that can be considered as part of it.

In comparison with the state-of-the-art, the contributions of this paper are:

- *Several pose-based GEIs from a gait cycle.* The method here proposed computes four different partial GEIs from a gait cycle. As they capture different short gait segments, they are expected to show more accurately some discriminant information concerning static and dynamic characteristics.
- *Decision-level fusion of pose-based GEIs.* In the classification stage, the four pose-based GEIs are individually classified. Then, their results are fused by weighted voting to produce a more robust and reliable decision.

Experiments on two large gait databases have tested this method under the gender classification task. Since both databases are unequally distributed with respect to the number of men and women, an imbalanced-driven solution based on an ensemble of classifiers that learn from balanced subsets was implemented. Results show that the proposed method is able to obtain a better performance than the original GEI method for both databases, and that this improvement comes from both the pose-based GEIs and the management of imbalance.

2   Methodology

2.1   Phases and Key Poses within a Gait Cycle

In a normal pattern of walking, a gait cycle is composed of two series of two phases called double and single stance respectively. In the second series, limbs interchange their roles with respect to the first one (see Figure 1). *Double stance* comprises the period of time in which both feet are on the ground for the transfer of body weight from the support limb to the other. Conversely, *Single stance* consists of a larger period of time in which only one limb is touching the ground and supporting the entire body weight, while the other limb is swinging. These two phases can be divided into eight main poses focusing on movements of a target limb, as depicted in Figure 1.

2.2   Fundamentals of the Proposal

The pose-based strategy here proposed is supported by three main hypotheses:

Hypothesis 1. Focusing on Fig. 1, the two halves of a normal gait cycle are expected to be symmetric. Therefore, the step can be chosen as the gait cycle measure instead of the stride (unlike most of the related works [3, 4, 8]) and four poses could summarize a gait pattern.

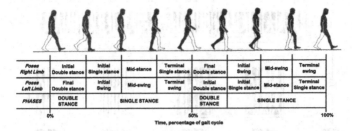

Poses Right Limb	Initial Double stance	Initial Single stance	Mid-stance	Terminal Single stance	Final Double stance	Initial Swing	Mid-swing	Terminal swing
Poses Left Limb	Final Double stance	Initial Swing	Mid-swing	Terminal swing	Initial Double stance	Initial Single stance	Mid-stance	Terminal Single stance
PHASES	DOUBLE STANCE	SINGLE STANCE			DOUBLE STANCE	SINGLE STANCE		

0%   50%   100%
Time, percentage of gait cycle

Fig. 1. Phases and poses within the gait cycle. The target limb is the black one.

Hypothesis 2. By using a partial GEI per each pose, the body parts' shape might be more accurately represented than in a unique standard GEI. In addition, pose-based GEIs might also better show some dynamic features, such as the length of the stride or the extent of arm swing.

Hypothesis 3. Given a gait sequence composed of several gait cycles, most works [3, 4, 8] compute a different GEI for each gait cycle. However, a more robust representation might be obtained by comprising all cycles in a unique GEI. By jointly considering the hypotheses 2 and 3, pose-based GEIs can benefit from the use of a higher number of frames.

Under these assumptions, given a test gait video sequence, the standard GEI of the whole sequence and four pose-based GEIs (GEI_{DS}, GEI_{ISS}, GEI_{MS} and GEI_{FSS}) are obtained (see Figure 2). The former image is computed by averaging all silhouettes, while the other four partial GEIs are obtained by averaging only those silhouettes that belong to the corresponding pose. The four poses considered are: i) *Double Stance* (DS), where both legs are spread and touching the ground; ii) *Initial Single Stance* (ISS), where the front leg is on the ground and the rear leg is swinging towards it; iii) *Mid-Stance* (MS), where legs are closest together; and iv) *Terminal Single Stance* (TSS), where the supporting leg is now the rear one, and the swinging leg appears as the front leg.

An overview of the new method (see Fig. 2) can be summarized as follows:

1. *Classification of silhouettes in poses.* Silhouettes are classified into one of the four poses (see Sec. 2.3). Then, they are normalized and horizontally aligned.
2. *Creation of pose-based GEIs.* All preprocessed silhouettes of a same pose are averaged to create its pose-based GEI. Formally, given a set of silhouette images $\{I_t\}$ with $1 \leq t \leq N$, the GEI is computed as $GEI = \frac{1}{N} \sum_{t=1}^{N} I_t$.
3. *Learning.* Pose-based classifiers learn from their corresponding partial GEIs.
4. *Classification.* Pose-based GEIs of a test sequence are separately classified.
5. *Decision-level fusion.* The four pose-based decisions are fused by a majority voting strategy, looking for a more robust joint prediction. Since the even number of classifiers could lead to a tie, weights per poses are computed (ω_{DS}, ω_{ISS}, ω_{MS} and ω_{FSS} in Fig. 2) as regards their discriminative powers, and the joint prediction is re-estimated by a weighted voting scheme.

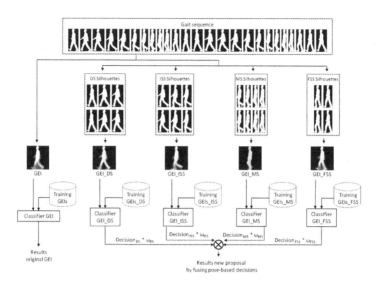

Fig. 2. General solution scheme

2.3   Classification of Silhouettes in Poses

Given a side-view gait sequence, the classification of each silhouette in a land-mark pose is based on the periodic signal provided by the silhouette width as a function of time [9]. The following procedure summarizes the classification of silhouettes (before preprocessing) into gait poses:

1. **DS.** This pose involves the silhouette with the local-maximum width w^+, and those neighbor silhouettes whose widths belong to $[w^+ - \delta, w^+ + \delta]$.
2. **ISS.** This pose considers all frames located between the last frame of each DS and the first frame of the next MS pose.
3. **MS.** This pose gathers the frame with the local-minimum width w^- and those neighbor silhouettes whose widths belong to $[w^- - \delta, w^- + \delta]$.
4. **TSS.** This pose collects all frames located between the last frame of each MS and the first frame of the next DS pose.

An example of silhouette classification into poses can be seen in Fig. 3. Note that frames before the first peak and those after the last peak are ignored (I).

2.4   Dealing with Imbalance in a Gender Classification Task

In general, the class-conditional distribution for the benchmark gait databases is significantly skewed in favor of the men class (see Tab. 1). Some works [2, 3, 7] have dealt with similar problems by using small balanced subsets with an equal number of subjects per gender, but their results strongly depend on the particular subsets selected and they might not consider all samples.

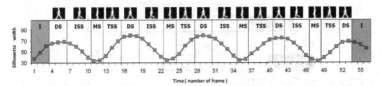

Fig. 3. Classifying frames in poses by their width

Table 1. Details about some of the largest gait databases

Name	#Subjects	#Men	#Women	#Sequences used
CASIA	124	93	31	744
SOTON	115	91	24	690

In this paper, the gender imbalance problem is tackled by an ensemble of classifiers learning from balanced subsets [11] as shown in Fig. 4. Given an imbalanced database, a number of balanced subsets are generated, each one containing all samples of the minority class (women) and as many randomly selected samples (with replacement) of the majority class (men) as needed to obtain a balanced subset. An odd number of individual classifiers are trained from the same number of balanced subsets, whose decisions are combined by simple majority voting. In the solution scheme of Fig. 2, this combined strategy would replace each pair of classifier and training set when dealing with imbalance.

3   Experiments and Results

3.1   Databases

Experiments have been conducted on two public large gait databases: CASIA [12] - Dataset B and the Southampton HID Database (SOTON) [13] - Set A. Table 1 summarizes their number of subjects (men and women) and sequences involved. Sequences from both databases were recorded under controlled indoor conditions and subjects appear walking in their side view without any covariate factor. The well-segmented silhouettes provided by them are used as inputs to compute the corresponding GEIs and pose-based GEIs. Note that the gender-conditional distribution of both databases are 3:1 for CASIA and 4:1 for SOTON.

The pose-based GEIs are built following the procedure outlined in Sec. 2 using the parameter $\delta = 2$. Since the GEI pixels are considered as features, the high dimensional GEI space has been projected by *Principal Component Analysis* (PCA) onto a smaller one that accounts for a 95% of the variance.

3.2   Experimental Setting

Evaluation protocol. A stratified 10-fold cross validation scheme is repeated 10 times to estimate robust recognition rates. Each gallery and probe folds

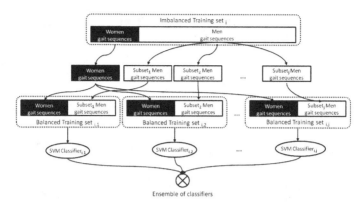

Fig. 4. Ensemble of classifiers for dealing with class imbalance in the gender classification tasks

are not overlapped (all samples of a subject are in the same fold). Besides, gallery and probe sets have the same subject order across all poses to support decision fusion. When imbalance is handled, nine balanced subsets are extracted from each imbalanced gallery fold (see Sec. 2.4) and used to feed the classifiers of the ensemble.

Classifier. The Support Vector Machine (SVM) classifier is used here due to its common high performance in two-class problems. The setting is the simplest one, i.e., a linear kernel with the parameter C=1. In case PCA is applied, the resulting features are Z-normalized to mitigate the impact of their different variances.

Performance measures. Unlike previous related works [2, 3, 7], this paper uses three measures which are sensitive to imbalance effects: the True Positive and True Negative rates (*TPr* and *TNr*), and the geometric mean of these class accuracies (*Gmean*) for providing a global unbiased performance assessment.

Pose-based weights. Weights for pose-based decisions over some probe fold across all poses are computed as the *Gmean* values obtained from a *leaving-one-out* scheme (leaving all samples of a person out each time) performed on the related gallery folds. When imbalance is managed, this process is applied to each balanced subset, and the average result is given as the *Gmean* of the fold. Finally, *Gmean*-based weights are normalized by their sum.

3.3   Results and Discussion

Experiments aim at assessing the effectiveness of the pose-based approach when compared to the plain use of the standard GEI method in a gender classification task. Four different experiments are conducted by considering all combinations of two aspects: the gait representation (standard GEI or pose-based GEIs) and whether imbalance of databases is managed or not. The averaged results (10×10-fold cross validation) are shown for both databases in Fig. 5, which also depicts their 95% confidence intervals. Four analysis are then carried out:

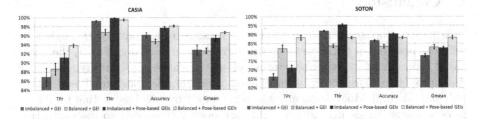

Fig. 5. Results of experiments for CASIA (left) and SOTON (right) databases

Analysis 1: Imbalanced+GEI vs. Balanced+GEI

When imbalance is managed, there is a clear tendency to significantly improve the success rate of the women class (*TPr*), along with a degradation of that for the men class (*TNr*). It produces a degradation of *Acc* because it is biased to the recognition rate of the majority class (men). However, an improvement of the unbiased *Gmean* can be achieved if the increase of *TPr* is higher than the degradation of *TNr*, as happens with SOTON.

Analysis 2: Imbalanced+GEI vs. Imbalanced+Pose-based GEIs

When imbalance is not managed, results show that the pose-based ensemble significantly outperforms the standard GEI results for both databases and all performance measures. Even so, while class performances for CASIA are pretty good (almost all the men and more than 91% of women are correctly classified), in the SOTON database, 95% of men are correctly classified but this rate drops to 71% for women. The main reason might be the influence of imbalance, which is higher in SOTON.

Analysis 3: Balanced+GEI vs. Balanced+Pose-based GEIs

In contrast to Analysis 2, a comparison of both gait representations is performed when imbalance is managed. Results demonstrate that the pose-based method significantly overcomes the standard GEI for all measures and databases. In addition, higher and more balanced class rates are obtained as compared to those of Analysis 2. In particular, more than 88% of men and women are correctly classified in SOTON.

Analysis 4: Imbalanced+GEI vs. Balanced+Pose-based GEIs

This analysis summarizes the results of this paper. It compares the standard GEI method on the original imbalanced databases (a baseline solution) with the imbalance-driven pose-based method here proposed. Thereby, the joint benefit provided by the two contributions are studied. The proposed method significantly outperforms the baseline solution for both databases. In the case of CASIA, the overall performance of the former is close to 97%, what involves almost all the men and a 94% of women correctly classified. On the other hand, a *Gmean* value higher than 88% with similar recognition rates for both genders is obtained for SOTON. Note that these improvements are mainly due to the gait pose-based representation, although the management of imbalance also contributes significantly in SOTON.

4   Conclusion

This paper proposes a new method to represent a gait pattern through four different pose-based GEIs. In comparison to the standard use of GEI, the pose-based representation seems to capture biometric shape cues and dynamic gait descriptors in a more accurate way. Given a test sample, four pose-based classifiers provide individual decisions, which are fused by weighted voting to obtain a more robust single decision. Weights are positively related to discriminative powers of the poses. This approach is assessed on a gender classification task, which introduces the problem of imbalance regarding samples per gender. It is tackled by an ensemble of classifiers learning from balanced subsets. Results from two large gait databases (CASIA and SOTON) show that the pose-based fusion significantly outperforms the standard GEI, being most of the improvement due to the new representation although managing imbalance also contributes.

References

1. Cutting, J., Kozlowski, L.: Recognizing friends by their walk: Gait perception without familiarity cues. Bulletin of the Psychonomic Society 9, 353–356 (1977)
2. Huang, G., Wang, Y.: Gender Classification Based on Fusion of Multi-view Gait Sequences. In: Yagi, Y., Kang, S.B., Kweon, I.S., Zha, H. (eds.) ACCV 2007, Part I. LNCS, vol. 4843, pp. 462–471. Springer, Heidelberg (2007)
3. Yu, S., Tan, T., Huang, K., Jia, K., Wu, X.: A study on gait-based gender classification. IEEE Transactions on Image Processing 18(8), 1905–1910 (2009)
4. Li, X., Maybank, S., Yan, S., Tao, D., Xu, D.: Gait components and their application to gender recognition. IEEE Trans. SMC-C 38(2), 145–155 (2008)
5. Kozlowski, L., Cutting, J.: Recognizing the sex of a walker from a dynamic point-light display. Perception & Psychophysics 21, 575–580 (1977)
6. Makihara, Y., Mannami, H., Yagi, Y.: Gait Analysis of Gender and Age Using a Large-Scale Multi-view Gait Database. In: Kimmel, R., Klette, R., Sugimoto, A. (eds.) ACCV 2010, Part II. LNCS, vol. 6493, pp. 440–451. Springer, Heidelberg (2011)
7. Lee, L., Grimson, W.: Gait analysis for recognition and classification. In: Proc. 5th IEEE Int'l. Conf. on Automatic Face and Gesture Recogn., pp. 155–162 (2002)
8. Han, J., Bhanu, B.: Individual recognition using gait energy image. IEEE Transactions on Pattern Analysis and Machine Intelligence 28(2), 316–322 (2006)
9. Collins, R.T., Gross, R., Shi, J.: Silhouette-based human identification from body shape and gait. In: FG, pp. 366–371 (2002)
10. Perry, J.: Gait Analysis: Normal and Pathological Function. SLACK Incorporated (1992)
11. Martín-Félez, R., Mollineda, R.A., Sánchez, J.S.: A gender recognition experiment on the CASIA gait database dealing with its imbalanced nature. In: Int'l Conf. Computer Vision Theory and Applications (VISAPP), vol. 2, pp. 439–444 (2010)
12. CASIA: CASIA Gait Database (2005), http://www.sinobiometrics.com
13. Shutler, J., Grant, M., Nixon, M.S., Carter, J.N.: On a large sequence-based human gait database. In: Proc. 4th Int'l Conf. on RASC, pp. 66–71 (2002)

Comparison of Key Point Detectors
in SIFT Implementation for Mobile Devices

Karol Matusiak and Piotr Skulimowski

Technical University of Lodz, Institute of Electronics
piotr.skulimowski@p.lodz.pl
http://www.eletel.p.lodz.pl

Abstract. The paper presents a comparison of key point selection methods used for recognition of objects in scenes recorded by a built-in mobile phone camera. The detected key points include corners and line crossings. An application for Android smartphones was developed utilizing the Features from Accelerated Segment Test (FAST) and Scale-Invariant Feature Transform (SIFT), which was specially modified for processing low resolution images. The implemented algorithm computes descriptors which are invariant to image acquisition settings such as: rotation, noise, scale and brightness variations. The proposed image classification algorithm is based on pairing key points based on similarity of their descriptors.

1 Introduction

The aim of the presented project was to compare two algorithms of key point detection in terms of their repeatability and computation cost for use in an object recognition application designed for blind or visually impaired users. In [1] it was shown, that Scale-Invariant Feature Transform (SIFT) descriptors (as proposed in [2,4]) can be used on mobile devices. Smartphones were chosen as the target platform due to the capabilities they offer, e.g.: built-in high-resolution cameras, large tactile displays and fast dual core processors (1.4 GHz or even more) for performing advanced calculations. Despite of the growing computation performance of smartphones there are still not as efficient as PCs. That is the reason why object recognition with mobile devices needs algorithms with lower computation costs and lower effectiveness loss in comparison with PCs equivalents. The application was designed for the Android operating system. The creators of the system delivered a very useful software development environment, providing ease of debugging and running of applications. What is more, it has a strong market position – according to Gartner in the fourth quarter of 2011 it has had more than 50% of the smartphone market [3].

The task of object recognition in images recorded by the mobile phone camera is not trivial. The required algorithm must be insensitive to image registration conditions, such as: brightness, rotation, scale, changes in lighting and backgrounds, etc. Classic methods of image recognition (such as template matching [5]), do not meet the requirements set out in this work. That is why we decided to

L. Bolc et al. (Eds.): ICCVG 2012, LNCS 7594, pp. 509–516, 2012.

use the SIFT algorithm, which allows to extract image features that are distinctive, invariant to scale, rotation and partially to illumination[2,4]. A difficulty with using SIFT is that it utilizes a Difference of Gaussian (DoG) algorithm to detect key points which is computationally expensive for mobile devices. In this work, FAST (Features from Accelerated Segment Test [6]) algorithm of corner detection was added to the application and modified to have similar capabilities to Difference of Gaussian. According to [6], it is one of the fastest corner detectors (even several times faster than Harris detector). The tests of feature detection and object recognition with these two algorithms were performed and presented in this paper.

2   Image Recognition Algorithm

The most important steps of the proposed algorithm implemented on Android OS are illustrated in Figure 1. First, a color image is captured by the mobile phone using default settings (with auto-focus). The resolution of the image is set to 384×512 pixels. Second, the image is converted to greyscale and key point detection is performed (either using FAST or Difference of Gaussian). Next, the descriptors for the located key points are calculated. When creating new reference patterns the descriptors are added to the local database in the phone's memory, otherwise they are compared, using nearest neighbor classifier, with descriptors of the reference images. The database may contain descriptors determined for multiple images of the same object.

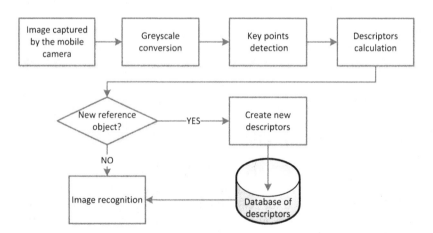

Fig. 1. The proposed method for object recognition in scenes recorded by a mobile phone camera

2.1   Features from Accelerated Segment Test

The FAST algorithm was first proposed by [7]. In this method, a candidate point p is compared to points located on a Bresenham circle of radius r.

The point p is considered as corner if at least n continuous points are all brighter or darker than point p with a predefined threshold value. The results of feature detection depend on the circle radius and the n parameter, e.g.: in the case of the radius equal to 3, only values of n equal to 9 or greater can prevent the detection of points lying on the edge instead of a corner. The problem with this method is that it can detect a lot of clustered features. To prevent this, there is a need to define the area where only one and the most distinctive corner will be detected. There are several versions of the algorithm in use, depending on which parameter is the most important in a given implementation (performance speed, robustness, insensitivity to rotation etc.).

For the FAST implementation the radius of the Bresenham circle $r = 3$ was used, but only 8 pixels with odd indexes on the circle are tested with parameter $n = 7$. What is more, a number of new improvements similar to Difference of Gaussian were added: the algorithm is applied not for the original image registered by mobile device, but for a Gaussian pyramid with two octaves with one image per octave. It results with the decreasing of the influence of noise and object scaling on the feature detections.

2.2 Difference of Gaussian

Difference of Gaussian (DoG) is the method that was originally used in the SIFT algorithm to detect stable and repeatable features [2]. To compute this algorithm, the source image is first used to produce a set of images of various scales. Every image is convolved with Gaussian filters with different variances σ^2. Such a stack of images is called a Gaussian pyramid. The numbers of smoothed and resampled images are parameters of the algorithm. In our work we used two octaves with four images per octave. Next, adjacent image scales are subtracted. Candidates for key feature points are points that are local extremes of neighboring difference of Gaussian images: each point is compared with its 8-point neighborhood in the current image and with the adjacent (in scale) images. The maximum number of comparisons for every single point is 26. Afterwards, candidates for key points are verified in order to determine whether they can be stable characteristic points. The conditions to be satisfied are high contrast and large gradient values in both horizontal and vertical direction.

An approximated approach of separated Gaussian functions was used to calculate the Gaussian filter matrix. The method consists of representing a 2D Gaussian blur with two 1D Gaussian functions. This results in decreasing the number of calculations for an N-sized matrix from N^2 additions and $N^2 - 1$ multiplications to $2^N - 1$ additions and $N + 2$ multiplications.

2.3 Key Point Descriptors

In both cases (DoG and FAST) the original SIFT descriptors are used. This means that for each neighborhood of a key point, image gradient magnitudes and orientations are used to form an orientation histogram; the highest peak in the histogram gives the orientation of the key point. In this implementation each histogram has 8 bins. Key points are described by a set of gradient magnitude histograms for a number of directions around the key point. In our implementation 16 4 × 4 pixel regions were used to calculate 16 histograms.

The histograms are stored as a function of orientation parameters calculated for a neighboring group of pixels for the given scale. Independence on rotation is achieved by shifting all the histograms to begin with the angle which corresponds to the key point orientation found in the previous step. Moreover, the pixel coordinates used for description calculation must satisfy the equation 1,

$$
\begin{aligned}
x_n &= x sin\left(\theta\right) + y cos\left(\theta\right) + x_{kp} \\
y_n &= x cos\left(\theta\right) - y sin\left(\theta\right) + y_{kp}
\end{aligned}
\tag{1}
$$

where x_n, y_n are pixel coordinates for description calculation, x_{kp}, y_{kp} are key point coordinates of orientation equals θ and x,y are pixel coordinates in the coordinate system associated with the key point for $\theta = 0$.

2.4   Key Point Selection

This step is needed to ensure the detected key points are stable. In the classic SIFT algorithm the key points lying along the edges are removed as described in [4]. Next, the value of key points from the Gaussian image are compared with a contrast threshold parameter to reduce the number of unstable key points. Examples of key points found for two images with different contrast thresholds are shown in Figure 2.

In case of the FAST algorithm, key point verification also depends on the contrast threshold value. Results for two images with different values of this parameter are shown in Figure 3. The main disadvantage of the FAST algorithm is finding clusters of key points (points are often localized very close to each other). Moreover the FAST method needs a higher threshold than DoG to find a similar number of points. The DoG detector found 111 and 45 key points for contrast values 5 and 10, whereas for the FAST detector 77 and 43 for threshold values 20 and 35.

2.5   Key Point Pairing

In order to find pairs of key points Euclidean distance is calculated between each pair of descriptors of the reference and the test image. Please note, that descriptors are invariant to rotation. For every key point from the reference image, the ratio of the two lowest distance values is calculated. If it is greater than the predefined threshold value, the pair is considered to be correct. Next, the average distance between the detected pairs of key points is calculated and used in the classification procedure. The reference image should contain key points which are chosen in a manner less restrictive than in the test images, because varying capturing conditions may result in the detection of only a small subset of all the possible key points.

Fig. 2. Key points (marked by squares) detected by DoG in the "phone" image for two different contrast parameters (5–left and 10–right)

Fig. 3. Key points (marked by squares) detected by FAST in the "phone" image for two different contrast parameters (20–left and 35–right)

3 Example Results

Two aspects of the results were considered during tests: performance cost (time) and correct classification of objects. The tests were done using the HTC Desire HD smartphone with a 1Ghz CPU unit and 768 MB RAM memory. Example results of time performance for full algorithm processing (from image capture to calculating the final descriptors) are shown in Table 1.

Table 1. Example results for time performance of the algorithms

Method	Image Id	Number of key points	Performance time[s]	Time per key point[s]
DoG	1	69	5,97	0,0865
DoG	2	177	6,51	0,0367
DoG	3	134	6,23	0,0464
DoG	4	62	5,84	0,0941
	Avg.:	110,5	6,1342	0,0659
FAST	1	106	2,042	0,0193
FAST	2	120	2,152	0,0179
FAST	3	131	2,142	0,0163
FAST	4	142	2,213	0,0155
	Avg.:	124,75	2,137	0,0172

Process time for each image depends on the number of detected key points. Due to this, results are shown in a form that includes ratio relationships between the calculation time and the number of key points. It can be noticed that using the SIFT image descriptor with the modified FAST algorithm is about three times faster than using DoG.

Table 2. Classification results for FAST and DoG key point selection methods

Test class	FAST				DoG			
	Reference class							
	A	B	C	D	A	B	C	D
A1	**0.4863**	0.7150	0.7286	0.6317	**0.5698**	0.7190	0.6315	0.8012
A2	0.6990	0.6886	0.6932	*0.5903*	0.7168	0.7326	0.7735	*0.7115*
A3	**0.5272**	0.6774	0.7040	0.6340	**0.5655**	0.7705	0.7494	0.8231
B1	0.7745	**0.5206**	0.8818	0.6643	0.6884	**0.4532**	0.7903	0.8758
B2	0.6953	**0.6660**	0.7950	0.7103	0.7466	**0.5660**	0.6407	0.6386
B3	0.6790	0.5526	0.8009	*0.5051*	0.7027	**0.4939**	0.7597	0.7826
C1	0.6779	0.7919	**0.5113**	0.6546	0.8178	0.8549	**0.5823**	0.9011
C2	0.7413	0.8169	**0.7125**	0.7933	*0.6071*	0.7758	0.6745	0.9151
C3	0.6197	0.7883	**0.5542**	0.6746	0.7363	0.8147	**0.6126**	0.7191
D1	0.7626	0.6393	0.7728	**0.4774**	0.7208	0.6986	0.7589	**0.5108**
D2	0.7178	0.6483	0.7205	**0.5744**	0.7108	0.6669	0.7632	**0.5158**
D3	0.6764	0.7091	0.7187	**0.4969**	0.6928	0.7087	0.7006	**0.4791**

For the classification tests a database of three classes (one photo for each) was prepared. Object recognition tests were performed three times (with different rotation, scale, localization in the captured image) for each object. The results for the FAST and DoG key point detection methods are shown in Table 2. The values in the table are mean distances between the reference class descriptors and the test images' descriptors. The value of the lowest distance is marked bold if the classification result is positive. A negative result is marked by italics.

Figure 4 shows the results of pairing key points from reference and test images based on the values of their descriptors. It can be noticed that most of the points are paired correctly despite of different capturing conditions.

Fig. 4. Example result of pairing key points (test class D3, reference class D). The lines connect the corresponding points.

4   Summary

A comparison of key point detection and selection methods was described in this paper. All the algorithms were implemented in Java for Android OS. Despite of the slightly worse classification results for key points found using the modified FAST algorithm it has a significant advantage in the form of reduced computation times. This method is employed in the object recognition application dedicated for the visually impaired. Additionally, the proposed recognition algorithm can be extended for checking the relationship between the mutual position of the detected key points.

Acknowledgement. This work has been partially supported by the Ministry of Science and Higher Education of Poland research grant no. NR02-0083-10 in years 2010–2013.

References

1. Matusiak, K., Skulimowski, P.: Object Recognition in scenes recorded by mobile devices. Young Scientists Innovations Forum (2011), http://www.fimb.p.lodz.pl ISSN 2082-4831
2. Lowe, D.: Object Recognition from Local Scale-Invariant Features. In: International Conference on Computer Vision, pp. 1150–1157 (1999)
3. Gartner: Gartner Says Worldwide Smartphone Sales Soared in Fourth Quarter of 2011 With 47 Percent Growth (2012),
   http://www.gartner.com/it/page.jsp?id=1924314
4. Lowe, D.: Distinctive image features from scale-invariant key points. International Journal of Computer Vision 60, 91–110 (2004)
5. Pratt, W.: Digital Image Processing. John Wiley & Sons Inc. (2001)
6. Rosten, E., Drummond, T.: Machine Learning for High-Speed Corner Detection. In: Leonardis, A., Bischof, H., Pinz, A. (eds.) ECCV 2006. LNCS, vol. 3951, pp. 430–443. Springer, Heidelberg (2006)
7. Rosten, E., Drummond, T.: Fusing Points and Lines for High Performance Tracking. In: Tenth IEEE International Conference on Computer Vision ICCV 2005, vol. 2, pp. 1508–1515 (2005)

Estimation of Position and Radius
of Light Probe Images

Przemysław Mazurek

West Pomeranian University of Technology, Szczecin
Department of Signal Processing and Multimedia Engineering
26–Kwietnia 10 Str. 71126 Szczecin, Poland
przemyslaw.mazurek@zut.edu.pl
http://www.media.zut.edu.pl

Abstract. Image Based Lighting technique needs light probe images. Light probe images are measurements of the scene light. Spherical and hemispherical mirrors (light probe measurement devices) and camera are used for the light probe image acquisition. In the paper is proposed and analyzed computational requirement of position and radius estimation of the hemispherical mirror with stripe pattern flange. Proposed solution reduces computation cost and allows processing of 4k image in 3 minutes.

Keywords: Light Probe, Pattern Recognition, Image Based Lighting.

1   Introduction

Image Based Lighting is one of the most important techniques for the acceleration of rendering [2]. Rendering is computationally very demanding, so optimization techniques that may replace raytracing and similar techniques are necessary. Approximation techniques are used for the reduction of the rendering cost.

The composition of the real and CG (Computer Graphic) footage needs fitting of the light. The light sources of the real scene should be modeled using CG. Differences between them will be visible for the viewer what is a source of confusion, without lights fitting. The modeling of the light is possible using a trial and test technique. It is time consuming operation, if a lot of light sources are in the real scene. Moreover, the complexity of the light sources is much higher then typical point, linear and area sources.

The best way for the complex light modeling is the technique based on the measurements of the real light in scene [2]. The obtained measurement (the light probe image) is used for the direct applications as a single spherical light source [3]. The CG scene is inside this sphere. Obtained measurements are a kind of the spherical filter placed between outer spherical area light source and the scene. This is very simple technique for desired realistic rendering. The cost of computations is low, what is important advantage over other techniques.

The light probe is the rectangular image with a specific mapping of the spherical probe. The mapping method is not important for the rendering quality if the image resolution is high.

L. Bolc et al. (Eds.): ICCVG 2012, LNCS 7594, pp. 517–524, 2012.

2   Light Probes Measurements

The light probe means generally the image of light measurements and one of the devices used for measurements. The light probes (image) are obtained using a few techniques. The measurements of the light are used typically. The painting of the light probe image is also used, especially in the motion picture productions. The light probes are also generated using CG software. Dedicated tools for the light probe generations are available, but the typical CG rendering tools are used typically.

The measurement based light probe images are obtained using different devices. The spherical or hemispherical mirrors are used in many movie productions. The spherical panorama recordings (Fig. 1) using a digital still camera and wide angle lenses are used, also. Special digital cameras for spherical panorama recordings are available. Multiple camera, robotic heads and special panoramic lenses are used for reduction of the acquisition time. The light probes images are LDR (Low Dynamic Range) or HDR (High Dynamic Range). The HDR images are preferred light probes due to quality measurements of the Sun, bright light sources and dark areas together [11,12].

Fig. 1. Example of Light Probe Image

Calibration of the light probe and movie footage is necessary, if both of them are recorded using different cameras. The mirror based technique allows recording of the both of them using the same camera and the same camera settings. It this case the calibration is not necessary and this variant is preferred in movie production.

Static light probe are used if the scene is static. The dynamic light probe (light probe movie) is necessary if the scene is dynamic, also [13,14]. One of the interesting applications of CG and light probes is the replacement of actor's body parts. Movement of the actor or camera changes position in the scene of desired CG elements. Light measurements should follow position of the actor, so multiple pass technique (actor and light probe) is necessary for the adequate lighting.

3 Estimation of Position and Radius Using the Hough Transform

Estimation of the position and radius of the light probe mirror are simple for short time footages. Manual extraction of the light probe is necessary from every frame. Longer footages should be automatically processed with reasonable time. Multiple takes of the actor and light probe of the single scene are filmed, so fast and reliable technique is necessary for automatic extraction.

This operation, without additional knowledge about image content, is extremely difficult or even impossible. In [6] is proposed flange based hemispherical mirror. The flange does not occupy large area of the image and does not disturb of light probe reflections. The flange has blue color and chroma keying techniques are possible to use for the separation from image. The chroma flange will fail for specific environments and much better technique is proposed in [6] that uses combination of the chroma keying and the dual edge detection (inner and outer part of the flange). The Hough Transform (HT) [1] is applied for the estimation of the position for different radiuses. The HT is computationally demanding so GPGPU implementations are proposed [7]. The GPGPU based implementation of the HT algorithm allows processing of the single image frame (512x512 resolution, 300 radiuses) takes 3 seconds [7]. Tracking of the light probe is also important for computation cost reduction [8]. Obtained estimates are used for more precised extraction of the light probe area.

The following formula is used for HT computations:

$$H(x, y, r) = \sum_i I\left(x + r\sin\left(\alpha_i\right), y + r\cos\left(\alpha_i\right)\right) \tag{1}$$

and the result of the estimation is obtained using the next formula:

$$(x, y, r)_{est} = \arg\max_{x,y,r} H\left(x, y, r\right) \tag{2}$$

where x and y is the position, r is the radius, α_i is the particular angle. The number of angles depends on the desired estimation quality. Dense sampling of the circle reduces estimation, error but increases computation time, unfortunately.

4 Estimation of Position and Radius Using the Stripe Pattern

In this paper is proposed another light probe device (Fig. 2) that is based on the stripe pattern flange instead single color flange around hemispherical mirror. It is expected that faster algorithm will be obtained.

The aim of the striper pattern and thresholding is the forcing of the black and white areas in the image. The stripe pattern is tested with less sampling points in comparison to the HT approach. Overall processing scheme is depicted in Fig. 3.

Fig. 2. Light Probe with circular stripe pattern – color and thresholded images

Fig. 3. Processing scheme of the estimation of the stripe pattern

The circular stripe pattern (Fig. 2) detection is based on the HT algorithm principles. The stripe pattern flange algorithm uses testing of the pattern located on the circle using reduced set of the sampling points. The number of the stripes N is known a priori and the sampling expects that desired value is obtained. It is a kind of the result's control. The HT accumulates values, so it is unknown the expected value of accumulations. The stripe pattern allows the checking pattern during the sampling of the circle. The incorrect result allows rejection of the circle without testing all samples.

The following formulas are used for stripe pattern testing:

$$S(x,y,r) = \sum_{i=0}^{N-1} I\left(x + r\sin\left(\alpha_i\right), y + r\cos\left(\alpha_i\right)\right) \oplus \ldots \qquad (3)$$
$$\ldots I\left(x + r\sin\left(\alpha_{i+1}\right), y + r\left(\alpha_{i+1}\right)\right)$$

where: $\alpha_0 = \alpha_N$. Maximal Hamming distance $d_{l1} = N$ that is a priori known as expected. The detection is achieved when the following formula is fulfilled:

$$S\left(x,y,r\right) = N \qquad (4)$$

The detection needs dual sampling of the circle due to sampling theory limits. The number of the stripes is known N and the number of samples is equal to this number. The sampling point series may test boundaries between stripes that are not reliable depending on the phase between samples and stripe patterns. Test using two circle samples point series are necessary. The first series uses sampling point defined as:

$$\alpha_i = i\frac{2\pi}{N} \qquad (5)$$

and the second uses in between locations:

$$\alpha_i = i\frac{2\pi}{N} + \frac{2\pi}{2N} \tag{6}$$

Example results of the S–space for the image from in Fig. 2 are presented in Fig. 4 and the white point is the maximal S value. The maximal S value is depicted only, because the S–space is three dimensional. The peak value corresponds to the estimated position of the center of flange and light probe hemisphere. Multiple peak values with value equal to the N are obtained due to size of the stripe pattern.

Fig. 4. Maximal values of the S–space for position only

5   Results

The proposed technique of the estimation of position and radius of the light probe device was tested for 4096x2048 image resolution. Tests are performed using the Pentium 4 processor (2.4GHz clock), DDR2 666MHz memory, GCC 4.4.5 compiler (-O3 level of optimization) using Debian Linux operating system.

Two code variants were tested. The first variant is the exhaustive search without validation of the bit pattern and is adequate to the HT computation cost. There are 40 samples per circle. Two phases of pattern are used.

The second variant is based on the runtime validation of the bit pattern. The expected pattern is compared with current sample. The tests of the next circle samples are rejected if incorrect sample value is obtained. The correct pattern is known (1010101 ... or 0101010 ... depending on the phase between stripe patterns and sampling points located on the circle), so expected bit value is defined. Two phases of pattern are used, also.

It is possible another variant also. The detection of the N of correct samples is adequate to the detection of the flange, so processing of the next circles could be abandoned. This is an aggressive strategy, and it is not guaranteed that estimated position and radius is a true flange.

The synthetic images are used for tests intentionally. The output of the uniform random noise generator is filtered using 2D low–pass filter and added to the synthetic flange image ($N = 40$ is assumed). Threshold technique is applied for the conversion of the grayscale image to the binary. An example synthetic image for small resolution 640x480 is shown in Fig. 5. Such tests allow testing at high degree of possibility of the detection of false pattern.

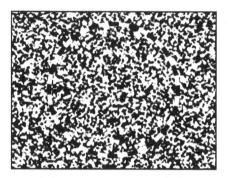

Fig. 5. Example synthetic test image – stripe flange ring and noise background

The reference processing using of the first variant is extremely slow and it take almost two hours of computations for 100 of radiuses. The total number of tested circles is 2x800M. Reduction of the spatial density allows reduction of the computations. The flange has own size, so multiple solution are possible around optimal one. It allows the reduction of processing time almost linearly. The sampling of single pixel instead all pixels in every 3x3 block gives the reduction

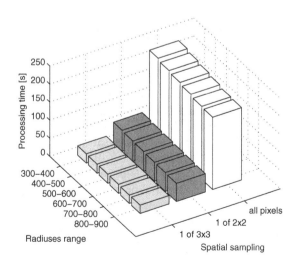

Fig. 6. Processing time depended on the spatial sampling and radiuses range

about 9 times. The computation takes a lot of time due to non optimal usage of the processor. The SSE instruction code will be much faster in comparison to the direct C–language based reference code. The much more efficient, even if C–language is used, is the second variant. The reduction of the computation by testing of the pattern on every new sample allows significant improvement. In Fig. 6 are shown results for circles with different radiuses.

6 Discussion

Processing of the large set of circles needs code optimization and algorithm optimization techniques for the particular processing platform. The first variant is inefficient and not adequate for the application. Initialization steps, processing at last two frames, are necessary for the application of flange tracking algorithms [9,10]. Manual selection for the initialization step is more optimal instead automatic search.

The optimization of the algorithm, but the rejection of the circles with incorrect patterns allows significant reduction of the computation cost, below to half minute per 100 radiuses (one sample per 3x3 block mode). These results are statistical for the assumed background synthesis. The computation of the all possible radiuses (100–900 pixels) takes about 3 minutes.

Obtained positions and radiuses should be used by the tracking algorithms (like the Benedict–Bordner or Kalman filter [9,10]). Tracking allows the reduction of the search space and it allows reduction of the processing time. The motion picture footage sometimes may have not light probe at the beginning and ending frames so exhaustive search will be used for larger number of frames also. The computation cost is almost linear for radiuses range and spatial sampling. Smaller radiuses need a large processing time in comparison to the larger, but the difference is not significant. Estimation for the second variant depends on the image content, but not on the position or radius of the flange.

7 Conclusions

Automatic extraction of the light probe image from hemispherical mirror using proposed device and algorithm is possible. Tests based on the synthetic pattern allow estimation of the processing time for particular processing device.

The algorithm estimation of the position and radius of the flange using reduced number of sampling points is proposed in this paper. It is desired for the reduction of the computations and memory transfers. The expected value of the S–space is predefined so the robustness of the estimation is obtained from the estimated values also. It is not available for the HT calculation due to noises and light variations in the flange image. Analysis of the shape of stripes using shape analysis techniques [4,5], allows estimation of the quality of estimation, due to light changes. It is interesting for the adaptive threshold selection. The GPGPU based implementation of the proposed algorithm is possible. It is expected linear reduction of the processing time depending on the number of processing units. Parallel processing does not need close cooperation between units. It is very important property of the proposed algorithm that allows reduction of the computation to real–time.

Acknowledgment. This work is supported by the UE EFRR ZPORR project Z/2.32/I/1.3.1/267/05 "Szczecin University of Technology – Research and Education Center of Modern Multimedia Technologies" (Poland).

References

1. Hough, P.V.C., Arbor, A.: Method and Means for Recognizing Complex Patterns, US Patent no. 3,069,654 (1962)
2. Debevec, P.: Rendering Synthetic Objects into Real Scenes: Bridging Traditional and Image-based Graphics with Global Illumination and High Dynamic Range Photography. In: SIGGRAPH 1998, pp. 189–198 (1998)
3. Debevec, P.: Light Probe Image Gallery, http://www.pauldebevec.com/Probes/
4. Frejlichowski, D.: An Experimental Comparison of Seven Shape Descriptors in the General Shape Analysis Problem. In: Campilho, A., Kamel, M. (eds.) ICIAR 2010, Part I. LNCS, vol. 6111, pp. 294–305. Springer, Heidelberg (2010)
5. Frejlichowski, D.: Analysis of Four Polar Shape Descriptors Properties in an Exemplary Application. In: Bolc, L., Tadeusiewicz, R., Chmielewski, L.J., Wojciechowski, K. (eds.) ICCVG 2010, Part I. LNCS, vol. 6374, pp. 376–383. Springer, Heidelberg (2010)
6. Mazurek, P.: Estimation of position of the light probe device for photorealistic computer animation purposes, Elektronika – Konstrukcje, Technologie, Zastosowania, 42–44, R. LII nr.1, 2011
7. Mazurek, P.: Circle parameters estimation using Hough transform implemented on GPGPU. Measurement Automation and Monitoring 57(8), 886–898 (2011)
8. Mazurek, P.: Light estimation using light probe devices. Electrical Review (in print, 2012)
9. Blackman, S., Poupoli, R.: Modern Tracking Systems. Artech House (1999)
10. Brookner, E.: Tracking and Kalman Filtering Made Easy. Wiley Interscience (1998)
11. Myszkowski, K., Mantiuk, R., Krawczyk, G.: High Dynamic Range Video. Morgan and Claypool Publishers (2008)
12. Reinhard, E., Ward, G., Pattanaik, S., Debevec, P.: High Dynamic Range Imaging. In: Acquisition, Display, and Image–Based Lighting. Morgan Kaufmann (2005)
13. Unger, J., Gustavson, S., Ollila, M., Johannesson, M.: A Real Time Light Probe. In: Proceedings of the 25th Eurographics Annual Conference, Short Papers and Interactive Demos, pp. 17–21 (2004)
14. Unger, J., Gustavson, S., Kronander, J., Larsson, P., Bonnet, G., Kaiser, G.: Next Generation Image Based Lighting. In: SIGGRAPH 2011, Talk, Vancouver, Canada, Vancouver, Canada, August 7–11 (2011), http://webstaff.itn.liu.se/~jonun/web/papers/2011-Siggraph/SiggraphTalk2011.pdf

Gait Identification Based on MPCA Reduction
of a Video Recordings Data

Agnieszka Michalczuk[1], Adam Świtoński[1,2], Henryk Josiński[1,2],
Andrzej Polański[1,2], and Konrad Wojciechowski[1,2]

[1] Polish-Japanese Institute of Information Technology
Aleja Legionów 2, 41-902 Bytom, Poland
{aswitonski,hjosinski,apolanski,kwojciechowski}@pjwstk.edu.pl
http://www.pjwstk.edu.pl
[2] Silesian Univercity of Technology, Akademicka 16, 44-100 Gliwice, Poland
{adam.switonski,henryk.josinski,andrzej.polanski,
konrad.wojciechowski}@polsl.pl
http://www.iinf.polsl.pl

Abstract. The scope of this article is gait identification of individuals
on the basis of reduced sequences of video recordings data. The gait sequences are considered to be the 3rd-order tensors and its dimensionality
is reduced by Multilinear Principal Component Analysis with different
values of variation covered. Reduced gait descriptors are identified by
the supervised classifiers: Naive Bayes and Nearest Neighbor. CASIA
Gait Database 'dataset A' is chosen to verify the proposed method. The
obtained results are promising. For the Naive Bayes and attributes discretization almost 99% of classification accuracy is achieved, which means
only one misclassified gait out of eighty validated.

1 Introduction

We can point three basic approaches to motion data classification: features extraction of the time sequences, Dynamic Time Warping and Hidden Markov
Models.

In feature extraction approaches the classification is based on the feature set,
calculated for the motion data sequences. For instance in [10] the first two lowest
Fourier components are chosen. In [2] four types of features are proposed for gait
paths classification: statistical, histogram, Fourier transform and timeline.

Dynamic Time Warping tries to synchronize two motions by warping their
time domains, which makes the motions faster or slower in the following moments. Matching of the synchronized motions estimates the similarities between
them. To classify motions the nearest neighbors classifier can be applied. In [3]
and [4] DTW is applied for the reduced pose descriptors of motion capture data
and binary silhouettes of CASIA dataset, respectively. In [5] the unsupervised
learning is performed on the basis of the DTW distance function.

In the approaches based on Hidden Markov Models pose sequences are considered to be Markov chains. The training phase calculates parameters of HMM

L. Bolc et al. (Eds.): ICCVG 2012, LNCS 7594, pp. 525–532, 2012.

separately for each person. On the basis of estimated human models, the one with the greatest probability of generating identified sequence of poses has to be found for the classification. In [6] the special pose descriptor called P-style Fourier Descriptor is built and their sequences are classified by HMM. The method proposed in [7] transforms the sequences of silhouettes into low dimensional embedding by manifold learning before modeling their dynamics with HMM.

There is multiple research done on the dimensionality reduction of motion data. The classical approaches do the work at the level of the pose descriptors. In [4] on the basis of distances between the selected body parts, the feature vectors of binary silhouettes are extracted and the first two principal components are chosen. In [6] linear PCA and in [7] nonlinear manifold learning is applied prior to the classification with HMM. In [3] and [4] DTW follows by the reduction of pose descriptors by PCA of feature vectors calculated for video and motion capture data, respectively. In [8] a modified ICA is used for skeletons of binary silhouettes. Other examples can be found in [9], [10] and [11].

Recently the multilinear reduction methods for tensor objects have gained more attention. They allow to reduce multi-dimensional objects indexed by multiple indices. The motion sequences are addressed by the frame number and spatial coordinates, which means that the entire sequences can be reduced, not only the pose descriptors. In [1] the MPCA method is used for the detected cycles of binary silhouettes and the classification is performed by selected distance functions. The MPCA reduction is also extended by LDA method. The application of MPCA to the classification of motion capture data by supervised learning can be found in [15]. In [12] mutlilinear ICA and in [14] uncorrelated MPCA are applied to face recognitions. Another example of MPCA usage to music genre classification is presented in [13].

2   Multilinear Principal Component Analysis

Multilinear principal component analysis, proposed in [1] is the multilinear extension of classical PCA method. The input and output data are considered to be tensor objects and contrary to PCA dimensionality reduction operates directly on tensors rather than its vectorized form.

A tensor is a multidimensional object, whose elements are addressed by indices. The number of indices determines the order of the tensor, where each index defines one of the tensor modes [1]. In MPCA an elementary matrix algebra is extended by two operations: tensor unfolding and the product of a tensor and matrix. The unfolding transforms a tensor into a matrix according to a specified mode. The tensor is decomposed into column vectors, taken from the perspective of a specified mode, see Fig. 1. The tensor X multiplication by the matrix U according to mode n $\tilde{\mathcal{X}}_m \times_n \mathbf{U}$ is obtained by the product of the unfolded tensor and the matrix U. To go back to a tensor space, an inverse unfolding operation is applied. In other words, the mode n of the tensor X is projected into the matrix U.

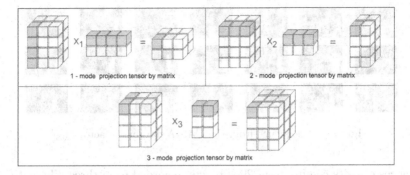

Fig. 1. 1,2 and 3-mode tensor matrix product

The MPCA algorithm consists of the following steps:

1. Preprocessing - the normalization of input tenor samples to zero mean value.
2. Learning phase of MPCA - a loop with specified number of iterations,
   - Initialization - for each mode k:
     - set matrix: $\Phi^{(k)*} = \sum_{m=1}^{M} \tilde{\mathbf{X}}_{m(k)} \mathbf{X}_{m(k)}^{T}$, where $\Phi^{(k)*}$ denotes the desired matrix and $\mathbf{X}_{m(k)}$ is the mth input tensor sample in the k-mode vector subspace, determined by unfolding operation.
     - Eigen-decomposition of the matrix $\Phi^{(k)*}$,
     - Selection of P_k most significant eigenvectors which form a projection matrix $\mathbf{U}^{(k)}$. Eigenvectors are evaluated by corresponding eigenvalues and the number of selected eigenvectors is determined by the variation cover $Q = \frac{\sum_{i_k=1}^{P_k} \lambda_{i_k}^{(k)*}}{\sum_{i_k=1}^{I_k} \lambda_{i_k}^{(k)*}}$, where I_k specifies the dimensionality of mode k and λ_{i_k} is i-th eigenvalue of matrix $\Phi^{(k)}$.
   - Local optimization - for each mode update tensors: $\tilde{\mathcal{Y}}_m = \tilde{\mathcal{X}}_m \times_1 \mathbf{U}^{(1)} \times_2 \mathbf{U}^{(2)} \times_3 \cdots \times_{(k-1)} \mathbf{U}^{(k-1)} \times_{(k+1)} \mathbf{U}^{(k+1)} \times_{(k+2)} \cdots \times_n \mathbf{U}^{(n)}$
3. Reduction phase of MPCA - calculate the output tensors by their projection on the determined matrices $\mathbf{U}^{(k)}$.

Our implementation of MPCA is based on Jama-1.0.2 library[1], supporting matrix operations and eigen decomposition.

3 Gait Data Representation

Portions of the research in this paper use the CASIA Gait Database collected by the Institute of Automation, Chinese Academy of Sciences[2]. The database contains raw video recordings as well as extracted binary silhouettes by background subtraction (see Fig. 2). CASIA dataset A is chosen. It contains 240

---

[1] http://math.nist.gov/javanumerics/jama/
[2] CASIA Gait Database, http://www.sinobiometrics.com

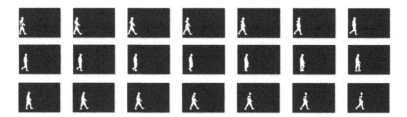

Fig. 2. Gait sequence from the CASIA database - actor "ljg"

sequences of gaits coming from 20 subjects, recorded from three different camera perspectives: i.e. parallel, 45 degrees and 90 degrees to the image planes. Subjects walk forward in two opposite directions. To improve the reduction and obtain directly comparable MPCA components, which simplifies classification, gaits are unified. We select only the parallel view and reflected horizontally gaits of opposite direction. To make classification independent from gait location and to remove useless data, a bounding box of every video frame is determined. It has fixed 100x180 resolution, adjusted to the tallest subject, and is centered to silhouette geometric centroid.

Gait sequences are considered to be the 3rd-order tensors with modes determined by spatial coordinates and time domain. The MPCA requires the same mode dimensionality of all tensors which is satisfied for spatial coordinates, but because of a different number of frames of video recordings the time domain mode has to be normalized. We applied linear scaling with a number of frames determined by an average video size.

4   Results

We examined two approaches in motion data dimensionality reduction:

- single dataset - all gait sequences are involved in learning - determining the eigenvalues and eigenvectors.
- train set and test set: the gait database is divided into the train and test sets - two sequences of each actor are included in the train set and the remaining two in the test set. Similarly to the supervised classifiers, MPCA uses only the train set in the learning phase.

The second approach, the more restrictive one, is more efficient in practical applications in terms of time and memory. To reconstruct the working of the "single dataset" approach directly, time consuming learning phases of MPCA and subsequent supervised classification have to be called separately for each newly classified gait. In the second approach learning is executed only once during the system initialization based on the supplied train set. However, removing some instances from the train set makes it less representative and makes learning much more difficult, especially in the case of small size train set.

In Fig. 3 the relationship between variation cover Q and obtained number of MPCA components is presented. This reduction was carried out for both proposed approaches - the single dataset with 80 gaits sequences and the train set containing half the data - 40 sequences. For the maximum considered parameter Q = 0.99, each of gait sequences is reduced approximately twice from the initial size of 900 to about 500 thousands of attributes in both cases. A single attribute is obtained when Q is less than 0.08. The compression rate is very similar for both analyzed train datasets.

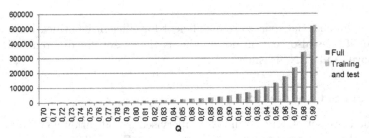

Fig. 3. Dimensionality reduction after applying MPCA algorithm

The reduced data is classified by two statistical WEKA[3] classifiers. It is a Naive Bayes (NB) with normal distribution and distribution estimated by kernel based method and the 1-nearest neighbor (1NN) classifier. The classification was repeated twice for both proposed reduction approaches. In case of the "single dataset", 10-fold cross-validation is used to split data into the train and test parts. To evaluate the classification accuracy we calculated the percentage of correctly classified gaits out of the test set.

4.1 Single Dataset

The detailed classification results are shown in Fig. 4. The mean classification accuracy for all considered Q values of 1NN classifier is 42.94% and the best result is 73.75% obtained by Q = 0.19 and Q = 0.20. In other cases, accuracy never exceeds 60%. There is a noticeable downward trend for the increasing Q parameter. More MPCA components undoubtedly contain more individual data, but also more noise.

The situation is quite different for Naive Bayes, which has a higher average score: 53.32% Beside the cases of strongly reduced gaits, ranging to Q = 0.48 with 358 MPCA components, it is much more precise. There is a very clear extreme for Q = 0.78 and 9064 attributes, in which the best classification accuracy of 86.25% is obtained. More MPCA components not only do not improve classification, but very strongly decrease it, to the worst performance of 16.25% for Q = 0.99. Naive Bayes is more robust in case of noisy data in comparison to 1NN and individual gait features are probably scattered in many different attributes.

---

[3] http://www.cs.waikato.ac.nz/ml/weka/

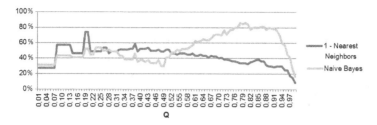

Fig. 4. 1NN and NB classification results for the single dataset approach

Thus, low dimensional spaces are insufficient for efficient identification and high dimensional ones also contain noise. This is the reason for differences between Naive Bayes and 1NN classifiers.

4.2 Train Set and Test Set

When the train set of MPCA and the supervised classification contain only half the data, the results are much worse as shown in Fig. 5. The performance does not exceed 30% and 43% of classification accuracy for Naive Bayes and 1NN classifiers, respectively. It is much better than random guessing, which gives only 5%, but still very poor. We suppose that it is mainly caused by the weak representativeness of input and reduced spaces because of the small size of the train set. Only two gait instances of each class are insufficient for effective probability estimation of high dimensional continuous spaces, necessary in statistical classification. To improve the classification we applied supervised discretization of reduced feature spaces, which should make statistical estimation easier. Because calculating distances in discrete spaces seems to be much less accurate than in the continuous ones, which is a crucial step of 1NN, we repeated the tests only for Naive Bayes classifier. In discretization we applied MDL method proposed by Fayyad and Irani [17]. The results shown in Fig. 6 are even better than we expected. Regardless of the poor representativeness of the train set, the maximum accuracy is 92.50% for Q=0.67 and 0.85, which means only three misclassified gaits. We can locate extreme once again. However the influence of noise in high dimensional spaces is weaker, for Q=0.99 accuracy is still higher than 60%.

Because of such promising results obtained by the classification based on discretized spaces for the "train set and test set" approach, we evaluated the influence of discretization on classification performance for the single dataset

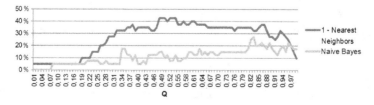

Fig. 5. 1NN and NB classification results for the train set and test set approach

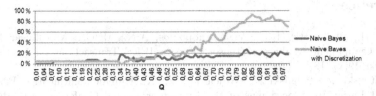

Fig. 6. Naive Bayes classification results for continuous and discretized spaces for train set and test set approach

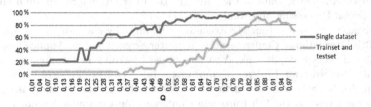

Fig. 7. Naive Bayes classification results for discretized spaces

approach. As seen in Fig. 7, the results have once again improved noticeably. The maximum precision is 98.75% for a wide range Q values starting from 0.76. It is always the same gait of the same subject, which is wrongly misclassified.

5   Conclusions

Multilinear principal component analysis is an effective method of reducing the dimensionality of tensor objects. Its application to gait sequences of video recordings data gives satisfactory results. The reduction preserves individual gait features, what allows us to identify humans precisely. In case of 84% of MPCA variation cover and the supervised discretization of reduced space, the Naive Bayes has 98.75% percentage of correctly classified gaits. It means that only one gait out of eighty validated is misclassified.

The more restrictive approach where the input data prior to the reduction of dimensionality is rigidly divided into two equinumerous sets - the train and test sets, was examined. The approach has important advantages from the point of view of practical deployments. It does not require separate computation associated with the learning phases of MPCA and with the supervised classification for each newly classified gait. Thus real-time identification has much lower computation requirements. Regardless of the small size of the train set - only two sequences for each actor, the 92.50% precision is achieved.

Discretization of continuous high dimensional spaces makes the classification much easier and in case of gait data, it does not remove individual features.

Acknowledgment. This paper has been supported by the research project OR00002111: "Application of video surveillance systems to person and behavior identification and threat detection, using biometrics and inference of 3D human model from video."

References

1. Lu, H., Plataniotis, K.N., Venetsanopoulos, A.N.: MPCA: Multilinear Principal Component Analysis of Tensor Objects. IEEE Transactions on Neural Networks 19(1), 18–39 (2008)
2. Świtoński, A., Polański, A., Wojciechowski, K.: Human Identification Based on Gait Paths. In: Proceedings of the 13th International Conference on Advanced Concepts for Intelligent Vision Systems (2011)
3. Świtoński, A., Polański, A., Wojciechowski, K.: Human Identification Based on the Reduced Kinematic Data of the Gait. In: 7th International Symposium on Image and Signal Processing and Analysis (2011)
4. Benbakreti, S., Benyettou, M.: Recognition Human by gait using PCA and DTW. In: 3th International Conference on Computer Science and its Applications (2011)
5. Kulbacki, M., Segen, J., Bak, A.: Unsupervised learning motion models using dynamic time warping. In: Proc. Symp. Intell. Inf. Syst., pp. 217–226 (2002)
6. Iwamoto, K., Sonobe, K., Komatsu, N.: A Gait Recognition Method using HMM. In: Proceedings of the 9th European Conference on Computer Vision, vol. 2, pp. 1936–1941. IEEE (2003)
7. Cheng, M.-H., Hoa, M.-F., Huanga, C.-L.: Gait analysis for human identification through manifold learning and HMM. Pattern Recognition 41(8), 2541–2553 (2008)
8. Pushpa R., M., Arumugam, G.: An efficient gait recognition system for human identification using modified ICA. International Journal of Computer Science & Information Technology 2(1) (2010)
9. Sminchisescu, C., Jepson, A.: Generative Modeling for Continuous Non-Linearly Embedded Visual Inference. In: ICML (2004)
10. Tacoob, Y.: Parameterized Modeling and Recognition of Activities. Computer Vision and Image Understanding 73(2), 232–247 (1999)
11. Liang, W., Tieniu, T., Huazhong, N., Weiming, H.: Silhouette Analysis-Based Gait Recognition for Human Identification. IEEE Transactions on Pattern Analysis and Machine Intelligence 25(12) (2003)
12. Vasilescu, M., Terzopoulos, D.: Multilinear Independent Components Analysis. In: Proceedings of the IEEE Computer Vision and Pattern Recognition Conference (2005)
13. Panagakis, Y., Kotropoulos, C., Arce, G.R.: Non-Negative Multilinear Principal Component Analysis of Auditory Temporal Modulations. IEEE Transactions on Audio, Speech, and Language Processing 18(3), 576–588 (2010)
14. Lu, H., Plataniotis, K.N., Venetsanopoulos, A.N.: Uncorrelated Multilinear Principal Component Analysis through Successive Variance Maximization. IEEE Transactions on Neural Networks 20(11), 1820–1836 (2009)
15. Josiński, H., Świtoński, A., Jędrasiak, K., Kostrzewa, D.: Human Identification Based on Gait Motion Capture Data. In: Proceeding of the International Multi-Conference of Engineers and Computer Scientists, vol. I (2012)
16. Witten, I.H., Frank, E.: Data Mining: Practical Machnine Learning Tool and Techniques
17. Fayyad, U.M., Irani, K.B.: Multi-interval discretization of continuousvalued attributes for classification learning. In: Thirteenth International Joint Conference on Articial Intelligence, pp. 1022–1027 (1993)

Canny Edge Detection Algorithm Modification

Wojciech Mokrzycki and Marek Samko

Faculty of Mathematics and Informatics
University of Warmia and Mazury, Olsztyn, Poland
Żonierska 14 10-561 Olsztyn, Poland
{mokrzycki,samko}@matman.uwm.edu.pl

Abstract. In this paper the novel modification of the well known Canny edge detection algorithm is presented. The first section describes the goal to be achieved by using the new algorithm. The second section describes theoretical basis of Canny algorithm and its practical implementation. Next, basics of the Ramer–Douglas–Peucker algorithm used for reducing the number of points in the curve are presented. The extension of the Canny algorithm and its implementation are presented in the fourth section. The next section shows the results of the new algorithm implementation for various images and presents statistical data to report effectiveness of the proposed algorithm modification.

1 Introduction

One of the most famous and commonly used edge detectors is Canny edge detector. Apart from simple filtering of the input image, the algorithm has a few optimization stages that make edges one-pixel wide and remove spaces between edge fragments to make them continous. The purpose of the researches was to extend Canny algorithm so that detected edges are prepared to be stored in beamlets structures.

Beamlets are a special dyadically organized collection of line segments, exhibiting a range of lengths, positions and orientations [1]. This collection is stored in multiscale pyramidal structure used for analysing linear features in two dimensional space. Relatively few line segments stored in beamlets could build quite general curves [1].

To prepare detected edges for storing in beamlets, the algorithm extension should make detected edges approximated by polygonial curve. Secondary result of this modification is reducing the number of pixels describing the edge. The algorithm extension, which uses Ramer–Douglas–Peucker algorithm, is started while the last stage of Canny algorithm (binarization with hysteresis) is performed.

2 Canny Edge Detector

2.1 Ideal Step Edge Detector

The goal of the Canny's researches was to find an ideal detector of the step edges. Canny assumed that such an ideal detector should satisfy the following conditions [2]:

L. Bolc et al. (Eds.): ICCVG 2012, LNCS 7594, pp. 533–540, 2012.
© Springer-Verlag Berlin Heidelberg 2012

1. Low level of the edge detection errors. The probability that the pixel, which does not belong to the edge in the input image, is marked as an edge pixel should be as low as possible. The probability of omitting (not marking) a pixel that is really an edge pixel should also be low. This criterion is mathematically represented by the following formula:

$$SNR = \frac{A \left| \int\limits_{-W}^{0} f(x)dx \right|}{n_0 \sqrt{\int\limits_{-W}^{W} f^2(x)dx}} \tag{1}$$

where: A – step edge amplitude, n_0 – standard deviation of the white gaussian noise, f – impulse response of the filter.

2. Good localization of detected edge. Dislocation between the detected edge and the real edge in the input image should be as small as possible. Thus, pixels marked by the detector as edge pixels should be placed as close to the center of the real edge as possible. Mathematical representation of this criterion is:

$$Localization = \frac{A|f'(0)|}{n_0 \sqrt{\int\limits_{-W}^{W} f'^2(x)dx}} \tag{2}$$

where: $f'(x)$ – first derivative of the filter impulse response.

3. Single response for single edge in the image. For each edge in the input image there should be exactly one response of the detector. This constraint is already included in the first criterion (low level of detection errors) – when a single edge gives two responses, one of them is incorrect. The following formula describes this criterion:

$$x_{zc} = \pi \left(\frac{\int\limits_{-\infty}^{\infty} f'^2(x)dx}{\int\limits_{-\infty}^{\infty} f''^2(x)dx} \right)^{\frac{1}{2}} \tag{3}$$

where: $f''(x)$ – second derivative of the filter impulse response.

Having considered the criteria depicted above, Canny found the filter which maximizes the first and the second criterion and satisfies single response for single edge limitation. Due to the fact that the resultant filter was too complex to have analytic solution, Canny proposed its effective approximation. This is the first derivative of gaussian operator:

$$\nabla G(x,y) = \left(\frac{1}{\sigma\sqrt{2\pi}} \exp\left(-\frac{x^2+y^2}{2\sigma^2} \right) \right)' \tag{4}$$

2.2 Algorithm Implementation

The first step of the Canny algorithm is the input image convolution with the found operator (4). In practical implementations instead of convolving image with first derivative of gaussian, convolution of image with gaussian followed by derivative calculation is often performed. Both operations are equal which results from convolution properties:

$$\nabla I'(x,y) = \nabla(I(x,y) * G(x,y)) = I(x,y) * \nabla G(x,y)$$

In this paper the second way of convolving (convolving with gaussian and calculating derivative) in Canny algorithm is used. Thus, the algorithm starts with image smoothing using gaussian:

$$I'(x,y) = I(x,y) * G(x,y)$$

where: $I(x,y)$ – resultant smoothed image, $I(x,y)$ – input image, $G(x,y)$ – gaussian operator.

Convolving image with two-dimensional gaussian is computationally complex. That is why it is commonly approximated by image convolution with one-dimensional gaussian in two perpendicular directions.

Next, differentiation in x and y directions is performed for a smoothed image:

$$\nabla_x I(x,y) = \frac{\partial I'(x,y)}{\partial x}, \ \nabla_y I(x,y) = \frac{\partial I'(x,y)}{\partial y}$$

On the basis of the calculated partial derivatives of the smoothed image $I'(x,y)$ the gradient module and direction are determined:

$$M(x,y) = \sqrt{(\nabla_x I'(x,y))^2 + (\nabla_y I'(x,y))^2} \tag{5}$$

$$\Theta(x,y) = \arctan \frac{\nabla_y I'(x,y)}{\nabla_x I'(x,y)} \tag{6}$$

where: $M(x,y)$ – gradient module, $\Theta(x,y)$ – angle between $M(x,y)$ vector and x axis of coordinate system.

The next stage of the algorithm is so called non-maximal suppression. It is performed to ensure one-pixel wide edge on the output of the algorithm. In direction perpendicular to the edge only one pixel with maximal gradient module value is preserved as the candidate edge pixel. Other pixels are suppressed – their value is set to background value. This operation is performed by testing 3x3 neighbourhood of each pixel and comparing the gradient module value of the central pixel with the values of the neighbour pixels in the gradient direction (perpendicular to the edge). If the central pixel has the maximum value, it is marked as the candidate edge pixel, otherwise its value is set to the background value.

The last stage of the algorithm is binarization. To avoid discontinuous edge on the output, Canny proposed binarization with hysteresis. This method consists in setting two thresholds. The candidate edge segment is added to the resultant edge map if at least one of its pixels has gradient module value greater or equal to high threshold T_H and other pixels have gradient module value not less than low threshold T_L:

$$L'(x,y) = \begin{cases} 0, \text{ if } L(x,y) < T_L \\ s, \text{ if } T_L \le L(x,y) < T_H \\ 1, \text{ if } L(x,y) \ge T_H \end{cases} \tag{7}$$

where: $L(x,y)$ – pixel value in source image, $L'(x,y)$ – pixel value in resultant image, T_L – low threshold, T_H – high threshold, $s = 0$ – if pixel does not neighbour with edge pixel, $s = 1$ – if pixel neighbours with edge pixel.

3   Ramer–Douglas–Peucker Algorithm

The purpose of the algorithm is to reduce the number of points describing the curve. Let the curve C_1 be described by the set of points $A = \{n_1, n_2, \ldots, n_p\}$. We want to find curve C_2 that is described by the set of points $B \subset A$ with the assumed accepted error ε.

The algorithm is illustrated in figure 1 and implemented as follows [3]:

1. The first and the last point of the curve C_1 are connected with the segment: $|n_1 n_p|$ (fig. 1b). Points n_1 and n_p are added to resultant set B.
2. From among other points of the curve $\{n_2 \ldots n_{p-1}\}$ point n_k is found, whose distance x from the segment $|n_1 n_p|$ is the largest (fig. 1c).
3. If $x \le \varepsilon$ then the algorithm is finished. In this case set $B = \{n_1, n_p\}$ and new curve C_2 is a segment $|n_1 n_p|$. Otherwise point n_k is added to B and algorithm is recursively started for curves: C_{1k} described by $\{n_1 \ldots n_k\}$ and C_{kp} described by $\{n_k \ldots n_p\}$ (fig. 1d).

4   Canny Algorithm Modification

As it was shown in the introduction, the goal of the algorithm modification is to reduce the complexity of the edges description and describe edges in the form proper to store them in a tree-based structures like beamlets. The first already implemented step consists in reducing number of pixels describing edges. This is achieved by using Ramer–Douglas–Peucker algorithm for edges detected by the standard Canny algorithm. On the output of the modified algorithm we get edges represented by curves that could be easily prepared for being stored in the beamlet. In this chapter the implementation of the proposed extension is described in more detail.

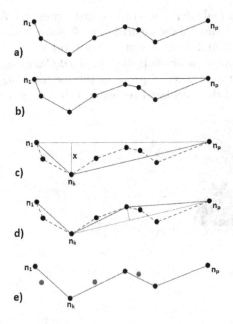

Fig. 1. Input curve, specified stages of the Ramer–Douglas–Peucker algorithm, output curve with reduced number of points

As it was shown earlier, the last stage of the Canny algorithm is binarization with hysteresis. The implementation of this stage starts with scanning pixels of the image and checking their value. When the first pixel with value greater or equal T_H is found, it is marked as an edge pixel. Next, eight of its neighbours are checked and their value is compared to the T_L. The pixel that has value greater or equal to T_L is marked as an edge pixel and recursively its neighbours are scanned. Thanks to this procedure, the chain of neighbouring pixels forming an edge is obtained. After reaching the last edge pixel, the algorithm looks for other edges using the same procedure. Having obtained a set of edges, each formed by a chain of pixels, the algorithm labels every single edge.

Now every labeled edge consists of a set of neighbouring pixels. The number of pixels is then reduced by passing the set of pixels to the input of Ramer–Douglas–Peucker algorithm for specified error level ε. On the output we get an edge described by the reduced number of points and represented by polygonal curve. This procedure is repeated for all labeled edges.

5   Experiments

Several experiments on various pictures were conducted during the research. In the real pictures the number of pixels describing edges was significantly reduced. Even with the minimal error $\varepsilon = 1$ the number of pixels was not bigger than 50% of the pixels obtained in the standard Canny algorithm. The obtained edges are represented by polygonal curves and can be easily prepared for storage in beam-lets structures. The results of the algorithm performance for sample pictures are shown in figures 2, 3 and 4. Also statistics are presented in table 1. It shows error level ε, the number of pixels in the standard Canny algorithm output P_C (before reduction), the number of pixels in the modified algorithm output P_M (after reduction) and the calculated reduction rate for all input images.

Fig. 2. Castle–input image, output of standard Canny algorithm and output of modi-fied algorithm for $\varepsilon = 10$, $\varepsilon = 5$ and $\varepsilon = 1$ respectively

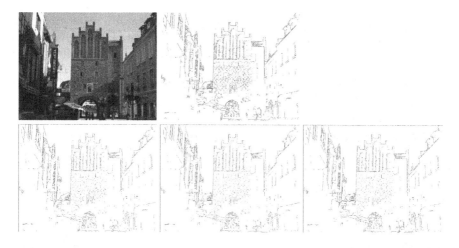

Fig. 3. Gate–input image, output of standard Canny algorithm and output of modified algorithm for $\varepsilon = 10$, $\varepsilon = 5$ and $\varepsilon = 1$ respectively

Fig. 4. Town hall–input image, output of standard Canny algorithm and output of modified algorithm for $\varepsilon = 10$, $\varepsilon = 5$ and $\varepsilon = 1$ respectively

Table 1. Statistic data of the modified alorithm performance

Image	ε	P_C	P_M	Reduction rate
Castle	10	14075	5034	35.77%
	5	14075	5040	35.81%
	1	14075	5694	40.45%
Gate	10	24237	5950	24.55%
	5	24237	5970	24.63%
	1	24237	6775	27.95%
Town hall	10	9112	2337	25.65%
	5	9112	2345	25.74%
	1	9112	2617	28.72%

6 Conclusions

The paper described Canny algorithm and its implementation. It presented modification of the Canny algorithm and its implementation followed by descriptions and the results of experiments based on various pictures. The modification included using Ramer–Douglas–Peucker algorithm to reduce the number of pixels and present the edges as polygonal curves which allow storing edges in beamlets. Although this article constitutes a discussion on the modification of Canny algorithm, due to limited resources the subject has not been fully examined and thus needs more investigation.

References

1. Donoho, D., Huo, X.: Applications of Beamlets to Detection and Extraction of Lines, Curves and Objects in Very Noisy Images. Nonlinear Signal and Image Processing (NSIP), Baltimore (2001)
2. Canny, J.: A computational approach to edge detection. IEEE Transactions on Pattern Analysis and Machine Intelligence PAMI-8 (1986)
3. Internet resource, `http://en.wikipedia.org/wiki/Ramer-Douglas-Peucker_algorithm` (accessed April 24, 2012)
4. Heath, M., Sarkar, S., Sanocki, T., Bowyer, K.: Comparison of Edge Detectors. Computer Vision and Image Understanding 69(1), 38–54 (1998)

Determination of Road Traffic Parameters Based on 3D Wavelet Representation of an Image Sequence

Wieslaw Pamula

Silesian University of Technology, Krasinskiego 8, 40-019 Katowice, Poland
wieslaw.pamula@polsl.pl

Abstract. This paper addresses the problem of providing traffic data for traffic control systems especially local traffic controllers, which optimize control sequences based on traffic loads at intersections. Optimization procedures require reliable data on preceding traffic changes for calculation of control commands. 3D wavelet representation of the road image sequence is proposed for use as an equivalent of traffic stream. Coefficients of this representation map with sufficient accuracy such traffic parameters as traffic density, traffic flow intensity and derivates. The level of wavelet decomposition is determined by the size and speed of the observed objects. Computation of the wavelet transform (3D DWT) may be easily performed using logic based circuits, which is an attractive solution for incorporation into local traffic controllers.

1 Introduction

The problem of determining parameters of moving objects in a sequence of images is tackled using several approaches. These are conditioned by the complexity of the algorithms, variability of the observation scene, required accuracy and speed of processing [1] [2]. The approaches may be broadly classified into two groups: segmentation based and feature based methods. The first group covers algorithms that segment the images extracting objects and then calculating their movement parameters. Feature-based methods analyse image pixels in context, extracting the spectral, temporal and spatial characteristics of neighbouring pixels and processing these instead of moving objects.

The idea of extracting moving objects uses the notions of background and foreground representing, respectively, elements that are permanent fixtures of the observed scene and elements of interest that change locations [3] [4]. Foreground elements constitute sought moving objects. Subtraction of the background from the current contents of the image frame gives moving objects. As the background changes, a reliable model is required to represent the changes. There are background models in the domain of intensities or features. The means by which the models properties are updated is characteristic of the particular methods. Techniques, such as average, median filtering, were the first applied to derive a background [5]. The reference background is the result of filtering a number

L. Bolc et al. (Eds.): ICCVG 2012, LNCS 7594, pp. 541–548, 2012.

of consecutive frames. A restrictive assumption had to be made that at least 50 % of the time no moving objects were present in the scene. This method is computationally simple, but sensitive to noise and changes of ambient lightning. The median filter may be approximated using the sigma-delta filter which significantly reduces memory requirements in implementation solutions [6].

To cope with complex light changes, pixel intensities are modelled using a mixture of Gaussian distributions [7] [8] [9]. An arbitrarily chosen number of parameterized distributions represent pixel intensity. Each incoming image frame contents updates the parameters of the distributions. Running averages and standard deviations are calculated. The current pixel value belongs to the foreground when it does not satisfy thresholds limited by distribution parameters. When changes in the background are fast, variance values of the Gaussian distributions become large and lead to a reduction in responsiveness.

Representing moving objects in the domain of features and aggregating these instead of segmenting images encompasses methods using feature detectors, salient points detection and methods based on processing transform coefficients [10] [11] [12]. Wavelet-based transforms prove attractive to apply as they preserve spatial relations among pixels and characterize these at different scales of examination. Temporarily related data that is important for movement description is obtained by subtraction of, consecutive in time, image coefficients or by taking time as the third dimension for processing.

Differencing in the transform domain is proposed in [13] [14]. The wavelet transform of consecutive image frames is calculated. Coefficients corresponding in space at several decomposition levels are subtracted each from the other. The difference values represent level-dependent motion detections and fused they denote movement in the observation field [15]. The differencing method was refined by introducing double change detection, an approach corresponding to double differencing used in background subtraction methods [16].

Image frames coming at consecutive time intervals constitute a 3D data object. A two dimensional representation is constructed by converting the frame contents into a pixel vector and assembling, consecutive in time, vectors into a 2D surface [17]. This surface depicts objects' movements in the frame in time as distinct strips.

The current work proposes a 3D analysis of the video stream. Digital wavelet transform is used for its advantageous calculation characteristics. This paper is divided into four parts. First, the characteristics of wavelets are briefly presented emphasizing DWT features, which are significant for the proposed analysis. The next section introduces the concept of an occupation index corresponding to traffic stream and shows the results of determining traffic density and traffic flow intensity. The concluding part summarizes the results and proposes further research topics.

2   Properties of 3D Digital Wavelet Transform

The choice of wavelet functions for representation is conditioned by the required accuracy and speed of calculation [18]. In this study this is further limited to interpolating transforms, which have simple algorithmic expressions suitable for integer based calculations easily implemented in logic-based circuits. Table 1 presents functions examined for representation of image sequence contents. The functions are built as pairs of prediction and update filters. The lifting scheme is used for streamlining the calculations. The lifting step consists of:

$$d_{n,i} = d_{n-1,i} + \sum_k P(k)s_{n-1,i-k},$$
$$s_{n,i} = s_{n-1,i} + \sum_k U(k)d_{n,i-k}, \tag{1}$$

$d_{n,i}$ - high pass coefficients, $s_{n,i}$ - low pass coefficients of the nth level of decomposition, $P(k)$ - prediction, $U(k)$ - update functions (mappings).

The listed transforms are separable, which facilitates separate calculation of coefficients for each dimension.

Table 1. Wavelet transforms using Deslauriers-Dubuc scaling functions

type	lifting steps of integer versions
(1,1)	$d_{1,i} = s_{0,2i+1} - s_{0,2i}$
	$s_{1,i} = s_{0,2i} + \lfloor d_{0,2i}/2 \rfloor$
(2,2)	$d_{1,i} = s_{0,2i+1} - \lfloor (s_{0,2i} + s_{0,2i+2})/2 + 1/2 \rfloor$
	$s_{1,i} = s_{0,2i} + \lfloor (d_{1,i-1} + d_{1,i})/4 + 1/2 \rfloor$
(4,4)	$d_{1,i} = s_{0,2i+1} - \lfloor 9(s_{0,2i} + s_{0,2i+2})/16$
	$\quad - (s_{0,2i} + s_{0,2i+4})/16 + 1/2 \rfloor$
	$s_{1,i} = s_{0,2i} + \lfloor 9(d_{1,i-1} + d_{1,i})/32$
	$\quad - (d_{1,i-2} + d_{1,i+1})/32 + 1/2 \rfloor$

Spatial and temporal resolution. The numbers of vanishing moments of the filters of the transforms determine the neighbourhood of pixels, which is involved in the calculation of coefficients. This characteristic, together with the level of decomposition, defines the resolution of the representation of the image sequence contents. The size of the neighbourhood S is expressed as the function of the level of decomposition n and the number of vanishing moments N is:

$$\begin{aligned} for\ N = 1 \quad & S = 2^n 2^n 2^n \\ for\ N > 1 \quad & S = (2^n + (2N - 1)(2^n - 1))^3 \end{aligned} \tag{2}$$

This neighbourhood defines the range of gathering the measure of spatio-temporal characteristics, which is manifested by the value of the wavelet coefficient. As such, it determines the resolution of analysis. The resolution limits the size and speed of detected moving objects.

The mapping of pixel distances to real world distances determines spatial resolution. Temporal resolution depends on the frame rate of the image sequence. At the third level of decomposition the neighbourhood for the (1,1) transform encompasses 8x8 pixels in eight consecutive frames, whereas in the case of the (4,4) transform it spreads over patches of 29x29 pixels in 29 consecutive image frames in all 24389 pixel values.

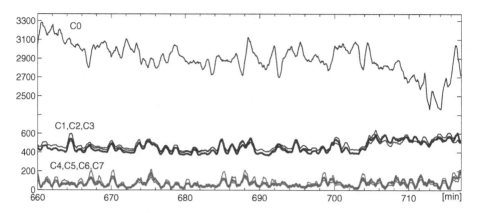

Fig. 1. Graphs of 3D wavelet coefficients

Three dimensional transform. 3D DWT based on Deslauriers-Dubuc scaling functions assigns sets of eight coefficient values to each pixel neighbourhood [19]. The (1,1) transform proved to be most efficient for performing calculations. It processes neighbourhoods of pixels that do not overlap eliminating multiple accesses to the same memory locations or enabling shortening of processing pipelines.

The coefficients values represent combinations of high and low pass filter responses at different dimensions of the image data stream. Values C_0, C_1, C_2, C_3 give spatial responses in the horizontal and vertical axes with low pass temporal responses: these are the middle graphs in the fig. 1. The C_4, C_5, C_6, C_7 show the high pass temporal response related at most to object motion: these are the lower graphs in fig. 1.

Coefficient C_0 is the outstanding coefficient and is the low pass response in all dimensions: the top graph in fig. 1. This coefficient tracks the mean light level in the neighbourhood also related to the overall colour of moving objects. Coefficient C_7 on the other end of the range of values represents high pass responses in all dimensions and is most robust to ambient light changes.

Coefficients C_1, C_2, C_3 represent average intensity changes in time, whereas C_4, C_5, C_6 highlight mean changes in space. Coefficients at subsequent levels of decomposition describe the characteristics of coefficients at previous levels, which in effect means enlarging the size of the pixel neighbourhood being characterized.

3   Road Traffic Parameters

The idea of the study is to determine coefficients, which at best model the characteristics of traffic parameters. The traffic density and traffic flow were chosen for investigation.

Density shows the number of vehicles moving on a stretch of a road. Traffic flow gives the number of vehicles travelling through a cross section of a road in a given time period. Treating coefficient streams as traffic streams leads to the proposition of defining a synthetic measure of behaviour such as an occupancy index O_i of the detection field:

$$O_i = 1/k \sum_k |C_i| \qquad (3)$$

The sum of absolute values of the coefficients is used as the synthetic measure of occupancy. This value is further normalized using the number of coefficients k describing the detection field. The resultant index maps the features of the traffic stream and thus enables the calculation of its parameters. For evaluating traffic density, it is proposed that the detection field encompasses a traffic lane - a dashed quadrangle in fig. 2a. For traffic flow calculation, in order to detect whole objects, a detection field of the size of the object is proposed for calculating occupation indices - a quadrangle in fig. 2b. The detection fields are fixed for a specific field of view of the road traffic camera.

Fig. 2. Occupancy fields defined on an image frame for calculating O_i, for determination of: a) traffic density, b) traffic flow intensity

3.1 Traffic Density Estimation

3D wavelet coefficients indicate moving objects. When a traffic lane is filled with vehicles occupancy indices vary in value. Experiments were carried out to determine the most representative index for tracking the traffic density. The ability to indicate congestion conditions, which means vehicles stopped in a queue along the whole length of the lane was also a desired property of the index. Indices O_2 and O_7 proved to be the best candidates. Index O_2 was chosen as it marked congestion conditions distinctly. Fig. 3 shows the performance of O_2. The graph plots the index averaged over 40 second periods to smooth the process of queue build up and discharge. The values were also scaled to the size of measured values of traffic density. Congestion may be detected by thresholding, a bias line gives an aproximate position of the threshold.

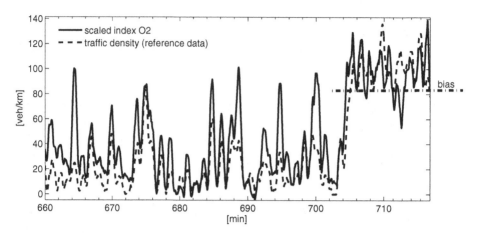

Fig. 3. Scaled index O_2 and traffic density graphs

Simple scale changes prove a high correlation between occupancy indices and traffic density values. These were achieved for a range of video streams containing rainy, sunny and cloudy traffic observations. In all, experiments were caried out with more than 30 hours of traffic films.

3.2 Traffic Flow Estimation

Detection of moving objects is achieved by analysis of the rate of change of pairs of occupancy indices. The peak of O_7 signals object movement which is confirmed by the extremum of O_0 or O_1. Peaks not confirmed indicate stopping objects, consecutive peaks are generated when objects resume motion.

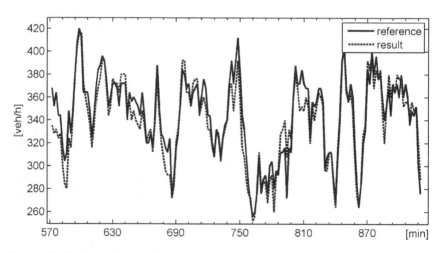

Fig. 4. Traffic flow calculated using occupancy indices (result) and refernce traffic flow intensity values (reference)

Fig. 4 shows traffic flow intensity calculated from the occupancy graph versus reference data acquired by manual measurements. The two graphs almost cover each other. Wavelet-based estimation gives lower values in some periods. Some erratic behaviour is also observed in highly congested traffic. The experiments were carried out using the same data base of traffic films as in the case of traffic density measurements. The mean error of determining traffic flow intensity was not higher than 3.5%.

Similar results are obtained when the occupation index is the sum of squared values of coefficients instead of absolute values.

4   Conclusions

The experimental results prove the feasibility and usefulness of the proposed method of determining road traffic parameters such as traffic density and traffic flow intensity, using 3D wavelet transform of image sequences. Analysis of coefficient values, which represent mixed spatial and temporal features, allows for robust determination of movement and requires no ambient light tracking in various conditions.

The fusion of coefficient behaviour data from adjacent levels of wavelet decomposition may be considered for enhancing the measuring algorithm.

References

1. Wu, Y., Shen, J., Dai, M.: Traffic object detections and its action analysis. Pattern Recognition Letters 26, 1963–1984 (2005)
2. Bugeau, A., Prez, P.: Detection and segmentation of moving objects in complex scenes. Computer Vision and Image Understanding 113, 459–476 (2009)
3. Piccardi, M.: Background subtraction techniques: A review. In: Proc. IEEE Int. Conf. Syst., Man, Cybern., vol. 4, pp. 3099–3104 (2004)
4. Li, L., Huang, W., Gu, I.Y.H., Tian, Q.: Statistical modeling of complex backgrounds for foreground object detection. IEEE Transactions on Image Processing 13, 1459–1472 (2004)
5. Cucchiara, R., Grana, C., Piccardi, M., Prati, A.: Detecting moving objects, ghosts, and shadows in video streams. IEEE Tram. on Pattern Anal. and Machine Intell. 25, 1337–1442 (2003)
6. Vargas, M., Milla, J.M., Toral, S.L., Barrero, F.: An Enhanced Background Estimation Algorithm for Vehicle Detection in Urban Traffic Scenes. IEEE Transactions On Vehicular Technology 59(8), 3694–3709 (2010)
7. Stauffer, C., Grimson, W.: Adaptive background mixture models for real-time tracking. In: Proc. IEEE Conf. Comput. Vis. Pattern Recog., vol. 2, pp. 246–252 (1999)
8. Stauffer, C., Grimson, W.: Learning patterns of activity using realtime tracking. IEEE Trans. Pattern Anal. Mach. Intell. 22(8), 747–757 (2000)
9. Harville, M.: A Framework for High-Level Feedback to Adaptive, Per-Pixel, Mixture-of-Gaussian Background Models. In: Heyden, A., Sparr, G., Nielsen, M., Johansen, P. (eds.) ECCV 2002, Part III. LNCS, vol. 2352, pp. 543–560. Springer, Heidelberg (2002)

10. Li, J., Allinson, N.M.: A comprehensive review of current local features for computer vision. Neurocomputing 71, 1771–1787 (2008)
11. Ilea, D.E., Whelan, F.P.: Image segmentation based on the integration of colour texture descriptors. A review. Pattern Recognition 44, 2479–2501 (2011)
12. Płaczek, B.: A Real Time Vehicle Detection Algorithm for Vision-Based Sensors. In: Bolc, L., Tadeusiewicz, R., Chmielewski, L.J., Wojciechowski, K. (eds.) ICCVG 2010, Part II. LNCS, vol. 6375, pp. 211–218. Springer, Heidelberg (2010)
13. Cheng, F.-H., Chen, Y.-L.: Real time multiple objects tracking and identification based on discrete wavelet transform. Pattern Recognition 39, 1126–1139 (2006)
14. Baradarani, A., JonathanWu, Q.M.: Wavelet-based Moving Object Segmentation From Scalar Wavelets to Dual-tree Complex Filter Banks. In: Herout, A. (ed.) Pattern Recognition Recent Advances. InTech (2010)
15. Anti, B., Crnojevi, V., Ulibrk, D.: Efficient wavelet based detection of moving objects. In: Proceedings 16th Int. Conf. on Digital Signal Processing, DSP 2009, Santorini, Greece, pp. 1–6. IEEE (2009)
16. Huang, J.-C., Su, T.-S., Wang, L.-J., Hsieh, W.-S.: Double-change-detection method for wavelet-based moving-object segmentation. Electronics Letters 40, 798–799 (2004)
17. Pamula, W.: Wavelet-based data reduction for detection of moving objects. Machine Graphics and Vision 20, 67–78 (2011)
18. Calderbank, A.R., Daubechies, I., Sweldens, W.: Wavelet Transforms that Map Integers to Integers. Applied and Computational Harmonic Analysis 5, 332–369 (1998)
19. Andreopoulos, Y., Munteanu, A., Van der Auwera, G., Cornelis, J.P.H., Schelkens, P.: Complete-to-Overcomplete Discrete Wavelet Transforms: Theory and Applications. IEEE Transactions on Signal Processing 53, 1398–1412 (2005)

Detection of Voids of Dental Root Canal Obturation Using Micro-CT

Rafał Petryniak[1], Zbisław Tabor[2], Anna Kierklo[3], and Małgorzata Jaworska[3]

[1] Institute of Applied Informatics, Cracow University of Technology
Al. Jana Pawła II 37, 31-864 Cracow, Poland
[2] Institute of Computer Science, Jagiellonian University
prof. Stanisława Lojasiewicza 6, 30-348 Cracow, Poland
[3] Department of Dentistry Propaedeutics Medical University of Bialystok
Jerzego Waszyngtona 15 A, 15-274 Bialystok, Poland
rpetryniak@gmail.com, zbislaw.tabor@wp.pl, Anna.Kierklo@umb.edu.pl

Abstract. In the present paper an algorithm for the detection of voids of dental root canal obturation in microCT images of the root is described. The algorithm consists of segmentation of the filling material, based on histogram analysis, detection of the voids surrounded by the filling material, detection of voids at the interface of dentine and root canal filling and final processing. The segmentation requires selecting two threshold levels and involves histogram thresholding followed by region growing. To detect the voids at the interface of the filling material a variant of a hit-or-miss filter is proposed. The performance of the algorithm is tested, based on a set of microCT images.

1 Introduction

A necessary condition of a successful therapy of a root canal is to adequately obturate the prepared root canal space [5,1,6]. The goal of the root canal obturation is to provide a complete filling of the canal.

Recently, a novel method of evaluating the quality of the root filling was proposed [4,2,3,7]. The method, which involves microCT scanning of a tooth, is nondestructive and provides three-dimensional data, the quality of which is determined mainly by the features of the microCT scanner. While the application of microCT scanners becomes a standard in the endodontic research, there is a challenge to develop image analysis tools to effectively and reliably examine the microCT data. The quantities, which determine the quality of root canal obturation, like the volume fraction of voids which are entirely surrounded by the filling material and those located at the interface of the root canal filling, can potentially depend on the features of the image processing procedures. Thus, to enable fair comparison between different studies and different endodontic procedures, a standard method of analyzing microCT data should be developed.

The aim of the present study was to develop an algorithm for the detection of the two types of voids in the root canal filling, based on three-dimensional microCT data. The algorithm depends on a small number of parameters.

L. Bolc et al. (Eds.): ICCVG 2012, LNCS 7594, pp. 549–556, 2012.

A rules of selecting these parameters are formulated and the performance of the proposed algorithm is demonstrated.

2   Materials and Methods

2.1   Materials

Ten extracted single-canal human mandibular premolars of similar size and root shape, with almost straight roots were used. The teeth were decoronated with a high-speed diamond discs and their root canals were prepared manually. The canals were irrigated with 2% sodium hypochlorite and 17% ethylenediaminete-traacetic acid (EDTA) for removing the smear layer, and finally, with saline solution. After drying, the root canals were obturated by thermomechanical condensation using gutta-percha and zinc oxide-eugenol-based sealer Tubli-seal (Kerr, Italy). Subsequently the roots were stored at 37°C with 100% humidity for 7 days to allow the sealers to set completely.

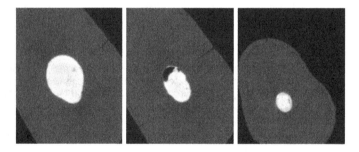

Fig. 1. Sample horizontal sections of a microCT image of a root with an obturated root canal. From left to right: top, middle and bottom parts of a root. A void is visible in the middle image.

An X-tek (Nikon) Benchtop CT160Xi high-resolution micro-CT scanner was used to scan the teeth. The settings of the microCT scanner were fixed for all samples. The X-ray tube was operating at 110kV and 50uA current. The samples were scanned with a pixel size of 10.6 micrometers, rotational step of 0.2 degree, rotational angle of 360 degrees and a 0,708 second exposure time. A 0,25 Copper filter was used to suppress beam hardening artifacts and a ring artifact minimizing algorithm was applied to the data. The original microCT images were coded with 32-bit float numbers. Prior to processing, the images were converted to 8 bit gray-level scale.

2.2   Methods

The algorithm developed for detection of voids consists of the following procedures, described below in detail: segmentation of the filling material, based on histogram analysis, detection of the voids surrounded by the filling material

($S - voids$), detection of voids at the interface of dentine and root canal filling ($I - voids$) and final processing. These procedures are applied sequentially to the initial microCT image.

Initial Segmentation of the Root Canal Filling. In all cases the histogram of gray level intensities of microCT images (Fig. 1) contained three well separated modes (Fig. 2), the left mode corresponding to the background (air), the middle mode corresponding to the dentine and the right mode corresponding to the filling material. Because the air and the dentine regions are homogeneous, the modes corresponding to these regions can be very well approximated with a Gaussian curves. The root canal filling contains two materials: sealer and gutta-percha and the mode corresponding to the canal root filling can be in principle approximated by a sum of two Gaussians.

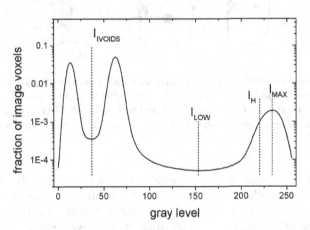

Fig. 2. Histogram of gray-level intensities of a microCT image of a root with an obturated root canal

Detection of the voids in the root canal filling, described below in detail, requires selecting two threshold levels I_{LOW} and I_{HIGH}. Threshold levels are determined, based on the analysis of the histogram of the gray-level intensities. The low threshold I_{LOW} was selected at the minimum between the modes corresponding to the dentine and the filling material. To avoid noise-related artifacts, I_{LOW} was determined for a histogram smoothed with a running average method. For smoothing a box with a size equal to eleven data points was used. To determine the high threshold I_{HIGH}, the difference between the gray-level intensity I_{MAX} of the maximum of the root canal filling mode and the gray-level intensity $I_H < I_{MAX}$ corresponding to the half of that maximum was found. The threshold I_{HIGH} was equal to:

$$I_{HIGH} = I_{MAX} - F * (I_{MAX} - I_H) \qquad (1)$$

where F is a user-adjusted parameter. After selecting the threshold levels, all voxels of the analyzed image with gray-level intensity less than I_{LOW} were assigned to the background (gray-level intensity equal to 0 - black) and the remaining voxels were assigned to the foreground (gray-level intensity equal to 255 - white). The value of I_{HIGH} is used to further process the regions associated with voids, as described in the following section.

Detection of the Voids. The $S - voids$ are defined as the black connected regions entirely surrounded by white voxels. A schematic draw of a root canal filling with an $S - void$ and $I - voids$ is shown in Fig. 3a. Thus, the detection of the $S - voids$ is equivalent to the standard hole filling procedure, defined within the framework of mathematical morphology.

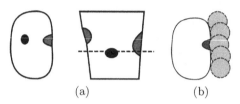

(a)   (b)

Fig. 3. (a) A schematic drawing of a horizontal (left) and longitudinal (right) cross-sections of a root canal filling with an $S - void$ (black region) and $I - voids$ (gray regions). (b) Detection of $I - voids$, based on the ball brush filter - the interior of the $I - void$ cannot be contained in sufficiently large gray balls which do not intersect the filling material.

The gray-level intensities of the medium within the $S - voids$ should be, in an ideal case, in a similar range as the density of soft tissues and lower than the density of dentine. However, because of the partial volume effect, one can expect that the range of the gray-level intensities of the voxels within the $S - voids$ is shifted to the higher values. Thus, segmentation utilizing I_{LOW} threshold only can potentially underestimate the volume of the $S - voids$. To (partially) correct for the partial volume effect, a region growing procedure is applied to the segmented image. For that purpose, starting from the connected regions corresponding to the $S - voids$, it is tested if the gray-level intensities of the foreground neighbours of the $S - voids$ are lower than I_{HIGH}. If that condition is fulfilled for some foreground neighboring voxel V, than V merges the processed $S - void$ and the procedure is repeated until convergence. Some arguments for the proposed procedure are given in the *Discussion* section. In the course of the region growing procedure, some $S - voids$ can merge the background, thus losing their $S - void$ status. Thus, to correctly distinguish $S - voids$ and $I - voids$, the hole filling procedure is repeated after finishing the region growing procedure. Finally, $S - voids$ are labelled and stored for further purposes.

The $I - voids$ (Fig. 3a) are roughly defined as cavities within the external surface of the foreground region, filled with background voxels. In an ideal case these cavities should contain voxels characterized by gray-level intensities in the range typical for soft tissues or fluid. However, because of the partial volume effect mentioned above, this need not be the case, especially for smaller cavities.

Because a rigorous definition of $I - voids$ can hardly be given, a semi-automatic procedure, utilizing an expert knowledge, is implemented to detect these voids. First, an initial cavity detection is performed, as described below in detail, and candidate $I - void$ voxels are found. Then, clusters of candidate $I - void$ voxels containing voxels characterized by gray-level intensity smaller than some user defined threshold I_{IVOIDS} are marked automatically. Next, the user is requested to put markers at the clusters of candidate $I - void$ voxels not marked automatically but recognized by the user as $I - voids$. Finally, the $I - voids$ are reconstructed from the set of all markers. The threshold level I_{IVOIDS} was selected at the minimum between the modes corresponding to the dentine and the air. As in the case of $S - voids$ detection a smoothed version of the gray-level histogram was used.

To detect candidate $I - void$ voxels a variant of a hit-or-miss filter (referred to as a ball brush filter) was implemented and applied to background voxels only. At the beginning of the procedure all background voxels are unmarked. Next, to launch the filtering procedure, a spherical structural element is defined with a radius R specified by a user. Then, for every background voxel V it is tested if all the voxels of the structuring element centered at V are contained within the background (Fig. 3b). If the condition is fulfilled then all the voxels in the structuring element are marked. Otherwise none voxel is marked. To speed up the procedure it can be noted that voxels whose distance from the foreground is larger than R must be certainly marked after finishing the filtering, while applying the filter to voxels at smaller distance would have no effect. Thus, before applying the ball brush filter to the image, an Euclidean distance from the foreground is calculated for all background voxels. Voxels at the distance $d > R + D$ are marked at the beginning and filtering is applied only to voxels at distance d such that $R - D \leq d \leq R + D$, where D is some buffer value (in all the calculations $D = 2$ was used). All background voxels which remain unmarked are labelled as candidate $I - void$ voxels.

In some cases the connected clusters of $I - void$ voxels can be composed of a bulk of voxels, contained within a cavity in the interface of a seal and flat tabs emerging from the bulk and merged to the interface outside a cavity. To correct for that effect, a morphological opening filter is applied to the segmented image, using a structuring element with type and size defined by the user. The filter is applied to $I - void$ voxels only and to 2D images in the set S_k, given in Eq. (2-4). Because as the result of filtering some tabs can decouple from the bulks of $I - void$ voxels, the reconstruction of $I - voids$ from the markers must be repeated after filtering.

3   Results

Horizontal sections of a microCT image of a sample tooth with an obturated root canal are shown in Fig. 1. Three mutually perpendicular sections of the reconstructed 3D image of the tooth are shown in Fig. 4. Clusters of dark voxels surrounded by bright voxels of the filling material are voids, which should

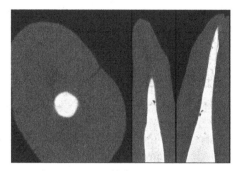

Fig. 4. Mutually perpendicular cross-sections of the reconstructed 3D microCT image of a sample tooth. Voids in the filling material manifest themselves as clusters of dark pixels surrounded by bright pixels.

be detected. The histogram of the gray-level intensities of the sample tooth is presented in Fig. 2. The values of I_{IVOIDS}, I_{LOW} and I_{HIGH} (for $F = 4$) are equal to 37, 153 and 175, respectively. The consecutive stages of the $S - voids$ detection are demonstrated in Fig. 5. Two axial cross-sections of a microCT image of a root are shown in the top panel of the figure. Two $S - voids$ detected after initial thresholding are marked with a gray color (middle panel). One of the voids (middle panel, right side) is localized close to the seal interface and after region growing this void merges black background and loses its $S - void$ status (bottom panel). The other void grows only marginally and does not change its

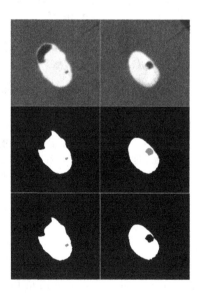

Fig. 5. Top - original 2D section of a microCT image of a tooth. Middle - images after initial thresholding and hole filling procedure. Bottom - images after region growing and final hole filling - final stage of S-voids detection

status of an $S - void$. A huge cavity - potentially an $I - void$ - is present in the top part of the filling material (right side images).

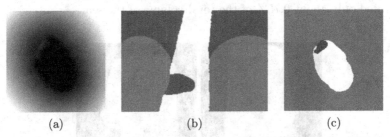

(a)   (b)   (c)

Fig. 6. (a) Euclidean distance from the foreground. (b) An intermediate stage of applying ball brush filter - horizontal section. (c) An intermediate stage of applying ball brush filter - longitudinal section.

The consecutive stages of the $I - voids$ detection, based on the ball brush filter are shown in Fig. 6. Because the size of the largest cavities in the interface of the filling material was of the order of 30-40 voxels, the radius of the structuring element was equal to 40. After computing the Euclidean distance from the foreground (Fig. 6a), filtering is applied to voxels at the distance in the range from 38 to 42 voxels. An intermediate step of the ball brush filtering is shown in Fig. 6b and Fig. 6c. Marked voxels are drawn with light gray and unmarked ones (candidate $I - void$ voxels after finished filtering) with dark gray colours. A flat tab artifact is present in the middle-right part of the interface of the seal in Fig. 6c. 3D renderings of the result of ball brush-based detection of candidate $I - void$ voxels is shown in Fig. 7.

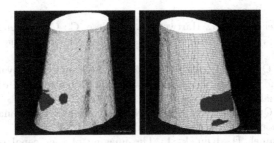

Fig. 7. 3D renderings of the root canal filling after ball brush filtering. Tab artifact manifest themselves as irregular clusters of bright and dark voxels on the surface of the seal. The $I - voids$ are visible as homogeneous gray regions.

After detecting candidate $I - void$ voxels, to correct for the tab artifacts, a set of markers was prepared. In the case of the part of the sample tooth (Fig. 5 - Fig. 7), markers were found automatically for the two largest $I - void$ clusters and the other three clusters were marked by the operator. After reconstructing $I - void$ clusters from the markers and applying morphological opening with a structural element size equal to 2 pixels, the tab artifacts disappeared (Fig. 8). The total volume of the $S - voids$ present in the filling of the sample tooth was 4 times smaller than the total volume of $I - voids$. The total volume of voids constituted only about 0.75% of the total volume of the seal.

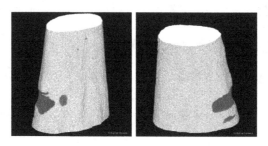

Fig. 8. The final result of ball brush-based detection of voids. After applying morphological opening and reconstruction from markers, tab artifacts disappeared.

4   Summary

In the present paper an algorithm for the detection of voids of dental root canal obturation in microCT images of the root was described. The performance of the algorithm was tested on a set of ten images. The correctness of the detection of the voids was approved visually. Because a large part of the endodontic research is focused on assessing the quality of root canal obturation a detection standard which delivers qualitative data related to the voids is highly expected.

References

1. Epley, S.R., Fleischman, J., Hartwell, G., Cicalese, C.: Completeness of root canal obturations: Epiphany techniques versus gutta-percha techniques. J. Endod. 32, 541–544 (2006)
2. Hammad, M., Qualtrough, A., Silikas, N.: Three-dimensional evaluation of effectiveness of hand and rotary instrumentation for retreatment of canals filled with different materials. J. Endod. 34, 1370–1373 (2008)
3. Hammad, M., Qualtrough, A., Silikas, N.: Evaluation of root canal obturation: A three - dimensional in vitro study. J. Endod. 35, 541–544 (2009)
4. Jung, M., Lommel, D., Klimek, J.: The imaging of root canal obturation using micro-CT. Int Endod J. 38, 617–626 (2005)
5. Oliver, C.M., Abbot, P.V.: Correlation between clinical success and apical dye penetration. Int. Endod. J. 34, 637–644 (2001)
6. Wu, M.K., Fan, B., Wesselink, P.R.: Diminished leakage along root canals filled with guttapercha without sealer over time: a laboratory study. Int. Endod. J. 33, 121–125 (2000)
7. Zaslansky, P., Fratzl, P., Rack, A., Wu, M.-K., Wesselink, P.R., Shemesh, H.: Identification of root filling interfaces by microscopy and tomography methods. Int. Endod. J. 44, 395–401 (2011)

Stafflines Pattern Detection
Using the Swarm Intelligence Algorithm

Weronika Piątkowska, Leszek Nowak, Marcin Pawłowski, and Maciej Ogorzałek

Faculty of Physics, Astronomy and Applied Computer Science
Jagiellonian University
Kraków, Poland

Abstract. This paper demonstrates the application of the Swarm Intelligence (SI) algorithm to recognize the specific patterns that are present in the digital images of handwritten music scores. The application introduced in this paper involves the detection of stafflines using particle swarm. The introduced solution described in this paper is a new approach to the problem, and illustrates how optimization algorithm can be modified and successfully applied in different subjects such as pattern recognition. The developed algorithm can be used as a first stage in Optical Music Recognition (OMR) that is followed by the staffline removal phase. It is worth pointing out, that contrary to most state-of-the-art algorithms, the proposed method does not require a binarization step in the preprocessing stage.

1 Introduction

Ant Colony Optimization (ACO) is one of a wide variety of computational methods used for solving global optimization problems. ACO algorithms are a part of Swarm Intelligence (SI) algorithms, which distinctive feature is the fact that they do not require any knowledge about the character of the solved problem. This means that no prior assumptions about the solution are necessary. In SI algorithms, the possible problem solutions are represented by the swarm of points (particles) that are located on the search space. These particles, in most cases are using a simple formula to calculate their fitness value. A number of particles are used in SI to search the solution space for the most optimal result. In the each iteration of the algorithm, these particles can change their position according to a set of rules. Depending on the applied rule set, there can be algorithms like: Particle Swarm Optimization (PSO), Ant Colony, Glow Swarm Optimization (GSO) etc. Most of those algorithms are based on real life swarm behavior examples [11]. Although SI algorithms have been proven effective in searching large solution spaces, they do not guarantee reaching an optimal result. Additionally, if the starting conditions are randomized, the algorithms can give different results each time. Taking into account SI characteristics, an assumption was made that it is possible to apply the particle swarm algorithm to the digital images processing problem where desired result is detection of specific patterns. This paper demonstrates, how particle swarm, using a simple rule set can explore two dimensional images in search of staffline patterns.

L. Bolc et al. (Eds.): ICCVG 2012, LNCS 7594, pp. 557–564, 2012.

2   Stafflines Detection and Extraction Problem

According to common music western notation, staffs can be treated as a two-dimensional system, in which the vertical coordinate indicates the pitch of notes, while horizontal coordinate - temporal features. Furthermore, staffs also can be used to determine the average size of music notation. This kind of information is crucial in the music recognition process. Therefore, the problem of detection of the staffs on music scores is a fundamental preprocessing step in Optical Music Recognition Systems.

Fig. 1. Binarized image of music manuscript; green lines represent staffline height and desired staffspace height; red lines represent the detection objective

Before the detection step can begin, parameters such as staffline height and staffspace height need to be estimated. Figure 1 illustrates an example image for which such estimation is done, and the desired detection result is marked. In most OMR Systems, the detection of stafflines is followed by the task of their removal; however few authors ignore stafflines after the localization step. The positions of staffs are firstly estimated according to the horizontal projections threshold value, along with the parameters of stafflines thickness and staffspace height. After that, the removal step can be seen as the image segmentation task, where pixels belonging to the staff are segmented from the background. In this paper an algorithm is introduced that uses a swarm of semi-intelligent particles that are able to move through the search space of the digital image that is a representation of the scanned music score. Each of these particles makes its own decisions concerning which route it should follow. Particles are able to find staffs and follow them. This can be done on the low quality images, without the necessity of preprocessing, and can solve the problem when standard projection thresholding fails.

3   State of the Art

3.1   Swarm Intelligence

A swarm is a collection of agents doing simple tasks to achieve complex results. Currently there are several approaches for modeling swarm behavior like Ant Colony Optimization (ACO), Stochastic Diffusion Search (SDS) or Particle Swarm Optimization (PSO). As shown in Fig. 2, clusters of particles are concentrated near the maxima of the two-dimensional search space. This is the result of running the example Glow Swarm algorithm, the objective of which was to find maximal values on the search surface.

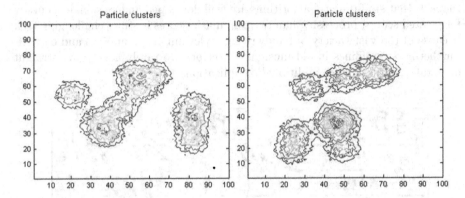

Fig. 2. Clusters of particles formed as a result of searching for the maximal values on the two dimensional space

Ant Colony Optimization uses an approach inspired by biological insects; ants are collaborating with each other to obtain food using the best (shortest) possible route. Like natural ants, agents leave trails of "pheromone" which are signals to other agents (stigmergic communication). This kind of model is used mostly in swarm robotics, traffic management and graph coloring. ACO method is also successfully applied in the task of contour matching in 2D [9]. The Stochastic Diffusion Search algorithm uses independent agents that examine space searching for the best solution of the previously assigned problem model. Every agent uses inexpensive methods to determine the answer for the given part of the problem. After obtaining the information an agent, sends gathered data to other agents. This algorithm is used with great effectiveness in text searching or object recognition [10]. Particle Swarm Optimization uses a little bit different approach than previous ones. Basically it starts by randomly setting up agents and modifies their behavior in the next steps to achieve the optimal solution.

3.2   Staffline Detection

The staffline detection problem is considered to be one of the crucial and fundamental preprocessing steps in Optical Music Recognition Systems. In western music notation, staffs are groups of five horizontal, equidistant and parallel lines, which define some kind of system, where notes and other symbols of music notation must be placed (not only on staffs, but also above and under each of them). Since staffs along with clefs and accidentals determine appropriate pitch of notes, it is crucial to localize them accurately on music scores. However, due to the fact that stafflines either touch or intersect notes, they remain a considerable obstacle in musical symbol localization and recognition. Hence, after correct detection of stafflines is done and information of corresponding notes pitch is gathered, the main effort is to isolate symbols of music notation from staffs. There are few authors, who ignore stafflines after the detection stage, nevertheless, most of them focus on removing staffs from music scores [2]. Despite the fact, that staff removal algorithms are well developed and gain high accuracy for printed scores, processing handwritten music scores is still a challenging task because of the vast variety of handwriting styles among composers and copyist. Furthermore, stafflines in old music manuscripts are rarely horizontal, straight or parallel, which induce additional complications.

Fig. 3. Fragment of an example image of scanned handwritten old music manuscript

As observed in Fig. 3, while processing old music manuscripts, the main problem is the poor quality and degradation of paper and ink. One of the most widely used technique for stafflines detection is finding the local maxima in the horizontal projection of the black pixels of the image, which correspond to staffline positions [1]. Another approach is based on vertical scan lines and Line Adjacency Graph (LAG), where potential lines are examined according to aspect ratio, connectedness and curvature criteria [2] [3]. Moreover, staff detection algorithms also use the Run-Length Coding method for the estimation of parameters such as staffline thickness and staffspace height (the distance between neighboring stafflines within a particular staff) [1]. Stafflines are determined on a basis of thickness, distance and position of grouped vertical columns on the image [4]. Other methods for staff detection employ line tracing, vertical and horizontal linkage of staff segments or rule-based classification [5] [6] [7]. The detection of stafflines is considered also as a global optimization problem [8]. Assuming that the image can be treated as a graph and stafflines can be considered as connected paths between margins, the problem is to find the shortest path.

4   Particles Swarm in Stafflines Detection

The proposed algorithm used to detect staffline pattern is inspired by PSO algorithms and in greater part the Ant Colony base concept. Although the original idea was similar to the first ACO algorithm, due to the course of research it has been modified. The modification is related to the pheromone trail, which no longer is a parameter that influences the behavior of other particles (ants).

4.1   Data Set Used for Testing

Images that were used in the development of the algorithm originated from the CVC-MUSCIMA database of handwritten music score images [12]. Music scores were scanned at 300 dpi and 24 bits per pixel. The size of each image was 3479x1290 pixels (containing multiple sets of stafflines), and for the detection process only a fragment of the original image was taken (containing a set of 5 stafflines). As a result, the size of the processed image was 3479x260 pixels in gray scale. This was done for easier result verification and shorter processing times.

4.2   Image Processing Stages

Each image is processed according to the following steps:

- Preprocessing done prior to running the algorithm involved only splitting the original scanned images into smaller fragments and conversion to grayscale.
- Generation of the starting particle swarm was the stage where each particle was placed in a random position on the image. The size of the swarm varied depending on the image size. The ratio used in the algorithm was 1 particle per 1000 pixels of the processed image.
- The execution of the rule set for each particle was done in a loop that needed to be repeated between 300 to 1000 times. Assuming that the particle speed is constant and is equal to 1 pixel per cycle, which ensures that each particle was, moved the same number of pixels as the loop cycles.
- The projection calculation is done on pheromone data that was generated by particles in the rule execution loop. The maxima of the projection plot Fig. 5 represent the position of the stafflines in the original image.

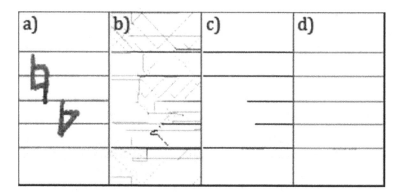

Fig. 4. Fragment of a testing image: a) original image; b) particle path trace; c) pheromone data; d) detected stafflines

4.3   Particle Behaviour Rules

To determine the behavior of the particles a data structure describing each of them was used:

- Position of the particle composed of X and Y component.
- Direction of movement. With 8 possible directions South, South-East, East, and so on.
- Persistence of the particle described how long the particle is moving in the same direction. The value of persistence increased if the particle moved in the same direction for more cycles.

In addition to the data structure, each particle was given a set of decision rules that influenced their behavior. These rules included:

- The particle can change direction of movement only by 45 degrees (e.g. moving south, particle can turn to south-east or south-west). This rule prevents "looping".
- The particle is "rewarded" (persistence parameter is increased) if it has been moving in the same direction as in previous step. This encourages following straight lines (e.g. stafflines) and ensures that if the staffline is "broken" the particle will be able to cross the "gap".
- The particle calculates three possible paths (turn left, go straight, turn right) two steps ahead. Then the best (darkest image pixels) path is selected.
- If all three paths have the same value, the path is selected at random.
- The particle is awarded higher persistence or moving east or west.
- The pheromone trail is generated Fig. 4c if persistence exceed threshold value.

These simple rules allow input image to be processed and the returning pheromone data allows easy calculation Fig. 5 of the staffline positions.

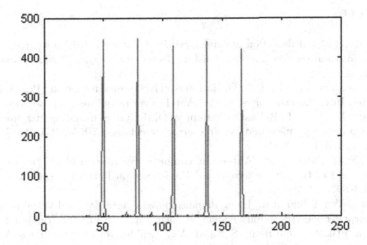

Fig. 5. Projection of the pheromone data

5   Discussion

As the previous section of this paper shows, it is possible to detect stafflines using particle swarms without the necessity of binarization or image enhancement. The introduced method is flexible and works well with images containing .jpg compression artifacts, or low contrast images where the staffline is printed in much brighter color than music notes. Example results are illustrated on Fig.6.

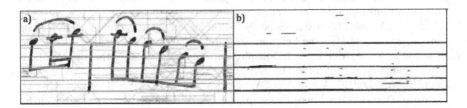

Fig. 6. Results of detection process: a) original image and particles paths (in green), b) pheromone data and detected stafflines (in red)

Taking into account the image compression and artifacts for 100 selected images from the database the algorithm detected stafflines with 99% success rate Fig. 6b. The computational complexity of the algorithm is expressed by the function $O(n)$ where n is the number of particles.

6   Conclusion

This method can easily be modified to be used in images where stafflines are drawn with a variable angle. And by extending the rule set, this algorithm can be applied to more complex patterns, or even music notes.

References

1. Fujinaga, I.: Staff detection and removal. In: George, S. (ed.) Visual Perception of Music Notation: On-Line and Off-Line Recognition, pp. 1–39. Idea Group Inc. (2004)
2. Bellini, P., Bruno, I., Nesi, P.: Optical music sheet segmentation. In: Proceedings of the First International Conference on Web Delivering of Music, pp. 183–190 (2001)
3. Rossant, F., Bloch, I.: Robust and adaptive OMR system including fuzzy modeling, fusion of musical rules, and possible error detection. EURASIP J. Appl. Signal Process., 160–160 (2007)
4. Reed, K.T., Parker, J.R.: Automatic computer recognition of printed music. In: Proceedings of the 13th International Conference on Pattern Recognition, vol. 3, pp. 803–807 (1996)
5. Roach, J.W., Tatem, J.E.: Using domain knowledge in low-level visual processing to interpret handwritten music: an experiment. In: Baird, Bunke, Yamamoto (eds.) Dorothea Blostein and Henry S. Baird, A Critical Survey of Music Image Analysis, vol. 6, pp. 405–434. Springer (1992)
6. Miyao, H., Okamoto, M.: Stave extraction for printed music scores using DP matching. Journal of Advanced Computational Intelligence and Intelligent Informatics 8, 208–215 (2004)
7. Mahoney, J.V.: Automatic analysis of music score images. B.Sc thesis, Department of Computer Science and Engineering, MIT. In: Baird, Bunke, Yamamoto (eds.) Dorothea Blostein and Henry S. Baird, A Critical Survey of Music Image Analysis, in Structured Document Image Analysis, pp. 405–434. Springer (1992)
8. Cardoso, J.S., Capela, A., Rebelo, A., Guedes, C., Da Costa, J.F.P.: Staff detection with stable paths. IEEE Transactions on Pattern Analysis and Machine Intelligence 31(6), 1134–1139 (2009)
9. Kaick, O., Hamarneh, G., Zhang, H., Wighton, P.: Contour correspondence via ant colony optimization, pp. 271–280. Computer Society (2007)
10. Gadat, S., Younes, L.: A stochastic algorithm for feature selection in pattern recognition. Journal of Machine Learning Research 8, 509–547 (2007)
11. Floreano, D., Mattiussi, C.: Bio-inspired artificial intelligence: theories, methods, and technologies. MIT Press, Cambridge (2008)
12. Fornés, A., Dutta, A., Gordo, A., Lladós, J.: CVC-MUSCIMA: A Ground-truth of Handwritten Music Score Images for Writer Identification and Staff Removal. International Journal on Document Analysis and Recognition (preprint), doi:10.1007/s10032-011-0168-2

Disparity Map Based Procedure for Collision-Free Guidance through Unknown Environments

Maciej Polańczyk and Przemysław Barański

Institute of Electronics, Technical University of Łódź
Wólczańska 211/215, 90-924 Łódź, Poland
maciej.polanczyk@gmail.com

Abstract. The paper presents an algorithm for building a map of obstacles and guiding an autonomous mobile platform in an unknown and changing environment. Depth images captured from a stereovision camera are used to detect objects and denote their location on the obstacle map. The depth images acquired from the stereocamera are encumbered with artefacts which poses the main problem in detecting obstacles. We propose a two-step filtering algorithm which is based on morphological operations and Bayesian inference. Experimental results proved the efficiency of the solution in the real environment wherein both static and mobile obstacles are present.

1 Introduction

The major task of control systems driving mobile platforms is the ability to detect and avoid static an moving obstacles. In many applications, where robots are programmed to explore an unknown environment, the map of the terrain with obstacles cannot be provided beforehand. Such a map needs to be built in run-time. Visual Simultaneous Localization And Mapping (VSLAM) is an algorithm which can guide a robot in an unknown and changing environment as well as built the model of the terrain.

As the robot explores new areas, the model of the environment is updated. The map is also used for estimating the robot's location. Moving obstacles are detected and included in the map. Their movements with respect to the robot position are traced to avoid collisions. Hence, the algorithm needs to work in real-time and reliability of positioning is of significant importance.

In this paper, a procedure for detecting obstacles and collision avoidance is presented. The mobile platform used in the trials housed a stereocamera. The information about the environment is obtained from depth images, which are compromised by many errors. This impairs correct identification of obstacles. An algorithm based on spatial filtering and Bayesian approach is employed. The trial results showed that the method is able to reliably navigate a robot in an unknown indoor and outdoor environment.

L. Bolc et al. (Eds.): ICCVG 2012, LNCS 7594, pp. 565–572, 2012.

2   Related Work

Research literature has extensively addressed the problem of building an up-to-date map. Majority of publications focus on a laser rangefinder, augmented with monocular or stereo vision [1],[2],[3] or sonar sensors [4], as a source of information of the environment. Such complex systems are characterized by high precision and reliability but are costly. Therefore, many researches focus on stereovision-only based systems that are more error-prone but much cheaper [5],[6].

The errors in depth images from stereovision systems can be corrected with a help of an image from a monocamera. For example the sub-pixel displacement methods [7] to enhance the accuracy of disparity have been developed. In [6] depth discontinuities in U-V-disparity domain are used to confirm the existence of obstacles.

The proposed method for building reliable obstacle maps uses only depth information. A general environment perception is estimated from a corrupted disparity map. Errors are corrected by both spatial and Bayesian filtering. The obtained map of obstacles devoid of artefacts is used for path-planning. The proposed platform-guidance system provides reliable mapping of an environment, correct short-term estimation of the platform's current position and real-time operation.

3   Proposed Solution

The proposed method consists of three processing stages: (I) camera motion estimation, (II) building a map of obstacles and (III) path planning - as presented on the flowchart in Fig. 1. Detailed description of the implemented algorithm for camera motion estimation can be found in the previous authors' papers [10]. Path planning is based on the well-known Lee's algorithm [11].

3.1   Preliminary Obstacles Detection

Using a stereovision depth image, 3D coordinates of points in the image are determined. Next, the points that are located further than Z_{max} (10m) from the camera are discarded. This decreases the location estimation error. (Disparity for closer points can be estimated more accurately). Points representing obstacles are assumed to have the Z coordinate in the range of 0-H_{max} (H_{max}-platform's height, 2m). Such assumption enables to eliminate points lying on the surface on which mobile platform is moving and located on hanging obstacles that have no impact on safety platform motion (note that to adopt this assumption the camera needs to be mounted parallel to the ground). Finally, points that belong to the considered volume are transformed from the camera coordinates to a 2D map of obstacles (Fig.1c)). The transformation is done according to the formula (1).

$$\begin{bmatrix} X_m \\ Z_m \end{bmatrix} = \begin{bmatrix} \cos(\beta) & \sin(\beta) \\ -\sin(\beta) & \cos(\beta) \end{bmatrix} \cdot \begin{bmatrix} X \\ Z \end{bmatrix} + \begin{bmatrix} X_c \\ Z_c \end{bmatrix} \tag{1}$$

where X_m, Z_m are the coordinates in the map, X_c, Z_c - the coordinates of a point in the real world, X, Z - the camera's current position in the map, β - the direction of the camera movement.

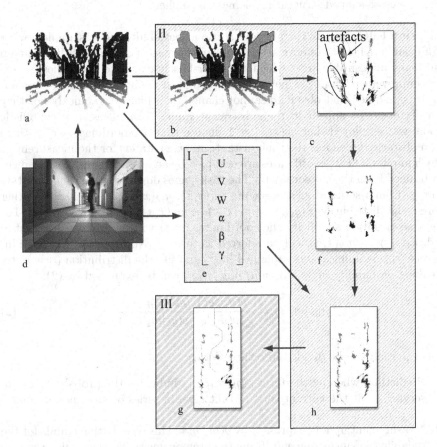

Fig. 1. The flowchart of the proposed algorithm. (a) Right image. (b) Disparity image with marked potential obstacles. (c) Potential obstacles points transformed to 2D map. (d) Depth image. (e) Motion vector. (f) Preliminary map of obstacles (c) after erosion. (h) Final map of obstacles. (g) Path. (I) Camera motion vector estimation. (II) Building map of obstacles. (III) Path planning.

3.2   Building Reliable Up-to-Date Map of Obstacles

A preliminary map of obstacles created in the previous step contains artefacts introduced by errors in disparity calculation (Fig.1c). These artefacts have to be filtered out since they cause difficulties in path planning (Fig. 2c). Therefore an algorithm employing spatial and Bayesian filtering is used. Points preliminarily classified as belonging to an obstacle undergo filtration (Fig. 1f, 1c) described in two next sections.

Spatial Filtering. Artefacts mainly consist of single points (Fig.2c). The probability that only one point was detected on the obstacle is considered as very low thus such a point can be neglected. Based on this assumption, the 3x3 erosion with the cross-shaped structuring element is applied.

Bayesian Filtering. In the previous section, spatial filtering was applied, what significantly helped to remove artefacts from the map of obstacles. Still, the map had many undesirable areas which stood for falsely calculated obstacles. A further improvement can be achieved by applying constraints on obstacles' dynamics. It is assumed that obstacles cannot change their places too quickly nor they can disappear or appear in the subsequent frame. The Bayesian probabilistic model was employed. Let $q_k(x, z) = 1$ denote that at coordinates (x, z) there is an obstacle. k denotes the time instant. $m_k(x, z)$ stands for the measurement which implies if (x, z) coordinates are occupied by an obstacle. The measurement is obtained from the stereocamera. The task comes down to estimating the state $q_k(x, y)$ from a series of measurements $m_1(x, z)$, $m_2(x, z)$, ... $m_k(x, z)$. In other words, the distribution $p(q_k(x, z)|m_1(x, z) \ldots m_k(x, z))$ needs to be found. For the sake of notion simplicity the coordinates (x, z) will be dropped hereinafter and $m_1(x, z) \ldots m_k(x, z)$ will be referred as to $m_{1:k}$. Applying the Bayesian inference with simplifications explained in [8] and [9], the distribution (or strictly speaking probability mass function) $p(q_k|m_{1:k})$ can be expressed by (2).

$$p(q_k|m_{1:k}) = \frac{p(m_k|q_k)p(q_k|m_{1:k-1})}{\sum\limits_{q_k} p(m_k|q_k)p(q_k|m_{1:k-1})} \tag{2}$$

This equation can be divided into three terms:

1. Prediction, whereby the term $p(q_k|m_{1:k-1})$ indicates the probability of observing q_k at the current time instant given a series of past measurements $m_{1:k-1}$.
2. Measurement update expressed by $p(m_k|q_k)$. This distribution stands for the reliability of measurements from the stereocamera. For example, $p(m_k = 1|q_k = 0)$ symbolizes the probability that the stereocamera indicates the presence of an obstacle, whereby in fact there is no obstacle in this place. The map of obstacles after spatial filtering incorporated such artefacts, hence the value $p(m_k = 1|q_k = 0)$ is greater than 0. Conversely, $p(m_k = 0|q_k = 1)$ implies the probability that the stereocamera could not detect the obstacle presence, e.g. the surface of an object was devoid of any texture.
3. Normalization which is expressed by $\sum\limits_{q_k} p(m_k|q_k)p(q_k|m_{1:k-1})$. The probability of q_k assuming 0 or 1, given a series of measurements $m_{1:k}$ should be a sure event. In other words, at given coordinates, there is or there is no obstacle, i.e. $p(q_k = 0|m_{1:k}) + p(q_k = 1|m_{1:k}) = 1$.

Consequently, if $p(q_k = 1|m_{1:k}) > 0.5$ it is assumed that an obstacle is present at given coordinates (x, z). Empirically, the history of 3 pasts measurements sufficed in the presented application to render good results. Thus, $p(q_k|m_{1:k})$

gets simplified to $p(q_k|m_{k-2:k})$ and $p(q_k|m_{1:k-1})$ to $p(q_k|m_{k-2:k-1})$, what greatly spares the memory.

All the coefficients in equation (2) are of empirical values and need to be selected by trial and error, depending on the stereocamera at hand and other factors like environment, lighting conditions, the penalty of overlooking an obstacle etc.

Map Update. While the stereovision camera explores 3D scene, a new obstacle can appear and other can change their positions. Therefore, to register the changes in the surrounding environment, a global map of obstacles must be built. All points with $p(q_k = 1|m_{1:k}) > 0.5$ are assumed to be obstacles and are added to the global map. All points existing in the global map, located within the camera visual proximity (defined as the 10m-long rectangular area in front of the camera restricted by a 100-degree camera's view angle), which are missing for last three measurements are labelled as "potentially to remove" and a follow-up procedure is done. In subsequent steps, it is verified whether these points are missing because the obstacles are not valid any more and should be removed or they were occluded by another obstacles. In order to do this, the disparities are compared. If the disparity is:

1. larger than the one resultant from the distance, it means that the obstacle was occluded by another object and should not be removed from the global map (closer objects have larger disparities).
2. otherwise it means that the object changed its position and has to be removed from the previous location on the map (some farther object is now within the camera's view range).

Disparity calculation based on the data from the global map is not a trivial task as the map is two-dimensional. Only information about X and Z coordinates is stored. To cope with this problem, disparities for all points in the range of Y: $0.0\text{m-}H_{\max}$ are computed and compared. Such updated global map of obstacles is an entry point for the path planning algorithm.

4   Experimental Results

In order to increase computational efficiency, the proposed algorithm is implemented in four parallel threads. The threads are responsible for: capturing stereovision images and calculating disparity, estimating the camera motion vector, obstacles detection and path planning, controlling the mobile platform.

To validate the proposed solution the Bumblebee2 stereovision camera was used [12]. This camera was mounted on the test mobile platform and several image sequences, for indoor environment, were captured. Fig. 2 presents the experimental results. In Fig. 2a the right image captured by the stereovision camera is shown. Fig. 2b presents the disparity image. Darker colours stand for farther localized points. Points marked with white could not be localized. Regions marked with slanted lines correspond to potential obstacles. In Fig. 2c

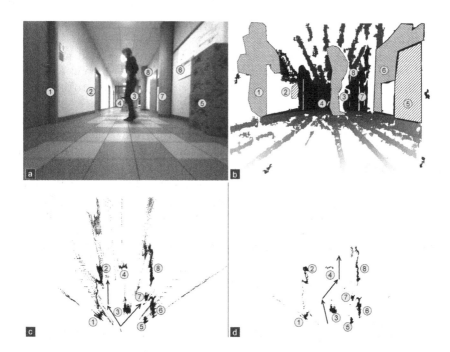

Fig. 2. The experimental results of proposed solution. (a) The frame captured form stereovision camera. (b) Disparity image; points being analyzed are marked with slanting lines; the darker color the further localized point; point for which disparity could not be calculated are marked white. (c) Potential obstacles points transformed to 2D map. Artifacts are visible. The thick dark arrows shows the impossibility of path planning. (d) Map of obstacles after spatio-bayesian filtering. The thick dark arrow shows the optimal path.

the preliminary map of obstacles is shown. Obstacle points (labelled 1-7) and artefacts are visible. The thick dark arrows show the impossibility of path planning. Most of the artefacts are removed after spatial and Bayesian filtering, c.f. Fig. 2d. The thick dark arrow shows the optimal path. In Fig. 3a larger global map of obstacles, built during the process of exploration, is presented. The thick dark line shows an optimal path. The A-B labels mean respectively: A) obstacles outside the camera vision range; B) obstacles within camera vision range.

Since the process of detecting objects and building a map is based only on a disparity image, homogeneous obstacles can get missed. A possible solution to this problem is to analyse data from an additional source like a monocamera's image.

In Table 1 the average computation times for every stage of the proposed algorithm are presented. The resolution of the images was 640x480. All calculations were performed using a 2.5GHz quad core computer. It can be noted that the image acquisition and disparity calculations are a weak point of the proposed solution. In order to cope with this problem, a disparity map could be calculated using a graphic card. Comparing the performance with other solutions tested on

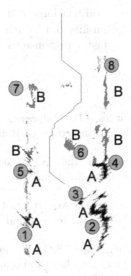

Fig. 3. Global map of obstacles with found path, A - obstacles outside the camera vision range, B - obstacles within camera vision range

similar equipment (the same camera, 2.4GHz processor), a significant improvement can be observed (the average computational time for images of 640x480 resolution for the proposed algorithm does not exceed 135ms. The algorithm in [8] operating on 320x240 images requires 230ms). Therefore, the proposed algorithm is more reliable and is able to avoid obstacles in a dynamically changing environment.

Table 1. Average times of computation

Stage	Time [ms]	Thread
Image acquisition and disparity calculation	60	1
Camera motion estimation	40	2
Obstacles detection	15	3
Map updating	20	3
Path planning	5	3
Mobile platform control	<1	4

5   Conclusion

An algorithm for building a map of obstacles based on stereovision was presented. The proposed method uses spatial and Bayesian filtering to deal with artefacts in the disparity map. The results proved that the described method greatly improves the quality of the maps. The precision of obstacles' localization allows to plan collision-free paths. The estimation of the camera motion is performed with ca. 17 frames per second and map building with ca. 28 frames per second. The average delay between the path update is ca. 130ms.

Further research will focus on modifications of the path planning procedure. A cost function based on the probability of obstacle occurrence will be used to plan a path. This will allow for a faster response to changes in the scene.

References

1. Castellanos, J.A., Neira, J., Tardos, J.D.: Multisensor fusion for simultaneous localization and map building. IEEE Transactions on Robotics and Automation 17(6), 908–914 (2001)
2. Murarka, A., Modayil, J., Kuipers, B.: Building Local Safety Maps for a Wheelchair Robot using Vision and Lasers. In: 3rd Canadian Conference on Computer and Robot Vision, vol. 25 (2006)
3. Labayrade, R., Royere, C., Gruyer, D., Aubert, D.: Cooperative Fusion for Multi-Obstacles Detection With Use of Stereovision and Laser Scanner. Autonomous Robots 19, 117–140 (2005)
4. Xue-Cheng, L., Cheong-Yeen, K., Shuzhi, S.G., Al Mamun, A.: Online map building for autonomous mobile robots by fusing laser and sonar data. In: Mechatronics and Automation, vol. 2, pp. 993–998 (2005)
5. Agrawal, M., Konolige, K., Bolles, R.C.: Localization and Mapping for Autonomous Navigation in Outdoor Terrains: A Stereo Vision Approach. Applications of Computer Vision 7 (2007)
6. Bai, M., Zhuang, Y., Wang, W.: Stereovision based obstacle detection approach for mobile robot navigation. In: International Conference on Intelligent Control and Information Processing (ICICIP), pp. 328–333 (2010)
7. Young-Chul, L., Chung-Hee, L., Soon, K., Woo-Young, J.: Distance Estimation Algorithm for Both Long and Short Ranges Based on Stereo Vision System. In: Intelligent Vehicles Symposium, pp. 841–846 (2008)
8. Cappe, O., Godsill, S., Moulines, E.: An overview of existing methods and recent advances in sequential Monte Carlo. Proceeding of the IEEE 95, 899–924 (2007)
9. Arulampalam, M., Maskell, S., Gordon, N., Clapp, T.: A tutorial on particle filters for online nonlinear/non-Gaussian Bayesian tracking. IEEE Transactions on Signal Processing 50(2), 174–188 (2002)
10. Polaczyk, M., Baraski, P., Strzelecki, M.: The application of Kalman filter in visual odometry for eliminating direction drift. In: International Conference on Signals and Electronic Systems, pp. 131–134 (2010)
11. Lee, C.Y.: An algorithm for path connection and its applications. IRE Trans. on Electronic Computers EC-10(3), 346–365 (1961)
12. BumbleBee2, http://www.ptgrey.com/products/bumblebee2/index.asp

Real-Time Hand Pose Estimation
Using Classifiers

Mateusz Półrola and Adam Wojciechowski

Institute of Computer Science, Technical University, Łódź, Poland
mateusz.polrola@gmail.com,
adam.wojciechowski@p.lodz.pl

Abstract. Development of human-computer interaction methods tends
to exploit more and more natural human activities like thoughts, body
posture or hands gesticulation. While most of authors improve whole
body tracking this paper concentrates on hand's poses analysis. Due to
the usage of the depth image based object recognition approach to hand
pose estimation a very precise method was obtained. Additionally thanks
to decision forest implemented on GPU a real-time processing is possible.

1 Introduction

Development of new human-computer interaction (HCI) methods, when computers are part of our everyday life, is nowadays one of the most important
tasks. Standard input devices such as a mouse and a keyboard are unnatural for
humans and in some cases cannot be used e.g. in a sterile operating room, and
everywhere computers tend to be transparent to users. Then much more intuitive
and recomended solution is communication using hand gestures, especially hand
poses. Hands are one of the most effective ways of nonverbal communication between people. Ability to determine hand pose can be very useful in hand gesture
recognition [14] or virtual objects' selection and manipulation. In this paper we
describe a method for real-time, image depth based, hand pose detection.

2 State of Art

Hand pose detection comes down to determining its skeleton joints positions. The
most efficient and accurate way to determine hand pose requires data gloves
equipped with tracking system [1], but they are expensive and inconvenient
solution to the user.

An alternative to data gloves are computer vision based methods. These methods can be classified by the type of used image. The most commonly used are
standard RGB images, but use of depth map images are popular too. In computer vision based methods of hand pose detection we can identify common
phases: localization of the hand and extraction of its features [14].

The purpose of hand localization is to extract image elements that belong only
to the hand. One way to achieve that is skin colour segmentation [4,9,10,22,28],

L. Bolc et al. (Eds.): ICCVG 2012, LNCS 7594, pp. 573–580, 2012.

or in case of using depth images, segmentation by thresholding depth values [19]. Other commonly used methods involve removing of background either by static background subtraction [2,8] or by the use of adaptive background models [3,4]. Common approach to the problem of hand localization is use of classification, usually in the form of a cascade of classifiers [11].

The features extraction phase aims to find the characteristic features such as position of fingers and palm centre. For this purpose, the hand contour analysis is often used. In these methods the hand position is calculated as a center of gravity of the contour [12], or as a point that maximizes distance to the nearest point of the contour [4,6,7]. Localization of the fingers can be done by finding local maxima of the hand contour curvature [2,8,9] or by the use of correlation methods using templates from real images [5,3]. Another approaches used in hand features extraction are machine learning [13,15] and object recognition [16]. There are also methods that try to fit the 3D hand model to the image [17,18] using optimization methods.

Our method uses depth images, because they provide more information than standard RGB images and it simplifies segmentation process. Additionally depth maps allow our method to recognize hand parts positions even when the hand is closed, which was only possible with data gloves or with use of 3d model fitting methods. For features extraction our method uses machine learning approach. Proposed method was inspired by Shotton work [20]. We employ the same object recognition approach applied to individual pixels, but instead of detecting body parts we construct classifier which detects hand parts. Contrary to Shotton we use integral image to find local modes of probabilities which are result of classification, instead of mean shift algorithm.

3   Method

The proposed method assumes usage of the object recognition approach to detect hand pose. The method exploits classifier that assigns labels of corresponding hand parts to individual pixels of depth image. Similarly like in Shotton method randomized decision forest is used as a classifier. As a result of that classification we get per pixel probabilities for each class, but unlike in Shotton's method we do not use mean shift to generate final joints proposals from this probabilities. The classifier is trained on pixels of real, hand labelled depth images.

Recognition of hand positions based on depth map consists of the following steps: hand segmentation, classification, hand joints pose determination and filtering.

As a depth map camera we use Microsoft Kinect, which provides depth maps of 640×480 pixels resolution with depth range from 0.4 m to 3.5 m. Depth accuracy is about 1 cm at distance of 2 m, which is a maximum working distance for our method. Hand pose recognition from larger distances is problematic because of small size of hand in depth map at that distances, but distance of 2 m creates comfortable workspace for user.

Hand has been divided into seven classes - five representing individual fingers, one representing centre of the hand and one representing rest of the hand.

Both the training and testing images were collected manually using the Microsoft Kinect and hand labelled. Labelling process was done using custom application that allows to "paint" labels on already captured depth maps. Images contain different hand configurations (number of visible fingers, open/closed hand) and some popular gestures: "thumb up", "victory sign", "okay sign", etc.

3.1   Hand Segmentation and Classification

Proposed method uses depth maps with segmented hands as an input. Segmentation process is not part of the method, but is needed by the method to work properly. We use very simple segmentation method that assumes that there are no other objects between user and depth camera. Additionally upper body part of the user is visible to the camera. Based on these assumptions, segmentation by simply thresholding depth values, was performed. The threshold is calculated as the lowest depth value of most bottom row of depth image[1]. To all pixels with depth value greater than that threshold, large constant value is assigned. This kind of segmentation can give many failures but it is only used to present essential part of the method. Fact of using Kinect creates possibility to exploit existing methods of tracking human body and use this additional information in segmentation process.

As mentioned earlier, the classification is done with a randomized decision forest, which is a composition of several decision trees. This approach, called boosting [24], is often used in machine learning to create a "stronger" classifier by means of few "weaker" ones. The classification algorithm has been implemented on graphic card processor (GPU), which significantly speeded up the process, and allowed to detect hand pose in time of about 5 ms.

Individual trees that form the randomized decision forest are trained using randomly selected pixels from the training images, this approach is known in the literature as bagging [25]. The trees are trained using Quinlan [23] method. During the training, each tree node contains some of the training samples and tries to select the most appropriate training samples split criterion. This will result in the separation of training data into two more homogeneous parts. By homogeneity we understand that most or all of samples in given part have the same label. At the beginning all training samples are assigned to root node of tree. The Shanonn entropy is used to measure training data homogeneity (eq. 1)

$$H(Q) = - \sum_i^n p(x_i) log\, p(x_i) \qquad (1)$$

where n is the number of classes in training data and $p(x_i)$ is the ration of number of training samples in node Q belonging to the class i to number of all samples in node Q.

Training samples are split into two sets defined as in equations 2 and 3

$$Q_L(u, v, \tau) = \{(I, x) | f_{u,v}(I, x) < \tau\} \qquad (2)$$

---

[1] For the distance of 2 m bottom row of depth image will always contain part of the user eg. torso or hips.

$$Q_R(u, v, \tau) = \{(I, x) | f_{u,v}(I, x) \geq \tau\} \tag{3}$$

where x are coordinates of pixel from image I, u and v are offset vectors and τ is a threshold value. The triple (u, v, τ) is the split criterion. The function $f_{u,v}(I, x)$ is called pixel feature and is defined like in Shotton (eq. 4).

$$f_{u,v}(I, x) = d_I(x + \frac{u}{d_I(x)}) - d_I(x + \frac{v}{d_I(x)}) \tag{4}$$

where d_I is the depth value of pixel x from image I. As Shotton reported "the normalization of the offsets by d_I ensures the features are depth invariant" [20]. These features are inexpensive to calculate and allow for efficient implementation on GPU.

The node Q has assigned the split criterion θ^* (eq. 6), from set of all split criterions generated randomly for each node, that maximizes information gain.

$$G(u, v, \tau) = H(Q) - \sum_{s \in \{L, R\}} \frac{|Q_s(u, v, \tau)|}{|Q|} H(Q_s(u, v, \tau)) \tag{5}$$

$$\theta^* = \arg\max_\theta G(\theta) \tag{6}$$

where $\theta = (u, v, \tau)$. The two sets $Q_L(\theta^*)$ and $Q_R(\theta^*)$, defined by equations 2 and 3, are assigned to respectively left and right child node of current node and whole process is repeated for them. After number of divisions, resulting from assumed tree height, normalized histogram of classes calculated from training samples, that reached this node, is saved in each leaf node.

Process of classification starts from root node. Examined pixel coming from depth map I and having position x is tested using test from equations 2 and 3 using split criterion stored in current node. According to result of that test process is repeated recursively for left or right child node of current node. Process stops when pixel reaches leaf node which stores information about probabilities that examined pixel belongs to selected classes. Final probability of pixel belonging to each hand part is calculated as average of results from each tree in forest. Middle column of figure 1 shows classification results[2].

3.2 Hand Parts Position Determination

Positions of the parts of analyzed hands are calculated based on the image pixels probability distribution belonging to the class of a given hand part. Rectangular areas of fixed size with summed probability of pixels, belonging to it, above some threshold are searched in the image. This searching is done using integral image [11], which helps to speed up the process.

Points representing centres of these areas are then clustered using k-means algorithm with constant $k = 2$. This allows to correctly find hand parts when the image contains both hands. For each of this two groups centres a closest region is

---

[2] Pixel is assigned to class with the highest probability

found. The distance between these two regions must be above some distance to prevent reporting two, the same, parts of hands in case the image contains only one hand. If the distance is below the threshold, the region with higher summed probability is chosen to represent hand part position (right column of fig. 1).

Fig. 1. Steps of the method: left column - test images with labels, middle column - results of classification, right column - final hand parts positions

The depth of the part is calculated based on pixels in region as weighted average of pixels depth values with weights equal to probability of pixels belonging to given class. Afterwards hand parts are assigned to left/right hand accordingly. Additionally hand parts positions can be filtered using double exponential filter, what assures reasonable tradeoff between smoothness and latency [26]. Another useful feature of this kind of filtering is prediction. It can be used to prevent flickering caused by not finding hand parts for some reasons in selected frames.

4   Experiments

The method was trained with 2500 labelled depth images and tested with 500 images. Unless otherwise specified, forest training parameters were: 3 trees, height 20, 500 pixels samples from each training image, 2000 pairs of u, v offsets in range of 300 pixels, 50 τ threshold values which gives 100000 split criterions.

We have tested classification and hand's parts position accuracy, that means that presented results are not the accuracy of recognition of specific hand poses. For classification we have measured accuracy as average per-class accuracy. For parts' positions we have measured average distance from part position calculated as described in section 3.2 and part position calculated using the same method but using test image labels as classification results. We have tested influence of different parameters of forest training on accuracy of the method.

Number of pixel samples. Figures 2 and 3 show influence of number of pixel samples, chosen randomly from each training image, on classifier accuracy and average parts positions estimation. Increasing the number of samples, the parts positions estimation error decreases, but time needed to train classifiers increases. The tradeoff between time of classifier training and low position estimation error is achieved for 100-400 samples per image.

Depth of trees. Figures 4 and 5 show influence of tree depth on classifier accuracy and average parts positions estimation. As can be seen increasing depth of tree parts positions estimation error decreases and saturates for depth of 16 levels. For this value the classifier accuracy is the highest. Although higher depth values decrease classifier accuracy, they still decrease position estimation error.

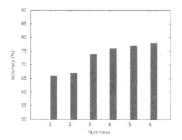

Fig. 2. Influence of number of image pixel samples on classifier accuracy

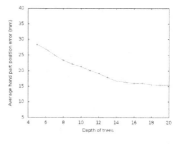

Fig. 3. Influence of number of image pixel samples on position error

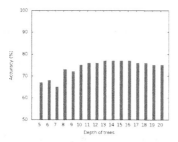

Fig. 4. Influence of trees depth on classifier accuracy

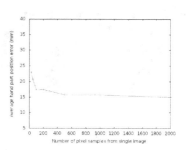

Fig. 5. Influence of trees depth on position error

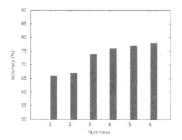

Fig. 6. Influence of number of trees on classifier accuracy

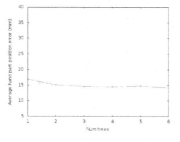

Fig. 7. Influence of number of trees on position error

Number of trees. Figures 6 and 7 show influence of number of trees in forest on classifier accuracy and average parts positions estimation. As can be seen, the more trees, the overall forest accuracy is higher, but it does not decrease position estimation error. On the other side the time needed for classification is linearly dependent on the number of trees. Good tradeoff is 2-3 trees in a forest.

5   Conclusions and Future Work

Created method proves that machine learning techniques, based on depth information, yield in very good results in the hand pose estimation field. Obtained results show that average error of individual hand parts positions estimations is about 15 mm for hand poses similar to the training set. Additional GPU [27] method implementation assured its real-time processing (5 ms per frame on notebook). Although maximum limit for current depth cameras is 30 fps, we must remember that proposed method will be mainly used as an input layer by other applications, which will have their own processing time requirements e.g. games, medical visualization systems.

Currently, in training set, there are images without or with very small rotation of hands, therefore method has some difficulties with pose recognition for rotated hands. Results of method can be further used to gesture recognition or sign language recognition by use of other artificial intelligence methods e.g. neural networks.

Another improvement, that can be applied, is method training with artificial images generated from 3d hand model [16]. It allows to create a bigger and a more representative training set with more accurate labels. Currently method can detect only positions of hand parts that are visible to the camera, however regression approach instead of classification could improve results due to correct positions estimation of not visible hand parts [21].

References

1. Sturman, D.J., Zeltzer, D.: A survey of glove-based input. IEEE Computer Graphics and Applications 14 (1994)
2. Malik, S., Laszlo, J.: Visual touchpad: a two-handed gestural input device. In: ICMI 2004: 6th International Conference on Multimodal Interfaces (2004)
3. Letessier, J., Berard, F.: Visual tracking of bare fingers for interactive surfaces. In: 17th Annual ACM Symposium on User Interface Software and Technology (2004)
4. Mo, Z., Lewis, J.P., Neumann, U.: Smartcanvas: a gesture-driven intelligent drawing desk system. In: 10th International Conference on Intelligent User Interfaces (2005)
5. O'Hagan, R., Zielinsky, A.: Finger Track - A Robust and Real-Time Gesture Interface. In: Sattar, A. (ed.) Canadian AI 1997. LNCS, vol. 1342, pp. 475–484. Springer, Heidelberg (1997)
6. Koike, H., Sato, Y., Kobayashi, Y.: Integrating paper and digital information on enhanceddesk: a method for realtime finger tracking on an augmented desk system. ACM Transactions on Computer Human Interaction 8 (2001)

7. Abe, K., Saito, H., Ozawa, S.: 3D drawing system via hand motion recognition from two cameras. In: IEEE International Conference on Systems, Man, and Cybernetics, vol. 2 (2000)
8. Segen, J., Kumar, S.: Gesture VR: vision-based 3D hand interface for spatial interaction. In: Sixth ACM International Conference on Multimedia (1998)
9. O'Hagan, R.G., Zelinsky, A., Rougeaux, S.: Visual gesture interfaces for virtual environments. Interacting with Computers 14 (2002)
10. Kjeldsen, R., Kender, J.: Toward the use of gesture in traditional user interfaces. In: International Conference on Automatic Face and Gesture Recognition (1996)
11. Viola, P.A., Jones, M.J.: Robust Real-time Object Detection. International Journal of Computer Vision (2001)
12. Jo, K.H., Kuno, Y., Shirai, Y.: Manipulative hand gesture recognition using task knowledge for human computer interaction. In: Third International Conference on Face and Gesture Recognition (1998)
13. Mackie, J., McCane, B.: Finger detection with decision trees. In: Image and Vision Computing, IVCNZ (2004)
14. Erol, A., Bebis, G., Nicolescu, M., Boyle, R.D., Twombly, X.: Vision-based hand pose estimation: A review. Computer Vision and Image Understanding (2007)
15. de Campos, T.E., Murray, D.W.: Regression-based Hand Pose Estimation from Multiple Cameras. Computer Vision and Pattern Recognition (2006)
16. Keskin, C., Kirac, F., Kara, Y.E., Akarun, L.: Real Time Hand Pose Estimation using Depth Sensors. In: IEEE International Conference on Computer Vision Workshops, ICCV Workshops (2011)
17. Oikonomidis, I., Kyriazis, N., Argyros, A.A.: Efficient model-based 3D tracking of hand articulations using Kinect. In: Proceedings of the 22nd British Machine Vision Conference, BMV 2011 (2011)
18. Appenrodt, J., Handrich, S., Al-Hamadi, A., Michaelis, B.: Multi Stereo Camera Data Fusion for Fingertip Detection in Gesture Recognition Systems. In: International Conference of Soft Computing and Pattern Recognition, SoCPaR (2010)
19. Raheja, J.L., Chaudhary, A., Singal, K.: Tracking of Fingertips and Centres of Palm using KINECT. In: Third International Conference on Computational Intelligence, Modelling and Simulation, CIMSiM (2011)
20. Shotton, J., Fitzgibbon, A., Cook, M., Sharp, T., Finocchio, M., Moore, R., Kipman, A., Blake, A.: Real-Time Human Pose Recognition in Parts from Single Depth Images. In: Computer Vision and Pattern Recognition (June 2011)
21. Girshick, R., Shotton, J., Kohli, P., Criminisi, A., Fitzgibbon, A.: Efficient regression of general-activity human poses from depth images. In: International Conference on Computer Vision (2011)
22. Guzek, K., Napieralski, P.: Measurement of noise in the Monte Carlo point sampling method. Bull. of the Polish Academy of Sciences Tech. Sc. 59(1) (2011)
23. Quinlan, J.R.: C4.5: Programs for machine learning. Morgan Kaufmann (1993)
24. Schapire, R.E.: The strength of weak learnability. Machine Learning 5(2), 197–227 (1990)
25. Breiman, L.: Random forests. Machine Learning 45(1), 5–32 (2001)
26. LaViola, J.J.: An experiment comparing double exponential smoothing and Kalman filter-based predictive tracking algorithms. In: Virtual Reality (2003)
27. Szajerman, D., Pietruszka, M.: Real-time ice visualisation on the GPU. Journal of Applied Computer Science (2008)
28. Lipiński, P.: Watermarking software in practical applications. Bulletin of the Polish Academy of Sciences: Technical Sciences 59(1), 21–25 (2011)

Facial Expression Recognition Using Game Theory and Particle Swarm Optimization

Kaushik Roy and Mohamed S. Kamel

Centre for Pattern Analysis and Machine Intelligence,
University of Waterloo, ON, Canada N2L3G1
kaushik.roy@uwaterloo.ca

Abstract. Robust lip contour detection plays an important role in Facial Expression Recognition (FER). However, the large variations emerged from different speakers, intensity conditions, poor texture of lips, weak contrast between lip and skin, high deformability of lip, beard, moustache, wrinkle, etc. often hamper the lip contour detection accuracy. The novelty of this research effort is that we propose a new lip boundary localization scheme using Game Theory (GT) to elicit lip contour accurately from a facial image. Furthermore, we apply a feature subset selection scheme based on Particle Swarm Optimization (PSO) to select the optimal facial features. We have conducted several sets of experiments to evaluate the proposed approach. The results show that the proposed approach has achieved recognition rates of 93.0% and 92.3% on the JAFFE and CK+ datasets, respectively.

Keywords: Facial expression recognition, lip contour detection, game theory, feature selection, particle swarm optimization.

1 Introduction

The accuracy of Facial Expression Recognition (FER) heavily depends on the correct detection of lip contour [1,2]. Many researchers have proposed different lip contour detection schemes [2], including model-based, color/gray level analysis-based, and level set-based approaches. The performance of model based approaches may not provide satisfactory performance due to poor contrast between lip and skin color. The color/gray level analysis-based approaches are computationally efficient. However, these methods result in large color noise and are sensitive to color contrast. The level set-based methods mainly rely on the image gradients and thus, are highly sensitive to the presence of noise and poor image contrast, which can lead to inaccurate lip detection results. In this paper, we propose a lip boundary localization scheme using Game Theory (GT) to extract lip contour from a facial image. We apply a parallel game-theoretic decision making procedure by modifying Chakraborty and Duncans algorithm [3], which integrates (1) the region-based segmentation and gradient-based boundary finding methods, and (2) fuses the complementary strengths of each of these individual methods. This integrated scheme forms a unified approach, which

L. Bolc et al. (Eds.): ICCVG 2012, LNCS 7594, pp. 581–589, 2012.

is robust to noise and poor localization, and is less affected by weak lip/skin boundaries. Previous work on FER has focused mainly on the issues of feature extraction and facial pattern classification. However, less effort has been given to the critical issue of feature selection which plays an important role in automatic facial expression detection system. In this effort, Particle Swarm Optimization (PSO) is deployed to reduce the dimensionality of the facial feature vector [4,5]. The proposed PSO-based feature selection algorithm is utilized to search the feature space for the optimal feature subset where features are carefully selected according to a well defined discrimination criterion. Evolution is driven by a payoff function that minimizes the within-class distance and maximizes the between-class distance [5].

2   Lip Contour Detection Using Game Theory

For each input image, we apply Viola and Jones method [6] to detect the presence of a human face. Prior to applying the GT-based lip contour detection process, an Active Shape Model with Local Features (ASMLF) [7] is applied to find a set of 60 facial feature points from the detected face image, which are used to delineate the regions of interest. Then, we apply the H-minima transform to reduce all minima in the image of delineated mouth region whose depth is less than a threshold. Watershed transformation is used to divide the image into several catchment basins, which consist of its own regional minimum [2]. This process is shown in Fig. 1. Finally, we apply a parallel game-theoretic decision making procedure by modifying the Chakraborty and Duncans algorithm [3], which combines the region-based segmentation and the boundary finding methods for the optimal estimation of lip boundary. The game is played out by a set of decision makers (or players), which in our case, corresponds to the two segmentation schemes, namely, the region-based and the gradient-based boundary finding methods [3]. The lip segmentation problem can be formulated as a two-player game. If p^1 is the set of strategies of the Player 1, and p^2 is the set of strategies of the Player 2, then each player tries to minimize the payoff function, $F^i(p^1, p^2)$. The main objective is to find the Nash Equilibrium (NE) of the system (p^{-1}, p^{-2}), such that:

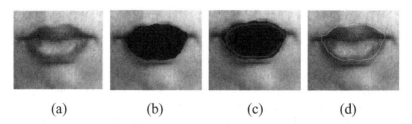

| (a) | (b) | (c) | (d) |

Fig. 1. Lip contour detection using GT. (a) Delineated mouth region from an original face image using ASMLF. (b) Image after H-minima transform and watershed segmentation. (c) Contour initialization. (d) Final contour.

$$F^1(p^{-1}, p^{-2}) \leq F^1(p^1, p^{-2}), \ F^2(p^{-1}, p^{-2}) \leq F^2(p^{-1}, p^2) \tag{1}$$

If we move toward the NE iteratively by taking t as the time index, we can formulate the game as:

$$p_{t+1}^1 = \arg\min_{p^1 \in P1} F^1(p^1, p_t^2); p_{t+1}^2 = \arg\min_{p^2 \in P2} F^2(p_t^1, p^2) \tag{2}$$

Chakraborty and Duncan [3] proved that there is always existing NE solution if F^1 and F^2 are of the following form:

$$F^1(p^1, p^2) = f_1(p^1) + \alpha f_{21}(p^1, p^2) \tag{3}$$

$$F^2(p^1, p^2) = f_2(p^2) + \beta f_{12}(p^1, p^2) \tag{4}$$

where α and β are scaling constants, F^i is bounded in $p^i \in P^i$, F^i is continuously second-order differentiable in $p^i \in P^i$, and there is an existing closed neighborhood of $u_i \subseteq p_i$ such that F^i is strongly convex in u^i. In the region-based method, the image is partitioned into connected regions by grouping the neighbouring pixels of similar intensity levels. The adjacent regions are then merged under some criteria involving the homogeneity or sharpness of the region boundaries. Now, if $y_{i,j}$ is the intensity of a pixel at (i, j) of the original image and $x_{i,j}$ is the intensity of a pixel at (i, j) of the segmented image, then, a common approach is to minimize an objective function of the form:

$$E = \Sigma_{i,j}(y_{i,j} - x_{i,j})^2 + \lambda^2 \left(\Sigma_{i,j} \Sigma_{i_s, j_s} (x_{i,j} - x_{i_s, j_s})^2 \right) \tag{5}$$

where, i_s and j_s are indices in the neighborhood of pixel $x_{i,j}$ and λ is a constant. In the above equation, the first term on the right-hand side is a data fidelity term, and the second term on the right-hand side enforces the smoothness. To detect the boundary of the lip, the objective functions are described as follows:For the region-based module (Player 1):

$$F^1(p^1, p^2) = \min_x \left[\Sigma_{i,j}(y_{i,j} - x_{i,j})^2 + \lambda^2 (\Sigma_{i,j}(x_{i,j} - x_{i-1,j})^2 + \right.$$
$$+ \Sigma_{i,j}(x_{i,j} - x_{i,j-1})^2) \right] +$$
$$\left. + \alpha \left[\Sigma_{i,j \in A_p}(x_{i,j} - u)^2 + \Sigma_{i,j \in \bar{A}_p}(x_{i,j} - v)^2 \right] \tag{6}$$

where, $y_{i,j}$ is the intensity of the original image, $x_{i,j}$ is the intensity of the segmented image given by p^1 as mentioned earlier, u is the intensity inside the contour given by p^2, and v is the intensity outside the contour given by p^2. A_p corresponds to the points that lie inside the contour, and $\bar{A}_p$ represents those points that lie outside the contour. The first term on the right-hand side of (6) minimizes the difference between the pixel intensity values and the obtained region, as well as enforces continuity. The second term tries to match the region and the contour. In the region growing approach, we select an initial area within

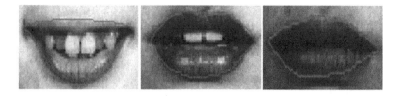

Fig. 2. Lip contour detection using GT on JAFFE database

the region of interest for the lip boundary detection. At each iteration, the neighbouring pixels are observed and the value of E is measured from (5). The pixels, for which the value of E is less than a predefined threshold, are accepted into the region. The objective function of the Player 2 (i.e., the boundary finding module) is as follows:

$$F^2(p^1, p^2) = \arg\max_{\boldsymbol{p}} \left[M_{gradient}(I_g, \boldsymbol{p}) + \beta(I_r, \boldsymbol{p}) \right] \tag{7}$$

where, $\boldsymbol{p}$ denotes the parameterization of the contour given by p^2, I_g is the gradient image, I_r is the region segmented image, and β is a constant. In this paper, we apply a Variational Level Set (VLS)-based active contour model to parameterize and represent the lip contour data during the game-theoretic propagation [8]. Fig. 2 shows the lip segmentation results. For feature extraction, a discrete set of log-Gabor kernels is used that contains 4 spatial frequencies and 6 different orientations from 0 ° to 180 °, differing in 30 steps that makes a filter bank of 24 different Gabor filters. These log-Gabor filters are deployed to each of the images and filter responses are obtained only at the selected fiducial points [9]. Therefore, the facial expressions in an input image are represented by a feature vector of length 1440 elements (60 fiducial points, 24 filter responses per point).

3   Facial Feature Selection Using Particle Swarm Optimization

PSO is a population-based search technique that can be applied to a wide range of problems [4]. The PSO algorithm is adaptive in nature and can be initialized with a population of random solutions called particles. Each particle represents a possible solution to the underlying optimization problem. Particle Swarm contains two primary operators: velocity update and position update. At each iteration, a new velocity value for each particle is measured based on its current velocity, the distance from its previous best position, and the distance from the global best position. The next position of the particle in the search sapce can be calculated from the the new velocity value. This process is then iterated a set number of times, or until a minimum error is achieved.

Each particle represents a point in an n-dimensional feature space. The i-th particle can be represented as $X_i = (x_{i1}, x_{i2}, \ldots, x_{in})$. Each particle memorizes the best previous position (pbest, the position providing the best fitness value) of any particle that is recorded and represented as $P_i = (p_{i1}, p_{i2}, \ldots, p_{in})$, where P denotes the size of the population. The position of the best particle among all the particles in the population is represented by the symbol gbest. The velocity for i-th particle is denoted as $V_i = (v_{i1}, v_{i2}, \ldots, v_{in})$. The particles are updated according to following equations:

$$v_{id} = w * v_{id} + c1 * rand()(p_{id} - x_{id}) + c2 * rand()(p_{gd} - x_{id}) \tag{8}$$

$$\text{if } \left(rand() < \frac{1}{1 + e^{-vid}} \right) \text{ then } x_{id} = 1; \text{ else } x_{id} = 0; \tag{9}$$

where $d = 1, 2, \ldots, n$. The value of the inertia weight, w is set to 1 to provide a balance between global and local exploration, and to gain a faster convergence to find a sufficiently optimal solution[1]. $c1$ and $c2$ in (8) are the acceleration constants and are set to 2. $rand()$ is the random number between $(0, 1)$. Particles velocities on each dimension are set to a maximum velocity, $V_{\max}$, and minimum velocity, $V_{\min}$. The (8) is used to measure the particles new velocity according to its previous velocity and the distances of its current position from its own best experience (position) and from the groups best experience. The experience is evaluated using the fitness function. In this paper, we propose the following payoff function that minimizes the within-class distance and maximizes the between-class distance:

$$\min(u(F)) = \min(W_l) + \min\left(\frac{1}{B_l + 1}\right) \tag{10}$$

In (10), W_l denotes the within-class distance and can be defined as

$$W_l = \frac{1}{n_l} \sum_{k=1}^{n_l} (X_k^l - m_l)^T (X_k^l - m_l) \tag{11}$$

where $l = 1, 2, 3, \ldots, c$ and m_l is the mean vector of class l. B_l in (10) denotes the between class distance and can be defined as

$$B_l = \sum_{l=1}^{c} p_l \times (m_l - m)^T (m_l - m) \tag{12}$$

where m is the mean vector of all samples.

4   Performance Evaluation

Extensive experiments were conducted on the following two databases, namely, JAFFE [10], and Cohn-Kanade Version 2 or Ck+ [11]. Fig. 3 exhibits the results of facial feature tracking using the ASMLF with the game-theoretic approach. From the Fig. 3, we can find that the applied shape guided approach with the local features robustly tracks the feature points on both of the databases.The game-theoretic lip contour detection process, further, enhances the feature tracking performance. An extensive set of experiments was conducted on all the datasets, and the coupling coefficients, α and β were set to 0.27 when the game-theoretic integration module was used. To obtain the contour data of the lip boundary during game-theoretic evolution, the selected parameter values using the VLS algorithm were set to $\mu = 0.001, v = 2.0, \lambda = 5.0$ and time step $\tau = 3.0$. The number of models in the shape models was 21 and 35 for the JAFFE and CK+ databases, respectively.

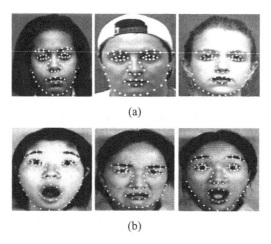

(a)

(b)

Fig. 3. Facial point detection results. (a) Cohn Kanade database. (b) JAFFE database.

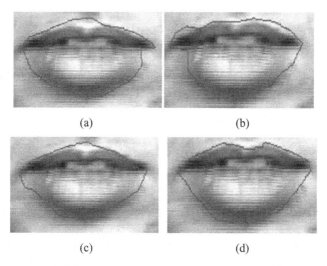

(a)   (b)

(c)   (d)

Fig. 4. Comparison of different lip contour detection methods. (a) GAC, (b) ASM, (c) ASMLF, and (d) ASMLF with GT

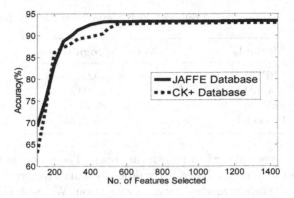

Fig. 5. Feature selection using PSO

To show the effectiveness of the lip contour detection process, we compared the proposed GT-based lip contour detection scheme with Geodesic Active Contour (GAC) [12], ASM proposed by Cootes et al. [13] and ASMLF [7] as shown in Fig. 4. The GT-based scheme substantially improves the robustness of lip

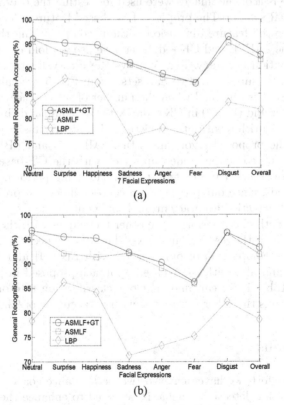

Fig. 6. Comparison of different FER methods. (a) Cohn-Kanade database. (b) JAFFE database.

Table 1. Comparisons of different FER methods on JAFFE database

Methods	7-class recognition (%)
LBP [1]	78.60
Boosted-LBP+SVM [1]	81.00
PCA [9]	87.51
Proposed	93.00

feature tracking, especially when mouths are open. The reason is that our proposed scheme uses the region-based information as well as the gradient data with the game-theoretic fusion method for lip localization. We used Support Vector Machine (SVM) [14] to classify 7 categories of expressions, namely, neutral, happiness, sadness, surprise, anger, disgust, and fear. In order to analyze the performance of the classifier in recognizing individual expression, a training set of 70 images is produced from the JAFFE database. The training set contains 7 images for each of the 10 expresser, one image per expression. The other images are then used for testing. For CK+ database, we used a set of 120 facial images for training and the rest of the images were used for testing the overall accuracy of the proposed FER system. The proposed PSO-based feature selection approach is used to reduce the feature dimension without compromising the recognition accuracy. For the JAFFE and CK+ datasets, we use a 4-fold crossvalidation to obtain the validation accuracy. Fig. 5 shows the crossvalidation accuracies of the selected feature subsets on two datasets. From Fig. 5, we can see that the reasonable accuracy is obtained when the number of selected features is (a) 485 in JAFFE dataset and (b) 570 in CK+ datasets. We compared the performance of the proposed algorithm with other existing FER algorithms. Fig. 6 shows the comparison of the proposed algorithm with ASMLF [7] and LBP [1]. We can find that the proposed shape guided approach with the GT-based lip contour detection process shows a better feature point tracking performance than the other two methods, since our proposed lip contour detection process enhances the feature point detection accuracy around the mouth region. We can find from Fig. 6 that our method outperforms the other techniques with the accuracies of 93.0% and 92.3% on the JAFFE and CK+ datasets, respectively. Table 1 also demonstrates the comparison of our method with LBP [1] and Boosted LBP reported in [1], and also with PCA-based approach proposed in [1] on JAFFE dataset. From Table 1, we can find that our classification rate on the JAFFE dataset outperforms the other techniques with an accuracy of 93.0%.

5   Conclusions

In this research effort, we have achieved two performance goals. First, a game-theoretic lip contour detection scheme is deployed to enhance the performance of lip localization method. The GT-based algorithm brings together the region-based and boundary-based methods and operates different probability spaces into a common information-sharing framework. The proposed algorithm localizes the lip boundaries from the delineated mouth regions that may be affected by low image intensities, poor acquisition process, opening of the mouth, variability in speaking style, teeth, wrinkles, and by the occlusions of beard and moustache. Second, PSO is used to find the subset of informative texture features. Further analysis of our results indicates that the proposed feature selection framework is capable of removing redundant and irrelevant features.

References

1. Shan, C., Gong, S., McOwan, P.: Facial expression recognition based on Local Binary Patterns: A comprehensive study. Image and Vis. Comput. 27(6), 803–816 (2009)
2. Li, K., Wang, M., Liu, M., Zhao, A.: Improved level set method for lip contour detection. In: IEEE Intl. Conf. Image Process., pp. 673–676 (2010)
3. Chakraborty, A., Duncan, J.: Game-theoretic integration for image segmentation. IEEE Trans. Pattern Anal. and Machine Intell. 21(1), 12–30 (1999)
4. Raghavendra, R., Dorizzi, B., Rao, A., Hemantha, G.: PSO versus AdaBoost for feature selection in multimodal biometrics. In: Proc. IEEE Intl. Conf. on Biometrics: Theory, Appl., and Syst., pp. 1–7 (2009)
5. Kennedy, J., Eberhart, R.: Particle swarm optimization. In: Proc. IEEE Intl. Conf. on Neural Networks, pp. 1942–1948 (1995)
6. Viola, P., Jones, M.: Robust Real-Time Face Detection. Intl. J. Comp. Vis. 57(2), 137–154 (2004)
7. Ginneken, B., Frangi, A., Staal, J., Romeny, B., Viergever, M.: Active shape model segmentation with optimal features. IEEE Trans. Medical Imaging 21(8), 924–933 (2002)
8. Li, C., Xu, C., Gui, C., Fox, M.: Level set evolution without re-initialization: a new variational formulation. In: Proc. IEEE Intl. Conf. Comp. Vis. and Pattern Recog., pp. 430–436 (2005)
9. Bashyal, S., Venayagamoorthy, G.: Recognition of facial expressions using Gabor wavelets and learning vector quantization. Intl. J. Engg. App. of Artificial Intell. 21(7), 1–9 (2008)
10. Lyons, M., Budynek, J., Akamatsu, S.: Automatic classification of single facial images. IEEE Trans. Pattern Anal. and Machine Intell. 21(12), 1357–1362 (1999)
11. Lucey, P., Cohn, J., Kanade, T., Saragih, J., Ambadar, Z.: The extended Cohn-Kanade dataset (CK+): A complete dataset for action unit and emotion-specified expression. In: IEEE Intl. Conf. Computer Vis. and Pattern Recog. Workshop, pp. 94–101 (2010)
12. Paragios, N., Deriche, R.: Geodesic active contours and level sets for the detection and tracking of moving objects. IEEE Trans. Pattern Analysis and Machine Intelligence 22(3), 266–280 (2000)
13. Cootes, T., Taylor, C., Cooper, D., Graham, J.: Active shape models their training and application. Computer Vis. Image Understand. 61(1), 38–59 (1995)
14. Vapnik, V.: Statistical Learning Theory. John Wiley and Sons, New York (1998)

Multibiometric System Using Distance Regularized Level Set Method and Particle Swarm Optimization

Kaushik Roy and Mohamed S. Kamel

Centre for Pattern Analysis and Machine Intelligence,
University of Waterloo, ON, Canada N2L3G1
kaushik.roy@uwaterloo.ca

Abstract. This paper presents a multibiometric system that integrates the iris, palmprint, and fingerprint features based on the fusion at feature level. The novelty of this research effort is that we propose a feature subset selection scheme based on Particle Swarm Optimization (PSO) with a new fitness function that minimizes the Recognition Error (RR), False Accept Rate (FAR), and Feature Subset Size (FSS). Furthermore, we apply a Distance Regularized Level Set (DRLS)-based iris segmentation procedure, which maintains the regularity of the level set function intrinsically during the curve evolution process and increases the numerical accuracy substantially. The proposed iris localization scheme is robust against poor localization and weak iris/sclera boundaries. Experimental results indicate that the proposed approach increases biometric recognition accuracies compared to that produced by single modal biometrics.

Keywords: Multibiometrics, distance regularized level set, feature level fusion, particle swarm optimization.

1 Introduction

Unimodal biometric authentication systems generally suffer from limitations such as noisy input data, limited degrees of freedom, intraclass variability, and nonuniversality [1]. Multibiometric systems overcome these limitations by combining the information presented by multiple biometric traits. The accuracy of multimodal biometric system heavily depends on the selection of appropriate fusion strategy. In the case of multibiometric system, fusion of information can be performed at four different levels: sensor level, feature level, matching score level and decision level. Much work in biometric fusion has been done in the sensor, match score and decision levels. However, less attention has been given to the fusion at the feature level. In this research effort, we perform fusion at the feature level by considering three biometric modalities: iris, fingerprint and palmprint [2]. Recent work [3] indicates that feature level fusion outperforms the match score fusion because of the availability of more and richer information at earlier stage of processing. However, the feature level fusion may lead to the curse of dimensionality due to the large size

L. Bolc et al. (Eds.): ICCVG 2012, LNCS 7594, pp. 590–599, 2012.

of the combined feature vector [4]. Addressing the above problem, a feature selection scheme based on Particle Swarm Optimization (PSO) is deployed to reduce the dimensionality of the fused feature vector. For PSO-based feature subset selection, we propose a new fitness function that minimizes the Recognition Error (RR), False Accept Rate (FAR) and Feature Subset Size (FSS). Most existing iris recognition algorithms focus on the processing and recognition of the ideal iris images that are captured in a cooperative environment [5,6]. In this paper, we process the non-ideal iris images that are acquired in an unconstrained situation and are affected by eyelid and eyelash occlusions, non uniform intensities, motion blurs, reflections, etc. We apply a Distance Regularized Level Set (DRLS) [7]-based iris segmentation procedure, which maintains the regularity of the Level Set (LS) function intrinsically during the curve evolution process. The LS-based curve evolution process is derived as the gradient flow that minimizes an energy functional with a distance regularization term and an external energy that drives the motion of the zero LS toward the inner and outer boundaries of the iris. DRLS also allows the use of more general and efficient initialization of the LS function and uses relatively large time steps in the finite difference scheme to reduce the number of iterations, while ensuring the stability of curve propagation process towards the iris/pupil contour. The iris boundary represented by the variational LS may break and merge naturally during evolution, and thus, the topological changes are handled automatically. In [6], region-based active contour model was used for iris/pupil localization. However, in the current effort, DRLS is used with an edge-based active contour model for the accurate segmentation of iris region [7]. The proposed variational model is also robust against weak inner/outer boundaries and shows better localization performance. Fig. 1 shows the block diagram of the proposed multibiometric system. This research effort mainly focuses on accurate iris segmentation and optimal feature subset selection of the fused feature vector.

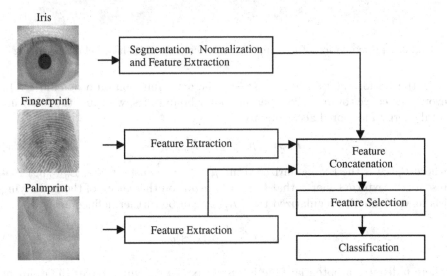

Fig. 1. Block diagram of the multibiometric system

2   Preprocessing and Feature Extraction

In this section, we focus on DRLS-based iris segmentation, distinctive feature extraction and fusion at feature level. We propose a three stage iris segmentation approach. First, we detect the strong and weak reflection areas by deploying a simple thresholding approach [5]. We also remove the specular reflection spots that occur inside the pupillary region as reported in [5]. In the second stage, prior to applying the curve evolution approach, we deploy Direct Least Square (DLS)-based elliptical fitting to approximate the pupil boundary. The DLS-based elliptical fitting returns five parameters $(p_1, p_2, r_1, r_2, \varphi_1)$: the horizontal and vertical coordinates of the pupil centre (p_1, p_2); the length of the major and minor axes (r_1, r_2); and the orientation of the ellipse φ_1. Similarly, to approximate the outer boundary, we apply the DLS-based elliptical fitting again, and obtain five parameters $(I_1, I_2, R_1, R_2, \varphi_2)$: the horizontal and vertical coordinates of the iris center (I_1, I_2); the length of the major and minor axes (R_1, R_2); and the orientation of the ellipse φ_2. This method, thus, provides the rough estimation of iris and pupil boundaries. Fig. 2 shows the approximated iris/pupil boundary. Based on the approximation of the inner and outer boundaries, the curve is evolved by using the DRLS method, reported in [7], for accurate segmentation of the pupil and iris areas. In the following paragraph, the DRLS evolution method is discussed briefly.

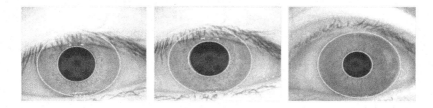

Fig. 2. Approximation of iris/pupil boundaries using DLS-based elliptical fitting

In the LS formulation, let $\varphi : \Omega \to \Re$ be a LS function on a domain Ω. To evolve the curve towards the inner and outer boundaries, we apply the following total energy functional according to [7]:

$$E(\varphi) = \mu R_p(\varphi) + E_{g,\lambda,v}(\varphi) \tag{1}$$

where $R_p(\varphi)$ is the LS regularized term, $\mu > 0$ is a constant, and $E_{g,\lambda,v}(\varphi)$ represents the external energy that heavily depends on the nature of the underlying iris images. The LS regularized term $R_p(\varphi)$ can be further defined as

$$R_p(\varphi) \triangleq \int_{\Omega} p(|\nabla \varphi|) dx \tag{2}$$

where p denotes a potential function $p : [0, \infty) \to \Re$, which forces the gradient magnitude of LS function to one of its minimum points, and thus, maintains a desired shape of LS function. The LS-based curve evolution is derived as a gradient flow that minimizes the energy functional of (1). In the LS propagation, the regularity of the LS formulation is maintained by a forward-and-backward diffusion derived from the distance regularization term [7]. Therefore, the distance regularization term completely eliminates the costly reinitialization process and avoids the undesirable side effect induced by numerical errors. The DRLS is implemented with a simpler and more efficient numerical scheme than the conventional LS formulations. Most importantly, relatively large time steps can be used to significantly reduce the number of iterations and computation time in the curve evolution process, while assuring sufficient numerical accuracy. In (1), g denotes the edge detector function and is defined by

$$g(I) = \frac{1}{1 + |G_\sigma * I|^2} \tag{3}$$

where G_σ is the Gaussian kernel with a standard deviation denoted as σ, and I denotes an iris image. The convolution in (3) is used to smooth the iris image and to reduce the effect of noise. We can further define the external energy term $E_{g,\lambda,v}(\varphi)$ of (1) as

$$E_{g,\lambda,v}(\varphi) = \lambda L_g(\varphi) + v A_g(\varphi) \tag{4}$$

where $\lambda > 0$ and v are constants, and the terms $L_g(\varphi)$ and $A_g(\varphi)$ in (4) are respectively defined as follows [7]

$$L_g(\varphi) \triangleq \int_\Omega g\delta(\varphi)|\nabla\varphi|dx \tag{5}$$

$$A_g(\varphi) \triangleq \int_\Omega gH(-\varphi)dx \tag{6}$$

where δ is the univariate Dirac function, and H is the Heaviside function. The energy functional $L_g(\varphi)$ measures the length of the zero LS curve of φ, and $A_g(\varphi)$ is used to speed up the curve evolution. Now, the energy functional of (1) can be approximated by

$$E_\epsilon(\varphi) = \mu \int_\Omega p(|\nabla\varphi|)dx + \lambda \int_\Omega g\delta_\epsilon(\varphi)|\nabla\varphi|dx + v \int_\Omega gH_\epsilon(-\varphi)dx \tag{7}$$

where δ_ϵ and H_ϵ denote the approximated Dirac delta and Heaviside functions, respectively. The energy functional (7) can be minimized by solving the following gradient flow

$$\frac{\partial\varphi}{\partial t} = \mu \, div\big(d_p(|\nabla\varphi|)\nabla_\varphi\big) + \lambda\delta_\epsilon(\varphi) \, div\left(g\frac{\nabla_\varphi}{|\nabla_\varphi|}\right) + vg\delta_\epsilon(\varphi) \tag{8}$$

The (8) is the desired evolution equation of the LS function. The first term on the right had side of (8) is associated with the distance regularization energy, while second and third terms on the right-hand side of (8) represent the gradient flows of the energy functional and are responsible for driving the zero LS-curve towards the inner/outer boundaries of the iris. In order to estimate the exact boundary of the pupil, we initialize the active contour φ to the approximated pupil boundary, and evolve the curve in the narrow band of ± 10 pixels. We evolve the curve from inside the approximated inner boundary to avoid the effect of reflections that may occur just outside the pupil. Similarly, for computing the outer boundary, the active contour φ is initialized to the estimated iris boundary, and the optimal estimation of the iris boundary is computed by evolving the curve in a narrow band of ± 20 pixels. In this case, the curve is evolved again from inside the approximated iris boundary to reduce the effects of the eyelids and the eyelashes. Fig. 3 shows the iris segmentation results using DRLS method.We deploy the eyelid and the eyelash detection techniques as used in [5]. We use a mask based on the extracted eyelids and eyelashes to detect the iris region without noise. However, the extracted iris boundaries are not exactly circular/elliptical and may be of any kind of curves. Therefore, to solve this size inconsistency, a simple method based on the connection of the adjacent contour points is deployed as reported in [5,6]. In order to compensate for the elastic deformation in iris texture, we unwrap the extracted (and localized) iris region to a normalized block of fixed size 60×60 by converting from the Cartesian coordinates to the polar coordinates [5]. In this paper, we deploy 1D log-Gabor transform, which uses 4 different scales and 8 orientations, to extract the distinctive features from the normalized iris, palmprint and fingerprint images of size 60×60 (See Fig. 3). First, we apply the log-Gabor filters to iris image, x_{iris} and obtain the log-Gabor transformed image, x_{Lg_iris} of size 240×480. To decrease the computational complexities, we downsample each transformed image by a ratio equal to 6. Thus, the transformed image, x_{Lg_iris} is reduced to a size of 40×80, and can be represented by the feature vector, $\hat{x}_{Lg\_iris}$ of size 3200×1.Similar approach is employed for the normalized palmprint and fingerprint images. We obtain

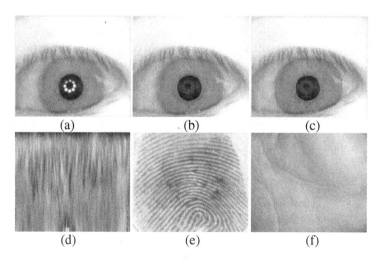

Fig. 3. (a) Original iris image, (b) Pupil detection, (c) Iris detection, (d) Normalized iris image, (e) Normalized fingerprint image, and (g) Normalized palmprint image

the palmprint feature vector, $\hat{x}_{Lg\_palm}$ of size 3200×1 and also, the fingerprint feature vector, $\hat{x}_{Lg\_finger}$ of size 3200×1. We concatenate $\hat{x}_{Lg\_iris}$, $\hat{x}_{Lg\_palm}$ and $\hat{x}_{Lg\_finger}$ and get the fused feature vector, $\hat{x}_{Lg\_iris\_palm\_finger}$ of size 9600×1. The z-score normalization technique is then deployed on $\hat{x}_{Lg\_iris\_palm\_finger}$ to ensure that the feature values across three modalities are compatible.

3   Feature Selection Using PSO

PSO is a population-based optimization scheme, which tries to find a solution to an optimization problem in a search space [8]. In this research effort, we propose to use PSO algorithm to perform feature selection from the fused feature space. PSO is initialized with a population of random solutions, denoted as particles, distributed over the search space. Each particle represents a point in an n-dimensional feature space. The i-th particle can be represented as $X_i = (x_{i1}, x_{i2}, \ldots, x_{in})$. Each particle memorizes the best previous position (pbest, the position providing the best fitness value) of any particle that is recorded and represented as $P_i = (p_{i1}, p_{i2}, \ldots, p_{in})$, where P denotes the size of the population. The position of the best particle among all the particles in the population is represented by the symbol gbest. The velocity for i-th particle is denoted as $V_i = (v_{i1}, v_{i2}, \ldots, v_{in})$. The particles are updated according to following equations

$$v_{id} = w * v_{id} + c1 * rand()(p_{id} - x_{id}) + c2 * rand()(p_{gd} - x_{id}) \qquad (9)$$

$$\text{if}\left(rand() < \frac{1}{1 + e^{-vid}}\right) \text{ then } x_{id} = 1; \text{ else } x_{id} = 0; \qquad (10)$$

where $d = 1, 2, \ldots, n$. w represents the inertia weight. The value of the inertia weight is set to 1 to provide a balance between global and local exploration, and to gain a faster convergence to find a sufficiently optimal solution[1]. $c1$ and $c2$ in (9) are the acceleration constants that represent the weighting of the stochastic acceleration terms that pull each of the particles towards pest and best positions. Both of acceleration constants are set at 2. $rand()$ is the random number between $(0, 1)$. Particles velocities on each dimension are set to a maximum velocity, V_{max}, and minimum velocity, V_{min}. The (9) is used to measure the particles new velocity according to its previous velocity and the distances of its current position from its own best experience (position) and from the group's best experience. The experience is evaluated using the fitness function. Based on the nature of our problem, we propose the following fitness function that optimizes the three performance issues, RE, FAR and FSS

$$u(F) = W_1.RE + W_2.FAR + W_3.\left(\frac{FSS}{\text{Total Features in Fused Feature Space}}\right) \qquad (11)$$

where, W_1, W_2 and W_3 are constant weighting parameters which reflect the relative importance between RE, FAR and FSS.

4   Performance Evaluation

Extensive experiments are conducted on CASIA Version 3 Interval Iris dataset [9], Fingerprint Verification Competition (FVC) 2000 dataset [10], and CASIA Palmprint dataset [11]. For the single sample recognition, we draw out the sample subsets of same size from these three databases. We select 110 classes from each of the databases, and each of these selected classes contains 8 samples. The first 3 samples of each class are used for training and the remaining samples are used for testing. In this paper, we use SVM for iris-palmprint-fingerprint pattern classification [12]. For the iris segmentation, we have applied the DRLS-based approach, and the segmentation results are shown in Fig. 4. We can find from this figure that our segmentation scheme performs well, despite the fact that the iris and the sclera regions are separated by a blurred boundary. An extensive set of experiments are conducted using DRLS evolution, and the selected parameter values are set to $\mu = 0.04, v = -3.0, \lambda = 5.0, \epsilon = 1.5$ and time step $\nabla_t = 3.0$.

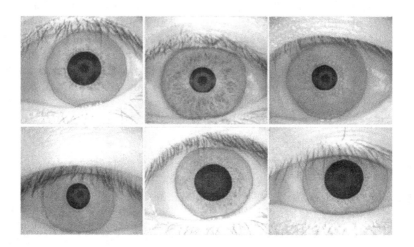

Fig. 4. Iris segmentation results on CASIA Version 3 Interval dataset

The proposed PSO-based feature selection approach is used to reduce the feature dimension without compromising the recognition rate. For the combined dataset, we use a 4-fold crossvalidation to obtain the validation accuracy. Fig. 5 shows the crossvalidation accuracies of the selected feature subsets for the PSO approach. From Fig. 5, we can see that the reasonable accuracy is obtained using the PSO scheme when the number of selected features is 2350 with an accuracy of 97.20%. The performance increases with the number of features selected with PSO up to 2350 and stabilizes afterwards. To demonstrate the effectiveness of the proposed feature selection scheme, we compare PSO-based scheme with Genetic Algorithms (GAs) [13] by deploying the same fitness function used in (11), and also, with Mutual Information (MI) [14]. GA achieves an accuracy of 97.00% when the selected feature subset size is 3120. Also, from Fig. 5, we can find

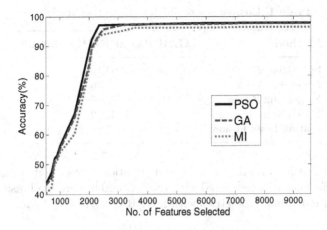

Fig. 5. Comparison of different feature selection schemes

that the performance curve of the MI-based approach starts to level off at 3560 feature elements with an accuracy of 96.23%. Therefore, we can find that the PSO-based feature reduction method outperforms the other two feature selection schemes and reduces the fused feature space by roughly 75%. The values of three weighting parameters, W_1, W_2, and W_3 are set at 2000, 150 and 1000, respectively.

From the ROC curve of Fig. 6 and Table 1, we can observe that the performance of the iris recognition scheme alone outperforms the fingerprint and palmprint recognition approaches with a Genuine Accept Rate (GAR) of 95.10% at the fixed FAR of 0.001%, while the achieved GARs of fingerprint and palmprint recognition schemes are 75.50% and 73.30%, respectively, at the same FAR of 0.001%. Furthermore, we apply the match score fusion strategy using a weighted SUM rule and compare with the proposed feature level fusion scheme. We can

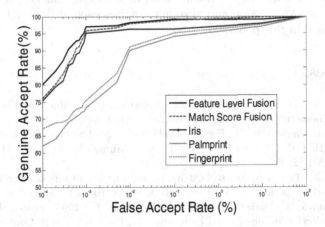

Fig. 6. ROC curve shows the comparison of different methods

Table 1. Comparison of different biometrics modalities

Methods	GAR (%) at FAR of 0.001%
Iris Alone	95.10
Palmprint Alone	73.30
Fingerprint Alone	75.50
Match Score Fusion	95.72
Feature Level Fusion	97.18

observe that feature level fusion of three modalities shows a significant improvement in performance as compared with that of match score level fusion and also with that of individual biometrics with a GAR of 97.18% at FAR= 0.001%.

5   Conclusions

In this research effort, we have achieved two performance goals. First, PSO is used to find the subset of informative texture features by minimizing three performance issues, RE, FAR and FSS. Further analysis of our results indicates that the proposed feature selection framework is capable of removing redundant and irrelevant features. Second, a DRLS-based iris segmentation scheme is deployed to enhance the performance of iris localization method. The proposed algorithm performs the accurate localization of the iris regions from degraded eye images, which may be affected by diffusion, non linear deformation, low intensity, poor acquisition process, eyelid and eyelash occlusions and small opening of the eyes. Also, the proposed iris localization scheme based on DRLS avoids over-segmentation and performs well for blurred iris/sclera boundary. We develop a virtual multibiometric database and validate the performnace of the proposed scheme. It is found from the experimental results that the fusion of iris, palmprint and fingerprint features at the feature level improves recognition accuracy over the match score level fusion and also, outperforms each of the single biometric traits discussed in this paper.

References

1. Liau, H., Isa, D.: Feature selection for support vector machine-based face-iris multimodal biometric system. Expert Syst. with Appl. 38(9), 11105–11111 (2011)
2. Ross, A., Govindarajan, R.: Feature level fusion using hand and face biometrics. In: Proc. SPIE Intl. Conf. on Biometric Tech. for Human Identification II, vol. 5779, pp. 196–204 (2005)
3. Rattani, A., Tistarelli, M.: Robust multimodal and multiunit feature level fusion of face and iris biometrics. In: Proc. Intl. Conf. on Biometrics, pp. 960–969 (2009)
4. Raghavendra, R., Dorizzi, B., Rao, A., Hemantha, G.: PSO versus AdaBoost for feature selection in multimodal biometrics. In: Proc. IEEE Intl. Conf. on Biometrics: Theory, Appl., and Syst., pp. 1–7 (2009)

5. Roy, K., Bhattacharya, P., Suen, C.: Iris segmentation using variational level set method. Optics and Lasers in Engg. 49(4), 578–588 (2011)
6. Roy, K., Bhattacharya, P., Suen, C.: You. J.: Recognition of unideal iris images using region-based active contour model and game theory. In: Proc. IEEE Intl. Conf. on Image Process., pp. 1705–1708 (2010)
7. Li, C., Xu, C., Gui, C., Fox, M.: Distance regularized level set evolution and its application to image segmentation. IEEE Trans. Image Process. 19(12), 3243–3254 (2010)
8. Kennedy, J., Eberhart, R.: Particle swarm optimization. In: Proc. IEEE Intl. Conf. on Neural Networks, pp. 1942–1948 (1995)
9. CASIA-Iris Version 3 dataset found at,
   http://www.cbsr.ia.ac.cn/IrisDatabase.html
10. FVC 2000, dataset found at
    http://bias.csr.unibo.it/fvc2000/databases.asp
11. CASIA-Palmprint dataset found at
    http://www.idealtest.org/dbDetailForUser.do?id=5
12. Vapnik, V.: Statistical Learning Theory. John Wiley and Sons, New York (1998)
13. Goldberg, D.: Genetic algorithms in search, optimization, and machine learning. Addison-Wesley Professional (1989)
14. Makrehchi, M., Kamel, M.: Aggressive feature selection by feature ranking. In: Liu, H., Motoda, H. (eds.) Computational Methods of Feature Selection, pp. 313–330. Chapman and Hall/CRC Press (2007)

A Supremum Norm Based Near Neighbor Search in High Dimensional Spaces

Nikolai Sergeev

Institute for Neural Information Processing
nikolai.sergeev@uni-ulm.de

Abstract. This paper presents a new near neighbor search. Feature vectors to be stored do not have to be of equal length. Two feature vectors are getting compared with respect to supremum norm. Time demand to learn a new feature vector does not depend on the number of vectors already learned. A query is formulated not as a single feature vector but as a set of features which overcomes the problem of possible permutation of components in a representation vector. Components of a learned feature vector can be cut out - the algorithm is still capable to recognize the remaining part.

Keywords: Near neighbor search, information retrieval.

1 Introduction

The object recognition system the new algorithm was developed for [Sergeev and Palm, 2011] produces feature vectors which consist of similar permutable components. So it requires a machine learning algorithm invariant to possible permutations of components in a request feature vector. Unfortunately the standard machine learning algorithm as artificial neural networks [Rosenblatt, 1962, Bishop, 2007], support vector machines [Vapnik, 1998], regression estimators [Gyofri et al., 2002] or nearest neighborhood search algorithms [Shakhnarovish et al., 2005] do not offer this property. Additionally a machine learning algorithm feasible for robotics should be able to learn a new object in time as less dependent on the number of objects as possible. These two properties were the main motivation to develop the algorithm to be described in this paper.

The new algorithm is a r-near neighbor search. For a query it looks for all stored vectors lying in a r-ball in a metric space $\mathbb{R}^d$. The metrics used in this case is derived from supremum norm. A typical near neighbor search is either based on space partition [Berchtold et al., 2000] using e.g. Voronoi diagram or data partitioning [Guttman, 2000, Ciaccia et al., 1997] using R-trees or M-trees.

The core algorithm of the new algorithm is based on space partitioning. The vector representation of the core algorithm is a spacial case of vector quantization [Pratt, 2001]. Classic vector quantization algorithms map a vector to a single subset of $\mathbb{R}^d$, whereas the new one maps a single vector to a set of subsets. Normally a search space is partitioned in a finite number of subsets. The new

L. Bolc et al. (Eds.): ICCVG 2012, LNCS 7594, pp. 600–609, 2012.

representation uses an infinite partitioning, which results in a better performance and higher flexibility.

There are some interesting properties of the algorithm resulting immediately from the definition, which are worth to be mentioned. Time demand to learn a new vector is independent of the number of vectors already learned. It makes the algorithm suitable for robotics. A query gets processed with 100% precision. High dimensional vectors consisting of similar components can be handled. Admittedly time complexity grows exponentially to the size of a single component but at the same time just linearly to the number of components in a single query vector. Another property of the algorithm is its robustness to the partial occlusion. Components can be cut out. The algorithm still recognizes the remaining part.

Under artificial and purely theoretical conditions time demand to process a single query vector does not change with the number of stored vectors. These conditions are not given in real life tasks. Nevertheless the reality is placed somewhere between the worst case and the best one. In the worst case time complexity is linear to the number of stored points, in the theoretical case it is independent of it.

The paper consists mainly of three parts. Part one builds the core search function f used to construct the actual near neighbor search F. Part two describes the implementation of F. Part three gives an application example of the algorithm, which is a simplified version of the new object recognition system.

In this paper it will be assumed that time complexity of saving and accessing of an element of hash map is independent of the number of elements already saved. It simplifies description omitting unnecessary details.

2   Core Algorithm

For $d, K \in \mathbb{N}, \varepsilon > 0$ and a sequence of vectors $v \in \prod_{k \in \{1, ..., K\}} \mathbb{R}^d$ the function $f : \mathbb{R}^d \to P(\{1, ..., K\})$ with

$$f(x) = \{k \leq K | \ \|x - v_k\|_{\max} \leq \varepsilon\} \tag{1}$$

has to be implemented. The following interpretation of v makes the definition of f comprehensible: $v_k \in \mathbb{R}^d$ is an encoded description vector of the label $k \in \{1, ..., K\}$. $f(x)$ returns all labels whose code is similar to x. In this section a fast implementation of f will be described.

At first several encoder E^i with $i \in \{1, ..., 6\}$ are to be introduced. The $E^1, ..., E^5$ are auxiliary functions used to define E^6.

For $\delta > 0$ the encoder $E^1_\delta : \mathbb{R} \to \mathbb{Z}$ is defined as

$$E^1_\delta(x) = \left\lceil \frac{x}{\delta} \right\rceil. \tag{2}$$

with $\lceil \cdot \rceil$ standing for ceiling. For example $E^1_\delta(0) = 0$ for all $\delta > 0$. The encoder $E^2_\delta : \mathbb{R} \to \mathbb{Z}$ is defined as

$$E^2_\delta(x) = E^1_\delta \left(x + \frac{\delta}{2} \right). \tag{3}$$

For example $E_\delta^2(0) = 1$ with $\delta > 0$. The encoder $E_\delta^3 : \mathbb{R} \to \mathbb{Z}^2$ is defined as

$$E_\delta^3(x) = \left(2E_\delta^1(x), 2E_\delta^2(x) + 1\right)^T. \tag{4}$$

Obviously $E_\delta^3(0) = (0, 3)^T$. The encoder $E_{d,\delta}^4 : \mathbb{R}^d \to \mathbb{Z}^{2 \times d}$ is defined as

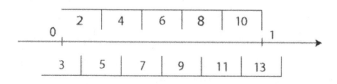

Fig. 1. Mapping behavior of $2E_{1/5}^1(\cdot)$(above) and $2E_{1/5}^2(\cdot) + 1$(under)

$$E_{d,\delta}^4(x) = \left(\left(E_\delta^3(x_j)\right)_i\right)_{(i,j) \in \{1,2\} \times \{1,\dots,d\}}. \tag{5}$$

For $d = 3$ and $x = (0, 0, 0)^T$ $E_{d,\delta}^4(x) = \begin{pmatrix} 0 & 0 & 0 \\ 3 & 3 & 3 \end{pmatrix}$. The encoder $E_{d,\delta}^5 : \mathbb{R}^d \times \{1, 2\}^d \to \mathbb{Z}^d$ is defined as

$$E_{d,\delta}^5(x, y) = \left(\left(E_{d,\delta}^4(x)\right)_{y(i),i}\right)_{i \in \{1,\dots,d\}}. \tag{6}$$

For example $E_{d,\delta}^5(x, y) = (0, 3, 0)^T$ with $d = 3, x = (0, 0, 0)^T$ and $y = (1, 2, 1)^T$. An outcome of $E_{d,\delta}^5(x, y)$ will be typically referred as *sample*. Finally the encoder $E_{d,\delta}^6 : \mathbb{R}^d \to P\left(\mathbb{Z}^d\right)$ is defined as

$$E_{d,\delta}^6(x) = \left\{ E_{d,\delta}^5(x, y) \,\middle|\, y \in \{1, 2\}^d \right\}. \tag{7}$$

To implement $f(x) = \{k \le K | \; \|x - v_k\|_{\max} \le \varepsilon\}$ the following type of storage $s : \mathbb{Z}^d \to P(\{1, \dots, K\})$ has to be defined

$$s(x) = \left\{ k \in \{1, \dots, K\} | x \in E_{d,\delta}^6(v_k) \right\} \tag{8}$$

with $\delta = 2\varepsilon$. In Java notation the storage can be implemented as follows:

```
Map<List<Integer>, Set<Integer>> s;
for (int k = 1; k <= K; k++)
  for (List<Integer> y : E^6_(d, delta)(x))
    if (s.containsKey(y))
      s.get(y).add(k);
    else {
      s.put(y, new HashSet<Integer>());
      s.get(y).add(k);
    }
```

Now $f(x) = \{k \leq K| \|x - v_k\|_{\max} \leq \varepsilon\}$ can be implemented as

$$f(x) = \left\{ k \in \bigcup_{y \in E^6_{d,\delta}(x)} s(y) \,\middle|\, \|x - v_k\|_{\max} \leq \varepsilon \right\}. \tag{9}$$

This implementation can be realized in the following way:

```
Set<Integer> f(x);
for (List<Integer> y : E^6_{d, delta}(x))
  for (Integer k : s.get(y))
    if (|| x - v_k ||_max <= epsilon)
      f(x).add(k);
```

It can be easily shown that

$$\|x - v_k\|_{\max} \leq \varepsilon \Rightarrow k \in \bigcup_{y \in E^6_{d,\delta}(x)} s(y) \tag{10}$$

and

$$k \in \bigcup_{y \in E^6_{d,\delta}(x)} s(y) \Rightarrow \|x - v_k\|_{\max} \leq 2\varepsilon. \tag{11}$$

In other words all $k \in \{1, ..., K\}$ with $\|x - v_k\|_{\max} \leq \varepsilon$ are definitely contained in the preliminary response $\bigcup_{y \in E^6_{d,\delta}(x)} s(y)$. But for some $k \in \bigcup_{y \in E^6_{d,\delta}(x)} s(y)$ one still has $\varepsilon < \|x - v_k\|_{\max} \leq 2\varepsilon$. Such $k \in \{1, ..., K\}$ have to be sifted out through explicit check $\|x - v_k\|_{\max} \leq \varepsilon$. Though not similar enough wrong v_k are still pretty similar to x. For that reason the number of false positives cannot be too large in an average case. It is important for the running time of the algorithm. The trivial implementation of $f : \mathbb{R}^d \to P(\{1, ..., K\})$ makes the explicit check $\|x - v_k\|_{\max} \leq \varepsilon$ for all $k \in \{1, ..., K\}$. The introduced algorithm makes the explicit comparison only for such v_k, which are pretty similar to x in sense of $\|x - v_k\|_{\max} \leq 2\varepsilon$. This aspect is responsible for the acceleration of $f(x)$ calculation.

The calculation of $f(x)$ consists of two parts. Part one determines the set of samples $E^6_{d,\delta}(x)$. Part two checks for all elements of $\{k \in s(y)|y \in E^6_{d,\delta}(x)\}$ if $\|x - v_k\|_{\max} \leq \varepsilon$ and adds k if necessary to $f(x)$. The time demand to calculate $E^6_{d,\delta}(x)$ is $O(2^d)$ and independent of K. The time demand of the second part is obviously $O(|\{k \in s(y)|y \in E^6_{d,\delta}(x)\}|)$. But the finite set of labels $\{1, ..., K\}$ is evenly distributed among infinitely many possible samples. For that reason $|s(y)|$ of a single sample $y \in E^6_{d,\delta}$ is small. Therefore $\{k \in s(y)|y \in E^6_{d,\delta}(x)\}$ is small. Time demand for a single check $\|x - v_k\|_{\max} \leq \varepsilon$ and addition to $f(x)$ is also small. All in all the implementation of $f(x)$ is fast.

Storage space demand estimation is trivial for this algorithm. In the worst case to save a new $v_k \in \mathbb{R}^d$ one needs 2^d sample vectors $y \in E^6_{d,\delta}(x) \subseteq \mathbb{Z}^d$ and 2^d copies of the label k for each sample. Space complexity is obviously linear to the number of saved vectors v_k. In big O notation it is $O((2^d d + 2^d)K) = O(2^d dK)$.

The time demand to store an additional vector v_k is independent of the number of the vector K already saved. In other words it is $O(1)$.

Running time of $f(x)$-calculation depends on $\max_{x \in \mathbb{Z}^d} |s(x)|$. Assuming v_k evenly distributed over entire $\mathbb{R}^d$ we get a finite set of K labels distributed over infinitely many samples from $\mathbb{Z}^d$. In this purely theoretical situation the running time does not change with growing K in an probabilistically average case.

3 Near Neighbor Search

Let $FS = \{X \in P(\mathbb{R}^d) | \|X| < \infty\}$ denote the set of finite subsets of $\mathbb{R}^d$. The function

$$F : FS \to \mathbb{N} \times P(\mathbb{N}) \tag{12}$$

to be implemented in this section is closely related to the previous one. It analyzes not just a single vector but a set of vectors. To construct f a sequence of vectors $(v_k)_{k \in \{1,...,K\}} \subseteq \mathbb{R}^d$ is used. For F a sequence of combinations $(c_k)_{k \in \{1,...,K\}}$ of such vectors with

$$c_k \in \underbrace{\mathbb{R}^d \times ... \times \mathbb{R}^d}_{l_k} \tag{13}$$

with $l_k \in \mathbb{N}$ is needed. c_k don't have to be of equal length. Let $l : \{1, ..., K\} \to \mathbb{N}$ denote the lengths of the combinations $(c_k)_{k \in \{1,...,K\}}$. Now $F(X)$ with $X \in FS$ will be defined in several steps. For each $k \in \{1, ..., K\}$ let $m_k \in \mathbb{N}_0$ denote the maximal integer, for which a subsequence $\pi : \{1, ..., m_k\} \to \{1, ..., l_k\}$ and a combination $x \in X^{m_k}$ exist with

$$\max_{i \in \{1,...,m_k\}} \|c_{\pi(i)} - x_i\|_{\max} \leq \varepsilon. \tag{14}$$

For $M = \max_{k \in \{1,...,K\}} m_k$ the function $F : FS \to \mathbb{N} \times P(\mathbb{N})$ is defined as

$$F(X) = (M, \{k \in \{1, ..., K\} | m_k = M\}). \tag{15}$$

The storage s needed to implement F is built in the following way:

```
Map<List<Integer>, Map<Integer, Set<Integer>>> s;

for (int k = 1; k <= K; k++)
\\ number of combination
  for (int i = 1; i <= l_k; i++)
  \\ number of component
    for (List<Integer> x : E^6_{d, delta}(c_k(i)))
      if (s.containsKey(x))
        if (s.get(x).containsKey(i))
          s.get(x).get(i).add(k);
        else {
          s.get(x).put(i, new HashSet<Integer>());
          s.get(x).get(i).add(k);
        }
```

```
      else {
        Map<Integer, Set<Integer>> map =
          new HashMap<Integer, Set<Integer>>();
        s.put(x, map);
        s.get(x).put(i, new HashSet<Integer>());
        s.get(x).get(i).add(k);
      }
```

Now $F(X)$ can be implemented in the following way:

```
Map<Integer, Set<Integer>> sub;
\\ sub - recognized subcombinations
\\ Integer k in sub.get(k) stands for the number of
\\ recognized combination.
\\ Integer i element of Set<Integer> sub.get(k) stands for
\\ the number of recognized component.
for (List<Double> x : X)
  for (List<Integer> y : E^6_{d, delta}(x))
    if (s.containsKey(y))
      for (Integer i : s.get(x).keySet())
        for (Integer k : s.get(i))
          if (||x - c_k(i)||_max <= epsilon)
            if (sub.containsKey(k))
              sub.get(k).add(i);
            else {
              sub.put(k, new HashSet<Integer>());
              sub.get(k).all(i);
            }
Map<Integer, Integer> m;
for (Integer k : sub.keySet())
  m.put(k, sub.keySet.size());
```

After having gained m_k the remaining part of implementation is trivial.

Replacing K through $N = \sum_{k=1}^{K} l_k$ in the estimation of space complexity of the first implementation one gains corresponding estimations for the second implementation: $O(2^d dN)$.

4   An Application Example

Now a simplified version of the new object recognition system will be used to demonstrate the way the new algorithm can be applied. The original system utilizes half ellipses. The simplified one utilizes straight edges.

An object is represented as a set of combinations of edges. From an image to analyze the simplified system extracts a set of edges. For each learned combination the system searches for a combination as long as possible consisting of the edges from the set, which can be approximately transformed into the learned combination through rotation, translation, scaling.

The simplified representation to be introduced is rotation, translation and scaling invariant. It will be built in three steps. For the set of complex numbers

$\mathbb{C} = \mathbb{R}^2$ and $x, y \in \mathbb{C}$ with $x \neq y$ the first representation function $R^1_{x,y} : \mathbb{C} \to \mathbb{C}$ is defined as

$$R^1_{x,y}(z) = \frac{z - x}{y - x}. \tag{16}$$

With the set of edges $E = \{e \in \mathbb{C} | e_1 \neq e_2\}$ and $e \in E$ the second representation

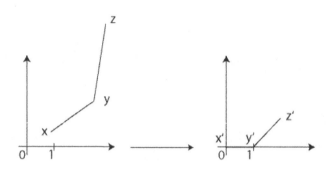

Fig. 2. Geometric meaning of $R^1_{x,y}(z)$

function $R^2_e : \mathbb{E} \to \mathbb{R}^4$ is defined as

$$R^2_e(\tilde{e}) = (R^1_{e_1,e_2}(\tilde{e}_1), R^1_{e_1,e_2}(\tilde{e}_2))^T. \tag{17}$$

For the set of combinations of edges $C = \bigcup_{n \in \mathbb{N}} E^n$ the third representation function $R^3 : C \to \bigcup_{n \in \mathbb{N}} \mathbb{R}^{4n}$ is defined as

$$R^3(c) = R^3((e_i)_{i \in \{1,...,n\}}) = (R^2_{e^1}(e^i))_{i \in \{1,...,n\}}. \tag{18}$$

The task of the simplified system can be now formulated in the following way. The system learns a sequence of K combinations of edges. The length of each combination $(e^k_i)_{i \in \{1,...,l_k\}} \subseteq E$ is l_k with $k \in \{1, ..., K\}$. Let $X \subseteq E$ denote the finite set of edges extracted from an image to analyze. For each learned combination $(e^k_i)_{i \in \{1,...,l_k\}} \in C$ the system looks for maximal $m_k \in \{1, ..., l_k\}$ and subsequence $\pi : \{1, ..., m_k\} \to \{1, ..., l_k\}$ with $\pi(1) = 1$ for which a combination of extracted edges $(\tilde{e}_i)_{i \in \{1,...,m\}} \subseteq X$ exists with

$$\left\| R^3 \left(\left(e^k_{\pi(i)} \right)_{i \in \{1,...,m\}} \right) - R^3 \left((\tilde{e}_i)_{i \in \{1,...,m\}} \right) \right\|_{\max} \leq \varepsilon. \tag{19}$$

For $M = \max_{k \in \{1,...,K\}} m_k$ the set

$$I = \{k \in \{1, ..., K\} | m_k = M\} \tag{20}$$

should be determined.

To implement the task the function $F : FS \to \mathbb{N} \times P(\mathbb{N})$ should be used. At first a sequence of feature vectors $(c_k)_{k \in \{1,...,K\}}$ with $c_k \in \prod_{i \in \{1,...,l_k\}} \mathbb{R}^4$ defined as $c_k = R^3(e^k)$ should be produced. After having built the storage for F from

$(c_k)_{k\in\{1,\ldots,K\}}$ find $F(X_e) = (M_e, I_e)$ with $X_e = \{R_e^2(\tilde{e})|\tilde{e} \in X\}$ for each $e \in X$. For $M = \max_{e\in X} M_e$ the required set is

$$I = \bigcup_{M_e=M} I_e. \tag{21}$$

To evaluate the original object recognition system the well known database COIL-100 (Columbia Object Image Library) was used. The data set is described in [Nene et al., 1996]. It contains 7200 color images of 100 3D objects. One image is taken per 5° of rotation.

The computer used in the experiments has a processor Intel(R) Core(TM)2 Duo CPU P8600 @2.40 GHz 2.40 GHz and 4.00 GB RAM. The system is implemented in Java.

There were made 2 experiments with slightly different parameter settings.

In the first experiment 18 views(1 per 20°) were used to learn each object. The remaining 5400 images were analyzed. A recognition rate of 99.2% was reached. The time demand to learn all objects is 277 seconds. The average time demand to analyze one image is 980 milliseconds.

In the second experiment 8 views(1 per 45°) were used to learn an object. The other 6400 were analyzed. A recognition rate of 96.3% was reached. The system needs 142 seconds to learn all objects. The time demand to analyze a single image is 1593 milliseconds.

The Table 1 compares the system with alternative methods. It is based on the results described in [Yang et al., 2000], [Caputo et al., 2000] and [Obdrzalek and Matas, 2011].

Table 1. Comparison with alternative results

Method	18 views	8 views
LAFs	99.9%	99.4%
Near Neighbor	99.2%	96.3%
SNoW / edges	94.1%	89.2%
SNoW / intensity	92.3%	85.1%
Linear SVM	91.3%	84.8%
Spin-Glass MRF	96.8%	88.2%
Nearest Neighbor	87.5%	79.5%

5   Conclusion

The application example shows how some properties of the new algorithm can be used. As feature vectors may be of varying length, objects to learn may be of varying complexity. The error tolerance makes the system robust to deformation up to an explicitly set ε-barrier. As the time demand to learn a feature vector and therefore a new object does not depend on the amount of information already learned, the system can be used in robotics or for a content based image retrieval system. Occlusion robustness of the algorithm makes the system highly robust to partial occlusion.

Despite several advantages the algorithm has some constraints. A feature vector should consist of similar permutable components. The dimension $d \in \mathbb{N}$ of the components should not be too high as time and space complexity grow exponentially with d.

References

[Berchtold et al., 2000]   Berchtold, S., Keim, D.A., Kriegel, H.-P., Seidl, T.: A new technique for nearest neighbor search in. IEEE TKDE (2000)

[Bishop, 2007]   Bishop, C.: Neural Networks for Pattern Recognition. Oxford University Press (2007)

[Caputo et al., 2000]   Caputo, B., Hornegger, J., Paulus, D., Niemann, H.: A spin-glass markov random field for 3d object recognition. In: NIPS (2000)

[Ciaccia et al., 1997]   Ciaccia, P., Patella, M., Zezula, P.: M-tree: An efficient access. In: VLDB (1997)

[Guttman, 2000]   Guttman, A.: R-trees: A dynamic index structure for spatial. In: SIGMOD (2000)

[Gyofri et al., 2002]   Gyofri, L., Kohler, M., Krzyzak, A., Walk, H.: A Distribution-Free Theory of Nonparametric Regression. Springer (2002)

[Nene et al., 1996]   Nene, S.A., Nayar, S.K., Murase, H.: Columbia Object Image Library, COIL-100 (1996)

[Obdrzalek and Matas, 2011]   Obdrzalek, S., Matas, J.: Object recognition using local affine frames. In: BMVC (2011)

[Pratt, 2001]   Pratt, W.: Digital Image Processing. Wiley (2001)

[Rosenblatt, 1962]   Rosenblatt, F.: Principles of Neurodynamics. Spartan, New York (1962)

[Sergeev and Palm, 2011]   Sergeev, N., Palm, G.: A new object recognition system. In: VISAPP (2011)

[Shakhnarovish et al., 2005]   Shakhnarovish, Darrell, Indyk: Nearest-Neighbor Methods in Learning and Vision. MIT Press (2005)

[Vapnik, 1998]   Vapnik, V.N.: Statistical Learning Theory. Wiley, New York (1998)

[Yang et al., 2000]   Yang, M.-H., Roth, D., Ahuja, N.: Learning to Recognize 3D Objects with SNoW. In: Vernon, D. (ed.) ECCV 2000. LNCS, vol. 1842, pp. 439–454. Springer, Heidelberg (2000)

APPENDIX

The following Lemma 1 makes the approximation properties of the algorithm comprehensible.

Lemma 1. *For $\varepsilon > 0$ set $\delta = 2\varepsilon$. Then we have:*

$$\forall x, y \in \mathbb{R} : |x - y| \leq \varepsilon \Rightarrow E_\delta^1(x) = E_\delta^1(y) \vee E_\delta^2(x) = E_\delta^2(y)$$

Proof: It's enough to show that

$$E_\delta^1(x) \neq E_\delta^1(y) \wedge |x - y| \leq \varepsilon \Rightarrow E_\delta^1\left(x + \frac{\delta}{2}\right) = E_\delta^1\left(y + \frac{\delta}{2}\right).$$

For $n_x = E_\delta^1(x)$ and $n_y = E_\delta^1(y)$ we will see at first

$$|n_x - n_y| \leq 1.$$

Considering

$$n_x - 1 < \frac{x}{\delta} \leq n_x$$
$$\wedge$$
$$n_y - 1 < \frac{y}{\delta} \leq n_y \Leftrightarrow -n_y \leq -\frac{y}{\delta} < -n_y + 1$$

we get

$$n_x - n_y - 1 \leq \frac{x - y}{\delta} \leq n_x - n_y + 1$$

$$\Rightarrow -1\frac{1}{2} \leq -1 + \frac{x - y}{\delta} \leq n_x - n_y \leq \frac{x - y}{\delta} + 1 \leq 1\frac{1}{2}.$$

Now it will be shown

$$E_\delta^1\left(x + \frac{\delta}{2}\right) = E_\delta^1\left(y + \frac{\delta}{2}\right).$$

Without loss of generality assume $x < y$.

$$\frac{y}{\delta} - n_x \leq \frac{y}{\delta} - \frac{x}{\delta} \leq \frac{1}{2} \Rightarrow \frac{y}{\delta} + \frac{1}{2} \leq n_x + 1 = n_y$$

$$n_x - \frac{x}{\delta} < \frac{y}{\delta} - \frac{x}{\delta} \leq \frac{1}{2} \Rightarrow n_x < \frac{x}{\delta} + \frac{1}{2}$$

$$\square$$

Using ASM in CT Data Segmentaion for Prostate Radiotherapy

Andrzej Skalski[1], Artur Kos[2], and Tomasz Zieliński[2]

[1] AGH University of Science and Technology,
Department of Measurement and Electronics,
Al. Mickiewicza 30, 30-059 Kraków, Poland
skalski@agh.edu.pl
[2] AGH University of Science and Technology,
Department of Telecommunications,
Al. Mickiewicza 30, 30-059 Kraków, Poland
{kosar,tzielin}@agh.edu.pl

Abstract. A novel method of prostate segmentation in a new CT data making use of explicit knowledge about the prostate is proposed. The segmentation procedure is based on active shape statistical model (ASM) of the prostate, calculated using available data base of CTs annotated by medical doctors. In the paper the problem of automatic calculation of **corresponding** prostate landmarks in **different** CTs, which are absolutely necessary for the ASM, is solved in a new manner by: 1) finding parameters of affine and B-spline transformations in groupwise registration framework ensuring pixel-based registration of all available CTs in one common co-ordinate system, 2) performing forward affine and B-spline transformation of the annotated prostate contours into this co-ordinate system, 3) averaging them - interpolation & re-sampling, 4) propagation (projection) of mean landmarks, obtained in common co-ordinate system, to the training CTs using the backward transformation. Having the same prostate landmarks in set of CTs, the ASM of the prostate is calculated (its mean shape and tendencies to its direction variations). The result of matching ASM to the data is treated as the prostate segmentation result. Obtained results are presented and discussed in the paper.

1 Introduction

Prostate cancer is one of the most common tumors in men. For example, in 2008, 37051 new cases were in UK and the Western European Age-Standardized (AS) Incidence Rates was equal 93.2 per 100,000 population [1]. In prostate cancers therapy [2] typically surgery treatment is used for younger patients and radiotherapy for older people, very often accompanied by hormone-therapy. In radiation therapy planning, the most important, difficult and time-consuming part is precise manual slice by slice anatomical organ delineation. From this reason development of special, fast, data-robust, automatic or semi-automatic CT data segmentation methods is a crucial and the most challenging research topic

L. Bolc et al. (Eds.): ICCVG 2012, LNCS 7594, pp. 610–617, 2012.
© Springer-Verlag Berlin Heidelberg 2012

in image-guided radiotherapy. It is not an easy task due to low signal-to-noise ratio, poor image contrast and organ deformations [3]. The main segmentation problem in prostate radiotherapy is low quality of the CT data causing that indicating a border between such anatomical structures like bladder and prostate is very difficult. Since a priori information can significantly help interpret new data that are analysed, nowadays segmentation algorithms are supported by additional explicit knowledge, very often in the form of medical models and atlases, and work much better than simple unsupervised solutions. Segmentation of a new CT can be guided by pixel-type or contour-type information extracted from available CT databases (the same modality) [3–7] or MRI (different modality in which soft tissue is better visible) [8–11]. Active shape models (ASM) [12] and active appearance models [13, 14] are knowledge extraction (approximation) methods used for building statistical generalisations of collected data coming from different realisation of the same or similar objects, e.g. human faces. ASMs have been already widely applied in 3D medical image segmentation [15]. The main problem making their application difficult is required consistent (strict correspondent) medical landmark placement over a large database (e.g. medical annotation of the same points of the same human organ in many CTs of different patients).

Some solutions to this problem has been already proposed and applied [16–21] but the problem is still opened. In [7] method [20] for automatic landmarks generation by training data sets re-sampling has been applied to prostate and rectum segmentation.

In this paper we address a problem of prostate segmentation in CT data, supervised (aided) by explicit statistical active shape model of the prostate build by ASM (mean value and its perpendicular deviations). We follow (and slightly modify) the landmarks labelling method of Frangi et al. [16–18], originally applied to heart not prostate, not the re-sampling method of Chen et al. [7], originally used for prostate. The segmentation was performed using the classical version of ASM [22]. Consistent placement of prostate landmarks in many CTs, required by ASM, has been solved in novel way. First, all CTs has been registered in group-wise manner using the free form deformation method with B-splines (global and local voxel adjustment). Then, all medical prostate annotations from the input CTs have been transform into one co-ordinate system using deformation fields found in the previous registration step, then they were averaged with interpolation & re-sampling and, finally, transformed back using inverse deformation field with geometrical correction. This way sets of strictly corresponding landmarks were obtained, used further by ASM to statistical prostate shape calculation. Manual landmarks' sets generation on mean CT is also possible.

The paper consists of introduction, brief state-of-the art problem description, presentation of the proposed method (training data generation, statistical prostate model construction and ASM-based segmentation), presentation of obtained results and their discussion.

2 State of the Art

Due to different types of exploited data, solution of the problem of segmentation of anatomical structures laying in the pelvis neighbourhood can be divided into three groups. In the first group, anatomical structures segmentation is based on CT data only [4–7]. The main problem appearing in this approach is very big difficulty in precise indication of borders between soft tissues, e.g. prostate and bladder. Therefore in the second group of methods [8–11] additional information is exploited during CT segmentation that comes from other modalities, like MRI, where soft tissue structures are more visible. In all methods some kind a priori knowledge about the object being segmented is taken into account. The main problem existing in application of the 3D ASM technique is appropriate creation of corresponding (consistent) landmark sets of training data. It is a direct consequence of the requirement that each landmark marked in one training data should correctly correspond to the same point in other training data. This feature is very difficult to obtain from practical point of view since users mark arbitrarily sets of landmarks and the landmark consistence (correspondence) should be obtained in large database, especially in 3D. Otherwise an incorrect parametrisation of the object would result. Another solution is to generate correct sets of landmarks automatically. Frangi et al. [16, 17] proposed registration of the analysed data to the available atlas using quasi-affine rigid global transformation and local non-rigid elastic transformation. Landmarks themselves are put in the atlas data, copied to the registered analysed data and then projected back to the atlas aligned-coordinates using inverse of the known elastic transformation. Next ASM can be performed on consistent sets of landmarks associated with data of interest. In [18] the same authors proposed to realise jointly the rigid global and elastic local transformations using B-Spline free-form deformation (FDD) of Ruecket et al. [23]. Application of the landmark generation method of Frangi is presented in [19]. Different approach of automatic landmarks creation was proposed by Jeong and Radke [20] in which all training data were re-sampled into the same number of slices by interpolating elliptic Fourier descriptor (EFD) coefficients. It was shown in [21] that consistent sets of landmarks can be obtained automatically by using point distribution models obtained from CT and simulating image generation.

3 Proposed Method

3.1 Methodology

We address the prostate segmentation in the CT data using ASM technique [22] in connection with groupwise registration [24] in order to receive automatic landmark creation. Differences in our approach in respect to [16–18] and [7] were stated in the introduction. In the first part of the research a prostate statistical model was built. Available CT images of prostates of the different patients were registered to one arbitrary chosen co-ordinate system in voxel-to-voxel manner,

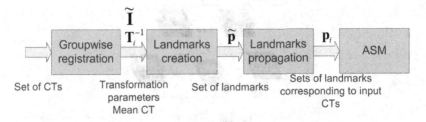

Fig. 1. Block diagram of presented method

i.e. each CT image was processed by a global affine and B-spline transformations (FDD method) [24]. Using found values of transformations' parameters prostate contours annotated (drawn) by medical doctors were transformed from input CTs to the common co-ordinate system, then averaged and interpolated (re-sampled). The resultant approximation was next transformed back to each input CT. Then, geometrical correction to medical contours was made. This way a set of CTs with corresponding prostate landmarks was obtained. Its possession is absolutely necessary on input of active shape modelling (ASM) procedures but usually is it very difficult to get. Finally, the ASM of the prostate based on Kroon's implementation [25] was built: its mean statistical shape and variances of its points in perpendicular direction to the surface. In the second part, exemplary automatic segmentation of prostate images for 4 patients was done. Block diagram of the segmentation method proposed in the paper is shown in fig. 1. First, geometrical "statistical" prostate model is generated by ASM, then it is used for new CT data segmentation.

3.2 Training Data Generation

Idea of the applied training data generation for the ASM is presented in fig. 2. First, automatic group-wise registration is performed, i.e. each image is registered to one coordinate system and its deformation field $\mathbf{T}_i$ in respect to this system is found. The coordinate system (reference) is not defined explicitly, but is calculated implicitly by constraining the average deformation to be the identity transform [24]. In groupwise registration framework, we chose the B-spline Free Form Deformation (FFD) in 3-level multiresultion scheme, proposed by Ruecket et al. [23] to registration of MRI breast images. Non-rigid B-Spline FFD was combined with affine transformation:

$$\mathbf{T}\left(x, y, z\right) = \mathbf{T}_{\mathbf{local}}\left(\mathbf{T}_{\mathbf{global}}\left(x, y, z\right)\right) \tag{1}$$

where $\mathbf{T}_{\mathbf{global}}$ is an affine transform and $\mathbf{T}_{\mathbf{local}}$ is a deformation model based on B-splines. The affine transform allows to compensate patients body pose while the B-splines - local deformation between the data. Calculation of deformation fields was done using implementation given by Balci et al. [24].

Then, set of M $\widehat{\mathbf{p}} = [\widehat{x_1}, \widehat{y_1}, \widehat{z_1}, \widehat{x_2}, \widehat{y_2}, \widehat{z_2}, \dots, \widehat{x_M}, \widehat{y_M}, \widehat{z_M}]$ landmarks on gradient of the mean CT $\widehat{\mathbf{I}}$ was calculated (i-th are landmarks coordinates). Knowing

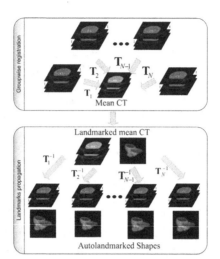

Fig. 2. Block diagram of training data generation. Description in the text.

N forward transformations of N CT data sets we can calculate inverse (backward) transformations $\mathbf{T}_i^{-1}$ (i=1..N) what allows to mapped landmarks from mean CT to individual data used to the mean CT creation. Resulting positions were corrected based on distance to doctors contour. Finally, we receive N vectors of landmarks correlated with the training data with correspondences between them kept:

$$\mathbf{p_k} = \mathbf{T_i^{-1}}\left([\widehat{x_1}, \widehat{y_1}, \widehat{z_1}, \widehat{x_2}, \widehat{y_2}, \widehat{z_2}, \ldots, \widehat{x_M}, \widehat{y_M}, \widehat{z_M}]\right) \tag{2}$$

3.3   Model Construction

During prostate model construction the following quantities were computed:

– mean shape $\overline{\mathbf{P}}$ of landmarks $\mathbf{p_k}$:

$$\overline{\mathbf{P}} = \frac{1}{N}\sum_{k=1}^{N}\mathbf{p_k} \tag{3}$$

– covariance matrix S:

$$S = \frac{1}{N-1}\sum_{k=1}^{N}\left(\mathbf{p_k} - \overline{\mathbf{P}}\right)\left(\mathbf{p_k} - \overline{\mathbf{P}}\right)^T \tag{4}$$

– eigenvectors ϕ_k of S (using principal component analysis (PCA)):

$$S\phi_k = \lambda_k\phi_k, \mathbf{\Phi} = [\phi_1, \phi_2, \ldots, \phi_{2M}] \tag{5}$$

– vector $\mathbf{b}$ such that for any π the following equation is true:

$$\pi = \overline{\mathbf{P}} + \mathbf{\Phi}\mathbf{b} \tag{6}$$

Vectors ϕ_k and $\mathbf{b}$ represent, respectively, main directions of the *mean* model changing and variances along these directions. Since eigenvectors with higher indexes have smaller deviations, only $\mathbf{t}$ largest eigenvalues were retained which allows to reduce dimensionality of the model. The final model was described by:

$$\pi \approx \overline{\mathbf{P}} + \mathbf{\Phi_t b_t} \tag{7}$$

As most shapes are within the range $\pm 3\sigma$, knowing vectors $\mathbf{\Phi_t}$ and $\mathbf{b_t}$ a new shape ϕ can be generated which is not derived from the training data.

3.4 ASM-Based Segmentation

Matching the statistical prostate model to the prostate target in a new image is based on Active Shape Model algorithm introduced by Cootes [12, 13]. The result of matching is treated as the prostate segmentation result. To initialise the ASM algorithm the statistical prostate model is approximately fitted to the image data by a global transformation $\mathbf{T_{global}}$ which gives:

$$\mathbf{\Pi} = \mathbf{T_{global}} \left(\overline{\mathbf{P}} + \mathbf{\Phi_t b_t} \right) \tag{8}$$

in local or image coordinates description. The first step is a local optimisation which starts near the target. In each landmark point a normal to boundary is inspected to find points with higher intensity gradients. These points are marked as the best candidates for new positions for corresponding landmarks. Then, a model pose is adjusted to achieve the best fit of the current landmarks to the target. Finally, new values of model vector $\mathbf{b}$ are computed to provide the best match of the model in a new pose to the target. These three steps are realized to minimize the function:

$$f\left(\mathbf{b}, \mathbf{\Pi_c}, \mathbf{s}, \mathbf{\Theta}\right) = \left| \mathbf{\Pi} - \mathbf{T_{global}} \left(\overline{\mathbf{P}} + \mathbf{\Phi_t b_t}; \mathbf{\Pi_c}, \mathbf{s}, \mathbf{\Theta} \right) \right|^2 \tag{9}$$

where $\mathbf{\Pi_c}, \mathbf{s}, \mathbf{\Theta}$ are, respectively: current model landmarks, scale and rotation. There steps are repeated until differences are repeated until differences between the model and the target becomes negligible.

4   Discussion and Results

All images (coming from 14 patients) which were used to build the atlas came from the same CT device what in consequence allowed us to use a simple similarity measure function - Sum of Squared Differences (SDD). The validation set were consisted of data of 4 patients to be treated for prostate cancer, who underwent a planning CT scan. All CT scans were acquired without contrast enhancement. The image size in axial plane was 512 by 512 pixels with 1 mm resolution for 5-mm thick slices. For each patient the prostate was manually contoured by the same medical doctor. In figure 3 exemplary segmentation results obtained for real prostate cancer CT data are presented. In order to validate

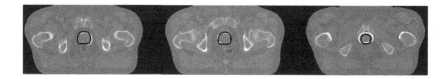

Fig. 3. Exemplary results; White contour - doctors outline, Black contour - results from proposed method

the results, the Dice's coefficient was calculated. Its average value for 145 slices coming from 4 CT data of prostate cancer patients not included to the model was equal 0.8015 with standard deviation = 0.0201.

The method of automatic landmarks propagation and segmentation algorithm of prostate in CT data has been proposed in the paper. Its efficiency has been confirmed by the visual inspection and comparison with outlines provided by an expert.

Acknowledgements. The work was supported by Polish grant founded by Polish Ministry of Science and Higher Education/National Science Centre, project NN 518 497739. The authors would like to express their gratitude to dr. hab. Pawel Kukolowicz and dr. Piotr Kedzierawski from the HolyCross Cancer Center, Kielce, Poland for making the available the CT date used in the reported research.

References

1. Cancer Research UK, Prostate cancer - UK incidence statistics,
   http://info.Cancerresearchuk.org/cancerstats/types/prostate/incidence/
2. Horwich, V.A., Parker, C., Kataja, V.: Prostate cancer: ESMO Clinical Recommendations for diagnosis, treatment and follow-up. Annals of Oncology 20, iv76–iv78 (2009)
3. Skalski, A., et al.: Computed Tomography - based radiotherapy planning on the example of prostate cancer: Application of Level-Set segmentation method guided by atlas-type knowledge. In: Conf. ISABEL 2011. ACM Digital Library (2011) ISBN 978-1-4503-0913-4/11/10
4. Pekar, V., McNutt, T.R., Kaus, M.R.: Automated model-based organ delineation for radiotherapy planning in prostatic region. Int. J. Radiation Oncology Biol. Phys. 60(3), 973–980 (2004)
5. Acosta, O., Dowling, J., Cazoulat, G., Simon, A., Salvado, O., de Crevoisier, R., Haigron, P.: Atlas Based Segmentation and Mapping of Organs at Risk from Planning CT for the Development of Voxel-Wise Predictive Models of Toxicity in Prostate Radiotherapy. In: Madabhushi, A., Dowling, J., Yan, P., Fenster, A., Abolmaesumi, P., Hata, N. (eds.) MICCAI 2010. LNCS, vol. 6367, pp. 42–51. Springer, Heidelberg (2010)
6. Lu, C., et al.: An integrated approach to segmentation and nonrigid registration for application in image-guided pelvic radiotherapy. Med. Image Anal. 15, 772–785 (2011)
7. Chen, S., Lovelock, M., Radke, R.J.: Segmenting the prostate and rectum in CT imagery using anatomical constraints. Med. Image Anal. 15(1), 1–11 (2011)

8. Klein, S., et al.: Segmentation of the prostate in MR images by Atlas Matching. In: 4th IEEE Int. Symposium on Biomedical Imaging From Nano to Macro, pp. 1300–1303 (2007)

9. Pasquier, D., et al.: Automatic segmentation on pelvic structures from Magnetic Resonance images for prostate cancer radiotherapy. Int. J. Radiation Oncology Biol. Phys. 68(2), 592–600 (2007)

10. Martin, S., Daanen, V., Troccaz, J.: Atlas-based prostate segmentation using an hybrid registration. International J. of CARS 3(6), 485–492 (2008)

11. Dowling, J., Lambert, J., Parker, J., Greer, P.B., Fripp, J., Denham, J., Ourselin, S., Salvado, O.: Automatic MRI Atlas-Based External Beam Radiation Therapy Treatment Planning for Prostate Cancer. In: Madabhushi, A., Dowling, J., Yan, P., Fenster, A., Abolmaesumi, P., Hata, N. (eds.) MICCAI 2010. LNCS, vol. 6367, pp. 25–33. Springer, Heidelberg (2010)

12. Cootes, T.F., Cooper, D., Taylor, C.J., Graham, J.: A trainable method of parametric shape description. Image Vision Comput. 10(5), 289–294 (1992)

13. Cootes, T.F., Taylor, C.J.: Statistical models of appearance for computer vision. Technical Report. University of Manchester (2004)

14. Gao, X., Li, et al.: A review of Active Appearance Models. IEEE Trans. on Systems, Man, and Cybernetics - Part C: Applications and reviews 40(2), 145–158 (2010)

15. Heimann, T., Meinzer, H.P.: Statistical shape models for 3D medical image segmentation: A review. Med. Image Anal. 13, 543–563 (2009)

16. Frangi, A.F., Rueckert, D., Schnabel, J.A., Niessen, W.J.: Automatic 3D ASM Construction via Atlas-Based Landmarking and Volumetric Elastic Registration. In: Insana, M.F., Leahy, R.M. (eds.) IPMI 2001. LNCS, vol. 2082, pp. 78–91. Springer, Heidelberg (2001)

17. Frangi, A.F., et al.: Automatic construction of multiple-object three-dimensional statistical shape models: application to cardiac modeling. IEEE Trans. Med. Imaging 21(9), 1151–1166 (2002)

18. Ordas, S., et al.: A statistical shape model of the whole heart and its application to model-based segmentation. In: SPIE Medical Imaging: Physiology, Function, and Structure from Medical Images, vol. 6511. SPIE (2007)

19. van Assen, H.C., et al.: SPASM: a 3D-ASM for segmentation of sparse and arbitrarily oriented cardiac MRI data. Med. Image Anal. 10(2), 286–303 (2006)

20. Jeong, Y., Radke, R.: Reslicing axially sampled 3D shapes using elliptic Fourier descriptors. Med. Image Anal. 11(2), 197–206 (2007)

21. Tobon-Gomez, C., et al.: Automatic Construction of 3D-ASM Intensity Models by Simulating Image Acquisition: Application to Myocardial Gated SPECT Studies. IEEE Transactions on Medical Imaging 27(11), 1655–1667 (2008)

22. Cootes, T.F., Cooper, D., Taylor, C.J., Graham, J.: Active Shape Models - Their Training and Application. Computer Vision and Image Understanding 61(1), 38–59 (1995)

23. Rueckert, D., Sonoda, L.I., Hayes, C., et al.: Nonrigid Registration Using Free-Form Deformations: Application to Breast MR Images. IEEE Trans. on Med. Imag. 18(8), 712–721 (1999)

24. Balci, S.K., Golland, P., Wells, W.M.: Non-rigid Groupwise Registration using B-Spline Deformation Model. The Insight Journal (2007), doi: http://hdl.handle.net/1926/568

25. Kroon, D.-J.: Active Shape Model (ASM) and Active Appearance Model (AAM), http://www.mathworks.com/matlabcentral/fileexchange/ 26706-active-shape-model-asm-and-active-appearance-model-aam

A System for Analysis of Tremor
in Patients with Parkinson's Disease
Based on Motion Capture Technique

Magdalena Stawarz[1], Andrzej Polański[1,2], Stanisław Kwiek[3],
Magdalena Boczarska-Jedynak[4], Lukasz Janik[1],
Andrzej Przybyszewski[5], and Konrad Wojciechowski[1,2]

[1] Silesian University of Technology, Institute of Computer Science,
Akademicka 16, 44-100 Gliwice, Poland
{Magdalena.Stawarz,Andrzej.Polanski,
Lukasz.Janik,Konrad.Wojciechowski}@polsl.pl
[2] Polish-Japanese Institute of Information Technology,
Aleja Legionów 2, 41-902 Bytom, Poland
{Andrzej.Polanski,Konrad.Wojciechowski}@pjwstk.pl
[3] Departament of Neurosurgery, Medical University of Silesia,
Central University Hospital, Medyków 14, 40-752 Katowice, Poland
skwiek@csk.katowice.pl
[4] Department of Neurorehabilitation, Departament of Neurology,
Medical University of Silesia, Central University Hospital,
Medyków 14, 40-752 Katowice, Poland
m.boczarska@gmail.com
[5] University of Massachusetts Medical School, Dept Neurology,
55 Lake Av, Worcester, MA01655, USA
Andrzej.Przybyszewski@umassmed.edu

Abstract. Resting tremor is one of the primary motor symptoms of
Parkinsons Disease. In this paper we analyze the occurrence of tremor
in Parkinsons disease by using a system for measurements of kinematic
data of upper limbs. The experimental group includes seven PD patients
during standing. Analysis is based on kinematic measurements done by
using multimodal motion capture (MOCAP) system for registration of
3D positions of body markers, ground reaction forces and electromyography signals. All patients taking part in examination have undergone
deep brain stimulation surgical treatment. Examination involved comparisons of tremor parameters across four conditions, where stimulator
was turned ON/OFF and medication was ON/OFF. Obtained results
confirm statistically significant differences of certain tremor parameters
between different experimental conditions.

Keywords: motion capture, tremor, parkinson disease.

1 Introduction

Tremor is an involuntary oscillatory - type motion of parts of human body resulting from uncontrolled contraction and relaxation of certain muscles. Tremor

L. Bolc et al. (Eds.): ICCVG 2012, LNCS 7594, pp. 618–625, 2012.

is known to be associated to a number of diseases, especially to diseases associated with neurological disorders [1]. A disease whose symptoms are very closely related to tremor is Parkinson's Disease (PD). Therefore analyses of tremor are very often pursed in studies devoted to diagnosis, treatment plans, estimation of different treatment results of PD, e.g. [3][4]. Depending on the type of motion, features and cause of origin tremors are classified into several further categories[2]. Resting tremor (RT) is the type of tremor observed when patient is not performing any motion activity. It is most often localized in patient's forearms and hands. Among several types of tremor, resting tremor is the one most often observed in PD patients and belongs to basic indexes for diagnosis and evaluation of patients responses to treatments. This paper is devoted to the design of a system for experimental analysis of resting tremor in patients with Parkinson disease. Experimental setup was based on multimodal MOCAP measurement system. All measurements have been made in Human Motion Laboratory located in Polish Japanese Institute of Information Technology in Bytom, Poland. In our kinematic movement recording set-up 10-camera, 3D motion capture system (Vicon) have been used. Examination involved a group of Parkinson Disease (PD) patients who have undergone the therapy based in implanting Deep Brain Stimulator (DBS) for improving his motoric skills. The patients taking part in the research was treated in Neurology Clinic Medical University of Silesia, with DBS stimulators implanted in Department of Neurosurgery, Medical University of Silesia [5][7][8]. Examination scenario of PD patient involved tremor measurements for four experimental conditions (called sessions) defined by medication and DBS stimulation (S1 - MedOFF StimOFF, S2 - MedOFF StimON, S3 - MedON StimOFF, S4 - MedON StimON, where StimON/OFF means that stimulator was turned on/off before experiment, while med ON/OFF means that patient was under the influence of drugs or not).

2   Methods

A basic standard for recording MOCAP data, used in the performed experiments was NIH MOCAP file format c3d [9][10]. C3d file is a binary file containing spatial positions of all body markers and all additional signals collected during a MOCAP session. As a part of experimental setup a software was developed for transforming contents of c3d file to text format. Then text files were used to create Matlab data files including all experimental results. All further data processing operations were carried out in Matlab environment. Kinematic data were collected from markers located on left and right wrists during normal standing, with eyes open. Time window with a width of 15 [s] was used in the analyzes.

Analyses of tremor signal included several steps are described below:

2.1   Constant Component and Trend Removal

As can be easily seen in Fig. 1, apart from tremor signal, X, Y and Z coordinates of the recorded signals LFIN and RFIN include constant and trend components.

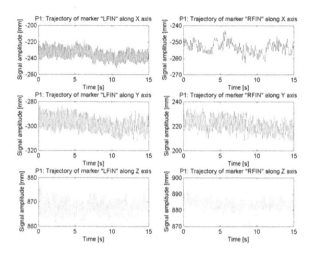

Fig. 1. X, Y and Z trajectories of c3d markers LFIN and RFIN recorded for a PD patient. Recorded signals include constant and trend components.

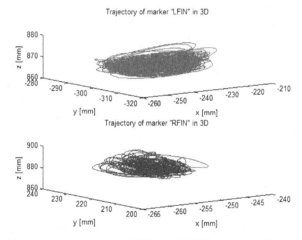

Fig. 2. Trajectories of c3d markers LFIN and RFIN recorded for a PD patient in 3 dimensions

In order to remove constant and trend components from the X ,Y and Z coordinates of the signals from LFIN and RFIN markers, the algorithm implemented as function 'msbackadj' from Matlab bioinformatics toolbox was used. This function uses recursive histogram algorithm in order to assess the signal background. The main idea is to retrieve the mean of the noise distribution, by using the method of a histogram [6]. The first step of the algorithm is estimate the baseline within multiple shifted windows, which width was set on 100 separation units. After that it regress the differing baseline to the window points using a spline approximation. Finally it adjusts the baseline of the peak signals provided by positions of c3d marker [11].

Results of removal of constant and trend components by the above algorithm are shown in Fig. 3.

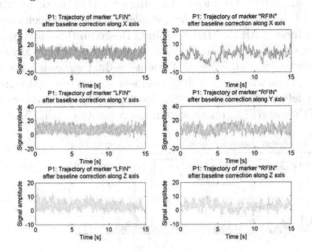

Fig. 3. Results of removal of constant and trend components of X, Y and Z coordinates of LFIN and RFIN signals

2.2   Resultant Spatial Signal

The resultant 3D spatial signal across X, Y and Z axis was calculated as Euclidean distance between the actual position of the marker and its centroid (rooted sum of squares, RSS). Application of this operation led to obtaining two 3D tremor signals corresponding to LFIN and RFIN markers. Time plots of amplitudes of these signals are shown in Fig. 4.

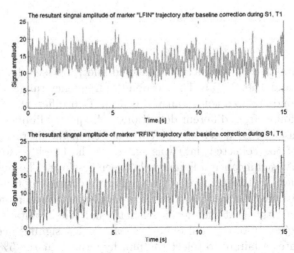

Fig. 4. Time plots of amplitudes of 3D tremor signals corresponding to LFIN and RFIN markers

2.3   Frequency Analysis

To find out how amplitude of tremor is changing across the frequency, Fast Fourier Transform (FFT) has been applied. Amplitude spectra have been calculated for the 15 [s] time course, with 100 [Hz] sampling. Based on this maximal and mean amplitude of the signal and the area under curve of spectrum in range of 3-7 [Hz] and 4-6 [Hz] were calculated. For each Patient residual values for 4 sessions were obtained. The residual value is calculated as mean across trials performed during each session for left and right separately. Examples of amplitude spectra corresponding to LFIN and RFIN tremor signals are presented in Fig. 5.

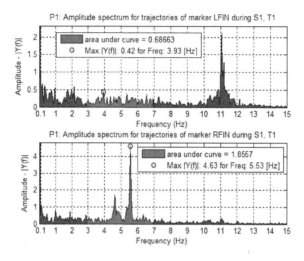

Fig. 5. Amplitude Fourier spectra of 3D tremor signals corresponding to LFIN and RFIN markers

3   Results

All features computed on the basis of collected and processed data are summarized in Tab. 1 and Tab. 2. Tab. 1 correspond to frequency range 3-7 [Hz], while Tab. 2 corresponds to frequency range 4-6 [Hz]. Two different versions of frequency ranges follow from different definitions of frequency limits corresponding to resting tremor in PD, which can be encountered in the literature [2]. Statistical analysis of the collected data was based on the t-test performed to find out if there exist significance differences between sessions. The null hypothesis assumes that data in two compared sessions are independent random samples from normal distributions with equal means and equal but unknown variances, against the alternative that the means are not equal. The resultant value $h = 1$, it indicates a rejection of the null hypothesis at the 5% significance level, while $h = 0$, it indicates a failure to reject the null hypothesis at the 5% significance level. The results of applied statistical tests are presented in Tab. 3 and Tab. 4.

Table 1. Mean $|Y(f)|$, Mean $|Y(f)|$ and area under spectrum between 3-7 [Hz] for left and right side for 7 patients across 4 sessions

Side	Patient	Mean Amplitude				Max Amplitude				Area under spectrum			
		S1	S2	S3	S4	S1	S2	S3	S4	S1	S2	S3	S4
	P1	0.24	0.02	0.18	0.11	0.64	0.07	0.52	0.14	0.86	0.08	0.61	0.51
	P2	0.03	0.01	0.22	0.08	0.04	0.01	0.28	0.11	0.11	0.03	0.90	0.35
	P3	0.05	0.01	0.05	0.09	0.12	0.01	0.08	0.12	0.20	0.02	0.23	0.38
Left	P4	0.78	0.55	0.55	0.65	4.25	1.76	1.77	2.34	2.18	1.52	1.61	1.78
	P5	0.03	0.01	0.02	0.39	0.07	0.02	0.05	0.45	0.15	0.04	0.10	1.64
	P6	0.30	0.04	0.11	0.03	1.69	0.06	0.16	0.11	0.81	0.15	0.47	0.14
	P7	0.04	0.02	0.03	0.01	0.16	0.05	0.05	0.02	0.27	0.09	0.15	0.04
	P1	0.24	0.02	0.18	0.11	0.64	0.07	0.52	0.14	0.86	0.08	0.61	0.51
	P2	0.03	0.01	0.22	0.08	0.04	0.01	0.28	0.11	0.11	0.03	0.890	0.35
	P3	0.05	0.01	0.05	0.09	0.12	0.01	0.08	0.12	0.20	0.02	0.23	0.38
Right	P4	0.78	0.55	0.55	0.65	4.25	1.76	1.77	2.34	2.18	1.52	1.61	1.78
	P5	0.03	0.01	0.02	0.39	0.07	0.02	0.05	0.45	0.15	0.04	0.10	1.64
	P6	0.30	0.04	0.11	0.03	1.69	0.06	0.16	0.11	0.81	0.15	0.47	0.14
	P7	0.04	0.02	0.03	0.01	0.16	0.05	0.05	0.02	0.26	0.09	0.15	0.04

Table 2. Mean $|Y(f)|$, Mean $|Y(f)|$ and area under spectrum between 3-7 [Hz] for left and right side for 7 patients across 4 sessions

Side	Patient	Mean Amplitude				Max Amplitude				Area under spectrum			
		S1	S2	S3	S4	S1	S2	S3	S4	S1	S2	S3	S4
	P1	0.24	0.02	0.18	0.11	0.63	0.07	0.52	0.14	0.49	0.05	0.37	0.28
	P2	0.03	0.01	0.22	0.08	0.03	0.01	0.28	0.11	0.05	0.02	0.43	0.16
	P3	0.04	0.01	0.05	0.09	0.09	0.01	0.08	0.12	0.09	0.01	0.10	0.18
Left	P4	0.84	0.55	0.55	0.65	4.25	1.76	1.77	2.34	1.73	1.12	1.27	1.41
	P5	0.03	0.01	0.02	0.39	0.06	0.02	0.05	0.45	0.06	0.02	0.04	0.78
	P6	0.30	0.04	0.11	0.03	1.68	0.06	0.16	0.11	0.62	0.07	0.22	0.07
	P7	0.03	0.02	0.03	0.01	0.09	0.05	0.05	0.02	0.07	0.03	0.06	0.02
	P1	0.77	0.06	0.34	0.03	3.28	0.19	1.19	0.06	1.57	0.12	0.70	0.34
	P2	0.02	0.02	0.29	0.07	0.03	0.03	0.37	0.10	0.04	0.04	0.58	0.14
	P3	1.20	0.01	0.12	0.02	3.95	0.02	0.19	0.03	2.44	0.02	0.25	0.05
Right	P4	0.77	0.29	0.36	0.17	4.56	0.72	1.53	0.43	1.58	0.58	0.81	0.54
	P5	0.02	0.02	0.04	0.67	0.04	0.03	0.06	0.82	0.05	0.03	0.08	1.35
	P6	0.62	0.08	0.12	0.32	4.14	0.20	0.21	1.58	1.28	0.6	0.24	0.64
	P7	0.28	0.10	0.05	0.01	0.59	0.20	0.08	0.03	0.55	0.20	0.10	0.02

Table 3. Presents the results for t-test. performed to find if there exist differences between values of mean $|Y(f)|$, max $|Y(f)|$ in range 3-7 Hz, for each pair of sessions

Mean Amplitude				Max Amplitude			
Session	Session	h	p-value	Session	Session	h	p-value
S1	S2	1	**0.018**	S1	S2	1	**0.009**
S1	S3	0	0.111	S1	S3	1	**0.026**
S1	S4	0	0.170	S1	S4	1	**0.026**
S2	S3	0	0.137	S2	S3	0	0.271
S2	S4	0	0.181	S2	S4	0	0.353
S3	S4	0	0.880	S3	S4	0	0.955

Table 4. Presents the results for t-test. performed to find if there exist differences between values of mean $|Y(f)|$, max $|Y(f)|$ in range 4-6 Hz, for each pair of sessions

Mean Amplitude				Max Amplitude			
Session	Session	h	p-value	Session	Session	h	p-value
S1	S2	1	**0.018**	S1	S2	1	**0.011**
S1	S3	0	0.099	S1	S3	1	**0.032**
S1	S4	0	0.146	S1	S4	1	**0.033**
S2	S3	0	0.137	S2	S3	0	0.271
S2	S4	0	0.181	S2	S4	0	0.353
S3	S4	0	0.880	S3	S4	0	0.955

4   Conclusion

The size of the group of PD patients in the experiment performed in this study was rather small, it included only 7 subjects. Nevertheless statistically significant differences between amplitudes of tremor in Session S1 (no medication no stimulation) and three remaining sessions S2, S3 and S4 were observed. In the future research we plan to re-analyze the experimental results for larger group of PD patients, including 30-40 subjects and to develop the experimental design by several new features of the tremor, amplitude asymmetry, phase difference between LFIN and RFIN.

Acknowledgments. This work has been partly supported by the European Union from the European Social Fund (UDAPOKL.04.01.01-00-106/09-00 M. Stawarz, L. Janik) and by The Polish National Science Center (NN518289240 A. Polański; NN516475740 K. Wojciechowski).

References

1. Jankovic, J., Fahn, S.: Physiologic and pathologic tremors. Diags. mechanism. and management. Ann. Intern. Med. 93, 460–465 (1980)
2. Findley, L.J.: Classification of tremors. J. Clin. Neurophysiol. 13, 122–132 (1996)

3. Grimaldi, G., Manto, M.: Neurological tremor: sensors. signal processing and emerging applications. Sensors 10, 1399–1422 (2010)
4. Rao, G., Fisch, L., Srinivasan, S., et al.: Does this patient have Parkinson disease? JAMA 289, 347–353 (2003)
5. Kwiek, S.J., Boczarska, M., Swiat, M., Kodowska-Duda, G., Kukier, W., Slusarczyk, W., Antonowicz-Olewicz, A., Szajkowski, S., Suszyski, K., Bażowski, P., Opala, G.: Deep brain stimulation for Parkinson's disease. Experience of Silesian Interdisciplinary Centre for Parkinson's disease treatment in Katowice. 39 Zjazd Polskiego Towarzystwa Neurochirurgów i Sekcji Pielêgniarskiej PTNCh z udziaem Greckiego Towarzystwa Neurochirurgicznego, September 17-20, Mikoajki, Poland (2009)
6. Andrade, L., Manolakos, E.S.: Signal background estimation and baseline correction algorithms for accurate DNA sequencing. Journal of VLSI Signal Processing 35, 229–243 (2003)
7. Kwiek, S.J., Kłodowska-Duda, G., Wójcikiewicz, T., Ślusarczyk, W., Kukier, W., Baowski, P., Zymon-Zagrska, A., Buszta, H., Konopka, M., Giec-Lorenz, A., Opala, G.: Stereotactic stimulation and ablative procedures for therapy of movement disorders. Own experience. Acta Neurochir 148(10), 42 (2006)
8. Kwiek, S.J., Kłodowska-Duda, G., Wójcikiewicz, T., Ślusarczyk, W., Kukier, W., Bażowski, P., Zymon-Zagórska, A., Buszta, H., Konopka, M., Kiełtyka, A., Opala, G.: Simultaneous targeting and stimulation of STN and VIM in tremor predominant PD patients. Pro's and Cons. Acta Neurochir. 148(10), 36 (2006)
9. http://c3d.org (accessed: March 15, 2012)
10. Lander, J.: Working with motion capture file formats. Game Developer 5(1), 30–37 (1998)
11. http://www.mathworks.com/help/toolbox/bioinfo/ref/msbackadj.html (accessed: March 20, 2012)

Multimodal Segmentation of Dense Depth Maps and Associated Color Information

Maciej Stefańczyk and Włodzimierz Kasprzak

Warsaw University of Technology, Institute of Control and Computation Eng.,
Nowowiejska 15/19 00-665 Warsaw, Poland
stefanczyk.maciek@gmail.com, w.kasprzak@elka.pw.edu.pl
http://robotics.ia.pw.edu.pl

Abstract. An integrated segmentation approach for color images and depth maps is proposed. The 3D pointclouds are characterized by normal vectors and then grouped into planar, concave or convex faces. The empty regions in the depth map are filled by segments of the associated color image. In the experimental part two types of depth maps are analysed: generated by the MS-Kinect sensor or by a stereo-pair of cameras.

Keywords: depth map, integrated image segmentation, surface segmentation, 3D point clouds.

1 Introduction

There is a long history of 3D data acquisition technology, ranging from stereo-vision, laser scanners to structured light processing techniques [1], [2]. But only when Microsoft's project Natal (now known as Kinect) became reality, the use of depth maps (or now more often called as 3D pointclouds) has became more and more popular on many fields, including computer entertainment, robotics, etc. [3]. This paper focuses on segmentation methods of dense depth maps produced by such a sensor, and using an RGB image aligned with it. Our aim is to use the segments extracted by the proposed method as the input for a model-based 3D object recognition system, with applications in service robotics [1].

In section 2 some methods of gathering pointclouds are described and a synthetic comparison of them is given. In next section, a method of enhancing the raw depth map by additional information - the normal vector per point - is proposed. Section 4 presents the actual segmentation process, that makes use of many modalities (depth, normal vector, color, etc.). Then section 5 describes various features that can be calculated for obtained segments, the 3D point subsets. The explanation of approach is in-place illustrated by experimental results. The paper ends with a summary.

2 Acquisition of Pointcloud Data

All methods of gathering 3D scene information can be divided into groups, depending on used hardware – from cheap, highly-available cameras, through those

L. Bolc et al. (Eds.): ICCVG 2012, LNCS 7594, pp. 626–632, 2012.

supported by specialized projectors, to the dedicated, highly-sophisticated hardware and laser scanners. Another criterion is the method of information acquisition – a passive registration of light from environment or the usage of active scene illumination. This comparison focuses on practical features of three presented approaches – one that uses an active distance sensor, a second one that uses a stereo-pair of cameras and a third one based on structured light illumination.

The first approach is using traditional distance sensors, such as rangefinders or laser scanners [1]. Mounting them on pan-tilt rotatable units allows the acquisition of a series of single scans, that can be merged to form a full 2D depth map. Precision ranges from single millimeters to centimeters, and depends on the quality of applied sensors and the precision of pan-tilt units. This method is rather slow, as a single scan of the whole scene can take up to few seconds. Very often, there is a need for an additional color camera to get a color image of scanned scene.

Another method is stereo vision, an image processing approach that uses two cameras. The depth of a point in space in front of them is calculated while computing the disparity between its two projections in both images. Most of the stereo-matching algorithms are based on point features detected in the images, so they behave well for outdoor scenes, where many natural characteristic points can be found. In interiors, where many objects with homogeneous surfaces exist (like walls and furniture fronts), there is a need for some active illumination to help the stereo-matching algorithm [2]. The generated depth map is usually automatically aligned with one of the images, so there is no need for separate color image acquisition. Also, this method can be pretty cheap, even classical web cameras can give good results. Drawbacks of this method are relatively high computational load and moderate framerates.

Another type of approaches that requires strong image analysis is based on structured light illumination. A camera observes the scene, which is illuminated by a well-known light pattern, and the depth map is created by pattern deformation analysis. This method actively uses illumination, so it is well suited for indoor environments, but in outdoor scenes, with high sun exposure, it usually fails. In cases where projected pattern uses visible light, the same camera can be used for depth and color registration, so both maps are perfectly aligned. On the other hand, using visible light can be uncomfortable if working in common space with people, so some infrared projectors and cameras are used instead. In this case, there are at least two cameras needed, and a separate step for aligning depth and color images is necessary. One of popular sensors using structured light is Microsoft Kinect, which was quickly hacked by open-source community [3]. This sensor was chosen for this work, because nearly the whole acquisition processing is done in hardware and the scene coverage is very high (sample images can be seen on fig. 1). We have also implemented a stereo-vision approach, but it is working much slower than Kinect, with an acquisition rate of 8 frames per second only.

Finally, the last type of 3D data acquisition approaches is using time-of-flight cameras [4], where the light is emitted from a projector and the arrival time (or

Fig. 1. Comparison of depth maps generated from MS Kinect and stereo vision algorithm from OpenCV library

light phase) is measured after it bounces back from objects on the scene. Again, to get an additional color image information there is a need for another camera and a depth map-to-image registration step. A summary of described methods and their main features is presented in table 1.

Table 1. Comparison of selected methods of generating 3D scene image

Method	CPU load	Acquisition time	Resolution	I/O[a]	HW cost
2D sensors	moderate	1s-3s	180x256px	●/●	˜1000USD
Stereo vision	high	0.1s-1s	640x480px	◖/●	˜100USD
Proj. texture stereo	high	0.1s-1s	640x480px	●/◖	˜400USD
MS Kinect	low	0.03s	640x480px	●/○	˜100USD
TOF cameras	low	0.01s-0.04s	176x144px	●/○	˜8000USD

[a] I - works well indoors, O - works well outdoors

3   Extending the Depth Data

Let us observe, that to rely only on the raw depth map could be insufficient in many applications. For example, a box located on a desk could be left undetected while using the depth map, because no real depth discontinuity is observed. Therefore, from this depth map some more information of different modality need to be extracted.

3.1   Normal Vector Map

The most straightforward extension is to obtain the normal vector map – at each depth map element we estimate a normal vector while taking into account the local neighborhood of given point in the depth map. The depths in the neighborhood are assumed to sample the unknown surface. Most often two kinds of algorithms are applied: based on numerical optimizations or on Voronoi diagrams [5]. The algorithms may work either on raw depth map (with distance from camera to object held in each pixel), or on its pointcloud representation (3D coordinates in some fixed frame held in each pixel). There are many challenges associated with normal estimation, such us handling the measurement noise and discontinuities in depth. For example, to avoid generating false normals indicating presence of wall, see fig 2. Using normal vector maps, objects mentioned earlier can be easily segmented – even if there are no discontinuities in depth, there will be visible edges in the normal image.

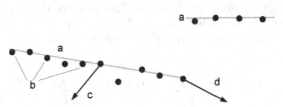

Fig. 2. Some caveats of estimating normals from sampled points; a - parts of real surfaces, b - sampled points, c - incorrect normal due to presence of noise, d - incorrect normal on edge of surface

3.2 Surface Curvature

Another modality that extends the depth map is the curvature factor of underlying surface [6]. This kind of information can be directly computed from the raw depth map. It can greatly enhance the detection of fuzzy boundary points, where the normal vectors show approximately continuous distribution, but where different surfaces cross (for example a bottle could be segmented into it's cylinder-like main part and sphere-like top, fig. 4a,b). There are of course visual differences between mentioned maps, that can be easily observed when looking at the image containing flat surfaces and spheres. In the normal vector map, both object types are filled with some gradient (in case of flat surface not parallel to camera plane), but it's hard to tell whether surface is really flat or distinguish a sphere from a cone (fig. 4c). Every flat surface, on the other hand, is filled with uniform color on normal maps (and curvature maps), independent of it's orientation (normal vectors of surface are the same in it's every point). Also sphere-like regions can be easily distinguished from cone-like regions in the depth map, but to tell exactly, where the border between sphere and cylinder is one must look at the curvature map (fig. 4d).

4   The Pointclouds Segmentation Approach

4.1   Similarity of Points

Our segmentation approach is based on a region growing technique, but instead of working on a single intensity image, we feed it with all the image maps mentioned earlier (hence the name of this approach – *multimodal segmentation*).

These input maps are aligned with each other, so pixels can be immediately sampled from all of them when segments are created. Because of using multiple images as input, similarity function has to be expanded accordingly.

Another modification of the classical region-growing segmentation is that in our approach points can be compared not only to mean values of already segmented ones, but also only to border pixels (pixels are compared only to currently considered ones, to be precise). This allows to detect slowly changing surfaces as single segments, that would be broken into smaller parts by a standard comparison criterion w.r.t. the mean value.

Our point similarity function (1) has four parameters, defining how close each of components has to be in both pixels, T_R, T_D, T_N and T_C, where R stands for normalized RGB, D for depth, N for normal vector and C for curvature, respectively:

$$S(p_x, p_y) = FUN\left(\frac{d_R(p_x, p_y)}{T_R}, \frac{d_D(p_x, p_y)}{T_D}, \frac{d_N(p_x, p_y)}{T_N}, \frac{d_C(p_x, p_y)}{T_C}\right) \quad (1)$$

The final value can be calculated by substituting FUN with either sum or max function, each giving slightly different results. Distances are calculated by associated d functions. Color comparison is done by calculating Euclidean distance between the normalized RGB values (i.e. R/L, G/L, B/L, where L means luminance) of both points, and T_R is the maximum allowed difference.

The location distance of points is calculated also as a Euclidean distance between their 3D coordinates, and T_D is expressed in meters. Normal vectors could be treated similarly to maps mentioned earlier, but it will be counterintuitive, so we calculate the angle between both vectors (2) using their dot product:

$$d_N(p_x, p_y) = \arccos(normal(p_x) \cdot normal(p_y)) \quad (2)$$

Observe, that both vectors are already normalized, so it's unnecessary to divide the distance by their length. T_N is then given in degrees, which is much more convenient.

The last component in (1) is a curvature, which is expressed as radius of sphere fitted to the point's local neighborhood. Hence, a simple comparison of curvature is needed only, like comparing two numbers.

4.2   Processing Pipeline

The pointclouds segmentation processing pipeline is shown on fig. 3 (the blocks represent components, the arrows represent data flows between the components). Along with the real data acquired by the Microsoft sensor, there is also a component for generating test scenes, consisting of some simple shapes, with a possibility of adding synthetic noise. This component is applied for testing whether algorithms works as expected on (almost) perfect data.

The segmentation approach has been implemented in DisCODe data processing framework [7], using the OpenCV library and the data acquisition module of the Kinect device.

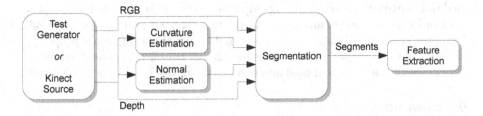

RGB

Depth

Fig. 3. The proposed segmentation processing pipeline

5 Multidimensional Segment Descriptors

The usability of raw segments, without having any specific information about them, is rather low. That's why we add another step to the processing pipeline – the feature extraction step. Apart from using widely known image moments [8], there are also popular features that are based on histograms of geometric distances from some fixed point (like center of mass) [9].

We propose another approach to feature extraction, that uses not only point coordinates, but also makes use of other information, their normal vectors specifically. For every point in given segment we calculate the angle between its normal vector and vector from this point to segment center of mass. All angles are accumulated and the mean value along with standard deviation are calculated. Based on those two factors we can classify a segment into planar (when the mean

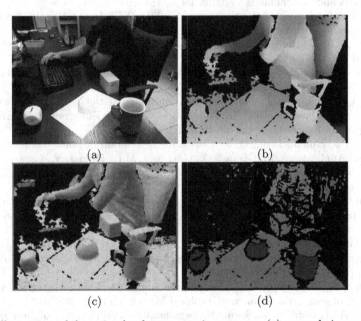

(a)   (b)

(c)   (d)

Fig. 4. Illustration of the pointcloud segmentation process: (a) example image, (b) the raw depth map, (c) normal vector map, (d) segmented point clouds

angle is close to 90°, green color in fig. 4d), concave (mean is lower than $90° - \epsilon$, blue color in fig. 4d) or convex surface (mean is larger than $90° + \epsilon$, red color in fig. 4d). Using the standard deviation value one can decide if the segment has proper parameter values – a high deviation value means that the current pointcloud set has not been sufficiently decomposed into segments and that it has to be further split.

6   Summary

We have proposed an integrated segmentation approach for dense depth maps and associated color images. Differently than in a typical Delaunay triangulation approach the raw 3D pointclouds are first characterized by their normal vectors, estimated on base of the point's local neighborhood. In the segmentation process, the subsets of 3D points are easily grouped into planar, concave and convex faces. In future work, we are going to implement a more detailed surface patch classification step that is based on the superquadrics approach to surface modeling [10]. The empty regions in the depth map are assumed to belong to a distant background and they are filled by segments of the associated color image. This step can also be enhanced in the future by assigning texture patterns, detected in the color image, to the surfaces, detected for 3D pointclouds.

References

1. Surmann, H., Nüchter, A., Hertzberg, J.: An autonomous mobile robot with a 3D laser range finder for 3D exploration and digitalization of indoor environments. Robotics and Autonomous Systems 45(3), 181–198 (2003)
2. Konolige, K.: Projected texture stereo. In: 2010 IEEE International Conference on Robotics and Automation (ICRA), pp. 148–155. IEEE (2010)
3. Giles, J.: Inside the race to hack the Kinect. The New Scientist 208(2789), 22–23 (2010)
4. Lange, R., Seitz, P.: Solid-state time-of-flight range camera. IEEE Journal of Quantum Electronics 37(3), 390–397 (2001)
5. Dey, T., Li, G., Sun, J.: Normal estimation for point clouds: A comparison study for a Voronoi based method. In: Point-Based Graphics, Eurographics/IEEE VGTC Symposium Proceedings, pp. 39–46. IEEE (2005)
6. Miao, Y., Feng, J., Peng, Q.-S.: Curvature Estimation of Point-Sampled Surfaces and Its Applications. In: Gervasi, O., Gavrilova, M.L., Kumar, V., Laganá, A., Lee, H.P., Mun, Y., Taniar, D., Tan, C.J.K. (eds.) ICCSA 2005. LNCS, vol. 3482, pp. 1023–1032. Springer, Heidelberg (2005)
7. Kornuta, T., Stefańczyk, M.: DisCODe: component-oriented framework for sensory data processing (PL). Measurements, Automation and Robotics 16(7-8), 76–83 (2012)
8. Giordano, P., De Luca, A., Oriolo, G.: 3D structure identification from image moments. In: IEEE International Conference on Robotics and Automation, ICRA 2008, pp. 93–100. IEEE (2008)
9. Mahmoudi, M., Sapiro, G.: Three-dimensional point cloud recognition via distributions of geometric distances. Graphical Models 71(1), 22–31 (2009)
10. Jaklic, A., Leonardis, A., Solina, F.: Segmentation and Recovery of Superquadrics. Computational imaging and vision, vol. 20. Kluwer, Dordrecht (2000)

Segmentation-Free Detection of Comic Panels

Martin Stommel[1], Lena I. Merhej[2], and Marion G. Müller[3]

[1] Artificial Intelligence Group, Universität Bremen, Germany
mstommel@tzi.de
[2] Art, Art History and Visual Studies, Duke University, Durham NC, USA,
VisComX, Visual Communication and Expertise, Jacobs University Bremen
l.merhej@jacobs-university.de
[3] Mass Communication, School of Humanities & Social Sciences,
Jacobs University Bremen, Germany
m.mueller@jacobs-university.de

Abstract. The detection of comic panels is a crucial funcionality in assistance systems for iconotextual media analysis. Most systems use recursive cuts based on image projections or background segmentation to find comic panels. Usually this limits the applicability to comics with white background and free space between the panels. In this paper, we introduce a set of new features that allow for a detection of panels by their outline instead of the separating space. Our method is therefore more tolerant against structured backgrounds.

1 Introduction

The understanding of the narrative is one of the most important aspects that artists, art historians and scholars of visual studies pursue in the analysis of iconotextual sequences such as comics and serialized graphics (e.g. poster series or newspaper advertising). The development of dedicated imaging software systems has simplified primarily the technical side of the production process. Tools such as Comic Life (Freeverse Software), Manga Studio Debut (Smith Micro Software Inc.), and Comic Book Creator (Planetwide Games) support the design of graphics and text, online publishing and page layout. Few tools, however, exist to support the analytical side. Audio and video annotation tools such as ELAN[1], ANVIL[2], and KIVI[3] allow for the labelling of the time-line and the creation of multiple views on the data. Unfortunately they do not support the specific structure of a comic where multiple panels with graphical and textual parts (cf. Fig. 1) are arranged in *multiframes* [1] and represented on single or double pages.

A basic functionality of a tool for the analysis of the narration of comics is to automatically extract the panels of the comic pages and display them in reading order. It is the prerequisite for the annotation of the time-line of a comic

---

[1] Language Archive Organization, http://www.lat-mpi.eu/tools/elan/
[2] Michael Kipp, http://www.anvil-software.de/
[3] http://keyvisuals.jacobs-university.de/kivi.html

L. Bolc et al. (Eds.): ICCVG 2012, LNCS 7594, pp. 633–640, 2012.
© Springer-Verlag Berlin Heidelberg 2012

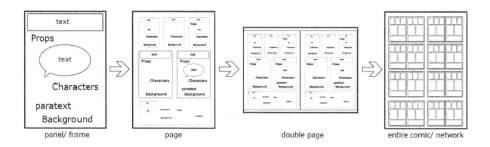

Fig. 1. Structure of a comic book

and therefore the analysis of causal and other dependencies or the rhythm and development of the narrative.

In this paper, we present a method for the automatic detection of comic panels that exploits multiple sources of local and global image information. As a consequence, it is possible to relieve some of the constraints that are usually imposed on the appearance of the panel separations.

2   Related Work

Algorithmic approaches to detect comic panels are related to document structure analysis [2] and image segmentation [3,4]. By assuming that the backround is predominantly white and homogeneous, it can be identified by tresholding, watershed segmentation [5] or region growing [4,6]. The remaining foreground areas are considered as the comic panels. Small connections between panels (caused e.g. by overlapping text balloons) can be broken up to a certain degree by morphological operations [4,6]. For simple layouts, the reading order of the panels can be estimated by first sorting according to the vertical position, then by horizontal position within a row [5].

Since segmentation algorithms are sensitive even to small connections between panels, many systems use top-down approaches [3,4,6]. Pages are recursively split into segments based on detected separating stripes. The lack of visual features of the stripes is compensated by the assumption of a certain length, straightness, and homogeneity. These properties are most frequently measured by axisparallel [7] or omnidirectional [3] projections of the intensity or the gradient [8]. The ordering of the recursive splits plays an important role, since errors manifest in split, missed, or merged panels. Tanaka et al. [8] therefore introduce a dedicated detector for T-joints of separating stripes. Han et al. [9] improve the noise robustness of the traditional X-Y recursive cut algorithm [10] by reducing the document page to a set of candidate splitting points. The splitting points are detected by a multilayer perceptron. The method is suited for disjoint panels with horizontal and vertical borders. Corner detectors are occasionally used to increase the accuracy of the detected panel positions [11].

3   Proposed Features and Procedural Pathways

As the examples from our data set (Fig. 2) show, the assumption of white background is often not appropriate to find the gaps between the panels. Instead, the background is often coloured. Overlapping text balloons make it difficult to distinguish between panel separations and elements within a panel. We therefore decided to focus on the detection of the panel outlines rather than the detection of homogenous gaps. As a simplification, we assume rectangular panels at the moment. This is of course not always fulfilled. In order to recognise the panel outlines, we developed five procedural pathways that deal with edges, corners, regions, globally dominant structures, and rectangles (cf. Fig. 3).

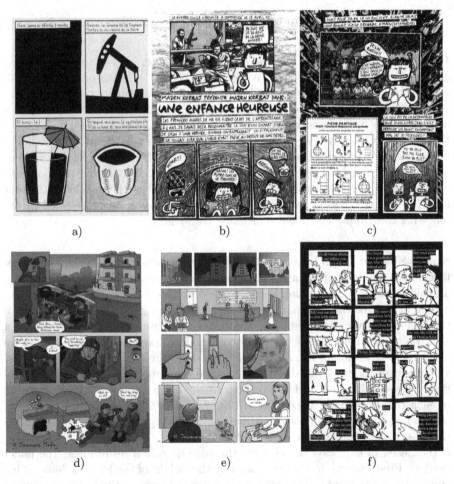

Fig. 2. Some pages from our data set: a) "Cola", b) + c) "Une Enfance Heureuse", d) + e) "Malaak", f) "Mission: Moon"

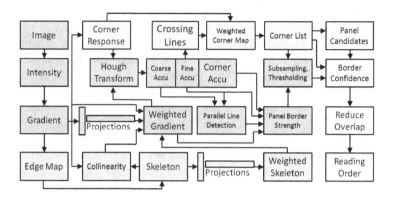

Fig. 3. Procedural pathways of the algorithm

Dominant Vertical and Horizontal Edges. After a grey scale conversion of the input image, the gradient is computed using the Sobel operator (Fig. 3, blue pathway). Then the horizontal and vertical projections of the gradient are computed, i.e. the mean gradient magnitude in each row and column. The aim is to detect rows and columns with long vertical and horizontal edges. To increase the selectivity, only those pixels are considered whose gradient orientation is perpendicular to the direction of the projection. Then for every pixel the gradient magnitude is weighted by the respective average gradient in one line or row, depending on the orientation. The weighted gradient is then scaled by a root function and normalised to the maximum. The two pathways described in the following contribute additional multiplicative weightings.

Stripe-Shaped Gaps between Panels. A skeletonisation is performed to detect homogeneous stripe-shaped gaps between the panels (Fig. 3, red pathway). To this end a coarse edge map is constructed by thresholding the gradient magnitude at half of the maximum. The skeletonisation gives the center pixels of the regions between the resulting edge pixels. For every local region around a skeleton point, the principle orientation of the local skeleton is computed, so we know the orientation of the respective region. We then compute horizontal and vertical projections of the skeleton analog to our procedure in the edge detection. By weighting each skeleton point with the mean number of skeleton points in each row or column, we emphasize horizontal or vertical skeleton lines corresponding to vertical or horizontal stripes. For every edge pixel, we determine the closest point on the skeleton as well as its orientation. The skeletonisation is then used in two ways to reinforce the edge detection results near the panel borders: First, we weight the edge pixel by the weight of the local skeleton. This emphasises edge pixels near horizontal or vertical stripes. Secondly, we weight the edge pixel by the collinearity between the edge direction and the direction of the local skeleton. This suppresses edge pixels which are not the outline of the separating stripe but regular panel contents.

Panel Corners and T-Junctions. The detection of panel corners is solved by a template matching algorithm with additional inputs from a Hough transform [12] (Fig. 3, green pathway). The motivation for template matching was a complete failure of the Foerstner [13] and Susan corner detectors [14]. This might be a result of the coarseness of the comic drawings. Unfortunately, it cannot be solved by downsizing the image because that would destroy strokes and smear gaps. Our template matching algorithm subdivides each local image region into a 3×3-grid and computes the mean vertical and horizontal gradient in each cell. By assigning a positive or negative sign to every cell and orientation and summing up the results of selected cells, we compute the response for the four panel corner directions and four directions of T-junctions. The Hough transform described in the following paragraph provides the accumulated strength of lines running through each corner coordinate. The weights of a possible vertical and a possible horizontal line are read from the accumulator of the Hough transform and multiplied with the response of the corner detector. This prefers corners on the panel borders over corners that lie on short edges or curved contours. A fixed number of the highest ranking local maxima in the corner response are chosen as discrete corner points. In our system the number is set to 80, which is near the maximum number of panel corners on the pages of our data base.

Mutual Reinforcement of Edges and Corners. A Hough transform [12] is used to compute histograms (called accumulators or accu, for short) of hypothetical line parameters (Fig. 3, brown pathway) that are plausible with the local gradient information. We compute accus with fine and coarse bin width. A comparison between the two accus indicates areas with parallel lines, for example in hatchings. Hatchings should be suppressed because they achieve high edge weights but rarely represent panel borders. The fine accu is also used in corner detection as mentioned before. For every line parameter, we also accumulate the corner weights where a line crosses the image. The types of corners accumulated along a line also indicate a panel border: For panel borders near mostly homogeneous stripes, T-junctions and corners to the inside of the panel are more likely. The maximum corner weight that is accumulated for a hypothesised panel border orientation is chosen to weight the gradient magnitude, together with the parallel line suppression. The result is a measure of the panel border strength. The panel border strength under the detected corners is used in an iterative process to threshold the result (see Fig. 4).

Rectangles and Reading Order. In the last part of the procedural pathway (Fig. 3, yellow), the thresholded border strength is converted to a list of rectangles. At first, a list of panel candidates is created by forming a rectangle between all diagonally opposite corners. The confidence of every side of a rectangle is estimated by accumulating the respective values in the thresholded map and searching for suitable corners. Rectangles that cross highly confident borders of other rectangles are discarded, unless they are crossed themselves by other rectangles. Generally unconfident rectangles are discarded. Then every rectangle

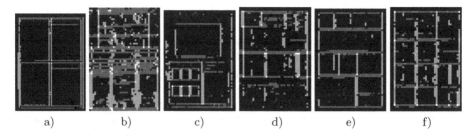

a)   b)   c)   d)   e)   f)

Fig. 4. Thresholded borders (red and blue depending on the orientation) and corners (blue) for the images in Fig. 1

that is intersected by a more confident rectangle is discarded. Intersections with the most confident rectangles are processed first. For the remaining rectangles the reading order is determined. To this end, the geometric relation 'upper left' describing a precedence in reading order is computed for every pair of rectangles. The final reading order is determined by iteratively selecting the first rectangle that is not blocked by other rectangles that have not been selected, yet.

4   Experimental Results

We tested our algorithm on the comics "Cola"[4] and "Une Enfance Heureuse" (2003) by Mazen Kerbaj, "Malaak" (2006) by Joumana Medlej[5], and "Mission: Moon", Ep. 1 by Ahmad Qatato[6] (Samandal Comic Book, issue 8). Figure 2 shows some examples. The combination of edge, corner and skeleton features together with the mutual reinforcement by the Hough transform leads to a robust emphasis of the panel borders with good background suppression. Although the strength of the detection varies over the image plane, the iterative thresholding is usually able to automatically find appropriate binarisation parameters. The corner detector reliably yields the strongest responses for the correct panel corners. Figure 4 shows the output of the feature extraction. False borders are sometimes detected for straight horizontal or vertical lines within the panels. Text balloons extending over the panel borders usually produce gaps in the detections. The same holds for adjoining panels, where the joint border has T-junctions in both directions. This case is difficult to distinguish from other straight lines within a comic.

   The analysis of the rectangles is able to resolve most conflicts that are caused by ambiguities and overlaps. As a result, many panels can be localised correctly. Figure 5 shows that most panels outlined by a rectangle have been found correctly. Panels without border do not yield detections (Fig. 5d). A lower recall here is tolerable because it is easier to manually add missing rectangles without having to delete spurious matches beforehand. The reading order is determined

[4] Kerbaj, M.: Cola. In: Le tour du monde en bande dessine, Vol.2, Delcourt (2009).

[5] http://www.malaakonline.com

[6] http://ahmadqatato.com

correctly. However, the filter heuristics are presently too simple to resolve two frequent ambiguities: 1. Small rectangles within a panel are preferred over the surrounding panel outline. This happens for example with rectangular text boxes (Fig. 5a, upper right panel, Fig. 5c, lower left panel). 2. Two adjacent rectangles with a low confidence of the adjoining side are not merged together. The resolution of these conflicts requires better heuristics or information by additional features. The speed of the algorithm is about 5s per image on a desktop computer (Intel Core2 Quad, 2.6GHz). A further speed up is easily possible by employing some of the known standard techniques for code optimisation (e.g. multithreading).

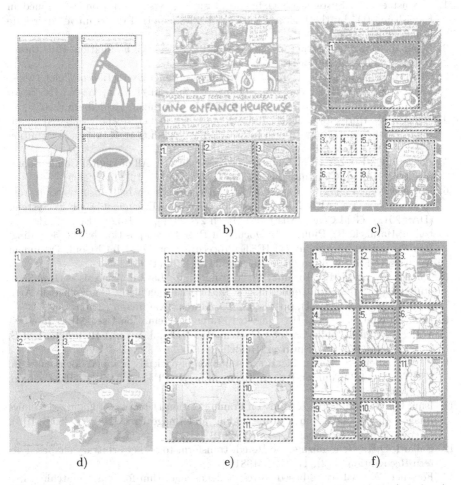

Fig. 5. Detected panels (dashed rectangles) and estimated reading order (numbers)

5 Conclusion

The detection of comic panels is a difficult problem if the panels are not separated by white background. In this paper we proposed a set of corner based, edge based, region based and global features that allow for the recognition of panels by their outlining rectangle instead of separating white regions. While the heuristics to resolve ambiguities in the assignment of correct rectangles serve basic visualisation needs, our experiments document a high reliability of the feature extraction steps even in difficult image material.

References

1. Groensteen, T.: Systéme de la bande dessinée ("System of Comics", issued in English in 2007 by the University Press of Mississippi). Presses universitaires de France, Paris (1999)
2. Liang, J.: Document Structure Analysis and Performance Evaluation. PhD thesis, University of Washington (1999)
3. Chan, C.H., Leung, H., Komura, T.: Automatic Panel Extraction of Color Comic Images. In: Ip, H.H.-S., Au, O.C., Leung, H., Sun, M.-T., Ma, W.-Y., Hu, S.-M. (eds.) PCM 2007. LNCS, vol. 4810, pp. 775–784. Springer, Heidelberg (2007)
4. Ho, A.K.N., Burie, J.C., Ogier, J.M.: Comics page structure analysis based on automatic panel extraction. In: 9th International Workshop on Graphics Recognition (GREC 2011), Seoul, Korea, September 15-16 (2011)
5. Ponsard, C., Fries, V.: Enhancing the Accessibility for All of Digital Comic Books. Int. J. on Human-Computer Interaction (eMinds) 1(5), 127–144 (2009)
6. Ho, A.K.N., Burie, J.C., Ogier, J.M.: Panel and speech balloon extraction from comics books. In: IAPR International Workshop on Document Analysis Systems (DAS 2012), Gold Coast, Australia, March 27- 29, pp. 424–428. IEEE (2012)
7. Ha, J., Haralick, R., Phillips, I.: Document Page Decomposition by the Bounding-Box Projection Technique. In: IEEE Proceedings of Third Int'l Conf. Document Analysis and Recognition (ICDAR), pp. 1119–1122 (1995)
8. Tanaka, T., Shoji, K., Toyama, F., Miyamichi, J.: Layout Analysis of Tree-Structured Scene Frames in Comic Images. In: International Joint Conference on Artificial Intelligence (IJCAI), pp. 2885–2890. Morgan Kaufmann (2007)
9. Han, E., Kim, K., Yang, H., Jung, K.: Frame Segmentation Used MLP-Based X-Y Recursive for Mobile Cartoon Content. In: Jacko, J.A. (ed.) HCI 2007. LNCS, vol. 4552, pp. 872–881. Springer, Heidelberg (2007)
10. Nagy, G., Seth, S.: Hierarchical representation of optically scanned documents. In: IEEE Comp. Int. Conf. on Pattern Recognition (ICPR), pp. 347–349. IEEE Comp. Soc. (1984)
11. Ishii, D., Watanabe, H.: A Study on Frame Position Detection of Digitized Comics Images. In: Workshop on Picture Coding and Image Processing (PCSJ/IMPS), Nagoya, Japan, December 7, pp. 1–2 (2010)
12. Ballard, D.H.: Generalizing the Hough transform to detect arbitrary shapes. Pattern Recognition 13(2), 111–122 (1981)
13. Förstner, W.: A feature based correspondence algorithm for image matching. ISP Comm. III, Rovaniemi, Int. Arch. of Photogrammetry 26(3/3) (1986)
14. Smith, S.M., Brady, J.M.: SUSAN – A new approach to low level image processing. Technical Report TR95SMS1c, Chertsey, Surrey, UK (1995)

Quantification of the Myocardial Viability Based on Texture Parameters of Contrast Ultrasound Images

Michał Strzelecki[1], Sławomir Skonieczka[1], Błażej Michalski[2], Piotr Lipiec[2], and Jarosław D. Kasprzak[2]

[1] Institute of Electronics, Technical University of Łódź, Wólczańska 211/215, 90-924 Łódź, Poland
[2] II Chair and Dept. of Cardiology, Medical University of Łódź, Kniaziewicza 1/5, 91-347 Łódź, Poland

Abstract. The aim of this research is to develop a method for classification of the degree of myocardial necrosis using texture parameters estimated for static ultrasound images. The study is performed for the color and monochrome contrast echocardiograms that allow the advanced evaluation of myocardial function. The analysis includes investigation of different texture feature selection methods and application of two neural networks with different architectures along with SVM for classification. The obtained preliminary results are promising; classification error in all investigated cases is lower than 20%. The results were presented and discussed, also direction of further research was outlined.

1 Introduction

The evaluation of early post-infarction (MI) myocardial viability is an important com-ponent of outcome assessment and long-term risk stratification of heart condition. Myocardial viability is defined as structural integrity enabling the cardiomyocytes to undertake systolic function. Resting echocardiographic examination allows for the identification of preserved contractility of myocardium. However, the heart segments, which are not presenting systolic function at rest may recover or remain non-functional - necrotic. Currently used methods are either utilizing inotropic stimulation (dobutamine) or are not suitable for bedside use (e.g. cardiac magnetic resonance - CMR or positron emission tomography - PET). Additionally, the high cost of CMR or PET makes them available only for a highly selected group of patients. On the contrary, contrast echocardiography is a novel, cost-effective, easy to perform imagining modality that allows the advanced evaluation of myocardial function and viability based on the integrity of microvasculature after the ischemic damage. It is, however, observer-dependent and requires additional post-hoc processing and quantification for the accurate and objective assessment. Therefore, an automatic or semi automatic method suitable for the analysis of contrast echocardiograms, which would enable to evaluate the myocardial viability in terms of echocardiographic texture, would

L. Bolc et al. (Eds.): ICCVG 2012, LNCS 7594, pp. 641–648, 2012.
© Springer-Verlag Berlin Heidelberg 2012

be very useful in the clinical practice. The objective of this work is to present such a texture analysis method, applied for classification of heart tissue with different necrosis degree in contrast echocardiograms. Texture represents properties of visualized objects and provides information about their structure. It is especially important in transformation of biomedical tissues into images. The proposed method is based on the assumption that image texture encodes important histological features of heart tissue and hence texture numerical parameters enable the discrimination of tissues with different myocardial viability. Usefulness of different texture features for evaluation of cardiomyopathy in animal models was already demonstrated [1].

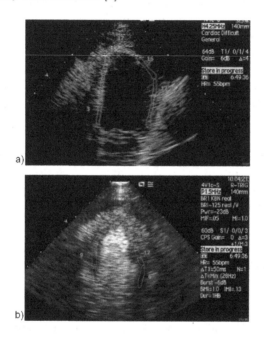

Fig. 1. Sample contrast echo images with marked regions of interests: monochrome (a) and color (b)

Ultrasound images suffer from several drawbacks, which impede their automatic analysis. Image information is highly anisotropic and position dependent, since the reflection intensity and signal to noise ratio depend on the depth and the angle of incident ultrasound beam. In addition, there are many artifacts present in echo images, resulting in local loss of anatomical information (shadowing, significant noise dropouts, side-lobes) [2]. Thus, analysis of such images is a rather difficult and challenging task. Many approaches to this problem covering application of texture features are proposed in the literature, e.g. neural network classifiers [3][4] or fuzzy reasoning [5] to discriminate between different types of heart cardi-omyopathy using, sparse linear classifiers for evaluation wall motion abnormalities [6], active snakes for segmentation and quantification of heart ventricles across a cardiac cycle [7] or classification of heart masses with application of oscillating networks [8]. In this study two different architectures of artificial neural networks (ANN) along with Support Vector Machine (SVM) were applied for data classification.

2   Materials and Methods

A contrast echocardiographic examination was performed using a Siemens Sequoia platform with the evaluation of myocardial perfusion after injection of stabilized microbubbles in the selected post-acute coronary syndrome patients. The patient group was selected from those undergoing a primary angioplasty treatment of their first myocardial infarction. 222 heart echo images (with dimensions of 1280x697 pixels) were acquired from 24 different patients. They were RGB color ones and native monochrome, both obtained after application of intravenous contrast agent; examples are shown in Fig 1. The color images are a richer source of medical information about blood flow in the heart muscle when compared to monochrome ones.

For regions of interest (ROIs) defined in each image by cardiologist, 298 image texture features were calculated (including those based on histogram, gradient matrix, run length matrix, and co-occurrence matrix, and wavelet transform) using the MaZda software [9]. Six classes of heart tissues with different amount of necrosis were defined, as presented in Table 1. The tissue vitality was evaluated based on MRI examination.

Table 1. Number of samples in each analyzed class with different degree of necrosis

Class	Number of samples	Necrosis [%]
0	128	0 (healthy tissue)
1	3	1-25
2	11	26-50
3	34	51-75
4	17	76-99
5	2	100

Due to uneven distribution of samples in classes, some of them were merged and finally three kinds of classifications were performed for the following cases: class 0 (healthy tissue) versus classes 1,2,3,4,5 (case 1); classes 0,1,2 versus classes 3,4,5 (case 2); and finally class 0 versus classes 1,2 versus classes 3,4,5 (case 3). Such experiments were suggested by the cardi-ologists as most important for clinical diagnosis of the heart tissue vitality. Feature selection was performed in two steps. First, the features minimizing ϵ in (1) were selected:

$$\epsilon = \frac{\sigma_f}{m_f} \cdot 100\% \qquad (1)$$

where m_f and σ_f are mean value and standard deviation of the feature f evaluated for given ROI type, respectively. The evaluation was performed separately for each ROI location (defined by numbers in Fig. 1) and for different vitality classes. Features with ϵ larger than 10% were discarded. Finally, such features were selected that both were common for all different ROI positions and necrosis classes and represented small ϵ value. In the second feature selection step different approaches were considered, including Fisher criterion, minimization of classification error along with average correlation coefficient (POE) [10] and evaluation of feature subsets (with 2 or 3 elements) that minimized classification error when the 1-nearest neighbor (1-NN) classifier was used. For classification of selected features two architectures of ANN were used. The first one was a two-layer perceptron with 4 (case 1and 2) or 6 neurons (case 3) in the hidden layer. The structure of a second network is shown in Fig. 2. Its second hidden layer contains two neurons. The second hidden layer was used to perform a nonlinear discriminant analysis (NDA) [11]. It transforms the input features into a new nonlinear feature space to provide further feature reduction and its linear separability [12]. The network output layer has two or three neurons corresponding to the number of analyzed classes. Another advantage of NDA is the reduction of the input data variance in the new space [8]. For network training, a backpropagation algorithm was applied [13].

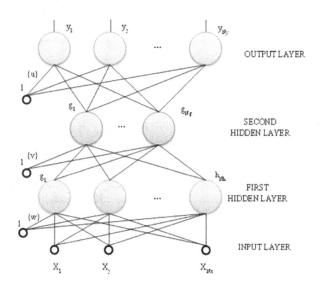

Fig. 2. The structure of NDA network

Finally, the SVM classifier was applied [14] using the LIBSVN for Weka software. LIBSVM supports various types SVM kernel functions for classification. In this study radial basis kernels were used and C-SVC classification type. The whole analysis process is summarized in diagram presented in the Fig. 3.

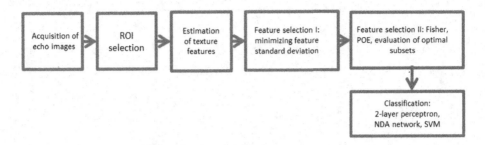

Fig. 3. The diagram of performed analysis

3 Experimental Results

The performed experiments demonstrated that the best classification results were obtained for red component of color RGB images and mochrome ones using feature selection technique based on evaluation of feature subsets that minimize the 1-NN classification error. Selected texture features included these estimated based on co-occurrence matrix (correlation), run length matrix (ShortRunEmphasis) and gradient matrix (the percentage of non-zero gradient elements). Classification results, obtained for different types of classifiers and both color and monochrome images, are summarized in Table 2. These results correspond to mean values of classification errors obtained after 5-fold network cross-validation. The same validation technique was applied in the case of SVM classifier.

Table 2. Classification errors for different types of classifiers obtained for red value of color RGB images and monochrome images. Cases indicate classification done for combination of classes with different necrosis, as described in Section 2.

Case	Two-layer perceptron		NDA network		SVM	
	Red value	Mono-chrome	Red value	Mono-chrome	Red value	Mono-chrome
#1	17,50	31,6	15,89	30	21,45	19,22
#2	23,60	31	21,46	28,5	17,45	15,19
#3	30,17	49,5	41,38	44,5	21,45	18,23

Fig. 4 presents a distribution of two NDA features, obtained for the input data by the use of the described neural network (sample validation sets, 3 classification cases as described in Section 2). The numbers represent feature vectors in NDA space and correspond to samples with different necrosis, as defined for given classification case.

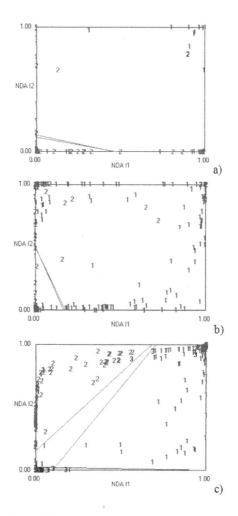

Fig. 4. Distribution of NDA features for input data: classification case 1 (a), case 2 (b), and case 3 (c)

4   Discussion and Conclusion

It was demonstrated that texture features are able to discriminate between diseased heart tissues in contrast echo images. These features were selected based on their minimal standard deviation estimated for different patients for similar heart regions and then for minimization of 1-NN classification error. Especially good results were obtained for discrimination of healthy and diseased heart tissues (case 1) as well as for separation of tissues with larger necrosis (case 2). Slightly larger classification error appeared when discrimination of 3 different necrosis degrees was considered (case 3). All three classifiers provided similar results, except for the case 3 where SVM outper-formed ANN approaches. Moreover,

SVM classifier is faster in implementation if compared to ANN (2.66 MHz Intel Core 2 Duo). Worse results obtained with ANN classifiers can be ex-plained by the fact that number of neurons in their hidden layer was reduced to maintain rea-sonable network size and avoid overtraining problem. It seems, however, that in the case of this particular classification problem appropriate feature selection mostly influences the discrimination results when compared to the choice of classification technique. Further work will include research on this topic considering different feature selection and reduction techniques. It was observed that texture parameters of tissue derived from both monochrome and red component of color ultrasonography images are important for heart regions classification. Other components (green and blue) of color RGB images were not useful for discrimination. This is probably linked with nonlinear mapping of gray levels onto colors performed by Siemens electrocardiograph, unfortunately the manufacturer does not provide any information on this issue. This requires further investigation to determinate the analytical form of this mapping. The preliminary obtained results are promising. However, further analysis of broader heart echo image dataset is required to validate the proposed approach and create a reliable tool to support evaluation of early post-infarction heart tissue viability.

References

1. Kerut, K.E., Given, M., Giles, T.: Review of Methods for Texture Analysis of Myocardium From Echocardiographic Images: A Means of Tissue Characterization. Echocardiography 20(8), 727–736 (2003)
2. Bosch, J., Mitchell, S., Lelieveldt, B., Nijland, F., Kamp, O., Sonka, M., Reiber, J.: Automatic Segmentation of Echocardiographic Sequences by Active Appearance Model. IEEE Trans. Med. Imag. 21(11), 1374–1383 (2002)
3. Du-Yih, T., Watanabe, S., Tomita, M.: Computerized analysis for classification of heart diseases in echocardiographic images. In: Proc. of the International Conference on Image Processing, pp. 283–286 (1996)
4. Kahl, L., Orglmeister, R., Schmailzl, K.J.G.: A neural network based classifier for ultrasonic raw data of the myocardium. In: Proc. of the IEEE Ultrasonics Symposium, pp. 1173–1176 (1997)
5. Tsai, D.-Y., Yongbum, L.: Fuzzy-reasoning-based computer-aided diagnosis for automated discrimination of myocardial heart disease from ultrasonic images. Electronics & Communications in Japan, Part 3: Fundamental Electronic Science 85(11), 1–8
6. Qazi, M., Fung, G., Krishnan, S., Jinbo, B., Rao, R., Katz, A.S.: Automated heart abnormality detection using sparse linear classifiers. IEEE Engineering in Medicine and Biology Magazine 26(2), 56–63
7. Watve, S., Sreemathy, R.: Segmentation of heart by using Gabor filter and principal component analysis. In: Proc. of the IEEE 3rd International Conference on Communication Software and Networks (ICCSN), pp. 644–648 (2011)
8. Strzelecki, M., Materka, A., Drozdz, J., Krzeminska-Pakula, M., Kasprzak, J.D.: Classification and segmentation of intracardiac masses in cardiac tumor echocardiograms. Comput. Med. Imaging Graph. 30(2), 95–107 (2006)
9. Szczypinski, P., Strzelecki, M., Materka, A.: MaZda - a Software for Texture Analysis. In: Proc. of ISITC 2007, Jeonju, Korea, November 23, pp. 245–249 (2007)

10. Mucciardi, A., Gose, E.: A comparison of Seven Techniques for Choosing Subsets of Pattern Recognition Properties. IEEE Trans. on Computers 9(20), 1023–1031 (1971)
11. Duda, R., Hart, P., Stork, D.: Pattern Classification, 2nd edn. Wiley (2001)
12. Mao, J., Jain, A.: Artificial Neural Networks for Feature Extraction and Multivariate Data Projection. IEEE Trans. on Neural Networks 6(2), 296–316 (1995)
13. Hecht-Nielsen, R.: Neurocomputing. Addison-Wesley (1989)
14. Vapnik, V.N.: The Nature of Statistical Learning Theory. Springer, New York (1995)

Analysis of the Abdominal Blood Oxygenation Signal of Premature Born Babies

Adam Szczepański[1], Marek Szczepański[2],
Krzysztof Misztal[1], and Ewa Kulikowska[2]

[1] AGH University of Science and Technology,
Faculty of Physics and Applied Computer Science,
Al. Mickiewicza 30, PL-30059 Kraków, Poland
{Adam.Szczepanski,Krzysztof.Misztal}@fis.agh.edu.pl
[2] Medical University of Białystok,
Department of Neonatology and Intensive Neonatal Care Unit,
Marii Skłodowskiej-Curie 24a, PL-15276 Białystok, Poland
szczepanski5@gazeta.pl, ekulikowska@wp.pl

Abstract. In this paper the analysis of the premature born babies abdominal blood oxidation values as a signal is conducted with the goal of acquisition of the basic parameters of the signal and establishing the reference parameters for further studies. The authors also study the behavior of the signal and determine the possibility of its prediction using ARIMA model. To authors' knowledge no such analysis of the signal from preterm babies was conducted yet, both from medical and computer science points of view, so in this paper they also try to answer the question whether the signal may be reliable for further studies on the possible use of it in monitoring and diagnosis of the preterm babies.

Keywords: Oximetry, abdominal blood oxygenation, preterm babies, statistical analysis, ARIMA model.

1 Introduction

Proper patients' diagnosis is the key to a successful hospital treatment, especially in the field of neonatology, because the premature born babies are the most fragile kind of the patients. That is why every new possibility of the preterm state monitoring may vastly improve the long-term outcome of the baby.

As far as the authors know, there were no research concentrating on abdominal blood oxidation of premature born babies and that is why the authors want to determine the possibilities of the usage of this signal in health monitoring and diagnosis of serious complications of prematurity (NEC - necrotizing enterocolitis).

The studies on children blood oxidation are rare in general and, typically, the researchers concentrate on the cerebral blood [1].

2 Acquisition of the Signal

The signal was acquired using noninvasive system INVOS Cerebral/Somatic Oximeter 5100C. The system uses near-infrared diodes attached to the skin of

L. Bolc et al. (Eds.): ICCVG 2012, LNCS 7594, pp. 649–656, 2012.

the patient, in this case the abdomen, to light the tissues of the body. Molecules of hemoglobin have a high level of absorption of this kind of light and the sensors, which are also attached to the body, analyze the absorption data to estimate the level of oxygen in the blood. The readings of the device shall be interpreted as the blood oxygenation.

The signals analyzed in this paper were acquired in the Department of Neonatology and Intensive Neonatal Care Unit of The Medical University of Bialystok Clinical Hospital. The measurements were carried out in 3 preterm babies born in 31.5 ± 1.05 week of fetal life and with a birth weight of 1363.33 ± 105.20 g. In the time of the measurement the babies were in their 38.33 ± 15.42 days of life and weighted 2256.67 ± 266.66 g. Total amount of collected data was around $3*72 = 216$ hours. The data was split into 9 files of similar length of around 24 hours, 3 files per patient, designated for example as I-01, II-03 where the first number identifies the baby (I, II and III) and the second number identifies the 24-hour period of the recording (01, 02 and 03). The signal have missing value which appeared when, for example, the sensors accidentally detached from the body. This values were approximated using Cubic Spline Interpolation, the method described in [2]. Exemplary signal is presented in Fig. 1.

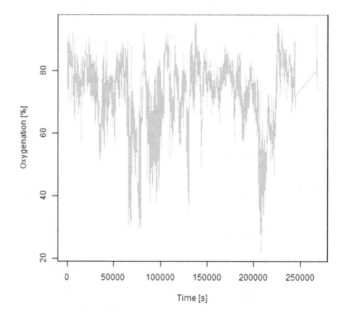

Fig. 1. The exemplary signal

3   Basic Parameters of the Signal

Most of the calculations are conducted using R software. The first step of the analysis was the establishment of the basic parameters of the signal. These parameters, such as mean, standard deviation, minimum, maximum and quartiles

Table 1. The basic parameters of the signal. Values of oxidation are given in percentage (%).

sample	mean	standard deviation	min	1 Q	2 Q	3 Q	max	max-min	max - 1 Q
I-01	75.28	12.16	24	68	79	84	95	71	27
I-02	72.57	10.73	22	68	75	79	95	73	27
I-03	79.63	5.55	46	76	80	84	95	49	19
II-01	75.70	6.03	44	72	76	80	93	49	21
II-02	71.54	7.59	15	67	73	77	95	80	28
II-03	74.04	7.28	37	70	75	79	95	58	25
III-01	79.55	6.93	46	76	80	84	95	49	19
III-02	79.11	6.71	49	75	79	84	95	46	20
III-03	79.10	5.61	49	76	79	83	95	46	19

(Q), are described in Table 1. All values of oxidation in this paper are given in percentage of oxygen level in blood although the mark "%" is omitted.

It is clearly noticeable that although the span between the minimum and the maximum is rather wide, the values of mean are near the values of the second quartile - the median. What is also worth noticing is that the mean and median from every 24-hour period for different patients are rather similar, from 71.54 to 79.63 for the mean and between 73 and 80 for median. This indicated that there is a possibility of establishing standard average values for long term statistics of abdominal blood oxidation of preterm born babies.

The values of the span between the first quartiles and the maxima is much lower than between minima and maxima, which may indicate that there is a factor which rarely lowers the blood oxidation value or there are some disturbances in the measurement. With this factors in mind the Locally Weighted Smoothing procedure, as described in [3], is applied. The influence of smoothing on the basic parameters of the signal is presented in Table 2 and the smoothed signal is presented in Fig. 2.

Compared to the original parameters, as expected, the span between minima and maxima is reduced and the mean is closer to the median. This means that the smoothing eliminated extremely low values.

The next conducted tests were Kendall [4], Spearman [5] and Pearson [6] correlation tests. The purpose of this tests was to check whether the smoothed signal preserved the information about the original signal trends. The results of these tests are present-ed in Table 3.

Pearson and Spearman tests show strong correlation between smoothed and nonsmoothed signal and the results of Kendall test indicate that the correlation is slightly weaker. Despite this the results are satisfactory and indicate that the smoothed signals keep the trend of the original ones and help to suppress the influence of unusually low values which may come from faulty measurement, so the rest of the analysis is conducted on the smoothed signals.

Table 2. The basic parameters of the signal after smoothing

sample	mean	standard deviation	min	1 Q	2 Q	3 Q	max	max-min	max - 1 Q
I-01	75.48	10.70	39.29	68.60	78.85	83.04	90.35	51.06	21.75
I-02	72.99	8.78	44.37	69.69	74.84	78.86	87.40	43.03	17.71
I-03	79.88	4.39	63.71	77.58	80.15	82.84	89.35	25.64	11.77
II-01	76.22	4.17	65.12	73.11	76.82	79.24	84.09	18.97	10.98
II-02	72.40	4.81	55.84	69.25	73.25	76.08	80.50	24.66	11.25
II-03	74.90	5.10	57.04	72.52	75.70	78.44	84.60	27.56	12.08
III-01	80.00	4.75	64.49	76.89	80.45	83.70	91.77	27.28	14.88
III-02	79.40	5.03	65.36	75.82	78.95	82.48	91.41	26.05	15.59
III-03	79.39	4.20	63.92	76.99	79.55	82.03	93.16	29.23	16.17

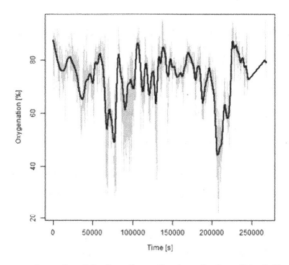

Fig. 2. The exemplary signal before (grey line) and after (black line) smoothing

Table 3. Correlation between the signals and their smoothed counterparts

sample	Pearson	Spearman	Kendall
I-01	0.8988401	0.8886314	0.7235258
I-02	0.8768277	0.8765876	0.7139501
I-03	0.8431869	0.8482798	0.6890805
II-01	0.7555782	0.7748078	0.5968241
II-02	0.7101319	0.7358794	0.5546853
II-03	0.7768175	0.7772261	0.6061792
III-01	0.7628201	0.7979778	0.6244874
III-02	0.7824477	0.7952157	0.6231035
III-03	0.7448219	0.7478320	0.5885563

4   Normality Tests

The next step of the analysis is the Shapiro-Wilk test [7] for the smoothed signal. Its results are presented in Table 4.

Table 4. Statistic and p-value of Shapiro-Wilk test

sample	statistic	p-value
I-01	0.77	2.78E-64
I-02	0.95	1.00E-38
I-03	0.95	6.35E-38
II-01	0.97	4.84E-32
II-02	0.89	3.79E-50
II-03	0.90	8.62E-50
III-01	0.97	5.65E-33
III-02	0.98	1.81E-24
III-03	0.91	1.13E-47

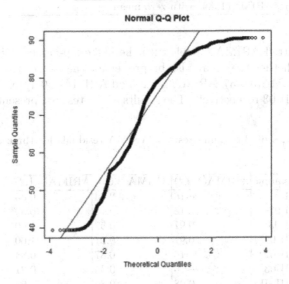

Fig. 3. Sample Q-Q plot of the smoothed signal

The p-value is extremely low, almost zero so the null hypothesis that the data is normally distributed is rejected. This is confirmed by the Q-Q plots of the signals (example in Fig. 3).

5   Autoregressive Integrated Moving Average (ARIMA) Model Fitting

The last question to answer in this paper is whether there is a possibility of simple forecasting of this kind of signal. For this purpose the Augmented Dickey-Fuller [8] and the Phillips-Perron Unit Root [9] tests were applied at first to check whether the data is stationary. Both tests for all signals confirmed this hypothesis so the procedure of finding the ARIMA model [10,11] for the signals was conducted. Results of this operation are presented in Table 5 along with Box-Ljung test [11] of ARIMA-s residuals corresponding p-values.

Table 5. Fitted ARIMA models and p-values of Box-Ljung tests of model residuals

sample	ARIMA model	Box-Ljung test p-value
I-01	ARIMA(3,0,2) with non-zero mean	0.17
I-02	ARIMA(3,0,4) with zero mean	0.78
I-03	ARIMA(0,0,1) with non-zero mean	< 2.2e-16
II-01	ARIMA(0,0,1) with zero mean	< 2.2e-16
II-02	ARIMA(3,0,3) with non-zero mean	0.86
II-03	ARIMA(5,1,2)	0.90
III-01	ARIMA(0,0,5) with non-zero mean	< 2.2e-16
III-02	ARIMA(0,0,5) with non-zero mean	< 2.2e-16
III-03	ARIMA(1,0,4) with zero mean	1.00

The three fitted ARIMA models with the highest p-values of Box-Ljung test are checked whether they may also be proper for the rest of the samples. This models are ARIMA(3,0,3), ARIMA(5,1,2) and ARIMA(1,0,4) for the samples II-02, II-03 and III-03 respectively. The results of the test are presented in Table 6.

Table 6. P-values of Box-Ljung tests of ARIMA residuals for three chosen ARIMA models

sample	ARIMA(1,0,4)	ARIMA(3,0,3)	ARIMA(5,1,2)
I-01	< 2.2e-16	< 2.2e-4	0.85
I-02	< 2.2e-16	0.78	0.99
I-03	0.97	0.57	1.00
II-01	0.97	0.21	1.00
II-02	< 2.2e-16	0.87	0.84
II-03	< 2.2e-16	0.35	0.91
III-01	0.98	0.86	0.94
III-02	0.99	0.80	1.00
III-03	1.00	0.69	1.00

Model ARIMA(5,1,2) fitted properly to all of the samples so the next step is the initial prediction of the signal. For this purpose the first two hours of each signals were used to predict the next two and ten minutes of the signals using ARIMA(5,1,2) model. The predicted values were correlated with the original signal values using Pearson method. The resulted correlation factors are presented in Table 7.

Most of the trends of the signals for 2 minutes ahead where predicted properly. For 10 minutes hardly any signal trend was predicted properly.

Table 7. The correlation factor between the predicted signals and the original values

sample	I-01	I-02	I-03	II-01	II-02	II-03	III-01	III-02	III-03
2 minutes	0.98	0.99	0.64	1.00	0.96	0.97	0.97	1.00	-0.97
10 minutes	-0.51	0.77	0.11	0.50	-0.85	0.79	-0.79	0.51	-0.92

6   Conclusions and Future Work

The authors of this paper have not found any average daily values of abdominal blood oxidation of premature born babies in any other publication, although the authors' initial results show that for three patients the average values are similar. To the authors' knowledge the under analysis subject is completely new and there were no publications about it both from medical and computer science points of view. It means that the average daily value of this statistic may be initially established at $76 \pm 5\%$. Further tests on more cases are necessary to determine more stable values of this average although due to the specific nature of the patients the acquisition of new data is more complicated than that from the older patients.

The values of oxidation are not normal, which means that there are possibly some external factors that influence them. The most probable reasons are the excitation before feeding and feeding of the babies and this will be the topic of the next studies of the authors.

The most surprising fact was, that in short terms the signal trend is predictable with the ARIMA model which leads to the conclusion that more complex prediction models may be able to determine the long term behavior of the signal and predict the moments of the needed feeding of the baby.

References

1. Denault, A., Deschamps, A., Murkin, J.: Cerebral Oximetry Monitoring in Anesthesiology. Anesthesiology Rounds 7(2) (2008)
2. O'Neill, C.: Cubic Spline Interpolation, http://www.golems.org/files/cubicspline.pdf (accessed May 28, 2002)
3. Cleveland, W.: Robust Locally Weighted Regression and Smoothing Scatterplots. Journal of the American Statistical Association 74(368), 829–836 (1979)
4. Puka, L.: Kendall's Tau. In: International Encyclopedia of Statistical Science, pp. 713–715. Springer, Heidelberg (2011)
5. Gooch, J.: Spearman Rank Correlation Coefficient. In: Encyclopedic Dictionary of Polymers, pp. 996–997. Springer, New York (2011)
6. Weisburd, D., Britt, C.: Measuring Association for Interval-Level Data: Pearson's Correlation Coefficient. In: Statistics in Criminal Justice, pp. 381–420. Springer US (2007)
7. del Barrio, E., Cuesta-Albertos, J., Matrn, C., Csrg, S., Cuadras, C., de Wet, T., Gin, E., Lockhart, R., Munk, A., Stute, W.: Contributions of empirical and quantile processes to the asymptotic theory of goodness-of-fit tests. Test 9(1), 1–96 (2000)

8. Said, S., Dickey, D.: Testing for Unit Roots in Autoregressive-Moving Average Models of Unknown Order. Biometrika 71(3), 599–607 (1984)
9. Phillips, P., Perron, P.: Testing for a Unit Root in Time Series Regression. Biometrika 75(2), 335–346 (1988)
10. Chatfiel, C.: The Analysis of Time Series: An Introduction, 6th edn. Chapman and Hall (2003)
11. Shumway, R., Stoffer, D.: ARIMA Models. Time Series Analysis and Its Applications, pp. 83–171. Springer, New York (2011)

The Smooth Quaternion Lifting Scheme Transform for Multi-resolution Motion Analysis

Agnieszka Szczęsna[1], Janusz Słupik[2], and Mateusz Janiak[1]

[1] The Silesian University of Technology, Institute of Informatics, Gliwice, Poland
{Agnieszka.Szczesna,Mateusz.Janiak}@polsl.pl
[2] The Silesian University of Technology, Institute of Mathematics, Gliwice, Poland
Janusz.Slupik@polsl.pl

Abstract. The representation and the thorough understanding of human motion is a crucial and challenging problem which has been raised in many scientific areas. This paper considers approaches in performing motion analysis with multi-resolution techniques based on rotations of joints over the time written in the form of a quaternion signal. The second generation wavelet transform constructed by the lifting scheme for the quaternion rotation representation can be used. Quaternions in terms of motion analysis are a more efficient representation of rotation than Euler angles. This paper presents the new quaternion lifting scheme building blocks for the smooth second degree transform based on the spherical cubic quaternion interpolation method (SQUAD). Also the possible applications of result multi-resolution representation as feature detection and compression are described.

1 Introduction

Human body motion synthesis and analysis are very challenging tasks and a very popular research domain. The most precise measurements of motion data are obtained by motion capture systems. We cooperate with a high tech motion capture laboratory having dedicated hardware capable of performing motion acquisition. To process so complex and big datasets the multi-resolution techniques can be used.

The main idea of the multi-resolution transformation is to represent a signal coarse to fine hierarchy. The input signal is decomposed into coarse base data (global pattern of signal) and a hierarchy of detail coefficients. The result multi-resolution representation can be base of many algorithms such as [1], [2]: denoising, filtering (smoothing, enhancement), compression, feature detection and multi-resolution editing. Such solutions can be used in many applications such as computer animation, motion analysis of the sick and athletes, motion synthesis, etc.

In this paper, we present our approaches in performing motion analysis with multi-resolution techniques based on rotations of joints over the time written in the form of quaternion signal. We use a second generation wavelet transform constructed by the lifting scheme for quaternion rotation representation. Using

L. Bolc et al. (Eds.): ICCVG 2012, LNCS 7594, pp. 657–668, 2012.
© Springer-Verlag Berlin Heidelberg 2012

the quaternion lifting scheme based on the quaternion algebra we can work directly on correlated motion data. This is in opposition to the methods presented in the literature, where the filters work on Euler angles as three non-correlated components. In this paper we describe a new smooth lifting scheme based on the spherical cubic quaternion interpolation method (SQUAD). Also, the example applications of multi-resolution representation of motion data such as feature detection and compression are presented.

Section 2 describes the main assumptions of multi-resolution analysis of motion data techniques and presents short review of solutions presented in literature. Section 3 presents our proposition of smooth quaternion lifting scheme. The next section 4 presents example application of result quaternion multi-resolution representation like feature detection and compression. The last section 5 is a summary.

2   Multi-resolution Movement Analysis Techniques

Multi-resolution methods for motion data are very often derived from classical digital signal processing techniques. Most of solutions are based on processing an orientation data of joints as a three non-correlated signals defined as Euler angles. Presented methods mostly focus on the correlation only in the time domain, without considering the correlation between joints. In [3] and [4] the spatial filters for orientation data are proposed. Similar solution based on the digital filter bank technique is presented in [5]. The B-spline wavelet for unit quaternion is used for smoothing the motion data in [6]. A similar work [7] concerns smoothing each component of a unit quaternion by soft and hard thresholding methods with the Daubechies wavelets (D_{10}). In [8] the rotation smoothing is formulated as a nonlinear optimization problem. The smoothing operators are derived from a series of fairness functionals defined on orientation data. In [9] a low-pass filter is applied to the estimated angular velocity of an input signal to reconstruct a smooth, angular motion by integrating filter responses.

Another application of multi-resolution representation can be feature detection. The generation of unique and robust correspondences between feature values and characteristics of motions is a major requirement for many problems in motion analysis. This is important for the reliable extraction of motion parameters and motion phases as well as for the reliable prediction of human motion. In [10] the Haar wavelet transform for the extraction of appropriate features from kinematic data (joint trajectories) are used. It combines a multiscale smoothing of input data with an extraction of features which characterize transitions between motion phases.

The multi-resolution techniques can be also the base of lossy compression of motion data. Generally most methods based on wavelet transform of the trajectories of the joint angles individually and next keeping higher frequencies (approximation coefficients) only for DOF (degree of freedom) that are more important. In [11] the cubic B-Spline wavelets was used. The combination of wavelet transform and forward kinematics was presented in [12]. In [13] the cubic interpolating bi-orthogonal wavelet basis implemented as the lifting scheme blocks are used for compression of skeletal animation data. This wavelet transform exploits a temporal coherence. In [14] each degree of freedom of a motion clip is smoothed by an anisotropic diffusion process and then divided into segments at feature discontinuities. Each segment of each degree of freedom is approximated by a cubic Bezier curve. The anisotropic diffusion process retains perceptually important high-frequency parts of the data, including the exact location of discontinuities, while smoothing low-frequency parts of the data. High level of compression comes at the expense of smoothing high frequency detail in the motion [15]. There the short clips of motion sentences can be also represented as cubic Bezier curves and perform clustered principal component analysis to reduce their dimensionality. This technique utilizes temporal coherence (fitting Bezier curves) and correlation between degrees of freedom.

3   The Smooth Quaternion Lifting Scheme Transform

The lifting scheme [16], [17] is a simple but powerful tool to construct a wavelet transform. The main advantage of this solution is the possibility of building wavelet analysis on non-standard structures of data (irregular samples, bounded domains, curves, surfaces) while keeping all powerful properties as speed and good ability of approximation [1], [18], [19], [20]. This generalizations are called as second generation wavelets [2]. They are not necessarily translation and dilation of one function (mother function). In this meaning, the lifting scheme also considers non-linear and data-adaptive multi-resolution decompositions.

A general lifting scheme consists of three types of operations:

- **Split:** splits input dataset into two disjoint sets of even and odd indexed samples. The definition of the lifting scheme does not impose any restrictions on how the data should be split nor on the relative size of each subsets.
- **Predict:** predicts samples with odd indexes based on even indexed samples. Next the odd indexed input value is replaced by the offset (difference) between the odd value and its prediction.
- **Update:** updates the output, so that coarse-scale coefficients have the same average value as the input samples. This step is necessary for stable wavelet transform [2].

These calculations can be performed in-place. In all stages input samples can be overwritten by output samples of that step. The reverse transform is easy to find by reversing the order of operations and flipping the signs.

Using the quaternion lifting scheme based on the quaternion algebra we can work directly on correlated motion data. This is in opposition to the methods presented in the literature where the filters work on Euler angles as three non-correlated components.

Input motion signal with length $n = 2^k$ is a set of normalized quaternions. In the split block this signal is divided into even and odd indexed samples: $..., o_i^j, e_i^j, o_{i+1}^j, e_{i+1}^j, ...$ The upper index j indicates the scheme step (the level of resolution) where j is a lower resolution level than $j+1$. The j level is obtained after removing every second sample from the signal in the $j + 1$ resolution. This paper presents the next quaternion lifting scheme method $SQUAD$. In our previous paper we have presented [21]: Haar and spherical linear ($SLERP$) quaternion lifting schema.

In lifting scheme the goal of the prediction step is to produce values as close as possible to the given data. It means the smaller the difference (detail coefficient), the better the prediction step is. In $SQUAD$ the result detail coefficients are vectors in tangent space. By the exponent we can have quaternion detail value. The update step smooths quaternion signal of lower resolution level.

Let us assume, that a signal consists of quaternions:

$$q_1, q_2, \ldots, q_n$$

where $q_i \in \mathbb{H}_1$ and $n = 2^k$ for some $k \in \mathbb{N}$.

We assume, that the signal has been processed by the selective negation, i.e. every quaternion q_i ($i > 1$) is converted to $-q_i$ if $\langle q_i, q_{i-1} \rangle < 0$. It means that arcs on the hipersphere $\mathbb{H}_1$ between adjacent quaternions are the shortest.

Note that, for any quaternions $p, q \in \mathbb{H}_1$ we have equation (1) where $LERP$ is a linear quaternion interpolation method.

$$SLERP(p, q, 0.5) = \frac{LERP(p, q, 0.5)}{||LERP(p, q, 0.5)||} = \frac{p + q}{||p + q||} \approx \exp\left(\frac{\log(p) + \log(q)}{2}\right) \tag{1}$$

Thus, the $SLERP$ middle point is obtained as the exponent of the average from logarithms of quaternions. Now, we compute logarithms of all quaternions from the signal. The results are elements of the tangent space, i.e. this are points from $\mathbb{R}^3$. We compute the average of these points and we obtain one point which we transform by exponent to $\mathbb{H}_1$. We assume that such quaternion is the average of the signal (equation (2)). The lifting scheme has to preserve that average.

$$average = \exp\left(\frac{1}{n}\sum_{i=1}^{n}\log(q_i)\right) \tag{2}$$

The $SQUAD$-method is derived from transformation of Bezier arc to the hipersphere $\mathbb{H}_1$. For all points $p_1, p_2 \in \mathbb{R}^3$ and control points $X, Y \in \mathbb{R}^3$ we can describe the arc by the formula (3):

$$bezier(p_1, p_2, h) = lin(lin(p_1, p_2, h), lin(X, Y, h), 2h(1 - h)) \tag{3}$$

where $h \in [0, 1]$. The point in the middle of the arc we can compute for $h = 0.5$ (equation (4)).

$$bezier(p_1, p_2, 0.5) = 0.5 * ((0.5 * (p_1 + p_2) + 0.5 * (X + Y)) = \frac{p_1 + p_2 + X + Y}{4} \tag{4}$$

For any points $p_i \in \mathbb{R}^3$ $i = 1, \ldots, n$, the smooth interpolation based on Bezier arcs can be obtained by assuming the following control points: for the arc between points p_i and p_{i+1} we have

$$X = p_i + \frac{1}{4}(p_{i+1} - p_{i-1}) \quad Y = p_{i+1} - \frac{1}{4}(p_{i+2} - p_i)$$

Now, we assume that the signal is transformed to the tangent space, already. The $SQUAD$ lifting scheme can be defined as follows. We have points in $\mathbb{R}^3$ (values of logarithms) split into two parts (**split block**):

$$\ldots, e_i^{j+1}, o_i^{j+1}, e_{i+1}^{j+1}, o_{i+1}^{j+1}, e_{i+2}^{j+1}, o_{i+2}^{j+1}, e_{i+2}^{j+1}, \ldots$$

The predict step is obtained by the rule presented on Fig. 1.

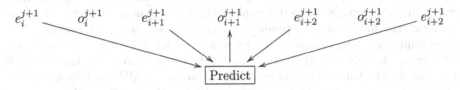

Fig. 1. The diagram of calculations in predict step

The in **predict block** we have equation (5).

$$o_{i+1}^j = o_{i+1}^{j+1} - 0.5625 \cdot e_{i+1}^{j+1} - 0.5625 \cdot e_{i+2}^{j+1} + 0.0625 \cdot e_i^{j+1} + 0.0625 \cdot e_{i+3}^{j+1} \quad (5)$$

The **update step** (equation (7)) is obtained in order to preserve the equality (average of the signal) as in equation (6).

$$\frac{1}{n}\sum_i (e_i^{j+1} + o_i^{j+1}) = \frac{2}{n}\sum_i e_i^j \quad (6)$$

$$e_{i+1}^j = e_{i+1}^{j+1} + 0.5 \cdot o_{i+1}^j \quad (7)$$

In natural way we can define the reverse lifting scheme. First, we have **undo update** step (equation (8)).

$$e_{i+1}^{j+1} = e_{i+1}^j - 0.5 \cdot o_{i+1}^j \quad (8)$$

Next the **undo predict** block (equation (9)).

$$o_{i+1}^{j+1} = o_{i+1}^j + 0.5625 \cdot e_{i+1}^{j+1} + 0.5625 \cdot e_{i+2}^{j+1} - 0.0625 \cdot e_i^{j+1} - 0.0625 \cdot e_{i+3}^{j+1} \quad (9)$$

Clearly, the average is preserved by the scheme if the signal is periodic (missing points at the ends we get from the other end of signal). This guarantees the inversion of the scheme. In practice, signals are not periodic and such method generates distortions at the ends of signals. For the purposes of analysis a duplication of end points is better method. We interpret this: the average is preserved in the interior of the time interval.

4   Results

4.1   Input Data and Implementation

For analysis the data from the motion acquisition laboratory *Human Motion Laboratory* at *Polish-Japanese Institute of Information Technology* in Bytom was used. Data are the motion description of human joints sampled with 100Hz during the walk pass. Data is delivered through the dedicated *Human Motion Database* for storing motion data in the form of the most popular motion industry standards like: C3D, ASF/AMC, BVH, VSK, AVI (video). Most of the calculations were done in a form of plugin for the EDR software. This is a modular software allowing users to prepare and use custom data types, data sources, data processors and data visualizers. For tests data source and data processor were implemented. For quaternion representation *Open Scene Graph* (OSG) quaternion implementation was used. Many extensions to this implementation were done: the template class for lifting scheme, resolution specific data sample picker (assuming periodic data or multiplying border samples), compact interpolator and predictor objects for different quaternion lifting schemes. Processed data are delivered in EDR defined type based on H-Anim (hierarchical skeleton structure). It allows accessing quaternion time series for particular joints and then loading them after modifications not affecting global model translation and without any concerns about segments configurations (connections, lengths, hierarchy).

4.2   Result Multi-resolution Representation

The result multi-resolution representation of joint knee data with 800 samples is presented in Fig. 2. Where we can see plot of original data in the highest resolution presented as three rotation angles (Fig. 2a). To better visualize the motion data we have chosen the Euler angles plots after their extraction from obtained quaternions. Next there are three levels of resolution with details (wavelet coefficients). Because the details in the *SQUAD* lifting scheme are computed as points in the tangent space, here details are presented as length of vectors in that space.

4.3   Joint Motion Data Analysis

The extraction of characteristic features is one of the key tasks for a detailed analysis and classification of human motion.

The analysis of signals of the knee joint was performed. We compare signals of healthy and sick joints (Fig. 3). Figures present first three levels of details for sick (Fig. 3b) and healthy knee joint (Fig. 3a). For clarity, the distance (in the tangent space) between details and $(0, 0, 0)$ point is presented (i.e. the lengths of vectors). Values at the first level are small, thus the predict step is properly defined. We can observe the sick joint detail signal contains few long peaks. This can be used to a lesion detection, but first, we are going to work on appropriate indicators, based on the multi-resolution representation, use in identifying the characteristics of movement.

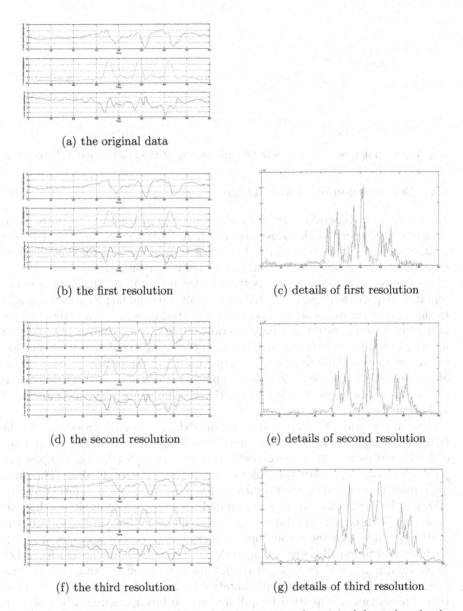

(a) the original data

(b) the first resolution

(c) details of first resolution

(d) the second resolution

(e) details of second resolution

(f) the third resolution

(g) details of third resolution

Fig. 2. The multi-resolution transform of the knee joint - the original data, three levels of resolution and detail coefficients

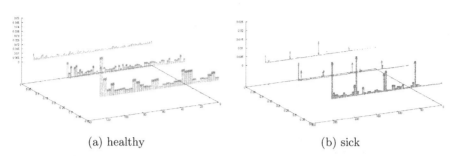

(a) healthy   (b) sick

Fig. 3. The first three levels of detail length vectors of the healthy and sick knee join

4.4 Compression of Motion Data

Motion data are generally huge data sets composed of translation and rotation description. Current work focuses on rotation, as it can be presented in the quaternion form. It is also possible to discuss translation, but for that the dual quaternions are required and it will be covered in our further work.

Rotations can be represented as three Euler angle values. Quaternion representation requires four values - three for rotation axis and one for rotation angle. In the wavelet compression method instead of storing signal in its original form as a plain rotation data series only relevant lifting scheme coefficients (data on lower resolution level) are stored. The detail coefficients used to reconstruct signal are set to zero. Although this compression is lossy - no perfect reconstruction of the original data is possible - the compression rates are high and for reasonable compression levels it is hard to notice the difference between compressed and original move.

Now a new way of compression motion data (rotations) based on the information about particular joints characteristics is presented. Let J be a set of joints and assume that move contains $n = 2^k, k \in \mathbb{N}$ rotation samples per joint. Such data represented in Euler angles requires $J * n * 3$ values. The same quaternion representation requires $J * n * 4$ values. Application of lifting scheme allows to limit the amount of data required for each joint individually. Instead of storing plain quaternion data series one could store them in the form of the particular lifting scheme resolutions coefficients (which are also quaternions). Such representation allows removing irrelevant resolutions detail coefficients. Let $R_j \subseteq \{0, 1, 2, .., k - 1\}$ be a set of resolutions not cut off by compression algorithm for j-th joint. This data representation requires values defined by equation (10). This is general equation for full quaternion lifting scheme, where we can have the details coefficients also as a quaternions. In $SQUAD$ method we have details as a R^3 points. But for general analysis of compression we define this as a four component value to store.

$$4 * \sum_{j \in J} \sum_{k \in R_j} 2^k = 4 * \sum_{j \in J} \left(n - \sum_{k \in R_j} 2^k \right) \tag{10}$$

Comparing equation (10) with Euler angles representation $3 * \sum_{j \in J} n$ gives the compression ratio r equal to (11).

$$r = 100 * \left(1 - \frac{4 * \sum_{j \in J} \left(n - \sum_{k \in R_j} 2^k \right)}{3 * \sum_{j \in J} n} \right) \tag{11}$$

The higher resolutions detail coefficients are removed the higher compression ratio is achieved. In practice it means that for periodic moves like simple walk such method should provide very good results, as high resolutions details do not bring any relevant data to move (only noise and some unnoticed movement details).

The compression algorithm was tested using a walk of a healthy, twenty four years old male. Move duration was about 4.5 second and data contained 1024 samples. For each joint the details of the same resolutions levels were cut off, so equation (10) can be refined to (12).

$$r = 100 * \left(1 - \frac{\sum_{j \in J} 4 * \left(n - \sum_{k \in R} 2^k \right)}{\sum_{j \in J} 3 * n} \right) = 100 * \left(1 - \frac{4 * \left(n - \sum_{k \in R} 2^k \right)}{3 * n} \right) \tag{12}$$

Removing the details from last resolution level for all joints will produce the following compression ratio:

$$r = 100 * \left(1 - \frac{4 * (1024 - 2^9)}{3 * 1024} \right) = 33,(3)\% \tag{13}$$

As it can be noticed the best compression ratio was around 91% for the highest four resolutions. The data difference was hard to notice comparing skeletons during the move. The example move before and after cutting off the highest three resolutions details are presented in Fig. 4. Reconstructed rotations after cut off of the four highest resolutions details presented as Euler angles reveled greater difference and for analysis of motion data such compression ratio could be assumed as too high (removing too much data) but it might be more then enough for entertainment applications. Even if only the highest resolution details are removed the compression ratio is equal $33,(3)\%$ (as in equation (13)) and data after decompression is almost identical with input data. Our future work will cover other lifting schemes and different coefficient configurations for each joint. Studding compression allows discovering important data resolutions for each joint independently, which will also lead to a better understanding of their move.

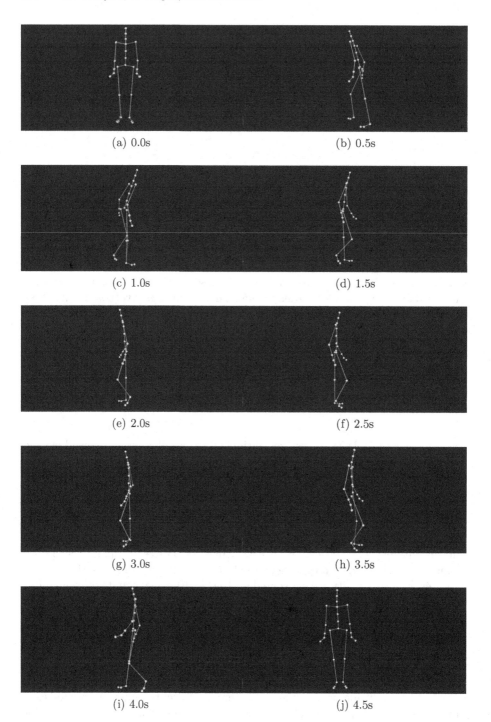

(a) 0.0s

(b) 0.5s

(c) 1.0s

(d) 1.5s

(e) 2.0s

(f) 2.5s

(g) 3.0s

(h) 3.5s

(i) 4.0s

(j) 4.5s

Fig. 4. The visual comparison of compressed move (after decompression) by removing details of three highest resolutions levels and its original version

5 Summary

We have presented, with results of our experiments, the new smooth quaternion lifting scheme method SQUAD. Applying the quaternion algebra properly, following quaternion space laws data correlation would be caught at each resolution. This gives a chance for better understanding of move than Euler angles as all information is closed in one structure instead of three independent values.

The result multi-resolution representation can be also a base for different motion processing algorithms as a generalization of signal processing tools. Examples can be feature detection and compression algorithms. Also the filtering (for example on the base of the threshold method) and editing algorithms can be proposed.

Our method use only temporal correlation. Next step can be the lifting scheme based on all skeletal joints which allows to find temporal and spatial correlations.

Acknowledgment. This work was partly supported by the European Community from the European Social Fund (*UDA-POKL.04.01.01-00-106/09*).

References

1. Stollnitz, E.J., De Rose, T., Salesin, D.H.: Wavelets for Computer Graphics: Theory and Applications. Morgan Kaufmann (1996)
2. Jansen, M., Oonincx, P.: Second Generation Wavelets and Applications. Springer (2005)
3. Lee, J., Shin, S.Y.: A coordinate-invariant approach to multiresolution motion analysis. Graphical Models and Image Processing 63(2), 87–105 (2001)
4. Lee, J., Shin, S.Y.: General construction of timedomain filters for orientation data. IEEE Transactions on Visualization and Computer Graphics 8(2), 119–128 (2002)
5. Bruderlin, A., Williams, L.: Motion signal processing. In: Proceeding SIGGRAPH of the 22nd Annual Conference on Computer Graphics and Interactive Techniques (1995)
6. Hsieh, C.-C.: B-spline wavelet-based motion smoothing. Computers and Industrial Engineering (2001)
7. Hsieh, C.-C.: Motion Smoothing Using Wavelets. Journal of Intelligent and Robotic Systems 35, 57–169 (2002)
8. Lee, J., Shin, S.Y.: Motion fairing. Proceedings of Computer Animation 96, 136–143 (1996)
9. Fang, Y., Hsieh, C.C., Kim, M.J., Chang, J.J., Woo, T.C.: Real time motion fairing with unit quaternions. Computer-Aided Design 30(3), 191–198 (1998)
10. Beth, T., Boesnach, I., Haimerl, M., Moldenhauer, J., Bos, K., Wank, V.: Characteristics in Human Motion - From Acquisition to Analysis. In: IEEE International Conference on Humanoid Robots (2003)
11. Ahmed, A., Hilton, A., Mokhtarian, F.: Adaptive Compression of Human Animation Data. In: Proceedings of the Annual Conference of the European Association for Computer Graphics, Eurographics (2002)
12. Li, S., Okuda, M., Takahashi, S.: Compression of Human Motion Animation Using the Reduction of Interjoint Correlation. Journal on Image and Video Processing - Anthropocentric Video Analysis: Tools and Applications, 2:1–2:15 (2008)

13. Beaudoin, P., Poulin, P., Panne, M.: Adapting wavelet compression to human motion capture clips. In: GI 2007 Proceedings of Graphics Interface (2007)
14. Lin, Y., McCool, M.D.: Nonuniform Segment-Based Compression of Motion Capture Data. In: Bebis, G., Boyle, R., Parvin, B., Koracin, D., Paragios, N., Tanveer, S.-M., Ju, T., Liu, Z., Coquillart, S., Cruz-Neira, C., Müller, T., Malzbender, T. (eds.) ISVC 2007, Part I. LNCS, vol. 4841, pp. 56–65. Springer, Heidelberg (2007)
15. Arikan, O.: Compression of Motion Capture Databases. ACM Transactions on Graphics - Proceedings of ACM SIGGRAPH, 25(3) (2006)
16. Sweldens, W.: The lifting scheme: A construction of second generation wavelets. SIAM J. Math. Anal. (1997)
17. Sweldens W.: The Lifting Scheme: A new philosophy in biorthogonal wavelet constructions. In: Wavelet Applications in Signal and Image Processing III (1995)
18. Daubechies, I., Guskov, I., Schröder, P., Sweldens, W.: Wavelets on Irregular Point Sets. Royal Society (1999)
19. Guskov, I., Sweldens, W., Schröder, P.: Multiresolution Signal Processing for Meshes. In: Computer Graphics Proceedings (1999)
20. Szczęsna, A.: The Multiresolution Analysis of Triangle Surface Meshes with Lifting Scheme. In: Gagalowicz, A., Philips, W. (eds.) MIRAGE 2007. LNCS, vol. 4418, pp. 274–282. Springer, Heidelberg (2007)
21. Szczesna, A., Slupik, J., Janiak M.: Quaternion Lifting Scheme for Multi-resolution Wavelet-based Motion Analysis. In: The Seventh International Conference on Systems ThinkMind, ICONS 2012 (2012)

Eye Blink Based Detection
of Liveness in Biometric Authentication Systems
Using Conditional Random Fields*

Mariusz Szwoch and Paweł Pieniążek

Gdansk University of Technology,
Department of Intelligent Interactive Systems, Poland
szwoch@eti.pg.gda.pl, pawpieni@student.pg.gda.pl

Abstract. The goal of this paper was to verify whether the conditional
random fields are suitable and enough efficient for eye blink detection in
user authentication systems based on face recognition with a standard
web camera. To evaluate this approach several experiments were carried
on using a specially developed test application and video database.

Keywords: biometrics, liveness detection, anti-spoofing, conditional random fields.

1 Introduction

Biometrics is an emerging technology that is used for human identification basing
on a set of physiological and behavioral human characteristics, such as fingerprints, DNA, iris, face, voice timbre, or a style of writing [1]. As each of these
biometric features can be used alone, or in combination with others, to unambiguously identify a human, many different biometric systems have already been
developed for access granting to different resources such as bank accounts, restricted areas, computer systems and others. Using biometric systems generally
easies and speeds up that access and also gains it up to another level where
access granting is not connected with passwords, tokens, or identity documents
but directly with a granted person.

Though, using biometrics in security and protection systems offers many advantages it can also have some drawbacks and threatens [2]. In order to be useful,
biometric systems must not only offer high reliability and positive recognition
rate but they should also be resistant to attacks of unauthorized persons. This
can be achieved in several ways such as using specialized hardware, forcing the
user to cooperate with a verification system, combining several multimodal attitudes, or creating more sophisticated and robust algorithms.

Rapid development of a computational power of digital systems allows for
creation of on-line biometric authentication systems operating on video stream

* This work was supported in part by Polish National Science Centre research project
no. N N516 367936 and by departmental grant no. 020206.

from a camera. Such systems uses face recognition methods as well as other human facial features to locate and identify the observed person. One of the most probable kind of attacks against such systems are spoofing attacks that use some kind of hardware copy of human image such as photography, video recording, 3D head models or even masks [2]. As the latter attitudes are somewhat troublesome, getting a facial photography of a given person is quite easy, capturing by hidden or telephoto camera or simply downloading from the Internet.

This paper presents an attempt to provide a reliable liveness detection subsystem that could assist face recognition systems to resist spoofing attacks with photographs. Its evaluation should point out whether such a subsystem can be used in user authentication systems based on face recognition. The described attitude does not require any additional hardware, except of standard web camera, nor any collaboration of a user. Instead, the algorithm uses some preprocessing and segmentation results from the face recognition process in order to improve its efficiency and reliability. The proposed attitude is presented in the next chapter.

Detection of Face Liveness. Liveness detection may be a significant factor in user authentication systems for access granting [3]. In normal situation this task is very easy for a human observing somebody's face with depth of view (DOV) information, possibility of combining other information such as voice and comprehensive knowledge about human's physiological face activities. However, liveness recognition becomes harder for computer systems when scene is observed with only one camera with narrowed field of view and no DOV information.

There have been proposed several attitudes to create anti-spoofing subsystem. Some of them use additional or specialized hardware such as high-resolution camera [4] to detect smooth appearance changes of a real face, additional near infrared camera to detect facial vein map or thermograph infrared camera to detect correct thermal map of the face [5]. These attitudes give good and reliable results in most cases but cannot be applied on standard platforms using ordinary web cameras. Another possibility is combining video and audio input into multimodal subsystem [6] or asking a user to do some facial activities, such as turning his or her head or closing eyes. Unfortunately this forcing of collaboration may be not convenient for the user.

Finally, in the third approach, some specific characteristics of live person in video recording are investigated to distinguish real face from a photo. Some attempts focus on recreation of the third dimension of a scene by analysis of the head movements or the face illumination. Unfortunately, these attitudes are sensitive to lighting conditions. Other attitudes concern temporal human activities such as natural head moving and turning, facial expressions, and blinking. In this paper just the eye-blinking human activity is used to confirm liveness in video image input that was proposed in [7].

Eye-Blink Characteristics. Eye-blink is a physiological activity of closing and opening the eyelids. Though the blink frequency may vary in quite wide range depending on many elements the time of spontaneous blinking lasts about 250ms [7]. As the web camera captures video at the minimum frequency of 15 fps, and typically at 30 fps, it means that the whole average blink can be recorded on at least 4 frames and typically on about 7 frames. This amount is enough for eye-blink noticing and using this phenomenon for liveness detection.

Usage of eye blinking gives some advantages, as it does not require any additional nor specialized hardware and it does not require user collaboration either. Thus, this attitude may be used in order to distinguish live face from its photography supporting an authentication process. Of course this attitude would not help in case of more sophisticated attacks with video face recording or using a mask, which are however less probable.

There have been only few works published concerning eye blink detection and usage. Ji et al [8] attempted to use an active IR camera to detect eye blinks for prediction of driver fatigue. Pan et al uses eye blink detection with a generic web camera for anti-spoofing [7]. In this attempt a special "eye closity" measure is used to initially label the eye state. Then, conditional random fields CRF [9] are used to detect the blinking activity in a time sequence of video frames. In this paper the same approach is evaluated in order to verify its usefulness for real time authentication systems [10].

2 Methodology

In general, face recognition process consists of several stages. The final recognition efficiency highly depends on successful realization of the very first stages such as face localization in the image and detection of characteristic features such as eyes, nose and mouth. Most of this information may also be reused in liveness detection subsystem which result can influence on, and determine the result of user authentication process (Fig.1).

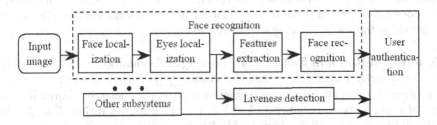

Fig. 1. User authentication based on face recognition and liveness detection subsystems

Eye-blink liveness detection is generally based on recognition of eyes states in the subsequent input frames. There are general two main states of an eye, which are *opened* and *closed* states. As closing and opening of an eye are continues processes one can also distinguish the transitional states that cannot be unambiguously classified as any of the main states. After [7] we can define a vocabulary set for eye states $Q = \{\alpha - opened, \gamma - closed, \beta - ambiguous\}$. Given a properly detected eye region almost any classifier can be used to recognize the current eye state. Unfortunately, the practical experiments show [7][11] that the efficiency of such classifier is not perfect due to many factors such as temporal problems in localization of eye region, varying light conditions, user movements and many others. As these misclassifications concern usually single frames it is possible to filter them out using classification results from neighboring frames.

The current state of the real eye blink is a temporal process observed on subsequent video frames captured by a camera. This process can be expressed in terms of changing of the eyes state as a sequence of transitions [7]:

$$\alpha \rightarrow \beta \rightarrow \gamma \rightarrow \beta \rightarrow \alpha \tag{1}$$

Thus, there are evident local dependencies between neighboring states of an eye. Proper modeling of these dependencies allows for using of context information to correct possible errors in classification of the current state of eye.

Hidden Markov Models. (HMM) are commonly used for modeling the temporal sequences of observations x_t, which are connected with some hidden, or unknown, states y_t of the observed object [12]. Properly created HMM model allows for successful reasoning about the underlying sequence (y_t) of the object's states on the base of the sequence (x_t) of observations. In order to model the joint probability $p(y, x)$ HMM makes two dependence assumptions [12]:

1. Each state y_{t+1} depends only on the previous state y_t (Markov property)
2. Each observation x_t depends only on the current state y_t

Unfortunately, generative approaches such as HMM, compute a model of $p(x)$, which can be complex and in fact is not needed for classification. Moreover the HMM assumptions 1. and 2. are too restrictive for the eye blinking model (1) and does not allow to benefit from the local context information available in the neighboring frames of blinking sequence.

Conditional Random Fields. (CRF) belong to the family of conditional models that directly model conditional distribution $p(y|x)$ that allows for using in classification rich global features as well as context dependencies. Formally, the pair of probability distributions (X, Y) is a CRF, when conditioned on X, the random variables Y and X obey the Markov property with respect to the graph $G = (V, E)$ in which Y is indexed by the vertices V [9]. In general, graph G can have any topography; though, to model temporal sequences a linear chain structure is usually used. The joint conditional distribution over the label sequence Y given observation X may be expressed in the following form [7]:

$$p_\theta(y|X) = \frac{1}{Z_\theta(X)} \exp\left(\sum_{t=1}^{T} \Psi_\theta(y_t . y_{t-1}, X)\right) \tag{2}$$

where the $Z_\theta(X)$ is a normalizing factor summed over all state sequences. The potential function $\Psi_\theta(y_t.y_{t-1}, X)$ is the sum of CRF features at time t that can depend on the previous state y_{t-1} and on any non empty set of labels x_i:

$$\Psi_\theta(y_t.y_{t-1}, X) = \sum_i \lambda_i f_i(y_t, y_{t-1}, X) + \mu_i g_i \sum_i (y_t, X) \qquad (3)$$

with parameters $\theta = \{\lambda_1, \ldots, \lambda_A, \mu_1, \ldots, \mu_B\}$ that should be estimated from a training data. The f_i (transitional) and g_i (state) feature functions can be defined in any way, possible taking into account local and global context dependencies. In that aspect CRF surpass HMM allowing considering a temporal window of frames, which would contain the whole eye blink.

3   Experiments

The goal of the experiments was to verify whether detection of eye blinks using CRF is enough reliable and efficient to be used in user authentication systems based on face recognition with a standard web camera [7].

To evaluate the approach two databases were used, both containing indoor recordings captured at 30 fps and 320 × 240 pixels. ZJU Eyeblink Database [7] consists of 80 video recordings captured for 5 seconds in good lighting conditions. For 20 different persons four clips were captured covering frontal view with two kinds of glasses, without glasses and with person looking upward [7]. The second database consists of 30 indoor recordings consisting of real faces in average light conditions (Fig. 2a) and five spoofing attacks with a high quality photographs that were moved, twisted, rotated, and bent.

Face and Eyes Localization. The developed test application accepts input video stream with dimensions of 320 × 240 pixels that can be acquired directly from a camera or read from a database. It uses AdaBoost cascade classifier from OpenCV (Open Source Computer Vision Library) [13] to localize a user face on a screen. The classifier uses Haar like features included in OpenCV sources. In general, face localization was successful except some videos from ZJU Database with persons looking upward. Though it is possible to create own Haar like features detector to find rotated faces in an image, these images were not further processed in our evaluation, as this case is rather rare in authentication systems.

After successful detection of the face in the video frame, application searches for eyes localization using the same AdaBoost algorithm. This time, classifier uses two detectors, different for each eye. Each detector was trained with 7000 positive samples normalized to the size 18 × 12 pixels. As initial efficiency of eyes localization was only 56%, several additional improvements to the algorithm were implemented:

- Face region was divided into left and right part and each eye was searched independently in the proper region. This prevents finding both eyes in the same part of the face that had happened occasionally before.

- Each eye (with its own Haar detector) is initially searched inside the region with top margin of 1/5 of the face height and bottom margin of 2/5 of the face height. If an eye is found then the searching region for the next frame is limited to the area of eye's position broadened by 15 pixels in each direction.
- If one eye is found in the next frame the predicted position of the other eye:
  - is located at the same place as in previous frame, in case when the found eye didn't change its position;
  - is searched in the region translated according to the eye's movement vector between subsequent frames. If the eye is still not found, its position is set according to the other eye's movement so the distant between the eyes would remain unchanged.
- If no eye is detected but the face is positively localized, the eyes locations are at first search in a new region, depending on a new face position. If this doesn't help, the eye position is set in relationally the same position within the face rectangle. Otherwise, if face is not detected on an image the application will wait for the next two frames to detect the face. If no face is detected, the algorithms exits with no real face detected message.

Recognition of Eye State. CRF algorithm needs some real valued feature functions to describe the (hidden) state of an eye. In [7] a single feature function eye closity $U(I)$ is proposed that should be discriminative enough to perform blink recognition and simple enough to do it in real time. Though, this feature function could be defined in many ways the authors used AdaBoost classifier trained for the open and closed eyes.

In our research we also describe the state of an eye by one measure but it is determined by SVM classifier. The measure is counted for rectangular area of an eye (20×10 pixels) preprocessed by SQI filter and binarized (Fig. 2b).

1300 training examples for opened eyes and 500 for closed eyes collected in various lighting condition from 30 people were used to create SVM model [14]. The output of the SVM classifier is a single floating-point number that allows determining, to which class (open or close eyes) belongs the tested eye and in what extent. As CRF algorithm needs labels defined for each classification value, the proper thresholds have been evaluated: a value greater than 1.0 means an opened eye, a value below 0.1 means a closed eye, and finally, values between those thresholds means an ambiguous state.

Using CRF to Detect Eye-blink. In our experiments HCRF 2.0b library [15] was used that implements both CRF and HCRF algorithms. The test application was coded in C++. Several experiments were performed including different window width, e.g. taking into account not only a current frame but also its neighboring frames - previous as well as next ones. The experiments show that taking into account the local context significantly improves the efficiency of blinking detection. The width of the context window should correspond to the frequency of video recording and the average time of the blinking. For the frequency of 30 fps and the blinking time of about 250 ms, the best window size

a)   b)   c)

Fig. 2. Sample image from a testing database with marked regions of interest (a), sample eye crops from a training set (b), and efficiency of blinking recognition for different sizes of context window for propriety database (upper line) and ZJU database

is 9 frames when algorithm reaches 84% of efficiency (Fig. 2c). This generally confirms the results achieved in [7] that the window frame is most efficient, when it covers the number of frames which show the blinking phenomenon.

Experiments confirmed also that in this case CRF works as a kind of low-pass filter and decreases the number of errors generated by SVM classifier. Three typical behaviors have been observed:

- Filtering of random changes – e.g.: $\alpha\alpha\beta\alpha\alpha\beta\alpha\alpha$ is converted to $\alpha\alpha\alpha\alpha\alpha\alpha\alpha$.
- Smoothing of an eye blink – e.g.: $\alpha\gamma\gamma\gamma\gamma\gamma\alpha$ is converted to $\alpha\beta\gamma\gamma\gamma\beta\alpha$.
- Recreation of an eye blink – e.g.: $\alpha\beta\beta\beta\beta\beta\alpha$ is converted to $\alpha\beta\beta\gamma\beta\beta\alpha$.

For the best window size of 9 frames the test of algorithm resistance to spoofing attack was performed. 80% of attacks were rejected which confirms quite high resistance of this attitude. Rotating, moving and bending of photography were ineffective. It occurs that the best way to cheat the system is to use photo on glossy paper, and use light reflection to make false blink. It could be done due to predicting eyes position. To eliminate this kind of attack the application should reduce the allowed number of frames when no eyes are detected.

Very important aspect of real time liveness detection subsystems is their performance as they are only a part of more complex user authentication systems. The measured time of frame processing in our experiment is about 35 ms per frame on 4-core 2,67 GHz Intel i5 based PC. This time allows for almost real time processing of video signal from standard web camera at the frequency of 30 fps and the size of QVGA. It is worth to mention that almost 88% of processing time is consumed for face and eyes location, which should be performed anyway in user authentication systems based an face recognition algorithms. This means that the liveness detection (mostly determining the state of an eye) lasts only 4 ms per frame that makes it usable in real time applications.

Additional experiments proved that the system performance could be further improved by omitting the face location phase in case when one or both eyes are successfully detected. This is true for video recording with only small movements or rotations of a user face, which is the most probable case.

4   Conclusions

In this paper the usage of conditional random fields for liveness detection in user authentication systems was verified. The performed experiments confirm that CRF is an interesting mechanism for recognition of context dependent phenomena in time series. Using CRF for eye blink detection is nowadays possible in real time applications using standard web camera. The only drawback of CRF is usage of symmetrical context time window, which means that the classification results for a currently processed frame can obtained after capturing and processing future frames belonging to that window. This situation is analogous to video encoding with MPEG coders that operate interframe movement prediction. Fortunately, the delay of three frames, e.g. about 100 ms, is of no meaning in user authentication systems.

Further research will focus on incorporating of this liveness detection subsystem into a user authentication system [10] and improving the system tolerance for non-standard user poses such as turning the head or its movements towards the camera.

References

1. Ross, A., Nandakumar, K., Jain, A.K.: Handbook of Multibiometrics. Springer (2006)
2. Schuckers, S.: Spoofing and Anti-Spoofing Measures. Information Security Technical Report 7(4), 56–62 (2002)
3. Bigun, J., Fronthaler, H., Kollreider, K.: Assuring liveness in biometric identity authentication by real-time face tracking. In: IEEE Conf. on Computational Intelligence for Homeland Security and Personal Safety (CIHSPS 2004), pp. 104–111 (2004)
4. Tian, Y., Kanade, K., Cohn, J.F.: Recognizing Action Units for Facial Expression Analysis. IEEE PAMI 23(2), 97–115 (2001)
5. Socolinsky, D.A., Selinger, A., Neuheisel, J.D.: Face Recognition with Visible and Thermal Infrared Imagery. CVIU 91(1-2), 72–114 (2003)
6. Chetty, G., Wagner, M.: Multi-level Liveness Verification for Face-Voice Biometric Authentication. In: Biometrics Symposium 2006, Baltimore, Maryland (2006)
7. Pan, G., Sun, L., Wu, Z., Lao, S.: Eyeblink-based Anti-Spoofing in Face Recognition from a Generic Webcamera. IEEE (2007)
8. Ji, Q., Zhu, Z., Lan, P.: Real Time Nonintrusive Monitoring and Prediction of Driver Fatigue. IEEE Trans. Vehicular Technology 53(4), 1052–1068 (2004)
9. Lafferty, J., McCallum, A., Pereira, F.: Conditional Random Fields: Probabilistic Models for Segmenting and Labeling Sequence Data. In: ICML 2001, pp. 282–289 (2001)
10. Smiatacz, M., Przybycień, K.: A Framework for Training and Testing of Complex Pattern Recognition Systems. In: IEEE Conference on SIPA, Kuala Lumpur (2011)
11. Szwoch, M.: Conditional Random Fields in Liveness Detection. Technical Report No 19/2011, Gdansk University of Technology (2011)
12. Li, S.Z.: Markov Random Field Modeling in Image Analysis. Springer (2001)
13. OpenCV web site, Internet (2012), opencv.willowgarage.com/wiki
14. Gański, T., Jankowski, B.: Eyeblink-based liveness tests. Engineer thesis, Gdansk University of Technology (2011)
15. Morency, L.P.: HCRF 2.0b library. Internet (2012), sourceforge.net/projects/hcrf

On Directionality
in Morphological Feature Extraction

Michał Świercz and Marcin Iwanowski

Institute of Control and Industrial Electronics
Warsaw University of Technology, Warsaw, Poland
Koszykowa 75, 00-662 Warszawa, Poland
{swierczm,iwanowski}@ee.pw.edu.pl

Abstract. Morphological feature extraction allows obtaining a feature vector that can be used in pattern recognition. It is a two stage process, based on the extraction of morphological spatial classes and class distribution functions in order to obtain a feature vector. In this paper, we discuss two ways of considering directionality within this process. The first approach is based on division of the image space into sectors, in which the spatial classes are computed. The second makes use of directional structuring element used by morphological operators. Example applications and test results are also presented in the paper.

1 Introduction

Morphological feature extraction method [1] allows extracting from the binary image sets of pixels belonging to pre-defined *spatial classes*. These sets consist of pixels characterized by particular morphological properties. Depending on the class being detected, various class extractors can be defined, based on morphological image processing operators. All the operators leading to extraction of spatial classes are using a single parameter – the structuring element. By applying structuring elements of increasing size when extracting spatial classes, *class distribution functions* can be obtained. They are expressing the dependence of the number of pixels belonging to a given spatial class (or, alternatively, their ratio to the total number of image pixels) on the size of the structuring element. The shape and characteristics of class distribution functions depend on the pattern for which they are computed. In a majority of cases, such features do not allow to consider the directional properties of a shape. In this paper we consider the issue of directionality within the scope of morphological feature extraction. In the methods presented in this paper, we modify this procedure to take into account the directionality of the shape features in the image. Two approaches to directionality-aware morphological feature extraction are presented. The first one splits the whole image area into a given number of sectors, in which morphological spatial classes are separately extracted. The sectors are located around the centroid of binary shape. The second approach makes use of a directional structuring element that replaces symmetrical one used in the

L. Bolc et al. (Eds.): ICCVG 2012, LNCS 7594, pp. 677–684, 2012.
© Springer-Verlag Berlin Heidelberg 2012

traditional approach. Morphological spatial classes are extracted with different spatial orientations of the structuring element.

2   Morphological Classification and Feature Extraction

Morphological image operators [6,10] apply the structuring element to modify the content of an image. Thanks to their structure-oriented properties they also allow for extraction of features from digital images [9]. Morphological classification [1,3,2,5,4,7] allows classifying binary image pixels into pre-defined spatial classes as well as extracting morphological feature vectors allowing recognition of the whole binary objects. It is based on the fact that morphological non-increasing operators can be seen as a tool for extracting, from a binary image, the subsets of pixels characterized by particular spatial property. These subsets of pixels are referred to as *morphological spatial classes* of the binary image F. Depending on the particular spatial class characteristics, various morphological operators should be applied to extract it. The only parameter used in the class extraction process is a structuring element B. In the current study four spatial classes are taken into account:

1. *Core* – region consisting of foreground pixels that are separated from the boundary of F obtained as:

$$\Psi_{cr}(F, B) = F \ominus B, \tag{1}$$

   where $\ominus$ stands for erosion operator, F – for input image and B for the structuring element.

2. *Core boundary* – region of pixels that are located inside the initial object that do not belong to the core region and are not farther from the core than the distance implied by structuring element B. This class can be obtained as a difference between opening (denoted by $\circ$) and erosion:

$$\Psi_{cb}(F, B) = (F \circ B) \setminus (F \ominus B) \doteq (F \circ B) \setminus \Psi_{cr}(F, B). \tag{2}$$

3. *Corridors* – groups of pixels which are neither core nor core boundary and which connect two disjoint core regions. A single object (connected component of foreground pixels) can contain more than just one core region. A connector between all cores of a single object that does not belong to core boundary is a corridor. Contrary to core boundary pixels, the corridor pixels are in a distance from the cores greater than implied by B. This class can be obtained by means of anchored homotopic skeletonization [6] of the input image with core pixels considered as anchor ones:

$$\Psi_{co}(F, B) = (F \setminus (\Psi_{cr} \cup \Psi_{cb})) \bigtriangleup SKH(F, \Psi_{cb}), \tag{3}$$

   where $SKH(F_1, F_2)$ stands for the anchored homotopic skeleton of F_1 with anchor pixels F_2 (arguments of Ψ functions that are equal to (F, B) has been omitted for simplicity reasons), and $F_1 \bigtriangleup F_2$ – for morphological reconstruction with mask F_1 and markers F_2.

4. *Branches* – groups of pixels which are neither core nor core boundary but are attached to a single core region (dead-ends of pattern):

$$\Psi_{br} = F \setminus (\Psi_{cr} \cup \Psi_{cb} \cup \Psi_{co}).\tag{4}$$

The example of classification into four above classes is shown in Fig. 1.

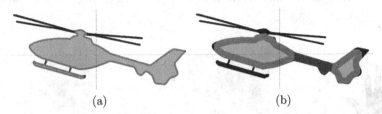

(a)   (b)

Fig. 1. Binary pattern classified into four classes: *core* – yellow, *core boundary* – green, *branches* – blue, *corridors* – red. Results in (a) and (b) were obtained using different structuring elements.

The choice of structuring element used in the classification process greatly influences its result. Depending on the form of the structuring element, various image regions may be classified as branches, corridors etc. Fig. 1 presents result of morphological classification with two different structuring elements B and shows that the result of classification strongly depends on the choice of B.

The structuring element can be chosen to be strongly direction-enforcing. The simplest example of such a structuring element is a thin, one-pixel wide line oriented spatially at a certain angle. The length of this line is the size of such a structuring element.

The dependence of the number pixels of given class (or their ratio to the total sum of pixels) on the size n of the structuring element $B^{(n)}$ is described by *class distribution function* which characterizes the shape of binary object. Based on these functions for all classes being considered, the morphological feature vectors are created. In order to obtain feature vectors of constant length the class distribution function is interpolated using splines and then sampled into a given number of samples.

3   Considering the Directional Shape Properties

3.1   Sector-Based Approach

Spatial classes describe properties of object shape considering object as a whole. In many situations however, also the position of given shape detail within the shape should be considered. For example, a shape resembling letter 'V' can be described as two branches oriented upwards. The same shape rotated 90 degrees clockwise has not only a different meaning ("smaller-than" symbol) but also different description. This time the same two branches are oriented to the left.

When computing morphological spatial classes as described in previous section, the representation of object by the quantity of pixels in given class is both cases the same. Sector-based directionality refers to the position of pixels of particular spatial class in reference to the center of gravity of an object. To consider such kind of directionality, the whole image is divided into angular sectors in which the pixels of particular class are separately calculated. The description of such a part is based on the angular sector centred at the center of gravity of the object denoted (c_x, c_y).

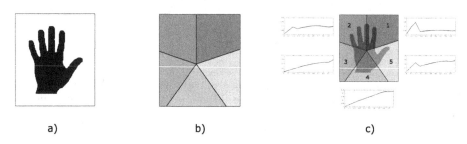

a)   b)   c)

Fig. 2. Sector division (b) of a binary shape (a), and sector distribution function examples (c)

Extracting from the initial object F pixels that are located within the area of certain orientation is based on the transformation of pixels' Cartesian coordinates into polar ones. Consequently, pixel coordinates (p_x, p_y) are transformed to (p_θ, p_r), where p_θ stands for the angular coordinate (angle) and p_r stands for radial coordinate (radius). Since, in our case, the orientation of pixel in relation to the center of gravity is considered, only the angular coordinate is taken into account. The angular coordinate of pixel p is computed, assuming that the center of coordinate system was shifted to (c_x, c_y), using the following equation:

$$p_\theta = \arccos\left(\frac{p_x - c_x}{\sqrt{(p_x - c_x)^2 + (p_y - c_y)^2}}\right) \mathrm{sgn}(p_y - c_y). \tag{5}$$

The above transformation produces angular coordinate within the range $[-\pi, +\pi]$ and allows one to extract from the initial binary object its part based on angular criterion. The angular cut operator is defined as follows:

$$\mathcal{A}_{[\alpha,\beta]}(F) = \{p : (\alpha + \pi) < p_\theta \leq (\beta + \pi)\}, \tag{6}$$

where $0 \leq \alpha < \beta < 2\pi$ stand for the range of angular coordinates. Obviously $\mathcal{A}_{[0,2\pi]}(F) = F$.

Operator $\mathcal{A}$ is used to extract from the original spatial class only those pixels that are located in particular location relative to the center of gravity of investigated object. For example $\mathcal{A}_{[0,\pi/2]}(\Psi_{cb}(F, B))$ stands for the set of such *core boundary* class pixels that are located in the upper-right part of the shape of F.

Classification of pixels using supplementary information on their position thus allows for more precise description of given shape. For example, helicopter shape from Fig. 1 is characterized by branches in the upper part (rotor) that appear in case of both smaller and bigger structuring elements, by branches in the lower part that are present only in case of bigger structuring element used (landing skids) and big corridor in the right-hand part (tail). The center of gravity of helicopter shape and four angular sectors are marked in Fig. 1 using horizontal and vertical thin black lines.

The angular class distribution function of a given binary image F has two arguments: structuring element size n and the number of angular sectors m and is defined as:

$$\mathcal{D}_{CL,m}(n) = \left| \mathcal{A}_{[(2\pi m/k)+\epsilon,(2\pi m/k)-\epsilon]} \left(\Psi_{CL}(F, B^{(n)}) \right) \right| \cdot l, \qquad (7)$$

where k stands for the number of sectors into which the round angle is divided, ϵ – for the angle range of each sector, and finally l is the normalization factor. The result of Eq. 7 with $l = 1$ is not scale invariant – when scaling the object, its number of pixels is changing respectively. Obtaining the scale invariance in the values of class distribution functions is possible by putting $l = |F|^{-1}$ i.e. by dividing the number of pixels of class CL in given sector by the total number of pixels of the object.

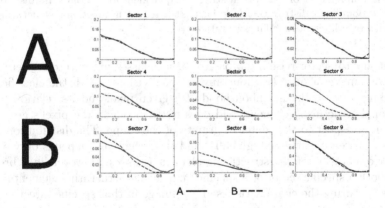

Fig. 3. Class distribution functions of two objects "A" and "B" in sectors

The round angle is divided in the proposed approach into k sectors. Sectors can cover the whole range of round angle either with or without overlapping. In the first case $\epsilon = \frac{\pi}{k}$, in the second one the angle range can be wider and $\epsilon > \frac{\pi}{k}$. The overlap range equals in such case $\epsilon - \frac{\pi}{k}$. In case $k = 1$, which means that there exists only one sector, the spatial classes are calculated globally and no directionality is considered.

3.2   Directional Structuring Element-Based Approach

Directional characteristics of the shape can also be captured into distribution functions using an alternative approach. Instead of using a non-direction-distinctive structuring element such as a disk, a line structuring element is used. The angle of the structuring element becomes therefore an additional parameter, along with the element's size. In the simplest case, such a directional structuring element consists of a central pixel and its neighbour(s) located in particular orientation, along a certain line, but can also be an ellipse or a oriented rectangle. The influence of directionality of the structuring element is shown in Fig. 4.

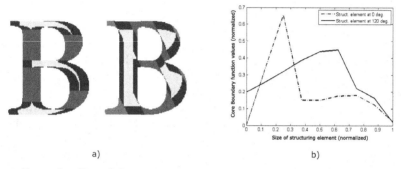

a)   b)

Fig. 4. Example effect of directional structuring element on spatial class distribution (a), 'Core Boundary' distribution functions extracted with directional structuring element with two different angular orientations (b)

Contrary to sector-based approach, spatial classes are extracted here from the whole image at once (without any sector divisions), with the classification depending only on the neighbourhood of a given pixel and its relation to the directional structuring element, and does not depend on the pixel's geometric position in respect to the center of gravity of the shape. The distribution functions are therefore extracted 'globally' and their character depends only on the angular orientation of the structuring element (Fig. 4). However, in a broader sense, both a specific sector or a specific angle of the structuring element can be seen as capturing the characteristics of the image in that specific direction.

4   Validation and Tests

In order to validate the robustness of directional morphological features and their usefulness for shape recognition, several classification experiments were performed, employing nearest-neighbour classifier and a set of artificial images.

As a training set for the classifier, we used a collection of binary images of the capital letters of the English alphabet. The set consisted of 25 letters, with each letter coming in five font variants and sizes, for a total of 125 images. The test set consisted of 2700 distinct letter images, with an average of 108 images per letter. All the elements of the test set were computationally generated, basing on a seed set of additional letter images from outside the training set. Distortions such as small rotations (5 degrees in both directions) and scaling were introduced to each member of the final testing set. No additional processing of the images was performed.

In the first round of testing, the feature vector consisted of only pixels of one of the classes *core, branch, core boundary* and *corridor*. For each sector, 12 samples were extracted, so the length of the feature vector totalled 108 elements for each shape in case of 9-sector division, up to 180 elements in case of 15-sector division. In the second round of testing, the feature vector was constructed from a single pixel class, e.g. *core* or *branch*, and with unchanged sampling parameters, the length of the feature vector totalled 108 elements for each shape in case of 9-sector division, up to 180 elements in case of 15-sector division.

The sector-based method yielded best results – over 96% recognition accuracy, with a relatively large number of sectors (15) and the feature vector consisting of only the 'Core' pixel class (Table 1). Other pixel class configurations produced worse results. For a larger number of sectors the results were either on par or worse than the results for 15 sectors, as effects such as image rotations played a more significant role. One of the other significant factors was the size of the shapes, with small shapes being misclassified more often, as sector distribution functions become distorted due to a small number of pixels.

The directional structuring element method was subjected to the identical testing procedure (with the feature vector being constructed from distribution functions from consecutive angular positions of the structuring element, instead of consecutive sectors of the image) and yielded similarly satisfying results - over 96% recognition accuracy. The best results were achieved with 5 angular positions (0, 72, 144, 216, 288 degrees). The results of this round of testing are also presented in Table 1.

Table 1. Shape recognition accuracy of sector-based method and directional structuring element method, using 'Core' pixel class

Sector method		Directional elem. method	
Sectors	Accuracy	Angular variants	Accuracy
9	92.3%	3	94.4%
12	95.4%	5	96.5%
15	96.1%	9	93.1%

The experimental results show that the sector-distributed morphological features are a highly distinguishing trait and can be successfully used in classification tasks, even employing a relatively simple classifier.

5   Conclusions

In the paper, two methods of considering directionality when classifying binary patterns were proposed. Both methods are based on the classification of pixels belonging to binary patterns into four spatial classes, which is performed using morphological image processing. By performing this classification with structuring elements of increasing sizes, the spatial class distribution functions are produced. These functions were normalized and sampled in order to obtain feature vectors of constant length. A nearest-neighbour classifier was applied to these feature vectors to distinguish between different shape types with high accuracy. Directionality is taken into account by either dividing the image into sectors and computing the class distribution functions in each sector individually, or by using a direction-enforcing structuring element and computing the class distribution functions in different angular orientations of the element.

The tests confirm that the proposed methods are robust and effective tools for binary pattern recognition. The methods are very flexible and can be optimized for a specific set of shapes in several ways, such as choosing a different shape of sector masks or predefined set of specific angles of the structuring element. Moreover, morphological operations performed during feature extraction can be computed in parallel to a large extent, allowing for significant reduction of processing time and can be easily adapted for specialized hardware, such as GPUs.

References

1. Iwanowski, M., Swiercz, M.: Pattern Recognition Using Morphological Class Distribution Functions and Classification Trees. In: Soille, P., Pesaresi, M., Ouzounis, G.K. (eds.) ISMM 2011. LNCS, vol. 6671, pp. 143–154. Springer, Heidelberg (2011)
2. Soille, P., Vogt, P.: Morphological segmentation of binary patterns. Pattern Recognition Letters 30, 456–459 (2009)
3. Iwanowski, M.: Morphological Classification of Binary Image Pixels. Machine Graphics and Vision 18, 155–173 (2009)
4. Iwanowski, M.: Binary Shape Characterization using Morphological Boundary Class Distribution Functions. In: Kurzynski, M., et al. (eds.) Computer Recognition Systems 2. AISC, vol. 45, pp. 305–312. Springer, Heidelberg (2007)
5. Vogt, P., Riitters, K., Iwanowski, M., Estreguil, C., Kozak, J., Soille, P.: Mapping Landscape Corridors. Ecological Indicators 7(2), 481–488 (2007)
6. Soille, P.: Morphological image analysis. Springer (1999, 2004)
7. Swiercz, M., Iwanowski, M.: Image features based on morphological class distribution functions and its application to binary pattern recognition. Electrotechnical Review (2), 132–135 (2012) Sigma-Not
8. Vincent, L.: Morphological grayscale reconstruction in image analysis: applications and efficient algorithms. IEEE Trans. on Image Processing 2(2), 176–201 (1993)
9. Iwanowski, M., Szostakowski, J., Skoneczny, S.: Image features extraction using mathematical morphology. In: Proc. of: SPIE Int. Symposium on Optical Science, Engineering and Instrumentation Applications of Digital Processing XX (SPIE Proc.), vol. 3164, pp. 565–572 (1997)
10. Serra, J.: Image analysis and mathematical morphology, vol. 1. Academic Press (1983)

Level-Set Based Infrared Image Segmentation for Automatic Veterinary Health Monitoring

Tom Wirthgen[1], Georg Lempe[2], Stephan Zipser[1], and Ulrich Grünhaupt[3]

[1] Fraunhofer IVI, Zeunerstr. 38, 01069 Dresden, Germany
Tom.Wirthgen@ivi.fraunhofer.de
[2] Technische Universität Dresden, Institute of Biomedical Engineering
Georg-Schumann-Str. 9, 01187 Dresden, Germany
[3] Karlsruhe University of Applied Science
Electrical Engineering & Information Technology
Moltkestr. 30, 76133 Karlsruhe, Germany

Abstract. Modern livestock farming follows a trend to higher automation and monitoring standards. Novel systems for the health monitoring of animals like dairy cows are under development. The application of infrared thermography (IRT) for medical diagnostics was suggested long ago, but the lack of suitable technical solutions still prevents an efficient use. Within the R&D project VIONA new solutions were developed to provide veterinary IRT based diagnostic procedures. Therefore a reliable object detection and segmentation of the IR images is required. Due to the significant shape variation of the objects of interest advanced segmentation methods are necessary. The level set approach is applied to veterinary IR images for the first time. The special features of the thermal infrared spectrum require extensive adaptations of the approach. The suggested probability based shape prior and results of the successful application on IR images of dairy cows are presented.

1 Motivation

The trend to higher automation and monitoring standards in modern livestock production as well as more restrictive legal requirements for animal welfare support the development of novel systems for the automatic health monitoring of livestock [1]. Infrared thermography (IRT) is a promising approach for the health monitoring of animals. The use of IRT for medical diagnostic systems has already been suggested in 1956 [2] by Lawson. In spite of many investigations IRT is still rarely applied in veterinary medicine. Knížková gives a short application orientated survey [3]. In human medicine, the IRT measurement and diagnostic standards were established in the last years [4,5]. In contrast veterinary IRT still suffers from the lack of defined technical and procedural standards.

Therefore the interdisciplinary R&D project VIONA was established whereat scientific and industrial partners are developing and evaluating a novel system for an automatic IR based health monitoring [6,7]. The VIONA project is focused on the automatic monitoring of dairy cows under typical farming conditions

L. Bolc et al. (Eds.): ICCVG 2012, LNCS 7594, pp. 685–693, 2012.

(moving animals and varying ambient conditions). Two essential parts of an automatic monitoring system are the IR based temperature measuring system and the image processing to provide the temperature of anatomic objects of interest based on the image segmentation.

Within the newly developed IR based temperature measuring system two IR cameras[1] record the images of automatically identified animals. For a precise absolute temperature measurement a reference body was introduced and the ambient conditions were considered [8].

For an automatic diagnosis a robust and precise segmentation of anatomic structures, such as the udder quarters or the claws of the cow, is required. These segmentations are fundamental for the subsequent feature extraction and diagnosis. Two promising segmentation methods have been developed and evaluated. The modified Active Shape Model described in [9] shows good results for the parallel segmentation of larger anatomic structures (as the udder for the diagnosis of mastitis) even in case of partial occlusions. The IR based monitoring of the health of the animals locomotor system requires an automatic and precise segmentation of the claw (see IR image Fig.1). The limited applicability of the Active Shape Model to smaller anatomic structures (as the claws) and the comparatively high complexity of the model generation lead to the development of the level set (LS) based approach discussed in the following.

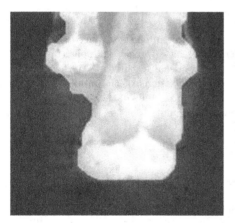 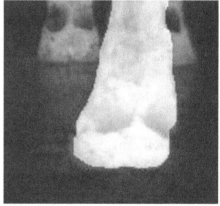

Fig. 1. segmentation with the state of the art level set approach

Fig. 2. segmentation with the novel shape prior

The paper gives a short introduction to the state of the art of the LS algorithm and the resulting segmentation for veterinary applications. The introduced model for shape prior knowledge as well as the optimisation of the segmentation quality are described. The paper concludes with the results and a short outlook to further works.

---

[1] DIAS Infrared: PYROVIEW 640L, 640×480 pixels, spectral range 8-14 μm, measurement uncertainty $\pm 2.0\,K$, temperature resolution $< 0.1K$.

2   Level Set Based Image Segmentation

Level Set Methods, introduced by Stanley and Osher in 1988, are based on the concept of dynamic, implicit surfaces [10,11]. For image segmentation the basic idea is the definition of a relief map Φ (3D data) on the image (2D). Setting a height in the relief map generates two regions (above/background and below/foreground) that can be interpreted as segmentation. The relief map is adapted iteratively. A velocity field F that depends on the images content deforms the surface:

$$\frac{\partial \Phi}{\partial t} = F\,|\nabla \Phi|\,. \tag{1}$$

The state of the art LS algorithm is based on the previous work of Waibel and Matthes [12]. It comprises two alternatives of the velocity field function F

$$F_1 = F_g + \nu F_c + \mu F_{sp} \quad \text{and} \tag{2}$$
$$F_2 = F_{gs} + \nu F_c + \mu F_{sp} \tag{3}$$

as a combination of terms describing different properties. The term F_g drives the contour in a way, that regions of similar grey values are enclosed [11]. F_{gs} is a statistical approach and takes the distribution of the grey values into account as well [13]. The term F_c limits the circumference of the relief map and therefore smoothes the segmentation by restricting the resolution of small details [14]. Finally F_{sp} takes an a priori defined parametric shape model into account. The weight parameters μ and ν tune the algorithm to the specific conditions.

3   Specific Modifications and Parameter Optimisation

The level set algorithm was combined with an environmental temperature based pre-filtering of the images. This step becomes necessary due to the high influence of the environmental temperature on the image contrast [9]. With optimised parameters the algorithm generally shows good results. But the investigation of the standard LS approach shows the following drawbacks:

- blooming of the segmentation due to overlapping areas of similar structure and temperature (front and back claws) as seen in Fig. 1 and
- difficult optimisation and interpretation of the tuning parameters in (2) that vary with the image scale.

Therefore an adapted LS model was developed comprising:

- a new probability based shape prior model,
- a new normalisation of the velocity field function,
- introduction of assessment and convergence criteria.

Finally the results of the parameter optimisation are discussed.

3.1 Normalized Velocity Field Function

As mentioned above the addends of the velocity field function F have different dimensions and vary in scale depending on the specific image content. This is disadvantageous for the parameter optimisation which is consequently depending on the image content as well. Therefore the normalisation (4) was introduced. With (4) follows that the weight parameters α, μ and ν of (5) are comparable.

$$F_i^* = \frac{F_i}{\|F_i\|_\infty} \tag{4}$$

$$F = (1 - \alpha)F_g^* + \alpha F_{gs}^* + \mu F_{sp}^* + \nu F_c^* \tag{5}$$

Furthermore this allows the merge of the two grey value based parts F_g and F_{gs} of (2) and (3) by the parameter α, which leads to a more detailed tuning that is advantageous for the segmentation quality (see section 3.5).

3.2 Shape Prior Representation

The parametric shape description for the veterinary application is complex, time consuming and therefore not practicable. Inspired by [15] a method which is based on a probability map Ψ derived from a training set of 100 manually labelled images is suggested. For the velocity field function this operates like a stamp that imprints characteristic shape features into the level set function.

The shape prior Ψ is created by the following algorithm [16]:

step 1. crop the region of interest $\mathcal{T}$ from the training images,
step 2. align all training set regions $\mathcal{T}$ by their area centre,
step 3. count the frequency a pixel is covered by the training set regions $\mathcal{T}$ and
step 4. normalize the frequency map by the number of training sets.

Figure 3 shows an example of the resulting probability map of the shape prior Ψ. The analyses indicate that the shape prior affects the shape of the level set significantly with a local benefit or loss of segmentation quality. The introduction of a weight map W (6) addresses this problem. For the application a gradation in vertical image direction shows good results. Figure 4 depicts the resulting shape prior Ψ_w.

$$\Psi_w = W \circ \Psi \tag{6}$$

The application of this stamp like shape prior necessitates the alignment of the shape prior. This comprises at least the translation t_x and t_y:

$$F_{sp}^* = \Psi_w(t_x, t_y). \tag{7}$$

Scaling and rotation can be performed but are not necessary due to the fixed configuration of the scene.

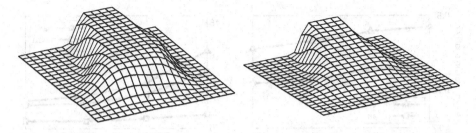

Fig. 3. Example of the weighted shape prior Ψ_w (left claw)

Fig. 4. Example of the original shape prior Ψ (left claw)

3.3 Assessment Criteria

To quantify the benefit of the modifications and parameter optimisations a criterion for the segmentation quality (SQ) was derived. Different criteria based on the segmentation $\mathcal{R}$ and the reference segmentation $\mathcal{T}$ (100 manually labelled test images) were compared to their sensitivity against small differences between $\mathcal{R}$ and $\mathcal{T}$ (with regards to the problem with overlapping areas). The following criterion showed the best results:

$$SQ = \frac{a\left(\mathcal{R} \cap \mathcal{T}\right) - a\left(\mathcal{R} \cap \bar{\mathcal{T}}\right)}{a\left(\mathcal{R} \cup \mathcal{T}\right)}, \tag{8}$$

where $a(\mathcal{S})$ represents the area of the segmentation $\mathcal{S}$. To provide online image analyses a low run time of the algorithm is a further objective. The denoted run time has been compared/optimised on one hardware platform[2] with an implementation using the image processing environment HALCON.

3.4 Convergence Criterion

In order to avoid further iteration steps with an almost adapted LS function the convergence criterion ρ monitoring the "amount of change" was introduced. If the change falls below a limit ρ :

$$\int_j \frac{\partial \Phi}{\partial t} \mathrm{d}j < \rho \tag{9}$$

the iteration is aborted and continued in the next resolution level. In this way the criterion has a negative influence on the SQ and a positive influence on the run time as shown in Fig. 5.

The final selection of ρ is a trade-off between quality and run time and depends on application constraints.

---

[2] CPU: Intel Core i5 3.33 GHz; RAM: 8GB.

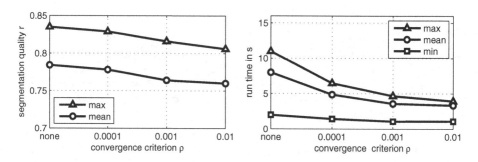

Fig. 5. Influence of the convergence criterion on the segmentation quality and run time

3.5 Optimisation and Application Results

The LS algorithm comprises several parameters effecting the SQ and the run time. The following relevant parameters are discussed in detail:

- weight parameters α, μ and ν of the normalised velocity field function (5),
- the number of down sampling levels (pyramidal levels) λ and
- the convergence criterion ρ.

These parameters are not independent, which makes the parameter optimisation more complex. For the optimisation a parameter space based on reasonable intervals is tested to identify the optimal solution. The tested intervals are $\alpha \in [0; 1]$, $\nu; \mu \in [0; 1.5]$, $\lambda \in [0; 5]$ and $\rho \in \{none, 10^{-4}, 10^{-3}, 10^{-2}\}$.

The balancing parameter α of the grey value based parts and the weight parameter ν of the curvature term have minor influence on SQ. The typical improvement is $< 2\%$. The influence of α on the run time is negligible. The effort of calculating the curvature term is not worthwhile compared to the low benefit in the SQ.

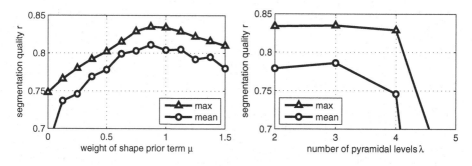

Fig. 6. Influence of the weight parameter μ and pyramidal level λ on the segmentation quality

The weight parameter of the shape prior μ and the pyramidal level λ have a major influence on SQ (Fig. 6). In contrast the convergence criterion ρ (Fig. 5) mainly shortens the run time as described above. The result improves even further when the algorithm is applied to image sequences. For sequences of about 30 images the run time decreases by factor 6 compared to a single image. The introduction of the new weighted shape prior considerably improves the SQ by avoiding the undesired blooming of the segmentation for overlapping objects (Fig. 2). For the pyramidal level it is remarkable that $\lambda > 4$ shows a significantly decreasing SQ due to the poor depiction of the considered object. The calculation of levels below $\lambda = 2$ is very time consuming and therefore rejected due to practical bounding conditions.

Table 1 shows the results of the optimised reference algorithm (state of the art) compared to the novel level set approach.

Table 1. Selected Results of the Parameter Optimisation

Algorithm	α	μ	ν	λ	ρ	run time in s	segmentation quality SQ
reference	0	0	0.5	2	n. a.	6.37	0.747
	0	0	0	2	n. a.	4.04	0.735
	1	0	0	2	n. a.	3.98	0.720
	1	0	0.875	2	n. a.	7.33	0.718
modified	0.2	0.875	0	2	0.001	3.15	0.804
	0.6	1	0	2	0.001	3.12	0.800
	0.4	1	0	3	0.001	3.02	0.795

n. a. ... not applied

The novel LS algorithm improves the segmentation quality as well as the run time.

4   Conclusion and Future Work

Within the VIONA project the LS approach was successfully applied to veterinary IR images for the first time. The proposed LS approach gives reliable segmentations of anatomic structures. The introduction of the new shape prior model effectually avoids the blooming of the segmentation for similar overlapping areas. This leads to a segmentation quality that is adequate for automatic health monitoring of the claws. The optimised algorithm was successfully tested during a measuring campaign under practical conditions. Thereby more then $\frac{3}{4}$ million images were processed.

Compared to the previously evaluated Active Shape approach the modified LS algorithm shows a higher segmentation quality for small anatomic objects (as the claws) and is less complex (easier training of the shape prior and lower run time consumption). In contrast to the primary assumption that the LS approach gives high segmentation quality without a trained shape prior the investigation shows that a shape prior is necessary to avoid undesired blooming. Limiting the parameter optimisation to the weight parameter of the shape prior μ reduces the time and effort to tune the algorithm to different scenes and anatomic objects. The other parameters are less sensitive and can be chosen heuristically near the middle of their domain of definition.

The development of an efficient implementation that can cope with the high throughput required for an online health monitoring of large groups of livestock requires further work. In addition the segmentation of the claws for walking animals and the simplification of the generation of the shape prior are the topic of further investigations.

Acknowledgement. These investigations were accomplished within the scope of the interdisciplinary VIONA project (www.viona-system.net) financed by the German Federal Ministry of Education and Research (BMBF, ID 03WKP04B). The authors are grateful to the industry partners: DIAS Infrared GmbH, Ralle Landmaschinen GmbH, and Yoo GmbH as well as the hosting farm Methauer Agro AG and Großdrebnitzer Agrar GmbH.

References

1. Büscher, W.: Current developments in livestock farming technology. Yearbook Agricultural Engineering 2011 23, 7–15 (2011)
2. Lawson, R.: Implications of surface temperatures in the diagnosis of breast cancer. Canadian Medical Association Journal 75(4), 309 (1956)
3. Knizkova, I., Kunc, P., et al.: Applications of infrared thermography in animal production. J. of Agric. Faculty of Ondokuz Mayis University 22(3), 329–336 (2007)
4. Diakides, N., Bronzino, J.: Medical infrared imaging. CRC press (2008)
5. Ring, E.F.J., McEvoy, H., et al.: New standards for devices used for the measurement of human body temperature. J. Med. Eng. Technol. 34(4), 249–253 (2010)
6. Franze, U., Geidel, S., Heyde, U., Schroth, A., Wirthgen, T., Zipser, S.: Evaluation of the potential of infrared thermography for automatic animal health monitoring systems in milk production. In: European Conference of Information Systems in Agriculture and Forestry Prague (2011)
7. Wirthgen, T., Zipser, S., Geidel, S., Franze, U.: Automatic infrared based temperature measuring system for health monitoring in veterinary applications. IEEE Sensors (2011)
8. Wirthgen, T., Zipser, S., Franze, U., Geidel, S.: Precise ir-based temperature measuring - a case study for the automatic health. In: SENSOR+TEST - IRS^2 (2011)
9. Wirthgen, T., Zipser, S., Franze, U., Geidel, S., Dietel, F., Alary, T.: Automatic Segmentation of Veterinary Infrared Images with the Active Shape Approach. In: Heyden, A., Kahl, F. (eds.) SCIA 2011. LNCS, vol. 6688, pp. 435–446. Springer, Heidelberg (2011)
10. Osher, S., Sethian, J.: Fronts propagating with curvature-dependent speed: algorithms based on hamilton-jacobi formulations. Journal of Computational Physics 79(1), 12–49 (1988)
11. Osher, S., Fedkiw, R.: Level set methods and dynamic implicit surfaces, vol. 153. Springer (2003)

12. Matthes, J., Waibel, P., Keller, H.: A new infrared camera-based technology for the optimization of the waelz process for zinc recycling. Minerals Engineering (2011)
13. Cremers, D., Rousson, M., Deriche, R.: A review of statistical approaches to level set segmentation: integrating color, texture, motion and shape. International Journal of Computer Vision 72(2), 195–215 (2007)
14. Chan, T., Vese, L.: Active contours without edges. IEEE Transactions on Image Processing 10(2), 266–277 (2001)
15. Cremers, D.: Dynamical statistical shape priors for level set-based tracking. IEEE Transactions on Pattern Analysis and Machine Intelligence 28(8), 1262–1273 (2006)
16. Lempe, G.: Anwendung von level-set-verfahren zur segmentierung der wärmebilder von milchkühen. Diplomarbeit, Hochschule Karlsruhe - Technik und Wirtschaft (2011)

Improving Density Based Clustering
with Multi-scale Analysis

Erdal Yenialp[1], Habil Kalkan[1], and Mutlu Mete[2]

[1] Suleyman Demirel University, Isparta, 32260, Turkey
eyenialp@akdeniz.edu.tr, habilkalkan@sdu.edu.tr
[2] Texas A&M University
mutlu.mete@tamu.edu

Abstract. Clustering in 2D space can be adapted as a segmentation method in images. In this study, we improve one well-known clustering algorithm, DBSCAN, to tackle pattern recognition problems in natural images. In DBSCAN, the details of objects are lost because of the noise in the scene or boundary regions. We overcome this problem using multi-scale approach to collect the salient features at different scales for better clustering. We use Gaussian kernel to smooth an image since multi-scale approaches are shown to be a well modeled with this kernel. Comparing with manually segmented images as gold standard, we show that the proposed multi-scale framework outperforms the segmentation of objects obtained with DBSCAN.

1 Introduction

Image segmentation is basically defined as locating the objects, lines or curves etc. by assigning a label for each pixel in image. It is widely used computer vision applications as a main task or a preliminary task prior to recognition. Traditional edge detection and image segmentation algorithms perform on a specific scale. However, image structures, such as edges, ridges, lines and corners, can be observed in the image at different scales where each scale may reveal a particular type of structure. Therefore, the structure detectors were developed to run at multiple scales of images [1].

The representation of images at various scales can be basically obtained by different distortion operator, such as Gaussian smoothing filter, in which increasing the smoothing level, called scaling level also, suppress the details and reveals the hard-to-catch structures in the images. Smoothing removes noise and also blurs edges, which make structure localization difficult [2]. Therefore, a multi-scale approach can finely localize the structures in the image. The multi-scale information of a given pixel can be obtained by simply concatenating the representation obtained at different scales. This approach not only increases the data dimension but also generates the irrelevant representation at a certain pixel. The challenging decision throughout evaluation of different scales is to find the locally most appropriate scale(s) for better representation of objects in an image

L. Bolc et al. (Eds.): ICCVG 2012, LNCS 7594, pp. 694–701, 2012.
© Springer-Verlag Berlin Heidelberg 2012

A well-known scale-space framework was introduced by [3] to detect the locally appropriate scale for images. This framework principally represents an image in different scales using Gaussian filtering and selects the local scales giving either the minimum or maximum output. The scale-space phenomena can be motivated from the biological visual perception [4] also. A similar framework is evaluated on Old Monkey's and it is seen that the biological visual systems analyze the scene first on coarse scale and then tunes to the appropriate fine scale to see the details.

Similar to visual system, machine vision systems also benefits from the multi-scale model to visualize the salient structures in images. Sumengen and Manjunath [2] used an iterative anisotropic diffusion based approach for multi-scale edge detection and segmentation. Liu et al. [5] used multi-scale autoregressive model with Support Vector Machines for clustering the satellite images. A more interesting application comes from M. Balafar et al. [6]. They have developed a multi-scale Fuzzy C-Mean (FCM) based image clustering algorithm for medical images. However, these methods mostly come with computationally expensive training steps.

In this study, we proposed a multi-scale Density Based Spatial Clustering Algorithm with Noise (MS-DBSCAN) that is an extension of scale space theory of [3]. The developed algorithm does not include a training phase, so computationally efficient solutions could be reached to segment region-of-interest. The proposed algorithm represents the images in multiple scales by using Gaussian smoothing functions and evaluates a density matrix for each scale. The density matrices in each scale are then fused to capture salient features in each scale. Later on, we applied MS-DBSCAN algorithm using the fused representation to achieve better clustering results.

The following section presents the DBSCAN [7] as base algorithm and then proposed multi-scale clustering algorithm. Section 3 details the result of quantitative and qualitative experimental results. Section 4 concludes the paper and presents the directions for the future research.

2   Methods

2.1   DBSCAN Algorithm

The algorithm of *Density-Based Spatial Clustering of Applications with Noise (DBSCAN)* was proposed in 1996 by Ester et al. [7], and effectively used for segmentation purposes in various image applications [8,9]. DBSCAN algorithm considers the density population of the corresponding nodes (pixels in image data) to form and expand the clusters. The algorithm requires two parameters, ε and *MinPts*, where ε is the radius of the density-reachable neighborhood and *MinPts* is the minimum number of the instances to call them a cluster under given parameters.

In general, the algorithm starts by selecting an unvisited arbitrary point - instance p from the dataset. Then ε-neighborhood of p is retrieved and the number of points detected as member of a particular cluster is assigned to the corresponding location. If the number of points in an ε-neighborhood is higher than *MinPts*, the visited point is regarded as core point of a cluster. If a point is retrieved in ε-neighborhood of a point where *MinPts* requirement is not satisfied, it is regarded as non-core point or border point. Non-core points can be reached by one or many core points of same cluster. Being not a core point, border points are also part of a cluster. The other points that are not in ε-neighborhood of a core point are regarded as noise; therefore, they are not added into any clusters. The border points are assigned to a cluster in a first-come first-serve basis.

In DBSCAN, the selection of the input parameters, ε and *MinPts*, significantly affects the clustering performance as expected. In the case of a big ε, all the points could be covered by one cluster. In opposite, if the ε is set so small, the number of the clusters may increase or decrease to zero. Thus, the selection of parameters may vary depending on the application and operators are expected to run multiple set of parameter pairs before a successful clustering.

2.2   Multi-scale DBSCAN Algorithm

Scale space theory provides a methodology to approach the image representation problems where scale is an important scale operator. The multi-scale image representation can be obtained by linear or Gaussian scale spaces [1,3]. In this work, we preferred Gaussian kernel since the standard deviation, σ, of kernel is directly related to the scale which the image is represented. Given an image $L : \mathbb{R}^2 \to \mathbb{R}$, the multi-scale image representation $L : \mathbb{R}^2 + \mathbb{R}^+ \to \mathbb{R}$ is obtained for the images, i.e., they are blurred with Gaussian filter g_σ at different scale of $\sigma\epsilon$ $\{1,2,...K\}$. The scale space representation of the image l is more formally defined as

$$L(x, y; \sigma) = (l * g_\sigma)(x, y) \tag{1}$$

where g_σ is a Gaussian kernel defined as

$$g_\sigma(u, v)) = \frac{1}{\sqrt{2\pi}} exp(-\frac{u^2 + v^2}{2\sigma^2}) \tag{2}$$

where *(u,v)* is the spatial location of the filter. Let *L(x,y,0)* represent the raw image *l(x,y)* and *L(x,y,1)* be the image obtained at scale $\sigma = 1$. Then, the Gaussian scaled images are transformed into binary image, $\hat{L}(x, y, \sigma)$ where the density reachable pixels are represented as one and the remaining pixels are represented with zero. In this study, We have embedded the notion of 'density matrix', $M(x, y, \sigma)$, into DBSCAN algorithm in order to easily shift to multi-scale framework. The so-called density matrix is at same size with the underlying image and each location in $M(x, y, \sigma)$ is simply the number of density reachable points in ε-neighborhood of the corresponding pixel *(x,y)* in binary image $\hat{L}(x, y, \sigma)$ and it is calculated as

$$M(x, y, \sigma) = \sum_{(i,j)\,\in\,\epsilon-neigh} \hat{L}(i, j, \sigma) \tag{3}$$

Since, we are interested in a single density matrix for representing the image, we automatically select the scale giving the maximum density over scales and assign that density for that location as:

$$\hat{M}(x,y) = max_{\sigma=1,2,...,K} M(x,y,\sigma) \tag{4}$$

Then the image location (x,y) is assigned to the cluster if the corresponding density in $\hat{M}(x,y)$ satisfied the condition defined in Section 2.1. The proposed algorithm is summarized in the flowchart of Fig.1.

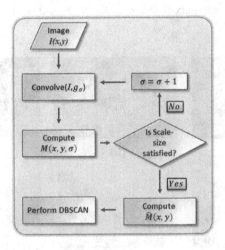

Fig. 1. Flowchart of MS-DBSCAN algorithm

3   Experimental Results

The proposed MS-DBSCAN algorithm is experimented for image segmentation purposes. In particular, single object segmentation is demonstrated considering the need for a specific cluster locater as objects or structures in tissues [8,10] for pattern recognition problems. We have evaluated the results on three different images from Berkeley segmentation database [11] where the scenes are manually clustered by human experts. (Figure 2-a, e, i). Each image is transformed into gray scale in the preprocessing step. DBSCAN detected the targeted segment given in an intensity range. The proposed algorithm can be performed in RGB scale as well. However, more expert knowledge should be required for the codebook for RGB images. Therefore, we performed on gray scale to obtain less expert dependent result.

The gray-scale image is represented in six different scales by using a Gaussian filter with zero mean and σ standard deviation where the σ takes values between one and six, $\sigma = 1, 2, ..., K$. The spatial size of the filter is empirically selected as 10x10. DBSCAN algorithm with $\sigma = 3$ is applied to the obtained Gaussian filtered images at different scales and a density matrix is obtained for each individual scales. The pixels in density matrix $\hat{M}(x, y)$ indicate the number of pixels assigned for clusters in σ neighborhood. Then a combined density matrix is obtained as given in Equation 3 and the pixels corresponding to the densities in density matrix $\hat{M}(x, y)$ which is higher than 15 *MinPts* is assigned to the cluster. Other *MinPts* values were also tried but the value of 15 was detected as the best threshold for six-scale range. Fig. 2 (b, e and h) shows the clustering obtained by a DBSCAN algorithm. It is observed that the DBSCAN algorithm falls short on assigning the points on the boundary of overlapped objects. However, this mis-clustering is mostly removed with the proposed MS-DBSCAN algorithm using multi-scale approach with six scales $\sigma = 1 - 6$ (Fig. 2 -c, f, i).

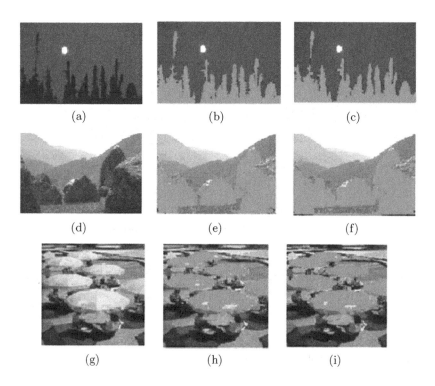

Fig. 2. a, d and g: Raw image; b, e and h: clustered image with $M(x,y,0)$ matrix of DBSCAN; c, f and i: multi-scale clustered image with six scales $\hat{M}(x, y)$

The multi-scale approach able us to capture the salient structures present is different scales. This can be better observed in rock image (Fig. 3) where the effect of scale-based approach is compared to the results obtained by fine ($\sigma = 1$) and coarse scale ($\sigma = 6$) segmentation. For example, at lower scales, some of the bright pixels on the rock objects are not assigned to the rock segment (Fig. 3-a). Whereas, these pixels are correctly assigned to the right cluster at the higher

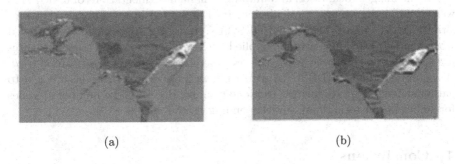

(a)   (b)

Fig. 3. a: clustered image in fine scale with *M(x,y,1)* matrix (b) clustered image in coarse scale with *M(x,y,6)* matrix

scale ($\sigma = 6$) (Fig. 3-b) while preserving the background pixels between the rocks. On the other hand, the proposed multi-scale DBSCAN (MS DBSCAN) combines the superiority of each scale (Fig. 2-f) at clustering.

In addition to visual comparison, in Table 1 sensitivity (recall) and F-measure are used to determine how much similarity obtained in the results of DBSCAN and MS-DBSCAN referencing the manual clusterings in images. In information retrieval, F-measure, precision and recall are used to analyze the test's accuracy. In pattern recognition field, these metrics are defined by TP (True Positive), TN (True Negative), FP (False Positive) and FN (False Negative) where recall and precision are defined as the rate of TP over (TP+FN) and (TP+FP), respectively.

Whereas, F-measure is the harmonic mean of recall and precision. In other words, Recall is the number of correctly clustered pixels divided by the number of pixels that should have correctly clustered and Precision is the number of correctly clustered pixels divided the number of all pixels assigned to the cluster.

Table 1. Sensitivity and F-measure of compared methods on three images. Bold typesetting indicates the best measures in respective group.

Image	Method	Recall	F-Measure
Rock	DBSCAN	0.86	0.915
	DBSCAN ($\sigma = 1$)	0.86	0.918
	MS-DBSCAN ($\sigma = 1 - 3$)	**0.88**	**0.918**
	MS-DBSCAN ($\sigma = 1 - 6$)	**0.88**	**0.918**
Trees	DBSCAN	0.82	0.899
	DBSCAN ($\sigma = 1$)	0.83	0.904
	MS-DBSCAN ($\sigma = 1 - 3$)	**0.85**	**0.915**
	MS-DBSCAN ($\sigma = 1 - 6$)	**0.85**	**0.917**
Umbrella	DBSCAN	0.72	0.834
	DBSCAN ($\sigma = 1$)	0.75	0.854
	MS-DBSCAN ($\sigma = 1 - 3$)	**0.78**	**0.870**
	MS-DBSCAN ($\sigma = 1 - 6$)	**0.79**	**0.873**

For the images rock, trees, and umbrella, manual segmentations of user #1105 were used in the accuracy calculation. It is presented in the Table 1 that sensitivity (recall) and F-measure of DBSCAN clustering are marginally improved when the DBSCAN algorithm is applied with ($\sigma = 1$). However, these measures are significantly improved when the proposed MS-DBSCAN algorithm is used. It is observed that MS-DBSCAN algorithm with only three scales is sufficient to gather salient structure for this particular image. However, the number of scales for sufficient clustering may vary depending on the image.

4   Conclusions

A multi-scale density based image clustering framework is proposed to analyze the image from coarse to fine details. Inspired by the Lindeberg's scale space selection approach, the developed algorithm represents the image in different scales and selects the scale that maximizes the joint density matrix. The algorithm exploits the salient structures in different scale to obtain better clustering results compared to DBSCAN algorithm. The proposed multi-scale framework also performs supervised clustering, which is regarded as one of the most restricting features in pattern recognition. Future studies should be conveyed on unsupervised clustering algorithm combined by scale space approach. Additionally, an automated scale increasing scheme might be easily adapted to the proposed approach by iteratively increasing the scale if more information is added to the joint density matrix.

Acknowledgments. This study was partly supported by a Texas A&M University-Commerce Research Grant and by the project SDU-BAP 2915-YL-11.

References

1. Romeney, T.H.: Front-End Vision and Multi-Scale Image Analysis. Kluwer Acedemics (2002)
2. Sumengen, B., Manjunath, B.S.: Multi-scale edge detection and image segmentation. In: Proceedings of European Signal Processing Conference (2005)
3. Lindeberg, T.: Feature detection with automated scale selection. International Journal of Computer Vision 30(2), 79–116 (1998)
4. Bredfeldt, C., Ringach, D.: Dynamics of spatial frequency tuning of macaque. The Journal of Neuroscience,1976–1984 (2002)
5. Liu, T., Wen, X.B., Quan, J.J., Xu, X.Q.: Multiscale SAR Image Segmentation Using Support Vector Machines. In: Congress on Image and Signal Processing (2008)
6. Balafar, M.A., Ramli, A.R., Saripan, M.I., Mahmud, R., Mashohor, S.: New Multiscale Medical Image Segmentation based on Fuzzy C-Mean (FCM). In: Proceedings of the IEEE Conferences on Innovative Technologies (2008)

7. Ester, M., Kriegel, H.P., Sander, J., Xu, X.: Density-Based Algorithm for Discovering Clusters in Large Spatial Databases with Noise. In: IEEE International Conference on Knowledge Discovery and Data Mining, pp. 226–231 (1996)
8. Mete, M., Xu, X., Fan, C.Y., Shafirstein, G.: Automatic Delineation of Malignancy in Histopathological Head and Neck Slides. BMC Bioinformatics, 7–17 (2007)
9. Celebi, E., Aslandogan, M.A., Bergstresser, P.R.: Mining Biomedical Images with Density-based Clustering. In: Int. Conf. on Inf. Tech.: Coding and Computing (2005)
10. Boucheron, L.E., Manjunath, B.S., Harvey, N.R.: Mining Biomedical Images with Density-based Clustering. In: Proceedings of the IEEE ICASSP (2010)
11. David, R.M., Charless, F., Doron, T., Jitendra, M.: A Database of Human Segmented Natural Images and its Application to Evaluating Segmentation Algorithms and Measuring Ecological Statistics. In: Proceedings of the ICCV, pp. 416–425 (2011)

Comparing Image Objects
Using Tree-Based Approach

Bartłomiej Zieliński and Marcin Iwanowski

Institute of Control and Industrial Electronics
Warsaw University of Technology, Warsaw, Poland
Koszykowa 75, 00-662 Warsaw, Poland
{bartlomiej.zielinski,marcin.iwanowski}@ee.pw.edu.pl

Abstract. In this paper, we propose a tree-based approach to represent and compare image objects. Upon objects separated from images trees are constructed. The key observation is that from similar objects similar trees are produced. On the other hand, upon dissimilar objects unlike trees are created. Additionally, the degree of dissimilarity between objects is proportional to the degree of dissimilarity between the trees. Hence, it is possible to express the difference between two objects as the difference between the trees. The paper presents algorithms of creating and comparing trees as well as results, which confirm usefulness of the approach.

1   Introduction

In many computer vision areas, one needs to process image objects that have been extracted from the original image by means of some segmentation technique. In this paper, we present a method which allows comparing such objects. It is based on a novel tree-based scalar similarity measure. Usually, when designing a similarity measure, the challenge is to determine a scalar value which would express how two images—or their parts—are alike (or unlike). Normally, such a measure should meet a number of requirements. First of all, it should correspond with human visual system. Moreover, invariance to scaling, rotation and basic image transformations is desired. There are many image processing areas where the need for image similarity measures comes from. The measures are extensively applied in image retrieval systems, which aim at browsing and finding images in datasets. Furthermore, the measures are useful tools in target detection, object recognition and—generally—image classification. They can also be used for evaluating image processing algorithms e.g. image coding, halftoning, compression, restoration, denoising, segmentation or image registration.

Many image comparison approaches have been proposed so far. There are methods which assume that considered images are of the same size. Comparison is performed pixel-wise and overall similarity depends on relation between pairs of corresponding pixels. Mean square error can be calculated this way. Such algorithms are usually fast, but vulnerable to scaling, rotation, image alterations and distortions. Other methods [1,2] initially determine pixel correspondence

L. Bolc et al. (Eds.): ICCVG 2012, LNCS 7594, pp. 702–709, 2012.

between images, with one-to-many relation possible. This approach allows comparing images of different size and proportions, but is highly time consuming. Some methods compare various features extracted from images, like shape [3,4], curves [5,6], edges [7], object contours [8] etc.

All the approaches proposed to date are limited in some way. Most perform well in a narrow class of problems. In this paper, we present an approach eligible for determining similarity between objects extracted from images. The task is difficult, since compared objects can be rotated, can differ in scale, brightness and contrast. Moreover, they may be blurred, distorted by compression, noisy etc. Presented solution is robust to these basic image alterations. To illustrate the method, we evaluate it on the set of images depicting airplanes.

The paper is organized as follows. The next section describes the algorithm of creating a tree upon an image object. In Section 3 the issue of comparing trees is discussed. Experimental results are presented in Section 4. Finally, Section 5 concludes the paper.

2 Tree Representation of Color Image Object

A color image I is usually perceived as a rectangular matrix of vectors of non-negative elements. The elements describe color component intensities of pixels. Image object is defined as a subset of image pixels belonging to the original image. Such subset may be obtained from the image segmentation result. In the proposed algorithm, the elements of such a subset (denoted as S) are defined as vectors consisting of pixel coordinates and a norm of a vector representing pixel value, i.e. $S = \{(p, \|I(p)\|)\}$, where p stands for pixel coordinates and $I(p)$ represents pixel value. The norm of vector $I(p)$ may be computed according to various approaches. The most popular are the following:

– squared Euclidean distance:

$$\|I(p)\|_2^2 = I_1(p)^2 + I_2(p)^2 + I_3(p)^2 \tag{1}$$

where I_1, I_2 and I_3 are particular color components of an input pixel. Since the distance is used to compare vectors, the square root is omitted to reduce the computational complexity.

– Manhattan distance:

$$\|I(p)\|_1 = |I_1(p)| + |I_2(p)| + |I_3(p)| \tag{2}$$

– Weighted average:

$$\|I(p)\| = 0.2989\, I_1(p) + 0.5870\, I_2(p) + 0.1140\, I_3(p) \tag{3}$$

where $I_1(p)$, $I_2(p)$ and $I_3(p)$ stand for values of color pixel in bands red, green and blue, respectively.

A rooted tree is a connected acyclic graph, with one vertex designated as a root. The proposed algorithm allows describing the subset of image pixels as a rooted tree. In successive steps of the algorithm, subsets of the input set are created. For the input set and its every subset, *characteristic elements* are calculated. The tree is constructed by connecting the characteristic elements, which become tree nodes. In order to apply the algorithm, one has to provide the input image subset, a function which determines the characteristic element, a criterion which allows constructing subsets upon a set and the height of the output tree. Algorithm 1 presents the idea.

Algorithm 1. Constructing Tree T

1: **procedure** $T \leftarrow \text{Set2Tree}(f, c, S, h)$
2:     $\text{root}(T) \leftarrow f(S)$
3:     **if** $h > 0$ **then**
4:         $(S_1, S_2, \ldots, S_n) \leftarrow c(S)$
5:         **for all** $i \in \langle 1, n \rangle$ **do**
6:             $T_i \leftarrow \text{Set2Tree}(f, c, S_i, h-1)$
7:             $\text{parent}(\text{root}(T_i)) \leftarrow \text{root}(T)$
8:         **end for**
9:     **end if**
10:     **return** T
11: **end procedure**

Input of the algorithm consists of function f, criterion c, set S and height value h. Function f is any function which determines a characteristic element for the set S. The characteristic element does not have to be a member of S. Criterion c extracts n subsets of S, such that $S_1 \cup S_2 \cup \ldots \cup S_n = S$ and $\forall_i S_i \neq \emptyset$. Value h influences height of the output tree T. The greater h is, the more precisely is S represented by T. Certainly, for finite S there is no point in increasing h over some value, because all subsets will finally be singletons.

The algorithm successively applies function f to determine characteristic elements for consecutive sets produced with use of criterion c. The process stops when the tree reaches the desired level i.e. h is negative.

Criterion c is defined with use of the median value. Let $m = \text{median}(\{\, \|I(p)\|\,\})$ of all $(p, \|I(p)\|) \in S$, thus m stands for median of intensity of all pixels belonging to S. Let $c(S) = (S_1, S_2)$, where $S_1 = \{(p_i, \|I(p_i)\|)\} \subseteq S$, such that $\|I(p_i)\| \leq m$ and $S_2 = \{(p_i, \|I(p_i)\|)\} \subseteq S$, such that $\|I(p_i)\| \geq m$. Thus, S_1 and S_2 contain only pixels of values smaller or equal than the median and greater or equal than the median, respectively. It is worth pointing out, that S_1 and S_2 may not be disjoint. In such a case, their intersection contains pixels of intensity equal to the median. Since there are two subsets created in a single iteration of our procedure, $n = 2$ and tree T is a perfect binary one, which means $|T| = 2^{h+1} - 1$. We apply median, because it ensures similar cardinality of subsets, which are represented by nodes on the same tree level.

The characteristic element of a set is computed as a mean coordinate of all pixels belonging to S, i.e. $f(S) = \text{mean}(\{p\})$ of all $(p, \|I(p)\|) \in S$. In other words, the function computes coordinates of the centroid—understood as the first moment of area—of a shape defined by indices of pixels of S. The coordinates are bound with corresponding vertices of T. This way, every tree vertex is represented by a centroid.

Height of the tree h should, on the one hand, be great enough to ensure that an image is minutely represented, on the other hand it should be small to save size of the representation as well as computation time of creating a tree. In addition, coordinates of centroids bound with vertices of successive tree levels are more dependent on distortions. Therefore, when working on highly distorted images, great h is inadvisable.

3   Comparing Images

Determining how any two objects are alike (or unlike) is possible by matching trees that represent them. In case of different objects, depicting different content, criterion c will produce unlike subsets and therefore corresponding distances among centroids will differ. On the other hand, centroids of corresponding vertices of trees created upon similar image objects will remain in similar configuration, due to similar subsets returned by criterion c. On the basis of this observation, we assume that the more similar objects are, the more similar are the trees. Besides, we go one step further. We assume that the more similar the trees are, the more similar have to be objects upon which the trees have been created. Thus, we claim that object similarity (or dissimilarity) can be expressed by tree similarity (or dissimilarity). We can estimate the extent of dissimilarity between two trees and therefore conclude upon the degree of difference between the objects. By comparing we mean determining a single scalar value which expresses the dissimilarity between the trees, and consequently between the images.

The way of creating a tree effects strict structure of the tree. As a result, while investigating differences between two trees, nodes can be compared pairwise, as every node has its corresponding one in another tree (this obviously holds for trees of the same height). The rule makes the issue of comparing trees a simple one. Difference between trees is a sum of differences between all pairs of vertices.

3.1   Comparing the Trees

Let T_1 and T_2 be trees of height h_1 and h_2, respectively. Comparing the trees is performed as shown in Algorithm 2, where δ_i stands for the difference of vertex pair i, $l = 2^{h+1} - 1$ with $h \in \mathbb{N}_+$ and $h \leq \min(h_1, h_2)$. This means that vertices of $h + 1$ successive tree levels are taken into consideration.

Algorithm 2. Calculating a Difference Between Trees

1: **procedure** $D \leftarrow \text{TreeDifference}(T_1, T_2, \alpha, s, l)$
2:     align T_1 and T_2
3:     $T_1 \leftarrow$ rotate T_1 by angle α
4:     $T_1 \leftarrow$ scale T_1 by factor s
5:     $D \leftarrow \sum_{i=1}^{l} \delta_i$
6:     **return** D
7: **end procedure**

The algorithm accepts trees T_1 and T_2, angle α and values s and l. First of all, trees are aligned. It is done by translating all the vertices of a tree by the same vector applied to translate the root of the tree to the origin of the coordinate system. Then, tree T_1 is rotated and scaled. This is achieved by transforming coordinates of all vertices of the tree to the polar coordinate system, in which each point is determined by an angle from a fixed direction and a distance from the pole. For every vertex of the tree, the angle is increased by α and the distance is multiplied by s. This way, a new tree T_1 arises. Next, the difference D between T_1 and T_2 is calculated.

The goal is to find such an angle α and a scale s, that the difference D is minimal. Then, D specifies the dissimilarity of trees, thus the dissimilarity of image objects. When comparing trees created upon the same objects (even if rotated or scaled), D equals 0 (or almost 0 due to rotation and scaling approximation). The difference between the trees increases along with the growth of the difference between the objects and is—theoretically—unlimited. Therefore, $D \in \langle 0, \infty)$. Determining angle α and scale s is a nonlinear optimization problem. In order to solve it, we use the particle swarm optimization (PSO) method [9], [10], which performed better than classical optimization approaches.

Optimizing the two parameters ensures invariance to affine transformations. If there was a need to compare trees of objects subjected to geometrical transformations other than mere scaling and rotation, then, an important advantage of the proposed tree representation method arises. That is, any geometrical transformation which can be applied to an image, can be performed on a tree as well. Therefore, one can design a tree matching method which uses any tree transformation e.g. widening, mirror flip or projective transformation, in order to satisfy desired goals, driven by specific applications.

3.2   Difference of Pair of Vertices

The difference δ_i [in line 5 of Algorithm 2] can be viewed as a "work" needed to translate a centroid of a vertex i to the position of centroid of corresponding vertex of another tree and vice versa. Term "work" is an analogy to the physical quantity, which is directly proportional to the force and the distance. The distance is naturally the Euclidean distance between the centroids of a pair of corresponding vertices. The force is proportional to the number of pixels z_{ei}

upon which the centroid for a vertex i in tree T_e is calculated. This reasoning leads to the following formula:

$$\delta_i = \left(\frac{z_{1i}}{Z_1} + \frac{z_{2i}}{Z_2} \right) d_i \qquad (4)$$

where $Z_e = \sum_{i=1}^{l} z_{ei}$ and d stands for the distance. (Note that Z_e may not necessarily equal a multiple of the total number of pixels in the object. Simple assignment Z_e as the total number of pixels would cause D to increase along with the number of vertices l).

Obviously, while comparing scaled objects, the same results of dissimilarity should be produced, regardless of the scale σ. In order to achieve this, Z_e must be raised to the power of 1.5 and the distance in T_1 component must be divided by scale s. This way, the final formula takes the following form:

$$\delta_i = \left(\frac{z_{1i}}{Z_1^{1.5}} \frac{1}{s} + \frac{z_{2i}}{Z_2^{1.5}} \right) d_i \ . \qquad (5)$$

The function ensures symmetry and gives the same results regardless of scaling. Both properties can be easily proven.

4   Experimental Results

In order to confirm the usefulness of presented algorithm, it has been subjected to experiments. We have tested the method on a dataset of images depicting airplanes separated from the background. Images of different aircrafts (see Fig. 1) have been evaluated—airliners, interceptors, transport aircrafts etc. There are 20 classes of images in the dataset. Every class consists of an original image of an airplane and its 4 variants, hence, there are 100 images in the dataset. Every variant has been created by rotating the original object by a random angle in range $\langle -\pi/4, \pi/4 \rangle$ (see Fig. 1e and 1f) and scaling by a random factor in range $\langle 0.5, 2 \rangle$. Moreover, the variants have been corrupted; each variant with one randomly chosen from among the following distortions (with $\|I(p)\| \in \langle 0, 255 \rangle$):

- with increased brightness by $b = 30$ or $b = -30$, according to the saturation arithmetic formula $\|I(p)\|' = \|I(p)\| + b$, where $\|I(p)\|'$ stands for output pixel value,
- with modified contrast with factors $a = 0.8$ or $a = 1.2$, according to the saturation arithmetic formula $\|I(p)\|' = a(\|I(p)\| - 255/2) + 255/2$, where $\|I(p)\|'$ stands for output pixel value,
- gamma-corrected with exponent of 0.5 or 2,
- contaminated with Gaussian white noise of mean 0 and variance 260.1,
- contaminated with salt and pepper noise of density 0.08.

Each distortion was used only once in a class.

We performed experiments with 3 versions of the dataset. In each version, images were coded in different color spaces, namely RGB, HSV and L*a*b*

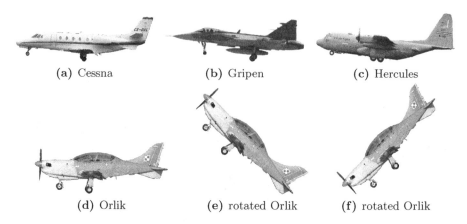

(a) Cessna   (b) Gripen   (c) Hercules

(d) Orlik   (e) rotated Orlik   (f) rotated Orlik

Fig. 1. Images of aircrafts

color space. For every image, various norms were applied. Then, object trees were created.

Evaluation procedure ran as follows. For a dataset, every possible pair of trees was compared. As a result, we obtained square matrix of dissimilarity values. If a reliable dissimilarity measure was used, then a simple condition was met. That is, the values calculated for objects of the same class were small, whereas those calculated for objects from among different classes were greater. To reason about the quality of the measure, we subjected the matrix of dissimilarity values to cluster analysis. Clustering was performed with use of k-medoids algorithm [11]. We express the reliability of the approach as the percentage of correctly clustered images. Table 1 presents the results for various color spaces, norms and height of trees. Several times, the algorithm performed slightly worse for larger values of h. This is because coordinates of centroids associated with nodes of successive levels of a tree are more vulnerable to distortions. Moreover, we take advantage of randomized methods, namely PSO and k-medoids algorithms, which effectiveness varies in different runs.

Table 1. Percentage Results of Tree-Based Dissimilarity Measure

Space	Norm	Height			
		$h = 2$	$h = 3$	$h = 4$	$h = 5$
RGB	(1)	87	99	99	100
	(2)	85	99	99	98
	(3)	91	99	97	97
HSV	(1)	88	99	99	97
	(2)	89	98	99	96
L*a*b*	(1)	79	83	80	82
	(2)	96	98	99	99

5   Conclusions

In this paper, we have addressed the problem of image object comparison. Presented approach is based on tree representation of objects. Instead of comparing objects themselves, it is possible to create trees upon them. Then, the difference between objects can be expressed as the difference between the trees. We argue that the method is effective and robust to noise, basic image alterations like brightness and contrast change, as well as invariant to scaling and rotation. To evaluate the approach we provide experimental results, which confirm the usefulness of proposed solution. We consider the method as a universal and generic tool in the field of image object comparison.

References

1. Belongie, S., Malik, J., Puzicha, J.: Shape matching and object recognition using shape contexts. IEEE Transactions on Pattern Analysis and Machine Intelligence 24(4), 509–522 (2002)
2. Grigorescu, C., Petkov, N.: Distance sets for shape filters and shape recognition. IEEE Transactions on Image Processing 12(10), 1274–1286 (2003)
3. Veltkamp, R.: Shape matching: similarity measures and algorithms. In: SMI 2001 International Conference on Shape Modeling and Applications, pp. 188–197 (May 2001)
4. Ankerst, M., Kriegel, H.P., Seidl, T.: A multistep approach for shape similarity search in image databases. IEEE Transactions on Knowledge and Data Engineering 10(6), 996–1004 (1998)
5. Sebastian, T., Klein, P., Kimia, B.: On aligning curves. IEEE Transactions on Pattern Analysis and Machine Intelligence 25(1), 116–125 (2003)
6. Latecki, L., Lakamper, R.: Shape similarity measure based on correspondence of visual parts. IEEE Transactions on Pattern Analysis and Machine Intelligence 22(10), 1185–1190 (2000)
7. Prieto, M., Allen, A.: A similarity metric for edge images. IEEE Transactions on Pattern Analysis and Machine Intelligence 25(10), 1265–1273 (2003)
8. Jia, L., Kitchen, L.: Object-based image similarity computation using inductive learning of contour-segment relations. IEEE Transactions on Image Processing 9(1), 80–87 (2000)
9. Kennedy, J., Eberhart, R.: Particle swarm optimization. In: Proceedings of the IEEE International Conference on Neural Networks, vol. 4, pp. 1942–1948 (November/December 1995)
10. Eberhart, R., Kennedy, J.: A new optimizer using particle swarm theory. In: Proceedings of the Sixth International Symposium on Micro Machine and Human Science, MHS 1995, pp. 39–43 (October 1995)
11. Kaufman, L., Rousseeuw, P.J.: Finding Groups in Data: An Introduction to Cluster Analysis. Probability and Statistics. Wiley–Interscience, New York (1990)

A Fast Lesion Registration to Assist Coronary Heart Disease Diagnosis in CTA Images

Maria A. Zuluaga[1,2], Marcela Hernández Hoyos[2], Julio C. Dávila[3], Luis F. Uriza[4], and Maciej Orkisz[1]

[1] Université de Lyon, CREATIS, CNRS UMR5220, INSERM U1044, INSA-Lyon, Université Lyon 1, France
[2] Grupo Imagine, GIB, Universidad de los Andes, Bogotá, Colombia
[3] DIME, Clínica Neurocardiovascular, Cali, Colombia
[4] Hospital Universitario San Ignacio, Pontificia Universidad Javeriana, Bogotá, Colombia

Abstract. This work introduces a 3D+t coronary registration strategy to minimize the navigation among cardiac phases during the process of ischaemic heart disease diagnosis. We propose to register image sub-volumes containing suspected arterial lesions at two cardiac phases, instead of performing a registration of the complete cardiac volume through the whole cardiac cycle. The method first automatically defines the extent of the sub-volumes to be aligned, then the registration is performed in two steps: a coarse rigid alignment and a deformable registration. Our method provides comparable results and is computationally less expensive than previous approaches that make use of larger spatial and temporal information.

1 Introduction

Ischaemic heart disease (IHD) is the main cause of mortality worldwide. Although invasive coronary angiography still remains the clinical gold standard in its diagnosis, computed tomography angiography (CTA) has dramatically progressed so that a reliable visualization of the coronary artery lumen and the identification of coronary plaques are now feasible. However, the diagnostic value of the cardiac CTA images depends on the image quality, which can be strongly affected by the coronary artery motion during the heart beat. Motion patterns differ between the left and right coronary systems and often also between proximal and distal portions of the same artery. The velocity of the arteries also varies along the cardiac cycle and among patients. Such heterogeneous movements and deformations of the coronary arteries lead to motion correction problems and motion artifacts in CTA images. Consequently, the clinicians use at least two cardiac phases (time points), typically one at the diastole and another one at the systole, in order to find an optimal representation of each arterial segment and create a mental image of the whole coronary tree. Searching for every structure of interest in each evaluated phase is time consuming and prone to errors.

L. Bolc et al. (Eds.): ICCVG 2012, LNCS 7594, pp. 710–717, 2012.

An alternative to reduce the navigation through the cardiac cycle might be an automatic registration of the arteries at different time points. However, this is a challenging task. The correspondence and alignment ambiguities are inherent to the task of automatically registering 3D images of tubular shapes [1]. The registration process is further complicated by the fact that vessels are typically surrounded by larger organs that swamp the similarity metric. In a first attempt [2], arterial landmarks have been followed through different time points of the cardiac cycle, using local vascular characteristics. The reported results are interesting, but the method has only been tested on simulated data and on a few points in two real sequences. More recently, a non-rigid registration strategy has been adapted to obtain a 4D deformation model of the coronary arteries on CTA images at different phases [3]. A non-rigid image registration algorithm has also been used to segment and track the coronary arteries in 3D+t sequences [4]. Both approaches have been aimed at estimating the coronary motion in order to subsequently exploit it in surgery planning. Since such a procedure is carried out "off-line", the computational time has not been a critical factor. In applications such as daily clinical diagnosis faster methods are required.

In this paper, we propose a 3D+t coronary artery registration strategy that minimizes the navigation and facilitates the evaluation of coronary lesions. Our approach mimics the procedure followed by physicians: after detecting a potential lesion in a particular time point of the cardiac cycle, the physician seeks the lesion in another time point to confirm the initial diagnosis. For this matter, only specific volumes of interest (VOI) in the arteries containing potential lesions are registered instead of the whole CTA volume. We demonstrate that our proposal can achieve good results without requiring information of the complete cardiac volume nor of the complete cardiac cycle.

2   The Method

The method first automatically defines the extent of the sub-volumes to be aligned. The aim of this step is to construct a VOI that encompasses the lesioned vessel segment at two different time points to be registered. Then the registration is performed in two steps. A coarse rigid alignment first reduces the displacement between the structures of interest (vessels with lesions) in both images. Subsequently, a deformable registration is applied to capture vessel deformations. Further details of each stage are provided in the subsequent sections.

2.1   VOI Definition

Let $I_M(x)$ denote the image at one time point, which will be locally deformed to fit the image from another time point, denoted $I_F(x)$. The below-described procedure is repeated for each structure of interest (*i.e.* potential lesion) located in I_F. The identification of the structures of interest is not the focus of this paper and can be performed either manually or by means of a lesion detection algorithm [6,5].

We define a VOI I_F^* that is expected to be discriminant, *i.e.* contain enough information about the lesioned vessel, so that the latter can be unambiguously identified. The algorithm seeks for the volume that best matches I_F^* within a VOI of I_M denoted I_M^*. The size of both I_F^* and I_M^* is a trade-off. While a too small I_F^* generally leads to the so called aperture problem, a too large I_F^* is likely to contain a predominant proportion of other structures (*e.g.* heart ventricles) that may swamp the similarity metric. Similarly, I_M^* is expected to entirely encompass the structure of interest defined in I_F^*, but be not too large to avoid long computations and possible confusion with other similar structures located nearby.

For this purpose, we construct a parallelepipedal I_F^* by adding up a thickness D_F around the bounding box of the suspected lesion. Similarly, the construction of I_M^* starts by mapping the spatial location of I_F^* to I_M, then a thickness D_M is added to build up I_M^*. This parameter corresponds to the maximum displacement magnitude observed on a coronary branch during the cardiac motion [7]. Both thickness parameters D_F and D_M were determined empirically, then fixed for the remaining experiments.

2.2 VOI Registration

Let us first recall that image registration seeks to deform one image, denoted the moving image, to fit another image, denoted the fixed image, by applying a transformation $\mathbf{T}(x)$ to the moving image. The registration problem is formulated as an optimization problem that seeks to minimize a metric $\mathcal{S}$ with respect to the transformation $\mathbf{T}(x)$. Under this premise, our registration stage is a combination of two transformations $\mathbf{T}(x)$: a (coarse) rigid one and a deformable one.

The coarse rigid registration algorithm is applied to perform an initial alignment of I_F^* and I_M^*. Its result is used as an input to a subsequent stage where deformations of the lesioned vessels are captured. The deformable registration consists of a non-rigid transform using a free form deformation (FFD) model based on B-cubic splines [8]. The rigid registration is performed at a single resolution, whereas the deformable registration uses a coarse-to-fine multi-resolution strategy. For every resolution, at most 500 iterations are executed by an adaptive stochastic gradient descent optimizer [9]. On every optimization iteration, 2048 samples are obtained from I_F^* using a random sampler [9] and a linear interpolator is used to evaluate the transformed I_M^* for both rigid and deformable registrations. A 3rd order B-spline interpolator is employed to apply the final deformation transform to I_M^*.

The above-described framework can be used with various similarity metrics $\mathcal{S}$ at both rigid and non-rigid registration stages. The choice was done by a careful empiric evaluation, which will be described in the next sections.

3   Experimental Setup

3.1   CTA Data

A total of 92 images from patients undergoing CT coronary angiography at the Hôpital Louis Pradel (Bron, France) were used. The datasets were acquired on a 64-row CTA scanner (Brilliance 64 − Philips Healthcare, Cleveland, OH) with a standard scan protocol. According to their quality, images were classified as poor (25), moderate (26) or good (41). This information was used to assess the performance of the method as a function of the image quality. Twenty paired datasets (systole/diastole pairs) were randomly selected and vessel centerlines were manually traced on three arteries: the right coronary artery (RCA), left anterior descending artery (LAD) and left circumflex artery (LCX). The annotated pairs of centerlines were used to evaluate the quality of the registration by measuring the distance between the reference and the registered artery. The remaining datasets were used in additional optimization and evaluation stages of the work.

3.2   Experiments

We first tested various values of the parameters D_M and D_F, respectively ranging from 1.0 to 2.5 cm and from 0.5 to 1.5 cm. I_F^* and I_M^* were respectively built in end-diastolic and end-systolic images, after a manual choice of the arterial segments of interest. These were selected from three coronary arteries (RCA, LAD and LCX) in the proximal (P), distal (D) and intermediate (O) part of each artery. The selection of D_M and D_F was assessed through a visual inspection by means of a user interface that allows the user to simultaneously navigate in both images [10].

Subsequent experiments aimed at the selection of the most appropriate similarity metric amongst the following: Mean Squared Differences (MSD), Normalized Correlation Coefficient (NCC), Mutual Information (MI) and Normalized Mutual Information (NMI). For this matter, 90 pairs I_F^*, I_M^* were generated: 3 locations per artery on 3 arteries in 10 datasets.

Once a metric selected, an experiment was performed to evaluate whether the direct registration of two time points (end-systole and end-diastole) degrades the quality of the results compared to an incremental registration strategy [3,4], in which a time point t is registered to time point $t + 1$, the resulting transform is used to initialize the registration between phases t and $t + 2$ and so on. From the available data, two datasets containing all the cardiac time points were used for incremental registration. Afterwards, a direct registration was performed between time points 40% and 75% to compare with the results of the incremental registration.

Registration results assessment was done by evaluating the displacement between the registered lesioned vessel and the corresponding vessel in the fixed image. For this matter, we used previously annotated vessel centerlines as an evaluation criterion. The transformation obtained from the registration of I_F^*

and I_M^* was used to deform the centerline from I_M^*. The distance between the deformed centerline from I_M^* and the one from I_F^* was then measured as an indicator of vessel displacement. Let C_F be the vessel centerline from I_F^* and C_M the deformed centerline from I_M^*, the average distance between centerlines [4] is defined as:

$$D(I_F^*, I_M^*, \mathbf{T}) = \frac{1}{N_F} \sum_{i=1}^{N_F} \|\mathbf{v}_i - l(\mathbf{v}_i, \mathbf{T}(I_M^*))\|$$
$$+ \frac{1}{N_M} \sum_{j=1}^{N_M} \|\mathbf{p}_j - l(\mathbf{p}_j, I_F^*)\|,$$

(1)

where N_F and N_M are the total numbers of vertices in C_F and C_M, respectively. For each vertex $\mathbf{v} \in C_F$, the function $l(\mathbf{v}, \mathbf{T}(I_M^*))$ calculates the closest vertex to $\mathbf{v}$ on C_M. Similarly, for each vertex $\mathbf{p} \in C_M$, the function $l(\mathbf{p}, (I_F^*))$ calculates the closest vertex to $\mathbf{p}$ on C_F.

4   Results and Discussion

VOI Selection. Results obtained from a visual inspection of the generated VOIs I_M^* showed that $D_M = 1$ and 1.5 cm were not enough to capture the movement between end-diastole and end-systole. VOIs formed with $D_M = 2$ and 2.5 cm succeeded in always containing the structure of interest. Since our goal was to reduce the amount of processed information $D_M = 2$ cm was selected. Visual inspection of different I_F^* VOIs showed that $D_F >= 1$ cm achieves the construction of a VOI with sufficient information. In this case, we preferred to conservatively keep a value larger than the lower limit and defined $D_F = 1.5$ cm for the remaining experiments.

Time Point Registration. Registration results in terms of average centerline distance (Eq. 1) using different metrics are presented in Figure 1. As a reference, the initial displacement of the arteries (no registration) was also computed. In general, the best results were obtained when using mutual information, so this metric was kept for the subsequent experimentations.

An analysis of the final vessel displacement in terms of image quality (Fig. 2) showed that the initial displacement has a higher incidence in the results than the image quality. The algorithm performs well on poor quality images but cannot recover excessively large displacements. We consider that the registration does not compensate the initial displacement when the final distance between centerlines is above the average maximum vessel diameter.

Table 1 compares the results obtained by direct and incremental frame registration on two datasets. In 9 cases the direct frame registration outperforms incremental frame registration, while the latter is better in the remaining 9. Although the incremental approach performs better in most of the cases where the initial displacement between vessels is large (as in RCA and LCX segments), the method does not perform well for very large distances, where the direct approach also fails. From the obtained results it is not possible to say that one of the methods is better than the other. The incremental registration tends to produce smoother images (Figure 3) than the direct approach and to introduce distortion of important structures such as calcified plaques. This can be explained by

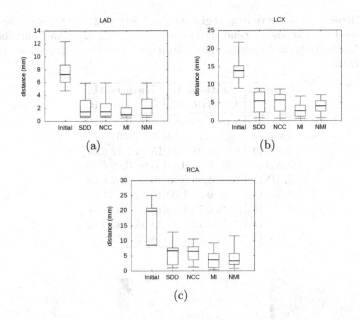

(a)   (b)

(c)

Fig. 1. Metric evaluation. Initial and final vessel centerline average distance (mm) after non-rigid registration using SSD, NCC, MI and NMI metrics for (a) LAD, (b) LCX and (c) RCA arteries.

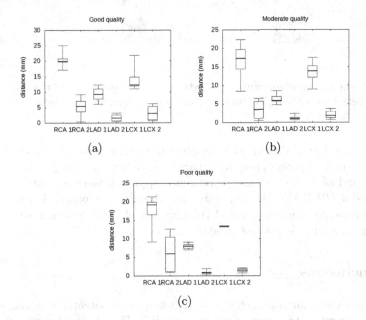

(a)   (b)

(c)

Fig. 2. Effect of image quality in the registration results - Final vessel centerline average distance (mm) in good (a), moderate (b) and poor (c) quality images. On each plot, 1 denotes initial displacement of the artery , and 2 the final one.

Table 1. Direct vs. incremental registration. Distance (mm) between the center-line at the end-diastole and the end-systole before applying any transformation (BT) and after directly (DR) and incrementally (IR) registering three segments of the RCA, LAD and LCX.

Segment	Dataset I			Dataset II		
	BT	DR	IR	BT	DR	IR
RCA P	9.18	1.20	3.61	14.98	0.55	0.50
RCA D	5.42	1.78	1.26	18.25	5.01	4.60
RCA O	6.31	1.31	2.48	15.03	7.82	6.68
LAD P	9.08	0.44	0.55	10.90	0.49	0.75
LAD D	7.98	1.96	0.98	8.67	0.52	0.68
LAD O	8.03	0.68	1.00	10.52	0.49	0.83
LCX P	13.33	0.73	1.15	14.21	1.03	0.80
LCX D	13.27	2.16	0.87	14.93	3.30	2.92
LCX O	13.31	1.54	1.07	14.72	2.81	2.75

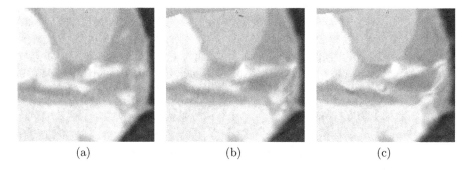

(a)   (b)   (c)

Fig. 3. Direct vs. incremental registration. The calcification and the vessel shape in (a) are better conserved with direct registration (b). Incremental registration results (c) are more blurred.

the higher number of deformations applied in the incremental registration approach. The overall process time for an artery segment was of 6 min in the direct approach and of 37 min for the incremental approach using a Pentium 4 with 3 GHz and 4 GB RAM. We can state that the direct approach is comparable to the incremental one, in terms of the final vessel displacement results, while remaining computationally less expensive.

5   Conclusions

We have presented an approach for the registration of potential vascular lesions in order to speed up the diagnosis process of IHD. The proposed approach registers the potential lesion and its surroundings to a corresponding vessel segment of the image reconstructed at a different time point. The quality of the results and the computational times obtained on a standard desktop PC make us believe that it is feasible to apply this approach in clinical practice.

Future work will focus in defining a metric to more formally validate the values of D_F and D_M, as well as in combining the method with a lesion detection algorithm [6,5] to provide the complete diagnosis pipeline.

Acknowledgements. This work has been partly funded by ECOS Nord C11S01, Uniandes Interfacultades 06-2010 and Colciencias 1204-519-28996 grants.

References

1. Aylward, S.R., Jomier, J., Weeks, S., Bullit, E.: Registration and analysis of vascular images. Int. J. Comput. Vision 55(2), 123–138 (2003)
2. Laguitton, S., Boldak, C., Bousse, A., Yang, C., Toumoulin, C.: Temporal tracking of coronaries in MSCTA by means of 3D geometrical moments. In: 28th IEEE EMBS Conf., New York City (USA), pp. 924–927 (2006)
3. Metz, C.T., Schaap, M., Klein, S., Neefjes, L.A., Capuano, E., Schultz, C., van Geuns, R.J., Serruys, P.W., van Walsum, T., Niessen, W.J.: Patient Specific 4D Coronary Models from ECG-gated CTA Data for Intra-operative Dynamic Alignment of CTA with X-ray Images. In: Yang, G.-Z., Hawkes, D., Rueckert, D., Noble, A., Taylor, C. (eds.) MICCAI 2009, Part I. LNCS, vol. 5761, pp. 369–376. Springer, Heidelberg (2009)
4. Zhang, D.P., Edwards, E., Mei, L., Rueckert, D.: 4D motion modeling of the coronary arteries from CT images for robotic assisted minimally invasive surgery. In: SPIE Med. Imaging, Orlando (USA), vol. 7259 (2009)
5. Zuluaga, M.A., Hush, D., Delgado Leyton, E.J.F., Hernández Hoyos, M., Orkisz, M.: Learning from Only Positive and Unlabeled Data to Detect Lesions in Vascular CT Images. In: Fichtinger, G., Martel, A., Peters, T. (eds.) MICCAI 2011, Part III. LNCS, vol. 6893, pp. 9–16. Springer, Heidelberg (2011)
6. Zuluaga, M.A., Magnin, I.E., Hernández Hoyos, M., Delgado Leyton, E.J.F., Lozano, F., Orkisz, M.: Automatic detection of abnormal vascular cross-sections based on Density Level Detection and Support Vector Machines. Int. J. Computer Assist. Radiol. Surg. 6(2), 163–174 (2011)
7. Shechter, G., Resar, J.R., McVeigh, E.R.: Displacement and velocity of the coronary arteries: cardiac and respiratory motion. IEEE Trans. Med. Imaging 23(3), 369–375 (2006)
8. Rueckert, D., Sonoda, L.I., Hayes, C., Hill, D.L.G., Leach, M.O., Hawkes, D.J.: Non-rigid registration using free-form deformations: application to breast MR images. IEEE Trans. Med. Imaging. 18(8), 712–721 (1999)
9. Klein, S., Staring, M., Murphy, K., Viergever, M.A., Pluim, J.P.W.: elastix: a toolbox for intensity-based medical image registration. IEEE Trans. Med. Imaging 29(1), 196–205 (2010)
10. Mattes, D., Haynor, D.R., Vesselle, H., Lewellen, T.K., Eubank, W.: PET-CT image registration in the chest using free-form deformations. IEEE Trans. Med. Imaging 22(1), 120–128 (2003)

Aesthetic-Driven Simulation of GUI Elements Deployment

Pawel Dabrowski[1,3], Sławomir Nikiel[2], Daniel Skiera[3],
Mark Hoenig[3], and Juergen Hoetzel[3]

[1] Institute of Control and Computation Engineering, University of Zielona Gora,
Podgorna 50, 65-246 Zielona Gora, Poland
P.Dabrowski@weit.uz.zgora.pl, Pawel.Dabrowski@de.bosch.com
[2] Institute of Control and Computation Engineering, University of Zielona Gora,
Podgorna 50, 65-246 Zielona Gora, Poland
[3] Bosch Thermotechnik GmbH Thermotechnology, Werk Lollar, Postfach 1161,
35453 Lollar, Germany

Abstract. We observe increasing complexity of Information Systems
that is seemingly in contrast to constant limits of human perception.
In order to handle this intricacy, various automated or semi-automated
methods for data visualization are implemented. Graphical User Interface design is very important for human-computer interaction since it
improves productivity and enhances human understanding. This paper
proposes the novel algorithm for estimation and deployment of the visual
elements of the GUI layout. The layout is composed of the blocks, that
eventually are replaced by the system dependent object representations,
e.g. visual metaphors of the heating system. The paper discusses the
theoretical background, the properties of proposed algorithms together
with the sample prototype application.

1 Introduction

Graphical User Interface greatly influences the overall user experience. Efficient
design of complex GUI systems should take into account the perception of people: how we see, understand, and think [1]. It is also necessary to understand how
information must be displayed to enhance human acceptance and comprehension [2], [3]. Good design is a crucial part of any CAD and diagnostic system and
must also consider the capabilities and limitations of the hardware and software
of the human-computer interface [4]. This limitation becomes particularly visible
in mobile systems, where using some automated tools in creation processes needs
special attention. Legible layout design, crucial for human-computer interaction
(HCI) should blend the results of above mentioned visual design research, knowledge concerning people, knowledge about the hardware and software capabilities
of the interfaces and artificial intelligence (AI) algorithms. During the GUI design process the individual elements are assigned a visual metaphors. The next
step is to organize and lay out those elements of GUI clearly and meaningfully.
Proper screen layout presentation and its background structure will encourage

L. Bolc et al. (Eds.): ICCVG 2012, LNCS 7594, pp. 718–725, 2012.

quick and correct information comprehension, the fastest possible execution of tasks and functions, and enhanced user acceptance [5], [6]. Usually, it is much harder to estimate numerically the information related to aesthetics that is actually perceived by user. There are some attempts to provide useful metrics [7]. This paper will present new metrics for the simulated GUI layouts, and some rationale and reasoning that explains why they are useful in numerical estimation of deployment of visual elements.

2   Layout Alignment

Many researchers have tried to find good interface and screen design methods and algorithms [8], [9], [10]. The methods range from minimalistic the rule of minimum design [11] to quite complex ones [12]. Aligning elements should make users eye movement through the screen much more obvious and reduce the distance it must travel. Screen organization should also be more consistent and predictable. Typically, the good alignment is achieved by creating vertical columns and horizontal rows of screen fields. Screen balance should be attained as much as possible. But how can we check whether the pattern created is consistent, predictable, and distinct? All symmetries are closely related to human sense of aesthetics, so one of the solutions is the visual complexity measure related to the estimation of the even deployment layout elements described in the following sections.

3   Aesthetic Deployment

In this paper the methodology to obtain the aesthetic deployment of GUI elements is presented. The aesthetic deployment is treated as even deployment of GUI[1] elements [13]. The Energy Algorithm is used for calculating the cost of a given deployment [14] with some modifications. The cost will be used as the returned value by the cost function for the Simulated Annealing Algorithm.

3.1   Preconditions

To solve the aesthetic deployment problem some preconditions were defined:

- the GUI elements have to be scalable e.g.: SVG[2] elements;
- the dimension of the deployment area is known;
- the GUI elements are treated as rectangles;
- the connections between GUI elements are not taken into account;
- the GUI elements can be deployed in the indiscrete deployment area (in the real examples it depends on the precision of the calculations);

---

[1] **GUI** – Graphical User Interface.
[2] **SVG** – Scalable Vector Graphics.

The result of aesthetic deployment is well if the deployment area is minimum two times bigger than the sum of all areas of GUI elements. For this example, described in this paper, the value is set to four. The ratio of the deployment area is fixed and is the same as the ratio of the given display. If the needed (determined) deployment area is smaller or bigger than the dimension on the display, the deployment area with the GUI elements can be scaled to the display size, because the dimension ratio is the same. In this case the GUI elements, shown on the display will be zoomed in or zoomed out. In Fig. 1 two examples of the same GUI elements are shown in two various ratios of the display.

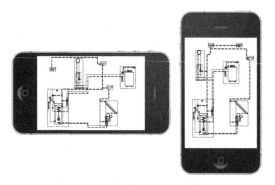

Fig. 1. An example of GUI elements on the display of a smartphone in the horizontal and the vertical position

3.2   Energy Algorithm

The Energy Algorithm can be used for aesthetic assessment of GUI elements deployment [14]. The idea of the algorithm is based on the calculation of energy between centers of elements. The energy between two GUI elements is calculated from the Eq. 1 [14].

$$E = \frac{a_1 a_2}{r^4} \tag{1}$$

where:
E – the energy between the centers of the GUI elements
a_1 – the area of the first GUI element
a_2 – the area of the second GUI element
r – the distance between the centers of the two GUI elements

The Energy Algorithm uses mirror elements to hold the distance to the edges of the deployment area. The distance to mirror elements is equal to two distances between center of GUI element and the suitable edge. The Fig. 2 shows the mirror elements for one chosen GUI element.

The sum of all energies, calculated between each pair of the GUI and the mirror elements is returned as the energy of the deployment [14].

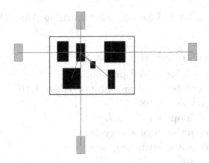

Fig. 2. The GUI element with all distances (the gray lines) to other GUI elements and to mirror elements (the gray rectangles) [14]

3.3   Simulated Annealing

The Simulated Annealing Algorithm is a meta-heuristics algorithm used in optimization problems, for which finding the optimal solution in an analytic way is not possible or the required computing time is too big [16]. The algorithm is based on the process of annealing (cooling) of metals [16], [17], [18]. It has been observed, that during annealing the particles of substances try to move to optimal places (this means that the particles structure of the substances should be regular) [17]. The power of the algorithm is that, it can with some probability accept worse solutions and in this way can leave the local minimums. The acceptable probability is decreased when running the algorithm [16], [17], [18].

For better understanding the terminology used in the Simulated Annealing Algorithm was created the Tab. 1. The table shows the analogy to the physical process.

Table 1. The analogy of physical process to Simulated Annealing

Physical process	Simulated Annealing
state of substance	solution of problem
temperature	probability
slow cooling	simulated annealing
assessment of structure	cost function

Modified Simulated Annealing Algorithm. The modification of the Simulated Annealing Algorithm is remembering of the best solution, which was found while running the algorithm. The Simulated Annealing Algorithm used in this research is shown in the Tab. 2. $N(S)$ is the neighborhood of the solution S. S' is the random neighborhood solution (the new configuration). If the new solution S' is accepted, the algorithm continues the search in the neighborhood $N(S')$.

Table 2. Modified Simulated Annealing Algorithm [15]

1:	generate initial solution S
2:	acceptable initial probability $W_S = 0.75$
3:	acceptable final probability $W_E = 0.01$
4:	factor $\alpha = 0.98$
5:	innerloop iterations $L = 10$
6:	acceptable probability $W = W_S$
7:	the best solution $S_B = S$
8:	**repeat**
9:	**for** $i = 0$ **to** L **do**
10:	generate random neighborhood $S' \in N(S)$
11:	$\Delta F = f(S') - f(S)$ // f – cost function
12:	**if** $\Delta F < 0$ **then**
13:	**if** $f(S_B) > f(S')$ **then**
14:	$S_B = S'$
15:	$S = S'$
16:	**else** generate random $\theta \in \langle 0, 1 \rangle$
17:	**if** $\theta < W$ **then**
18:	$S = S'$
19:	$W = \alpha \cdot W$
20:	**until** $W \leq W_E$
21:	return the best found solution S_B

Cost Function. For calculating the value of the cost function the Energy Algorithm is used but with some modification of distances to the mirror GUI elements. Experimentally it has been observed, that the GUI elements were grouped in the middle of the deployment area. It occurs, because the distances to mirror elements were too short. If the elements were placed in the middle of the deployment area the energy was smaller. A good returned result has been observed if the distances to mirror elements were increased three times.

The Energy Algorithm does not guarantee that the calculated energy will be considerably changed if the GUI elements overlapped [14]. To solve this issue additional values were used, equal to the sum of overlapped areas of GUI elements. In this case, if the GUI elements overlap, the deployment will be assessed less good through the cost function than a deployment without overlap. Finally the cost function is calculated as the sum of energy and the overlapped area of GUI elements (see the Eq. 2).

$$F = \sum_{0 < i < j}^{n} \frac{a_i a_j}{r_{ij}^4} + \sum_{i=1}^{n} \sum_{d=1}^{4} \frac{a_i^2}{(3r_{id})^4} + \sum_{0 < i < j}^{n} A_{ij} \qquad (2)$$

where:

F – the value of the cost function

n – the amount of GUI elements, $n \in N \setminus \{0\}$

$i, j \in N \setminus \{0\} \cap 0 < i < j$

a_i – the area of the i GUI element

a_j – the area of the j GUI element

r_{ij} – the distance between the centers of the i and j GUI elements

d – the direction to the GUI element (e.g.: $d = 1$ – means the left mirror element, $d = 2$ – means the top mirror element, etc.)

r_{id} – the distance between the i GUI element and the d mirror element

A_{ij} – the overlap area of the i and j GUI elements

Neighborhood. The initial solution S is generated by randomly choosing the location for each GUI element. To determine the neighborhood solution S' the genetics methods – mutation is use. The mutation is realised in to cases of placement modification [19].

1. The GUI element is selected at random and moved to a random location. If a location is forbidden (the GUI element with this position does not fit in the deployment area), then a new location is randomly selected.
2. The two GUI elements are selected at random and switched. If a switched location is forbidden, then a new random position for this GUI element is generated.

The choosing of the placement modification method is done by random with probability 0.6 for first method and 0.4 (1 minus the probability of the first method) for the second method.

4   Verification

The value of probabilities of choosing the two methods of generating the neighbourhood were experimentally determined, for three examples (the first example consisted 4 GUI elements, the second 7 and the third 14). The probability of first method started with 0.1 (the probability of second method was equals to 0.9 (1 minus the probability of the first method), next with 0.2 etc., to 1. For each probability 1000 deployments were generated and the arithmetic mean of the final values of the cost function was calculated. The results are presented in the graph in Fig. 3.

Fig. 4 shows two deployments of the same GUI elements (for the second example in the graph in Fig 3). The deployment with smaller final value of the cost function is more even.

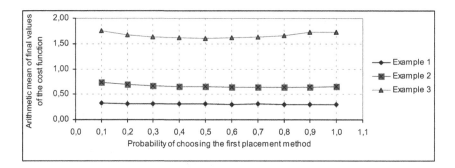

Fig. 3. The relation between arithmetic mean final values returned by the Simulated Annealing Algorithm and the probability of choosing the first placement method (the probability of second methods was equals to 1 minus the probability of the first method)

Fig. 4. Examples of two deployments of GUI elements. The final value of the cost function for the left deployment is equal to 0.5556 and for the right deployment is equal to 1.0614.

5 Conclusion

GUI design is very important in the field of Human Computer Interaction. The paper proposes the novel algorithms for estimation and deployment of the visual elements in the given GUI layout. Layout elements are obtained as the output of simulation placing rectangular blocks on a given layout area. The paper discusses alternative metric of visual aesthetics, based on the Energy Algorithm that is used in the simulation performed by the Simulated Annealing Algorithm. The authors plan to develop further the methods in order to support more complex mobile systems.

Acknowledgment. This study is supported by Bosch Thermotechnik GmbH, and the authors would like to thank the company for the cooperation and assistance rendered.

References

1. Winograd, T., Flores, F.: Understanding computers and cognition. Ablex Publishing (1986)
2. Miller, G.A.: The Magical Number Seven, Plus or Minus Two - Some Limits on Our Capacity for Processing Information. Psychological Review, 343–352 (1955)

3. Bodker, S.: Through the interface: a human activity approach to user interface design. Lawrence Erlbaum Associates (1991)
4. Wood, L.E.: User Interface Design: Bridging the Gap from User Requirements to Design. CRC Press (1997)
5. Gromke, G.: Digital Asset Management - der effektive Umgang mit Mediendaten. In: Proceedings, Intl. Conf. EVA 2007, Berlin, pp. 161–166 (2007)
6. Hoffmann, P., Lawo, M., Kalkbrenner, G.: Zur Aesthetik interaktiver Medien - Hypervideo im Spannungsfeld zwischen Usability und Design. In: Proceedings, Intl. Conf. EVA 2007, Berlin, pp. 117–123 (2011)
7. Gamberini, L., Spagnolli, A., Prontu, L., Furlan, S., Martino, F., Solaz, B.R., Alcaniz, M., Lozano, J.A.: How natural is a natural interface? An evaluation procedure based on action breakdowns. In: Personal and Ubiquitous Computing (2011)
8. Hartswood, M., Procter, R.: Design guidelines for dealing with breakdowns and repairs in collaborative work settings. International Journal on Human Computer Studies, 91–120 (2000)
9. Keppel, G., Wickens, T.: Design and analysis: a researcher's handbook. Pearson/Prentice Hall (2004)
10. Galitz, W.: The Essential Guide to User Interface Design. Wiley (2007)
11. Sirlin, D.: Subtractive design. Game Developer, 23–28 (2009)
12. Teo, L., Byrne, J., Ngo, D.: A Method for Determining the Properties of Multi-Screen Interfaces. International Journal of Applied Mathematics and Computer Science, 413–427 (2000)
13. Deussen, O.: Aesthetic placement of points using generalized Lloyd relaxation. In: Computational Aesthetics 2009, pp. 123–128 (2009)
14. Nikiel, S., Dabrowski, P., Skiera, D., Hoenig, M., Hoetzel, J.: Simulation of Visual Assessment for the Given Deployment of Graphical User Interface Elements. In: 26th European Conference on Modelling and Simulation - ECMS 2012, pp. 216–221 (2012)
15. Nikiel, S., Dabrowski, P.: Deployment Algorithm Using Simulated Annealing. In: 16th International Conference on Methods and Models in Automation and Robotics - MMAR 2011, pp. 111–115 (2011)
16. Puchta, M.: Optimierung von Problemstellungen aus der diskreten und der Prozess-Industrie unter Verwendung physikalischer Verfahren. PhD thesis, 16–17, 23–24 (2004)
17. Plaum, B.: Optimierung von ueberdimensionierten Hohlleiterkomponenten. PhD thesis, 74 (2001)
18. Emden-Weinert, T.: Kombinatorische Optimierungsverfahren fuer die Flugdienstplanung. PhD thesis, 26–53 (1999)
19. Koakutsu, S., Sugai, Y., Hirata, H.: Block Placement by Improved Simulated Annealing Based on Genetic Algorithm. In: Davisson, L.D., MacFarlane, A.G.J., Kwakernaak, H., Massey, J.L. (eds.) System Modelling and Optimization. LNCIS, vol. 180, pp. 648–656. Springer, Heidelberg (1992)

SmartMonitor: An Approach to Simple, Intelligent and Affordable Visual Surveillance System

Dariusz Frejlichowski[1], Paweł Forczmański[1], Adam Nowosielski[1],
Katarzyna Gościewska[2], and Radosław Hofman[2]

[1] West Pomeranian University of Technology, Szczecin
Faculty of Computer Science and Information Technology
Żołnierska 52, 71-210, Szczecin, Poland
{dfrejlichowski,pforczmanski,anowosielski}@wi.zut.edu.pl
[2] SmartMonitor, sp. z o.o.
Niemierzynska 17a, 71-440, Szczecin, Poland
{katarzyna.gosciewska,radekh}@smartmonitor.pl

Abstract. The paper provides fundamental information about the SmartMonitor – an innovative surveillance system based on video content analysis. We present a short introduction to the characteristics of the developed system and a brief review of methods commonly applied in surveillance systems nowadays. The main goal of the paper is to describe planned basic system parameters as well as to explain the reason for creating it. SmartMonitor is being currently developed but some experiments have already been performed and their results are provided as well.

1 Introduction

Nowadays the surveillance systems are becoming more and more popular. Their main functionality is associated with ensuring the safety of monitored people, buildings and areas by detecting suspicious behaviours and situations. The most commonly used monitoring systems require human support that can involve observation of multiple monitors and a need of quick reaction. Moreover, intelligent monitoring systems that utilize video content analysis algorithms are usually applied for monitoring wide areas or public places, such as airports or shops, where the number of moving objects is large. Such systems as well as required infrastructure are very specific, targeted and expensive. For those reasons they are unaffordable for individual clients and home use. Nevertheless, there is still a large number of people who want to ensure the safety of themselves and their assets in small areas. Additionally, a high demand on robust alarm systems with low percentage of false alarms and on systems requiring commonly available hardware exists. According to the lack of solutions designated for personal use, SmartMonitor is being developed to satisfy the mentioned needs.

The SmartMonitor is assumed to be an inexpensive security system designed to protect properties as well as to ensure personal safety. It will utilize common

L. Bolc et al. (Eds.): ICCVG 2012, LNCS 7594, pp. 726–734, 2012.

hardware that is available and affordable for individual users – personal computer connected with digital camera(s) (by USB, Ethernet or Wi-Fi), what will offer good image quality. SmartMonitor will analyse captured video stream in four predefined scenarios and in opposition to traditional monitoring systems it is intended to work without users control. The initial system calibration will be the only operation requiring human interaction. The system would react to every learned situation in pre-specified way. The most important advantage will come from system customizability. Each client will be able to decide about the system reaction, the region that is monitored and particular situations or objects (e.g. people, cars, pets, etc.) that must be detected and tracked. Therefore, it will allow for creating individual safety rules that meet ones actual requirements.

The SmartMonitor is related to the category of small-size surveillance systems (Closed Circuit Television, CCTV) that aim at increasing the safety and systems that analyse image content, usually with the use of background modelling methods (Video Content Analysis, VCA). The algorithms that will be employed belong to the state-of-art category, yet they are adopted and simplified to the characteristics of the system. Additionally, SmartMonitor could be integrated with available infrastructure in public areas and better PCs would manage to run more complex procedures. A simplified scheme of planned system modules is presented in Fig. 1.

Fig. 1. Simplified scheme of basic SmartMonitor system modules

The rest of the paper is organized as follows. The second section contains a brief review of visual surveillance systems as well as some methods and algorithms that are usually utilized. The third section presents main goals, functions and properties of the developed system. The fourth one provides sample experimental results and the last one concludes the paper.

2 Brief Review of Intelligent Monitoring Systems and Algorithms

Three main modules embedded in visual surveillance system are adaptive background model, object extraction and tracking. Each of them requires specific algorithms that can be utilized in real-time system in respect to computation time. Many current systems focus only on tracking people without the analysis of their behaviour. If the system is assumed to be an intelligent one, it should utilize more sophisticated solutions and during the tracking of particular objects the methods for removing false objects and classification have to be introduced as well. Below we present a set of visual monitoring systems characteristics and algorithms.

Intelligent monitoring system presented in [1] analyses human behaviour on the basis of the location, motion trajectory and velocity, and with the use of Hidden Markov Models (HMM). In order to recognize the type of behaviour, the probability of the similarity between a scene model and a scene actually processed is estimated. Unfortunately, learning process requires the preparation of large database and the involvement of qualified employee ([1]) what is unnecessary in SmartMonitor due to the assumed feature based methods and simple calibration.

In [2] the problem of object tracking was described. Discussed system is based on the generalization of MAPF (Memetic Algorithm Particle Filter) for tracking variable and multiple number of objects. It utilizes simple scenarios only for selected areas, such as enter/exit or restricted ones. That can be found as an important advantage in relation to less computation time ([2]) for SmartMonitor as well.

Another paper ([3]) is focused on problems of automatic monitoring systems with object classification, especially those analysing real video scenes. An approach for classifying objects as well as several features that distinct various classes were proposed. Authors assumed that the background is static and does not change during the video sequence. That is found as an important simplification but also a limitation because of background variability in real videos. Therefore, this approach cannot be introduced to SmartMonitor – the planned system scenarios are associated with very unpredictable scenes, e.g. due to changing weather conditions. Nevertheless, very valuable algorithms were described in [3]. Basic object features were represented in anumerical form as descriptors (e.g. geometric moments). That allowed for the utilization of threshold values during classification ([3]).

Moving object detection is usually based on background subtraction that utilizes algorithms for estimating background models. In reference to the literature, there are three categories of such methods. The first one includes models based on static background. In order to extract foreground image, current video frame is compared with previously prepared background image. That approach is simple but has low efficiency. In the second category the background image is obtained by averaging agroup of initial frames that is compared with currently processed average group of frames. This model is more adaptive but still do not adjust to the changes in lighting. Therefore, the background image can be obtained e.g. every hour or more frequently what gives at least partial adaptability ([4]). The third category includes adaptive background models such as Gaussian Mixture Models (GMM), found in the literature as the most efficient (e.g. [5–8]). In [5] a method for modelling each pixel value as amixture of Gaussians and on-line approximation for model adaptation is discussed. The background image is updated with every processed frame basing on Gaussian distributions – the most probable pixel distribution is considered as abackground. This model adapts to slow changes in lighting conditions and repetitive variations([5]). Despite all advantages, there are also some drawbacks. The first problem is related to the number of Gaussian distributions that represent every pixel. It was proposed in

[6] that it should be equalled to 3 to 5 models or can be modified adaptively. Additionally, false objects (artefacts) such as shadows, reflections or false detections can significantly influence the foreground region. A shadow is most often occurring false object. It moves with the real object and enlarges the detected foreground region. Basic GMM algorithm does not distinguish between moving objects and moving shadows. Hence, in [7] an improved GMM was proposed that is able to detect shadows and to improve final results by accelerating the learning process. Shadow areas can be eliminated by the analysis of HSV and YIQ colour spaces as well. It was proved that shadows change only the image intensity value without influencing the hue. Therefore, the comparison of foreground images estimated for H component of HSV colour space and Ycomponent of YIQ colour space excludes the shadow ([8]). In order to eliminate smaller false detections the morphological operations can be used. Additionally, models based on GMM are very sensitive to sudden changes in lighting. In order to avoid false detections the authors of [8] proposed the use of colour features as well as gradients.

According to variable backgrounds, GMM method proposed in [5] was chosen to be employed in the developed system. It allows for building background model adaptively on the basis of every following frame. In order to eliminate shadow areas the analysis of HSV and YIQ colour spaces described in [9] could be applied together with morphological operations. Moreover, the system could operate only on selected region what was proposed in [2] and object features could be analysed with the use of simple descriptors as it was presented in [3].

3 Parameters and Scenarios of the Developed System

Let us assume that the system will be implemented in several different places and will be aimed at different working conditions. Such combination of intended or predicted situation is called a scenario. Each scenario defines a group of functions and determines the types of algorithms used. Scenarios are system operational modes and are not overlapping each other. Only one mode can be active at the particular moment. Each mode is characterized by particular parameters and functions that are movement detection, object tracking, object classification, region limitation, object size, event detection, weather conditions and work time.

Usually, any detected movement induces the alarm while the lack of activity does not. However, while an ill person is supervised and does not move it can mean afainting. Every object that will be tracked by the system will move along a certain path, called the trajectory. System will follow an object, analyse its behaviour and decide which is a suspicious one. Typical monitoring system turns the alarm on independently from object type. The reaction of the system that includes classification module depends on the type or the size of monitored object. Therefore, it will be possible to specify groups of objects with particular characteristics that can enter observed area. Moreover, system will allow to limit the region that is under analysis or to determine the border (line) that could not be crossed by a moving object. That would reduce the computation time by excluding the regions with lower possibility of movement occurrence and could increase system efficiency in every scenario. Event detection will aim at dynamic analysis of object appearance during following frames. For instance, it will detect changes in object shape that could indicate suspicious behaviour or dangerous situation. Moreover, conditions in which the system will finally work are very important. Changing weather conditions could cause e.g. limited visibility, sudden changes in lighting or shadow occurrence. Those factors will make image analysis more difficult and will influence the final foreground region size. While working at night or in the case of insufficient lighting the use of artificial lighting will be necessary. The cost of infrared cameras is too high.

Each scenario has a specific role that simply results in utilized parameters. For instance, if the movement detection is a key issue, classification methods are redundant. SmartMonitor is planned to work in four independent modes:

- Scenario A: Home/surrounding protection against unauthorized intrusion,
- Scenario B: Supervision over ill person,
- Scenario C: Crime detection,
- Scenario D: Smoke and fire detection.

Scenario A is very similar to the scenarios realized in the traditional monitoring system that induces the alarm in the case of any detected movement. However, in the developed system we will introduce basic classification that will determine whether the moving object is a human or not. Then, object size could be a classification condition. In this mode, the main goal of the image analysis will be to indicate suspicious objects. Weather conditions will have to be taken into consideration as well.

In scenario B the movement and the behaviour will be analysed. Sudden changes in object features will be detected. That will concern e.g. a shape change or a lack of movement. Ill person supervision mode will utilize tracking without classification. Then, image analysis will aim at identifying possible untypical behaviour, e.g. diabetic fainting caused by low blood sugar level. The key issue will be to recognize a fall as well.

The third scenario is similar to the previous one – interiors will be monitored as well. Sudden changes in object trajectory and appearance that could indicate suspicious behaviours will be detected, such as raising hands up. Scenario C could be used for monitoring small shops or offices in the attack situations when the offender prevents from activating the alarm. System could recognize a danger and send information as well as camera image to the security services.

The last scenario is an additional one. System could work inside as well as outside the building where the lighting is changeable. The main task will be to detect the movement of specified objects with defined sizes and features (smoke and fire). The classification without tracking will be performed.

Such classification of scenarios makes it possible to select particular algorithms aimed at specific needs, thus it can help in tuning the whole system in order to make it much more precise. It means, that the system aimed at supervising potentially ill persons will not detect crime situations, while a guarding system will not be targeted at detecting fainting.

4   Description of the Experiments and Exemplary Results

A common task for all scenarios will be the analysis of video sequences captured
by cameras placed in various locations such as apartments, shops, gardens or
different types of buildings and their surroundings. In order to perform the development of the system it is very important that the test database reflects real
situations in which the system will finally work. Despite many benchmark solutions (e.g. [10–12]) there is no publicly available database that is universal, free
of charge and meets system requirements in full. They usually concern specified
applications and situations. Therefore, a set of video sequences containing real
scenes that match the system parameters and planned scenarios was prepared.

Some experiments were carried out in order to explore the efficiency of selected
algorithms. We present the results of foreground mask extraction that was

Fig. 2. Sample experimental results for scenario A – a person crossing the garden (the
description is given in the main text)

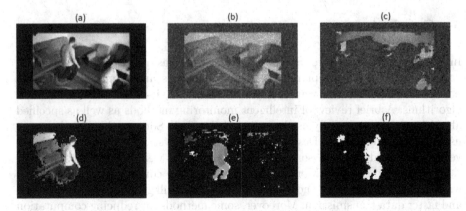

Fig. 3. Sample experimental results for scenario B – a person that is falling down (the
description is given in the main text)

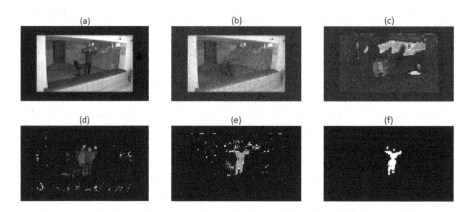

Fig. 4. Sample experimental results for scenario C – an attack situation (the description is given in the main text)

performed with the use of GMM background modelling method and the results of false object removal based on HSV and YIQ colour models analysis and morphological operations. Figures 2, 3 and 4 provide the results for sample frames and for scenario A, B and C respectively. Every following figure contains: (a) original image, (b) background image for Y component (luminance), (c) background image for H component (hue), (d) foreground image for Y component, (e) foreground image for H component and (f) a final foreground mask after false objects removal.

The experiments performed so far gave very promising results. Moving people were detected and extracted properly. Some additional regions that appeared on foreground masks were not taken into consideration on the basis of threshold values that determine minimal size. Binary form of the final image simplifies the application of shape measurements and basic classification.

5   Conclusions

In this paper the concept of SmartMonitor system was introduced. We provided basic information about planned system parameters and scenarios. Each scenario will determine the way the system will work, its functions and utilized algorithms. A brief review of intelligent monitoring methods as well as specified algorithms that are usually used was included as well. Some of them became very useful for SmartMonitor. Despite the fact that the system is being currently investigated and developed, some experimental results were presented.

Final version of SmartMonitor system will utilize commonly available hardware – personal computer and digital camera. That will give better image quality and faster data transmission. Moreover, some methods for reducing computation time could be introduced as well. That includes e.g. the limitation of the region that is under analysis. These all factors will influence the product availability and affordability for particular users. The most important advantage of the system will be the elimination of human factor – system will work independently, without human involvement. Only the initial system calibration will require it. However, that will be a benefit as well. The calibration will allow for setting individual safety rules that will be adjusted to the situation, monitored people and areas.

Since the system is not finished yet, a lot of future work can be done in order to prepare the final product version. Our aim is to utilize methods as simple as possible but also the most efficient ones. Nevertheless, in some cases more sophisticated algorithms can be taken into consideration, e.g. Histogram of Oriented Gradients (HoG). It detects and extracts objects from static images what is associated with detailed classification. HoG could be introduced to the system with some modifications and on several conditions, e.g. with time interval and on limited region. Additionally, it is important to define a group of methods for describing object features, e.g. using several shape, texture or colour descriptors.

Acknowledgments. The project *Innovative security system based on image analysis* — *"SmartMonitor" prototype construction* (original title: *Budowa prototypu innowacyjnego systemu bezpieczestwa opartego oanalize obrazu* — *"SmartMonitor"*) is the project co-founded by European Union (project number PL: UDA-POIG.01.04.0-32-008/10-00, value: 9.996.904 PLN, EU contribution: 5.848.800 PLN, realization period: 07.2011-01.2013). *European Funds – for the development of innovative economy (Fundusze Europejskie — dla rozwoju innowacyjnej gospodarki).*

References

1. Robertson, N., Reid, I.: A general method for human activity recognition in video. Computer Vision and Image Understanding 104, 232–248 (2006)
2. Pantrigo, J.J., Hernandez, J., Sanchez, A.: Multiple and variable target visual tracking for video-surveillance applications. Pattern Recognition Letters 31, 1577–1590 (2010)
3. Gurwicz, Y., Yehezkel, R., Lachover, B.: Multiclass object classification for real–time video surveillance systems. Pattern Recognition Letters 32, 805–815 (2011)
4. Frejlichowski, D.: Automatic localisation of moving vehicles in image sequences using morphological opertions. In: Pro. of the 1st IEEE International Conference on Information Technology, Gdansk 2008, pp. 439–442 (2008)
5. Stauffer, C., Grimson, W.E.L.: Adaptive background mixture models for real-time tracking. In: Proc. of the IEEE Computer Society Conference on Computer Vision and Pattern Recognition, pp. 2–252 (1999)
6. Zivkovic, Z.: Improved adaptive Gaussian mixture model for background subtraction. In: Proc. of the 17th International Conference on Pattern Recognition, vol. 2, pp. 28–31 (2004)
7. Kaewtrakulpong, P., Bowden, R.: An improved adaptive background mixture model for realtime tracking with shadow detection. In: Video Based Surveillance Systems: Computer Vision and Distributed Processing. Kluwer Academic Publishers (2001)

8. Javed, O., Shafique, K., Shah, M.: A hierarchical approach to robust background subtraction using color and gradient information. In: Proc. of the Workshop on Motion and Video Computing, pp. 22–27 (2002)

9. Forczmański, P., Seweryn, M.: Surveillance Video Stream Analysis Using Adaptive Background Model and Object Recognition. In: Bolc, L., Tadeusiewicz, R., Chmielewski, L.J., Wojciechowski, K. (eds.) ICCVG 2010, Part I. LNCS, vol. 6374, pp. 114–121. Springer, Heidelberg (2010)

10. CAVIAR, Context aware vision using image-based active recognition, http://homepages.inf.ed.ac.uk/rbf/CAVIAR

11. IEEE International Workshop on Performance Evaluation of Tracking and Surveillance (PETS), http://www.cvg.rdg.ac.uk/PETS2010/index.html

12. CLEAR, Classification of events, activities and relationships evaluation campaign and workshop, http://www.clear-evaluation.org

Biometrics Image Denoising Algorithm Based on Contourlet Transform

Monika Godzwon and Khalid Saeed

AGH University of Science and Technology,
Faculty of Physics and Applied Computer Science,
Al. Mickiewicza 30, PL-30059 Kraków, Poland
mika.go@interia.pl, saeed@agh.edu.pl

Abstract. This paper presents a new image denoising method based on contourlet transform and Lee filter. Classical contourlet transform methods are based on denoising procedure that processes the contourlet coefficients with a threshold in each subband. This is performed without considering the neighbourhood characteristics of the invariance of the contourlet transform which introduces some artifacts. In this work, however, Lee filter is used to solve this problem. The suggested algorithm is particularly useful when considering biometric images that need precise preprocessing.

1 Introduction

Image denoising is very important step in pre-processing images that eases further analysis of images in the fields of computer vision and image processing. Tradi-tional image denoising algorithms blur image losing information about the most important parameter in biometrical analysis, the edges. Due to lost of information the image denoising algorithms started developing in other domain than spatial. Nowadays the most exploited are wavelets [7], curvelets [8] and contourlets [12]. The curvelet transform and contourlet transform have their origin in wavelet trans-form.

2 The State of the Art

As shown in Fig. 1, there are two basic approaches to image denoising: spatial filtering methods and transform domain filtering methods [1].

2.1 Spatial Domain

All traditional denoising filters are placed in spatial domain, which can be divided into non-linear filters and linear filters. In Non-Linear Filters the denoised image is nonlinear combination of noised image pixels.

L. Bolc et al. (Eds.): ICCVG 2012, LNCS 7594, pp. 735–742, 2012.

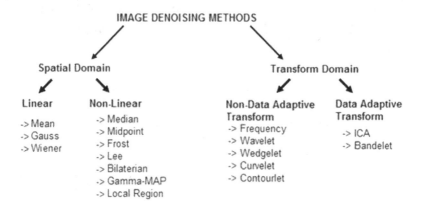

Fig. 1. Classification of denoising algorithms

Lee Filter. Lee filter is based on the assumption that the mean and variance of the pixel of interest is equal to the local mean and variance of all pixels within the user-selected moving kernel. The formula used for the Lee filter is:

$$S_{out} = M + K(S_{in} - M) \tag{1}$$

where M is the mean value of pixel intensieties in the moving window, S_{in} and S_{out} image pixels in noised image and output image.

$$K = \frac{var(x)}{M^2\sigma^2 + var(x)} \tag{2}$$

Where x is pixel intensities.

$$var(x) = \frac{\nu + M^2}{\sigma^2 + 1} - M^2 \tag{3}$$

where ν is a variance within the window.

In spatial domain the denoised image is combination of noised image pixels, so they blur sharp edges, destroy lines and other image details. In order to overcome those weakness were proposed new denoising schemes in transform domain.

2.2   Transform Domain

The transform domain filtering methods are based on function transform. The transform function can be classified into non-data adaptive and data adaptive transforms. One of the first filtering methods transform is frequency transform based on Fast Fourier Transform. Methods based on the frequency transform are time consuming and may produce artificial frequencies in the processed image. In wavelet domain the 2-D wavelet can capture only limited directional information and cant detect the smoothness along the contours. To overcome this problem Starck, Cands, and Donoho develop a new geometric transform: curvelet[9].

Unfortunately methods based on curvelet transform are in continuous domain, so it makes implementation for discrete images very difficult. To overcome this Do and Vetterli proposed contourlet tramsform[12].

3   Contourlet Transform

The contourlet transform is used to capture geometrical structure and offer a flexible multiscale and directional expansion from images. In classical contourlet transform, the Laplacian Pyramid(LP) is first use to capture the point discontinuities, then it is followed by Directional Filter Bank(DBF) to link point discontinuities into linear structures.

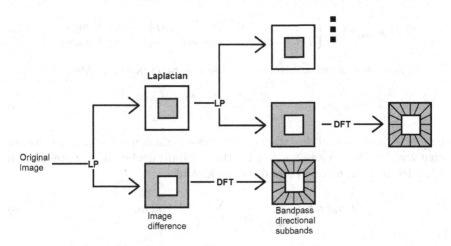

Fig. 2. Block diagram of contourlet transform

3.1   Laplace Pyramid

Laplace Pyramid is decomposition based on difference of low pass filters. The image is recursively decomposed into low pass and high pass bands. Each band of the Laplacian pyramid is the difference between two adjacent low-pass images gained by using Laplace filter and expands.

3.2   Directional Filter Banks

The original construction of the DFB in modelling the input image and using quincunx filter banks with diamond shaped filters. Figure 3 show wedge shaped frequency partitioning with to 2^l subbands gained by 2-D DFB via an l-level binary tree decomposition.

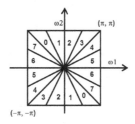

Fig. 3. Frequency partitioning

3.3 Threshold

This is the most important part of algorithm. In [15] is proposed thresholding contourlet coefficients $I(j, k, m, n)$ by using $I'(j, k, m, n)$:

$$I'(j, k, m, n) = \begin{cases} 0 & \text{if } \mid I(j, k, m, n) \mid < Th(j, k, m, n) \\ I(j, k, m, n) & \text{if } \mid I(j, k, m, n) \mid \geq Th(j, k, m, n) \end{cases} \quad (4)$$

Where j is domain scale, k direction, m and n is pixel position. Also:

$$Th(j, k, m, n) = \left(\frac{E_{mea}(j, k) - M_{mea}(j, k)}{I_{mea}(j, k, m, n) - M_{mea}(j, k)} \right) \lambda \xi_{jk} \sigma \quad (5)$$

where σ is the standard deviation of the white Gaussian noise, λ is a constant (often $\lambda = 4$ or $\lambda = 3$) and ξ_{jk} denotes the standard deviation of white noise in contourlet domain in scale j and direction k. And:

$$I_{mea}(j, k, m, n) = \frac{1}{N} \sum_{(m,n) \in B} \mid I(j, k, m, n) \mid \quad (6)$$

where B is neighbourhood square window around contourlet coefficient $I(j, k, m, n)$. $E_{mea}(j, k)$ denotes mean value of $I_{mea}(j, k, m, n)$, and $M_{mea}(j, k)$ denotes the minimum value of $I_{mea}(j, k, m, n)$.

3.4 Proposed Modification

Fig. 4 shows the scheme of the proposed modification, which is based on using Lee filter.

4 Results and Comparison

To present the results of the proposed image denoising algorithm, the authors have considered fingerprints as their input image. Biometric images are specific and need precise pre-processing [16]. Lee-Contourlet, were used on three different types of noise presented in Fig. 5. Fig. 6, however, shows how the suggested denoising method is filtering all of them.

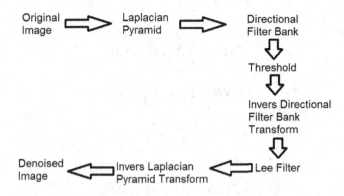

Fig. 4. Proposed modification scheme

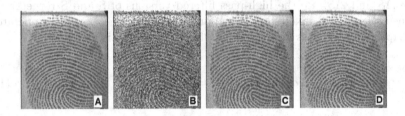

Fig. 5. Picture A is reference image, B - noisy image with paper-salt noise, C - noisy im-age with complex noise[3] and D is noisy image with photon noise

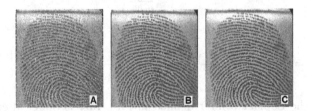

Fig. 6. Images denoised by the proposed algorithm: A denoised paper-salt noise, B - denoised and C denoised photon noise

In order to evaluate the result of filters quantitatively, the following six parameters are defined and calculated: Signal to Noise Ratio (SNR), Mean Square Error (MSE), Peak Signal to Noise Ratio (PSNR), β[4], Mean Absolute Error(MAE) and parameter proposed by authors named φ.

$$SNR = 10log_{10}(\frac{\sum_{i=1}^{K} S_i^2}{\sum_{i=1}^{K} (S_i' - S_i)^2}) \tag{7}$$

where S_i is the original image, S_i' the denoised image and K the image size.

$$MSE = \frac{1}{K} \sum_{i=1}^{K} (S'_i - S_i)^2 \tag{8}$$

$$PSNR = 10log_{10}(\frac{255^2}{MSE}) \tag{9}$$

$$MAE = \frac{1}{K} \sum_{i=1}^{K} |S'_i - S_i| \tag{10}$$

$$\beta = \frac{\Gamma(\Delta S - \Delta S', \Delta S - \Delta \bar{S}')}{\sqrt{\Gamma(\Delta S - \Delta \bar{S}, \Delta S - \Delta \bar{S})\Gamma(\Delta S' - \Delta \bar{S}', \Delta S' - \Delta \bar{S}')}} \tag{11}$$

where ΔS and $\Delta S'$ are the high-pass filtered versions of S and S respectively, obtained with a 3x3 pixel standard approximation of the Laplacian operator. The Laplacian high pass filter used here for this purpose is as follows:

$$LaplacianFilter = \begin{vmatrix} 0 & -1 & 0 \\ -1 & 4 & -1 \\ 0 & -1 & 0 \end{vmatrix}. \tag{12}$$

Also the operator Γ denotes:

$$\Gamma(S_1, S_2) = \sum_{i=0}^{K} S_{1_i} S_{2_i} \tag{13}$$

$$\varphi = \sum_{i=1}^{K} \frac{|L_{S'_i} - L_{S_i}| + |So_{S'_i} - So_{S_i}| + |R_{S'_i} - R_{S_i}|}{3 \times 255} \tag{14}$$

where L_S is the Laplacian filter defined in (12), So_S is Sobel filter and R_S is Roberts filter on image S. To get the best resulta values of MSE, MAE, β and φ must be near zero, in other hand SNR and PSNR need to be as large as they can.

Table 1. Comparing denoising methods for an image noised by complex noise

Filter/ Parameter	Noised Image1	Median	Midpoint	Lee	Authors'
SNR	25.17	16.55	14.79	15.61	18.86
PSNR	29.35	20.65	17.89	20.05	23.34
MSE	76	560	1056	753	301
MAE	4.00	16.35	24.58	20.77	11.21
β	0.32	0.85	0.88	1.10	0.46
φ	0.09	0.24	0.26	0.28	0.17

Table 2. Comparing denoising methods for an image noised by photon noise

Filter/ Parameter	Noised Image1	Median	Midpoint	Lee	Authors'
SNR	22.55	16.09	13.14	15.85	17.50
PSNR	26.32	19.81	15.66	19.88	21.70
MSE	152	679	1766	668	439
MAE	7.53	17.61	36.86	20.42	17.10
β	0.76	0.84	0.83	1.07	0.73
φ	0.38	0.24	0.24	0.28	0.25

5 Conclusions

A new algorithm for image denoising built on the basis of contourlet transform and Lee filter has been introduced in this work. Classical contourlet transform methods are based on processing the contourlet coefficients with a threshold in each subband. Lee filter has shown a significant improvement of the denoised image. Table 1 and Table 2 present results for image denoising by some known filtering methods. The authors proposed criterion and the worked out algorithm has shown good and promising results for all parameters. It can be developed for ex-ample by using Nonsubsampled Contourlet Transform to be modified like Contourlet Transform in Fig 3.

Acknowledgement. This work was supported by the Polish Ministry of Science and Higher Education.

References

1. Motwani, M., Gadiya, M., Motwani, R., Harris, F.: Survey of Image Denoising Techniques. In: Proceedings of GSP, Santa Clara, CA, September 27-30 (2004)
2. Schowengerdt, R.A.: Techniques for image processing and classification in remote sensing. Academic Press, New York (1983)
3. Lim, S.H.: Characterization of Noise in Digital Photographs for Image Processing. In: HP Laboratories 2008. ISandT/SPIE Electronic Imaging, vol. 6069 (2008)
4. Rajabi, M.A., Mansourpour, M., Blais, J.A.R.: Effects and Performance of Speckle Noise Reduction Filters on Active Radar and SAR Images (2006), http://people.ucalgary.ca/blais/Mansourpour2006.pdf
5. Maini, R., Aggarwal, H.: Peformance Evaluation of Various Speckle Noise Reduction Filters on Medical Images. International Journal of Recent Trends in Engineering 2(4), 22–25 (2009)
6. Judith, G., Kumarasabapathy, N.: Study and Analysis of Impulse Noise Reduction Filters. Signal and Image Processing: An International Journal, SIPIJ 2, 82–92 (2011)
7. Donoho, D., Johnstone, I.: Ideal spatial adaptation by wavelet shrinkage. Biometrika 81(33), 425–455 (1994)
8. Donoho, D.L., Duncan, M.R.: Digital Curvelet Transform: Strategy, Implementation and Experiments. Stanford University (1999)

9. Starck, J., Cands, E.J., Donoho, D.L.: The Curvelet Transform for Image Denoising. In: 6th IEEE Transaction on Image Processing, vol. 11, pp. 670–684. IEEE Press, New York (2002)

10. Bhadauria, H.S., Dewal, M.L.: Performance Evaluation of Curvelet and Wavelet based Denoising Methods on Brain Computed Tomography Images. In: IEEE Emerging Trends in Electrical and Computer Technology, pp. 666–670. IEEE Press, New York (2011)

11. Pennec, E., Mallat, S.: Sparse Geometric Image Representations With Bandelets. In: 4th IEEE Transaction on Image Processing, vol. 14, pp. 423–438. IEEE Press, New York (2005)

12. Do, M.N., Vetterli, M.: The Contourlet Transform: An Efficient Directional Multiresolution Image Representation. In: 12th IEEE Transaction on Image Processing, pp. 2091–2106. IEEE Press, New York (2005)

13. Xiaobo, Q., Jingwen, Y.: The Cycle Spinning-based Sharp Frequency Localized Contourlet Transform for Image Denoising. In: ISKE 3th Intelligent System and Knowledge Engineering, November 17-19, pp. 1247–1251. IEEE Press, New York (2008)

14. Eslami, R., Radha, H.: The Contourlet Transform for Image De-noising Using Cycle Spinning. In: IEEE Asilomar Conference on Signals, Systems, and Computers, November 9-12, pp. 1982–1986. IEEE Press, New York (2003)

15. Ding, Q., Song, H., Geng, W., Jiang, Z.: Image Denoising Algorithm Using Neighbour-hood Characteristics and Cycle Spinning. In: IEEE 2th Digital Manufacturing and Automation, August 5-7, pp. 614–617. IEEE Press, New York (2011)

16. Waluś, M., Kosmala, J., Saeed, K.: Finger Vein Pattern Extraction Algorithm. In: Corchado, E., Kurzyński, M., Woźniak, M. (eds.) HAIS 2011, Part I. LNCS, vol. 6678, pp. 404–411. Springer, Heidelberg (2011)

Multi-person Tracking-by-Detection
Based on Calibrated Multi-camera Systems

Xiaoyan Jiang, Erik Rodner, and Joachim Denzler

Computer Vision Group Jena
Friedrich Schiller University of Jena
{xiaoyan.jiang,erik.rodner,joachim.denzler}@uni-jena.de
http://www.inf-cv.uni-jena.de

Abstract. In this paper, we present an approach for tackling the problem of automatically detecting and tracking a varying number of people in complex scenes. We follow a robust and fast framework to handle unreliable detections from each camera by extensively making use of multi-camera systems to handle occlusions and ambiguities. Instead of using the detections of each frame directly for tracking, we associate and combine the detections to form so called tracklets. From the triangulation relationship between two views, the 3D trajectory is estimated and back-projected to provide valuable cues for particle filter tracking. Most importantly, a novel motion model considering different velocity cues is proposed for particle filter tracking. Experiments are done on the challenging dataset PETS'09 to show the benefits of our approach and the integrated multi-camera extensions.

1 Introduction

Multi-object tracking is important for various applications in computer vision, such as visual surveillance, traffic control, sports analysis, or activity recognition. Since cameras are getting cheaper and tracking definitely benefits from organized multiple cameras with different views, it is sensible to track multiple objects based on calibrated multi-camera systems. In general, tracking multiple objects in real-time in an accurate way is very challenging due to background clutter, occlusion between objects and background, and the appearance similarity between objects to be tracked. The difficulties additionally arise from the aspect of how to reliably fuse the information from individual cameras and how to perform robust global tracking in an efficient manner.

With the improvement of detection algorithms [1,2] both in accuracy and computational feasibility, tracking-by-detection is one of the most popular concepts for tracking [3,4]. Targets to be tracked can be initialized by continuously applying detectors to single image frames. Typically, the output of a detector is a set of image regions with confidence scores. Incorporating temporal context here is necessary due to the high amount of false positives and missing detections as shown in the left part of Fig. 1. Recent tracking approaches [3,4,5,6] try to associate the detections and track objects from uncalibrated single cameras.

L. Bolc et al. (Eds.): ICCVG 2012, LNCS 7594, pp. 743–751, 2012.

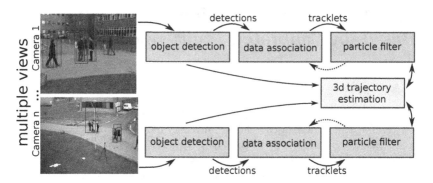

Fig. 1. Overview of our framework. Left images show outputs of a person detector [1] from two views of the PETS'09 database highlighting the necessity of tracking and 3D reasoning.

Additionally, multi-camera systems are also used for efficient tracking. Correspondences of observations of walking humans across multiple cameras can be established by geometric constraints like a planar homography [7]. The work of [8] reconstructs the top-view of the ground plane and map the vertical axes of a person in each view to the top-view to intersect at a single point that is assumed to be the location of the person on the ground. Many other papers also make full use of the ground plane assumption [9,10].

We intend to utilize two or more calibrated cameras and fuse the information in a joint tracking-by-detection framework without using homography restrictions or top-view images. As we will see later, this yields more precise results. In details, detections in single camera images with lower confidence scores which are considered to belong to the same objects are rejected first. Afterwards, detections are associated to form more reliable tracklets. Once tracklets are found, they are used to update the motion model as well as the target model for particle filter tracking. Secondly, global tracking based on estimating the 3D position is realized, where we focus primarily on occlusion reasoning from a geometrical point of view. Thirdly, particle filters are initialized with tracklets and the motion is estimated in subsequent frames.

The paper is structured as follows. The details of our algorithm are presented in Section 2. Experiments on PETS'09 [1] are evaluated qualitatively and compared to other state-of-the-art algorithms in Section 3. Finally, Section 4 concludes the paper with a summary and an outlook.

2   Tracking-by-Detection with Multi-camera Systems

A block diagram of our tracking approach is shown in Fig. 1. The algorithm mainly consists of three parts: data association, particle filters for tracking, and 3D trajectory estimation. First of all, we use data association techniques to

---

[1] http://www.cvg.rdg.ac.uk/PETS2009/

combine detections after k consecutive frames to form tracklets. Each tracklet is then associated with a particle filter. The key idea is that the particle filter additionally uses the estimated 3D trajectory to fuse the information from multiple cameras. Furthermore, back-projecting this 3D trajectory into every view allows for recovering from missed detections. To eliminate duplicate tracking results, we use several similarity measurements based on appearance features as well as geometry reasoning.

2.1   Data Association

Initializing a particle filter tracker for each detection directly in each frame may lead to unreliable tracking results. Therefore, we use an intuitive matching criteria to find corresponding detections in k subsequent frames. If such a correspondence is found, the detections in all k frames define a tracklet and are taken into account for particle filter tracking. This reduces the number of false positive detections to a large extent. The correspondences are found by greedy association, which showed results comparable to the assignment problem solved by the Hungarian algorithm [3]. We basically follow the work of [3], but modify it in two important aspects: first, we associate the detections in single cameras to get more reliable tracklets. Furthermore, a calibrated multi-camera system is used to estimate the 3D trajectory and use the projections in each camera to provide valuable cues especially in the case of occlusions and ambiguities.

To find the best associated detections in time t in camera i, we consider the Manhattan distance and the overlap ratio between each current detection d with the previous detection from a tracklet T using a gating function:

$$g(d, T) = \begin{cases} 1 & \text{if } o(d, T) \geq \sigma \text{ and } M(d, T) \leq \xi(T) \\ 0 & \text{otherwise} \end{cases} . \tag{1}$$

The value $g(d, T) = 1$ indicates that this detection belongs to the tracklet considered. In equation (1), the overlap ratio $o(d, T)$ between the two regions is defined as follows:

$$o(d, T) = 2 \cdot \frac{d \cap T}{|d| + |T|} , \tag{2}$$

where we interpret d and T as sets of image pixels. The parameter σ is set experimentally. The Manhattan distance $M(d, T)$ is thresholded depending on the size of the tracklet:

$$\xi(T) = \alpha \cdot [\text{height}(T) + \text{width}(T)] , \tag{3}$$

where the parameter $\alpha < 1$ is manually chosen.

If a detection passes the gating function, it will be associated to the corresponding tracklet. Furthermore, the input to the thresholding operation is a set of ranked detections of which the detections with higher scores that satisfy the conditions stated above will be selected primarily.

2.2   Data Fusion from Multiple Views

Fusing information from multiple views is done by reconstructing the 3D position of the centroid of the object. With the knowledge of epipolar geometry, it is known that a corresponding pair of points in two cameras is limited to epipolar lines [11]. The correspondence of detections is obtained by the combination of Euclidean distances between their centers to respective epipolar lines and appearance similarity between them. Afterwards, we estimate the 3D position of the object center from two views using triangulation [11].

3D Trajectory. After obtaining all possible 3D points from all the cameras, 3D points which are near to each other are considered to belong to the same object, which are merged by simple averaging of their 3D vectors. The 3D trajectory of an object is formed based on associating the 3D points frame by frame.

Occlusion Reasoning. The most challenging part of multi-object tracking is how to tackle tracking under occlusion. When there exists inter-object occlusion or the object is occluded by background objects, the target in some views will be partially (or totally) invisible. This might lead to the failure of both detection and tracking. Therefore, many works consider occlusion reasoning to improve the results [3]. The inter-object occlusion reasoning is done by considering the intermediate detection confidence as a part of the observation model of particle filters. In [12], occlusion is taken into account by calculating the visible parts of the object and trajectory estimation is achieved by energy function minimization.

   However, we want to take advantage of multiple views and intend to perform inter-object occlusion reasoning from a geometrical point of view. We assume two kinds of occlusion: first situation, if an object was trackable previously and there is another one or more trackable objects nearby, then we regard this object as occluded by another object, no matter how much proportion of the object is invisible; second situation, if one detection in a view has more than one corresponding detections in other views for several frames, then it is supposed that there is occlusion between these detections. After obtaining tracklets and the 3D trajectories of the objects, they are used to update the target model and the motion model of the particle filter, which is explained in the next section.

2.3   Kernel Based Particle Filter

In case of clutter environments, the assumption of Gaussian distributed object states does not hold. In contrast, particle filters are able to model flexible and multi-modal distributions, and are due to this reason better suited for tracking than Kalman filters [13]. Particle filters use a set of weighted samples, referred to as particles, to model the posterior distribution [13]:

$$\chi_t = \{\mathbf{x}_t^{[1]}, \mathbf{x}_t^{[2]}, ..., \mathbf{x}_t^{[M]}\} \ , \tag{4}$$

where M is the number of particles which is constant in our case and $\mathbf{x}_t^{[m]}$ (with $1 \le m \le M$) is a hypothesis of the 2D state (x, y, hx, hy) (object center and half of the width and height of the object) at time t.

Initialization and Termination. Initialization of trackers is done using two different sources: the newly assigned tracklets and the projections of 3D trajectories of the object which are within detections. We also check whether these cues have not been associated with any existing tracker. Initially, particles are distributed uniformly over the initial region with the same weight $1/M$.

The appearance model of a target or a candidate is a kernel-based RGB histogram [14]. The kernel assigns higher weights to the samples close to the target region centroid to reduce the effect of peripheral samples, which might be affected by occlusions from the background. After initialization, particles will be propagated to the new hypothesis states according to the motion model.

Propagation. In some papers like [3], people are assumed to walk with constant velocity and the motion model is empirically configured in advance. This assumption is not valid, when people stop walking during a period of time or increase speed. Furthermore, this leads to particles, which may converge to totally wrong positions or scale because of ambiguities in the scene. Therefore, we decide to utilize a robust motion model to guide the particles.

The motion model is composed of three different velocities:

$$\mathbf{v} = \beta \cdot \mathbf{v}_T + \eta \cdot \mathbf{v}_O + \gamma \cdot \mathbf{v}_S \quad \text{with} \quad \beta + \eta + \gamma = 1 \tag{5}$$

where $\mathbf{v}_T$ is the velocity of the associated tracklet at the current time step t, $\mathbf{v}_O$ is the velocity of the tracker at previous time step $t-1$, and $\mathbf{v}_S$ is the velocity of the back projection from the corresponding 3D trajectory at current time step t. In normal situations β, η, and γ are set equally. During occlusion, the detections associated with a tracker in a single view are considered to be unreliable. Thus, β is set to be lower, while γ is given higher weight to incorporate useful information from other cameras. Besides that, $\mathbf{v}$ should not be greater than a maximum velocity. For people who are walking, this maximum velocity could be defined by twice of the normal speed of a person. Otherwise, $\mathbf{v}$ equals to the previous velocity to reduce abrupt movement. One advantage of utilization of this motion model is that the particles can still propagate correctly even during occlusion by fusing useful cues from other cameras.

Observation. Given the propagated particles, the weights of individual particles are obtained by the Bhattacharyya coefficient [14] between the candidate and the target. Most importantly, the target model is updated by the associated detection which is totally visible and satisfies object appearance consistency. Appearance consistency is based on the reasonable assumption that the appearance of a person in two consecutive frames does not change significantly.

The final state is estimated by the combination of the mean and the maximum of the modeled posterior distribution:

$$\mathbf{x}_t = \frac{1}{2} \left(\sum_{m=1}^{N} w_t^{[m]} \cdot \mathbf{x}_t^{[m]} + \underset{m=1...N}{\arg\max} \; \mathbf{x}_t^{[m]} \right), \tag{6}$$

where $\mathbf{x}_t$ is the final state at time t and $w_t^{[m]}$ is the corresponding weight of the particle $\mathbf{x}_t^{[m]}$.

3 Experiments

Datasets. There are not many publicly suitable datasets for multi-person tracking in multi-camera systems. Since PETS09/S2.L1 contains different types of human movements, different types of occlusion, cameras located in different angles with different illumination and different resolutions, we choose this challenging dataset for testing our algorithm.

In all our experiments, we do not train the detector specifically for this dataset and do not perform background extraction. We use the detector of [1] and the corresponding source code and learned models. Furthermore, no special information of this dataset is used, which allows for applying our algorithm to other scenarios and datasets. The ground truth of the first view was provided by Anton Andriyenko[2].

Experimental Setup. We use the CLEAR MOT metrics [15] and the evaluation program of [6] to analyze the tracking performance. We compare our algorithm with the state-of-the-art results on PETS'09 S2.L1 in Table 1, where the performance of other methods are provided in [3]. MOTP considers the precision of estimated positions and MOTA takes misses, false positives, and mismatches into account [15]. The parameter k in this dataset is set to 3 and we use 1000 units in the world coordinate system [6] as a threshold to recognize 3D points belonging to the same object. Furthermore, 8 bins per color channel are used to compute the RGB histograms and σ is set to 0.4. $M = 100$ particles are used in one tracker.

Evaluation. Fig. 2 shows six sample images from the dataset. Different colors identify the different objects with corresponding 2D trajectories. From the images, we can see that most of the people can be tracked correctly even during occlusion. There are sometimes double or more assigned trackers to the same object, partially arised from initialization of trackers by back projected points of 3D positions that within detections or from missing detections that may separate long tracklets into several shorter tracklets. The precision of multi-camera system calibration has heavy effect on the final results, since the 3D positions of the objects has large impact especially during occlusion.

Evaluation results are shown in Table 1. We can see that our approach outperforms other methods with respect to the MOTP value. This is mainly due to the utilization of cues from multiple cameras, which is especially useful because of missing detections in the first view. Compared to other state-of-the-art methods, the MOTA value of our approach is lower. This is mainly caused by reassignment of the same objects or the model update of the particle filters when groups of people split and merge again. We plan to overcome these issues by not

---

[2] http://www.gris.informatik.tu-darmstadt.de/~aandriye/data.html

Fig. 2. Tracking results: top and bottom row show results in view 1 and 5, respectively

Table 1. Results of our approach on PETS'09/S2.L1 compared to state-of-the-art

Algorithm	MOTP	MOTA
Our approach	**78.8%**	60.8%
Breitenstein et al. [3]	56.3%	79.7%
Yang et al. [16]	53.8%	75.9%
Berclaz et al. [9]	60.0%	66.0%
Andriyenko et al. [6]	76.1%	**81.4%**

only considering the centroid of tracked objects but also the complete 3D shape to allow for a more exact data association.

Runtime Performance. The entire system is implemented in C++, except that the detection is the MATLAB source code of [1], without taking advantage of GPU processing. For tracking without considering the time used for detection, the average runtime is 2.6 seconds for each time step processing images from 7 cameras. Time measurements were done on a standard PC with Intel Core i5 2.8GHz processor.

4   Conclusion

In this paper, we proposed a tracking-by-detection framework for multi-camera systems. We showed that estimating the 3D position of the tracked objects can help to solve for ambiguities and provides more robustness to occlusions. Our framework is based on an efficient detection algorithm, several intuitive rejection rules, and the combination of several appearance as well as geometry cues. Specifically speaking, the performance during occlusion is improved by integrating cues from multiple cameras. This is reflected in the novel motion model incorporated in particle filters, where the importance from 3D trajectory is higher during occlusion.

For future research, we plan to integrate more complex motion models and uncertainties derived from 3D position estimation. Additionally, a more accurate target model is also worth to be considered for future investigation. Furthermore, we will record our own large-scale dataset within a challenging outdoor environment to allow for a more realistic evaluation.

Acknowledgements. We would like to thank our colleagues for their comments and suggestions.

References

1. Felzenszwalb, P., Girshick, R., McAllester, D.: Cascade object detection with deformable part models. In: CVPR (2010)
2. Dalal, N., Triggs, B.: Histograms of oriented gradients for human detection. In: CVPR (2005)
3. Breitenstein, M.D., Reichlin, F., Leibe, B., Koller-Meier, E., Gool, L.V.: Online muti-person tracking-by-detection from a single, uncalibrated camera. PAMI 10, 1–14 (2010)
4. Huang, C., Wu, B., Nevatia, R.: Robust Object Tracking by Hierarchical Association of Detection Responses. In: Forsyth, D., Torr, P., Zisserman, A. (eds.) ECCV 2008, Part II. LNCS, vol. 5303, pp. 788–801. Springer, Heidelberg (2008)
5. Wu, B., Nevatia, R.: Detection and tracking of multiple, partially occluded humans by bayesian combination of edgelet based part detectors. International Journal of Computer Vision 75(2), 247–266 (2007)
6. Andriyenko, A., Schindler, K.: Multi-target tracking by continuous energy minimization. In: CVPR (2011)
7. Khan, S.M., Shah, M.: A Multiview Approach to Tracking People in Crowded Scenes Using a Planar Homography Constraint. In: Leonardis, A., Bischof, H., Pinz, A. (eds.) ECCV 2006. LNCS, vol. 3954, pp. 133–146. Springer, Heidelberg (2006)
8. Kim, K., Davis, L.S.: Multi-camera Tracking and Segmentation of Occluded People on Ground Plane Using Search-Guided Particle Filtering. In: Leonardis, A., Bischof, H., Pinz, A. (eds.) ECCV 2006. LNCS, vol. 3953, pp. 98–109. Springer, Heidelberg (2006)
9. Berclaz, J., Fleuret, F., Fua, P.: Robust people tracking with global trajectory optimizaton. In: CVPR (2006)
10. Fleuret, F., Berclaz, J., Lengagne, R., Fua, P.: Multi-camera people tracking with a probabilistic occupancy map. IEEE Transactions on Pattern Analysis and Machine Intelligence 30, 267–282 (2008)
11. Hartley, R., Zisserman, A.: Multiple View Geometry. The United Kingdom at the University Press, Cambridge (2006)
12. Andriyenko, A., Roth, S., Schindler, K.: An analytical formulation of global occlusion reasoning for multi-target tracking. In: ICCV Workshops (2011)
13. Nummiaro, K., Koller-Meier, E., Gool, L.V.: Color features for tracking non-rigid object. In: ACTA Automatica Sinica (2003)

14. Comaniciu, D., Ramesh, V., Meer, P.: Kernel-based object tracking. PAMI 25, 564–577 (2003)
15. Bernardin, K., Stiefelhagen, R.: Evaluating multiple object tracking performance: The clear mot metrics. EURASIP J. on Image and Video Processing, 10 (2008)
16. Yang, J., Shi, Z., Vela, P., Teizer, J.: Probabilistic multiple people tracking through complex situations. In: IEEE Workshop Performance Evaluation of Tracking and Surveillance (2009)

Author Index